Nick Rider

short breaks in
NORTHERN FRANCE

'follow a sign right and you'll be
delivered into a green, narrow valley
that can feel like a lost world: the river is
a quick-flowing, burbling stream, and
hunkered down alongside it are villages
of white-walled, red-roofed cottages,
surrounded by the trademark flowers
of all the Artois valleys.'

CADOGANguides

Contents

About the author

Nick Rider's first experience of French food was a crêpe with jam from a stand in Brittany when he was six years old, made by a man with a beard in baggy brown shorts. Its impact has never been forgotten. More recently, he lived in Barcelona for ten years, and has travelled widely in Spain, France, Italy and Mexico, as well as writing, among other things, a Ph.D on Spanish history, a general index of movies, and articles on food, travel, history, music and art and design. He has also written the Cadogan Guide to the *Yucatan and Mayan Mexico*.

The author would like to thank P&O Ferries for their kind assistance in the preparation of this guide.

Cadogan Guides
Network House, 1 Ariel Way, London W12 7SL
info@cadoganguides.co.uk
www.cadoganguides.com

The Globe Pequot Press
246 Goose Lane, PO Box 480, Guilford,
Connecticut 06437–0480

Copyright © Nick Rider 1996, 2001, 2005

Book design by Andrew Barker
Cover photographs by © jonarnoldimages/
    Walter Bibikow, © jonarnoldimages/Alan
    Copson, © jonarnoldimages/Jon Arnold
    and © Kicca Tommasi
Maps © Cadogan Guides,
    drawn by Map Creation Ltd and
    Tracey Ridgewell
Managing Editor: Natalie Pomier
Editorial Assistant: Nicola Jessop
Proofreading: Elspeth Anderson
Indexing: Isobel McLean

Printed in Italy by Legoprint
A catalogue record for this book is available
    from the British Library
ISBN 1–86011–183–1

Introduction

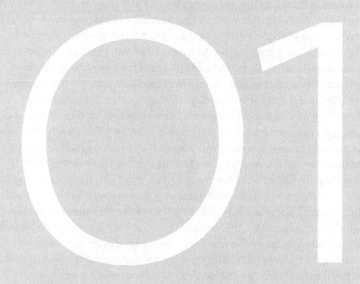

France is a country about which everyone has an opinion. Some still say it's an innately stylish place, the home of chic. No, say some, it's overrated. Some think the French are always hostile and unhelpful. No, say others, they're very charming. For British people, France is both well-known and unfamiliar. For it's true, the French have their ways of doing things. Contrary to a prejudice frequently aired in the British press, they don't cultivate these distinctive habits just to annoy other people, and in my experience are generally perfectly charming about explaining and showing off their customs to foreign visitors, in a neighbourly way. It's just that they have a long-established idea of how they like to do things. And individuality is a sign of character.

The distinctiveness of France, the multi-varied complexity of its culture and its determined ways of behaving, means that any visit there can give you an enjoyable blast of difference. Along the north coast of France or just a short distance inside the country there are small-town cafés, neat seaside towns that still shut up except 'in season', bustling weekly street markets, stylish city shopping streets and a natural, unbuilt-over countryside, all with the unequivocal stamp of Frenchness.

Visiting France has always been bound up with eating. *Restaurant* and *hotel* are both French words, and for foreigners and the French themselves the thousand varieties of French foods, how they are prepared and how they are eaten have long been essential parts of the nation's identity. For a long time French cuisine was considered the only proper cuisine, while all the rest was just food. More recently other places have come on a great deal, while it's often said that French restaurants have become immobile and complacent. There are of course mediocre restaurants in France as there are everywhere else. On the whole, though, the standard of French country and small-town restaurants – especially compared with similar areas else-where in Europe – is still very high. French diners may often be a tad conservative when it comes to the things they will try, but they are also extremely demanding with regard to quality. And when this quality is kept up it's done by staying true to certain basic and very valid principles – following the seasons, using only fresh ingredients, whenever possible using only local produce. Associated with this is a willingness to be near-endlessly painstaking, for perfectionism is one of the lesser-known but very marked French characteristics, and if France has been so important in the history of cuisine it is because it was the first country in Europe to institutionalize taking trouble over its food. And one other aspect is a sense of luxury, for France enjoys its pleasures, and a pampering opulence is still a prime feature of fine French food today.

This guide seeks to open up a range of attractive places within easy distance of the Channel coast, familiar and non-familiar – famous sites such as Monet's garden at Giverny or the great cathedrals of Amiens or Bayeux, beautifully tranquil countryside, cities and small towns. In restaurants, it does not aim to be any kind of guide to all the thousands of eating places across northern France, but to offer a selection. For this thoroughly revised new edition, the restaurants have all been revisited, and some left out, while some hugely impressive new ones – and fine places to stay – have been added. Among the featured restaurants there are some of the region's premier chefs, but also tiny inns lost in the countryside, small-town favourites, hip beach-resort brasseries. All, though, can provide a wonderful meal that's a rare pleasure.

The Food and Drink of Northern France

The distinctiveness of French cooking is very apparent but sometimes hard to define. One element is its special combination of tradition and flexibility: certain methods, dishes and styles – cooking with sauces, reductions and *demi-glaces* – are well established as 'the French way to eat', but at the same time the French tradition is so broad and has so many things in it that it offers endless space for variations and innovations. Moreover, there's scarcely any other country where even small-town chefs are under such pressure to be creative and leave their own personal stamp on their food, within their particular tradition, if they want to be considered true professionals. Related to this is perfectionism, a particular readiness to take trouble: fine French cooks go to extraordinary lengths to get the right fresh ingredients or create the right effect, with a slightly obsessive sense of craft that seems to come up from the collective undergrowth of French culture.

And another characteristic is variety from one place to another, essential to which is the concept of *terroir*, an authentic obsession in modern French food. *Terroir* means earth, or rather the particular piece of earth of each place or region. Every *terroir* in France, every region, sometimes each small locality, has its own specialities, based on the products most suited to its soil, climate, even the lie of the land, and it's assumed that wherever possible cooks should make use of them – fish or shellfish on the coast, apples or leeks inland – because the most local produce will always be the most fresh. There is just as much of a concern to follow the seasons, out of a desire for genuine, unadulterated freshness and respect for the *terroir*.

Freshness and quality of ingredients is everything in good French cooking. This is the opposite of the kind of attitude that expects to have strawberries, tomatoes or sugar snaps 365 days a year, flown in from any corner of the globe. There is still an enormous demand in France for local, premium-standard produce, even if it costs more, and despite the inexorable advance of agribusiness a substantial part of French agriculture, fishing and the distribution system – in short, the much-decried ways of the traditional French farmer – is still geared to satisfying this need. There is also a strong interest throughout France in obtaining fresh products directly from farms and independent producers, many of which are listed in this book. Such ingredients simply taste exactly as they should taste, and the difference this makes is exhilarating, so that even simply prepared dishes can be spectacular.

Because of the notion of *terroir*, food in France – above all rural France – is still tremendously regionalized, sometimes to extremes: in Picardy virtually every restaurant has *ficelle picarde* on its menu, while if you cross the little River Bresle into Normandy cider and cream sauces suddenly appear on every side. The importance given to *terroir* has even grown, as regional cooking has become more fashionable than the old *haute-cuisine* classics, and with the growth in ecologically-inspired concern for more authentic – so once again, local – foods rather than standardized industrial products. Like any fashionable concept *terroir* can be abused and trivialized, but at its best it creates a fascinating diversity. And in northern France it leads to local produce such as leeks, cabbage, carrots, meats and herbs being valued and used in a way that could well inspire restaurants in Britain that still dismiss them in favour of sun-dried tomatoes and shiitake mushrooms.

Pas-de-Calais and Artois

The Pas-de-Calais (chapters 4–6 and 9–11) is the closest part of France to Britain geographically and in its produce: northern vegetables such as cabbages, carrots, chicory, celeriac, shallots and leeks feature strongly. This has never been one of France's most admired cuisines, but dishes are often satisfying and subtle. Among meats, lamb and duck are often more prominent than beef, there is plenty of pork-based charcuterie, game and rabbit are popular in season, and one local speciality is *volailles de Licques*, free-range poultry from around Licques, south of Calais, which is known for its low fat content and full-bodied but delicate flavour. This usually means chicken (*poulet de Licques*) but there are also Licques turkeys (*dindes*). This is also a big fish-eating area, from wonderful sole, ling and sea bass to the many uses of mussels.

The most traditional drink is, as in Flanders, beer. One of the best of the local small-brewery labels is the deliciously full-bodied **Ch'ti**, brewed at Benifontaine near Lens.

Boulette d'Avesnes: A powerful hybrid cheese made with bits of Maroilles (*see* below) kneaded together with herbs and spices and then formed into a cone, coated in paprika and cured for another length of time, forming a very strong, spicy mix.

Caudière, chaudière, chaudrée: Fish stew, usually with sole and other types of fish, mussels, small eels, potatoes and white wine.

Flamiche, Tarte Flamiche, Flamique: Vegetable tart on a doughy base, rather like a quiche but often without the upturned rim, and frequently topped with leeks (*flamiche de poireaux*), cream and cheese. *Flamiches* are also found throughout Flanders and Picardy.

Maroilles: The classic cheese of northern France, with many variants. A strong cow's-milk cheese that's aged and washed for some time before eating, with a dark reddy-brown rind, a soft texture and (usually) a powerful smell. Some Maroilles is washed in beer during *affinage*, giving it extra strength in taste and odour.

Rollot: Another northern washed cheese, strong and spicy like Maroilles, with a lighter, yellower rind. It is often round or heart-shaped.

Flanders

French Flanders (chapter 7 and, to some extent, chapter 8, Lille) is something of an anomaly in this book, as the least 'French' part of the whole area from Belgium to Brittany. Flemish country food makes much use of beef, rabbit and chicken, carrots and leeks, with a certain un-French, hearty quality, and a lack of the usual Gallic complexity. Another 'oddity' of dining in Flanders is the *estaminet*, the time-honoured Flemish pub (*see* pp.59–61), which traditionally does not serve food in the standard French three-course, set-menu style but instead offers single-course dishes – open sandwiches, platters of cold meats, plates of stew with chips – served with beer, produced in one of the many excellent small local breweries (or just across the border in Belgium). Beer is much-used in local cooking, and is one of its most distinctive sources of flavour; another is the use of juniper, whether as juniper hips (*baies de*

Eating Out in France – a User's Guide

Timing and Opening Times
Very important: that the French are a nation of traditionalists is a statement that can be mulled over at length, but it certainly applies in one area: when to eat. A huge proportion of the population, and in rural areas just about everybody, sits down to lunch from about 12.30 to 1.15pm, and for dinner from 8.30 to 9pm, and anywhere called a restaurant expects to serve food only around these times. To avoid disappointment it's advisable to adapt to this as much as possible. In cities eating times are more fluid, and many restaurants may take orders until 10–11pm.

Restaurant **opening times** given in this book refer to the **hours of service, within which you can order a meal**; if a restaurant no longer takes orders after 1.45pm it does not mean you will have to leave shortly afterwards, for once you've sat down you can take as long as you like, and in fact are far less likely to be harassed off a table than in British restaurants where they hope to squeeze in a 'second sitting'.

Most restaurants close for at least one day a week, usually Monday, and not many are open on Sunday evenings. Most take a few weeks holiday in the slackest times of the year: for country and seaside places this is generally November or January, but some city restaurants close up some time in summer.

Restaurants and Brasseries
The traditional alternative to the French restaurant with its set timings has been the *brasserie*. Real city brasseries have a less formal style, have huge menus with snacks and one-course dishes as well as three-course meals, and are genuinely open *à toute heure*, at all hours, or maybe till 2–3am. In country districts, however, you may find that even in a place that calls itself a brasserie they look aghast at you if you try to order anything more than a coffee or a drink during the afternoon, so this flexibility cannot be relied on. One other aspect of regular eating habits is that Normans, especially, rarely snack between meals. This attitude changes in the north, where *frites* or chip stands are common, and in Brittany with the bargain institution of the *crêperie*.

Reservations
It is always a good idea to book in French restaurants, even if you only call ahead the same day to say you're coming. Gourmet restaurants expect it, and for anywhere that's popular and has a reputation it's pretty much essential from Friday to Sunday, and at holiday times. Brasseries traditionally have a looser style, but, if a place is popular, it can still be advisable to reserve, especially at weekends and holidays.

Menus, Formules *and the* Carte
The set menu is the most common way of ordering a meal in French restaurants, with three courses (or four, with cheese) and coffee for a fixed price. Wines and other drinks are usually charged separately. Most restaurants offer a range of *menus* of varying degrees of elaborateness, and this is nearly always the best-value way to eat. Ordering from the *carte*, which most restaurants also have, will always be more expensive. Brasseries generally list both set menus and a big range of single dishes.

Cheap, bargain menus are often called *formules*, and for lunch many cheaper restaurants also offer a low-priced *plat du jour*, a single-course dish of the day.

In more sophisticated restaurants, set menus will include *amuse-bouches* or *amuse-gueules* (appetizers) before the meal, sometimes a *pré-dessert* before the main sweets and petits fours at the end, plus, in Normandy, often a *trou normand* (see p.12) between courses. However, more flexible formulas are also increasingly popular. And, one thing to note is that French restaurants rarely object to anyone ordering just one or two courses – as many French people do, especially for lunch.

Salons de Thé *and* Crêperies
Salons de thé firstly serve tea, usually in attractive settings, but the name also tends to indicate they serve light, fresh one-course lunch menus of mixed salads, quiches, omelettes and so on – a style of eating ever more fashionable in France, especially with younger women. So far they're a fairly urban phenomenon, but they're also found in towns like Honfleur (*see* chapter 21). *Crêperies*, common in seaside towns and ubiquitous in Brittany, are another boon to anyone (i.e., some kids) resistant to other French food. Their menus divide between sweet and savoury (*see* p.12). *Salons* and *crêperies* have flexible daytime hours, but rarely open in the evenings.

Auberges du Terroir *and* Ferme-Auberges
An *auberge du terroir* is officially recognized as serving only fresh produce from the surrounding area, although the way it uses them may be notably sophisticated. A *ferme-auberge* is a farm-with-dining-room serving meals made only with produce from the farm itself, usually simple country cooking – but, again, the inventiveness of French farming families can amaze you. It is **essential** to book at *ferme-auberges*.

Wine and Water
You will usually be asked if you want *un apéritif* while ordering. Wine lists are often huge, but there are usually several bottles for more everyday consumption. Most people do not ask for mineral water with a meal but a *carafe d'eau*, a jug of tap water, which is free, and perfectly good quality. Branded mineral water is quite expensive.

Children and Children's Menus
Children are welcome in most French restaurants, although they are expected to know how to behave in them too. Many restaurants – even gourmet ones – and virtually all brasseries offer special children's menus, usually for €7–10.

Disabled Access
French restaurants are under considerable pressure to provide full access and toilet facilities – and many now do – but equally many, particularly if they're installed in old buildings, still do not. It's always worth calling ahead to check.

Tipping
By law, a service charge of 12–15 per cent is added to all restaurant bills in France. It's not uncommon to leave a few coins (€1–5) as well to acknowledge particularly good service, but this is entirely optional.

genièvre) or just as gin. Even conventional restaurants in Flanders are more likely to serve one-course dishes than is the case in most parts of France, and since the Flemish are big snackers (again in an un-French way) there are *frites* stands everywhere. In Lille, cuisine is much more Frenchified, and more sophisticated.

Carbonnade (de bœuf): Beef braised in beer with onions.

Coq à la bière: Chicken cooked in beer with mushrooms.

Mimolette: A round cheese with an orange flesh, similar to Dutch Gouda or Edam and with a grey rind, that is aged for over a year before eating. A powerful cheese (the strongest kind is called *Vieux Lille* or *Vieux Puant*, 'Old Stinker', for reasons that can be imagined). General De Gaulle loved the stuff.

Potjevleesch, potje'vleesh: Mixed terrine of rabbit, veal, chicken, pork or combinations of the above, served in slices cold with *frites*.

Tartine: Open sandwich on buttered bread or toast, with different toppings.

Waterzooi: Creamy stew of chicken or river fish with vegetables.

Picardy

The food of Picardy (chapters 12–13) is sturdy, country cuisine. Since a great deal of the area is wetland, duck is especially important, and features heavily on menus from autumn to spring. Around the Bay of the Somme, fish and shellfish caught inshore – shrimps, mussels, sole and *lieu* (pollack) – are spectacularly good. Most celebrated of all the Bay's produce is its lamb. The Somme Bay is one of two main areas in northern France (the other being the Bay of Mont St-Michel) where sheep can be raised on salt marshes. Salt-marsh lamb or *agneau de prés-salés* has unusually lean meat and a sparer, more delicate flavour than most lamb, and is highly prized. Ham and pork are also prominent, while around Amiens much is made of the vegetables grown in the *hortillons* or water gardens beside the Somme.

Belval: Mild cows'-milk cheese, made in flat disks.

Ficelle Picarde: The ubiquitous Picard dish: a savoury crêpe filled with ham, mushrooms and onions (and sometimes also chicken) and baked in a cheese sauce.

Soupe Maraîchère/des Hortillons: Fresh garden vegetable soup (Amiens).

Normandy

Normandy is the area most featured in this book (chapters 14–32) and Norman cooking is one of the *grandes cuisines* of France. Its very recognizable identity comes from its favourite ingredients, all drawn very visibly from the lush, green Norman *terroir*: apples – there are no uses for them that Normans have not researched – cider, cream and butter. This may sound pretty rich, but dishes need not be leaden or overpowering: all they require is an able chef, as fine Norman cooking is a real test of skill.

The apparently simple basic repertoire of Norman cooking can be applied to all kinds of ingredients and leaves enormous scope for variation. Peasant in origin, it also provides a base for dishes of great sophistication. *Normande* or *Vallée d'Auge* sauces can be used with chicken, veal, pork or other meats, while duck – as prominent here as in Picardy – might be served with a subtle reduction with just a hint of apple. Cattle in this dairy region are more often served to eat as veal, from male calves, than as beef. Duck also features in one of the richest of Norman dishes, characteristic of Rouen and the Seine-Maritime, *Caneton Rouennais*, in which the bird is cooked unbled so that the meat is supremely tender and has exceptionally dense flavour. In its most complete form, this is one of the most elaborate dishes of old-style *haute cuisine* (*see* p.186).

The most prominent Norman charcuterie are earthy varieties: *boudin noir* (black pudding) or *andouilles* and *andouillettes* (gut sausages), the very best of which come from the Vire area in southwest Normandy. Smoked meats are a speciality of the Cotentin, including delicious smoked ham. Normandy is also the source of some of France's finest foie gras, and one of its widest varieties of duck and goose terrines and *rillettes*. The Bay of Mont St-Michel, meanwhile, is one of the areas where the much sought-after *pré-salé* or salt-marsh lamb is raised.

Normandy also has a long coastline, and everywhere that fish and shellfish are landed there are restaurants that try to make the best of them. Sole has traditionally been the most highly regarded fish in Norman cooking, but turbot, *turbotin* (small turbot), sea bass and sea bream (*daurade*) are all popular. Mussels – often cultivated semiartificially on *bouchots* (posts driven into mud flats offshore) – are consumed in huge quantities. Shellfish are best around the Cotentin peninsula: the region's finest oysters come from St-Vaast-la-Hougue, followed by the Bay of Mont St-Michel and the Isigny coast, while lobsters are generally better in the western Cotentin. In winter, *coquilles St-Jacques* (scallops) take pride of place in coastal restaurants.

Given Normandy's huge importance in the cheese world, it's only natural that restaurants here tend to keep up the tradition of the cheese course, now under pressure in some more fashion-conscious parts of France. Desserts are another area where Norman cooking comes into its own, with, again, the classic ingredients: apples and cream, with liberal dashes of apple booze (calvados). *Tarte normande, tarte aux pommes, tarte tatin* or *tarte aux poires* (with pears) are found across the region.

Barbue à l'oseille: Brill in a sorrel sauce.

Douillon aux Pommes (or **aux Poires**): Fruit dessert in which a whole baked apple or pear is surrounded by a ring-like pastry case.

Jambon au Cidre: Ham baked or braised in cider.

Marmite Dieppoise: Fish and shellfish stew with white wine, leeks and cream. In Fécamp virtually the same dish is called a *Marmite Fécampoise*.

Moules à la crème (normande): Mussels cooked in white wine, onions and cream, sometimes with a touch of cider.

Poulet, veau, lapin Vallée d'Auge: Meat served with a *crème fraîche*, calvados and onion sauce, with sautéed apples and mushrooms.

Salade Normande: Mixed salad (usually) with ham, potatoes and hard-boiled eggs.

Sauce Normande: Sauce with a base of cider and *crème fraîche*.

Sole Normande: Sole poached in cider and cream with shrimps; in more refined versions, oysters, langoustines and other shellfish may be added.

Teurgoule: Norman baked rice pudding with thick cinnamon-flavoured crust.

Tripes à la mode de Caen: Classic Norman dish of beef tripe, onions, other vegetables and spices cooked in water, cider and calvados.

Normandy Cheeses

Camembert: The least historic of Norman cheeses, 'invented' in the 1790s (*see* p.256), but by far the best known. Camembert can now be made virtually anywhere, but the authentic *appellation d'origine contrôlée* (AOC) local product is identified as *Camembert de Normandie*. In good Camembert the rind should have some browny-red colour in it, and it should have a noticeable but not over-strong smell.

Livarot: A cows'-milk cheese with its own AOC (made only in the Pays d'Auge) that is one of the oldest Normandy cheeses, and quite pungent. With a thick yellowy-orange rind, it is always made in round disks wrapped in five strips of paper that are said to suggest military stripes, which is why it's sometimes called *Le Colonel*.

Neufchâtel: From the Pays de Bray (*see* p.175), and the only one of the classic Normandy cheeses from north of the Seine. It's one of the least known, but also one of the most satisfying, and different from cheeses from further south: it has a drier, powdery texture, a mild taste and a white, powdery rind. Neufchâtel is mentioned in documents from the early Middle Ages, but it only got its AOC in the 1970s. It's made in a variety of shapes: cylinders (*bondes*), rectangles (*briquettes* and *carrés*) and, most distinctively, hearts (*cœurs*). This doesn't affect the flavour, which depends on its age and whether or not it's *affiné*.

Cheese Lore: the Mysteries of *Affinage*

Among the most distinct and popular products of each *terroir* are its cheeses, for every French region has at least some of its own. There seems to be some doubt over the figure given in the famous quote from De Gaulle, as to how anyone can govern a country that produces x different kinds of cheese – the number varying from around 260 up to 400 – but there is certainly a vast variety.

Fine French cheeses are usually the result of two distinct processes, the actual cheese-making on the farm or at the cooperative, and the maturing or *affinage* that takes place in a cheese cellar. *Affinage* is one of the greatest of French inventions, the delicate process by which cheeses are aged by being washed in different liquids – *eau-de-vie*, brine, beer – in special cellars to create subtle flavours. Some farm producers mature their own cheeses, but the best are produced in the cellars of craft cheese merchants, identified as a *Maître Fromager Affineur*. Any good *fromager* will have a choice of cheeses from around the country, but the ones on most prominent display will be those from the local area. Cheeses are always *affiné* to reach their best at a certain time, and when buying cheese you will almost certainly be asked when you intend to eat it. Most Northern French and Norman cheeses are soft, and have a fairly short life – and so become pretty malodorous and acidic after about two weeks.

Virtually all traditional northern and Norman cheeses are made with cows' milk, but many farms now produce good-quality *brebis* (ewes'-milk cheese) and especially *chèvre* (goats'-milk cheese), generally based on more traditional southern varieties.

Pavé d'Auge: Very similar to Pont-l'Evêque, but stronger and with a darker rind.

Petit Lisieux or **Vieux Lisieux**: Another Pays d'Auge cheese related to Pont-l'Evêque, but possibly older and certainly spicier and stronger smelling. A very robust, rich cheese.

Pont-l'Evêque: A tender cows'-milk cheese from the northern Pays d'Auge, where the AOC area is centred, although it is now made all over Normandy. It has been known since at least the 16th century. Softer in texture than Camembert and milder in flavour, but still with a noticeable tang, it is made in squares, with a whiteish-brown rind. It should not have a very strong smell.

Cider, *Pommeau* and Calvados

Normandy is the largest region of France that does not contain a single vineyard. It does, however, have huge quantities of cider farms, and cider is the drink with Norman tradition behind it. Cider farms come in all sizes: the largest are in the northern Seine-Maritime – like the giant Duché de Longueville estate south of Dieppe, which represents Normandy cider in supermarkets around the world. In the Bessin, west of Bayeux, there are large, attractive and less 'industrial' farms, while in the Cotentin cider farms tend to be tiny smallholdings half-lost up winding lanes; in the Pays d'Auge there are farms of all sizes, except for big, high-production estates.

Many smaller producers only sell direct, not through shops, which gives an added interest to cider-hunting; tourist offices in cider areas have leaflets indicating local farms open for direct sales. Many Normandy farmers produce a relatively coarse cider in barrels (*cidre tonneaux*), which is sold in bottles with screw caps, but their best cider is always *cidre bouché* (corked cider), which has a light fizz or *pétillance* and is usually available either *doux* (sweet), *demi* or *brut* (dry). Traditionally the most prestigious cider-producing area in Normandy is the Pays d'Auge east of Caen, which – around Cambremer – is the only district with an AOC for ciders. Pays d'Auge ciders tend to be well-rounded, with a slightly more golden colour than many, and often even the *brut* ciders still have a touch of sweetness. If you prefer a drier, cleaner flavour try the more astringent ciders from the stonier soils of the Cotentin to the west. Also, ciders are very unpredictable, much more so than wines: apples are more susceptible than grapes to changes in the weather, so that, contrary to the sacred notion of *terroir*, ciders from the same patch of ground can vary a great deal from year to year. This only adds to the interest. The one rule is, hot weather, especially at the time of pressing, produces drier ciders, by evaporating more of the sugar.

The apple harvest runs roughly from mid-September to November. Once the apples have been gathered and crushed, the dryness of cider can be deliberately varied by how long it is left to ferment in the barrel, although cider apples more than six months old must by law be made into calvados. Cider, once bottled, does not change significantly with age. Some farms now bottle up some very sweet *cidre nouveau* for sale by Christmas, but purists scoff at this as a crude copy of the *Beaujolais nouveau* fad. *Demi* and *brut* ciders become available in March or April, so that the best time for tasting and buying is from mid-spring to early autumn. Large producers have ciders on sale all year round, but by October smaller farms may have sold out. Even very fine ciders, brought direct from the producers, are very cheap, at around €8–10 a bottle.

Very few Normandy farms produce only cider. Many also have **pommeau**, a cider-and-calvados mix that makes an enjoyable, smooth liqueur. It's quite sweet, and is used a good deal in cooking because of the tangy flavour it gives to meat. Farms also often sell *poiré* (pear cider, or old English perry), fine cider vinegars and fresh apple juice. And lastly but most importantly there is **calvados** itself, *calva*: distilled apple juice or apple brandy, perhaps Normandy's greatest culinary invention and still its favourite after-dinner *digestif*. There is a common British idea that calvados is all a bit rough, but this is a terrible mistake: good calvados is actually smoother than most whiskies or other spirits. Much more than with brandy or other *digestifs*, you drink it with your nose as much as your mouth, for this is the most fragrant of spirits, and in fine calvados what you notice first in the bouquet are the apples, not the alcohol.

As with ciders, calvados from the Pays d'Auge has traditionally been the most highly regarded, and there are two different AOC categories, one for calvados and another for *Calvados du Pays d'Auge*, which must be passed twice through the traditional pot still, a process called double distillation. Again, calvados is hugely variable, which leaves plenty of room for individual taste and discussion. Calvados also varies a great deal according to how long it is left to age in the barrel. 'Standard' calvados is aged for up to five years; beyond that it may be called *Hors d'Âge* or identified more precisely as ten, 15, 20 or up to 50 years old. Well-aged fine calvados is a superbly complex drink.

A final great Norman institution is the **trou normand**: a shot of calvados drunk between the first and second courses of a meal, to clear a 'hole' for the remaining courses. In Maupassant's time it was the custom at Norman country dinners for men at least to take a straight slug of calvados between every course, and some traditional folk may be stout enough to keep this up today. The most common version of the *trou* found in restaurants today, though, is a more refined equivalent: a little cup of apple sorbet, floating in calvados. There is a theory-and-practice to this too: take a spoonful of equal parts sorbet and calvados, put it in your mouth and hold the sorbet on your tongue, feeling the coldness; then, inhale before swallowing. The result is dazzling.

Brittany

Brittany features only briefly in this book, in chapter 33, on St-Malo. This being a port city, its best food has always been based on fresh fish and seafood, and the immediate differences between local cuisine and that of other Atlantic coast regions are not that marked, although compared to Normandy there is a noticeable decrease in the use of apples. Oysters, from Cancale, and cod, whether fresh (*cabillaud*) or salt cod (*morue*), have always been St-Malo specialities, at least until recent cod crises. One significant change is in the number of *crêperies*. There is one essential distinction to know in *crêperie* menus, between these two:

Crêpes (de froment): Thin wheatflour pancakes, often with sugar in the mix, served with sweet fruit, chocolate and cream fillings, often with cream on top.

Galettes (de sarrasin): Thicker, savoury buckwheat pancakes, served with savoury fillings such as mushrooms, ham, eggs, cheese and so on.

Practicalities

14 Practicalities

Getting There

By Air

From the UK and Ireland

Given the short distances involved and the range of land- or sea-bound alternatives, flying is not the most obvious choice for a short-break trip to the northern French coast, but there are some air routes that – especially if you're not starting out from southern England – are worth bearing in mind. **Ryanair** flies daily from Luton to **Dinard**, the airport for St-Malo (*see* chapter 33), and from Glasgow Prestwick, Dublin and Shannon to **Beauvais**, optimistically advertised as 'Paris-Beauvais'. It's actually 56km (35 miles) north of the capital, but is also well-located for anyone visiting Amiens and the Somme, Rouen, the Seine Valley and the Seine-Maritime (chapters 12–20), with good rail, bus and road links.

Little **Lyddair** also flies between Lydd airport, near Romney Marsh in Kent, and **Le Touquet** (*see* chapter 10), using 16-seater Trislander aircraft. There are flights every weekend all year, and more frequently in June-Sept; flight time is about 30 minutes. Aircraft are also available for private charters.

There are also of course many more flight options via the two main Paris airports, Charles de Gaulle and Orly. **Air France**, **British Airways**, **British Midland**, **bmibaby**, **Aer Lingus**, **easyJet** and **Flybe** all fly to one or the other from many airports around the UK and Ireland. Once there, the best way to get to Normandy or the coast is by train, but for a short trip this is a long way round.
Lyddair, **t** 01797 320 000, *www.lyddair.com*.
Ryanair, **t** UK 0871 246 0000,
t IR 0818 30 30 30, *www.ryanair.com*.

From the USA and Canada

There are frequent flights to Paris (usually Charles de Gaulle airport, north of the city, the main hub for long-haul flights) from many parts of North America. From there, you can explore France's northern regions by train or rental car. In off-peak seasons (such as any time in fall, winter and early spring) you can generally expect to find scheduled economy tickets from (for example) New York to Paris from around $350–$480. In summer scheduled prices rise, but many more direct charter flights become available.

However, for this area it can work out cheaper to fly to Britain – for which there is a bigger range of flights – and then continue your journey to France from there.

A big choice of charters and discount tickets to both France and the UK is available year-round. Check Sunday-paper travel sections for current deals, and the bargain-flight websites. A selection of sites that can be particularly useful is listed here:
www.bestfares.com
www.cheaptrips.com
www.eurovacations.com
www.expedia.com
www.hotwire.com
www.lowestfare.com
www.priceline.com
www.travelocity.com

By Sea

The opening of the Channel Tunnel transformed cross-Channel travel, but not in ways everyone expected. Instead of going out of business, ferry companies have been forced to become more competitive, so that they now offer a range of interesting deals in the hope of drawing passengers away from the Tunnel – especially for 1-, 3- or 5-day returns. At most times, ferry fares are now more flexible, and very often lower, than those of the Tunnel. Crossing the Channel can still be expensive at times – such as midsummer – but it's always worth checking the options, and looking to see if you can get a better fare deal by varying your travel dates. For more on how to get the best cross-Channel fares, *see* p.16.

There are now two types of Channel ferries, conventional ships, and large Seacat-style catamarans. The latter are significantly faster, but also cost more, and are more likely to be delayed or even cancelled by bad weather (some fast services operate April–Oct only). The disadvantage of all ferries against the Tunnel, of course, is that they take longer, especially since you normally have to check in at least 30–45 minutes before sailing. However, crossing by ferry with a car also has advantages. Modern ferries are fast and very comfortable, and provide a pleasant break in the journey; most companies also offer a range of perks for families, such as discounted rates for anyone travelling with kids aged 4–15, while under-4s travel for free. On longer routes, such as those in the western Channel to St-Malo or Cherbourg, it can be worth overnighting with a cabin (for an additional charge), particularly with children in tow.

Most ferry companies also still take **foot passengers**, and tickets are extremely cheap. If you only wish to visit one of the coastal ports like Calais or Dieppe, or anywhere easily accessible by public transport, this is worth taking advantage of. Even if you want to explore a bit further, another option to look into is taking a foot-passenger ticket across the Channel, and then renting a car in France (*see* p.18).

Ferry Routes and Companies

Car ferry routes currently available in areas covered by this guide are shown with crossing times below. There is still uncertainty about P&O's western Channel services, but the Portsmouth–Le Havre route may be taken over by Brittany Ferries. Passenger-only ferries run between the **Channel Islands** and several ports in the Cotentin Peninsula; *see* pp.319, 331.

> ### Average Crossing Times
> Not including check-in times.
> **Channel Tunnel** 35mins
> **Dover–Dunkerque** 2hrs
> **Dover-Calais** 55mins Seacat,
>   1hr 15mins–1hr 30mins standard ferries
> **Dover-Boulogne** 50mins
> **Newhaven–Dieppe** 2hrs Seacat,
>   4hrs standard ferries
> **Portsmouth–Le Havre** 5hrs 30 mins by day,
>   7hrs 15mins overnight
> **Portsmouth–Caen (Ouistreham)** 3hrs 30mins
>   fast ferry; 5hrs 45mins standard ferries by
>   day, 7hrs overnight
> **Portsmouth–Cherbourg** 3hrs fast ferry,
>   5hrs standard ferries by day, 6hrs overnight
> **Poole–Cherbourg** 2hrs 15 mins fast ferry,
>   4hrs 15mins standard ferry by day,
>   6hrs 45mins overnight
> **Rosslare–Cherbourg** 12hrs
> **Portsmouth–St-Malo** 10hrs 45mins, overnight
> **Poole/Weymouth–St-Malo** 4hrs 30 mins, or
>   8hrs with stopover in Channel Islands

Brittany Ferries, t 08703 665 333, *www.brittany-ferries.com*. Largest in the western Channel, with fast (*April–Sept*) and conventional ferry sailings **Portsmouth–Caen**, **Portsmouth** and **Poole** to **Cherbourg** and **Portsmouth–St-Malo**. May also take over the **Portsmouth–Le Havre** route.

Condor Ferries, t 0845 345 2000, *www.condorferries.com*. Fast-ferry sailings year-round from **Weymouth** and **Poole** to the **Channel Islands** and **St-Malo**; several St-Malo sailings go via Jersey or Guernsey, with a stopover in between. In summer (*June–Sept*) Condor also has ferries from **Poole** and **Portsmouth** to **Cherbourg**.

Hoverspeed, t 0870 240 8070, *www.hoverspeed.co.uk*. Fast Seacat services **Dover–Calais** and **Newhaven–Dieppe**. Prices are relatively high, but these are some of the fastest Channel crossings.

Irish Ferries, t IR 1 890 31 31 31, *www.irishferries.com*. Weekly overnight ferries between **Rosslare** and **Cherbourg**.

Norfolk Line, t 0870 870 1020, *www.norfolkline.com*. **Dover–Dunkerque**. A formerly freight-only line with passenger services since 2000. Not the quickest, but Norfolk offers some of the best fares, and the simple pricing structure – with only 5-day and open returns – is particularly good if you stay longer than a few days in France.

P&O Ferries, t 08705 20 20 20, *www.poferries.com*. Standard ferries **Dover–Calais**, with 3–4 sailings every hour, and many good fare offers. Also **Portsmouth** to **Le Havre** and **Cherbourg**; these routes will be discontinued at some point in late 2005: check with P&O on their current status.

Seafrance, t 08705 711 711, *www.seafrance.com*. **Dover–Calais** only, and sometimes the cheapest of the Dover ferries.

Speedferries, t 0870 220 0570, *www.speedferries.com*. **Dover–Boulogne**, a fast catamaran service that has brought some of the style of low-cost airlines into the Channel, with ultra-competitive pricing and many special offers. Speedferries do not take foot passengers.

Transmanche Ferries, t 0800 917 1201, *www.transmancheferries.com*. **Newhaven–Dieppe** only: slower than Hoverspeed, but also cheaper.

By Car

Putting your car on a Shuttle train through the **Channel Tunnel** has become the most popular way of getting to France from Britain. It takes only 35mins to get through the tunnel from Folkestone to Calais, and there are up to 4 departures an hour, 365 days of the year. Compared to ferries, the Tunnel has the added convenience of speed, and that it's not affected by the weather (a significant factor in winter). The same considerations apply to Tunnel and ferry tickets (*see* right) – so it's always worth checking on current rates, offers and so on.

The basic price for Shuttle tickets is per car no more than 6.5m in length, plus the driver and up to four passengers. In low season, a return tickets for over 5 days in France should cost around £140–250 return, rising to £300-plus at peak times. Fares vary by time of day, and are significantly cheaper if you book well ahead, and if you book online. While it is advisable to book on Eurotunnel, it's also possible just to turn up and wait for the next available space. **Eurotunnel, t** 08705 35 35 35, *www.eurotunnel.com*. For Shuttle bookings.

By Train

One of the most comfortable ways to get to France is on **Eurostar** trains from London Waterloo or Ashford in Kent. While the busiest route is to Paris, they also run direct to **Lille** (*see* chapter 8) in just under 2hrs. If you want to continue on by rail, at Lille you can change onto the French TGV high-speed network, with connections throughout the country.

Eurostar offers a range of packages and promotional fares. To get the best, you need to book at least 21 days in advance, and include a Saturday night in your stay. Also offered are **Eurostar Plus** deals, which include a Eurostar ticket and an internal French railways ticket to a range of destinations. On Eurostar you need to check in 20mins before departure.

Details and reservations are available via: **Eurostar, t** 08705 186 186, *www.eurostar.co.uk*. **Rail Europe** (UK), **t** 08705 848 848, *www.raileurope.co.uk*. **Rail Europe USA**, 226 Westchester Av, White Plains, NY 10064, **t** 1 800 438 7245, *www.raileurope.com*.

Getting the Best Fares

Whether for Tunnel or ferry, standard fares across the Channel can still seem surprisingly high at times. Fares vary wildly by season and demand, sometimes in ways that appear almost deliberately confusing. However, the arrival of new lower-cost operators such as Speedferries and Norfolk Line has brought a far wider range of fares, and it's always worth looking around for the best deals available. This can, though, involve some digging. All ferry operators and the Tunnel now prefer you to book online – and give discounts for doing so – and their brochures give only rough price guides; however, their websites frequently fail to present their company's current fares clearly, so that it can be a laborious operation to find out whether you might save money by travelling a few days (or even hours) later or earlier. This is one case where it's often best to phone, get through to a human being and ask for details of the cheapest fare available at any particular time (you can still then book online, to get the discount). One other benefit of the new competition, too, is that it is at last obliging the older companies to adopt much simpler, more transparent pricing structures.

Another relatively recent change is that most of the ferry companies now follow the Tunnel – which has always done so – in charging a flat fare for a car and up to 5 (or sometimes 6) passengers, instead of the old practice of having a basic fare for car and driver and then charging extra for each additional person. However, this is still not universal, and if you're travelling as a family or a group it's important to check, as you will do much better with a flat-rate fare. Also, however, be aware that some companies that do not always have flat-rate fares sometimes offer good-value mini-break fares for a car and a varying number of passengers.

The most expensive fare period runs from early July to mid-August; other peak-season times include Easter and some of the UK school holidays. Weekdays, and night crossings, are always cheaper than those at weekends. It's advisable to book as far ahead as you can – especially for peak times – and to look out for special offers. Drivers pay extra to bring a caravan or trailer, but like basic fares these charges vary by season.

Entry Formalities

EU citizens and holders of full US, Canadian, Australian and New Zealand passports do not need a visa to enter France for stays of up to 3 months. Anyone else should check on current requirements at the nearest French consulate.

Getting Around

By Car

Unless you are prepared to stick to towns with train connections, wait as long as it takes for buses, to cycle or walk, a car is the only way to explore remoter – and some of the loveliest – parts of the French countryside. Driving in France has great pluses, too: outside the main urban areas traffic densities are low, so there is very little congestion much of the time, and driving can be remarkably stress-free. This is in the face of traditional suspicions about the supposed manic aggressiveness of French drivers, as reflected in the high local accident rate. In fact, most French country drivers have two main requirements of other road users, especially foreigners: not to dither, and not to hog the middle of the road. If someone comes shooting up behind you, let them go by, and you need never bother each other ever again. Squatting in the outer lanes of main highways, on the other hand, as many British drivers seem determined to do, is an absolute no-no in France, and should you do it don't be surprised if you are determinedly tailgated.

Drivers must have their **driving licence, vehicle registration document** and up-to-date **insurance papers** in the car with them. Drivers with a valid licence from any EU country, the USA, Canada or Australia do not need an international licence to drive in France. If you take your own car to France, you should of course make sure you are properly insured. Under European law all UK motor insurance policies now include basic third-party cover for all EU countries, but it's advisable to get extended, fully comprehensive international cover, which most insurance companies provide for a limited extra premium. It's also advisable to have breakdown assistance, which many insurance companies can also arrange.

Cars from the UK or Ireland require **headlamp adjusters,** and also, under French law, you should have some things with you that are still not usual in Britain: **spare bulbs** for the car's main lights, and a **warning triangle,** which if you break down should be placed 50m behind the car. All cars in France are also required to have rear seat belts, which must be worn.

If you have a breakdown (*une panne*) on major roads or motorways, use the orange emergency phones to contact rescue services or the police. If you have a breakdown service, ring them; if not, ring the police, **t** 17. If you have an accident involving another driver, you will need to fill out an international incident form, which should have been supplied with your insurance papers. Note, though, that French insurance companies are very slow payers, so many drivers prefer to try and sort incidents out between themselves.

The main French *autoroutes* (motorways) are toll roads, but note that nowadays quite a few of them are not – among those that are free-access are the A16 between Calais and Boulogne, the A16–A25 from Calais to Lille, the A28 between Abbeville and Rouen and the A84 from Caen to Rennes, via Avranches. Where tolls do apply, rates vary, but Boulogne–Amiens by the A16, for example, costs about €9.50 in tolls. At motorway toll stations it's theoretically possible to pay by credit card, but this wastes a lot of time and it's really much easier to have cash. Cards are not accepted at the toll bridges over the Seine.

Speed limits are 130kph/80mph on *autoroutes*; 110kph/69mph on main highways; 90kph/55mph on other roads; and 50kph/30mph in urban areas. There are few speed cameras, but the police often set up radar traps in lay-bys. Fines are payable on the spot,

---

Driving Information
Autoroute information, *www.autoroutes.fr.* Has the current toll rates, in detail.
Road and traffic information, *www.bison-fute.equipement.gouv.fr.* The site of the French National Traffic Centre, which provides an amazing range of information on all aspects of driving in France – including weather conditions and current blockages – in French and English.

and begin at about €90 but can be far more, especially if you fail a breath test. A campaign against drink-driving has been under way for some time, and police traps are often set up after Sunday lunch. France also has a law against driving while using a mobile phone, which is actually quite rigorously enforced.

There are a few more points to note about driving in France. One is the famous *priorité à droite*, the old system whereby traffic coming from streets to your right, unless halted by a stop sign and/or a thick white line, automatically has right of way. This venerable rule has been disappearing in favour of a more international system whereby main roads automatically have priority, and its application is increasingly scarce, but some villages maintain it, and many older country drivers, in particular, seem blissfully oblivious of any changes in the law since they first learnt to drive. *Priorité à droite* does not apply at roundabouts, where you give way to cars already on them. Also, if you see little yellow triangle signs by the roadside, this means the (main) road you are on has priority even in villages it passes through; if, however, you then see a triangle with a black line through it, this means that *priorité à droite* has returned, and slow-moving vans may trundle out of even the tiniest lanes to your right without their drivers even looking. A good rule of thumb is to watch out for *Cédez le passage* (Give Way) signs, and to treat each intersection with care.

Another point is that French drivers rarely respect pedestrian crossings.

Road signs, though, are another plus point in driving in France. Two are particularly useful: when you're approaching any town, following *Centre Ville* signs will always take you to the middle of town by the most direct route, while if you're lost, or need to leave, *Toutes Directions* or *Autres Directions* signs will take you out of town equally logically, to a major road where you can get your bearings.

Petrol stations can be scarce in the countryside, and many keep shop hours, and are shut at night, on Sunday afternoons, on Mondays or for lunch. Unleaded fuel is *sans plomb*, and diesel may be called diesel, or *gazole* or *gasoil*. The cheapest places to buy fuel are the petrol stations attached to supermarkets; the most expensive are on motorways. Out of hours they are often self-service, but pumps do not usually accept cash or foreign credit cards, so it's best to fill up in normal opening times.

Hiring a Car in France

Car hire has been relatively expensive in France, but recently a much wider range of prices has become available, thanks in part to the emergence of local French rental chains such as Ada or RentaCar, which frequently offer very good deals for weekend or weekly rentals. All the major international car hire chains also operate in France, and are also increasingly competitive. Hence – depending very much on when you want to do it – it can be an economical option to get to France as a foot passenger or by air and hire a car there.

The minimum age for hiring a car in France varies from 21 to 25, and the maximum is 70, depending on the company. Some companies impose surcharges for drivers under 25. Rental conditions are now fairly standard, but check that the price quoted includes tax, full insurance and unlimited mileage.

Listed here are some car hire agencies in the main Channel ports and other regional entry points. All the agencies shown have websites that take bookings for offices throughout France: **Ada** (*www.ada.fr*); **Avis** (*www.avis.fr*): **Budget** (*www.budget.fr*); **Europcar** (*www.europcar.fr*); **RentaCar** (*www.rentacar.fr*)

Beauvais
Ada, 28–30 Rue Jeanne d'Arc, t 03 44 45 48 38
Europcar, Beauvais airport, t 03 44 15 05 03

Boulogne-sur-Mer
Ada, 211 Rue Nationale, t 03 21 80 80 82
RentaCar, 26 Rue de la Lampe, t 03 21 80 97 34,

Calais
Europcar, Car Ferry Terminal, t 03 21 96 73 40;
   22 Place d'Armes, t 03 21 34 81 00
Budget, Car Ferry Terminal, t 03 21 96 42 40;
   44 Place d'Armes, t 03 21 96 42 20

Cherbourg
Ada, 10 Av de Paris, t 02 33 20 65 65
Europcar, Ferry Terminal, t 02 33 44 53 85
RentaCar, 48 Quai Alexandre III,
   t 02 33 20 14 06

Dieppe
Ada, 48 Rue Thiers, **t** 02 32 44 50 70
Budget, 1 Av Normandie-Sussex,
  t 02 32 14 48 48
Europcar, 33 Rue Thiers, **t** 02 35 04 97 10

Le Havre
Ada, 25 Av du Général Archinard,
  t 02 35 22 94 31
Europcar, 51 Quai de Southampton,
  t 02 35 25 76 83

Ouistreham
Budget, Ferry Terminal,
  t 02 31 83 70 47
Europcar, Ferry Terminal, **t** 02 31 84 61 61

St-Malo
Ada, 77 Bd des Talards, **t** 02 99 56 06 15
Avis, Ferry Terminal, **t** 02 99 40 58 68,
Europcar, 16 Bd des Talards, **t** 02 99 56 75 17

By Train

Travelling by rail in France is very easy. French Railways (**SNCF**) trains are sensibly priced and well used. The stars of the network, the sleek TGV high-speed trains, allow you to nip, for example, from Paris to Rouen in just over an hour. There is also still a decent network of slower local trains serving destinations away from the main lines, and in some areas where rail links have been discontinued (as in the Seine-Maritime) SNCF buses have been supplied to fill in for former train routes. Train and bus services are linked, so that you can move painlessly from one to the other, rather than finding that the last bus left 5 minutes before your train pulled in.

When you board a train, you must stamp (*composter*) your ticket in the odd-looking orange machines by the platform entrances. This date-stamps your ticket, and if you forget to do it you're liable to a fine; also, if you break your journey you must re-*composter* the ticket. You can book train tickets online inside or outside France, and pay by credit card. For non-high-speed trains SNCF fares vary according to whether you travel in off-peak (*période bleue*, blue times) or white (*blanche*, or *période de pointe*) peak periods: Friday and Sunday evenings, and national holidays, nearly always fall in white periods. All stations dish out little calendars with the 'blue periods' clearly marked. The SNCF also offers many discount fares, especially for under-25s and over-60s, which make the fares still more reasonable: details are available at all stations. **SNCF information**, in France, **t** 08 36 35 35 35, *www.sncf.com*

By Bus

Bus services are much less extensive than the rail network. The Calvados *département* has its own quite efficient bus service, the *Bus Verts*, which can be notably useful for getting up and down the 1944 invasion beaches without a car, and in the Seine Maritime there is a fairly good bus route along the coast either side of Dieppe. Elsewhere, though, services are patchy, and many villages have a bus just once a week or not at all. Also, country bus schedules are often timed to fit in with local markets and schools, so buses leave a village very early in the morning and return in late afternoon. Most larger towns have a *Gare Routière* (bus station). For details of local buses, ask at the nearest tourist office.

By Bicycle

As is well-known, cycling is a major part of French culture, and France is an exceptionally bike-friendly country. Many SNCF trains (with a bicycle symbol on the timetable) carry bikes for free, sometimes in a designated carriage. Even if you don't have your own bike with you, cycles can also be hired from many SNCF stations in larger towns, and then dropped off at a different station, as long as you specify where this will be when you hire the bike. Elsewhere there are bike hire shops in just about every town, usually with rates of around €10 a day, and tourist offices will be able to point you to them. Hirers may also be asked for a deposit, or a credit card number. The common French word for a *bicyclette* is a *vélo*, and a *vélo tout terrain*, or *VTT*, is a mountain bike. If you rent, ask about insurance against theft, or check if your travel insurance covers you for theft or damage. Bike shops are plentiful, so it's easy to get spare parts.

It can be perfectly pleasurable just to cycle through the countryside on conventional minor roads, but French cycling-enthusiasm is also reflected in the great many *véloroutes* or dedicated cycleways sheltered from all motor traffic, often combined with footpaths and bridal paths. One of the most interesting is the **Avenue Verte** in the Seine-Maritime, a disused rail line that so far runs from Dieppe to near Forges-les-Eaux (*see* p.173). It is hoped to extend it to Paris, and it is 'twinned' with the Cuckoo Trail in East Sussex, so at some point it will in theory be possible to walk or cycle along green paths (but with a little water in between) all the way from London to Paris. Further west, the Manche *département* has a very extensive range of *véloroutes* and **Voies Vertes**, 'green ways' – some on the old pilgrim paths to Mont St-Michel – and in Ille-et-Vilaine a canal has been cleared providing a tranquil water, cycle and footpath route from the River Rance near St-Malo through Rennes to southern Brittany. All the *département* tourist boards (*see* p.22) have comprehensive – and very user-friendly – guides to all the 'green way' projects in their respective areas.

On Foot

France has over 60,000 kilometres of long distance footpaths or *sentiers de Grandes Randonnées* (GRs), and walking facilities are as keenly maintained as are cycle tracks – many paths, like the *Avenue Verte* or the Manche's *Voies Vertes* (*see* above), combine both. GR paths, indicated by red-and-white striped signs, are easy to find, and there are also many good map-guides to them available, such as the *Topoguides* series. In many places it's easy to walk a stretch of one, then cut off onto other paths to make a circuit. As well as GRs there are shorter *Petites Randonnées* (PRs), usually indicated by single yellow or green stripes, plus *sentiers de Grandes Randonnées de Pays* (GRPs), marked by a red and yellow stripe, and many variants between them. Some of the most beautiful routes are the coastal footpaths: the GR21 between Le Tréport and Le Havre (120km) takes in the cliffs of Fécamp and Etretat, and the wonderful GR223 goes all the way around the edge of the Cap de la Hague and the Cotentin peninsula.

As with cycle tracks, *département* tourist boards have full guides to all their footpaths, and the Manche has been especially enthusiastic in extending long-distance routes and re-opening pilgrim paths to Mont St-Michel.

In addition to these longer paths, every local tourist office has guides to attractive walks in their area, from short strolls to treks of a few kilometres. They're usually very well-produced, easy to use, and often available in English.

Disabled Travellers

France may have been relatively late in expanding access for all, but a great deal more has been done in the last few years. Of most interest to visitors is the fact that serious attention has been given to opening up accommodation for disabled people, and as a result many hotels and even many *chambres d'hôtes* B&Bs now offer fully adapted – and attractive – ground-floor rooms and so on. Tourist offices and the *chambres d'hôtes* agencies (see p.22) can provide details, and indicate disabled access in their brochures and listings.

For travelling to France, the Tunnel has great advantages, as all the ferries still have many steps, and often awkwardly-located lifts.

Health and Emergencies

In a medical emergency (*un cas d'urgence médicale*), take the person concerned to the local hospital. You can also call the local *SOS Médecin*s, the number of which will be in the phone book. If you have a minor emergency in a rural area, go to the nearest chemist, as pharmacists are trained in first aid. They also have addresses of local doctors (*docteurs* or *médecins*), with lists of those who speak English, and of emergency clinics (*services des consultations externes*).

All EU citizens are entitled to use the French health system, but to do so they should have an E111 form, which in the UK is obtainable free from health centres and post offices.

Emergency Numbers
Ambulance (SAMU), t 15
Police and ambulance, t 17
Fire, t 18

However, under the French system you, like most French people, still have to pay upfront for medical treatment, and later reclaim most of the cost. At the end of a consultation, make sure the doctor gives you the necessary form, properly filled out. The leaflet that comes with the E111 explains how to reclaim the money.

To avoid this sort of bureaucracy it can just be better to rely on private travel insurance, which also covers you for theft, lost property and other potential problems.

Money and Banks

French banks usually open Mon–Fri 8.30am–12.30pm (or 9–12 noon) and 1.30–4pm. Some branches open on Saturdays, in which case they will be closed on Monday. All close early the day before a public holiday, and on the holiday itself will be firmly shut. All banks with a *change* sign will exchange foreign currency or travellers' cheques for euros, usually at better rates than *bureaux de change* (and far better than in hotels); you will need your passport for any transaction. The cheapest places of all to change cash are main post offices, which don't charge commission.

However, the ample supply of ATM cashpoints often makes using them with a credit or debit card the most convenient – and often the cheapest – way of getting money. Major cards are very widely accepted, and used, across France. However, in smaller hotels and restaurants, and *chambres d'hôtes* (B&Bs), the owners may not take cards, so it's advisable to have cash, travellers' cheques or other source of money as well, and not rely on cards alone. Take note that self-service petrol stations and bridge toll booths do not accept foreign cards.

Opening Hours, Museums and National Holidays

Many **shops and supermarkets** now open continuously Tues–Sat 9/10–7/7.30, but businesses in smaller towns still close for lunch (12/12.30–2/3 or, in summer, till 4). With local exceptions, nearly all shops are also closed on Mondays. In many towns, Sunday morning is a big shopping period. **Markets** usually function mornings only, and pack up by about 1pm.

National Holidays

1 January New Year's Day
Easter Sunday March or April
Easter Monday March or April
1 May *Fête du Travail* (Labour Day)
8 May VE Day, 1945
Ascension Day usually end of May
Pentecost (Whitsun) and the following
  Monday end May or early June
14 July Bastille Day
15 August Feast of the Assumption
1 November All Saints'
11 November Remembrance Day
  (First World War Armistice)
25 December Christmas Day

Most **museums** close for lunch and on one day a week, nearly always **Monday** or **Tuesday**, and sometimes for all November or all winter. Hours change by season: longer summer hours begin in May or June and run to the end of September – usually. **Churches** are usually open all day, but might only open for Mass. On French **national holidays**, banks, shops and many museums close, but most restaurants will be open.

Post, Phones and Internet

Post offices, the *PTT* or *Bureaux de Poste*, are easily indentified by a blue-bird-on-yellow logo. In cities they open Mon–Fri 8am–7pm, and Sat 8am–12 noon; in villages, offices may open later, break for lunch, and close at 4.30–5pm. Stamps are also sold in *tabacs*.

Nearly all public telephones have switched from coins to *télécartes*, which you can buy at any post office or *tabac*, valid for 50 or 120 *unités*; 120 currently cost around €15. UK and Irish mobile phones work fine in France so long as they have a roaming facility, but check your service provider's charges.

The French phone system has eliminated area codes, so you must dial the whole 10-digit number wherever you are in the country. Mobile numbers begin with 06. To **call France from abroad**, the international code is 33, and then drop the first '0' of the number. To **call from France**, dial 00, then the country code (UK **44**; US and Canada **1**; Ireland **353**; Australia **61**; New Zealand **64**), and then the local code (minus the 0 in UK numbers) and number.

France has been peculiarly slow in opening up access to the **Internet**, and Net cafés are far scarcer (and more expensive) than elsewhere in Europe, and very rare outside cities. Don't expect to be able to check email with ease.

Tourist Information

France has some of the world's best visitor information services. Every city and town, and many villages, have an information office (*Office de Tourisme* or *Syndicat d'Initiative*). The main bodies coordinating their work are the **CDTs**, the tourist offices of each *département*, which produce a torrent of useful literature on everything possible in their area – walking guides, cycle hire, farm food producers – most of it now in English, and all for free. Some CDTs also coordinate interesting, good-value short break packages. It's now easy to contact CDTs directly, as all have good websites, in French and English. The CDTs listed here will be the best port of call when looking for extra information on areas covered in this guide.

CDTs –
Comités Départementaux de Tourisme
CDT-Pas-de-Calais, t 03 21 10 34 60,
    www.pas-de-calais.com. Chaps. 4–6, 9–11.
CDT-Nord, t 03 20 57 59 59, *www.cdt-nord.fr.*
    Chaps. 7–8.
CDT-Somme, t 03 22 71 22 71,
    www.somme-tourisme.com. Chaps. 12–13.
CDT-Seine-Maritime, t 02 35 12 10 10,
    www.seine-maritime-tourisme.com.
    Chaps. 14–19.
CDT-Eure, t 02 32 62 04 27, *www.cdt-eure.fr.*
    Chaps. 19–20.
CDT-Calvados, t 02 31 27 90 30,
    www.calvados-tourisme.com. Chaps. 21-27.
CDT-Manche, t 02 33 05 98 70,
    www.manchetourisme.com. Chaps. 28–32.
CDT-Haute-Bretagne-Ille-et-Vilaine, t 02 99 78
    47 47, *www.bretagne35.com.* Chap. 33.

French Tourist Offices Abroad
UK: Maison de France, 178 Piccadilly, London
    W1J 9AL, **t** 09068 244 123,
    www.franceguide.com
USA: 444 Madison Av, New York, NY 10022,
    t 410 286 8310, *www.francetourism.com*

Where to Stay

The accommodation listed in this guide can only be a selection: every place chosen has some particular attraction, from grand luxury to rustic character. Most divide into hotels or *chambres d'hôtes*, French bed-and-breakfast. One difference: **hotel prices** listed usually **do not include breakfast**, which is charged separately (usually for €6–9); in *chambres d'hôtes*, prices, **breakfast is nearly always included**.

France has a great many hotel chains. One worth recognizing is **Logis de France** (*www.logis-de-france.fr*), with its green-and-yellow chimney logo. *Logis* are not really a chain but an association, of independent, usually family-run hotels with resident proprietors. They can be luxurious, or quite basic, but *Logis* membership nearly always guarantees a reliable level of comfort and individual service.

Chambres d'hôtes – B&B

Chambres d'hôtes are enormously popular in France. They are often a better choice than hotels – they usually have much more character, are often in fabulous old houses in beautiful locations, and tend to be far better value. Many *chambres d'hôtes* are real labours of love. Beyond those listed in this guide, tourist offices have local lists, but the best sources of information are the main federations to which most (but not all) are affiliated, *Gîtes de France* and *Clévacances*. Officially, *Gîtes* are supposed to operate in the countryside, *Clévacances* in towns, but there is a lot of blurring between the two. Both have rating systems for their members, from 1–4 *épis* (ears of corn) or *clés* (keys) respectively. Anywhere with 3 or 4 of either is likely to be very enjoyable, and anywhere with the extra label *de charme* will be, well, charming. *Fleur de Soleil* is a recently created association limited only to *maisons de charme*. All these organizations have central booking services, but if you can handle any French it's best to call or email a B&B directly. Good *chambres d'hôtes* need to be booked well ahead, especially for summer.
Féderation Nationale Clévacances,
    t 05 61 13 55 66, *www.clevacances.com*
Fleur de Soleil, *www.fleur-soleil.tm.fr*
Gîtes de France, t 01 49 70 75 75,
    www.gites-de-france.fr

Unavoidable:
Calais

04

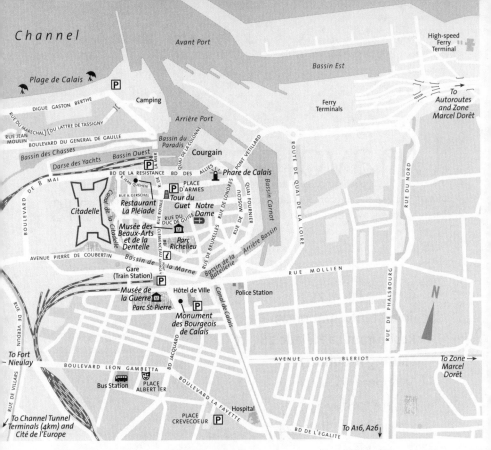

Ah, Calais. For Britain, the best-known, essential point of contact with France and Continental Europe. A city rarely praised and rarely loved.

It's a little strange that Calais should be so prominent as a gateway to France, a country so often associated with golden sunsets by southern rivers, café-lined neo-classical squares, Gothic cathedrals, tranquil country towns, a sense of style, chic and *je ne sais quoi* in all things. Calais doesn't fit in with any of the above. It's a gritty little working-class city, with a high level of unemployment and famously argumentative dockers, part of a workaday France without many airs and graces. Calais will never be put on any list of *villes de charme* or win any competition for the *ville plus belle* or *plus fleurie*. The rest of France has tended to regard it as a utilitarian facility even more than the British have, and craggy Calais has only gained a little more national prominence in the last few years through the efforts of its heroic football team, the oddly-named CRUFC (from *Calais Racing Union Football Club*), the still all-amateur side that has regularly taken on and defeated top-flight professional teams, providing a whole new source of local pride.

It's not that Calais isn't a historic town. Rather, Calais has suffered from an excess of history, of the violent kind that has swept away whole centuries of its architecture, often to be replaced by whatever could be put up most easily. And this history has always, inescapably, been bound up with Britain.

Most recently, of course, Calais is best-known in Britain as Europe's largest discount booze store, which only adds to its functional feel. If all you want to do in Calais is find the drinks warehouses, hypermarkets or shopping malls, fill up the car boot and leave, then modern Calais's road system is organized to make this very easy to do. However, if you take the time to wander into town, central Calais also offers plenty of things to see and do in a day. As well as its megastores it has rows of bars and cafés and their pavement terraces, and beneath the ferrytown surface there are all the everyday necessities of French life – *boulangeries, pâtisseries, traiteurs*, street markets. It has a lovely, unsung beach, stretching westwards through the dunes of Blériot-Plage to the cliffs of Cap Blanc-Nez. And one very good reason for lingering in Calais can be to sample food and cuisine that – even today – you just won't find done the same way at home, for the city has a quite exceptional range of fine places to eat, better than you might find in many higher chic-rated destinations, and enough to justify a visit all by themselves. Of the impressive selection, one of the very best is M Eric Mémain's **La Pléiade**, a discreet little restaurant in the heart of the old town.

Getting There

The **ferry terminals** are all on the east side of Calais harbour. From the main exit to the terminal area, follow the *Toutes Directions* sign to the first roundabout and take the exit right for *Centre Ville* to head directly for the old town centre and the Place d'Armes; to go straight to the big out-of-town stores, turn left at the same roundabout and follow the ring road east and then south instead. This road also leads very directly to a major intersection with the two *autoroutes* passing Calais, the A16 (for Dunkerque, Lille, Boulogne, Normandy) and the A26 (Arras, Paris).

The **Channel Tunnel** is west of the city at Coquelles. From the Shuttle terminal for cars, you have the option of heading straight into the Cité de l'Europe shopping centre, joining the A16 *autoroute* and the Calais ring road, or following *Centre Ville* signs into town.

The main artery of Calais's old centre is the north-south street that's called at different points Rue de la Mer, Rue Royale and Boulevard Clemenceau, and which crosses the main square, Place d'Armes. Parking is not usually that difficult in the city centre, and there are large car parks in Place d'Armes, on Boulevard de la Résistance and just behind the beach. Rue Jean Quéhen, where La Pléiade restaurant is located, is the first turning on the right off Rue de la Mer, heading away from the port and the sea.

Ferry companies provide complimentary or very cheap buses between their terminals and the town centre for **foot passengers**. Calais also has good **rail** links to Paris, the rest of France and other destinations from the Gare Centrale, near the Hôtel de Ville. Some London–Paris and London–Brussels Eurostar trains also stop at Calais-Fréthun station outside the city, just south of the Channel Tunnel; there are free bus transfers (as well as taxis) between the Gare Centrale and Fréthun.

Calais has plentiful **car hire** offices, mostly on or near Place d'Armes. For details of some companies, *see* chapter 3. **Taxis** are quite easy to find in the city centre, but you can also phone for a cab on **t** 03 21 97 13 14.

Tourist Information

Blériot-Plage: Route Nationale, **t** 03 21 34 97 98.
Calais: 12 Bd Clemenceau, **t** 03 21 96 62 40, *www.calais-cotedopale.com*.

Excursions

Navi-Boat, Port de Plaisance, Remparts de la Citadelle, **t** 03 21 19 65 45. Small boats and five-seater pedalos for hire to sail up and down on Calais's canals. Departure point is by the Citadelle and Pont Freycinet on Bassin de la Marne. *Open mid-Mar–mid-June, mid-Sept–mid-Nov Sat, Sun 2–7pm; mid-June–mid-Sept daily 10am–8pm.*

La Pléiade

32 Rue Jean Quéhen, t 03 21 34 03 70, f 03 21 34 03 13, www.lapleiade.com.
Open Tues–Sat 12–2.30 and 7.30–9.30; closed Sun (except special holidays)
and Mon. Menus €22–50; carte average €46.

The Rue Jean Quéhen is, to be frank, a typically plain street of plain, post-war central Calais, a curving grey line of offices and apartment blocks off the Place d'Armes. Look along it, though, and you can find – behind a shop-like frontage that does not initially look much more distinctive than the rest of the street – a little haven of delights, an opportunity to enjoy a whole array of rare pleasures. Inside La Pléiade, the traditional French restaurant comforts and customs are properly and smartly maintained: neat, classic décor, bowls of flowers on the tables, crisp linen, correct table settings. This traditionalism seems a little surprising, for Mme Delphine Mémain and her staff, who greet and serve with charm, style and attentiveness, are all young. The clientele – which usually includes a few Brits – is a wide mix, from families and business groups to young locals in jeans and sweaters who drop in for a quick but superior lunch.

Neither trendy nor inflexibly old-fashioned, it's a restaurant with a certain timeless sense of intimacy. The first introduction to chef-proprietor Eric Mémain's cooking comes with the *mises-en-bouche*, the appetisers. One could very enjoyably undertake a whole study of *mises-en-bouche* in fine French restaurants, which in a suitably idle moment you could argue are the true test of any cook who really wants to be an individual and creative chef. Often experiments on the way to the creation of new dishes, they can be little jewels of taste that leave you begging for more, wonderfully crafted miniatures that perfectly demonstrate all the dedicated trouble-taking over tiny details that is at the heart of the best French cooking. On a summer evening, M. Mémain's appetisers began with very fine, cheesy pastries, followed by a 'crab cappuccino', an exquisitely refined, multi-layered seafood reduction in a little cup.

A Calais native, Eric Mémain worked in Paris, Switzerland and various places around France before opening La Pléiade in the early 1990s. He is well schooled in the traditional dishes of northern France – fish stews, classic sauces – but is also always experimenting, trying out new combinations, with a style that can seem radical and too open-ended to some conservative locals. And, throughout, diners reap the rewards of the same hugely impressive attention to detail, an absolute refusal to cut corners, above all in sourcing the finest possible ingredients. Fine freshly-landed fish and seafood are among Calais's great assets, and a first course of superbly fresh langoustines steamed and marinated with *algues, nem de chou* and *laitue de mer* – different seaweeds – and an exquisite smoked seafood mousse tastes almost extravagantly of the sea. To follow, fillets of sea bream delicately arranged in *mille-feuille* are cooked with the lightest of touches to take nothing from the quality of the fish, and served with a spiced onion compote, a smooth *mousseline* of fennel and a little savoury mix of breadcrumbs and Corsican sausage, creating whole panoramas of flavour on the tongue. Meat main courses frequently feature the Pas-de-Calais's celebrated, strongly-flavoured Licques chickens, often artfully combined with seafood.

This is exceptionally refined, subtle food, made with an extremely skilful and delicate touch, imaginative but never trivial or unbalanced. And, while prices have risen in the last few years, it's also excellent value, given the painstaking care involved in every dish.

To go with them there's a well-selected list of wines, all perfectly served. The final details are as quietly sybaritic and original as the earlier courses. On my last visit, a cheese course that looked like a little oriental sculpture was followed by a *pré-dessert* of *écume des petits pois* with almond and mint pastries – a surprising (and enjoyable) use of peas in a pudding. The full dessert was a variation on pineapple, which arrived baked, candied, as a coulis, in a *beignet* fritter and in a truly fabulous sorbet, and fine coffee was accompanied by notably fruity petit-fours. And after that, when you finally leave this little pocket of luxury and head off into the streets outside you might find that poor old, much-decried Calais has taken on a whole new glow.

Touring Around

Calais has two main parts. The medieval city of Calais was a fortified town built on a patch of hard ground surrounded by some of the many unstable watercourses that crisscross northern France and Flanders, which long ago were made into solid canals that ringed the old city like a moat and converted it into a quite distinct little island, as can easily be seen on any map. Directly to the south and some way inland there grew up an initially entirely separate community of St-Pierre, centred roughly where the junction of Boulevards Jacquard and Lafayette is today, which expanded greatly with 19th-century industrialization. Both halves were officially joined together in one city in 1885, and since then have been surrounded by a large late-20th-century urban sprawl. The old city on the island is sometimes referred to as Calais-Nord, while the 'new' city in the former St-Pierre is Calais-Sud.

Not that either of them appears especially old to the visitor today. This is because Calais gives you a rapid and striking introduction to one of the less-publicized but pervasive features of northern France, 1940s reconstruction architecture. It is not widely appreciated in the English-speaking world just how much the north of France was devastated in the two World Wars. Whole cities from Normandy to Flanders were fought over and bombarded two or three times in just a few years, while others, especially transport hubs, were repeatedly bombed. The old quarters of the northern cities, based on brick and wood, burnt very easily when the firing started. Afterwards, some towns were the site of often astonishing restoration programmes – most remarkably Arras and St-Malo. Others were restored in large part, such as Rouen. After the Second World War, however, there were just too many places in urgent need of reconstruction and resources were too thin for this kind of work to go on everywhere, and entire districts or towns were rebuilt in a fairly uniform, practical style of straight lines, sloping tiled roofs and light grey stone or concrete walls. St-Lô and Tilly-sur-Seulles in Normandy are almost complete reconstruction towns. And one of the largest reconstruction cities is Calais.

Calais' particular catastrophe came in May 1940, when British and French troops were besieged within the city's centuries-old fortifications by relentless German air and artillery bombardment. The last-ditch defence of Calais significantly delayed the German advance, and played a major (some say essential) part in gaining time for the evacuation of the main Allied force from Dunkerque to the east. It was also one of the better examples of Franco-British cooperation, with heroic incidents such as that of the '1,000 volunteers of Calais', the French sailors who, offered the possibility of evacuation, volunteered to stay behind to fight as infantry; if France in general had not been so concerned to forget the whole sorry saga of 1940 they would be more widely commemorated. Calais was fought over again in September 1944, when Canadian troops ejected the Germans. By that time, virtually all of the historic architecture in the old city had been destroyed. Had this not happened, visitors to the city today, instead of complaining about its greyness, would probably praise the charms of a town that curiously contained the largest (and only) concentration of English Tudor architecture in France.

Calais is a relative latecomer among the Channel ports, and is first mentioned in documents, as a subsidiary community of the much more important town of Boulogne, in 1180. In 1223 Philippe *Hurepel* or 'Frizzy Hair', made Count of Boulogne by his father Philippe Auguste of France, first began to build up Calais as a fortified town, with a castle on its western side. It soon became an important link in the wool trade between England and Flanders, and grew fairly rapidly in the following century. More difficult contacts with the English came with the Hundred Years' War. In September 1346 Edward III, fresh from his victory at Crécy, besieged Calais. The city held out doggedly for all but a year until August 1347, when the starving *Calaisiens* asked for surrender terms. A vengeful Edward said that he would spare the people of Calais if six of its leading citizens, the famous 'Burghers of Calais', would come to present the keys of the city to him as beggars dressed only in their shirts. He sentenced the six to death, but was obliged to be merciful by the pleadings of his wife, Philippa of Hainault. Most of Calais' population, though, were expelled from the city, which would remain in English hands for the next 211 years.

It suffered a second, unsuccessful, siege in 1436, this time at the hands of the Duke of Burgundy, who had fallen out with his former English allies. It was still a significant English possession in the early 16th century, and both Henry VIII and Mary Tudor sponsored substantial building work in the city. Then in 1558 the Duke of Guise, in a surprise attack, took Calais for France, supposedly leaving Queen Mary to die with Calais written on her heart. This was not the end of Calais' travails, though, for it then became caught up in France's wars with the Spaniards in the Netherlands to the east. A Spanish army took Calais in a bloody assault in 1596, and it was attacked again in 1638 and 1651, before the French frontier moved a safe distance away under Louis XIV. It then settled into its role as a port of passage for the English, and further major changes did not come until after the Napoleonic wars, when Calais – or rather, at that time, St-Pierre – became an important centre for the making of lace, helped by several families of English lace-makers from Nottingham who settled here. The arrival of a railway line from Paris in the 1840s, ahead of those to its competitors, cemented its position as the busiest of the French Channel ports. It also developed considerably as a commercial and fishing port, and was an early hub of the French labour movement, hence those obstreperous dockers.

Any visit to central Calais today has a natural focus in the **'old' city**, and particularly Rue de la Mer–Rue Royale–Boulevard Clemenceau, the main shopping, café and restaurant thoroughfare. The main square, **Place d'Armes**, still has its historic name but is the kind of place in Calais that – try as you might – does little to help you be nice about it. Surrounded by grey shop-fronts, it never quite seems sure whether it's a real square or just a car park. A plaque by a patch of grass indicates the site of an English Tudor belfry that was built for Mary I and destroyed in 1940.

Looming up by the corner of Rue Royale there is a remarkable survivor of many battles, the battered but impressive watchtower the **Tour du Guet** (38.5m tall), which has a vaguely Gothic base that formed part of the first defences of Calais built for Philippe Frizzy Hair in 1224, but which leads up bizarrely to a completely out-of-style bell tower, added in 1770. From the platform on the first storey Jean de Vienne, Governor of Calais, announced Edward III's surrender conditions to the people during the siege of 1347. A short walk from the far right corner of the Place d'Armes (looking from Rue Royale) is the 14th–15th-century church of **Notre-Dame**, which has the distinction of being the only mainly English-perpendicular-style Gothic church in France. Altered many times over the centuries, it's another rare survivor from 1940–44, but was very badly damaged, and is often closed as part of its long-drawn-out restoration (check with the tourist office for any times when it may be open). General de Gaulle was married here, in 1921.

A few streets to the north on Boulevard des Alliés is Calais' lighthouse, the **Phare de Calais** (*open Oct–May Wed only 2–5.30, Sat, Sun and public hols 10–12 and 2–5.30; during winter school hols also open Mon–Fri 2–5.30; June–Sept Mon–Fri 2–6.30, Sat, Sun and public hols 10–12 and 2–6.30; adm*). Towering up strangely from the midst of the old town, it provides panoramic views over the port, the surrounding coast and cliffs and across the Channel to Kent, and is one of the most perennially popular local attractions. The triangular **Courgain** district, between Boulevard des Alliés and the harbour, was one of the most traditional fishermen's quarters of Calais, and in post-1945 reconstruction an attempt was made to conserve something of its community feel in its very unusual apartment blocks, linked by small squares and passageways. The area still contains several good small fish restaurants, especially along the *quais* facing the Bassin du Paradis, where there's also a small open-air fish market.

However, the greatest monument of old Calais is reached by cutting back to the main street and following any of the streets on the western side of Royale/de la Mer to the end. This will take you to a broad esplanade and the moat-canal surrounding the massive low walls of the **Citadelle**, reached by a bridge. It was begun by the Duke of Guise in 1560, taking over and extending the site of the old castle, to ensure that the English would not be able to win the town back again. Subsequent rulers and generals extended it several times. The defenders of Calais made their last stand here in 1940, when its walls, like those of many other old French fortresses, showed themselves remarkably able to survive 20th-century technology, even though most of

Shopping

For big-scale shopping, there are three major concentrations around Calais, with more stores scattered around the ring road and the main streets near the ferry port. The **Cité de l'Europe**, one of the continent's largest malls, is right next to the Tunnel terminal and has a Toys'R'Us, Tesco, Oddbins, Le Chais, a vast Carrefour hypermarket and many smaller shops. Near **Fort Nieulay**, roughly between the Tunnel and Calais town, lies another clutch of stores, including Sainsbury's and an Auchan hypermarket. A third area is in the industrial estates on the east side of the ring road, especially the **Zone Marcel Dorêt**, which you soon pass if you turn left from the ferry terminals (from the Tunnel, follow the A16 and the ring road in the opposite direction, anticlockwise). This is where you find the biggest discount wine warehouses, like Eastenders. In general, French-owned Calais wine stores concentrate on French wines, while British-owned outlets have the multi-national range seen in Britain.

Inside Calais, high-street shopping is concentrated mainly around Boulevards Jacquard and Lafayette, while there are many individual food shops on or around Rue Royale in the old town. Calais still holds traditional street **markets**, in Place d'Armes (*Wed and Sat mornings*), and (with more stalls) in Place Crèvecœur, off Bd Lafayette (*Thurs and Sat*).

Calais ✉ 62100

Le Bar à Vins, 52 Place d'Armes, **t** 03 21 96 96 31. For a complete change from the big wine warehouses search out this great little shop and convivial bar, where you can taste before you buy. Luc Gille stocks carefully chosen wines from small producers around France – including many organics – plus a still more select range of liqueurs and fine Normandy ciders. M Gille speaks good English and loves to talk wine; you won't find the obvious labels here, but can make great discoveries. Prices begin very low.

Le Chais, 40 Rue de Phalsbourg, **t** 03 21 97 88 56, *www.lechais-calais.com*. Long-established local wine merchant (also at Cité Europe) that has gone into the big-scale trade. The range of wines (with only a few beers) is entirely French and a bit conservative, but it's often Calais's best for classic burgundies and champagnes. *Open daily 10–8, Cité Europe 9.30–6.30.*

Charcuterie Goetgheluck, 39 Rue Royale, **t** 03 21 34 54 52. Bright traditional *charcuterie-traiteur* selling enticing prepared dishes, and a particularly good range of French sausages, all own-made.

Eastenders, 14 Rue Gustave Courbet, Zone Marcel Dorêt, **t** 03 21 34 53 33. The king of cash-and-carry, in a huge warehouse off the ring road (plus two other outlets): popular, high-turnover wines dominate, but it's hard to beat on price. *Open 24 hours daily.*

Gastronomie du Sud-Ouest, 111 Bd Lafayette, **t** 03 21 34 83 37. A very pretty and distinctive *épicerie* with fine-quality truffles, Armagnacs and other gourmet specialities of southwest France as well as more local northern cheeses and other treats.

La Maison du Fromage et des Vins, 1 Rue André Gerschel, **t** 03 21 34 44 72. Another alternative to the supermarkets: an attractive, individual shop just off the Place d'Armes that's a great place to stock up on high-quality cheeses, fine wines and other delicacies before boarding a ferry or Shuttle. The Crespo family also make up spectacular cheese platters to order. *Closed Tues.*

Marché aux Vins Perardel/Perardel Wine Market, Rue Marcel Dorêt, **t** 03 21 97 21 22, *www.perardel.com*. Very big French-run wine warehouse (with a few beers) that's part of a nationwide chain. Not many rare labels or *grand crus*, but it's one of the best for good mid-range French wines at very decent prices. *Open Mon–Sat 8.15–7.45, Sun 9–7.45.*

Royal Dentelle, 106 Bd Jacquard, **t** 03 21 96 68 40. For a very traditional souvenir of Calais: handkerchiefs, lingerie, veils and other gift items, and fine lace sold by the metre.

Wine & Beer World, Rue de Judée, Zone Marcel Dorêt, **t** 03 21 97 63 00, *www.wineandbeer.co.uk*. Part of the UK's Majestic Wines group, this British company has helpful staff, reliable quality and wines from every continent. Their special offers are always worth checking out, and you can pre-order online to pick up when you get to Calais. This is their largest Calais outlet (*open daily 7am–10pm*); there is another by the Tunnel at Coquelles (*open daily 8–8*).

the buildings within them were destroyed. Today it's a very atmospheric park: an idea of its awesome size can be gained from the fact that inside it there is an entire sports stadium, built in 1965. Calais also has another unusual fortress-park inside the 17th-century walls of **Fort Nieulay**, near the western end of the main through-road through town, not far from the Tunnel terminal (*open April–Oct only*).

The old city also contains the **Musée des Beaux-Arts et de la Dentelle** (*open Mon, Wed–Fri 10–12 and 2–5.30, Sat 10–12 and 2–6.30, Sun 2–6.30; closed Tues; adm exc Weds*), beside the Parc Richelieu at the southern end of Rue Royale, housed true to form in a dull 1960s building. The 'Museum of Fine Arts and Lace' is really three, not two, museums in one. Best-known is its sculpture collection, centred on the studies by Rodin for the *Burghers of Calais* monument nearby, which are interestingly exhibited alongside studies for similar monuments by more conventional sculptors of the time like Eude, Maillol and Carpeaux – making Rodin look all the more radical by comparison. The Rodin collection also includes an impressive set of small busts, with a very fine self-portrait and one of his protégée/lover Camille Claudel. Secondly, there is an unusual picture collection, from engagingly odd 17th- and 18th-century naive paintings from the Calais region to a few works by major artists such as Picasso and Dubuffet, although the museum's more important contemporary works often seem to be somewhere else on loan. It also hosts regular shows of contemporary art. The largest section of the museum, however, is that given over to lace-making. An enormous amount of information is given (in French) on the history and techniques of lace in general and Calais lace in particular, while on show there are beautiful pieces of 19th-century lace, entire Belle Epoque outfits, theatrical costumes, wedding dresses, underwear and examples of the use of lace by couture designers from Worth through Dior and Givenchy to Christian Lacroix, all of which could make it quite a sexy museum if it was displayed with a little more style. On a more industrial level there's a giant 19th-century Jacquard lace-maker's loom. And, oddly placed in the middle of the lace section, perhaps because there was no obvious other place to put it, is a remarkable 1904 relief model of Calais, showing the city as it was before 1940, and with the old and new towns still clearly separate.

From the museum a short walk southwards down Boulevard Clemenceau, past the tourist office, will take you to the large bridge that connects the old and new towns. Immediately visible on the other side and to the left is Calais's spectacular **Hôtel de Ville**, built in Flemish-revival style with a giant belfry and clocktower, visible for miles, which has long been a symbol of the city to ferry passengers arriving in the harbour. The town hall was begun in the 1890s to mark the joining of old Calais and St-Pierre, but was not finished until 1925; this was one building that was carefully restored after the Second World War. In the park-like square in front of it is Calais' most famous and precious monument, the first casting of Rodin's extraordinary statue of the six *Bourgeois de Calais*, the Burghers of Calais, unveiled in 1894. When the city fathers commissioned it at the time of the 'unification' of Calais they were probably hoping for a conventional piece of patriotic sculpture, exalting the heroism of the six citizens who were ready to sacrifice themselves for their community. They got something quite different: it has no conventional heroism in it at all, but an immense, quiet intensity. It is also completely different from conventional group monuments in that each of the six figures is entirely individual, and they seem almost to be choreographed against each other, and yet still form a whole with a special sense of drama. Especially awe-inspiring is the figure of the leader, Eustache de St-Pierre, who appears to loom out from among the others, like an emphatic figure of wisdom.

Across the street to the west there is another, more bizarre monument, a huge, lushly romantic **Monument aux Morts**, epitomizing the kind of melodramatic patriotic sculpture that Rodin avoided. It commemorates not the usual dead, since it was put up well before the First World War, but the fallen in all sorts of obscure colonial conflicts around France's empire during the 19th century, from Indochina to Madagascar, and passing by the Paris Commune of 1871. Behind the monument is the neatly maintained Parc St-Pierre, half-hidden inside which is the entrance to the **Musée de la Guerre** (*open mid-Feb–Mar Mon, Wed–Sun 11–5; April and Sept daily 11–5.30; May–Aug daily 10–6; Oct–mid-Nov Mon, Wed–Sun 12–5; last admission 45mins before closing; adm*), Calais' 1939–45 war museum. It is so hidden because it occupies the concrete bunker that was once the command post for the German Navy in the Calais sector, which gives it extra atmosphere. Inside, there's a huge amount to see, with memorabilia of the two battles of Calais in 1940 and 1944, life under the Occupation, the German coastal defences, Calais when it was a major British base during the 1914–18 war and many other aspects of the city in the World Wars.

Below the park and the Hôtel de Ville, Boulevard Jacquard and, further down, Boulevard Lafayette form the high streets of non-ferry orientated Calais, with all the everyday department stores and shoe and clothes shops that you find in an everyday French city. The two boulevards meet at **Place Albert Ier**, surrounded by busy, lively bars, which is better known to locals as Place du Théâtre because it is dominated by the very grand Beaux-Arts-style theatre, opened in 1905. In front of the theatre there is a very large and striking monument to Joseph-Marie Jacquard, whose invention of the Jacquard punch-card loom and its adaptation to lace-making made this district's fortune in the 19th century. The Jacquard loom was something of an Anglo-French collaboration, for he was greatly aided by two British engineers, Martyn and Ferguson, who are duly commemorated on the monument.

South of Boulevard Lafayette there are residential and shopping streets, and the stadium where the mighty amateur footballers of the CRUFC play their games. In general, though, there isn't much more to explore in the new town. It's a better bet on a decent day to head back through the old town to the beach, one of Calais's lesser-known attractions. It's a fine, old-fashioned strip of sand, with good restaurants and all the proper French crêpe- and *frite*-stands alongside it. There's no limit to it at the western end, where it runs into the less-developed beaches and dunes at Blériot-Plage and Sangatte, which are popular for sand-yachting. As the day draws in, if you're not due for a meal at one of the better restaurants in town, you can always head back to the Rue de la Mer, old Calais' bar and café row. It has English pubs, a place just called *Le Pub*, a giant brasserie called Le Bistrot, and a North African restaurant with belly dancers. It's not the most chic place in France, but it's far from dull.

Where to Stay

Calais ✉ 62100

Hôtel Meurice, 5–7 Rue Edmond Roche,
t 03 21 34 57 03, *www.hotel-meurice.fr*
(*double rooms €75–€120*). The classic Grand
Hotel of Calais, where the famous and the
eminently respectable have been stopping
over on their way to or from their ferries
since 1771 (although the present building is
mostly modern, constructed to replace the
original destroyed in 1940). It offers traditional, carpeted comfort, although the
rooms themselves have no great character.
It's popular mainly with an older, well-
heeled clientele. The similarly venerable-
looking, wood-panelled restaurant,
La Diligence, provides traditionally
elaborate *haute cuisine* (*menus €15–70*).
Le George V, 36 Rue Royale, **t** 02 21 97 68 00,
www.georgev-calais.com (*double rooms
€69–87*). Another of Calais's historic hotels,
providing reliable comfort and convenience
combined with a rather livelier and more
relaxed atmosphere than at the Meurice.
The 42 rooms are bright and spacious, and
come in two categories, *standard* and
supérieure (with bigger bathrooms). It has a
choice of two **restaurants** on the ground
floor (*see* p.34).
Hôtel Pacific, 40 Rue du Duc de Guise, **t** 03 21
34 50 24, *duhamel.marc@wanadoo.fr*
(*double rooms €30–46*). A popular small
hotel off Rue Royale that's one of the city's
best-value budget options. The 17 rooms,
spread around a rambling building that's
relatively old for central Calais (and with, so
far, no lift) are plain but comfortable, and
range from some small singles with shower
only to doubles with full bathrooms. There
are also family rooms (*€56 for four*) and a
warm, cosy breakfast room, and M and Mme
Duhamel are quietly hospitable. The Pacific
also has some indoor parking.

Blériot-Plage ✉ 62231

Hôtel Les Dunes, 48 Route Nationale,
t 03 21 34 54 30, *www.les-dunes.com* (*double
rooms €32–62*). A very pleasant small *Logis*
hotel a short walk from the broad and
bracing beach in the suburb of Blériot-Plage,
between Calais and the Tunnel, this is a
long-standing favourite with British
overnighters in the area. Rooms vary in size
and so price (most cost €55), but are all
bright and comfortable. Two rooms (a
double and an adjoining room with bunk
beds) can be let together as a family room
(*€87 for four, €103 for five*). Owners the Mené
family are quietly welcoming, the hotel has
a likably cosy feel, and there's also an
excellent **restaurant** (*see* p.34).

Hervelinghen ✉ 62179

La Leulène, 708 Rue Principale, **t** 03 21 82 47 30,
laleulene@aol.com (*rooms €49 for two, €87
for four*). A very pretty converted farm in this
tiny, quiet village, not far from Wissant
*c.*12km west of Calais between the A16 and
the coast. The friendly Mme Petitprez has
three charming B&B rooms, and guests can
relax in a cosy lounge or a lovely garden. A
very peaceful place to stay.

Marck ✉ 62730

Le Manoir de Meldick, 2528 Av du Général
de Gaulle, Le Fort-Vert, **t/f** 03 21 85 74 34,
jeandaniele.houzet@free.fr (*rooms €55 for
two, €70 family room for four*). Popular B&B
in an impressively large 1930s farm in a
peaceful location near the coastal dunes
just outside the hamlet of Fort-Vert (not in
Marck town itself) – but also only a few
minutes east of Calais. The five rooms
include an enormous four-person family
room; all are spacious and attractively
furnished, and there's a large lounge and
breakfast room and well-kept garden. M and
Mme Houzet take good care of their guests.

Peuplingues ✉ 62231

La Flamandrie, Route de Calais, **t** 03 21 85 22 63,
laflamandrie@gofornet.com (*rooms €45–50
for two, €70 for four*). High-standard B&B in
a grand old farm near Peuplingues village,
just a few kilometres west of the Tunnel. The
five very comfortable rooms differ in size but
are all rather like self-contained studios,
with kitchenettes.
Rental of horses and ponies can be arranged
from a centre nearby for rides along the
clifftops. M and Mme Mouchon have
many return customers, so rooms need to be
booked well ahead.

Eating Alternatives

Calais's hotel restaurants have quite a high reputation, notably **La Diligence** in the **Hôtel Meurice** (*see* p.33).

Calais ✉ 62100

Le Grand Bleu, 8 Rue Jean-Pierre Avron, Bassin du Paradis, **t/f** 03 21 97 97 98 (*menus €25–70*). A gourmet restaurant in a homely location, opposite the quayside fish market in the old fishing district of Courgain, on the east side of the port. Chef Michaël Olivier's bright, nautical restaurant serves almost entirely fish and seafood, making the best use of the local catch. The style is straight-forward and unstuffy, but the cooking is very superior. Traditional fish dishes of the Pas-de-Calais like *chaudière* are superbly done here, and there are fabulous *assiettes* and *plateaux* of *fruits de mer* (*from €16*), plus lighter dishes in a similar style for lunch. *Closed Sat lunch and (Oct–May only) Sun.*

Le George V, 36 Rue Royale, **t** 02 21 97 68 00, *www.georgev-calais.com* (*menus €22–46*). The main restaurant at the George V (*see* p.33) is a large, traditional, high-quality hotel dining room, serving classic French cuisine with some sophisticated touches. The hotel's ground floor is divided, though, between the main restaurant and a cheaper, perhaps more family-oriented alternative, **Le Petit Georges**, with a classic bistro-type menu that includes old favourites like duck *à l'orange*, grills or *moules marinières* as well as salads and lighter dishes. *Closed Sat lunch and Sun eve.*

L'Aquar'aile, 255 Rue Jean Moulin, **t** 03 21 34 00 00, *www.aquaraile.com* (*menus €22–38*). The big attraction of this *restaurant panoramique* is its odd location, five floors up at the top of a modern block behind the western end of Calais beach. The views are fabulous, right across the port, along the coast and across the sea to England (be sure to ask for a window table). The food is not always as impressive, but the exuberant platters of fresh seafood, dishes made with Licques chicken and – in the autumn-to-spring season – trout, game and forest mushrooms can be very enjoyable. *Closed Sun eve and Mon.*

Au Côte d'Argent, 1 Digue Gaston Berthe, **t** 03 21 34 68 07, *www.cotedargent.com* (*menus €17–36*). Unmissable at the 'town' end of Calais beach, this classic French seaside restaurant offers panoramic views and fine food. Fish and seafood are naturally highlights on chef Bertrand Lefebvre's menus, but there are also great meats, especially local poultry – Licques chicken, duck, or pigeon. It has many British regulars. *Closed Sun eve and Mon.*

L'Histoire Ancienne, 20 Rue Royale, **t** 03 21 34 11 20, *www.histoire-ancienne.com* (*menus €11–30*). Cosy restaurant with old-style brasserie décor and an able young chef, Patrick Comte, who provides both fine classic dishes and his own creations, such as cucumbers in *fromage blanc* with mint, or skate wings in cream sauce with grapefruit zest, pilau rice and chargrilled potatoes. Great value for such distinctive cooking. *Closed Sun.*

Café de Paris, 72 Rue Royale, **t** 03 21 34 76 84 (*menus €15–28*). Bustling brasserie beside the Place d'Armes that highlights local standbys – *moules frites*, quiches, fish grills, salads. Serving food all afternoon and late-night, it's a good bet for meals outside usual French hours. *Open daily until 1am.*

Au Calice, 55 Bd Jacquard, **t** 03 21 34 51 78 (*menus €13.90–25*). Big, snug and comfort-able brasserie, decorated slightly in Flemish *estaminet* style, that's a fine standby for quick snacks and lighter meals. On offer is a big range of local and Belgian beers, and set menus, *plats du jour* or *flamiches*, omelettes and salads. *Open daily until 2am.*

Blériot-Plage ✉ 62231

Hôtel Les Dunes, 48 Route Nationale, **t** 03 21 34 54 30, *www.les-dunes.com* (*menus €16–38*). M. Philippe Mené, owner of Blériot's Dunes hotel (*see* p.33), is also a highly regarded chef, and his restaurant is of a standard well above that you might expect in a modest *Logis* hotel. Classic local dishes feature strongly, from fresh fish and seafood to Licques chicken. The dining room is very comfortable, prices are reasonable, and after your meal you can clear the head with an enjoyable walk on the beach. *Closed Sun eve except public hols, and (Sept–July) Mon.*

Just Across
the Water:
Boulogne

05

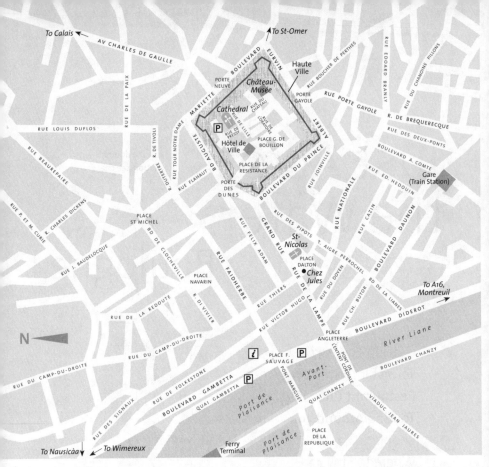

Most of the thousands of people who visit the Pas-de-Calais every year use it just as a supermarket, or as a place to pass through quickly on the way to somewhere else. Of those who want to linger and explore, many are not sure where to choose. Only just west of Calais and the Channel Tunnel, however, there is a beautiful, sweeping coastline of dunes, cliffs, wind-blown coarse grass and long beaches, labelled the *Côte d'Opale* because of the sometimes iridescent, milky-green colour of its waters. Along this coast there is a string of very individual, surprisingly out-of-the-way little beach towns. And just to the south is Boulogne, a town of real charm and personality.

Boulogne is the oldest of all the Channel ports: it was the main harbour for links with Roman Britain, and has at its heart the best-preserved medieval walled town in northern France. Today it's France's most important fishing port; it's also an excellent place to experience *la vie française* and a great shopping destination, with a wonderful, bustling street market and several gourmet specialists – including one of France's very finest cheese emporia – as alternatives to the hypermarket hustle.

And of course Boulogne and the *Côte d'Opale* have their special restaurants. To experience the life of Boulogne and its market square there's no place better than **Chez Jules**, a classic brasserie-restaurant that has been welcoming locals and visitors alike from early morning until late at night since the 1890s.

Getting There

The **ferry terminal** used by Speedferries is very near central Boulogne but is located, with the rest of the modern port, on the other side of the River Liane. From there look for signs for *Centre Ville*, which take you round in a loop to cross the river and come up the east bank quays from the south. Speedferries do not take foot passengers, but it's a short walk from the terminal into town across Pont Marguet.

Two roads lead from **Calais and the Channel Tunnel** to Boulogne, the A16 *autoroute* (toll-free as far as Boulogne) and the leisurely, pretty but slow D940 along the coast. Just north of Boulogne the exit road from the *autoroute* (exit 3) joins the D940, so that both bring you into town along boulevards Ste-Beuve and Gambetta, beside the river.

As you approach the town centre look out for an entrance on the right into a large car park along the quay, one of two good places to leave vehicles before exploring the town (the other is around the ramparts of the Haute-Ville, reached by following signs to St-Omer; either way, you have to do some walking uphill). From the quay walk up Rue de la Lampe to Place Dalton, where Chez Jules is impossible to miss on the downhill side.

For **car hire** information, *see* chapter 3. To phone for a **taxi**, call **t** 03 21 31 37 32.

Tourist Information

Boulogne-sur-Mer:
24 Quai Gambetta, **t** 03 21 10 88 10, *www.tourisme-boulognesurmer.com*. The office is by the quays, near Pont Marguet.
Wimereux: Quai Alfred Giard, **t** 03 21 83 27 17, *www.wimereux-tourisme.com*
Wissant: 1 Place de la Mairie, **t** 03 21 82 48 00, *www.ville-wissant.fr*.

Chez Jules

8–10 Place Dalton, **t** *03 21 31 54 12,* **f** *03 21 33 85 47.*
Open (service times) Sept–June Mon–Sat 9.30am–10pm, Sun 9.30am–2.30pm; July–Aug daily 9.30am–10pm. Closed 1–15 Sept and 23 Dec–5 Jan.
Menus €18.30–39.60; carte average €32.

Chez Jules is a local institution, with a jaunty rooftop sign that flashes out each night across Place Dalton. Across the façade below, another, positively brash 'Brasserie-Restaurant-Pizza' sign announces the *trois formules* Chez Jules proudly offers, so that there's something for everyone at all kinds of prices, from elaborate dishes to simple salads and pizzas, from full meals to snacks or a coffee and croissant. The bar-brasserie-pizzeria parts take up the ground floor, with plain tables and comfily padded seats, and an outside terrace in front for a close-up view of Place Dalton's comings and goings. By the bar, a big poster of Johnny Halliday in leathers lets you know you have arrived in *la France éternelle*. The smarter, pretty restaurant dining room is on the floor above, with a view over the square from some of its tables.

Throughout, there's the constant to-ing and fro-ing of a lively brasserie. As well as a fair number of British diners, a whole cross-section of Boulogne seems to come here, to be served by bluff waiters who appear to know half their clientele personally. A good deal of Chez Jules' movement centres around the wiry, effervescent owner, Claude Leleu, who seems to do so much meeting and greeting he might be mistaken for the mayor. While he presides behind the bar, his son Philippe is in charge in the kitchen. Restaurant and bar might be busy, but you never feel cramped or hurried. This is a place in which to get back in touch with the sociable side of eating, to settle into and linger for as long as digestion or conversation might require.

The menus are long, with loads of choices from the simple to the sophisticated: 'welsh rarebit', chicken and chips, pasta, pizzas, even paella. The Leleus take good advantage of Boulogne's unbeatable supply of fresh fish. Turbot, sole, skate or whatever is best that day can be had simply poached or steamed with a classic sauce, or in elaborate specialities such as *la pêche miraculeuse*, a marvellous brochette of succulent chunks of monkfish, scallops, salmon and prawns, a smoothly satisfying *blanquette de poisson* with monkfish, salmon, *sébaste* (ocean perch) and more, or the intricate starter *millefeuille de la mer* (*see* below). It can be just as good here, though, to go for the well-priced brasserie classics, made with an equally distinctive touch – like the *moules marinières à notre façon*, featuring the juicy small mussels special to the *Côte d'Opale* and a deliciously subtle sauce with celery and thyme.

Meats are not neglected, with dependably enjoyable standards like steaks, rack of lamb with thyme or duck in cider, and sometimes a bit of game in winter. The same energetic concern for quality is notable in everything, in the fresh strawberry petit-fours or the ample and ambitious wine list. And there's also excellent coffee, to help you sit back after a feast *chez Jules* and watch Boulogne go by.

Millefeuille de la Mer

Serves 6–8

650g/1½lb fresh prawns in their shells, and preferably with heads
500g/1lb 2oz leeks (white parts), well washed
150g/5¼oz butter
100g/3½oz crème fraîche
1kg/2¼lb spinach, stemmed, washed and shaken dry
30g/1oz ground almonds
2 carrots, cut into thin strips
2 courgettes, cut into thin strips
2 celery sticks, cut into thin strips
225g/8oz crab meat
8 large scallops without roe
6–8 sheets *feuilles de brick*, or filo pastry (*feuilles de brick* is slightly thicker)
chopped chervil
salt and pepper

For the sauce:
15ml/1 tablespoon olive oil
3 shallots, finely chopped
100ml/3½fl oz dry white wine
150g/5½oz crème fraîche or double cream
50g/1¾oz cold unsalted butter, diced

Peel the prawns, keeping the shells for the sauce. Reserve, covered, in the fridge.
For the sauce, heat the oil in a saucepan on a medium heat and add the prawn shells. Cook, stirring, until lightly coloured and beginning to stick. Add the shallots

Touring Around

If you get to France via Calais or the Tunnel and take the A16 south, turn off seawards at exit 7 until you come to a fork, from which one road leads to Cap Gris-Nez and the other, the D238, runs up to the little town of **Wissant**, half-swallowed up amid the sand dunes. The name comes from the old Flemish for 'White Sand', and in front and on either side is a vast expanse of white beach and dunes, now a magnet for sand-yachters and windsurfers. Wissant has a claim to being almost as old a Channel port as Boulogne, for it is believed that Julius Caesar used it for his second invasion of Britain in 54 BC; it was an important port in the early Middle Ages, and Thomas à Becket passed through here in 1170 on his last journey back to Canterbury. By the 16th century, however, its harbour had entirely silted up. Since then the fishermen have had to drag their distinctive little boats – *flobarts* – back and forth across the beach. Fewer locals work in fishing today, but they still haul their *flobarts* to and from the sea with tractors, and keep them in their back gardens the rest of the time. The town has a clutch of hotels and crêperies, *moules-frites* stands and pleasant bars.

and cook for a minute or two. Add the wine, let it bubble and pour in 1 litre/1¾pints water. Bring to the boil, reduce the heat and simmer for 25 minutes. Strain the stock into a clean saucepan, discarding the solids. Boil to reduce by half and stir in the cream. Continue boiling gently to reduce by one-quarter. Set the sauce aside.

Thinly slice the leeks. Melt half of the butter in a saucepan over a medium heat. Add the leeks and cook for about 5 minutes, stirring frequently. Add the crème fraîche and continue cooking until the cream is thick and reduced and the leeks soft. Season with salt and pepper and set aside.

Cook the spinach in a large saucepan until wilted in the water clinging to it, or steam or microwave it. Drain well, pressing to extract as much water as possible, and chop finely. Melt the remaining butter, add the spinach and ground almonds, season with salt and pepper and set aside.

Steam the carrot, courgette and celery strips until just tender.

Preheat the oven to 200°C/400°F/Gas Mark 6. Butter the bottom of a 23–25cm/9–10in springform mould. Mix the crab meat with 2–3 tablespoons of the sauce. Slice the scallops crossways into 3 discs each.

Cut the *feuilles de brick* into 6 rounds the size of your mould. Set the mould on a baking tray. Start with a round of pastry. Top with the crab meat mixture, spreading it out, another pastry round, spread the spinach, top with pastry, layer the prawns, another pastry round, the vegetable strips, pastry, and the scallop discs, the last pastry round and top with the leeks. Bake for 15–20 minutes, until nicely browned.

Meanwhile, finish the sauce. Whisk in the butter, bit by bit, to make a silky, thick sauce. Taste and season, if needed (if too salty, whisk in a little more cream or butter). Pour into a warm serving jug. To serve, spread a little of the sauce on a warm serving dish, transfer the mould to the dish and then remove the mould. Cover the *mille-feuilles* with sauce, and sprinkle it with chopped chervil. Serve cut into wedges.

The view along the beach at Wissant is framed at either end by **Cap Blanc-Nez** to the east and the much taller **Cap Gris-Nez** to the west, their white chalk cliffs a perfect mirror to the Kent cliffs that can usually be seen across the Channel. From Wissant there's a great walk to Cap Gris-Nez along the beach (for most of the way) or the GR coastal footpath, over dunes, grassy cliffs and bits of German blockhouses. A lazier alternative is to drive around to the cape on the D940 from Wissant. At Cap Gris-Nez there's a lighthouse, the modern Channel shipping control station with its thicket of aerials, great views and another fine sandy beach. At Audinghen, where the cape road meets the D940, there's a small **Musée du Mur de l'Atlantique** (*open June–Sept daily 9–7; Oct–Nov and Feb–May daily 9–12 and 2–6; closed Dec–Jan; adm*), centred on some massive concrete bunkers with, still in place, two of the huge German guns installed there in 1940–41 to bombard Dover.

The D940 rejoins the coast at **Audresselles**, a genuine, particularly tranquil, fishing village that seems remarkably remote from any of the larger towns nearby. Just to the south is **Ambleteuse**, a beach village among the dunes with a strip of shingle, sand and rock pools that's good for windsurfing, crabbing and windswept winter walks. It stands beside the estuary of the River Slack, which has created a small-scale salt-marsh, with lots of birds, that is now a protected nature reserve. The scene is dramatically topped off by **Fort Vauban** (*open for guided tours Easter–Nov with prior reservation*, **t** *03 21 32 60 44*), the castle atop a rock that dominates the seaward view. The Slack estuary had often been used as a landing point by English invaders, and in the 1680s Louis XIV's fortress-builder *extraordinaire* Marshal Vauban built this bastion here to prevent any further incursions. It's a wonderfully ghastly structure, the ideal kind of place in which to lock up a deposed prince for life. Ambleteuse also has a small private Second World War display, the **Musée 39–45** (*open April–15 Oct Mon–Sat 9.30–6, Sun 10–6; 16 Oct–Nov and Mar Sat, Sun 10–6; closed Dec–Feb; adm*).

Before it runs into Boulogne the coastal road meets **Wimereux**, a charming little *Belle Epoque* seaside resort – once optimistically promoted as 'the Nice of the North' – with a slightly raffish air. Compact and friendly, with a fine beach and great views out to sea from its long prom, Wimereux is a hugely relaxing place to spend a day or so, with some great places to eat and stay, and shop.

Wimereux almost runs into **Boulogne** itself. If you arrive in town on a Wednesday or Saturday morning, make straight for the Grande Rue, the main street, and – just to one side of it and presided over by the grey, war-battered church of St-Nicolas – **Place Dalton**, site of one of the best traditional markets in this part of France. Rows of stalls offer up fine cheeses, terrines, farmhouse sausages and a kaleidoscope of herbs, fresh flowers and pot plants; this being the north, the market is especially good for local vegetables – carrots, chicory, shallots and endives – and sweets, chocolates and biscuits. Boulogne has its hypermarkets, mostly near the *autoroute* or the N42 St-Omer road, but the main town-centre shopping area (especially good for chocolates) is just across the Grande Rue from the market, around **Rue Thiers** and **Rue Victor Hugo**. Anyone with the remotest liking for cheese will want to make the pilgrimage to the legendary *fromagerie* of Philippe Olivier on Rue Thiers (*see* p.43), which for some justifies a trip to Boulogne all by itself.

If Boulogne has more character than most other Channel ports, it is in good part because of its long history. Whatever the claims of Wissant, it is known with certainty that Caesar sailed on his first invasion of Britain in 55 BC from the mouth of the River Liane, and that after their definitive conquest of Britain the following century the Romans built a fortress-town near its banks as their main base for communications with the new colony. After the fall of Rome Boulogne was semi-abandoned, but it revived in the early Middle Ages as the seat of a line of independent counts. Though not a Norman, Count Eustache II, *As Grenons* ('Fine Moustaches'), of Boulogne went with William the Conqueror to Hastings; his son, Godefroy de Bouillon, was one of the leaders of the First Crusade. In 1214 Philippe Auguste of France established his authority over Boulogne, and from then on it was the main bastion of French power in the north, against challenges from the Counts of Flanders and, later, England and Spain. The king gave Boulogne to his second son Philippe *Hurepel* ('Frizzy Hair') who, in between plotting to take over the crown himself, substantially rebuilt the old town and gave it the present castle and ramparts (1227–31). Marshal Vauban made some changes to the ramparts in the 1680s, but today large sections of the walls look much as they did in the 13th century, especially the Porte des Degrés on the west side.

To get to the **Haute-Ville**, the old walled town, walk straight up the steep Grande Rue. Before entering through Vauban's **Porte des Dunes**, spare a glance for the plaque on the tower to the right dedicated to François Pilâtre de Rozier, an early adventurer in cross-Channel flight. Pilâtre made the world's first manned balloon flight in November 1783 – two months after the Montgolfier brothers' first experiment with a duck, a sheep and a cockerel – and, 26 years old, was a superstar of his day. He attempted to cross the Channel in June 1785, leaving from this same tower to gain height, but his balloon caught fire and plummeted into the ground near Wimereux. Beneath the ramparts to the left of the Porte des Dunes is a broad esplanade with a large, odd monument of a man in a fez on top of a pyramid. This is **Auguste Mariette**, the father of French Egyptology, one of several engaging figures who gave Boulogne a notably individual cultural and intellectual life in the 19th century.

Through the gate you enter the heart of the old town, **Place de la Résistance** and, just beyond it, **Place Godefroy de Bouillon**, on the site of the crossroads that formed the centre of Roman Boulogne. To the left are the neoclassical Palais de Justice and **Hôtel de Ville**, attached to a massive stone belfry that's partly 12th-century and so a rare survivor from before the arrival of Philip Frizzy-Hair. On the right in Place Godefroy de Bouillon is the **Hôtel Desandrouins**, an elegant 18th-century mansion that was used by Napoleon and Josephine as their residence during their extended stays in Boulogne while the Emperor sought the means to invade England.

The streets of the old town are narrow and cobbled, the tight ring of the ramparts creating an enclosed, hushed atmosphere. The **Rue de Lille**, the most important street running off Place Godefroy de Bouillon, was the *decumanus* of the Roman town. Today it contains antique and souvenir shops, restaurants and irresistible chocolate shops. No.58 is the oldest house in Boulogne, built as an inn for 16th-century travellers, and now occupied by a restaurant and the Vole Hole bar (*see* p.46). Above the gate a scallop shell indicates that it was used by pilgrims on their way to Santiago de Compostela.

Across the street is the **Cathedral**, the giant dome of which can be seen from miles around but which, close up, comes upon you almost by surprise. During the most radical phase of the French Revolution in 1793, Boulogne's revolutionaries were not content with just desecrating their 12th-century abbey church, but actually destroyed it; so, in the 1820s the Catholic Church, reinstated and in truculent mood, decided to put the Godless to shame with this colossal edifice. Completed in 1866, its interior seems extraordinarily huge – the dome above all – but impressive rather than beautiful.

At the end of Rue de Lille is another gate, the **Porte Neuve**, and one of many points where there are steps up to the **ramparts**, a circuit of which is a special part of a meander around the Haute-Ville – with old Boulogne inside, and outside views over the rest of the town and out to sea. In the eastern corner is the monolithic castle of Philippe Hurepel, now the **Château-Musée** (*open Mon–Sat 10–12.30 and 2–5, Sun 10–12 and 2.30–5.30; closed Tues and 23 Dec–20 Jan; adm*). The collection is a bit of a hotch-potch, put together from donations from local private collectors and savants, but the display areas were attractively renovated as part of the regional overspill from Lille's stint as European culture capital in 2004. The highlights are Egyptian mummies and relics left by the great Mariette, but the museum also has some fine 18th-century porcelain, and, oddest of all, a remarkable collection of Inuit and Native American masks acquired by a local anthropologist, Alphonse Pinart, in Alaska in 1871. The most interesting part of the castle itself is the *Salle de la Barbière*, a fine vaulted Gothic hall.

From the Haute-Ville, walk back down the hill into the shopping streets of the new town. At the river, turn right for a walk along the busy quays of the port. Unmissable at the seaward end is the modernistic geometry of Boulogne's most innovative attraction, the curiously named **Nausicaá** 'sea experience museum' (*open Sept–June daily 9.30–6.30; July–Aug daily 9.30–8; closed Dec 25 and three weeks Jan; adm*). A big hit since it opened in 1991, this modern aquarium succeeds in providing a wealth of ecological information about the sea in enjoyable form, through multimedia displays (with good provision for different languages), and theme-park-ride exhibits like the deck of a trawler in a storm, or a sealed 'tropical environment' in which to warm up in mid-winter. There's also a pool where kids can touch rays, skate and the like, if not the sharks that are always among the main attractions. A full visit takes at least two hours. Just next to the museum is Boulogne's fairly clean but often unnoticed beach.

On the north side of Boulogne, next to a British war cemetery, is another of the town's most visible landmarks, the **Colonne de la Grande Armée** (*check with tourist offices for opening times*), one of the greatest monuments ever raised to a non-event. From 1803 to 1804 Napoleon kept an army of 200,000 men encamped at Boulogne for months on end while he tried to work out a way of invading England, until he finally gave up the idea and marched them off to greater glory in Germany. The men, however, had had such a good time that they voted to erect a memorial to their stay, and all the officers chipped in to pay for this column, with a statue of the Emperor on top; it was completed under Louis-Philippe in 1841. At the bottom there's a small **museum** (*open mid-June–Sept daily 10–12 and 2–6.30; Oct–mid-June Sat, Sun 10–12 and 2–4; adm*). The column itself has been under repair and so often closed, but when you can it's worth scaling the 263 steps for panoramic views over Boulogne and the *Côte d'Opale*.

Shopping

The market aside, Rue Thiers, the Grande Rue and the Haute-Ville contain Boulogne's most interesting concentrations of shops. Rue Victor Hugo, parallel to Rue Thiers, contains rather duller fashion stores and banks. Boulogne's largest hypermarket, Auchan, is on the way out of town on the N42 towards St-Omer.

Boulogne-sur-Mer ✉ 62200

Boucherie du Centre, 48 Rue Thiers, t 03 21 32 02 93. A fine traditional butcher with superior local produce – especially Licques chickens and Le Touquet's Pérard fish soup, celebrated as the best in France (*see* p.104).

Charcuterie-Traiteur Bourgeois, 1 Grande Rue, t 03 21 31 53 57. A delightful traditional *traiteur* selling a wonderful range of ready-prepared dishes, and which is also packed with other enticing gourmet items – sausages like *boudin noir*, fine wines, quails' eggs and more. The window displays are magnificent in themselves, and the very courteous staff speak English.

Philippe Olivier, 43–45 Rue Thiers, t 03 21 31 94 74, f 03 21 30 76 57. The most famous – and most enterprising – *fromagerie* in northern France has around 300 varieties of cheese in stock at any one time, but both the shop and the *caves* beneath are surprisingly small, for M. Olivier believes that any change in scale could lead to a compromise on quality. All the cheeses – and the equally fine butter – are made with entirely non-industrial methods, and the range changes continually, for he is always looking for new varieties and producers. Olivier is especially strong in local northern French cheeses such as Maroilles and Rollot, but the stock covers the whole world of cheese. Staff are never too busy to answer queries, and to complete their cheese education clients can also receive a newsletter. Olivier now has branches (with their own *caves*) in Lille and Valenciennes.

Saveurs et Traditions, 26 Grande Rue, t 03 21 31 19 64. An unobtrusive little shop dedicated to showcasing the products of small producers from around the Pas-de-Calais, many of whom use little-known traditional recipes: M Hubert Delomel's *perlé* fruit 'champagnes' from Loison-sur-Créquoise

(*see* p.112), Artois ciders, natural lemonades, honeys and mead, waffles, farm-made terrines, jams and natural cosmetics.

Les Vins de France, 4 Rue de Lille, t 03 21 80 55 96. Boulogne has small traditional wine shops rather than Calais-style warehouses, and this highly-respected wine merchant has an excellent range of quality French labels. The company also has two larger branches in the newer parts of town, at 11 Rue Nationale and 26 Rue Brèquerecque.

Wimereux ✉ 62930

Les Chocolats de Beussent, 9 Rue Carnot, t 03 21 32 86 10. If you can't get to this company's little 'factory shop' in Beussent (*see* p.101), they also have several shops around the region to showcase their luxurious handmade chocolates. The Wimereux branch is actually larger than the one in Boulogne (at 56 Rue Thiers, t 03 21 92 44 00).

Saveurs et Couleurs, 68 Rue Carnot, t 03 21 32 35 75. An enticing shop with gourmet delicacies from all over France.

Where to Stay

Boulogne-sur-Mer ✉ 62200

Hôtel de la Matelote, 70 Bd Ste-Beuve, t 03 21 30 33 33, *www.la-matelote.com* (*double rooms €95–180, higher rates Sat, Sun and public hols*). The most luxurious hotel option in Boulogne town, opened by chef Tony Lestienne next door to his acclaimed restaurant (*see* p.45). Its 29 rooms offer superior facilities for business travellers, and extra comforts for those more at their ease. A drawback could be the rather out-of-the-way location, opposite the Nausicaá centre and a little way from the centre of town. There's no direct communication between hotel and restaurant, but *demi-pension* packages are available.

Enclos de l'Evêché, 6 Rue de Pressy, t 03 91 90 05 90, *www.enclosdeleveche.com* (*rooms €70–115 for two, €130 for four*). A distinguished 19th-century *hôtel particulier* next to the Cathedral in the Haute-Ville that has been transformed into a specially lovely *chambres d'hôtes*. Restoration and decoration of the house has clearly been a real labour of love for owners Thierry and Pascaline Humez, and their personal care and imagination are apparent throughout. The five rooms are each decorated with a different Boulogne-related theme: the 'Desvres' room is based on Desvres porcelain, while another is an Egyptian room to commemorate Boulogne's great Egyptologist Auguste Mariette. The Mariette room is also a family-sized suite, with a fully-separate twin-bed room as well as the main room. Delicious breakfasts are served in an airily spacious dining room, or the courtyard. The setting may be elegant but the atmosphere is relaxed and welcoming, and M and Mme Humez – mines of information on Boulogne and area – are exceptionally helpful. There is ample parking alongside, in the former *Enclos de l'Evêché* (Bishops' Courtyard) itself.

Par Hasard, Rue de la Providence, **t** 03 21 91 36 88, *www.par-hasard.net* (*rooms €50–55 for two, €70 for four*). A fine 18th-century house in the heart of the Haute-Ville – in a tiny street off Rue de Lille – with two very pretty *chambre-d'hôtes* rooms at the top of winding staircases. One is a snug double, the other is spacious enough to be a family room for up to four, and from their windows there are atmospheric views of the old town's backyards and roofscapes. The house has style and character, Mme Lise Noel is unfussily welcoming and there's a nice patio at the back for outdoor breakfasts when the weather suits. *Closed Oct and 1–15 Feb.*

Hesdin-l'Abbé ✉ 62360

Hôtel Cléry-Château d'Hesdin-l'Abbé, Rue du Château, **t** 03 21 83 19 83, *www.hotelclery-hesdin-labbe.com* (*double rooms €59–122 low season, €70–155 April–Oct*). A Louis XV château, in a village a few kilometres south-east of Boulogne, transformed into a smart country-house hotel. It stands in an extensive park: rooms are divided between the main château and the former stables. The very large 'Grand Confort' rooms and suites have a real touch of luxury; standard and 'Confort' rooms are more conventional, but still very comfortable. The hotel's lounges exude cosy opulence, and there's a fine if expensive restaurant, **Le Berthier**, with elaborate gourmet fare (*menus €25–48*).

Wierre-Effroy ✉ 62720

Ferme-Auberge de la Raterie, **t** 03 21 92 80 90, *www.ferm-auberge-laraterie.com* (*double rooms €45–95*). La Raterie, in the village of Wierre-Effroy around 10km northeast of Boulogne, may not immediately match your idea of a *ferme-auberge*: opened on a small scale in the 1980s, it now has 20 rooms (so that it qualifies as a hotel), and restaurant space for 160 diners. The farm is a huge, rambling assemblage around a courtyard, with a big garden for outdoor breakfasts: rooms vary according to where they are and when they were converted. The most attractive are in the main farmhouse; newer rooms in the former outbuildings don't have as much character, but offer good facilities for families, while some large rooms have massage showers. There is also an impressive farmhouse restaurant (*see p.46*).

Wimereux ✉ 62930

Hôtel L'Atlantic, Digue de Mer, **t** 03 21 32 41 01, *www.hotel.atlantic.fr* (*double rooms with sea view €84–117; land-side rooms €70*). With its smartly restored sky blue-and-white Art Deco façade presiding over Wimereux's seafront, and fresh, spacious lounges, L'Atlantic has a real feel of the seaside about it, and is run with style by chef-proprietor Alain Delpierre. It's best known for his esteemed restaurant (*see p.46*), but above it there are modern, brightly comfortable rooms with sea views and, in the best of them, balconies from which to watch the sunsets and survey all the activity on the prom.

Villa Tremail, 1 Bd Thiriez, **t** 03 21 30 33 58, *www.villatremail.net* (*rooms €80–90 for two*). On Wimereux's charming seafront, overlooking the beach and a marina, this *Belle Epoque* villa has been converted into a stylish modern *chambres d'hôtes* by Jérôme Avot (brother of Mary Avot of La Goelette, *see* below) and his wife Laurence. The very comfortable rooms are full of light: the three that face the sea take every advantage of the view, while a fourth room is big enough to accommodate a family of four. The breakfast room has an equally fresh, likeable feel, with an open log fire for whenever the weather draws in.

La Goelette, 13 Digue de Mer, t 03 21 32 62 44, *www.lagoelette.com* (*rooms €61–80 for two, rates are higher for Sat, Sun, public hols and in French school holidays*). A delightful *chambres d'hôtes* on Wimereux's seafront, run by the charming Mary Avot, a very good English-speaker who has redecorated this old seaside villa with style and flair, using wooden floors, antiques and bright linens. Two rooms facing the sea are spectacular, with wonderful views of the beach as you wake up. Two rooms on an interior patio are smaller and not so special (and so a bit cheaper), but still pretty and comfortable; taking both is a good option for families. Abundant breakfasts are served in a pretty room that faces the sea, and on arrival you'll find a chocolate bar on your pillow.

Hôtel du Centre, 78 Rue Carnot, t 03 21 32 41 08, *www.hotelducentre-wimereux.com* (*double rooms €51–80*). Long a favourite with Brits, the Centre couldn't look more like a classic French small-town hotel if it was a film set. Combined with this traditional feel are a full range of comforts, and the 23 rooms were fully renovated in 2001. The restaurant (*see* p.46) is equally popular, and there's a pretty garden terrace, but what regulars appreciate most is the warm atmosphere of this family-run hotel.

Eating Alternatives

Boulogne-sur-Mer ✉ 62200

Boulogne's restaurants make more provision than is usual in France for vegetarians – perhaps thanks to the number of British visitors passing through.

La Matelote, 80 Bd Ste-Beuve, t 03 21 30 17 97, *www.la-matelote.com* (*menus €25–71*). The Matelote is celebrated as Boulogne's premier restaurant, and its chef Tony Lestienne is one of the region's culinary stars. His great fortes are fish, and every day there's a choice of fabulously fresh varieties such as turbot, cod, sole, lobster and langoustines cooked several different ways, as well as exquisite new creations of his own. The restaurant is a little outside the centre on the quayside boulevard, opposite Nausicaá. There is now a Matelote hotel too

(*see* p.43), and Lestienne also oversees the simpler, brasserie-style but still high-quality **Restaurant de Nausicaá** (t 03 21 33 24 24) in the sea-life centre itself.

Estaminet du Château, 2 Rue du Château, t 03 21 91 49 66 (*menus €14.50–32*). An attractive, *sympa* and very well-priced small bistro in the Haute-Ville, in a narrow street between the cathedral and the château-museum. Between four different menus and the *carte* there's loads of choice, including *plateaux de fruits de mer* for a blowout, and a good range for vegetarians. The quality wine selection is good value too.

Aux Pêcheurs d'Etaples, 31 Grande Rue, t 03 21 30 29 29 (*menus €13–24*). A classic Boulogne experience. This outlet of the Etaples fishermen's cooperative opposite Place Dalton, couldn't declare its business more emphatically: the entrance is dazzling, since this is also a spectacular fishmongers', piled high with sole, turbot, red mullet, crab, langoustines, mussels and more, while along one wall there is a tank of multi-coloured tropical fish (not usually on the menu). Beyond is the bright and suitably nautical dining room. The menu offers plenty of options, whether you feel like spending a little or a lot: from *moules-frites* and a children's menu to gargantuan *plateaux de fruits de mer* (*from €28*).

Au Bon Accueil, 55 Rue de Lille, t 03 21 80 37 41 (*menus €12–25*). This long-running budget favourite in the Haute-Ville looks a bit like everyone's image of a traditional French bistro, but the mostly-female staff are young and bright. The cooking highlights straight-forward local favourites, with lots of choices and excellent-value menu options, especially the daily *formules du marché*. Meat dishes such as *côte de porc au maroilles*, variations on sole and skate, *moules*, steaks or omelettes with *frites* and vegetarian dishes all feature. *Closed Sun eve and Mon.*

La Cave du Fromager, 30 Rue de Lille, t 03 21 80 49 69 (*menus €9–20.50*). A cosy little café-restaurant that – as the name suggests – highlights every kind of dish made with cheese, including tasty snacks like *tartine* open sandwiches, quiches and cheese pastries as well as a few larger dishes. There's a bargain children's menu, and while *La Cave* closes early in the evenings it serves food through the afternoons. *Open 11am–7pm; closed Tues.*

The Vole Hole, 58 Rue de Lille, **t** 03 21 92 15 15. Occupying part of the oldest building in Boulogne, with scallop shell above the gateway alongside to show that it was once on the road to Santiago, this bar is a perennially popular stop-off for Boulogne visitors. To go with the ever-relaxed atmosphere there's a big choice of beers and fine wines, and a few small snacks.

Audresselles ✉ 62164

Au P'tit Bonheur, 2 Rue Jeanne d'Arc, **t** 03 21 83 12 54 (carte *average €28*). This almost beach-hut like restaurant off the seafront in the laidback fishing village of Audresselles is simple in every way, but is hugely recommended by locals for the quality of its fresh fish and seafood – carpaccio of coquille St-Jacques, roast sea bass with mushrooms, and more. There's usually a *carte* rather than set menus, but prices are eminently reasonable. One worth seeking out – but note, it's truly tiny, so be sure to book. *Closed Mon.*

Marquise ✉ 62250

Le Grand Cerf, 34 Av Ferber, **t** 03 21 87 55 05, *www.legrandcerf.com* (menus *€22–48*). Stéphane Pruvot is one of the most able chefs in northern France, the creator of beautifully inventive dishes such as his sublime *aumônières* (filo parcels) of crab in shellfish essences. His restaurant occupies a grand 18th-century coaching inn on the old road between Boulogne and Calais, with an imposing stone courtyard. At its best, a meal here is a truly memorable experience.

Pont-de-Briques ✉ 62260

Hostellerie de la Rivière, 17 Rue de la Gare, **t** 03 21 32 22 81, **f** 03 21 87 45 48 (menus *€27–50*). This smart little restaurant isn't in the most obvious location – in the suburb of Pont-de-Briques just south of Boulogne, very near the roundabout where the Montreuil and Le Touquet roads divide – but its young chef-owner Dominique Martin has a high standing among local food-lovers for his refined cooking. His specialities include *desserts à l'ancienne* – seductively extrava-

gant desserts at their very best. In summer, there are also tables outside in a pretty riverside garden. *Closed Sun eve and Mon.*

Wierre-Effroy ✉ 62720

Ferme-Auberge de la Raterie, **t** 03 21 92 80 90, *www.ferm-auberge-laraterie.com* (menus *€20–44*). La Raterie has developed beyond a simple farmhouse *auberge*, but Mme Coquerelle makes it clear that all the food served still makes use of the farm's own produce, and that she herself, in a *tour-de-force* of sustained energy, is still in charge of all the cooking. Her menus feature classic country cooking skilfully prepared – pork, chickens, duck and veg, in hearty dishes such as an *assiette de terrines*, or roast farm chicken (a staple). Diners not in a big group are served in a pretty farmhouse room. *Closed Sun eve and Mon.*

Wimereux ✉ 62930

Restaurant La Liègoise-Hôtel L'Atlantic, Digue de Mer, **t** 03 21 32 41 01, *www.hotel.atlantic.fr* (restaurant menus *€32–61; brasserie lunch menu €17.50*). Alain Delpierre's restaurant in the Atlantic hotel is one of the best-regarded on this coast. Local fish and seafood, and the traditional cuisine of the Pas-de-Calais, naturally rate strongly among his sources of inspiration; specialities include *panaché* of turbot, and red mullet with a *poêlée* of foie gras. The elegant main dining room, with a fine outlook over the sea, is on the first floor; the ground-floor bar-brasserie – with a big seafront terrace – offers a fine seafood-brasserie range and an exceptional-value lunch menu. Hence it's often packed, and on sunny days it's essential to book or to be there early to get a table.

Hôtel du Centre, 78 Rue Carnot, **t** 03 21 32 41 08, *www.hotelducentre-wimereux.com* (menus *€19–29*). Wimereux's Hôtel du Centre is a piece of old France, and the dining room accordingly looks just like the kind of bistro Jean Gabin might have hung out in in a 1930s movie. Its food is similarly traditional, with good-value versions of such staples as *magret de canard, moules, filet de cabillaud*, and so on. The atmosphere is relaxed and friendly, and loved by its British fans even more than by the locals.

The First Town in France:
St-Omer

06

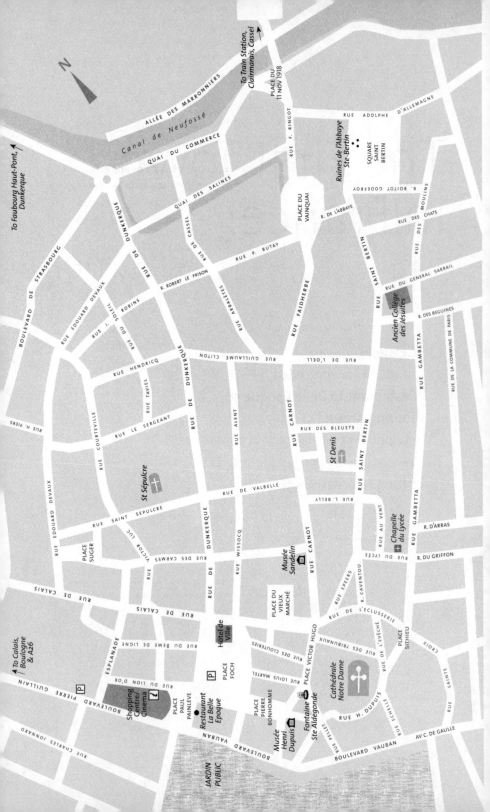

It's such a common impression there must be something to it: any number of people, having wandered across the Channel and come upon St-Omer, describe it as the first real French small town they've found within a short distance of the exits from Calais. It's not hard to see why: at its heart there is a broad, cobbled main square, with cafés around the sides and presided over by an imposing Hôtel de Ville, which hosts a vibrant weekly market; nearby are narrow streets with beautiful *pâtisseries, charcuteries* and other individual shops, a magnificent, oddly little-known Gothic cathedral and, dotted around the old town, ornate fountains and elegant *hôtels particuliers* from the days of the *Ancien Régime*. One such archetypically French 18th-century *hôtel* houses one of the region's best museums, recently reopened.

The idea that St-Omer should epitomize all that is French might seem strange, however, since it has only been part of France since 1678, later than any other part of Artois. For much of its history the town was attached to Flanders, and ruled successively by the counts of Flanders, the dukes of Burgundy and the kings of Spain, all of them in endless warfare with the kings of France. Like much of Flanders, St-Omer was partly built on water, and just to the east there is an atmospheric, silent landscape of marshes and polders, the *Marais Audomarois*, rich in wildlife, with a web of canals built up over centuries between reed beds and prolific vegetable gardens.

The produce from these marsh-gardens – leeks, chicory, carrots, cauliflowers – has always been among the staples of food in St-Omer. Others, typical of northern France and Flanders, are beef, rabbit, fresh fish from the nearby ports, and beer – for drinking and in cooking. Locals also noticeably share the region's love of chocolate and other things sweet. For fine versions of local dishes in St-Omer – plus others from a broader French range – you would have to look hard to do better than **La Belle Epoque**, an unassuming but very hospitable restaurant just off the main square.

Getting There

St-Omer is about 30mins from Calais by *autoroute*. Whether you go there direct on the old N43 Calais road or come in from Boulogne and the A26 *autoroute* via the N42, you will reach the same bypass around the town; follow signs for *Centre Ville* to come on to a long straight road along the north side of St-Omer, Avenue Joffre. From there, look for a broad turning to the right, also signposted *Centre Ville*, Boulevard Pierre Guillain.

Follow this road into town and you will come to the main square, Place Foch. Just off the *place* is another smaller square, Place Paul Painlevé, where the Belle Epoque is hard to miss. Place Foch is also usually the best place to **park** in St-Omer, except on market days (Sat), when it's better to try to park on Bd Guillain or around the Jardin Public.

St-Omer has frequent daily **train** services, on the Calais–Lille line, with some trains going on to long-distance destinations. The station is on the east side of the town, by the River Aa.

Tourist Information

Saint-Omer: 4 Rue du Lion d'Or, t 03 21 98 08 51, *www.tourisme-saintomer.com*. As well as providing all kinds of information this office, in the modern cinema and leisure complex on the north side of Place Painlevé, offers an extensive range of guided tours – including some to local monuments that otherwise are often closed – and sells tickets for La Coupole, the Eperlecques blockhouse and Marais boat trips. The website has details of current tour programmes.

Watten: 12 Rue de Dunkerque, t 03 21 88 27 78, *otwatten@aol.com*.

La Belle Epoque

Place Paul Painlevé, t/f 03 21 38 22 93. Open May–Sept Mon, Wed–Sun 12–3 and 7–10.30; Oct–May Mon, Wed–Sat 12–3 and 7–10.30, Sun 12–3; closed Tues. Menus €12–26; carte average €27.

Mme Dacheville does pretty much everything in the kitchen at the Belle Epoque – until very recently she did absolutely everything, but has now finally acquired a young assistant to pass her skills on to. Her husband, meanwhile, looks after front-of-house, with occasional help from two young waitresses. On some days, though, Madame also takes the orders, lays tables and serves as well, but will still agree very amiably to provide complex dishes at short notice late into the evening. On top of this, she also manages to remain utterly charming and welcoming throughout, and, most important of all, the results of her cooking are excellent. There's no sign of anything being skimped under pressure, and even the pâtisserie is homemade; everything is prepared with the same very personal care. Moreover, she is used to the inability of British visitors to observe proper French hours (and the needs of those arriving late from or on their way to the Tunnel or a ferry), and is willing to serve food well outside customary local closing times. Those given above are more like guidelines than strict timings; if the Dachevilles are there in mid-afternoon, she may well be prepared to cook something up for you.

Occupying two small 1900s townhouses, the restaurant is neatly comfortable, with plenty of flowers, white linen and smart red-plush bench seats. In summer, there are a

Carbonnade de Boeuf

Serves 6

1kg 200g/2lb 10 oz shoulder of beef (*paleron*)
600g/1 lb 5oz onions
2 slices *pain d'épice* or similar spiced bread
½litre/1 pint beer: a light, non-gassy lager (*bière blonde*) or similar
½litre/1 pint water
100g/3½oz butter
30ml/2 tablespoons olive oil
thyme and bay leaves
flour
salt and pepper

Cut the beef into large cubes, and slice the onions. Brown the meat in a casserole dish in the butter and half of the oil, then remove it and put on one side to dry. Cook the onions in the same mixture until just brown, then add the rest of the oil. Break up the *pain d'épice* and add to the casserole, then return the meat to the dish, stir together and stir in the water and the beer. Season with salt, pepper, thyme and bay leaves, stir well together and then simmer for around 1½ hours. Just before the casserole is finished, thicken with a little flour, to taste.

Serve with vegetables and, ideally, dauphinoise potatoes.

few open-air tables in front. Despite this being a one-woman band, menus and *carte* offer an ample choice. Rich meat dishes based on traditional local favourites and local produce are a prime speciality, but another is fish, with specials based on whatever's fresh that day, such as *dos de lieu à la moutarde ancienne*, pollack in a mustard sauce, or trout or other freshwater fish from nearby rivers. Other menu fixtures are meat grills – steaks, lamb chops, *andouillette* sausages – with a choice of moreish sauces. There are good options for a lighter meal too, with omelettes and generous mixed salads – plus, for a bigger change in style the Dachevilles' daughter Sandrine has opened a full-scale crêperie next door to the Belle Epoque, **L'Oasis**.

The Belle Epoque's set menus are equally generous, and impressive value. The €20 list might include, to start, a deliciously light but flavoursome *gratin* of Chavignol with bacon salad, or some wonderful homemade foie gras *parfumé aux sauternes*, infused with an elusive tang of sweet wine and served with a beautifully subtle grape and strawberry conserve. To follow you could choose one of Mme Dacheville's most popular specialities, rabbit with prunes and flambéd in armagnac, or the classic Flemish *carbonnade de bœuf*, a fine, strong beef-and-beer stew. Full-bodied flavours are a characteristic of her cooking, but there's a great deal of imagination and craft here too, as in her precisely-blended sweet-and-sour *magret de canard* with roast peaches.

The wine list is also sizeable, and decently priced, and the cheese selection includes some great, properly powerful local Rollot and Maroilles. More highlights arrive for dessert, like a formidably good strawberry tart – wonderfully fresh, and a perfect example of the Belle Epoque's likeable combination of home comforts and quality food. And you'll not be obliged to hurry over your coffee, if you're not rushing to get away.

Touring Around

The main square, officially **Place Foch**, is still very much the hub of St-Omer. Like many town squares in Flanders and Artois it is strikingly large, built to accommodate the market. Today it also looks as if it was created around the **Hôtel de Ville** that fills up one side, although the square is in fact much older, and was once even bigger. The town hall was only built in the 1830s, to replace a smaller Gothic hall that was on the verge of collapse. Designed by Parisian architect Pierre-Bernard Lefranc, the 'new' town hall is distinctly grand, and was intended to bring together all sorts of local amenities under one roof, including, at the back, a neat Italian-style **theatre**. Closed for years, this has been restored and is due to reopen for concerts and performances during 2005 (*for guided tours of Hôtel de Ville and theatre, enquire at tourist office*).

The biggest pavement cafés and bars are on the south, higher, side of Place Foch, with a balcony view over the rest of the square. It is busiest on Saturday mornings, when it's taken over by the **market** (there is also a smaller market on Wednesdays). The most eye-catching stalls display local products, notably fine chicory and other vegetables from the Marais, highly regarded because of the special qualities given by the rich soil of the drained marsh-gardens, which can produce several crops each year. In among the crowds there are stalls with fresh herbs or homemade biscuits, or piled up with northern cheeses such as the strong Maroilles, as well as others with all the non-food items that mark out a genuine town market, from baby clothes to books.

St-Omer was founded in 637 by Audomar (later St Omer), a monk sent to evangelize the pagan population of this region of bogs and swamps. He also founded an abbey, St-Bertin, which remained a powerful influence in the town until its dissolution during the Revolution. In the early Middle Ages St-Omer and Bruges were the two richest cities in Flanders, larger than Arras and many cities to the south; however, its position also put it in the middle of the area chosen by France, England and later Spain as their prime battleground for nearly 400 years. When St-Omer was finally secured for Louis XIV and France after a long siege in 1677, Marshal Vauban encased it in a massive set of ramparts as part of his *pré carré* or 'square field', the line of forts built to protect the new frontier. They held the town like a clamp for two centuries. South of Place Foch is St-Omer's main park, the **Jardin Public**, which incorporates the only remaining section of Vauban's ramparts, a monolithic screen of plain brick.

The long streets that lead northeast from Place Foch, especially Rue de Dunkerque, form St-Omer's main everyday shopping centre. The little streets that run off the square on the south side, on the other hand, lead into **old St-Omer**, a small area with a distinctive charm. Especially attractive are Rue des Clouteries, opposite the Hôtel de Ville, and the parallel Rue Louis Martel, two alley-like streets that now contain small, chic fashion shops mixed in with bakers selling superb fresh bread and *charcuteries* full of bulging red sausages. Throughout the town centre the sweet tooth of northern France is catered for in a markedly high number of chocolate and cake shops.

Rue des Clouteries and Rue Louis Martel lead into rectangular **Place Victor Hugo**. To the right there is an endearingly over-grand baroque fountain, the **Fontaine de Ste-Aldegonde**, erected to celebrate the birth of one of Louis XV's children in 1757. Leave the square to the left of the fountain, admiring its chubby cherubs on the way, and turn left again, and you will come to St-Omer's greatest monument, the **cathedral**.

It was begun around 1200 on the site of three earlier churches, and completed 300 years later, as the largest, grandest Gothic church in the Pas-de-Calais. Before going in, walk around the outside to get an idea of its monumentality: some of the lower, 13th-century sections are quite plain, almost similar to Romanesque, while the squared-off 15th-century tower is entirely a work of elaborate, *flamboyant* late Gothic. Most impressively sculptural of all is the *portail royal* at the end of the south transept, on the opposite side from Place Victor Hugo, flanked by two massive, soaring towers and with extraordinary, often bizarre carvings. The cathedral has many treasures, of which perhaps finest of all is the magnificent organ that fills the whole west end of the nave, a superb piece of baroque woodcarving from 1717 that manages to combine perfectly with its medieval surroundings. It is regularly used for concerts. In the north transept, look up to see a wonderful and very rare astrological clock from 1558 – a fine illustration of Renaissance ideas of the world, and still in working order – beneath an intricate *flamboyant*-Gothic rose window from the 1450s that, because the cathedral does not actually face due east as it should, beautifully catches the evening light.

Place Sithieu and the streets around it, down a steep slope from the eastern end of the cathedral, make up one of the oldest parts of St-Omer, a little knot of cobbled alleys full of fascinating, sometimes precarious-looking structures. The long streets to the north and east are a mix of plainish, largely 19th-century buildings, more elegant French 18th-century residences and some much grander brick edifices from the era when St-Omer was an important city of the Spanish Netherlands and a centre of the Catholic church. Rue Gambetta is straddled by the departments of the town *lycée*, the core of which is in the former buildings of a Jesuit seminary. On Rue du Lycée, off Rue Gambetta, looms up the giant mass of the **Chapelle du Lycée** or *Ancienne Chapelle des Jesuites* (*open Mon–Sat 9–12 and 2–5*), the seminary's extraordinary former chapel. Built in 1615–40 by the Jesuit architect Du Blocq, it's spectacular above all for its size, rivalling the cathedral, with a towering five-level façade combining Flemish traditions and Italianate Jesuit Baroque. Equally unusual are the two remarkably slim, flat-topped towers, difficult to appreciate from the street, at its eastern end. The interior – now often used for exhibitions – is in Flemish *hallekerk* style with no transepts.

Rue du Lycée meets Rue St-Bertin, where a right turn will lead to the **Ancien Collège des Jesuites**, also now part of the *lycée*. A plaque outside records that it was built as the English College, a reminder of a time when in England to be found to have come on a mission 'from St-Omer' was something like being discovered with credentials from the KGB at the height of the Cold War, and liable to much bloodier penalties. In 1592, as measures against Catholics in England tightened, English Jesuits sought help to found a new college to educate the sons of Catholic families on safe soil. It was the most important of several English Colleges on Spanish territory, and lavishly endowed by Spanish monarchs and governors. Expelled from France in 1762, the college survives to this day as Stonyhurst College in Lancashire, founded by former St-Omer pupils in 1794.

On the opposite side of Rue St-Bertin a small courtyard contains the simple 13th-century church of **St-Denis**, which has a *Last Supper* from 1523 attributed to Della Robbia, although this has been contested. Following its final absorption into France St-Omer acquired its more Gallic appearance with large *Ancien Régime* buildings, notably *hôtels particuliers* or town residences built for local notables. The soberly elegant **Hôtel de Bergues**, at 20 Rue St-Bertin, accommodated George V and the future Edward VIII on their visits to the front during the First World War. St-Omer's finest mansion, however, is the **Hôtel Sandelin** on Rue Carnot, a very elegant Louis XV-style residence built for Marie-Josephe Sandelin, Comtesse de Fruges, in 1777. Rising up behind an ample courtyard, it now houses the **Musée Sandelin** (*open Wed, Fri–Sun 10–12 and 2–6, Thur 10–12 and 2–8, closed Mon, Tues; adm*). One of the most engaging of northern France's museums, this was lost to view for years until long-drawn out renovation was finally completed in 2004. One benefit of the wait, though, is that far more of its collections can now be seen, in ideal conditions. A prime attraction is the house itself, with original, delicately prettified décor from the era of Marie-Antoinette, especially the lovely turquoise dining room, laid with fine blue 18th-century St-Omer china. The collection includes a spectacular display of other porcelain and ceramics – perfect for the setting – and French, Dutch and Flemish paintings, notably Jan Steen's provocative *La Ribaude* ('The Bawd'), but some of its greatest treasures are local, in the shape of medieval religious sculptures from abbeys near St-Omer. Finest of all is the *Pied de Croix de St-Bertin*, an extraordinary 12th-century crucifix-stand in copper, bronze and enamel. St-Omer has another museum, the **Musée Henri Dupuis** (*check at tourist office for opening times*), a curious collection combining birds, shells and other items amassed by the local naturalist after whom it is named and fine ceramics, but this too has been closed for renovation, although it may reopen during 2005.

At the very end of Rue St-Bertin, heading east, there is one more relic of medieval St-Omer, the ruins of the **Abbey of St-Bertin**, standing rather neglectedly within a small park. Built between 1326 and 1570 in emphatic Gothic style to replace St Audomar's first abbey, it was closed by the Revolution – when the saints on the façade all had their heads knocked off – and demolished piecemeal-fashion over the next century, leaving only the main façade and part of the nave still standing. Continue left of the abbey to reach the canals of the River Aa, where a left turn will take you towards one more of St-Omer's unusual mix of neighbourhoods, the **Faubourg du Haut-Pont**. This characterful district of 19th-century river-workers' cottages still has something of the feel of the French riverside communities seen in Jean Vigo's *L'Atalante* or the films of Jean Renoir.

Outside St-Omer there are two attractions that stand out, for curiosity value alone, among the many Second World War sites in the Pas-de-Calais, and which exert an awful fascination for anyone interested in the development of destructive technology. The St-Omer area was a hub of Hitler's plans to develop long-range missiles, and about 10km north near the village of Eperlecques is the **Blockhaus d'Eperlecques** (*guided tours every hour, daily Mar 2–6, April and Oct 10–12 and 2–6, May–Sept 10–7, Nov 2–5; closed Dec–Feb; adm*), one of the launching sites for V1 and V2 attacks on London in 1944. Five kilometres south of town between Helfaut and Wizernes is **La Coupole** (*open daily Sept–June 9–6, July–Aug 10–7; closed 22 Dec–4 Jan; adm*), another V2 bunker which hosts a state-of-the-art display. Highly popular, this exhibit deals not just with the Nazi rocket programme but also with the subsequent career of Doctor Werner von Braun and the development of space travel, while another section traces the story of the war and occupation in northern France, although the star of the show is the journey down into the giant concrete pit of La Coupole itself. A joint ticket is available for both sites.

For a complete contrast, from spring to autumn you can take a boat trip through the canals of the **Marais Audomarois**. Several companies run tours from villages around St-Omer, the most accessible of which is usually **Isnor** in Clairmarais (*t 03 21 39 15 15, www.isnor.fr, tickets also available from tourist office; 1hr tours April–June, Sept Sat, Sun and hols hourly 2–5; July–Aug daily 11am and hourly 2–5; adm*) on the east side of town, although in summer some tours also pick up at the Haut-Pont in St Omer. They use open boats (other companies' closed launches may be weather-proof, but have much less charm). To get to the main landing point, follow the road to the right of the railway station across the Aa from central St-Omer. Commentaries on the flora, fauna and many legends associated with this strange, flat space are given in English if there are enough people who require it. Canals to drain the marshes, known by their Flemish name *watergangs*, began to be built in Audomar's time, and have been added to ever since. It's a different, tranquil world of rushes, lilies and marsh flowers, inhabited by grebes, ducks and herons. During the day, there are also the *maraîchers*, the cultivators of the marsh allotments. Few now live full-time in the little houses along the banks, but they still take their produce to market in silent, punt-like boats.

Shopping

St-Omer has a choice of hypermarkets: Carrefour is north of town, by the main road from Calais and the *autoroute*; Auchan is to the south, by the main roundabout in the direction of La Coupole and the *autoroute* south (*both open Mon–Sat till 10pm*).

Saint-Omer ✉ 62500

Les Caves du Vieux Chai, 1 Place Pierre Bonhomme, **t** 03 21 12 59 03. Wine merchant Pierre Glaçon of Fressin (*see* p.112) has now opened this attractive St-Omer shop. As at their home base, the stock is especially strong in fine examples of classic French wines, especially Bordeaux, at very good prices. A charming place to build up one's wine rack.

Les Chocolats de Beussent, 30 Rue des Clouteries, **t** 03 21 12 66 82. Another outlet for the wonderful handmade chocolates from Beussent (*see* p.101).

Le Marché du Quai – La Ferme, 4 Quai du Commerce, **t** 03 21 39 62 36. Pass this barn of a store by accident, on the quay leading to the Faubourg du Haut-Pont, and you might dismiss it just as a supermarket. Inside, however, you'll find an excellent selection of local produce: regional cheeses, many from small producers, are a highlight, but there are also local marsh veg, meats – sausages, hams, Licques chickens – wines, liqueurs and a great stock of the region's fine beers.

Le Terroir, 31 Rue des Clouteries, **t** 03 21 38 26 51. An attractive little shop with a superior display of fine wines, fresh produce and other local delicacies.

Houlle ✉ 62910

Distillerie Persyn, 19 Route de Watten, **t** 03 21 93 01 71, *www.genievredehoulle.com*. A scent of gin wafts over the centre of the village of Houlle. This is because it is home to this tiny distillery, the only one in the Pas-de-Calais, where fine gins have been made since 1812. Visitors can take a tour (*Mon–Sat; reservation necessary; adm*), including a tasting – which can be a test, as there are over seven distinctive varieties and they won't let you get away with trying just one or two. You don't have to take the tour to buy at the distillery shop; bottles of gin cost from around €14.

Where to Stay

Saint-Omer ✉ 62500

Hôtel Le Bretagne, 2 Place du Vainquai, **t** 03 21 38 25 78, *www.hotellebretagne.com* (*double rooms €58–78*). A modern, slightly functional but decently comfortable 75-room hotel on the eastern side of St-Omer, near the ruins of St-Bertin abbey, around a 10–15min walk from the centre. The large ground floor **restaurant** offers both a brasserie list and a fairly sophisticated *carte* (*menus €14–29*).

Hôtel Saint-Louis, 25 Rue d'Arras, **t** 03 21 38 35 21, *www.hotel-saintlouis.com* (*double rooms €62*). This pleasant, unfussy and comfy small-town *Logis* hotel in a much-renovated old coaching inn is a short walk from the cathedral and Place Foch. Service is warm, and the St-Louis has a livelier restaurant, **Le Flaubert** (*see* p.56), than many *Logis* hotels.

Eperlecques ✉ 62910

Château de Ganspette, **t** 03 21 93 43 93, **f** 03 21 95 74 98 (*rooms €50 for two*). A big 19th-century country house – rather than a real 'château' – in ample, wooded grounds north of St-Omer. There are three *chambres d'hôte* rooms, each one comfortable and spacious. The estate also contains a campsite, with swimming pool and tennis courts, which gets busy in the summer season.

Muncq-Nieurlet ✉ 62980

Mme Françoise Breton, Ferme de la Motte Obin, Rue du Bourg, **t** 03 21 82 79 63 (*rooms €35 for two*). Mme Breton's farmhouse is reached from the road between the villages of Muncq-Nieurlet and Ruminghem, 15km north of St-Omer and 30km from Calais. Turn through the imposing gate into the farm and you enter a sweeping timber and brick courtyard, with the house in one corner and giant stables around the other sides. Mme Breton, an elderly widow, now lives in this venerable pile by herself, but this doesn't seem to faze her; she loves to have guests, to whom she talks at length (in French). The two rooms are big, characterful and comfortable, and each has space for kids' beds. With some advance notice she also serves ample country meals (*€16*), which are praised to the skies by former guests. *Closed Nov–Mar.*

Tilques ✉ 62500

Hôtel Château de Tilques, t 03 21 88 99 99, *www.chateautilques.com* (*double rooms €110–235, higher rates Fri–Sun and public hols*). The local luxury option, a very plush 53-room country-house hotel in its own grounds. The current château was built in the 19th century in mock-Flemish baronial style, but the manor on which it stands, just north of St-Omer, is centuries older. The 30 rooms in the château are traditional in style, while the bigger 'garden rooms' in an adjoining building are a little more modern; all offer every kind of comfort. In the former stables there's a much-admired restaurant (*see* below).

Zouafques ✉ 62890

La Ferme de Wolphus, Route Nationale 43, t/f 03 21 35 61 61, *ferme.de.wolphus@wanadoo.fr* (*rooms €38–42 for two, €64 for four*). A popular B&B off the N43 south of Ardres. It's a little functional but made welcoming by the friendly owners, and is great value for families. The three guest rooms are simply decorated in modern style; one has space for up to four and all have access to a kitchenette. There are also two fully self-contained *gîtes*. Owner Jean-Jacques Behaghel also sells wine and honey.

Eating Alternatives

Saint-Omer ✉ 62500

Le Cygne, 8 Rue Caventou, t 03 21 98 20 52 (*menus €13–42*). A pretty restaurant on one of the old streets just east of the cathedral, with rather fluffy bourgeois décor – lace curtains, white table settings. Chef Jean-François Wident's much-praised cuisine covers an interesting and sophisticated range, from local dishes such as cod baked in white beer or an excellent *salade maraîchère* with local vegetables to some with quite exotic touches.

Restaurant Le Flaubert, Hôtel Saint-Louis, 25 Rue d'Arras, t 03 21 38 35 21, *www.hotel-saintlouis.com* (*menus €12–34*). One half of this popular hotel restaurant is a conventional dining room, with a good-value range of substantial classic dishes. A hearty Alsatian meat *choucroute* is the house speciality, but there's also an ample

range of salads. The other half is a relaxed (and cheap) bar-brasserie-'sandwicherie', a favourite with students from the *lycée*.

Au Petit St-Pierre, 27 Quai du Haut-Pont, t 03 21 38 01 44 (*menu €14*). On the quay in the Faubourg du Haut-Pont, the bluff and basic St-Pierre is the place to go in St Omer to find really traditional, no-frills, northern, Artois and Flemish specialities. The €3 *plats du jour* are great value. *Lunch only*.

Clairmarais ✉ 62500

Auberge des Nénuphars, 60 Route de St-Omer, t/f 03 21 38 24 84 (*menus €10–15*). A laidback little *auberge* in the marshlands, easy to find on the D209 as it continues out from St-Omer past the Clairmarais boat landings. It stands alongside a big, placid *étang*, with ducks, geese and a landing stage for (occasional) boat trips, and the dining room is in a big glass conservatory that maximizes the view, with more tables outside. The food is simple, but enjoyable and fine value.

Houlle ✉ 62910

L'Auberge de l'Etang Poupart, 12 Impasse des Etangs, t 03 21 93 05 26 (*menu €19, Sat, Sun and public hols €22*). A winding (but sign-posted) lane leads out of the marshlands village of Houlle, 6km north of St-Omer, to end at this restaurant in a flower-bedecked old *marais* farmhouse, with – as the name suggests – a large *étang* (pond) at the back, beside which there are tables in summer. Chef-owner Jérôme Delplace concentrates on fine versions of traditional dishes – *carbonnade, andouilles*, fish soups – with, since this is a *restaurant du terroir*, a firm emphasis on fresh local produce.

Tilques ✉ 62500

Restaurant Le Vert Mesnil, Hôtel Château de Tilques, t 03 21 88 99 99, *www.chateautilques.com* (*menus €25–65*). The château's fine restaurant offers a suitably opulent repertoire, with a spectacular gourmet menu topped by a still more extravagant 'Seven Desires' list (at €65). Chef Patrick Hittos's style combines French *haute cuisine* with some exotic touches from Asia, the Pacific Rim and elsewhere. There's also a similarly refined wine list, and a wine shop.

In the Flemish Mountains:

Cassel and the Monts de Flandre

07

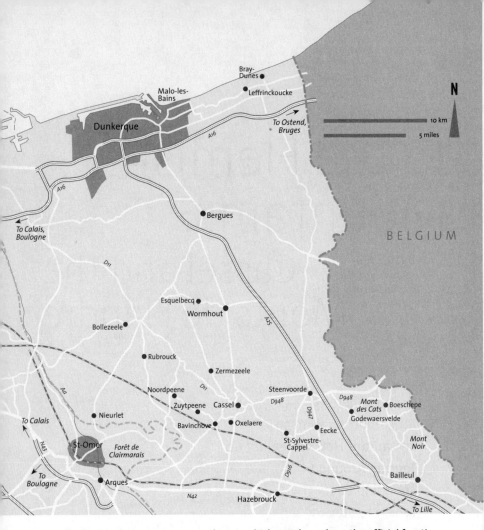

All over the European continent there are little patches where the official frontiers and the limits of the communities on the ground don't quite coincide, where the drawers-up of border lines, wrapped up in high politics, never took much care to ensure that speakers of one language were all on one side of a line while those of a neighbouring culture were all on the other.

Such a place is French Flanders, the compact strip of land between Lille, St-Omer, the sea and the Belgian border. A glance at the map and the place names – Zermezeele, Boeschepe, Godewaersvelde, all about as Gallic as Rembrandt's nose – is enough to show that this is not one of the historic heartlands of French culture. And yet this has been a part of France since the 1670s, when it was seized by Louis XIV. Today, it's a curious, distinct mix: French in language, but still Flemish in many of its customs.

Another thing that is known about Flanders is that it is flat. In France it is virtually obligatory in any reference to Flanders to quote from the Jacques Brel song *Le Plat Pays* ('The Flat Country'), which raised flatness to the level of a poetic image, a state

Getting There

The quickest road route from Calais and the Tunnel to the Monts de Flandre is via the A16 *autoroute* eastwards to Dunkerque, and then the A25 south, following signs for Lille. From Dunkerque ferry port, well-signed roads lead straight to the A25. Both *autoroutes* are toll-free in this area. Leave the A25 at junction 13 (Steenvoorde) for Cassel (7km). It's usually easy to get there in about 45mins. A more leisurely and rural route is to leave the A16 at junction 24, west of Dunkerque, head south on the D600 signposted to St-Omer for about 4km and then look for the little D11 to the left, for Cassel, via villages and flat Flanders fields.

This area has quite good local **train** services. Many trains from Calais or Dunkerque to Lille stop at Hazebrouck, and local Dunkerque–Lille trains also stop at Bailleul and Bavinchove, the station for Cassel, which is 3½km from the station on the top of its hill.

Tourist Information

There is a general website for all French Flanders, *www.coeur-de-flandre.com*. Local offices provide excellent free walking guides.
Bailleul: Office de Tourisme des Monts de Flandre, 3 Grand'Place, **t** 03 28 43 81 00, *www.montsdeflandre.fr*. The largest, most comprehensive tourist office for the whole area, on Bailleul's main square.
Cassel: 23 Grand'Place, **t** 03 28 40 52 55, *www.ot-cassel.fr*.
Esquelbecq: La Maison du Westhoek, 9 Place Bergerot, **t** 03 28 62 88 57, *maison.westhoek@wanadoo.fr*.
Hazebrouck: Hôtel de Ville, Grand'Place, **t** 03 28 49 59 89, *contact@ville-hazebrouck.fr*.
Steenvoorde: Maison de Flandre, Place Dr JF Ryckewaert, **t** 03 28 49 97 98, *si-steenvorde@wanadoo.fr*.
Wormhout: Place Général de Gaulle, **t/f** 03 28 62 81 23, *ot.wormhout@wanadoo.fr*.

of mind. And flatness is certainly its most overriding characteristic. However, Flanders does have some substantial hills, the *Monts de Flandre*, which are the reason why France wanted the area in the first place. Though all under 200m high, they are actually very steep, rising up out of the flat, wet Flemish plain. The abrupt contrast between the hills and the plains below creates a strangely awesome landscape, making the *Monts* a favourite with walkers.It also means they have wonderful views, and especially clear light and air that's kept alive by the uninterrupted winds. Their peculiar prominence has also given them a special role in the area's folklore, religion and war. And on top of the tallest of them all is the little walled hill town of Cassel, one of the most atypically characterful historic towns in northeast France.

The idiosyncratic identity of French Flanders is also illustrated by the huge windmills on many of the hills, standing out like giant sailed monuments against the sky. There is a distinctive architecture, of step gables, belfries, rectangular churches, small brick houses, painted shutters and lace curtains. There are traditional Flemish games, the *carillons* of little bells that peal from the belfries, and a dense folklore of Carnival and giants that is celebrated each year. And as soon as you cross the River Aa by St-Omer the food changes, taking on a much more straightforward heartiness in place of the usual French elaboration. The great drink of this *terroir* – as in Belgian Flanders – is fine beer, produced by small traditional breweries. There are also special places to sample it, together with the best of the local foodstuffs. France-proper has never had real pubs (nouveau-Irish bars not counting); but Flanders does have, its *estaminets*, snug little bars with wooden tables and adorned with all sorts of knick-knacks that curiously have become French Flanders' most cherished institution. Locals have their favourites, but the most celebrated *estaminet* of all is **Het' Kasteelhof**, at the very top of Cassel's hill.

Het' Kasteelhof

8 Rue St-Nicolas, Cassel, t 03 28 40 59 29. Open Thur, Fri, Sun 11am–10pm, Sat 11am–midnight. Closed Mon–Wed and three weeks Jan. Dishes €3–10.50.

As the 'peak' of Flanders, the summit of Mont Cassel has historically been topped by a castle, long demolished, and a windmill, placed there to make the most of the wind. Today it has another 'monument' in the shape of this small bar, the 'Castle Inn', in an ideal location across the road from the mill. Looking out from the windows of the bar, its rooftop balcony or the garden terrace it's easy to feel truly on top of the world, with the great green expanse of Flanders laid out below you to disappear into the soft horizon. Turn away from the panorama for a while and you can admire a positive overkill of all the accumulated bits and bobs that make up *estaminet* décor. Dangling from the roof there are bunches of hops and herbs, tin baths and all sorts of old pots; around the walls and shelves they are matched by an unclassifiable mix of paintings, old beer or chocolate adverts, Victorian figurines and other things harder to make out.

A drink and a convivial meal while contemplating the view at the Kasteelhof is a favourite reward for walkers and cyclists who have made their way up the hill. They are joined every weekend by a complete mix of the less energetic – young families, couples, pensioners, Lille metropolitan-types in need of fresh air – who get there by other means. Arch-traditional as this and other *estaminets* may seem, their current popularity is a fairly recent phenomenon. Twenty years or so ago, many *estaminets* were dying on their feet, dingy old places frequented only by elderly villagers, the local equivalent of the kind of English pub whose only idea of food was crisps and a Scotch egg. Their rediscovery has come as part of the general enthusiasm for anything with roots and the smack of authenticity, and the particularly French cult of *terroir*, the passion for the small-scale and for fresh, local food and drinks. And this revival owes a great deal in particular to Emmanuel de Quillacq, *patron* of the Kasteelhof, who first began to seek out and showcase the best of local beers, and to offer an ample range of finely prepared Flemish dishes and products rather than just a few snacks. This 'model' has now been followed by bars all across the region.

Emmanuel de Quillacq is an enthusiast for every other aspect of French-Flemish culture as well. The bar hosts regular folk-music and storytelling sessions, and at any time you can try out the often-bizarre Flemish bar-room games, like table skittles. It's also naturally a centre of activity during Cassel's special events, like the Carnival and the International Bagpipe Festival (yes, a bagpipe festival) each June.

Estaminet eating still doesn't conform to the usual patterns of French dining. In place of the structured courses of a classic French meal there are just dishes of varying sizes, so that you can put together a hefty meal, or a small snack. The sometimes compulsive intricacy of much *cuisine française* is largely absent too. Instead, there's a notable comfort-food quality, with many dishes that – served with obligatory heaps of *frites* – are more like satisfying, warming nosh, which incidentally means that they go perfectly with beer. Quality stems from the use of excellent fresh ingredients and proper care in preparation. At the Kasteelhof, for a snack or first course, you can choose from salads, soups, sausages, *tartines* (open sandwiches with cheese, pâtés, meats or other toppings) and a fine range of *flamiches* and quiches, such as the richly pork-and-apple-flavoured *cœur casselois*. For something larger, *potjevleesch* is French Flanders' best-known dish, but it's not for everyone: the usual translation 'terrine' doesn't sum it up nearly as well as the more literal 'pot of meat', a Brueghelesque mix of coarse-cut pork, veal and often other meats, served cold with chips and salad and eaten with lashings of mustard. There are plenty of less full-on alternatives, such as a smoothly satisfying beef-and-beer *carbonnade*, larger quiches, omelettes and a choice of *planches*, generous mixed platters of *tartines* with a variety of local cheeses, pâtés and other cold meats (plus the salad and chips). Desserts are not neglected either, with *crêpes*, fresh home-made fruit tarts and imaginative homemade ice-creams, including a sorbet made with beer.

The subtleties missing from Flemish food tend to be deferred to the beers, which are wonderful. The Kasteelhof is a beer-taster's heaven. The list offers over 50 varieties, all from small breweries in the Nord or the Pas-de-Calais – in contrast to those of some *estaminets*, which also stock better-known Belgian beers. One can spend a very pleasant afternoon here sat by the window and the view making discoveries – the soft, full-bodied Trois Monts from St-Sylvestre-Cappel, Cassel's own Zannekin, the wheaty Blanche de Cambrai – before finally heading off down the hill. As you leave, note that the bar has a small shop, with beers and other local produce to take away.

Touring Around

Cassel is the natural centre of the *Monts de Flandre*, perched atop Mont Cassel (176m), the highest point in Flanders. This may not seem much of a height by international standards, but as you climb the winding lanes that lead up from the plain it looks huge: the town is clustered together in almost unreal fashion at the top, behind its old fortified gates, to complete the theatrical impression. At its core there is an expansive Grand'Place, and, at the very peak, a remarkable windmill, a statue of Marshal Foch and the Kasteelhof. Around and below, the houses of Cassel are packed precipitously along the hillsides, their steep-sloped grey- and red-tiled roofs sometimes seeming impossibly close together, mixed in with vegetable allotments and footpaths, while all around the green and brown Flanders plains stretch away for ever.

The height of Mont Cassel in a flat country has always made it important in wars, which Flanders has probably seen more of than any other part of Europe. It was a stronghold of a Gaulish tribe called the Morins, and the Romans built a fortress here in the time of Julius Caesar. Cassel was fought over many times in the Middle Ages. Then, in the 1670s, as Louis XIV was driving French frontiers relentlessly eastwards, his generals informed him that the *Monts de Flandre*, which until then had with the rest of Flanders formed part of the Spanish Netherlands, were a strategic property France definitely needed to acquire. In 1677 a Spanish and Dutch army was defeated by the French at Zuytpeene, just to the west, and the following year western Flanders was attached to France for ever. For a long time this meant little to most of the population, who remained predominantly Flemish-speaking until the early 20th century.

This did not end Cassel's military role. In 1914 it was the headquarters of the French General (later Marshal) Foch in the Battle of the Yser, in which his armies halted the Germans' attempts to cut around the flank of the Allied lines. The last time Cassel saw fighting was in May 1940, when both its hill and the Mont des Cats to the east were strongpoints in British attempts to slow down the German advance on Dunkerque, and were only given up after a ferocious three-day battle. A British war cemetery is attached to the town cemetery, beside the Bailleul road on the east side of town.

The obvious place to begin exploring Cassel is the **Grand'Place**, which slopes up and down over different levels and terraces. It contains the town's most distinguished buildings, a mix of French *Ancien Régime* styles with others that are far more Netherlandish, as well as others in functional brick from the 1950s. Cassel is another town that needed a great deal of reconstruction after 1945 and, although not every-thing could be restored, the result is still impressive. Grandest of the mansions is the **Hôtel de la Noble Cour** on the west side (also known as the **Landshuys**), built under Spanish rule in the 16th century. Beneath a typically Flemish gable roof, it has an elegant, much more French-Renaissance-influenced main façade; its most curious features, though, are the grotesque heads carved at the foot of its windows, mythical beasts and figures that often look distinctly devilish. Originally the courthouse of the Lordship of Cassel, which had authority over the whole territory between St-Omer and Ypres, the Noble Cour now houses the **Musée de Flandre**, a folk and social history museum, but this has been closed for restoration and is unlikely to reopen for some time. Other façades on the Grand'Place provide a run-through of Cassel's history: the **Taverne Flamande** restaurant, built in 'neo-Flemish' style in the 1930s, stands next to a finely-proportioned Louis-XVI *hôtel*. One building that was irredeemably lost in 1940 was the famous 1634 town hall, which was replaced by the current plain brick Hôtel de Ville that houses the tourist office. All around the square there are attractive cafés and restaurants, with plenty of outside terrace-space when the weather's suitable.

One street back from the Grand'Place but dominating the view at the eastern end of the square is Cassel's main church, the **Collégiale de Notre-Dame**. Parts of this giant brick temple date from the 11th century, but the greater part of it is a sombre 16th-century Gothic *hallekerk* or hall-church, a huge rectangular space with three naves of equal length instead of the usual cross-pattern, a church style peculiar to Flanders that – prior to the French takeover – also spread westwards into Artois. Right behind Notre-Dame there is the impressive Flemish Baroque façade of the one-time **Jesuit Church**, which now provides a very grand (and odd) location for a garage. There are several more churches and small chapels around Cassel, which for centuries was an important pilgrimage centre; the tourist office has a full list.

From the main porch of Notre-Dame, a walk along the street sloping up to the right out of the Grand'Place, Rue de Bergues, will take you on a circuit around the line of Cassel's 16th–17th-century **ramparts**, which once enclosed the tiny fortified town. The corner of Route de Dunkerque, right next to the church, marks the site of the **Porte de Dunkerque**, now mostly demolished; further up Rue de Bergues, at the corner of Rue Profonde ('Deep Street'), there remains from the old **Porte de Bergues** a strange little watchtower, with wonderful views over a near-360° circle. As in much of Cassel atop its hill, it's often invigoratingly windy. Continuing along Rue de Bergues will take you into a big, sloping square that's now primarily a car park, **Place du Général Vandamme**, named after a Napoleonic commander born in the town. From there, the little alley of Rue St-Nicolas strikes up steeply toward the Kasteelhof and the very top of the hill.

The top of the hill naturally gives the very best **views** of all, especially from the eastern side by the Foch statue, where the Marshal, atop his horse, scans the horizon endlessly for signs of any new invading armies. According to a local saying, from the summit of Mont-Cassel it's possible to see five kingdoms: France, Belgium, Holland, Britain and the Kingdom of Heaven. Dominating the vista in a westerly direction is the magnificent 16th-century windmill, the **Moulin de Cassel** (*open June–Sept daily 10–12 and 2–6, Oct–May Sat, Sun and public hols 10–12 and 2–6; adm*), beautifully restored and now very much in use; you can even buy freshly ground flour. To the left of the mill

Watch out that the Giants don't get you: Flemish Festivals

Nearly every town and village in French Flanders has its set of **giants**, huge wood and papier-mâché figures commonly associated half-seriously with some legend of the origin of the community. Lovingly maintained, they are generally paraded around town during Carnival, in the spring, and on a few other set days each year, depending on each town's particular calendar of events. The parades are led by loopy-sounding marching bands in jokey outfits, which make their way around town amid general partying and much sampling of the local brew.

These festivals are also occasions for bringing to the fore the strange range of **Flemish games**, such as Flemish archery (firing an arrow straight up into the air to hit a target dangling from a crane), Flemish bowls (played with round slabs, which look a bit like uncut cheeses, instead of balls) and many more. There are also games that can be played at any time of year in *estaminets*, such as *putbak*, a quoits-like game that involves throwing balls into the mouth of a metal frog.

Listed here are just a few of the larger parades; Cassel in particular hosts several more events each year, and tourist offices have details of all of them.

Bailleul Carnival is one of the biggest and most boisterous; at its hub is *Gargantua*, Flanders' only sitting giant, whose parade is on the Sunday before Mardi Gras.

Cassel's giants are a couple, *Reuze-Papa* and *Reuze-Maman*. *Reuze-Papa*, who looks like a Roman soldier, makes his first appearance of the year on the Carnival Sunday before Shrove Tuesday, and both come out together on Easter Monday.

Hazebrouck's giant, Roland, comes out – unusually – in the middle of Lent, and has another, bigger, parade with his family, the *Tijse-Tajse*, on the first weekend in July.

Steenvoorde has several giants who appear several times each year, including *Yan den Houtkapper* (Jan the Woodcutter), who supposedly made a pair of clogs for Charlemagne, and was rewarded with a magic breastplate. Two other big occasions are the International Giants' Summer Carnival in late April, and the Hop Festival on the first Sunday in October.

Wormhout: The *Roi des Mitrons* parades with his band, the *Bande des Mitrons*, on Carnival Sunday.

is the site of the former château of Cassel, destroyed in the 18th century, and now a small park, the **Jardin Public**, containing the *Monument des Trois Batailles*, commemorating three conflicts in the hill's history, in 1071, 1328 and 1677. On one side of the esplanade there is also a large but now decayed 1920s building known as the 'casino'. Built in an attempt to give Cassel a Grand Hotel, but long closed, its main purpose today is to hold up the transmitters of a local bilingual radio station. Just below it, a path leads steeply down through the 1621 **Porte du Château**, flanked by two very solid turrets and the only substantial part of the old castle still standing. This path runs into the equally steep and narrow Rue du Château, which leads back to the Grand'Place.

Cassel is a town of alleys and courtyards, hidden spaces and gardens. To follow a popular route, head out of the inner ring of streets from Place Vandamme northwest down Rue Bollaert le Gavrian, the St-Omer road. A short distance from the *place* there is an opening on the left into a very narrow alley which, surprisingly, is the beginning of the **Chemin des Remparts**, a paved path that runs just below the line of the old fortifications along the western side of town, between houses and vegetable patches, with more superb views along the way. In Cassel the town fades away quickly into open country as soon as you leave the main streets. Along the way the ramparts path meets the **Chemin d'Aire**, with the **Porte d'Aire**, the most complete survivor of the

Shopping

Bailleul ✉ 59270
Ferme de Beck, Eeckelstraete, t 03 28 49 03 90, f 03 28 42 28 32. Christiane and Denis Beck brew a fine traditional beer, *Hommelpap*, at their farm on the outskirts of Bailleul, and also sell their own butter and other farm produce. Visitors can tour the farm and brewery, and at weekends traditional dinners are served to accompany the beer (*Mar–Nov only, Sat from 7pm, Sun from 5pm*).

Esquelbecq ✉ 59470
Brasserie Thiriez, 22 Rue de Wormhout, t/f 03 28 62 88 44, *www.ifrance.com/brasseriethiriez*. Often known just as the 'Brasserie d'Esquelbecq', Dominique Thiriez's village micro-brewery uses the best traditional Flemish brewing techniques. It produces four main beers, plus interesting special-occasion brews such as the spicy *Bière de Noël*, and another brewed in collaboration with the Swale Brewery of Sittingbourne, Kent. The brewery shop is also a charming little *estaminet*, where you can sample the product together with local snacks. *Open Mon–Sat 9–1 and 2–7, and some Sundays in summer; tours by reservation.*

Godewaersvelde ✉ 59270
Fromagerie du Mont des Cats, Le Mont des Cats, t (via L'Auberge) 03 28 42 51 44. All the fine cheese on sale at this shop next to the Auberge on top of the mount is made by the monks at the Abbey. It also has a small selection of farm-made biscuits, beers and other local produce. *Closed Sun am, Mon and Tues.*

Oxelaere ✉ 59670
Ferme des Templiers, La Place, t 03 28 40 50 37. Marie-Christine and Philippe Dubois produce a creamy, rich cheese, *Boulet de Cassel*, and the farm shop also sells their butter, jams and homemade waffles and biscuits, as well as local beers, *potjevleesch* and other *charcuterie*. The farm is signposted, near the centre of Oxelaere just south of Cassel.

St-Sylvestre-Cappel ✉ 59114
Brasserie St-Sylvestre, 1 Rue de la Chapelle, t 03 28 40 15 49, *www.brasserie-st-sylvestre.com*. One of the best of French Flanders' medium-sized traditional brewers, which produces the distinctively subtle *Trois Monts*, *Gavroche* and several other refined beers. There is a small brewery shop for direct sales. *Open Tues–Fri 8–12.30 and 2–5.30, Sat 8–12.*

17th-century gates. Beyond it, the path continues through more allotments and over a little bridge to emerge beyond the southeast corner of the Grand'Place, via another tiny alley. This is only one of many enjoyable walks in and around Cassel, all of which are marked out on the tourist office's very handy free leaflets.

Two roads lead east from Cassel. The D948 runs straight to **Steenvoorde**, where the eye is grabbed by two of the largest Flanders windmills, which dominate the town. An alternative is to take the Bailleul road southeast through St-Sylvestre-Cappel – site of one of Flanders' best breweries – and turn off left onto the country road that leads, via the attractive village of **Eecke**, to **Godewaersvelde**. As well as having one of the region's most incorrigibly un-French names, this little village 5km from the Belgian border is one of the most characteristically Flemish in the whole area, with a long winding street through the middle, a big hall-church and little brick and tile houses with lace curtains. It's a centre for French Flanders' mild-mannered nationalist movement which, fittingly, is based in a bar, the wonderful **Het Blauwershof**. With its green-white-and-red shutters, wood panelling, copper stoves and magnificent beer, this venerable place could even outdo the better-known Kasteelhof as an image of a traditional *estaminet*.

Just southeast of Godewaersvelde is the **Mont des Cats**, most dramatically steep of the *Monts de Flandre*, and reached via a narrow lane that winds up through the curious tiny village that clings to the green flank of the hill. The mountain's name does not have anything to do with cats but is derived from that of a Germanic people known as the *Cattes*, who made it their stronghold in the 5th century AD. The road turns through tight loops as it climbs to the top of the mountain (158m), where there are wonderful views into Belgium, and a massive, brick-faced monastery, the **Abbaye de Ste-Marie-du-Mont**. This is not a medieval foundation, but was established in 1826 as part of the restoration of Catholicism following the Revolution. Restored in turn after 1918 and 1945, the abbey has a neo-Gothic, dark-tower look, a cross between a cathedral, a castle and a Victorian textile mill. The mountain has been a religious centre since time immemorial, and is still home to a closed community of Trappist monks. The abbey has a visitor centre and shop (*open Mon 2.30–6, Wed–Sat 10–12 and 2.30–6, Sun 12.15–1pm and 2.30–6*). The monks particularly make their own cheese, which is also on sale at the shop next to the Auberge du Mont des Cats (*see* left).

Further on are more of Flanders' mountains. On the very line of the Belgian frontier is **Mont Noir**, famous to French readers as the childhood home of the novelist Marguerite Yourcenar. The château where she lived is no longer there – it was obliterated in the First World War – but the summit has been made into a delightful wooded park in her memory. Both Mont Noir and the Mont des Cats are wonderful for walking. On the way up to Mont Noir from **Boeschepe** there is also an especially magnificent windmill, the **Ondankmeulen** (*open April–June and Sept–Oct Sun and public hols 3–6; July and Aug daily 3–5.30; adm*), built in 1802 and still in regular use. Like others nearby, it is particularly impressive when the weather closes in and the wind strikes up, which happens fairly frequently around here.

The villages north and west of Cassel also have points to explore, amid a landscape that runs down from the hills to roll gently for a while before becoming completely flat. Little **Zermezeele**, about 4km north of Cassel, has the personal chapel of a 15th-century *seigneur* incorporated into its church; further north again is the fascinating village of **Esquelbecq**, built around an impressively large square with a very Flemish-looking château from 1606 on one side and a giant 16th-century *hallekerk* church with elaborate decorative brickwork – and a fine *carillon* – on the other. The château is not open to the public, but its exterior can well be appreciated from the square, all pepper-pot turrets that make it an ideal candidate for a ghastly grange. A barn near Esquelbecq was the site of the 'Wormhout Massacre' in May 1940, when some 80 British prisoners were massacred by German SS troops, and this event is commemorated by monuments in Esquelbecq and on the Esquelbecq–Wormhout road. Esquelbecq tourist office, the **Maison du Westhoek**, has a small folk museum, and information on the 1940 incident.

To the west, **Bollezeele** has an especially grand late-Gothic church, completed in 1606. About 3km south is **Rubrouck**, an ancient village full of medieval details that also has one of the region's most bizarre sights. This was the home of Friar Guillaume de Rubrouck, who in the 13th century travelled all the way to Mongolia, to the court of Genghis Khan. To commemorate its most distinguished son little Rubrouck now has a museum, the **Maison Guillaume de Rubrouck** (*open April–Sept Sat and Sun 2.30–5.30; adm*). As well as the tourist office it contains a display on Mongolian life and culture, but its *pièces de résistance* are outside the village, none other than two genuine round Mongol yurt tents, plonked in a Flanders field. Just south again are **Noordpeene** and **Zuytpeene**, site of the battle that secured Cassel for France in 1677.

Of the larger towns in the south of French Flanders, **Bailleul** was one of the wealthiest in Flanders in the Middle Ages, when it had particularly close links with England. It was devastated in the First World War, but a prodigious effort was made at restoration. Like all old Flemish merchant towns it has a very big Grand'Place or market square, which post-1918 regained a remarkable number of its Flemish stepped-brick façades. Above all, Bailleul's magnificent Gothic **Hôtel de Ville** was restored almost completely, together with its giant 13th-century tower-belfry, **Le Beffroi**, which can be climbed to enjoy the view (*open April–Sept Sat 3pm, Sun 11am, July–mid-Sept also Tues 11am, Wed and Fri 4pm; adm, tickets from tourist office*). Just off the square there is also a more than usually interesting local museum, the **Musée Benoît Depuydt** (*open Mon, Wed–Sun 2–5.30; adm*). As well as an impressive collection of Flemish furniture, costumes, lace and household items, it also contains Italian ceramics and a surprising picture collection, with fine works by many Flemish artists such as Gérard David and Pieter Brueghel the Younger. Bailleul is also one of the towns of French Flanders most dedicated to keeping up its traditions, in food, its Carnival, and its markets.

Hazebrouck, 13km west of Bailleul, was heavily knocked around in both the First and Second World Wars. Nevertheless, amid the modern town there are still many relics of old Flanders, such as the 15th-century church of **St-Eloi**, and the former **Augustinian Convent**, from 1518. Hazebrouck's main attraction, though, is its busy street activity, centred on one of the largest Flemish Grand'Places, dominated by a 19th-century neoclassical **town hall** that could easily be mistaken for a national parliament. The square is at its liveliest during the great weekly markets, which in both Hazebrouck and Bailleul, due to a curious Flemish tradition, are on Tuesdays.

Where to Stay

Cassel ✉ 59670

Hôtel Le Foch, 41 Grand'Place, **t** 03 28 42 47 73 (*double rooms €65–70*). Cassel has strangely few hotels, but this curiously old-fashioned little place has a great location on the main square. The recently-renovated rooms are still quite simple, but it's a decent weekend option. The Foch also has a traditional **restaurant** (*menus €15–32*).

Les Sources, 326 Rue d'Aire, **t** 03 28 48 26 26, *valejean@wanadoo.fr* (*rooms €48 for two*). Amid fields on the hill south of Cassel, this great *chambres d'hôtes* has a distinctively relaxing feel. The five airy, imaginatively decorated rooms (one with full disabled access) are subtly stylish in a low-key way, and owners Valérie de Poorter, Jean-Bernard Vincent and family are similarly welcoming. They also have an art space, for exhibitions and workshops. The rooms have delightful views – down over the plains on one side, up to the mill of Cassel on another – and it's exceptional value.

La Prairie, 1516 Route d'Hazebrouck, **t** 03 28 42 41 15, **f** 03 28 48 47 92 (*rooms €40 for two*). A comfortable B&B on the outskirts of Cassel, in a tranquil old farm with garden and pond. The two rooms, in a former barn, have good facilities. Owners M and Mme Woestelandt also have two fully self-contained *gîtes*.

Boeschepe ✉ 59299

Auberge du Vert Mont, Route du Mont Noir, **t** 03 28 49 41 26, *aubergevertmont@aol.com* (*double rooms €58–80*). An unusual *Logis* hotel in its own grounds on the slopes of Mont Noir, with tennis courts, spectacular views, and health farm facilities such as a sauna, hammam and massage treatments. The **restaurant** (*menus €13–29*) serves conventional local fare.

T'Heerenhuys, 340 Rue de la Gare, **t** 03 28 49 45 73, *www.boeschepe.com* (*rooms €60 for two*). Boeschepe's former manor house (which is what the name means in Flemish), this distinguished 19th-century mansion is now a superior B&B. The four high-ceilinged rooms have been carefully redecorated to match the style of the house, with antiques, paintings and elegant décor as well as all modern

comforts, and the breakfast room and lounge, with fine porcelain and original fireplaces, are just as attractive. There's an extensive garden, and M and Mme Maertens offer **evening meals** by arrangement (*€20–30*). It's very popular, so book early.

Bollezeele ✉ 59470

Hostellerie St-Louis, 47 Rue de l'Eglise, **t** 03 28 68 81 83, *www.hostelleriesaintlouis.com* (*double rooms €51–76*). A superior *Logis* hotel in a rambling 18th-century residence surrounded by a large garden. The well-equipped rooms are mostly in the 19th-century wings. The **restaurant** (*menus €23–50*) serves standard French and local dishes.

Le Pantgat Hof, 27 Rue de Metz, **t** 03 28 68 00 87, *http://pantgat.free.fr* (*rooms €45 for two, €73 for four*). An impressive *chambres d'hôtes* in a big courtyard-style farm 2km outside Bollezeele, with four spacious, pretty rooms, one of them a fully-family-sized two-room suite. **Evening meals** are available by arrangement (*€18*), there's a lovely garden, and the owners, M and Mme Chiloup-Gey, also run an art workshop and offer guided walks and pony rides.

Eating Alternatives

Thanks to the *estaminet* it's common to order food here as single dishes, often in mixed platters (*assiettes* or *planches*), in place of the usual French three-course set menu.

For anyone interested in really exploring Flanders' *estaminets*, local tourist offices have listings of all the traditional bars in the region, many in small villages. Take note, though, that *estaminets* are often closed early in the week, and/or may only serve food at weekends.

Cassel ✉ 59670

La Taverne Flamande, 34 Grand'Place, **t** 03 28 42 42 59 (*menus €11–16*). A comfortable restaurant in one of the most distinguished buildings on the square, with gable roof and flower-filled windows. The long dining room runs right through the building to end atop one of the flanks of MontCassel, giving a soaring view. The set menus are great value: regulars include a warming cheese *flamiche*, pork cooked with juniper, and juicy apple tarts. As well as the inevitable local beers, there's a decent wine list.

Kerelshof, 31 Grand'Place, **t** 03 28 42 43 02 (*dishes c. €6–11*). This roomy, perfectly relaxed *estaminet*-bar has all the classic fittings inside – old wood, odd metal pots, Flemish curiosities – plus, outside, the most characterful of the terraces that line Cassel's Grand'Place in summer, in pole position on the north side of the square. To eat there are generous platters of local favourites, with – of course – a superior range of fine beers.

Bavinchove ✉ 59670

In den Goedendag, 1 Kerke Plaetse, **t/f** 03 28 48 49 18 (*dishes c. €6–8*). In a little village south of Cassel, this is a classic country *estaminet*, with an ample choice of beers and (*Fri–Sun only*) good *tartines*, *potjevleesch* and other hearty dishes. *Closed Mon.*

Boeschepe ✉ 59299

De Vierpot, 125 Rue du Moulin, **t** 03 28 49 46 37 (*dishes c. €6–15*). Converted from a farm, this isn't the prettiest of Flanders' *estaminets*, but gains a special attraction from its location, right at the foot of Boeschepe's Ondankmeulen windmill. There's a big terrace outside from which to watch the sails go around, satisfying platters of Flemish favourites – particularly good cheeses and own-made fruit tarts – and the customary healthy range of beers to look through, with 48 varieties. Note the changing opening days. *Open Oct–Mar Fri–Sun and hols only; April–June and Sept Wed–Sun and hols only; July and Aug Tues–Sun and hols.*

Eecke ✉ 59114

Brasserie St-Georges, 5 Rue de Caestre, **t** 03 28 40 13 71 (*dishes c. €6–15*). The St-Georges retains the essential *estaminet* features and country feel, but is much bigger than the norm. It's a place for hearty meals and beer-sampling: there are over 60 bottled beers, and five on draught. The food range includes less common Flemish dishes such as ham in beer and *standevleesch* (cooked *charcuterie*, pork, melted Maroilles cheese and cumin, served with salad). *Open Sept–June Fri eve, Sat, Sun, public hols and eves of public hols only; July–Aug eves daily, and lunch Sat, Sun.*

Godewaersvelde ✉ 59270

L'Auberge du Mont des Cats, Le Mont des Cats, **t** 03 28 42 51 44 (*dishes c. €6–10*). This big eating-house by the abbey doesn't try to be adventurous in its country cooking – the *Assiette de l'Abbaye*, with bacon and Mont des Cats cheese, salads, Flemish sausages – but there are over 25 local beers and, as a prime attraction, a superb view from the dining room or the larger outside *terrasse*.

L'Auberge du Catsberg, 1487 Route de l'Abbaye, **t** 03 28 42 59 59 (*menus €7–15.50*). A little below the abbey on the north side of the Mont des Cats, but still with a fine view, this convivial bar-restaurant offers local classics like *carbonnade*, *potjevleesch* and *coq à la bière*. *Closed Mon, lunch only Tues–Fri.*

Au Roi du Potje Vleesch, 31 Rue du Mont des Cats, **t** 03 28 42 52 56 (*dishes c. €8–12*). Almost as pretty as the Blauwershof, with a slightly wider choice of Flemish specialities, especially meats and local *charcuterie*. It also has a shop selling meats, beers, cheese and other Flanders products. *Closed Mon.*

Het Blauwershof, 9 Rue d'Eecke, **t** 03 28 49 45 11 (*dishes c. €3–10*). A wonderfully relaxing bar where you can easily settle in for a whole afternoon. There are three beers on tap, close to 30 French and Belgian beers in bottles and a big choice of gins and spirits. The food is hearty: *coq à la bière*, *flamiches* and *tartines*, all served with huge bowls of *frites*. There's the full range of traditional Flemish bar games, and you can pick up leaflets about the area. *Closed Mon.*

Hazebrouck ✉ 59190

La Taverne, 61 Grand'Place, **t** 03 28 41 63 09 (*menus €13.50–23*). Unmissable on Hazebrouck's main square with its soaring Flemish gable façade, this is a combination of *estaminet* and town brasserie. It gets impressively bustling each lunchtime, but there's always room in the barn-sized, near-baronial interior, with its old dark woodwork and a ceiling inset with stained glass. Diners can choose between Flemish classics – especially good *flamiches* and quiches, many vegetarian-friendly – or more complex offerings, many made using local beer or gin. A great place on a wintry afternoon. *Closed Sun eve and Mon.*

Metropolitan France:

Lille

08

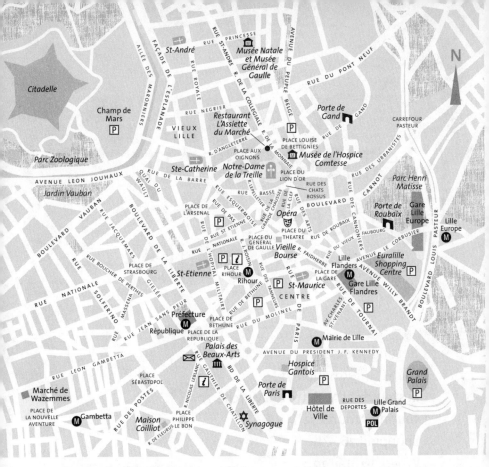

France's regional centres long lived in the shadow of Paris. Lille, fourth-largest city in the country, was once its great industrial textile centre, while around it was its largest coalfield. In the last few decades, however, the city has been comprehensively cleaned up, to reveal an elegant, still businesslike city beneath the old factory soot – a process that has reached a peak with Lille's year as European Capital of Culture in 2004. Lille is also a frontier city, the one-time capital of Flanders, and at its heart there is an old 16th–17th-century Flemish town of great charm. The Eurostar has transformed access to Lille from Britain, and a visit there provides an enjoyable immersion in French urban life. It's a lively, buzzy city, with a huge student population. At its core are three central squares, where, true to its old merchant heart, Lille holds the largest antiques and flea market in Europe each September, the *Braderie*. It has luxurious food shops, and is a shopping mecca in other ways too. Because of Lille's long position as a textile centre, it has a spectacular, positively Parisian, concentration of high-chic fashion stores.

In food, Lille offers all the diversity of a modern French city, where restaurant-going seems to be the number-one social activity. Local Flemish tradition – especially the superb beers – lives alongside a range of more eclectic French and international influences. One of the city's most imaginative modern restaurants is **L'Assiette du Marché**, combining fine quality with one of old Lille's most characterful settings.

Getting There

Eurostar **trains** from London or Brussels and TGV trains from Paris and most other parts of France arrive at **Lille-Europe** station, on the eastern side of the city centre. It's an easy walk from there to the heart of town, downhill along Av Le Corbusier, which leads in about 130 metres to the recently renovated older station, **Gare Lille-Flandres**, which handles all local routes. From there, along Rue Faidherbe, it's a few minutes' walk to Lille's central squares. A turn up any of the streets on the right will take you towards Vieux Lille.

If you **drive** to Lille on the A25 *autoroute* (toll-free from Calais or Dunkerque), leave the motorway at the *Lille-Centre* exit, which will take you via some twists onto Rue Nationale. From Paris and the south on the A1, follow signs to *Lille Périphérique-Sud*, then *Lille-Centre*. There are several central **car parks**; most convenient for Vieux Lille is usually Av du Peuple Belge.

Lille **airport**, 10km south, has French domestic and European flights (but as yet none from the UK). There are regular buses into the city.

Getting Around

Central Lille is easy to get around on foot, but **taxis** are plentiful and there is a good public transport system. There are two **Métro** lines, which cross each other at Gare Lille-Flandres, and many bus routes. Tickets are sold from automatic machines at Métro stations and some bus stops, and at the tourist office. The best ticket to get is the *Pass' Journée*, which gives unlimited travel on the Métro and buses for one day for €3.50, but there are also other discount and family tickets.

Tourist Information

Lille: Palais Rihour, Place Rihour, t 03 59 57 94 00, *www.lilletourism.com*. The city tourist office offers an interesting range of guided tours, many in English, and also sells transport tickets, and has a gift shop.
CDT-Nord: 6 Rue Gauthier de Châtillon, t 03 20 57 59 59, *www.cdt-nord.fr*. The tourist office for the Nord *Département* has a complete range of information on the whole area.

L'Assiette du Marché

61 Rue de la Monnaie, t 03 20 06 83 61, assiettedumarche@free.fr.
Open Mon–Thur 12–2.30 and 7–10.30, Fri, Sat 12–2.30 and 7–11; closed Sun.
Menus €15 (two courses), €20 (three courses); carte *average €30.*

The Rue de la Monnaie takes its name from the Hôtel de la Monnaie, one of the most elegant of Vieux Lille's mansions. Parts of it are from the 12th century, and it was the residence of high city officials before becoming a royal mint under Louis XIV. Turn off the street into its cobbled courtyard today, however, and you find the *hôtel* is now home to this equally striking contemporary restaurant, open since January 2004. Inside, original features that keep up a *Lillois* identity – grand old stone fireplaces, fine 17th-century woodwork, intriguing carved lions picked out in gold – combine with a minimalist dark-wood bar, clean-lined tables and ultra-comfortable leather seating. Go beyond the main room and you enter a glass-roofed internal courtyard that's another eye-catching piece of urban chic. Young waiters and waitresses bustle about not in waistcoats and buttoned-up whites but in modish loose black shirts.

Thomas Proye, owner of the Assiette du Marché, comes from the same family that runs Lille's most illustrious restaurant, L'Huîtrière, and the also highly-regarded Ecume des Mers (*see* p.80). In his own restaurant, though, he has struck out with an innovative, fresh, more informal style. One of the most noticeable features is in the pricing: the €20 set menu is quite exceptional value, and the outstanding, carefully assembled wine list equally offers many of the best current French labels at much lower-than-usual prices.

M. Proye explains that this reflects a deliberate decision, to aim for volume rather than big margins on each meal, and an intention to 'democratize' fine wines. This generous (and very popular) approach is combined with a proper awareness of how things should be done, encouraged no doubt by his family credentials: in any trendyish, designer-y restaurant it's common to feel that the waiters got the job on looks alone, but the staff here are not just pretty but also friendly, able, non-snooty and on the ball.

Most importantly, this same pairing of imagination and attention to essentials is there in the food. Northern French regional cooking provides the basis, but with each dish looked at anew and given an original, light touch. Many dishes feature subtle, unusual herbs and spices – although Thomas Proye and chef Patrice Patou maintain this isn't a real departure from French tradition, since things like cumin or saffron have always been used in some part of France. Above all, the 'du Marché' in the name reflects an absolute dedication to first-rate ingredients and market freshness – the menu changes every week – and it shows. From an early-summer menu, a *grand salade* was an absolute explosion of perfect spring vegetables, grilled, roast or raw – aubergines, carrots, asparagus, parsnips, mushrooms and more. *Souris d'agneau* featured beautifully tender, well-flavoured lamb shanks, cooked with a delicate trace of cumin.

Desserts hit the spot too, with a modern take on a meringue *vacherin glacé*, topped by superbly fresh strawberries. Many restaurants nowadays try to match up a special location, slick design, an informal atmosphere and quality food, but few do it so well.

Touring Around

The heart of Lille is its three main squares, and above all the **Grand'Place**, officially titled Place Général de Gaulle, in memory of the city's most famous son. On the north side, towards Vieux Lille, it's lined by an up-and-down row of old houses, all with different roof lines, while to the south the eye is grabbed by the giant façade of the Voix du Nord newspaper building, built in the 1920s in a curious Flemish revival-art deco style with a huge stepped gable in grey concrete. Next to it, Lille's main theatre, the **Théâtre du Nord**, is housed in the surprisingly elegant building designed in 1717 as the *Grand'Garde*, the main guardhouse for the city's French army garrison. In the middle of the square there is a patriotic monument, the column of the *Déesse*, commemorating the resistance of Lille during its siege by the Austrians in 1792.

The most striking building on the square, and Lille's greatest treasure, is the **Vieille Bourse** or 'Old Exchange' along the eastern side, now beautifully restored so that the red, ochre and black of its façades gleam out. Rising up through three floors to a grey slate roof, it's a classic of Flemish burgher baroque, a fascinating combination of solidity and tangled, intricate carvings, with caryatids and other mythical creatures. The work of local architect Julien Destrez, the Bourse was built in 1652–3, at the highest point of Lille's wealth and importance as a major city of the then-Spanish Netherlands. Crests sit above each of its four entrances: on the north side is a blue-and-yellow shield of the city's merchants; facing the Grand'Place is the white fleur-de-lys on red of the City of Lille itself; on the south side there is the black lion on gold of the Counts of Flanders; and above the Place du Théâtre entrance is the multi-quartered coat of arms of the Habsburg monarchs of Spain. The Bourse's ground floor consisted of 24 small shops that were occupied by the city's principal merchants, around a galleried courtyard which now contains stalls selling flowers and second-hand books (*daily exc Mon*).

The Grand'Place is always full of movement, but it comes particularly alive at certain times of the year. At the end of April it hosts a dazzling flower market, June sees the *Fêtes de Lille*, and in the first weekend of September each year the Grand'Place and Place Rihour are the centre of the **Braderie**, Lille's extraordinary flea market. The origins of this event are a medieval law that allowed servants to sell their masters' old clothes and other oddments on the street once a year: since then everyone in the city has had the right to set up a stall on these two days every September. Today, people selling piles of old junk rub shoulders with serious antique dealers from across Europe, together with an estimated one million visitors. All sorts of other events are organized to go with it, and this is also a traditional time to eat *moules* and *frites*. The square is also especially lovely around Christmas, when a **Christmas fair** takes over Place Rihour, and the Grand'Place, lined with lights, has as its centrepiece the *Grande Roue*, an ornate, grandly old-fashioned ferris wheel.

From the corner of the square by the Grand'Garde little Rue Rihour – lined with cafés and brasseries, and one of Lille's prime spots for watching the city go by – leads through to **Place Rihour**. The tourist office on its north side occupies the irregular remaining parts of the **Palais Rihour**, the sole architectural reminder of Lille's medieval era under the Dukes of Burgundy. It's a much-battered building: from the 17th century it served as Lille's town hall, but it was damaged by fires in 1700 and during the German occupation in 1916. It's hard to get a good idea of its overall structure from what's left, but some of its *flamboyant* Gothic features can be seen: the tourist office is in a former chapel. Overshadowing the Palais is Lille's huge, sombre war memorial, erected in the 1920s.

The third of the main squares, **Place du Théâtre**, is a more orderly space. Facing the Bourse are two giant buildings from among Lille's singularly quirky collection of early 20th-century architecture, both of them strangely by the same architect, Louis-Marie Cordonnier. The huge **Opéra** was designed to replace a smaller 18th-century theatre that had burnt down in 1903, in an extravagant neo-Louis XVI Baroque style that by the time it was completed – after the First World War – appeared completely out of its time. In the 1900s Cordonnier had also built the **Chambre de Commerce** further along the square, only this time in Flemish-revival style with a massive towering belfry.

The Grand'Place is one of the oldest parts of Lille, a market since its earliest days, but it was outside the early walled town. This was centred to the north, around a castle where Notre-Dame de la Treille is today, on a semi-island amid the streams of the River Deule (Lille and its Flemish name, *'T Rijsel*, both derive from words for island). Since then the Deule has been gradually confined in canals. Lille was first mentioned in documents in 1066, and became one of the chief towns of the independent Counts of Flanders. In 1369, the then-Count's daughter married the Duke of Burgundy, making Lille and Flanders part of the 'Burgundian Inheritance', which would also include modern Holland, Belgium and Luxembourg, and great chunks of eastern France. At the turn of the 16th century another set of marriages and deaths led to the Burgundian territories passing to the Habsburg Emperor Charles V, who was also King of Spain. Lille and Flanders would thus be drawn into the conflict between Philip II of Spain and the Protestant northern Netherlands, although strongly Catholic Lille, like most of the south, stayed loyal to the Spanish king. In the early 17th century peace and administrative reform in the Spanish Netherlands encouraged a rapid growth in trade and wealth. Lille in particular enjoyed something of a Golden Age, and the finest Flemish-style buildings of Vieux Lille and the Vieille Bourse itself all date from this time.

Louis XIV of France, however, was not prepared to let Spanish power stay in the region, and was pushing his frontiers eastward. In August 1667 his troops took Lille, after a 17-day siege. There was no enthusiasm in the city for being French; Louis's governors, though, set about Lille's transformation. Marshal Vauban built a vast citadel to ensure that it would never be lost to France, new, much more regular 'French' streets appeared, and officially-encouraged migration from the rest of France ensured the once-bilingual city became solidly French-speaking. Still more migrants arrived after Lille became a hub of French industry in the 19th century. This industrial muscle also gave Lille a particular place in French Socialist politics, which was one reason why, in the 1980s, President François Mitterand took special interest in the regeneration of Lille, as one of his *grands projets*. The renovation of Vieux Lille, the building of the Métro, the Eurostar and all their attendant infrastructure were all begun under the Mitterand aegis.

Vieux Lille, the oldest core of the city northeast of the three squares, has been the greatest beneficiary of Lille's clean-up. It's a great area for wandering in no particular direction, with charming narrow streets and old Flemish houses, most now beautifully restored, often with elaborate carved details picked out in reds, yellows, blues, greens and more. This is also Lille's most chic shopping area. The most historic route into the old town is to turn right at the north end of the Grand'Place along Rue de la Bourse to enter **Rue de la Grande Chaussée**, which began life as the main path between the walled town and the Grand'Place market. It meets Rue des Chats Bossus, where in front of you is **L'Huîtrière**, France's most magnificently ornate fishmongers' (*see* pp.76, 79). Another great street to wander up is **Rue Esquermoise**, north from the Grand'Place, with the **Pâtisserie Meert**, as fabulous a temple to cakes and chocolate as the Huîtrière is to fish. Rue Basse and Rue Lepelletier are two of the most attractive streets in the old town, with fashion by young designers, antiques, gift shops and great bars and restaurants.

From Rue Basse, a turn north up Rue du Cirque leads to the semi-circular space around Lille's curiously unknown cathedral, **Notre-Dame de la Treille**, the first sight of which may come as a shock, for it's easy to think that part of its west front is covered in plastic sheeting. A strange tale is attached to this building. Lille had never had a cathedral, and in the 19th century a competition was launched to find a suitable design. The winner was a scheme by two English architects, but when it became public that foreign architects had won the prize demands were made that French architects amend the design, and the process descended into chaos. Work stumbled to a complete halt in 1947, and for years the west front was simply bricked up. La Treille was finally given its west façade in 1999, to a design by PL Carlier so radical and so at variance with Victorian Gothic that the cathedral can still appear vaguely 'unfinished'. The 'plastic' façade is actually translucent glass, around a rose window by the artist Kijno, and, however odd it looks from the outside, the effect from inside the cathedral is stunning. Lately, though, this new façade has exhibited structural problems of its own.

Rue des Chats Bossus ends at the very pretty **Place du Lion d'Or**, where to the left is **Rue de la Monnaie**. As well as containing the Assiette du Marché restaurant, it has some of Vieux Lille's most charming Flemish ornamented gables, and the city's best fabric and interior design shops. Just above Place du Lion d'Or, the **Musée de l'Hospice Comtesse** (*open Mon 2–6, Wed–Sun 10–12.30 and 2–6; closed Tues; adm*) occupies a hospital founded in 1237 by Jeanne, Countess of Flanders. Most of the present building dates from the 15th and 17th centuries; one of its great attractions is its beautifully calm old Flemish interior, with a refectory, parlour and dormitories, and an enormous Gothic main hall. The baroque chapel from 1649 has a spectacular painted ceiling and a fine altarpiece, by Arnould Vuez. The museum's collection is an illuminating display of the arts and crafts of Lille and the Low Countries from the 15th to the 17th centuries – painting, faïence pottery, wood carvings, tapestries, and rare early musical instruments.

The Place du Lion d'Or runs indistinguishably into **Place Louise de Bettignies**. In the 17th century the strip of land now called Place du Peuple Belge was still an open canal, where goods were loaded and unloaded, making this one of the most important parts of the merchant city. The most striking of the square's 17th-century buildings is the **Maison de Gilles de la Boë**, built for a wealthy merchant in 1636, and now suitably occupied by a fashion shop. Designed by Julien Destrez, it looks almost like a miniature dry run for the same architect's Vieille Bourse of 15 years later. Away on the eastern side of Place du Peuple Belge is the **Rue de Gand**, with the 1621 **Porte de Gand** impossible to miss at its far end. Beautifully proportioned, this is the finest of Lille's Spanish gates. Rue de Gand is one of the liveliest streets of Vieux Lille, Lille's foremost restaurant row.

North of Place du Peuple Belge the streets have a different feel, because they are long and straight. This is part of Louis XIV's 'extension' of Vieux Lille, laid out after 1667. The lower end of **Rue Royale** is now a buzzing night-time bar and bistro area. In contrast just to the west is Lille's oldest church, **Ste-Catherine**, a Flemish *hallekerk* begun in 1288, with a monolithic 16th-century tower. A walk several blocks up Rue Royale and right on Rue Princesse leads to the **Maison Natale du Général De Gaulle**, a shrine to the great man who was born here in 1890 (*open Wed–Sun 10–12 and 2–5; closed Mon, Tues; adm*).

The areas of Lille south of the three main squares are mostly made up of other post-1667 extensions. To the east, beyond the dainty old **Gare Lille-Flandres** train station, is what could be called 'Mitterrand's Lille'. Looming up over the old station is the awesome mass of the 1994 **Euralille** shopping mall, behind which are the modernistic roofs of **Lille-Europe** station. Running due south from Place du Théâtre, **Rue de Paris** existed before 1667 but was largely rebuilt to form the central spine of the French additions in the south of Lille. It still contains some older, heavy-timbered houses, such as the 1460 almshouse the **Hospice Gantois** – now the **Hermitage Gantois** hotel (*see p.79*) – and at the north end is the 15th-century church of **St-Maurice**, the finest surviving Gothic building in the city and a model of the *hallekerk* style. Rue de Paris continues down to the **Porte de Paris**, a suitably Parisian Baroque arch erected in the 1680s to celebrate the French conquest of Lille. The Sun King's monument is now overshadowed, however, by the immensity of the quite extraordinary **Hôtel de Ville**. Despite initial appearances it

Shopping

Vieux Lille is the foremost area for window (and real) shopping, with a wonderful concentration of individual shops. Rue de la Grande Chaussée, Rue des Chats Bossus, Rue Basse and Rue Lepelletier are the essential fashion streets, with both famous names and cool little shops, while the best places to look for contemporary design items are Rue de la Monnaie and the little streets near Notre-Dame de la Treille.

For more everyday shopping the best areas are the streets south of the Grand'Place, and Rue Gambetta. And for complete convenience there's **Euralille**, but note that even this mega-mall doesn't open on Sundays. Many Lille shops are also closed on Monday mornings.

Lille ✉ 59000

Les Bons Pâturages, 54 Rue Basse, **t** 03 20 55 60 28. In the heart of Vieux Lille, a traditional master cheese merchant with an excellent range of local cheeses – Maroilles, Mimolette, Vieux-Lille – all skilfully *affinés* on the premises, as well as an inventive range of tarts, quiches and cheese terrines.

Boulangerie Leroy, 118 Rue Esquermoise, **t** 03 20 55 35 55. A wonderful array of fine fresh breads and pâtisseries, from old favourites like baguettes, *pains de campagne* and croissants to half-forgotten traditional breads like *carré de Lille*. Plus, an excellent range of local beers and gins.

Boulangerie Paul, 8-12 Rue de Paris, **t** 03 20 78 20 78. Impossible to miss on the corner of Rue de Paris, opposite the Vieille Bourse, this prestigious establishment covers the whole *boulangerie-pâtisserie-chocolaterie* field: superb breads, delicious gateaux, pastries and endless combinations of chocolate.

Le Cèdre Rouge, Parvis de la Treille, **t** 03 20 51 96 96, *www.lecedrerouge.com*. On the square next to the cathedral, this attractive shop has a big range of modern design and household items from beautifully elegant wooden furniture and striking lamps to fine glass, ceramics and smaller accessories.

A l'Huîtrière, 3 Rue des Chats Bossus, **t** 03 20 55 43 41, *www.huitriere.fr*. Considered both the premier restaurant in Lille (*see* p.79) and the most spectacular fish shop in France, this is an essential sight of the city even if you aren't buying (not, sadly, that so many people wish to see it that only a few visitors are allowed in at a time). The 1928 art deco tiling is extraordinary: on the façade are scenes of undersea life, grapes as symbols of abundance, and huge lobsters surrounded by curly mosaics of steam, while the interior, behind stained-glass windows, features Breton fishing scenes. Below them are some of the world's finest oysters, lobsters, prawns, sea bass and more. There are also non-seafood delicacies such as Licques chickens and other poultry, pâtés and terrines, the house foie gras, exquisite desserts and Périgord truffles.

Jean Maniglier, 89–91 Rue de la Monnaie, **t** 03 20 13 05 05. A home accessory shop that stands out for the sheer class and variety of its stock. It's an emporium of modern luxury: Toulemonde-Brochart contemporary handmade carpets, tableware, lighting, superb fabrics, oriental carpets, and also some smaller (and sometimes twee) gift items.

Pâtisserie Meert, 27 Rue Esquermoise, **t** 03 20 57 07 44. An astonishing temple to chocolate-and-cream indulgence, a piece of old-world luxury right down to the uniformed young lad to open the door for you. The 1839 décor wouldn't shame an opera house: elaborate ceiling mouldings, intricate metal balconies, wonderful mirrors and gilded cabinets. The all house-made chocolates, cakes, pastries and ice-creams on display are no less magical than the décor, and purchases are beautifully wrapped and presented. Should you wish to linger, there's also a *salon de thé*. Catch Meert's window displays before Christmas, when they are still more tastefully magnificent than ever.

Le Savour Club, 46 Rue Négrier, **t** 03 20 74 33 44, *www.le-savour-club.fr*. Lille's foremost wine repository, a branch of the Paris-based organization that French oenophiles swear by. You won't find the bargain offers of Calais wine dealers here, but you can discover very fine wines at still-reasonable prices. All the labels are selected by experts, and the shop staff are knowledgeable and helpful; there's also a superior selection of whiskies and liqueurs, and a respectable interest is even shown in non-French wines. Members of the 'club' receive a newsletter, discounts, special offers and other perks.

was only commissioned after the First World War and built in 1924–28, to replace the by-then unusable Palais Rihour. Its style could maybe be described as Flemish revival-art deco-modernist-Gothic, and topping it off there's the tallest of all Flanders' many belfries, 107 metres high, which has become one of the city's inescapable landmarks.

To the west is 19th-century Lille, made up of typically French broad, straight boule-vards, the most important of them **Boulevard de la Liberté**. Its centrepiece is **Place de la République**, flanked by two very large, equally typically French public buildings in the ornately bloated Beaux-Arts style favoured by official France from the Second Empire to the 1900s, the Préfecture to the north and the **Palais des Beaux-Arts** to the south (*open Mon 2–6, Wed, Thurs, Sat and Sun 10–6, Fri 10–7; closed Tues; adm*). Often described as the second-most important museum in France after the Louvre, Lille's Beaux-Arts was given a stylish and expensive renovation in the 1990s. It has several real masterpieces, but as with many French regional museums it's also very patchy. Many of its most impressive works have some local connection. Flanders' 17th-century Golden Age is heavily represented, with major works by Rubens and Van Dyck. Standing out among an otherwise rather routine display of French 18th-century painting is David's 1780 *Belisarius asking for alms*, which is credited with initiating the vogue for neoclassical history painting in France. The collection of French 19th-century painting is a very individual mix. The most celebrated pictures are Courbet's superb 1849 *Après Dîner à Ornans*, one of the groundbreaking works of realism, and Delacroix's lush *Medea*. The Impressionists are decently represented – Manet, several Monets, Sisley landscapes, a little-known Toulouse-Lautrec – and there's a fascinating display of the work of a far less well-known movement with strong Lille connections, the Symbolists, including a passionate 1868 *Le Baiser* ('The Kiss') by Lille-born Carolus-Duran, and highly sexually charged Romantic-Symbolist paintings by the also-*Lillois* Alfred Agache.

The non-French pictures are another varied bag, including an El Greco, a Veronese, a Raphael cartoon, Tintoretto's wonderful *Portrait of a Venetian Senator* and the finest pictures in the whole museum, its two ferocious Goyas, *Time (The Old Women)* and *The Letter (The Young Women)*. Beyond them, a few works by Sonia Delaunay, Léger, Braque, Picasso and other major 20th-century names come as a surprise in a museum dominated by historic art. The Beaux-Arts has a huge ceramics collection, covering all the renowned styles of the Netherlands (north and south) and northern France from the 17th and 18th centuries, and a vast stock of 19th-century monumental sculpture, although this rarely appeals to modern tastes except as kitsch. In the basement there are artefacts from ancient Greece and Egypt, some local Roman finds, and superb medieval and Renaissance art and craftwork. There is also an extraordinary collection of 17th–18th-century relief models of the fortified cities of northern France and the Netherlands. Made for military planners, these models – with streets, churches and houses faithfully reproduced – give a remarkable picture of these towns before the arrival of modern industry, and in some cases, as with Ypres or Calais, provide the only complete image of what they looked like before the devastation of 20th-century wars.

A short way west of the museum is the circular **Place Philippe Le Bon**, just off which on Rue Fleurus is another of Lille's architectural oddities, the **Maison Coilliot**, the city's only complete art nouveau building. It was designed in 1898 by Hector Guimard, author of the famous Paris Métro entrances, and is one of the most unusual of all his unusual buildings, curving and asymmetrical at every point, with a strange recessed façade, and great details in tile, glass and metal. Sadly it's now a bit neglected and in need of repair.

Place Philippe Le Bon is traversed by Rue Solférino, a walk up which and then left on Rue Gambetta will take you to the Wazemmes district and **Place de la Nouvelle Aventure**, home of Lille's celebrated flea market, held on Tuesday, Thursday and Sunday mornings and best-known as the **Marché de Wazemmes**. A little southwest on Rue des Sarrazins is an emphatic product of Lille's year as European Culture Capital, the **Maison Folie de Wazemmes**. The planners of Lille-2004 decided not to undertake any Mitterand-style giant projects in the city centre but instead to 'decentralize' culture by creating 12 multi-purpose arts and community centres around Lille's suburbs and the surrounding towns, the *Maisons Folie* or 'madhouses', often in former industrial buildings. In Wazemmes, an old textile mill has been transformed with high-tech materials and considerable éclat to house a theatre, cinema, restaurant, children's space, garden and all kinds of activities. Tourist offices have lists of all the *Maisons Folie*.

Further up Rue Solférino around the junction with Rue Nationale is the **Quartier Solférino**, Lille's main 'student quarter' and a favourite area for cheap socializing, with pubs, clubs, couscous houses, bargain bistros and other ethnic and budget eating-spots. At the top of Solférino and Liberté is Lille's largest open space, the parks and gardens around the huge **Citadelle**. A giant five-pointed brick star on the ground, 2,200m round, it was the largest of all the many fortresses built by the great Marshal Vauban, who declared it his 'Queen of Citadels'. The Citadelle itself is still a military establishment and can only be visited with tours from the tourist office (*April–June and Sept–Oct, Sun pm only*). Around it, though, there is a peaceful park and Lille's zoo, and there is a great 2km walk around the green, wooded line of the former moats, the **Circuit des Remparts**.

Outside central Lille the other towns of the Lille-Métropole conurbation have two big visitor attractions. In Villeneuve d'Ascq, just east of Lille, is the **Musée d'Art Moderne de Lille Métropole** (*open Mon, Wed–Sun 10–6; closed Tues; adm*), the region's contemporary art showcase. From Place Rihour take the Métro to Pont du Bois, and from outside the station take the 41 bus four stops to Parc Urbain-Musée; from there, take the sloping footpath behind the bus stop. Opened in 1983 in this otherwise unlovely suburb in an earlier effort to take culture to the masses, the museum stands in an attractive park which also functions as a sculpture garden, with impressive large pieces by Calder, Lipschitz and others. The low-standing brick museum is a tad severe from the outside, but makes a fine, intricate exhibition space within. It's extremely strong in Cubism, with Braque, Picasso and especially Léger, and there are fine works by Modigliani, Miró, Joaquim Torres-García, Rouault and Van Dongen, and lively contemporary installations. The star exhibit is the wonderful installation *Exploded Cabins V2-42* by Daniel Buren, three room-size wooden box structures with walls of multi-coloured plexiglass that produce fascinating, shifting colour effects. The other, newer attraction is **La Piscine – Musée d'Art et d'Industrie** (*open Tues–Thurs 11–6, Fri 11–8, Sat, Sun 1–6; closed Mon; adm*) in Roubaix (Métro Gare Jean Lebas). Even those not enticed by an industrial museum (although it does also have paintings, textile designs and other surprises) can be dazzled by its location, in a spectacularly converted 1930s art deco swimming pool.

Where to Stay

Lille ✉ 59000

L'Hermitage Gantois, 224 Rue de Paris, **t** 03 20 85 30 30, *www.hotelhermitagegantois.com (double rooms from €190)*. One of the most radical projects carried out prior to Lille's stint as European Culture Capital was the conversion of the 1460 Hospice Gantois, a classic of Flemish architecture, into this chic, spectacular luxury hotel. Behind its venerable façade there is now a sleek, emphatically contemporary lounge bar area; in the rooms, old beams and original details are artfully combined with modern comforts. The hotel also has a fine **restaurant** (*menus €24–39*) and a **bar-brasserie** for smaller meals.

Hôtel Carlton, 3 Rue de Paris, **t** 03 20 13 33 13, *www.carltonlille.com (double rooms from €165)*. The traditional luxury choice in Lille, an old-style grand hotel that has dominated one side of Place du Théâtre since the 1890s. Its 60 rather flowery rooms come with every modern comfort and perfect soundproofing, and the celebrated suites (*from €420*) are magnificent. Service is very smooth.

La Maison Carrée, 29 Rue Bonte Pollet, **t** 03 20 93 60 42, *www.lamaisoncarree.fr (rooms €120–160 for two)*. An imposing 1900s mansion in a quiet part of Lille transformed into a very special modern B&B. Every part of the interior has been individually and imaginatively designed, and the five rooms have all sorts of extras – fine linen, superb bathrooms, DVD players and stereos in each. Plus, they're deliciously comfortable, and not just laid out to impress. In the garden, there's a similarly sleek heated pool, and breakfasts are excellent, with lots of fresh fruit. It's on the west side of the city, near Cormontaigne Métro, about 15–20 mins from the centre.

Hôtel de la Treille, 7-9 Place Louise de Bettignies, **t** 03 20 55 45 46, *www.hoteldelatreille.fr.st (double rooms €86)*. A 40-room hotel in a great location on one of Vieux Lille's main squares, ideally placed for shopping and the restaurants of Rue de Gand: some rooms look out onto Place Louise de Bettignies, while others have views of Notre-Dame de la Treille. The completely modernized rooms have much less character, but are bright and functionally comfortable.

Hôtel Brueghel, 5 Parvis St-Maurice, **t** 03 20 06 06 69, *www.hotel-brueghel.com (double rooms €53.50–94.50)*. A quirkily charming mid-range hotel in a seven-storey building beside the church of St-Maurice, with wonderful views of its Gothic façade from several rooms; in the lobby, pot plants, bric-à-brac and an antique lift set the cosily original tone. Some rooms are all-white with sea-grass flooring, others are in colours with carpets. The bathrooms could be better laid out, but the hotel's attractions make up for its oddities.

Janine Hulin, 28 Rue des Hannetons, **t/f** 03 20 53 46 12 (*rooms €46.40 for two*). Mme Hulin is a candidate for the perfect B&B host: warm, chatty and endlessly helpful (she speaks some English). Her house, full of flowers and plants, is in a quiet area outside the centre, reachable in 10–15 mins by Métro and bus, but she goes to great lengths to explain the route, and will drive to the Métro station to pick up lost guests. There are two comfortable rooms, and breakfast is served in her bright kitchen by the garden.

M and Mme Goblot, 51 Rue Négrier, **t** 03 20 51 39 09 (*rooms €45 for two*). A charming two-room B&B in an 18th-century house just north of Vieux Lille. The rooms are packed with an unclassifiable mix of antiques, books and other objects, and the old house (with an original cellar, which guests can visit) is quite creaky, but the elderly Rémi and Any Goblot are kindness itself – to the point of having a video library for rainy days.

Eating Alternatives

Lille ✉ 59000

A l'Huîtrière, 3 Rue des Chats Bossus, **t** 03 20 55 43 41, *www.huitriere.fr (menu €43–122)*. One of France's grand culinary monuments, a place of pilgrimage for (sufficiently funded) seafood lovers for nearly a century. It's a little odd to see well-dressed diners walking through a fish shop to eat, but this is what happens here, as the plush dining room is at the back of the magnificent *poissonnerie*. L'Huîtrière is not a place to come to for experimental cooking, but to find supreme-quality fish and seafood in perfect versions of the most traditional styles – oysters, coquilles St-Jacques à la fleur de thym, lotte aux morilles, fabulous seafood salads. There are also meat dishes and the *maison*'s famed foie gras, but not to have seafood here seems to miss the point. Service, wines and so on are of a quality to match. *Closed Sun eve.*

La Terrasse des Remparts, Logis de la Porte de Gand, Rue de Gand, **t** 03 20 06 74 74, *www.terrassedesremparts.fr (menus €15 lunch, €24–42 dinner)*. A restaurant with a location to die for, in the former guardhouse of one of Lille's old Spanish city gates, the 1621 Porte de Gand. Inside, the old military brickwork has been imaginatively combined with modern design, and there's also a garden terrace with a rampart view. The food is not as striking as the setting, but features modern, light versions of northern French-based dishes, often with a few global touches such as Asian spicings.

L'Ecume des Mers, 10 Rue des Pas, **t** 03 20 54 95 40, *www.ecume-des-mers.com (menus €15 lunch, €20 dinner)*. In one of the streets north of the main squares, this is an offshoot of the legendary Huitrière (*see above*), which allows you to sample similar fine seafood but more simply presented and at a more mid-range price. The interior is bright and pretty, in nautical blue and white. The cooking is conservative, but extremely well done: typical dishes include fine oysters, John Dory in a ginger vinaigrette and a superb *plateau de fruits de mer (€38)*. *Closed Sun eve.*

Brasserie de la Paix, 25 Place Rihour, **t** 03 20 54 70 41 (*menus €15.50–23*). Most distinguished of the brasseries around Place Rihour, with a magnificent 1930s interior of mahogany, mirrors and tiles. The food is equally classic: *moules marinière*, soups, fish and meat grills, fine seafood. Note that, while La Paix has the class, other brasseries on the square have lower prices, and longer hours. *Closed Sun.*

L'Orange Bleue, 30 Rue Lepelletier, **t** 03 20 55 04 70 (*menus €14–22*). A bustling modern bistro in a fine Vieux Lille building, with ochre rag-rolled walls between 17th-century columns. The menu offers all the options favoured by younger French diners: fresh pastas, salads, lighter versions of traditional dishes, with fresh ingredients, and globally-influenced seasonings. Service can be slow, but it's very good value, and very popular. *Closed Sun.*

La Cave aux Fioles, 39 Rue de Gand, **t** 03 20 55 18 43 (*menus €12–33*). Great Old-Lille restaurant that ably combines the charm of its 18th-century building with a Gallic sense of bohemian cool, aided by a (sometimes live) jazz soundtrack. The fare combines classic local dishes with lighter things like mixed salads and others that experiment with sweet and sour flavours. The owners are welcoming, and there's an excellent wine selection. *Closed Sat midday and Sun.*

Les Compagnons de la Grappe, 26 Rue Lepelletier, **t** 03 20 21 02 79 (*menus €18–23*). A convivial bar-restaurant down a passageway off Rue Lepelletier, open late, and with a small courtyard with terrace tables. The good-value bistro-style food consists mainly of local favourites presented in a light modern way: *tarte au Maroilles*, salmon salads. Another asset is the carefully selected wine list, featuring many fine wines from little-known producers. *Open Mon–Sat till 2am; closed Sun.*

Estaminet 'T Rijsel, 25 Rue de Gand, **t** 03 20 15 01 59 (*menu €11*). 'T Rijsel is Flemish for Lille, and this is a city embassy for the traditional Flemish village *estaminet* (*see p.59–61*), with plain wooden bar, farmhouse furniture and old bric-a-brac around the walls. There's a great selection of local and Belgian beers, and the food consists of lightish versions of local classics, like the tasty *poulet au maroilles*, and traditional snacks. It's cramped and very popular, so get there early to grab a table; so successful is it the same owners now have a 'branch', **Chez La Vieille**, just up the street (60 Rue de Gand, **t** 03 28 36 40 06). They're more restaurants than bars, and so don't open in the afternoons. *Closed Sun, Mon, and Aug.*

La Ducasse, 95 Rue Solférino, **t** 03 20 57 34 10 (*dishes c. €6–12*). A cosy *estaminet*-style bar-restaurant, with the requisite wooden tables and antique fittings. To eat there are meaty local classics, *tartines*, *flamiches*, salads, seafood and some good vegetarian options.

L'Arrière Pays, 47 Rue Basse, **t** 03 20 13 80 07 (*dishes c. €5–12, menu €15*). An excellent option for a light lunch, a combination restaurant, *salon de thé*, bakery and grocery; the menu highlights are *tartines*, open sandwiches with varied fresh toppings, while the shop offers fine breads and an enticing choice of superior, often organic foodstuffs.

The Pleasures of the Grand'Place:
Arras

09

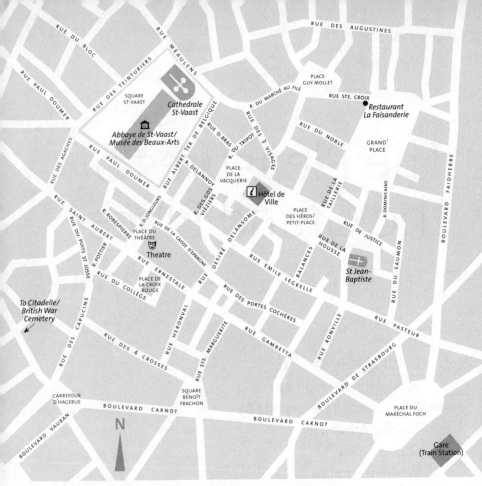

France's northern region has a jewel of a city, Arras. Its three great squares are an interlocking, harmonious ensemble of medieval and 16th-century buildings. Built to hold markets, they are a remarkable reminder of the years when the merchant cities of northern France and Flanders were the great trading centres of northern Europe. The capital of Artois, and always French-speaking, Arras nevertheless long looked to Flanders for its political allegiance, and many parts of the old city have a distinctly Flemish appearance, while others nearby have a more classical French elegance.

Restored with astonishing success after the First World War, the centre of Arras is full of unusual features. Beneath the squares runs a labyrinth of cellars and tunnels, used over the years as chalk mines, wine stores, refuse dumps or refuges. Above, Arras still hosts a giant, sprawling market of a kind that you might no longer expect in a modern city, as well as very individual shops. And around the squares, soberly beautiful on a winter's day or more animated when the market is in session, there is an appealing atmosphere in the cafés and restaurants beneath the arcades. Arras also has a special hedonistic attraction in **La Faisanderie**, right on the Grand'Place. Jean-Pierre Dargent is one of the premier chefs of northern France. Greatly admired by other chefs, a setter of culinary benchmarks, he remains constantly creative.

Getting There

Arras is about one hour's drive from Calais by the A26 *autoroute* (toll) or 1½hrs by slower roads. Whichever direction you approach from, you meet the ring of boulevards around the city centre. From the A26, shortly after joining the boulevards (here Av P. Michonneau), you come to a broad junction with a sign to the right indicating Grand'Place; from Boulogne on the N39, turn left at the boulevards and follow them round clockwise till you reach the same junction. This turning takes you abruptly into the great expanse of the square. Except on market days the Grand'Place is also the best place to **park** in Arras (pay and display).

Arras has good **train** connections to Calais, Amiens and several other cities and is on the Paris-Lille TGV line. The station is just outside the ring of boulevards on Place Foch, within easy walking distance of the central squares.

Tourist Information

Arras: Hôtel de Ville, Place des Héros, **t** 03 21 51 26 95, *www.ot-arras.fr*. The tourist office is the starting point for a range of tours around the city, and is also the ticket office for visits to the town hall Belfry and the *Boves* or caves beneath central Arras. *Open daily.*

La Faisanderie

45 Grand'Place, t 03 21 48 20 76, la-faisanderie@wanadoo.fr. Open Tues–Sat 12–2 and 7–9.30, Sun 12–2. Closed Mon and two weeks Feb, three weeks Aug. Menus €25 (Tues–Fri and Sat lunch only) and €40–65; carte average €80.

La Faisanderie occupies a venerable house on a corner of the Grand'Place, entered via a hallway with classic, pastel-shaded French bourgeois décor. To eat, you descend a spiral staircase into an elegantly restored, barrel-roofed cellar, one of the many *caves* beneath the square, with bare brick walls that give it a light, modern feel, and colour provided by paintings (for sale) and an abundance of flowers. It was once a stable, but you'd never know it. The staff are both smoothly professional and warmly welcoming. It's a place that always has a comfortable burr, a feel of pleasurable relaxation.

The restaurant's character reflects that of Jean-Pierre Dargent himself, an ebullient man without any notion of *grand chef* hauteur. Like his friend Roland Gauthier in Montreuil, he is originally from another part of France entirely – the Hautes-Pyrénées – but in pursuit of perfect freshness uses predominantly northern ingredients, and creates spectacular versions of traditional northern French dishes. The menu changes frequently with the seasons, and in over 15 years at the Faisanderie his cooking has never ceased to evolve and experiment; recently, he has gone back to his origins a little – which suits current tastes – with more use of stronger, southern French seasonings, like the Basque *espelette* peppers. In the vast wine list, as well as French bottles there are a few international wines, plus traditional beers from small local breweries.

The culinary innovations begin right away in the appetisers, which change every day – perhaps a beautifully delicate little quiche, with superb pastry and topped by a sliver of fried red mullet. While you're savouring this minor marvel the bread trolley arrives, offering a choice of seven superb freshly baked breads all made on the premises (it will come round again, so you can try a few of them).

For first courses, there might be langoustines in a herb *croustillant* with a citrus compote, or a terrine of scallops with cep mushrooms. Late autumn and early winter are especially good times to eat here, because Jean-Pierre Dargent does extraordinary things with mushrooms of all kinds. Earlier in the year the menu highlights spring vegetables, as in his *mousseline* of fresh asparagus with hazlenut and smoked eels – a true demonstration of what gourmet cooking is all about, a fabulous combination of subtly contrasting, deeply pleasurable tastes and textures. Eels, incidentally, are one of the historic staples of the Pas-de-Calais, and M. Dargent's many creative uses of them can convince even the most sceptical. Main courses might include a *poitrine de canette de challans* grilled with peppers and served with a *confit* of bitter oranges. Beneath the unfamiliar name this is a supreme interpretation of a dish that's less a classic than a cliché – duck *à l'orange*. It's the kind of fine cooking that writes a story on the tongue: the perfectly flavoured duck breast comes in a delicious, surprisingly strongly-spiced *croustillant*, which interplays wonderfully with the almost reflective flavour of the bitter oranges, infused with a trace of cocoa beans.

Tartelette de Crevettes à l'Œuf Poché, Crème de Maroilles

Serves 4

225g/8oz shortcrust or puff pastry
1 large leek, trimmed and washed
100g/3½oz small cooked and peeled shrimps or prawns
4 eggs
100ml/3½fl oz beer
50g/1¾oz butter, plus more for cooking
150g/5½oz Maroilles cheese without its rind, diced (or similar strong, soft cheese)
5ml/1 teaspoon Dijon mustard
cayenne pepper

Preheat the oven to 190°C/375°F/Gas Mark 5. Roll out the pastry on a lightly floured surface to a thickness of about 3mm/1/8in and use it to line 4 tartlet tins of 10cm/4in diameter. Prick the bases, line the pastry cases with foil and fill with baking beans. Place on a baking sheet and bake for 15mins until the edges are golden. Remove the foil and beans and continue baking for 5–7mins, until the pastry is deep golden brown. Cool on a wire rack.

Meanwhile, slice the leek thinly and steam until tender. Refresh in cold water and drain. Put the beer in a saucepan with the butter, the cheese and the mustard and set over a gentle heat. Cook, stirring constantly, until everything has melted and blended well together. Season with cayenne pepper.

Bring a saucepan of salted water to a simmer and add a splash of vinegar. Stir the water into a whirlpool and add the eggs, one at a time. Poach the eggs for a few minutes until the white is set, and the yolk still runny. Remove with a slotted spoon. Refresh in cold water, drain and trim off the trailing edges of white.

To serve, preheat the grill to a hot temperature. Melt a small knob of butter in a pan, add the leek and prawns, heat through and divide the mixture between the tartlet cases. Place an egg on each one and cover with the cheese sauce. Place under the grill to brown the tops, and then serve the tartlets at once on warm plates.

This is very clever food, but with cleverness for a purpose, for it's also hugely enjoyable. The cheese selection is also fabulous, but if you were tempted to come in for just one course, it might be dessert. Jean-Pierre Dargent's lemon ice cream *à la crème de thé vert*, infused with green tea, is pure nectar, and potentially addictive. In summer, a salad of strawberries and raspberries with a citrus dressing is a magnificently refreshing demonstration of what the French cult of market freshness is all about. And then, finally, with your coffee there arrives a plate of sybaritic petit-fours that's a real picture, as a final touch to a truly memorable meal.

Touring Around

When you first enter the **Grand'Place**, you are immediately knocked back by its size. It is lined by Flemish-style houses that are all four storeys high, with curving gables. Their first floors jut out over the pavement, supported by slender stone columns, creating arcades that once sheltered market traders and their wares from the rain. From the corner of the square furthest from the main traffic entrance a little street, Rue de la Taillerie, connects through into the more intimate **Place des Héros**, better known as the **Petit-Place**, which is dominated by the soaring Gothic Hôtel de Ville. Behind the town hall is the third historic square, the plainer **Place de la Vacquerie**.

A market was first recorded on the site of the Grand'Place in the year 828. The size of the square is an indication of just how important Arras was during its Golden Age, in the 14th and 15th centuries. Merchants from all over the continent came to buy and sell here, and Arras tapestries – such as the 'arras' behind which Polonius is hiding when he is stabbed in *Hamlet* – were prized luxuries as far away as Byzantium.

The *places* today look very much as they have done for the last few hundred years, but a great deal is actually reconstruction – perhaps the greatest of all the restoration projects carried out in France following the World Wars. During the First World War Arras had the misfortune of being part of the front line, and was incessantly pounded by German artillery – photographs in the town hall vividly reveal the extent of the devastation. As the dust settled the decision was taken to rebuild the town centre exactly as it had been, to the extent of recovering individual bricks from the rubble and returning them to their exact location. The result is extraordinarily effective.

The houses in the *places* are aligned with such simple harmony that at first sight they can appear quite uniform, but this impression rapidly disappears. Some have brick façades, others stone, and the spirals and other decoration on their gables are endlessly varied. Look above the arcades and you see all sorts of fascinating details: a mermaid on no.11 in the Petit-Place, the Three Kings in Rue de la Taillerie, a cauldron, probably once a shop sign, at 32 Grand'Place. The Grand'Place's north side is especially beautiful, with gables and façades that are all differently, and delicately, coloured. It contains the oldest house in Arras at no.49, now the Trois Luppars hotel, a wonderful semi-Gothic townhouse from 1467 with a watchtower in its stepped-gable roof.

The best times to see the *places* are Wednesday and especially Saturday mornings, when they regain their original function and some of their 14th-century bustle with one of the largest **markets** in France. It no longer fills the whole of all three squares, but is still huge, and enormously varied. Foods, farm-fresh vegetables, flowers, stacks of cheeses and even a few live chickens can be found in Place de la Vacquerie, where the countryside meets the city; in the Petit-Place there are rows and rows of cheap jackets and other clothing, more great cheese and flower stalls, and any number of stands to answer an apparently limitless local demand for spit-roast chicken, which throw out wafts of warmth in winter. In the Grand'Place, meanwhile, you might come across clothes, tableware, antiques, old buttons, more foods and many other stalls that defy categorization. Pre-Christmas, all three squares take on an extra gleam, with traders offering trees and bright mountains of decorations beneath the festive lights.

There are also interesting **shops** around the squares, notably the Leclercq family's **Fromager des Arcades** cheese palace on the corner of the Petit-Place and Rue de la Taillerie, and the **Côtellerie Caudron** for Arras blue porcelain (for both *see* p.89). A little clutch of interesting souvenir and oddments shops can be found by walking on past the Cotellerie, down Rue des Grands Viéziers and across Rue Paul Doumer.

The grandest piece of post-war reconstruction in Arras is the **Hôtel de Ville**, one of the finest pieces of civil Gothic architecture in Europe: grandest of all is the central section, built very quickly between 1502 and 1506 in a *flamboyant* style with elaborate traceries and pinnacles and a peppering of tiny dormer windows in the roof. The giant belfry behind it, celebrated in a poem by Verlaine, was built separately and took much longer (1462–1554). Both had to be painstakingly restored during the 1920s.

As you enter the main porch, look left to meet Arras' good-natured giants, Colas and Jacqueline and their daughter, who are paraded around the city during the main *fêtes* in June and at the end of August. The tourist office beneath the porch is also the place to obtain tickets for visits to the different parts of the Hôtel de Ville. A lift takes you – with some steps at the end – to the top of the **Belfry** (*open May–Sept Mon 10–6.30, Tues–Sat 9–6.30, Sun 10–1 and 2.30–6.30; Oct–April Mon 10–12 and 2–6, Tues–Sat 9–12 and 2–6, Sun 10–12.30 and 3–6.30; adm*), for a panoramic view. When you come down, you can wander around the town hall if there are no meetings in progress. Inside, no real attempt was made to duplicate the pre-1914 décor, but the 1920s substitutes have an engaging charm. The **Salle des Mariages** has pretty murals with Isadora Duncanesque Grecian maidens on the subject of 'Spring', which make it popular for nuptials; the beautiful main hall has still larger murals of 15th-century life in Arras by the artist Hoffbauer, in a style somewhere between Brueghel and Arthur Rackham.

From the basement of the Hôtel de Ville you can also take a tour of the **Boves** (*opening times as for belfry; book and check current times at tourist office; tours last c.30–45mins, approx hourly Mon–Fri, every 30mins Sat, Sun, and more frequently in summer; English-speaking guides available; adm*), the bizarre catacomb of tunnels that extends through the chalk beneath Arras. Some tunnels existed here in Roman times, and many more were opened up during the Middle Ages. They extend downwards through three levels, and without a guide you would easily get lost. Until 1982 everyone in Arras had a right of access to them. Since then the bottom levels have been closed for safety, except to tour groups, but many parts of the first level are still in private use, and entrances to these cellars can be seen all around the Grand'Place.

The *Boves* have been used for all kinds of different purposes. Their temperature and humidity make them perfect for storing wine, and many Arras porcelain merchants routinely threw all their damaged stock down them. During the Revolutionary Terror of the 1790s, Catholics held secret services here. The caverns were greatly extended in 1916–17 by British troops, who used them as a safe means of getting to the trenches east of Arras; long-forgotten sections of the wartime tunnels are still being discovered.

From the Hôtel de Ville it's a short walk west to Rue Paul Doumer and the **Musée des Beaux-Arts** (*open Mon, Wed and Fri–Sun 9.30–12 and 2–5.30, Thurs 9.30–5.30; closed Tues; adm*), in the former Benedictine **Abbaye de St-Vaast**, which somewhat surprisingly is a giant neoclassical edifice, vast by name and vast by nature, completed in 1783. Founded in the 7th century, St-Vaast abbey was one of the most important institutions in Arras throughout the city's history. In the 1740s, however, it was decided to knock down its early-medieval buildings and replace them with this all-new abbey. It is believed that one of the prime movers of the scheme was the Cardinal de Rohan, Abbot of St-Vaast and one of the most worldly clerics of the *Ancien Régime*, and it looks more like a palace than a monastery. The museum collection is mixed, with a sizeable amount of unexceptional painting. There is a beautiful collection of 18th-century Arras and Tournai porcelain, a major Brueghel (the *Census at Bethlehem*) and several landscapes by Corot, who often painted in Arras. The museum's greatest artefacts, though, are its medieval sculptures. The 1446 tomb sculpture of Guillaume Lefranchois, a Canon of Béthune, is extraordinary and still shocking: a decomposing skeleton, a classic product of the anguished late-medieval mind. Entirely different is the 14th-century *Head of a Woman*, also thought to be from a tomb, a timeless, serenely beautiful face. The museum has, though, only one Arras tapestry – there are very few still in existence – *St-Vaast and the Bear*, with a delightfully worked, almost abstract background.

Alongside the museum is the **cathedral**, in a similar neoclassical style. If the Cardinal de Rohan did not like Arras' antique abbey, he was no more taken with the Gothic abbey church, and in the 1770s work on a new one was begun by Constant d'Ivry, one of the most important architects of the day. Unfinished at the time of the Revolution, it was completed in 1833, and then had to be rebuilt after 1918. It's a huge building, plain and white, and frankly unwelcoming.

The architectural mix of Arras closely reflects its history. Originally a Roman town, from the 13th century it was ruled in turn by the counts of Artois, the dukes of Burgundy and the kings of Spain. Its incorporation into France in 1659 was initially highly unpopular. In the following decade Marshal Vauban arrived to give Arras a set of his ramparts, as a defence against invaders and to keep a check on the populace. In the 18th century, integrated as a French provincial capital, Arras acquired the *hôtels particuliers* and neoclassical piles of every other French city under the *Ancien Régime*. Arras was noticeably effervescent in the years before the Revolution. As well as the Cardinal de Rohan, it had many of the lawyers, officials and aspiring intellectuals who were the core of provincial cultural life, and chief enthusiasts for 'enlightened' ideas.

To enter another piece of 18th-century Arras, cross Rue Paul Doumer from the Beaux-Arts and veer left to come to the **Place du Théâtre**. As well as the gracious 1785 **theatre** itself, its fine buildings include the **Hôtel de Guînes**, a mansion that has been radically converted to become the **Maison Folie d'Arras**, one of the multi-use arts centres created for Lille's year as culture capital in 2004 (*see* p.78). Just off the square is the former home of one of the rising personalities of 1780s Arras, in the street named after him, **Rue Maximilien-Robespierre**. Robespierre lived in this house while he was establishing his reputation as a ferocious advocate, before going off to use his talents on a wider stage. Arras has never known quite what to do with its most famous son, or his house: being the home town of a man widely credited with the invention of modern totalitarianism is not easy to handle. For years the house was shut up, and the only voices calling for it to be made a memorial were those of the most incorrigible Stalinists in the French Communist Party. In 1999, however, the city ceded the house to the *Compagnons du Tour de France* – not a cycling club, but a craftsmen's friendly society – who use half of it for an exhibition on their own work and have opened the rest as the **Maison Robespierre** (*open May–Sept Tues–Fri 2–5.30, Sat and Sun 2.30–8.30; Oct–Mar Tues and Thurs 2–5.30, Sat and Sun 3.30–6.30*), with a few artefacts – clothes and documents – and information on the Revolutionary era.

Another 18th-century addition to Arras is the **Basse-Ville**, to the west past Place du Théâtre. The product of an early foray into town planning, begun in the 1750s, it has streets intersecting in a grid, centred on **Place Victor Hugo**, a wide, octagonal square with an obelisk in the middle, an idea quintessentially of the Enlightenment era. From there, continuing roughly in the same direction, you eventually come to the boulevards around the line of Marshal Vauban's ramparts, demolished in the 1890s. In the southwest corner, however, is his **Citadelle**, still in use by the French army.

To the northwest, the boulevard leads up to the only surviving part of Arras' walls, the **Bastion des Chouettes**, now landscaped into a tranquil park. Beside the boulevard midway between Bastion and Citadelle is the **First World War British Cemetery**, one of the largest and most overwhelming of so many in the area. It contains over 2,600 graves, and around the walls there are the names of nearly 40,000 men with no known grave, in lists that go on and on until it's impossible to take any more.

Arras and the areas to the east and north formed one of the most bitterly contested battlegrounds of the First World War, and there seem to be green-signposted Commonwealth cemeteries in virtually every village, as well as the giant French cemetery at Notre-Dame de Lorette (20,000 graves). Even those without any special interest in the Great War or military affairs can appreciate a trip out to **Vimy Ridge**, north of Arras off the N17 Lens road. Taken by the Canadian army in 1917, it is now the **Canadian National Memorial** (*open daily sunrise–sunset; tours April–Nov daily 10–6*). All war cemeteries were ceded by France in perpetuity, but no other country has made so much of this as Canada. Vimy Ridge is a Canadian National Park, a little piece of Canada: everything is rigorously bilingual, and the excellent free guided tours are given by French- and English-speaking Canadian students. The park is immaculately maintained: near the top of the steep ridge many of the trenches, terrifyingly close together, and grassed-over craters have been preserved, and from the peak, by the sombre 1936 memorial, you can well appreciate why it was considered strategic, for it has a view eastwards for miles over France's traditional industrial heartland, from this distance looking surprisingly green.

Shopping

Cave à Vins, 4 Rue du Marché au Filé, **t** 03 21 50 63 96. A very special wine emporium: a narrow entry leads down into a warren of 15th-century cellars, within which is an extraordinary wine collection, amassed over years. Local wine-lovers gather here to chat at weekends (the only days it's open), in cellars that seem to stretch into subterranean infinity: there are over 1,200 French wines, including, it's said, at least one from every year since 1833, and others from all over the world. *Open Fri 4–8, Sat 10–1 and 3–8*.

Le Cellier des Arcades, 8bis Rue de la Taillerie, **t** 03 21 23 09 28. Beer-enthusiasts without the time to tour northern France's small breweries need not go away disappointed. This little shop between the two main squares has a comprehensive collection of the fine beers of northern France and Belgium, plus several from other parts of the world. The friendly, English-speaking owner is an able guide to his huge stock.

Cotellerie-Porcelaine Caudron, 15 Place de la Vacquerie, **t** 03 21 71 14 23. Far more than just a tableware shop, Caudron is the sole current maker of the delicate blue-on-white *bleu d'Arras* porcelain for which the city was renowned in the 18th century. The Caudron family first opened their shop in 1845. All the pieces are made in their small workshops outside town: cheaper designs use ready-made plates, but the tableware series are entirely handmade and hand-painted. The charming old shop is worth a visit in itself, and also stocks silverware and fine glass.

Le Fromager des Arcades, 39 Place des Héros, **t** 03 21 71 47 85. Arras' premier master cheese-merchant, in a beautiful shop on the corner of the Petit-Place. All the cheeses are carefully matured in *caves* beneath the shop; there's a full range of northern cheeses, and many from other parts of France.

Pâtisserie Yannick Delestrez, 50 Place des Héros, **t** 03 21 71 53 20. One of the sights of the Petit-Place, this pastry and chocolate palace specializes in the city's own most traditional sweetmeats: *cœurs d'Arras* – spicy, heart-shaped almond biscuits – and chocolate *rats d'Arras* (the rat has been a symbol of Arras since the 14th century). The beautiful old shop also contains an eye-catching display of other chocolates and cakes, as well as fine *traiteur* dishes.

Where to Stay

Arras is a little short on hotels, and it's advisable to book rooms well ahead.

Hôtel de l'Univers, 3–5 Place de la Croix Rouge, **t** 03 21 71 34 01, *www.hotel-univers-arras.com* (*double rooms €90–130*). Occupying a grand town mansion on the site of a 17th-century convent, this is one of the region's classic hotels. Now affiliated to Best Western, it has been fully renovated with superior facilities and opulent, comfortable traditional designs. Service is excellent, and the elegant restaurant (*see p.90*) has its own fan club.

Ostel des Trois Luppars, 49 Grand'Place, **t** 03 21 60 02 03, *www.ostel-les-3luppars.com* (*double rooms €55–60*). The most characterful hotel in Arras, in the oldest building on the Grand'Place, a magnificent Flemish-Gothic townhouse from 1467 (now with lift). 'Luppars' is old Flemish for wolves, three of which are carved into the façade. All the 42 rooms, some squeezed into the eaves, have been well re-equipped with modern facilities. Service can be cranky, but it's still Arras' most engaging, and popular, hotel.

Aux Grandes Arcades, 8–12 Grand'Place, **t** 03 21 23 30 89, *aux.grandes.arcades @wanadoo.fr* (*double rooms €52–56*). Location is the big plus of this characterful old hotel on the main *place*. The rooms are straightforwardly comfortable, and come in different sizes: top-floor ones have impressive old beams, and the best to go for are naturally those with a Grand'Place view. The restaurant below (*see p.90*) is an excellent place to imbibe some city atmosphere.

Hôtel Astoria-Carnot, 10–12 Place Maréchal Foch, **t** 03 21 71 08 14, **f** 03 21 71 60 95 (*double rooms €51*). Big and bright, and one of a clutch of hotels on the square by the train station. Not a place with great character, but it's well run, with 29 modernized rooms. The big **brasserie** (*menus €17–40*) is open late, and handy for snacks and light meals.

Hôtel-Brasserie du Beffroi, 28 Place de la Vacquerie, **t** 03 21 23 13 78, **f** 03 21 23 03 08 (*double rooms €40–45*). Straightforward little hotel behind the Hôtel de Ville that's a good budget option. Some rooms share showers, but they're all light and well-kept, and the owners are friendly. The **brasserie**, with terrace on Place de la Vacquerie, has good-value classic dishes (*dishes c. €5–16*).

Fampoux ✉ 62118

M and Mme Peugniez, 17 Rue Verlaine, **t** 03 21 55 00 90 (*rooms €33 for two, €43 for four*). A big brick 19th-century farmhouse in the middle of Fampoux, 8km east of Arras, with five simple but spacious and cosy B&B rooms. Fampoux is a classic, quiet Artois village – with many First World War connections – with a big old brewery across the street from the farm.

St-Nicolas-lès-Arras ✉ 62223

Mme Antoinette Lesueur, Route de Roclincourt, **t** 03 21 55 27 85 (*rooms €33 for two*). Mme Lesueur offers three *chambres d'hôtes* rooms on her big old farm, standing up out of the Artois plain between the villages of St-Nicolas-les-Arras and Roclincourt. It's only around 3km north of Arras, but feels very rural. The rooms are simply comfortable: all have showers, but toilets are shared.

Thélus ✉ 62580

M et Mme Japsenne, 19bis Rue d'Arras, **t** 03 21 73 08 85, *http://victor.japsenne.free.fr* (*rooms €40 for two*). Two very comfortable B&B rooms in a modern house, with very large garden, in a quiet village 7km north of Arras, between the city and Vimy Ridge. The rooms connect, so it's well-suited to families.

Eating Alternatives

Arras ✉ 62000

Restaurant Le Clusius, Hôtel de l'Univers, 3–5 Place de la Croix Rouge, **t** 03 21 71 34 01, *www.hotel-univers-arras.com* (*menus €19.50 lunch only, €28–49*). The Hôtel Univers' highly regarded restaurant is a plush, pampering space where rather intricate, refined *haute cuisine* dishes are served. The

hushed, traditionally smart atmosphere will not be to everyone's taste, but its devotees love it, and it can be recommended for a particularly snug dinner for two.

La Coupole d'Arras, 26 Bd de Strasbourg, **t** 03 21 71 88 44 (*menus €24–29*). Like its Parisian namesake, a traditional brasserie in the grand manner, with ranks of tables, fast-moving waiters and a giant menu offering an unchanging choice of classics such as fish *choucroute*, steaks, mussels and a whole range of smaller dishes such as salads, onion soup and snacks. As usual in city brasseries, most people eat off the well-priced *carte*.

La Clef des Sens, 60–62 Place des Héros, **t** 03 21 51 00 50 (*menus €23–29*). A stylish, popular venue in a prime location on the Petit-Place, with a lively terrace, a brasserie at street level and in the *caves* and a more plush restaurant on the first floor. Both main menu and the brasserie list highlight satisfying northern French cooking, and its food keeps up a high standard.

Aux Grandes Arcades, 8–12 Grand'Place, **t** 03 21 23 30 89 (*menus €15–35*). Impossible to miss on the *place*, the giant Grandes Arcades – beneath the hotel (*see p.89*) – offers two complete dining rooms, one with set menus and an *à la carte* menu of French classics and gutsy northern specialities, the other with a big brasserie menu. The food holds no surprises, but the buzzing atmosphere, view of the *place* and terrace on the square make up for it. There's also a great wine stock, kept in a giant *cave* beneath the square.

La Rapière, 44 Grand'Place, **t** 03 21 55 09 92 (*menus €14.50 lunch only, €18–28*). In one of the old shop-fronts in the arcades, this good-value restaurant has modern décor and highly regarded food, an enjoyable mix of traditional local favourites like *andouillettes d'Arras* and some subtle, original modern touches. The staff are charming, and it's very popular.

Le Bateau du Ch'ti, 17 Place du Héros, **t** 03 21 23 20 38 (*menus €10–18*). A laidback little bar-brasserie by the Hôtel de Ville, popular with a young, studentish crowd. As well as bargain set menus there's a generous range of salads for around €9–12, and the excellent, wheaty Ch'ti beer, brewed at Benifontaine near Lens, is on tap.

Small Town Gem:
Montreuil

10

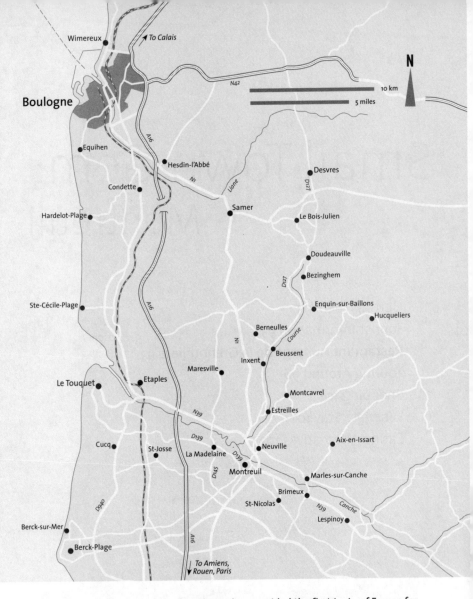

The countryside just south of Boulogne has provided the first taste of France for British travellers for a very long time. Its place names and those of the nearby seaside resort towns like Le Touquet can seem very familiar, and it might not seem an obvious area to look for the peace and timeless atmosphere associated with a classic image of the French countryside. Away from the main routes, though, there are any number of quiet villages with farmers going about their business, and lush, green valleys producing fine local meats and cheeses, and unusual specialities such as handmade chocolates. And, on a rock above the wooded valley of the Canche, there is Montreuil, called *sur-Mer* despite the absence of any sea, a historic little walled town still contained within its ramparts as it was in the 16th century, and showing no

Getting There

The A16 *autoroute* (toll road from Boulogne) passes between Montreuil and the sea. The road in from the motorway (exit 26) and all the other roads south join up just north of Montreuil in the N1, which makes an eastward loop around the town. Take the turn into Montreuil and carry on through the ramparts and the old town to the Abbeville road.

On the south side of Montreuil look for a sharp right turn, at a small roundabout, signed to La Madelaine-sous-Montreuil. In the village there is another right turn, with a sign for the Auberge de la Grenouillère.

Le Touquet **airport**, which has flights from Lydd in Kent (*see* chapter 3), is 9km from Montreuil. Information, **t** 03 21 05 03 99.

Tourist Information

Montreuil: 21 Rue Carnot, **t** 03 21 06 04 27, *www.tourisme-montreuillois.com*. The office is beside the grassy esplanade next to the Citadelle of Montreuil.

Berck-sur-Mer: 5 Av Francis Tattegrain, **t** 03 21 09 50 00, *www.opale-sud.com*.

Etaples: Bd Bigot Descelers, **t** 03 21 09 56 94, *www.etaples-sur-mer.com*.

Hucqueliers: 14 Grand'Place, **t** 03 21 81 98 14, *www.ot-hucqueliers.com*.

Le Touquet: Palais de l'Europe, Place de l'Hermitage, **t** 03 21 06 72 00, *www.letouquet.com*.

Vallée de la Course: 316 Rue du Village, Bernieulles, **t** 03 21 90 72 53. Bernieulles is 2km west of Beussent.

inclination to outgrow them. It receives its fair share of visitors, and yet nothing seems to disturb its placid pace and very refreshing small-town atmosphere.

Montreuil also makes an ideal destination for those in search of a pampering, utterly relaxing break within a very easy distance of a Channel crossing, since, thanks to its charms and well-established status as a travellers' rest, the town – and the deliciously lush countryside of the Course and Canche valleys around it – possess an exceptional range of places to eat and stay. In particular, just outside Montreuil, there is a superb restaurant-hotel in a quite ravishing location.

The **Auberge de la Grenouillère** ('The Froggery') is in La Madelaine-*sous*-Montreuil, a village at the bottom of Montreuil's crag with a special view up to the town's remarkable ramparts. It occupies a beautifully restored old farmhouse – with entirely unique décor – by the River Canche, amid woods and lush meadows. Inside, award-winning chef Roland Gauthier creates endlessly inventive, richly enjoyable dishes based on a supremely skilful working of seasonal, local ingredients. For a combination of pure pleasure, comfort and rural calm, it's hard to beat.

Auberge de la Grenouillère

La Madelaine-sous-Montreuil, **t** *03 21 06 07 22, www.lagrenouillere.fr.*
Open Sept–June Mon, Thurs–Sun 12–3.30 and 7.15–9.30, closed Tues and Wed;
July and Aug open daily. Closed Jan. Menus €30 (not available Sat eve, Sun,
public hols) and €50–70; carte average €80.

The winding lane that takes you down to the Auberge de la Grenouillère runs past the houses of the village of La Madelaine, eventually petering out beside the bright waters of the Canche. There are trees all around, and fine horses in a little field beside the river. The restaurant is just to your left, in a traditional Picard-style one-storey farmhouse, with red roofs and white walls, around a courtyard with tables, sunshades and flowers, a little pocket of plenty even in December. It is quite exceptionally pretty, and just as lovely and very comfortable inside, with dark wooden beams, tiles, more flowers and white linen. In winter, there's also a log fire. The unique feature of the décor is that the walls of the 'Froggery' are covered in whimsical pictures of very human-looking frogs – illustrating one of La Fontaine's fables about a frog who wanted to be as big as an ox and ate so much he exploded – painted in the 1930s by Frank Reynolds, once art director of *Punch*, who was a friend of the then owner. The combination of this very English period artwork with such a very French setting gives the main dining room an appealing eccentricity (book early and ask expressly for a table in the main room, as the other rooms don't have the same atmosphere).

Roland Gauthier worked at the Connaught Hotel in London before setting up on his own at La Grenouillère, where he has been in charge for nearly 25 years. His cooking has won great praise, but like any real first-rank chef he hasn't stood still in all that time, and has never ceased to create, adapt and explore. Keeping up a restaurant of this standing over many years isn't easy, and some ups and downs are unavoidable; recently, though, its devotees are agreed that the Grenouillère has again been on a very high note indeed. Roland Gauthier has been joined in the kitchen by his son Alexandre, who excels in light dishes such as an ultra-refreshing summer *tartare* of three kinds of tomatoes. In line with current tastes, father and son make increasing use of delicate distillations of flavours – so a certain amount of fashionable froth – and of ingredients once thought unusual in France such as ginger or coconut milk, tendencies which have further expanded the possibilities of a Gauthier trademark – apparently radical but very subtly-handled contrasts of ingredients within the same dish, so that in one meal you can feel you've been on a real journey through a whole series of surprising, very pleasurable flavours and taste combinations.

Through all these innovations certain traditional essentials are firmly adhered to: the monthly-changing menus are strictly seasonal, and are centred on entirely local, *du terroir*, ingredients. This means that in autumn they may heavily feature game and duck, and sea bass and other fish from local ports, while at other times they might highlight Boulogne or Somme Bay salt-marsh lamb, sole, langoustines or river fish. Many dishes are also based (albeit distantly) on traditional northern French dishes.

The subtlety of the cooking is already announced by the appetisers, which in summer consisted of a little pot of exquisitely juicy melon matched with strong dry-cured ham, followed by a delicate cup of asparagus soup. The main weekday menu is *du marché*, while the larger menu is currently called *saveurs du littoral*: both offer a range of enticing options. Among the first courses might be some fabulous langoustines grilled in their shells with ginger butter and a frothy coconut milk *bouillon*, a supremely delicate, almost Oriental concoction in which the main ingredients are set against a remarkable background of fragrant, often barely suggested flavours and textures, including both hot and sweet spices and herbs.

Seasonings and methods are complex, but never so much as to block out the rich, enjoyable flavours of main ingredients or the qualities of perfectly fresh fine produce. In a main course of a *piccata* of veal sweetbreads, for example, the ultra-tender meat and addictively rich gravy are both wonderful, but one could easily be tempted to set them aside and concentrate on the other things on the plate, the utterly superb cooked spring vegetables – spring onions, tomatoes, green beans, lettuce – and a magnificent little pot of *morilles* mushrooms, deglazed in white wine.

The cheeseboard is equally one to be explored, a hugely impressive all-regional selection that includes Vieux Boulonnais, Pavé du Nord, great *chèvre* from nearby Montcavrel and many other often-neglected northern cheeses instead of just the usual standards. There is also a pretty exhaustive, if expensive, all-French wine cellar. Anticipation could mount the most, nevertheless, as you get closer to the desserts, another Gauthier forte – he devotes special care to them, since, he says, as the *coup de grâce* of a meal, they are often what lingers most in the mind. First, before you're served your individual choice, there arrive some *pré-desserts* that are further bravura showpieces of the culinary arts – such as an astonishing cream of strawberries and rhubarb, with a touch of hot spice and extraordinary depth of flavour, followed by an ideally fruity *gelée* of peaches. After that the 'main' desserts could seem a tad superfluous, but Roland Gauthier's ice-cream-filled 'spring rolls' with explosively well-flavoured cherries, or the subtly bitter-sweet chocolate mousse, are the kind of things that it's hard to pass on.

Cerises en Rouleaux de Printemps, et Pistaches

Serves 4, with 4 rolls per person

For plum dough for the spring roll casings:

> 500g/18oz prunes or dried plums
> 75g/3oz sugar
> 100g/4oz flour
> 150g/5oz butter
> 250g/9oz egg whites

For the filling and garnish:

> 16 cherries, cut in half, for the ends of the rolls
> 16 cherries, to be pan-fried
> 400g/14oz pistachio ice-cream
> 400g/14oz almond ice-cream

Mix the dough ingredients together well, and with a circular pastry cutter (or a plate or glass) divide it into 16 small circles (four per person) and roll them flat on a baking tray. Cook in the oven for 12 minutes at 180°C/350°F/Gas Mark 4. As they come out of the oven, form into rolls on an aluminium cylinder, and allow to cool.

Stone all the cherries, keeping the stalks for later. Cut the first 16 cherries in half.

Fill the rolls with ice-cream, two with pistachio and two with almond for each person, and close up the end of each roll with a half-cherry. Arrange the rolls on plates, and sprinkle an even layer of sugar over the rolls. Just before serving, sauté the remaining cherries very quickly in butter, and pour them over the rolls.

Replace their stalks on each cherry, and for a final garnish, sprinkle over the rolls a little grated chocolate and a few drops of pistachio oil.

If the weather's suitable, go out into the courtyard for coffee and (similarly exquisite) petit-fours, and watch the breeze in the trees. Afterwards, take a wander down the path alongside the soothing river. And, for a longer rural idyll, take advantage of the Grenouillère's guest rooms, which need to be booked well in advance.

Touring Around

It's possible to get from Calais or Boulogne to Montreuil in about half an hour on the A16, or even on the N1 unless you get stuck behind a tractor or a line of trucks, but an incomparably more attractive route is the little D127 road that runs roughly parallel to the main roads down the valley of the **River Course**, just inland. To get on to it, turn off the N1 in Samer on to the road to Desvres, the D52, and then in a switchback section with great views north over the valley of the Liane look for a tiny lane off to the right, with signs to Doudeauville and Bois-Julien, that disappears into the trees straight up a steep hill. At the top, follow another sign right to Doudeauville and you will be delivered into a green, narrow valley that is immediately so different from the semi-industrial small towns straggling south from Boulogne that it can feel like a lost world. The river is a quick-flowing, burbling stream. Hunkered down alongside it there are villages of white, red-roofed one-storey cottages, surrounded by the trademark flowers of the Artois valleys.

The Course has been discovered by a fair number of British travellers (there are very *gentils* little signs here and there reminding you to drive on the right), but it manages to remain a very genuinely rural, sleepy stretch of French countryside, with tree-clad villages with old-fashioned bars and other more hidden attractions spread along the valley. Several have unfussy restaurants and small *auberge* hotels, which make great places to stop and take the atmosphere on board.

Near Enquin-sur-Baillons a road cuts eastwards up to the *Haut-Pays*, the flatter 'High Country' above the valley, centred around **Hucqueliers**, an attractive large village with some distinguished 16th–18th-century buildings. Further south back in the main valley there is **Beussent**, home of – to the left just before you enter the village from the north, and easy to miss – **Les Chocolats de Beussent**, a high-quality craft chocolate-maker that has become the Course valley's major 'industry' (*see* p.101). From Beussent another narrow lane turns off to the east and runs across the river and then away from the Course to enter a branch valley that seems almost wild and uninhabited, with only a few isolated farms such as **Le Fond des Communes**, producer of fine fresh *chèvre* and butter.

Further south, just past Estréelles, the Course valley road brings you back to the main N1. Just beyond the junction, a turn left (east) leads to the village of **Neuville-sous-Montreuil**, which has two distinctive monuments. One is the **Cimetière Hindou**, actually a Commonwealth war cemetery for Indian soldiers – both Hindu and Muslim – who died serving with the British Army during World War I. The other, just east of the village, is the **Chartreuse de Notre-Dame-des-Prés**, a giant former Carthusian monastery. Founded in the 1320s, it was closed during the Revolution but then reclaimed by the church and extensively rebuilt by the local neogothic architect Clovis Normand in the 1870s, only to be seized again by the French state in another argument with the Catholic church in 1901. For years it served as a mental hospital, but after this closed in 1990 an attempt was made once again to establish a religious community there. By 2002, however, the building was in such a decrepit and potentially dangerous state that these monks too, lacking the means to restore it themselves, were also obliged to leave. Since then the huge complex has been closed up and awaiting restoration, but it can occasionally be visited with tours from Montreuil tourist office (*enquire at office for details*).

Montreuil-sur-Mer is just a kilometre or so further south, the old *ville-haute* atop its impressively steep hill reached via a hairpin road from the main highway that brings you up to the main gate, the Porte de Boulogne, in the town ramparts. Beyond the gate the road winds round again to the right, as it has since the 19th century to avoid one of Montreuil's most famous streets, the **Cavée St-Firmin**, a precipitous cobbled incline, lined with quaint white houses with roofs each at a different level, which caused havoc among the carriages of 18th-century British travellers when they had to negotiate it en route to Paris.

It is believed that the site of Montreuil was already occupied in Roman times, although the town was actually founded some time in the 7th century by wandering monks. It grew to be of most interest, however, to the region's warriors, and the first fortifications appeared 200 years later. It's not hard to see why, for the crag on which the *ville-haute* stands has a commanding view in every direction, and especially along the valley of the Canche. It was also an important port, which is why, against all visible evidence, it still retains the title 'sur-Mer'. The harbour was one of the wealthiest in northern Europe during the 12th century, trading in grains, wines and wool, but the Canche had already begun to silt up, and by 1400 was virtually impassable. Today if you look from Montreuil out towards the sea, now 15km away, across the fields and thick woods where the port's traffic once came and went, you can only marvel at the capacity of this stretch of coast to shift and change.

Montreuil's position as a harbour and fortress long gave it a torrid and violent history. For two centuries it had the eccentric status of being the only port in France, for in the years when the theoretical 'kings of France' were consistently abused or ignored by over-mighty vassals such as the dukes of Normandy this was the only outlet to the sea under their direct jurisdiction. This situation ended after 1200 when King Philippe Auguste seized control of Normandy and Boulogne, but Montreuil nonetheless remained a much-desired stronghold in all the wars that crisscrossed the region. Its greatest catastrophe came during the wars between François I of France and the Holy Roman Emperor Charles V. In 1537 an Imperial army besieged Montreuil and destroyed virtually the entire town. After it was recovered, François I ordered it rebuilt in a radically different manner, abandoning the old lower town alongside the now-useless river and retreating to the *ville-haute* on top of the hill, which was to be surrounded by the ramparts that are now Montreuil's most exceptional feature. The townspeople were required to take part in the building work, which continued off and on for over a hundred years.

In the 17th century, though, as the French frontier moved away to the east and the sea receded further to the west, Montreuil was allowed to slip into being a quiet backwater, which is why most of the town, remarkably, is still contained within the 16th-century walls. It was still a stop for the Paris–Calais mail coaches, and as such was visited by Victor Hugo, who set part of *Les Misérables* here, as the town where Jean Valjean briefly achieves peace and prosperity under the name of M. Madeleine, and even becomes mayor. In the last few years, since the appearance of the musical, the town has taken much more notice of its *Les Miz*-potential, and a son et lumière show, *Les Misérables à Montreuil-sur-Mer*, is now presented each summer, on the last weekend in July and during the first weekend in August (*details available from tourist office*). Around 400 local residents get suitably dressed up to take part.

If you arrive in Montreuil on a Saturday morning, carry on straight along the main street past the town centre to the south side of the *ville-haute* and Place Charles-de-Gaulle, commonly called the **Grande-Place**, a wide, rambling square that's the site of the weekly **market**. This is a real small-town country market, with stalls in no apparent order offering excellent local vegetables, fresh herbs, very good, strong cheeses and terrines, farm eggs, CDs, computer games and shoelaces. Around the square there are plenty of bars and cafés, bustling with shouted conversations on market days, tranquil again after the stalls have packed up.

Overlooking the scene from one side of the square, perhaps with little admiration, is Field Marshal Sir Douglas Haig, atop a horse, a statue placed here in commemoration of the fact that for much of the First World War, from 1916 to 1918, little Montreuil was the headquarters of the British Army in France. One of the main buildings the army staff used was the one behind him, since converted into a rather odd-looking theatre. Haig himself stayed at the Château de Beaurepaire (*not open to visitors*), in St-Nicolas, a little way southeast of the town. He was a familiar figure in the countryside around Montreuil, for he used to exercise by going riding every morning, always accompanied by several officers and a troop of lancers, and preceded by another horseman carrying a Union Jack.

The market finishes in good time to go down through the gate in the ramparts on one side of the Grande-Place to the Grenouillère for lunch. Afterwards, or before lunch if it isn't market day, head back into the rest of Montreuil, north of the square. The intertwining streets and squares of the old town are narrow, small-scale and have enormous charm. As a town upon a hill it has a noticeably airy feel, an impression helped by its mostly whitewashed or light-grey stucco buildings. The little white cottages in the oldest streets sometimes look as if they should be in a fishing town, perhaps some kind of hangover from when it was 'sur-Mer'. The main streets are busy at the end of the school day, when crowds of children mill around waiting for buses to take them back to the surrounding villages. At other times the streets are often quiet as a mouse.

The main through street, the old Paris road that is now called Rue Pierre Ledent, runs through the western side of the *ville-haute*. Just off it is **Place Darnétal**, a very pretty square with lime trees and an engagingly twee fountain in the middle. The 16th-century half-timbered houses and Les Hauts de Montreuil hotel across on the other side of Rue Pierre Ledent are the oldest buildings in the town, parts of which may even be survivors from before 1537. From Place Darnétal a little street connects with the main square, **Place Gambetta**.

Montreuil has a curious range of churches. **St-Saulve** on Place Gambetta is the largest, a fine early-Gothic pile which, however, only half survived the great sack of 1537. The 15th-century main façade and nave are both beautiful, but the choir and the transepts were all destroyed, leaving the church only half its previous size, and the sections rebuilt or added at different times since then look like nothing more than attempts to put a brave face on things. Inside, though, its battered state can make it strangely atmospheric. Across the square, next to Montreuil's much-rebuilt old hospital, is the **Chapelle de l'Hôtel-Dieu**, its former chapel. It's usually only open to visitors during France's *journées du patrimoine* weekend in September, although this does not matter too much since its main features are all on the outside. Montreuil's hospital or *Hôtel-Dieu* was founded around 1200, but the chapel dates from the 15th-century. In the 1860s, while the hospital – which now houses the Hermitage Hotel (*see* p.101) – was rebuilt in the form we can see today, the restoration of the chapel was entrusted to Clovis Normand, a local architect and Gothic revivalist of the school of Viollet-le-Duc who undertook to save and restore many of the Canche valley's then-battered and neglected medieval buildings, including the monastery at Neuville. His very romantic idea of 'restoration', however, went far beyond anything that would be considered as such today, and at the Hôtel-Dieu he virtually rebuilt the entire chapel (only the main portal is wholly original). The result is a pure medievalist fantasy, with a mass of luxuriantly sculpted *flamboyant* Gothic details.

Go down the street to the right of the Hôtel-Dieu and you come to another quiet little square, with the **Chapelle de Ste-Austreberthe**, a simple, whitewashed late-medieval church. From there, Rue Porte Becquerelle and then Rue de Paon, to the right, will take you to the most picturesque part of Montreuil, with the little cobbled alleys of **Clape-en-Bas** and **Clape-en-Haut** huddled against the ramparts. The tiled roofs of the cottages that lean against each other along the steep streets seem almost to touch the ground, and each door is a different colour. Ungraciously, the names of the streets mean roughly Lower Drain and Upper Drain, referring to the gutters – the remains of open sewers – that still run down the middle of them. Several of the houses are used as craft workshops or bars in summer, which keeps the area lively, but on other days they can be as slow-moving as the rest of the town.

Montreuil also has its museums, although they're peculiarly elusive. The main local collection, the Musée Roger Rodière on Rue de la Chaîne, has fallen victim to another major renovation project and is closed until further notice. Summer afternoons are the only times you can see the **Hôtel Acary de la Rivière** (*open July–Aug daily 3–6; adm*) on Parvis St-Firmin, just off the main winding street into town. An elegant mansion built for a Napoleonic general in 1810, it was left to the town by its last, British, owners in 1978, and in their honour now houses the '*Musée de l'Espoir Frank et Mary Wooster*'. The greatest attraction is the house itself, with its gardens and near-complete original décor, but around the rooms there's also a well-matched collection of very fine 18th- and 19-century furniture, and an unpredictable mix of paintings.

Late afternoon, when the shadows are beginning to be more noticeable, is a good time to approach Montreuil's most special attraction, the walk around the **ramparts**, which are accessible from many streets in the town. They form an unbroken loop, and as you go around it the circuit seems to accentuate the smallness of Montreuil, confining it still more upon its hill. They extend for three kilometres, and the full walk takes about an hour, but along the way there are plenty of places to stop. And, despite the walls' original purpose, they are wonderfully peaceful, overgrown with grass and ivy along the top, with at some points a sheer drop beneath you. All around, the views are superb: inwards, over the streets of Montreuil; northwards, over lower Montreuil and the Canche; westwards, towards the sea, the lower Canche and superb, gold-lit sunsets. By the **Porte de Boulogne**, rebuilt in the 1820s, you look down over lush flowerbeds by the roadside, which soften the town walls' naturally forbidding glare.

In the northwest corner of the ramparts, beyond an especially attractive, grassy area that now also contains Montreuil's tourist office, a little bridge leads to the **Citadelle** (*open Mon, Wed–Sun Nov–Mar 10–12 and 2–5; April–Oct 10–12 and 2–6; closed Tues; adm*). It was built, still more than the rest of Montreuil, to dominate the approaches along the Canche, and so has a still better view. Since it was attacked, damaged, rebuilt and added to over the centuries, different parts of it vary in age enormously, from the first Montreuil of the 9th century, through two massive towers built for Philippe Auguste, and a 17th-century entrance by the ever-present Marshal Vauban. The **Tour de la Reine Berthe** is where one of France's least distinguished kings, Philippe I, is supposed to have confined his Dutch Queen Berthe in 1091 after he had repudiated her to marry another, Bertrade de Montfort.

After exploring old Montreuil it's worth wandering into the soft, green countryside of the lower Canche below La Madelaine, along the line of the one-time harbour. It's a curious landscape, visibly a low-lying dip and yet just as obviously an area that has been 'inland' for centuries, and with some deliciously pretty and calm villages among the woods and fields – especially **St-Josse** and **Cucq**. And a visit to Montreuil can also include a trip to the beach. At the end of the roads west there are coastal towns that are entirely different one from another, offering very clear options.

Etaples, on the north side of the mouth of the Canche, has a beach but is very much a working fishing port, quite rough and ready, and with great fish restaurants. To the south, and by complete contrast, is eccentrically glitzy **Le Touquet**, an artificial resort created in the 1890s as a rival to Deauville and other spots further south, and long successful with wealthy Brits. Its art deco architecture, casino and grand hotels give it a vaguely Noël Coward-ish air, but it still has obvious cachet, with giant houses among the pines that surround the town, and many fine shops. Recently, with its giant beach, superior golfing and sports facilities, flight links with Britain (*see* chapter 3) and indulgent feel Le Touquet has even enjoyed a noticeable expansion in its popularity.

To the south, the coast runs down through **Stella-Plage**, **Merlimont** and finally **Berck-sur-Mer**, all much more low-key, old-fashioned French holiday towns, each with the necessary long prom, *frites* stands and giant sandy beach (the sea departs for the horizon at low tide). Berck especially is very popular with windsurfers and sand-yachters, and a fun place to watch the sun go down over the Channel.

Shopping

An essential place of gourmet pilgrimage in this area is **Maison Pérard** in Le Touquet, for its legendary fish soups (*see p.104*).

Montreuil-sur-Mer ✉ 62170

L'Atelier du Goût, 9 Rue Pierre Ledent, t 03 21 86 41 44, *www.atelierdugout.fr*. Joanne Harris readers may well think this is what France is really for: an artisan *chocolatier* producing all sorts of utterly seductive handmade chocolates and other sweeties and gourmet treats, supplied to you in exquisite little gold-lined boxes. It also has very fine coffees and teas, and there's a little *salon de thé* as well so that you can sample the goods on the premises. *Closed Mon am and Wed.*

Vinophilie, 2 Rue du Grand Sermon, t 03 21 06 01 54, *www.vinophilie.com*. In an ancient alley near the Citadelle at the top of Montreuil, this modern wine merchant has an ample choice of quality French wines, displayed in renovated old *caves*. Particularly impressive are the *grands crus* and fine champagnes, plus spirits and liqueurs. *Open Mon–Sat 8–12.30 and 2–7, Sun 10–12.30.*

Berck-sur-Mer ✉ 62600

Le Succès Berckois, 56 Rue Carnot, t 03 21 09 61 30, *www.succesberckois.com*. A distinguished family firm, based in a lovely old shop one street back from Berck's seafront. *Succès* and *berlingots* are boiled sweets, and the Matifas family have made them to their own recipes since the 1920s, in a huge variety of fruit, herby and flower-based flavours – the range changes all the time, as they are continually introducing new mixtures. In traditional French style they have won many awards, including one for best sweet in France.

Beussent ✉ 62170

Les Chocolats de Beussent, 66 Route de Desvres, t 03 21 86 17 62, *www.choco-france.com*. A remarkably successful cottage industry, the Beussent *chocolaterie* produces a complete range of filled chocolates, pralines, chocolate bars, cooking chocolate and other goodies, all handmade in its village workshop. So successful is it that it now has outlets in Boulogne, Wimereux,

St-Omer and other towns, but this is the most charming place to try the range. *Open (shop) Mon–Sat 9–12 and 2–7; (tours) 14 July–Aug Mon–Sat 3.30, 4.30, 7.*

Montcavrel ✉ 62170

Le Fond des Communes, Route de Beussent, t 03 21 06 21 73. Eliane and Louise Leviel produce excellent *chèvre*, butter and cows'-milk cheeses on this remote farm in a side valley of the Course. Specialities are *aperichèvres*, appetisers on a *chèvre* base. They also sell at Le Touquet market (*Mon, Thurs, Sat*). To find it, take the lane across the river in Beussent (past the Restaurant Lignier), and then follow an even smaller hill road to the right, towards Montcavrel. *Farm tours by appointment Feb–Nov daily exc Sun.*

Where to Stay

Montreuil-sur-Mer ✉ 62170

Château de Montreuil, 4 Chaussée des Capucins, t 03 21 81 53 04, *www.chateaudemontreuil.com* (*double rooms €170–196, cottages, apartments €170*). The luxury option in Montreuil – although not really a château, but rather a very large, 19th-century villa, surrounded by a flower-filled garden with swimming pool. Chef-proprietor Christian Germain trained with the Roux brothers in England, his wife Lindsay is English and at any time half the clientele are likely to be so too. The great attraction is its complete comfort: the rooms, all different and with many special touches, are not cheap, but in return you get true luxury. There is also a very spacious apartment, and cottages around the garden. And to go with the rooms there is Christian Germain's renowned cooking (*see p.103*).

Hôtel Hermitage, Place Gambetta, t 03 21 06 74 74, *www.hermitage-montreuil.com* (*double rooms €115–170 high season, €70–120*). Montreuil's former hospital, founded in the Middle Ages and rebuilt in the 1860s, was thoroughly renovated once again in 2002 to house this impressive modern 57-room hotel. The rooms could have been decorated with more awareness of the setting – they're designed with an eye as much to business as to leisure travellers – but are spacious and have all contemporary comforts, and service is excellent. The hotel also has an innovative restaurant, **Le Jéroboam** (*see* right). Low-season rates apply roughly Nov–Mar, but several days during this time also qualify as high season.

Les Hauts de Montreuil, 21–23 Rue Pierre Ledent, **t** 03 21 81 95 92, *www.leshautsdemontreuil.com* (*double rooms €79–95*). The oldest house in Montreuil, said to date from 1537, is impossible to miss. Owner Jacques Gantiez works hard to make the most of his ancient pile, with a borderline-brashness that might horrify historic purists, and offers a whole range of eating options (*see* p.104). The renovated interior is not as venerable as the exterior suggests, but very cosy, and the atmosphere is convivial despite (or because of) the touristy touches. The 27 rooms have plenty of charm and very good facilities, and there are also ample suites (*from €134*).

M and Mme Louchez, 77 Rue Pierre Ledent, **t** 03 21 81 54 68, *louchez.anne@wanadoo.fr* (*rooms €50 for two*). A charming B&B with an ultra-convenient location right in the middle of Montreuil, in an 18th-century house that has plenty of antique character but is also very much the family home of Danièle and Michel Louchez and their family. Their five guest rooms (two doubles, two twins, one a double with an extra bed) are attractive and comfortable, and breakfasts are generous.

Beussent ✉ 62170

Le Ménage, 124 Route d'Hucqueliers, **t** 03 21 90 91 92, **f** 03 21 86 38 24 (*rooms €80 for two*). An outstanding *chambres d'hôtes* in an imposing 19th-century manor house standing amid its own grounds and woods on the high plateau east of Beussent. M and Mme Barsby are both artists, and have a studio and gallery in part of the house; the five very spacious, high-ceilinged guest rooms (all doubles) have been restored and redecorated with great taste and imagination. A special place to stay: to find it, cross the river from Beussent village, past the Restaurant Lignier, carry on to the top of the hill, and turn left.

Bezinghem ✉ 62650

Ferme-Auberge des Granges, **t/f** 03 21 90 93 19, *www.fermeaubergedesgranges.com* (*rooms €40 for two*). A rambling white-washed farm – still very much in operation – in the rural heart of the Course valley, with six B&B rooms (five doubles, one for three). They're simple, but attractively decorated, and well-priced. Mountain bikes can be hired for exploring the area. The **restaurant** offers fresh country cooking, especially traditional *tartes* cooked in a wood oven (*menu €13*). Meals must be booked in advance. *Restaurant closed Sun eves and Mon.*

Hucqueliers ✉ 62650

Le Clos, 19 Rue de l'Eglise, **t** 03 21 86 37 10, *http://clos.bertin.online.fr* (*rooms €55–65 for two*). A superior *chambres d'hôtes* in the centre of Hucqueliers, in the Haut-Pays above the Course valley. The 19th-century house was once home to the local notary, and has a front courtyard, stable blocks and walled garden. Four of the six rooms are more or less self-contained apartments, giving the option of B&B or self-catering; in another wing are two romantic double rooms. Facilities include a lounge, cable TV, music, books and games. Owners Alain and Isabelle Bertin (who speak very good English) take great care of guests, offering to babysit and book golf courses, taxis or anything else you may need.

Inxent ✉ 62170

Auberge d'Inxent, **t** 03 21 90 71 19, *auberge.inxent@wanadoo.fr* (*double rooms €64–70*). A lovely old Course valley inn, in one of the prettiest villages along the river, with a delightful garden and geraniums at every window. It was picked out as a model of a French country *auberge* years ago by no less than Elizabeth David, and its **restaurant** (*menus €13–37*) has continued to place a fine emphasis on fresh local produce. The six guest rooms have pretty, traditional décor, and views of the garden, village and river.

La Madeleine-sous-Montreuil ✉ 62170

Auberge de la Grenouillère, **t** 03 21 06 07 22, *www.lagrenouillere.fr* (*double rooms €75–90, apartment €100*). The Grenouillère's four utterly charming guest rooms are built into the eaves of the old farmhouse, and combine antique furniture with excellent bathrooms and fittings to create the feel of a romantic hideaway. One is a very relaxing suite-style 'apartment', with space for two adults and 1–2 children.

Maresville ✉ 62630

Ferme-Auberge des Chartroux, t 03 21 86 70 68, **f** 03 21 86 70 38 (*double rooms €56–79*). Mme Delianne's very peaceful *ferme-auberge*, deep in the country 7km northwest of Montreuil, is a member of *Logis de France* and so officially a hotel, but feels more like a warm farm B&B. The cosy rooms are spread about the former farm buildings and yard, and there's also an enjoyable **restaurant** (*see p.104*). *Closed two weeks Nov and two weeks Jan.*

Neuville-sous-Montreuil ✉ 62170

Ferme de la Chartreuse, t 03 21 81 07 31, *anne-fourdinier@wordonline.fr* (*rooms €46 for two*). A big old ivy-clad farm that was once part of Neuville's medieval abbey, just alongside it. Within walking distance of the village, it's a warm family home, with a pretty garden. Mme Fourdinier has two B&B rooms, one a double and one with three single beds, so it's well-suited to families.
Le Vert Bois, t 03 21 06 09 41, *etienne.bernard6@wanadoo.fr* (*rooms €43 for two*). A dramatic medieval fortified gate forms the entry into this magnificent old farm, in rather splendid isolation in the countryside about 1½km east of Neuville. Inside it, there's a massive courtyard, with duck pond and a variety of buildings of different ages. The two B&B rooms (one double, one twin) are more modern in style, and very well-kept. Very peaceful; a genuinely rural *chambres d'hôtes*.

St-Josse ✉ 62170

Le Manoir du Tertre, 50 Chaussée de l'Avant Pays, **t** 03 21 94 05 97, **f** 03 21 81 62 91 (*rooms €60–90 for two, €120 for five*). Amid over a hectare of green and wooded grounds, this fine old manor farm has been attractively converted to house three especially comfortable, suite-style B&B rooms. The house has a very welcoming feel, and all the rooms have

been furnished with a mix of modern features and traditional country décor, and have lovely views of the placid countryside. One is a family-size suite (with balcony), and all three can be booked at a group rate.
La Ferme du Tertre, 77 Chaussée de l'Avant Pays, **t/f** 03 21 09 09 13, *pretrealain@hotmail.com* (*rooms €49 for two, €75 for four*). A stylish, charming *chambres d'hôtes* in a former farm on the lane between La Madelaine and St-Josse, with distinctive blue-and-white gates. The four modern rooms, with excellent facilities, are in one of the ex-farm buildings, and each has its own French-window entrance from the garden. One room has space for four and a kitchenette, and there's also a *gîte* (for up to eight). Breakfast can be served in the garden, and there are ponds with ducks, swans and geese, and good fishing.

Eating Alternatives

Montreuil-sur-Mer ✉ 62170

Château de Montreuil, 4 Chaussée des Capucins, **t** 03 21 81 53 04, *www.chateaudemontreuil.com* (*menus €38 lunch only, €58–78*). Unreservedly top-drawer country-house hotel (*see p.101*), with a high reputation. Chef Christian Germain, worked with the Roux brothers in Britain for some years before coming to Montreuil; his cooking accordingly combines French traditions with original touches. Local meats, fish and seafood are often presented with adventurous spicings, and there is a formidable Philippe Olivier cheeseboard and a suitably comprehensive wine cellar.
Le Jéroboam, Hôtel Hermitage, Place Gambetta, **t** 03 21 86 65 80, *www.hermitage-montreuil.com* (*menus €15 lunch only, €28–58*). Montreuil restaurants tend to look fairly traditional, but Olivier Germain, son of Christian Germain of the Château (*see above*) has struck out in a new direction with this distinctly metropolitan modern brasserie in the Hermitage hotel (*see p.101*), but with its own independent entrance. The sleek décor is contemporary-minimalist style, in deep burgundy and dark wood; the food also departs from the French norm,

with global and (even) modern-British-influenced ingredients and seasonings. There's also a fine, equally contemporary wine collection. Prices are a bit high; service is informal and very charming.

Les Hauts de Montreuil, 21–23 Rue Pierre Ledent, **t** 03 21 81 95 92, *www.leshautsdemontreuil.com* (*menus €22–38*). This picturesque 16th-century inn offers a whole variety of possibilities: the main restaurant, a bar-brasserie, and the 'West Indies Bar Club', specializing in rare rums. For all the hard sell the restaurant has a good reputation, especially for local specialities – Licques chicken, duck and lamb, fish and seafood – and very unusually has a (rather cheesy) vegetarian menu. Les Hauts also has a shop with wines and local foodstuffs, and Montreuil's own beers.

Le Darnétal, Place Darnétal, **t** 03 21 06 04 87, *www.darnetal-montreuil.com* (*menus €18–34*). A popular restaurant in the centre of old Montreuil, with a snug dining room full of flowers and antiques. M and Mme Vernay extend a warm welcome. Highlights of their menus are refined fish and seafood dishes – *paupiette d'aile de raie aux poireaux et moules* – or poultry – fillet of duck in red wine with *baies de cassis*. There are four simple guest rooms (*double rooms €35–70*).

Berck-sur-Mer ✉ 62600

L'Auberge du Bois, 145 Av du Docteur Quettier, **t** 03 21 09 03 43 (*menus €13–30*). A very popular, simple place for bargain seafood specialities – especially *choucroute de la mer* and a still heftier *plâteau de fruits de mer* – other fine fish choices and some meat dishes. It's some way from Berck beach, on one of the avenues running inland.

Beussent ✉ 62170

Restaurant Lignier, Place de la Mairie, **t** 03 21 90 71 65 (*menus €20–35*). A long-established country restaurant by the banks of the Course, popular with locals. Beyond the old-fashioned bar are the riverside dining rooms, where you can choose from homemade terrines, local trout, game, and classic meat favourites grilled over a wood fire, along with superior cheese and wine selections. *Closed Sun eve and Mon.*

La Madelaine-sous-Montreuil ✉ 62170

Auberge du Vieux Logis, **t** 03 21 06 10 92 (*menus €17–26*). In the centre of La Madelaine, near the turn for La Grenouillère, this cosy village bistro doesn't compete in culinary sophistication but offers traditional food of a high standard, with generous menus and good salads and lighter dishes from around €7. There's a very pleasant terrace outside whenever the weather suits. *Closed Wed and eves Tues, Sun.*

Maresville ✉ 62630

Ferme-Auberge des Chartroux, **t** 03 21 86 70 68, **f** 03 21 86 70 38 (*menus €18–24*). A superior *ferme-auberge* in a rambling old farm that's also a *Logis* hotel (*see* p.103). The produce used – notably the renowned lamb – still comes from the farm, but the antique-filled dining rooms are neatly pretty as well as rustic, and Mme Delianne and her family run the place with sophisticated charm. Reservations essential. *Closed two weeks Nov and two weeks Jan.*

St-Josse ✉ 62170

Le Relais de St-Josse, Grand'Place, **t** 03 21 94 61 75 (*menus €21–50*). In a low, old inn that's clad in geraniums for much of the year, the Relais has a homely look, but its menus have an innovative, modern style. Local meats and fish are often mixed with global touches, such as ginger and Chinese pears. It's also a *salon de thé*, with nice light dishes.

Le Touquet ✉ 62520

Restaurant Pérard, 67 Rue de Metz, **t** 03 21 05 13 33, *www.restaurantperard.com* (*menus €17–26*). Pérard of Le Touquet is one of those French establishments that has gained the status of national institution, with the accolade of producing the finest *soupe de poisson* in France. Long known more as a shop, lately it has expanded its restaurant, terrace and oyster bar. *Carte* and menus feature only fish and seafood, of superb quality, including magnificent *bouillabaisse* and *plateaux* of different *fruits de mer*. There is still a *traiteur* shop attached, and French diners do not miss the chance to pick up a pot of soup (the crab and lobster are as celebrated as the fish) before leaving.

On the Back Roads of Artois:
Hesdin and the Sept Vallées

11

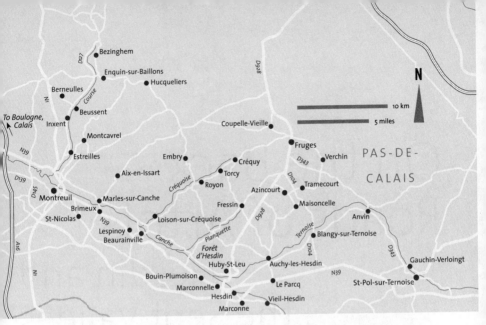

The countryside inland in the Pas-de-Calais, east of the main roads south, can at first glance look to be just a plain, open expanse of rolling downs, with few trees and giant fields patrolled by lonely tractors, and always wind-blasted when the winter weather sets in. Explore a little, though, and you find that the downland is divided by a string of sheltered, mellow valleys, some open, some steep-sided, lined by groves of trees and with fast-flowing rivers, babbling becks and large, placid ponds. Instead of feeling monotonous, the landscape suddenly seems abundant and varied.

Away from the main roads, this area – known as the *Sept Vallées* or Seven Valleys of Artois – is a place of villages of neat, whitewashed cottages with red-tiled roofs and window boxes packed with flowers, so peaceful they seem lost to the world. Each has its individual quirks and features – a tumbledown château glimpsed through trees, a bizarrely shaped church porch, even a piano bar in the middle of nowhere. And, like any other part of rural France, the region has its traditions and special foods – especially cheeses, *charcuterie* and unusual liqueurs.

For centuries this area was also part of Europe's greatest battleground, fought over time and again by France, England, Spain and other powers. Its towns and villages have been conquered and retaken many times, and this past is reflected in historic buildings found by market squares, or in battlefields such as Azincourt – aka Agincourt – still visible amid the rural quiet.

Roads wind up and around hills through the Artois valleys, interconnected by tiny, often sunken lanes, making them ideal for anyone who likes just wandering and taking each place as they find them. For thorough orientation, local tourist offices have plenty of informative literature, including lists of traditional food and craft outlets. And, as a focus when exploring, a natural point to aim for is Hesdin, the valleys' main town, which was built as a Spanish stronghold, and then became a garrison town of the *Ancien Régime*. It has several very enjoyable places to eat, and, in **L'Ecurie**, an excellent showcase for the region's produce and cuisine.

Getting There

To reach the *Sept Vallées* from Calais or Boulogne, follow the A16 *autoroute* or the N1 south to Montreuil. The main N39 Hesdin-Arras road turns off the N1 a little further south, but the most attractive routes to Hesdin are the two roads along the Canche valley, the D349 south of the river and the little D113 north of it. Lanes turn off these roads to go up the other valleys.

As you enter Hesdin on the D349, called Av François Mitterrand in town, you come to a triangular park with a war memorial and a car park; park here, and walk the short distance up Rue André Fréville to Place d'Armes, the main square and centre of town. L'Ecurie is a short walk away down Rue Jacquemont, one of the turnings off the square to the right.

Tourist Information

Hesdin: Office du Tourisme des 7 Vallées, Hôtel de Ville, Place d'Armes, t 03 21 86 71 69, *www.tourisme-7vallees.com*. The enterprising central information office for the whole of the *Sept Vallées*, prominently located in Hesdin's Hôtel de Ville.
Azincourt: 22 Rue Charles VI, t 03 21 47 27 53, *www.azincourt-medieval.com*.
Beaurainville-Vallée de la Créquoise: La Mairie, Beaurainville, t 03 21 90 30 63/03 21 81 03 54. *Special tourist information point open June–mid-Sept daily.*
Fressin: 8 Grande Rue, t/f 03 21 86 56 11.
Fruges: Hôtel de Ville, t 03 21 04 02 65, *ot-fruges@pas-de-calais.com*.
St-Pol-sur-Ternoise: Place de l'Hôtel de Ville, t 03 21 47 08 08, *www.ternois-tourisme.com*.

L'Ecurie

17–19 Rue Jacquemont, Hesdin, t/f 03 21 86 86 86.
Open Wed–Sun 12–2 and 7–9.30; closed Mon and Tues, and two weeks Jan, two weeks early June. Booking essential Sun eves.
Menus €15 (Wed–Fri and Sat lunch only), €23–30; carte average €35.

L'Ecurie occupies a 16th-century former stables (*écurie*) near Hesdin's Place d'Armes, which by the 1930s, as an old photograph on the wall shows, had moved on to house a garage at one end and a café at the other. The old building has been neatly restored, making good use of the plain brick and stone of its entrance to give an uncluttered sense of style. Inside, there's a small bar, and a combination of classic features – 19th-century prints, flowers, neat table settings – and more modern touches – lemon walls, wicker chairs, staff in casual clothes. The atmosphere is bright and airy. This mix of tradition and innovation is characteristic of the restaurant throughout.

The men behind L'Ecurie, chef Jean-Luc Lecoutre and maître-d Michel Cadet, are both from the *Sept Vallées* but worked in several first-rank restaurants around the north – including the august Huîtrière in Lille – before opening up here in 1997, believing that there was a space in Hesdin and the Valleys for a more imaginative, quality restaurant that made the most of local produce and culinary traditions. As Cadet puts it, they know that in a country setting they cannot be too experimental – there's no point in deliberately alienating a local clientele that tends to have firm opinions on what it likes – but nevertheless they always try to be creative in their approach to food. And this winning combination of satisfying but refined food presented in a relaxed style (and at very reasonable prices) has clearly hit the mark. It's a place that the whole town seems to enjoy – men in suits, families, men lunching on their own, pairs of elderly ladies or young women, and passing tourists.

As you wait to order, the arrival of some delicious freshly-baked bread rolls gives an indication of the Ecurie's attention to detail and quality. Menus and *carte* are all shortish and easy to handle, but still offer plenty of interesting possibilities – such as an omelette with mussels in the Basque *pipérade* style, with chopped red pepper, onions, garlic and tomatoes, from the €15 list. Jean-Luc Lecoutre presents inventive dishes rather than relying on old standards, but his cooking is very much based in northern French cuisine, with a liking for strong, vigorous flavours, a rich sense of meatiness and earthiness, and a great use of northern ingredients such as green vegetables, duck, beer, juniper berries and especially locally-caught fish, whether from nearby ports or the valleys' rivers. In autumn, the €23 *menu petit plaisir* might include a very original, highly enjoyable 'gateau' of salmon with leeks and local root vegetables – parsnips, turnip – followed among other meatier options by grilled salt cod combined with rich, no-nonsense *andouille* sausage. On the €30 list, meanwhile, you could go for a classic fillet of beef, precisely cooked and served with a great *méli-mélo* mixture of beautifully flavoured, wonderfully wintry forest mushrooms.

The cheese course covers all the essentials, with local favourites such as maroilles or rollot, and the wine list is, like the menus, shorter than some but skilfully selected. To finish, there are creamy and fruity desserts, and fresh-fruit sorbets. On a weekday at around 2pm many of your fellow diners will get up and go back to their business, but for those with no demands on their time there's no pressure to move on.

Touring Around

The valley of the **Canche**, running inland from Le Touquet past Montreuil, is the largest of the Artois valleys and the area's main artery. From Montreuil the D349 towards Hesdin runs parallel to the river, rolling up and down along the wooded banks through a line of occasionally busy villages, several of which have their particular attractions. The Canche here is quite wide and slow-moving, and at **Brimeux** forms several large, mysterious-looking ponds surrounded by willows and birches, and much-loved by local anglers (permits are required, obtainable from the town hall).

Everywhere there is colour, for the villagers of Artois are known for their love of flowers, and except in the very dead of winter virtually every house has bunches of geraniums, hydrangeas and wild flowers decorating their windowsills. Further east along the Canche in **Bouin-Plumoison** – or 'goose-pluckers', a reference to the villagers' early occupation – there is the **Musée de l'Abeille d'Opale**, a private display dedicated to maintaining interest in one of the Pas-de-Calais' oldest traditions, beekeeping. As Therry Apiculture, the same owners also produce fine honey and things derived from it, especially *hydromel* or fermented honey, otherwise known as mead. Billed here as 'the drink of the Gauls', it has been made in this area for centuries, and recently has enjoyed a mild revival. In the same village there is also **La Plume d'Oison**, a showcase for the work of the many craftspeople around the Seven Valleys.

Beyond Bouin the road approaches **Hesdin**, at the meeting-point of the Canche and Ternoise valleys. Although it now has the appearance of an historic old community, the capital of the Seven Valleys was once a 'new town', transplanted from its original location a few kilometres to the east in 1554 on the orders of the Emperor Charles V. The great Franco-Spanish wars that long dominated the life of Flanders and Artois began when Charles fortuitously inherited both Spain and Burgundy, so that his territories effectively surrounded France. For the next century and a half, every French king and minister took it as his aim to break this ring around them, a goal finally achieved between 1640 and 1680 by Richelieu, Mazarin and Louis XIV. A hundred years earlier, though, the great Charles carried all before him, and in 1553, after their French garrisons had obstructed his troops once too often, he ordered that both Thérouanne to the north and the first Hesdin be razed down to the last brick, and a new Hesdin created to the west. For the next decades, until a French army took it by siege in 1639, it would be the main bastion of Spanish power in Artois, face to face with the French stronghold at Montreuil, with regular skirmishes along the valley between them.

Hesdin today is a very attractive little town, with monuments that reflect its special history. The main square, **Place d'Armes**, which seems almost too big for the town, is dominated by a grand, Flemish-looking brick **Hôtel de Ville**, begun in 1572 and fronted by a magnificently sculpted two-level Baroque stone porch, from 1629. At the very top there is a *fleur-de-lys*, added in the 18th century, but the coat of arms at the centre of the balcony is that of Spain, flanked by those of Hesdin and Artois, and the figures on the sides of the upper level represent Philip IV of Spain and his French queen Isabelle, surrounded by the cardinal virtues. Nearby is the massive church of **Notre-Dame**, built between 1565 and 1585 in the Flemish *hallekerk* style as a rectangular hall instead of in the shape of a cross. Its brick façade is mainly very late Gothic, but it has an impressive Renaissance-style stone porch, surmounted, again, by the Spanish Habsburg arms. Inside, there is some very fine Baroque woodwork.

Next to the church is the River Canche, which runs through the middle of the town under little humpbacked bridges, sometimes disappearing under buildings and then re-emerging beside houses and the winding, cobbled streets. At No.11 Rue Daniel Lereuil is the birthplace of the **Abbé Prévost**, born 1697, famously un-devout and misbehaving priest and author of *Manon Lescaut*, while north of Place d'Armes in Rue Prévost is the **Hospice St-Jean**, formerly the Jesuit college where the future Abbé studied, begun in 1562 but with a distinguished neoclassical façade added in 1746.

Hesdin is busiest on Thursdays, when farmers from all around the valleys descend on the square for the area's most important and vigorous **market**. The town is also known for two kinds of food, a moreish crunchy chocolate called a *pavé hesdinois*, in the shape of an Artois roof tile, and charcuterie, often made with beer and honey, which can be found in the market and in many shops near the square. And, after wandering through the streets of Hesdin, you can also walk all the way around it along a lovely beech-lined footpath, the **Tour-de-Chaussée**, created in the 17th century by travelling merchants to avoid passing through the town and paying the dues it was entitled to charge.

From Hesdin it's possible to head out into the *Sept Vallées* in any direction. To follow a circular route, continue eastwards along the N39 road toward **St-Pol-sur-Ternoise**. On the way, pay at least some respect to tiny **Vieil-Hesdin**, site of what was, until it incurred Charles V's wrath, one of the region's richest towns. It also contained a famously palatial castle, the ruins of which are still visible, and the 'Park of Marvels', a giant pleasure garden created at the beginning of the 14th century by Richard, Count of Artois. Stretching all the way to the Ternoise, and landscaped to create all kinds of visual tricks, it contained exotic beasts, elaborate fountains, bizarre statues and even jokes such as bridges that gave way when you trod on them. Renowned throughout Europe, it was used by the dukes of Burgundy for extravagant entertaining, but later it, too, was obliterated on the Emperor's orders, and only the name of the village of **Le Parcq** remains. Not far away is another idiosyncratic village, **Auchy-lès-Hesdin**, with a 19th-century cotton mill – long closed down – built within the remains of a medieval abbey, and a superb Gothic church.

St-Pol-sur-Ternoise is a large, plain town, which had the misfortune to be badly battered twice the last time Artois was a battlefield, in 1940 and 1944. A turn north-west, though, onto the D343 signposted to Anvin will take you back into the **Ternoise**, a broad, misty valley with rambling, widely dispersed villages such as **Gauchin-Verloingt**, apparently lost in green tranquillity. **Anvin** and, further west, **Blangy-sur-Ternoise** both have fine, but very different, 16th-century churches, the former late Gothic, the second more eclectic. Blangy is also the place where Henry V of England and his army crossed the Ternoise in October 1415, on their way to Azincourt (better known in English spelt with a G), where they would defeat a French force five times larger in one rain-soaked day. It's now reached by turning north on to the little D104 in Blangy.

For years **Azincourt** had a small museum that, like the stand-up figures of medieval knights all around the village, was an entirely local initiative (governments rarely commemorate defeats). However, since 2000 local officialdom has swallowed its pride and recognized the potential of the site, and the village now has a state of the art **Medieval History Centre** (*www.azincourt-medieval.com; open Jan–Mar, Nov–Dec Mon, Wed–Sun 10–5; April–June and Sept–Oct daily 10–6; July–Aug daily 10–7; adm*). In a way this is a bit of a pity, since the old museum with its sometimes shameless use of any material the local organisers had to hand had a charm of its own, but the new one hosts a lively display that opens up the life of the time and tells the story of the battle (in French and English) highly effectively through videos, reconstructions and other exhibits. It's sometimes a tad wordy (in French museum style), but has excellent hands-on bits for kids, such as 'helmets' that give a vivid idea of just how much (or how little) a medieval knight could see once strapped into his armour. It's a good idea to visit the centre to get an idea of the main events of 1415 before walking or driving to the battleground. The Azincourt battlefield itself is remarkable: perhaps due to its compact size, it's possible to recognize the outlines of what happened there nearly 600 years ago more easily than at the sites of many far more recent events. The forests either side of the field, which hemmed in the French horsemen and made it impossible for them to use most of their strength, have gone, but the track along which carts ran – keeping the English archers supplied with arrows as they poured them into the French knights sliding and falling in the mud – is still there, now the road past the neighbouring village of **Maisoncelle**. Nowadays Azincourt also hosts a biennial international archery competition, next due in May 2006.

From Azincourt take the main D928 south towards Hesdin, then turn off right on to yet another tiny lane to enter another valley, the **Planquette**, and reach **Fressin**, known to students of French literature as the long-time home of Georges Bernanos and the background to many of his novels. Also, in among the trees just to the west, at the end of the village's long main street, there are the romantic ruins of a **castle** (*open April–Sept; adm*) that was once the seat of the Créquy, one of the grandest Artois families from the Middle Ages right up until the *Ancien Régime*, and servants at different times of both the kings of France and the dukes of Burgundy. Fressin has one of the finest of the Valley churches, **St-Martin**, most unusual because its interior is entirely washed down in white. Especially beautiful is the funeral chapel of the Créquys, first built by a widow, Jeanne de Roye, for her husband and two others of the clan who died at Azincourt, and with superb lattice-work Gothic carving. The rest of the church was actually built later, with almost English-style columns added by a 16th-century Créquy who was ambassador to England.

As you leave the church, not far away downhill on Fressin's main street are **Les Caves du Vieux Chai**, the Glaçon family's imposing, also-historic wine *cave*, now run by M. Paul Glaçon and his daughter. Buying wine here is a great, relaxed alternative to pushing a trolley around the ferry-port mega-warehouses.

North of Fressin a road winds on up to **Créquy** village, at the head of the **Créquoise**, perhaps the most idyllic of all the *Sept Vallées*. The valley sides wind and dip and are very green, while the river sparkles and rushes along the roadside and past the village churches and flowerbeds. Just outside Créquy to the north is the **Sire de Créquy** farm, which produces a unique cheese with the same name, after a 13th-century Créquy, Raoul, who went off to the Crusades, was captured and believed lost forever, and then returned to claim his 'widow' on the day she was due to remarry (this story is also re-enacted in a cute *son et lumière* pageant in Fressin in early July). Visitors can have meals at the farm's *auberge* as well as tasting and buying (*see* pp.112, 114).

A little way downriver in **Torcy** there is a piano bar and cabaret, **Le Baladin**, that's an original combination of nightspot and village *crêperie*; from there it's a further couple of kilometres to **Royon**, an exceptionally pretty village with the river running through the middle and a very fine *flamboyant*-Gothic church from the 1540s. If you take a turn right there through **Embry** (on the Hucqueliers road), look out for its very odd but engaging whitewashed chapel, with a 19th-century wrought-iron porch that looks almost like a gazebo. Back in the main Créquoise valley, the road eventually winds down to **Loison-sur-Créquoise**, with a 12th-century Knights Templars' manor, **La Commanderie**, that is now an exceptional B&B. Loison is also the sole home of another special product, *perlé de groseille* or *de framboise*, a kind of redcurrant or raspberry champagne, an enjoyably smooth, refreshing creation that's available at the **Maison du Perlé**, easy to find by the roadside. Owner Hubert Delomel also offers tours and bikes to hire to ride through the surrounding woods. Below Loison, the Créquoise runs into the Canche and the road meets the D113, which to the right will take you back to Montreuil along a leafier, emptier route than the D349, with the option of a detour up one more steep, intimate, wooded valley, the **Bras de Brosne**, via the beautifully out-of-the-way hillside hamlet of **Marles-sur-Canche**.

Shopping

Hesdin ✉ 62140

Distilleries Ryssen, 1 Rue de la Paroisse, **t** 03 21 81 61 70, *www.ryssen.fr*. Producers of a distinctive pastis since 1829, as well as an interesting range of fruity liqueurs. Their Hesdin shop, which shares space with the Wine Society, also sells a range of wines.

The Wine Society, 1 Rue de la Paroisse, **t** 03 21 86 52 07, **f** 03 21 86 52 13. Aimed squarely at the Brit trade – all signs are in English – but somewhat oddly located on Hesdin's very French market square. The selection not just French but also New World and other European wines, at French prices.

Aix-en-Issart ✉ 62170

L'Egouttoir, 26 Rue Principale, **t** 03 21 86 07 41, *www.legouttoir.fr*. Gilbert and Xavier Brunel produce wooden furniture large and small in their village workshop, in historic styles (especially Louis Philippe, Directory and Louis XV) as well as the traditional country styles that have never fallen from fashion in these parts. Each piece is beautifully finished, and items can be made to measure.

Bouin-Plumoison ✉ 62140

Musée de l'Abeille d'Opale/Therry Apiculture, 923 Route Nationale, **t** 03 21 81 46 24. The Therry family's curious, informal 'museum' tells you everything you ever wanted to know about beekeeping, tour of the hives included. The shop sells pollen, royal jelly, cosmetics, candles and mead (*hydromel*), and there's an annual 'Fête du Miel', usually on the first weekend in September. *Shop open Tues–Fri and Sun 2–7, Sat 10–7; museum open June–Sept Tues–Sat 2–7; Sept–June Sat, Sun and hols 2–7.*

La Plume d'Oison, 1395 Route Nationale, **t/f** 03 21 81 59 62. On the main road through Bouin, this shop has an attractive, often quite chic mix of craft work from around the Seven Valleys – pottery, wooden toys, leatherwork, painted textiles, country furniture – and other gifts and home accessories from further afield. At weekends it also becomes a pleasant *estaminet*-style **bar**, with enjoyable snacks (*c. €10–20*). *Shop open Tues–Sat 2.30–7; bar-café open lunch, dinner Fri–Sun.*

Fressin ✉ 62140

Les Caves du Vieux Chai, 20 Grand'Rue, **t** 03 21 90 61 43, *www.cavesduvieuxchai.com*. The Glaçon family have been in the wine trade, from their magnificent old *caves* in the middle of Fressin, for four generations. Their great speciality is Bordeaux, where they have a vineyard, but other French regions and champagnes are also well represented. They now also have a shop in St-Omer (*see* p.55), and can deliver to the UK. *Guided tours of the caves by reservation.*

Fruges and Créquy ✉ 62310

Les Brebis d'Esgranges, Ferme du Bois d'Esgranges, **t/f** 03 21 81 13 14. A small farm near Créquy that produces a variety of high-quality sheeps'-milk cheeses and yogurts. *Farm tours and tastings May–Oct daily 2–7.*

Le Sire de Créquy, Route de Créquy, **t** 03 21 90 60 24. This farm between Créquy and Fruges, which has an *auberge* restaurant (*see* p.114), produces its very own fine cheese, a variation on the region's traditional rollot, a pungent, spicy, strong cheese with an orange rind and a shortish life. Visitors can also tour the *fromagerie* and its *caves*.

Loison-sur-Créquoise ✉ 62990

La Maison du Perlé, 50 Rue Principale, **t** 03 21 81 30 85, *www.perledegroseille.com*. Simple fruit wines have been made by Artois farmers for centuries, but Hubert Delomel has refined the traditional recipes to create his unique *perlés de groseille* and *de framboise* – blackcurrant and raspberry champagnes. The shop also sells ciders, preserves, terrines and his *eau-de-vie-de-cidre*. Tours are provided, and there is a small creperie, to accompany tastings. Visitors can also use the *maison* as a base for walks or cycle rides into the countryside.

Verchin ✉ 62310

Ferme Bocquet, 25 Rue Maranville, **t/f** 03 21 04 43 66. Patricia Bocquet bakes wonderful breads, brioches, tarts and other delicacies on her farm north of Azincourt, using a truly historic wood oven. There's a picnic space for sampling the products on site, with local ciders and cheeses. *Open mid-Mar–mid-Nov daily; mid-Nov–mid-Mar closed Sun.*

Where to Stay

Hesdin ✉ 62140

Hôtel Les Flandres, 22 Rue d'Arras, **t** 03 21 86 80 21, **f** 03 21 86 28 01 (*double rooms €50–56*). Hesdin's once rather cranky *Logis* hotel – long popular with British guests – has been extensively modernized recently, so that its lounges and 14 rooms have greater comforts to add to their more venerable charms. Also much improved is the **restaurant** (*menus €14–24*), which now offers high-quality local cooking, especially meats. There's still a cosy bar, and service remains unfussily friendly.

Auchy-lès-Hesdin ✉ 62770

Auberge le Monastère, **t** 03 21 04 83 54, **f** 03 21 41 39 17 (*double rooms €35–58*). A convivial hotel-restaurant near Auchy's medieval church and old cotton mills. Best known for food (*see* p.114), it's also a *Logis* hotel with 10 simple, comfortable rooms and a garden.

Azincourt ✉ 62310

La Gacogne, **t**/**f** 03 21 04 45 61, *http://advs.online.fr/gacogne* (*rooms €46 for two*). This likeable *chambres d'hôtes* is on the edge of the Azincourt battlefield, and owners M and Mme Fenet are great local history enthusiasts. Their house, with a tower where breakfast is served, is 18th-century. The four rooms are in a pretty ex-farm building alongside, with its own lounge with fireplace.

Beaurainville ✉ 62990

Mme Bailey, 313 Rue du Mont Blanc, **t** 03 21 81 04 26, *orazio.cerrato@wanadoo.fr* (*rooms €61 for two, €95 for four*). In a lovely garden near the banks of the Canche, near several footpaths, this *chambres d'hôtes* is more like a *gîte*, as the one room has a double bed and two singles, and a well-equipped kitchenette – but breakfasts are still provided. Weekly rates are available.

Gauchin-Verloingt ✉ 62130

Le Loubarré, 550 Rue des Montifaux, **t** 03 21 03 05 05, *http://loubarre.com* (*rooms €44 for two*). M and Mme Vion's grand old manor house, with pointy turrets and neoclassical portico, has sections dating from the 17th to the 19th centuries, and is stuffed with

antiques and other curiosities; outside, there is a wooded garden with a few goats. The four B&B rooms, in a former outhouse, have simple, old-style country furniture. To find it, follow *chambres d'hôtes* signs through Gauchin village, via twists, turns and dips.

Loison-sur-Créquoise ✉ 62990

La Commanderie, Allée des Templiers, **t** 03 21 86 49 87 (*rooms €54–61 for two, €84 for four*). A gem of a *chambres d'hôtes*. The main house of this giant farm – the *Commanderie* itself – was originally a 12th-century lodge for the Knights Templar, and the hall-living room-games room is wonderfully baronial; the location, by the Créquoise river, is just as delightful. The four rooms are individually decorated, and have loads of fresh flowers; the magnificent suite is almost a self-contained *gîte*, with its own breakfast room with riverside view, and access to a kitchenette. Owner Marie-Hélène Flament runs her house with a distinctive, friendly style.

Marles-sur-Canche ✉ 62170

Manoir Francis, 1 Rue de l'Eglise, **t** 03 21 81 38 80, **f** 03 21 81 38 56 (*rooms €50 for two*). A ravishing B&B in a tiny village well-placed for both Montreuil and the *Sept Vallées*. The giant castle-like manor-farm, built in 1662, has a broad, circular yard, whitewashed walls and stone flags. The charming owner, Dominique Leroy, ensures it feels warm and homely. As well as collecting antiques, she rescues animals, so there is a varied collection of cats, dogs, ducks and other fauna. The three rooms all have different, atmospheric décor, and the breakfast room, kitchen and winding staircases are equally delightful.

Eating Alternatives

Hesdin ✉ 62140

La Bretèche, 19 Rue du Général Daullé, **t** 03 21 86 80 87 (*menus €16–50*). A relaxed, very comfortable traditional restaurant in the heart of Hesdin. Owners Fabien and Christine Oudart, though, are young, and make excellent use of local produce. It's long been a showcase for the region's own cuisine, so go for the *menu du terroir*, and specialities like chicken cooked with Créquy cheese and beer, or *croustillant d'andouillettes*. *Closed Sun eve and all day Fri.*

Café du Globe, Place d'Armes, **t** 03 21 86 82 65 (*lunch menu €11, plats du jour c. €7*). A near-inescapable presence on Hesdin's market square: an all-day bar-brasserie that serves coffee, snacks, crêpes and larger dishes at bargain prices, and sees all local life pass by.

Auchy-lès-Hesdin ✉ 62770

Auberge le Monastère, **t** 03 21 04 83 54 (*menus €22–48*). That the bar is also the village *café-tabac* gives some idea of the amiable feel of the Monastère. It's also a 'piano bar', since owner Jean-Robert Marecaux is a jazz fan, and plays the clarinet. Meals, served in a pretty old dining room with open fireplace, include both original creations and meaty *terroir* dishes, with generous menus. There are also guest rooms (*see* p.113). *Closed Mon.*

Azincourt ✉ 62310

Le Charles VI, 12 Rue Charles VI, **t** 03 21 41 53 00, *restaurantcharles6@wanadoo.fr* (*menus €13–31*). Rather smart new restaurant near Azincourt museum, with bar, large, airy dining room and a lovely garden terrace in summer. The seasonal menus are quite ambitious, and include a 'medieval menu' based in historic dishes. The wine collection is impressive, too. *Closed Sun eve and Wed.*

Cavron St-Martin ✉ 62140

Estaminet Chés 2 Agaches, **t** 03 21 81 49 16 (*dishes c. €6–15*). A popular, convivial bar in Cavron, a little northwest of Hesdin, with straightforward *planches* of local fare, *estaminet* games and very fine local beers. *Open 4–8pm July–Aug Tues–Sun, Easter–June Sat and Sun, Sept–Easter Sun only.*

Coupelle-Vieille ✉ 62310

Le Fournil, Route de St-Omer, **t** 03 21 04 47 13 (*menus €15–35*). On the D928 north of Fruges, this pleasant roadside inn, much recommended by locals, offers interesting fare at decent prices. Traditional favourites are to the fore, but there's no lack of imagination in their versions of such things as *suprême de pintade aux prunes*, and the quality wine list. *Closed Sun eve and Mon.*

Fruges and Créquy ✉ 62310

Auberge du Sire de Créquy, Route de Créquy, **t** 03 21 90 60 24, **f** 03 21 86 27 72 (*menus €9.60–23*). A big old farm on a hill a little north of Créquy towards Fruges, which has a huge, simply decorated dining room and menus of stout, often cheesy country dishes – renowned *flamiches*, *carbonnades*, duck with walnut sauce – made with fresh produce, mostly from the farm itself. The farm also produces a unique cheese, Sire de Créquy (*see* p.112). Reservations essential.

Huby St-Leu ✉ 62140

La Garenne, 52–54 Rue du 8 Mai 1945, **t** 03 21 86 95 09 (*menus €28–62*). Nothing quite prepares you for the discovery of La Garenne in the middle of the Artois countryside. At first sight it seems to be a simple white-fronted country cottage, but enter the leafy garden and you find it packed with a Disney-twee collection of gnomes and other details; inside the house, there's an extravagant combination of French *bourgeois* comfort and theatrical camp – pink linen, photos of theatre and movie stars, grand open fireplaces, loads of flowers, and much more. On a more prosaic note there are comfortable lounges, with log fires, where crêpes and drinks can be served outside restaurant hours. The food, like the décor, is more elaborate than the rural norm: fine fish and game are specialities, and the seafood salads are fabulous. *Closed Mon.*

Torcy ✉ 62310

Le Baladin, 62 Rue Principale, **t** 03 21 90 62 51, *www.lebaladin.fr* (*dishes c. €8–25*). One of the surprises of the Artois valleys, in a great old barn-like building beside the road in Torcy, overlooking the tumbling Créquoise. This enterprising café-crêperie-music bar hosts a non-complacent range of music on many Saturdays all year (every Sat in summer): jazz, blues, folk, rock, even African hip-hop, together with magic acts, art shows and theatre. At other times, there's a laid-back atmosphere, good beers and enjoyable crêpes, *galettes*, salads and other one-course dishes. *Open Sept–June Fri and Sat from 6pm, Sun and hols from noon; July and Aug Tues–Sat from 6pm, Sun and hols from noon.*

Land, Sea and Sky:
Baie de la Somme

12

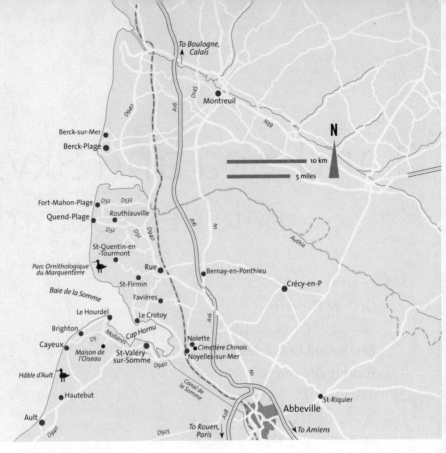

To Boulogne, Calais

Montreuil

Berck-sur-Mer
Berck-Plage

N

10 km

5 miles

Fort-Mahon-Plage
Quend-Plage
Routhiauville
St-Quentin-en-Tourmont
Parc Ornithologique du Marquenterre
Rue
Bernay-en-Ponthieu
Crécy-en-P
St-Firmin
Baie de la Somme
Favières
Le Hourdel
Le Crotoy
Brighton
Cap Hornu
Cayeux
Nolette
Maison de l'Oiseau
St-Valéry-sur-Somme
Cimetière Chinois
Noyelles-sur-Mer
Hâble d'Ault
St-Riquier
Hautebut
Canal de la Somme
Abbeville
Ault
To Rouen, Paris
To Amiens

Seventy miles south of Calais there is a special, misty landscape of sand flats, water, dunes, salt marshes, giant skies and unbreakable stillness that is one of the least populated, least developed areas anywhere on the coast of France. The Bay of the Somme is a broad arc where at low tide the sea recedes for miles, and the placid channels, sandbanks and expanses of coarse grass, rushes and marsh lavender present a subtle, ever-changing, mix of colours fading into the horizon. It's a landscape for lovers of the horizontal: borders between earth, sea and sky are often hard to distinguish, and the light in the Bay has an opaque quality celebrated by writers from Jules Verne to Colette, and painters such as Degas and Seurat. The Bay is also exceptionally rich in bird life, and beloved by walkers and birders.

The quiet little towns around the Bay can sometimes seem lost in the immensity of the landscape, left behind by history as much as they have been by the tide. They include, though, some of the oldest towns in France. St-Valery-sur-Somme, the largest, stands on a site occupied since the Stone Age, on one of the few rocky outcrops around the Bay. Locals believe William the Conqueror's enemy Harold of Wessex was imprisoned here, and the Conqueror himself passed through in 1066. Later St-Valery became a fishing port, a weekend retreat for the Amiens bourgeois and, briefly, a British military camp. Nowadays, the main qualities of the ancient town are a sleepy tranquillity and an idiosyncratic charm.

Getting There

The coast road south from Calais and Boulogne via Le Touquet, the D940, runs directly to the Bay of the Somme, arriving in Le Crotoy and eventually St-Valery. If you are travelling on the A16 *autoroute* (toll-road south of Boulogne) or the main N1 road inland via Montreuil, turn off either road westwards near Bernay-en-Ponthieu (exit 24 on the A16), towards Rue, to join the D940.

About 3km south of Rue there is a turning left signposted for Favières. Coming from the south, there is a turn for Favières on the right from the D940 as it curves around the Bay near Noyelles. In Favières, La Clé des Champs is easy to find in the middle of the village.

From Dieppe, follow the D925 along the coast to Eu, then the D940 to St-Valery.

The only Bay towns with conventional **train** services are Noyelles and Rue, both stops on the Amiens–Abbeville–Boulogne local line. Many longer-distance trains stop at Abbeville, where you can change onto local services.

Tourist Information

For the steam railway around the Bay, and organizations that provide guided walks and facilities for cycling, kayaking, sailing and other activities, *see* p.122. There is also a joint bay website, *www.baiedesomme.org*.

St-Valery-sur-Somme: 2 Place Guillaume-le-Conquérant, **t** 03 22 60 93 50, *www.saint-valery-sur-somme.fr*. Easy to find at the point where the road into town turns to run along the quay, by the mouth of the Somme Canal.

Ault: 4 Place de l'Eglise, **t** 03 22 60 57 15, *officedutourisme.ault80@wanadoo.fr*.

Cayeux-sur-Mer: 1068 Bd du Général Sizaire, **t** 03 22 26 61 15.

Le Crotoy: 1 Rue Carnot, **t** 03 22 27 05 25, *www.tourisme-crotoy.com*.

Fort-Mahon: 1000 Av de la Plage, **t** 03 22 23 36 00, *www.fort-mahon-plage.com*.

Quend-Plage: Place du 8 Mai, **t** 03 22 23 32 04, *www.quendplagelespins.com*.

Rue: 54 Rue Porte de Bécray, **t** 03 22 25 69 94, *www.ville-rue.fr*.

The Baie de la Somme is also an area celebrated for its special produce – lamb raised on the salt marshes (*prés-salés*), duck when in season, leeks, celery and other greens, and fish and shellfish caught close offshore, shrimps, mussels, cockles, sole and *lieu* (pollack). It might be expected that in somewhere so apparently remote this food would be presented very simply, but, this being France, the Bay also has its well-tended restaurants. And, most surprising of all, deep in the marshes north of the Bay in the little village of Favières there is one, **La Clé des Champs**, where you can find a rare combination of the best of local produce, traditional Picard cooking and very sophisticated culinary skill, flair and imagination.

La Clé des Champs

Place des Frères Caudron, Favières, t 03 22 27 88 00, f 03 22 27 79 36.
Open Wed–Sun 12.15–2 and 7.30–9.30; closed Mon and Tues,
1–15 Jan, two weeks Feb, third week Aug.
Menus €13.73–€19.82 (both weekdays and Sat midday only), €24.40–€32.

The narrow lanes that lead to Favières twist and bend and then bend again between low-lying fields, hedges and bunches of trees standing out against the flat horizon. Like most of the marshland communities it's a rambling place that doesn't have the closely defined centre usual in French villages, more a collection of farms and houses spread out along paths and roads. A few modern alterations aside, most are in the traditional style of the *maison picarde*, long, single-storey cottages with whitewashed walls and roofs of thatch or red tiles that hang down like sleep-heavy eyelids. And, in the area most like a centre that Favières does have, near the church, is La Clé des Champs, in one of the biggest Picard houses, clearly indicated by its own signposts. On Sundays the grass verges and the little triangular space in front that serves as a car park suddenly fill up, but on most days there will scarcely be any traffic around except maybe the occasional chugging tractor.

Inside, traditionally pretty décor of muted pinks and greens offsets the giant old farmhouse fireplace, and carefully selected arrangements of seasonal wild flowers beautifully catch the afternoon light. The young weekend staff lack the polish of more metropolitan waiters, but service still follows all the proper rituals. A massive and superior wine list (all French, naturally) and original, very refreshing *mises-en-bouche* of little mixed carrot and sweet onion salads on fresh bread add immediate confirmation, if any were needed, that this is no backwoods operation.

Chef Bruno Flasque is as much a part of the *terroir* as the ingredients he uses, for he was actually born in this same house, when it was just the village *bar-tabac*, with a few crêpes cooked by his mother available at weekends. He has never worked outside the Baie de la Somme: after studying at the regional *Hôtellerie* school he cooked for a few years at Chez Mado in Le Crotoy, before taking over La Clé from his parents in 1985 with his wife Isabelle. He describes himself modestly as something of an auto-didact, in which case, he must have made a very good teacher. Both he and his wife display plenty of the untiring care for detail that is a cornerstone of traditional French catering, seen in the homemade breads, or the choice of different coffees from around the world. Traditional Picard dishes are an essential part of his repertoire, along with classic French styles, but he's also highly imaginative. His cooking doesn't dither: strong, unabashed flavours turn up frequently, but his dishes are also subtle,

Assiette de Poissons de Petits Bateaux du Crotoy

Serves 4

1 medium carrot, cut into very thin strips *julienne*-style
1 celery stick, cut into very thin strips *julienne*-style
1 leek (white part), cut into very thin strips *julienne*-style
120ml/4fl oz Muscadet (dry white wine)
12 mussels, cleaned and debearded
400ml/14fl oz fish stock
1 shallot, finely chopped
4 plaice fillets, about 80g/3oz each (cut large fillets in half lengthways)
4 sole fillets, about 80g/3oz each (cut large fillets in half lengthways)
4 small turbot fillets, about 80g/3oz each (cut large fillets in half lengthways)
4 scallops
120g/4oz small raw prawns, shelled
200ml/7fl oz crème fraîche or double cream
100g/3½ oz cold butter, diced
salt and pepper

delicate, refined and perfectly balanced. And, of course, he knows exactly where to find the very best products of the Bay, from salt-marsh lamb or sole and shrimps from Le Crotoy to celery, cress and summer asparagus.

There is no *carte*, only a series of set menus, but they offer a very broad choice, and – with the most sumptuous list still at €32 – are also quite phenomenal value. The €13.73 menu provides a delicious light, fresh meal, usually including a pretty definitive version of the local favourite *ficelle picarde*, along with a fresh fish of the day. In summer wonderful use is made of the local asparagus, as in (from the €24.40 list) a fabulous *delicat d'asperges* that features both simply cooked asparagus and an exquisitely flavoured warm mousse – a perfect combination of subtlety and country freshness. Fish is spectacular here, and one of the restaurant's prime staples is local fish *de petits bateaux*, caught inshore from small boats, which are served up in a constantly changing range of combinations such as Le Crotoy sole with sancerre and Somme Bay prawns, or pollock with ginger and leeks. Nowadays the number of small-boat fishermen operating out of Le Crotoy is sadly dwindling, but M. Flasque knows all of them, he says, and where to find the best catch.

A meal at La Clé des Champs makes an excellently sybaritic restorer after a walk around the Bay, with extra notes of luxury available should you wish – such as, between the first and main courses, the offer of an 'Interlude', a glass of sorbet with calvados, like a *trou Normand*, and the excellent cheeseboard. Before desserts comes a *pré-dessert*, perhaps a remarkable, fragrant orange and chocolate mousse. The 'real' desserts include both light, modern options and Bruno Flasque's delicious versions of classic French puddings like *fraises Sarah Bernhard*, a highly moreish strawberry and ice-cream crumble. After which, and the choice of coffees, you can take a wander beneath Favières' waving poplars, to enjoy some more of the clean Bay air.

Steam the carrot, celery and leek separately until tender, for about 8 minutes. Season and set aside.

Put 30ml/2tbsp of the wine in a small stainless steel saucepan, add the mussels and set over a medium heat. Cook, tightly covered, for about 4 minutes or until the mussels open, shaking the pan occasionally. Strain off the liquid and reserve. Discard any mussels that fail to open.

Put the fish stock, shallot and remaining wine in a stainless steel saucepan and bring to a simmer. Season the fish fillets and scallops. Poach the fillets in the shallot and wine stock until they are opaque and cooked through (7–8 minutes), adding the scallops and prawns after 3–4 minutes' cooking time. Carefully remove the fish and shellfish onto a plate and cover to keep warm.

Boil this cooking liquid vigorously to reduce by half. Add the cream and the cooking liquid from the mussels, and bring to a gentle boil. Whisk in the butter bit by bit, lifting the pan from the heat if the butter melts before it can be incorporated. Taste and season the sauce with salt and pepper as needed. Add the chopped vegetables to the sauce, and heat through.

To serve, pour pools of sauce on four warmed plates, and divide the vegetables among them. Arrange the fish and scallops, and garnish with mussels and prawns.

Touring Around

St-Valery-sur-Somme makes a natural focus for any visit to the Bay of the Somme. Spread along the side of the Bay, it consists of two halves, the old Ville-Haute on its hill, and the port and 'new town' (much of which is a few centuries old itself) beneath it to the east. The harbour is a very low-key affair: there are no docks or breakwaters, just a long **quay** winding round the shoreline from the end of the Somme Canal, alongside which a surprising number of fishing boats and small pleasure craft are moored in line. For several hours each day they rest on sand, and the only water to be seen is a shallow channel running out of the Canal. The quayside is a beguiling place to walk along, with a little gentle, unhurried activity usually in progress. In the last few years the completion of the A16 *autoroute* has led to the Bay becoming much better known and even trendy as a weekend destination for Parisians and city-dwellers from the surrounding regions, as reflected in the appearance of a hipper style of shop and, above all, more bars and brasseries for taking in the scene along the quay, but this still hasn't had too radical an effect on the atmosphere. St-Valery's sense of calm is an essential part of its attraction, and – certainly outside of summer weekends – is still the pre-eminent characteristic.

The quay runs into **Place des Pilotes**, which fills up with the main market on Sunday mornings and with a slightly smaller gathering on Wednesdays. Beyond the square towards the sea the road is closed to vehicles, and becomes Quai Amiral Courbet, a tree-lined walkway where on Sunday evenings a large part of the town promenades up and down in positively Mediterranean fashion beside the water (or sand). Alongside it there are several endearingly grand 1900s houses and villas, some notably ornate and some more discreet – the Guillaume de Normandy hotel is far the most extravagant – from a time when St-Valery enjoyed a brief vogue as a summer residence for affluent families from Amiens and other towns inland. Beneath the old town, the promenade runs out into the sand flats – sometimes referred to hopefully as a 'plage' – and the footpath to Cap Hornu. At the point where the promenade ends, near the Tour Harold (*see* below), there is a pleasant little beach bar and outside terrace, **La Buvette**, that's great for a contemplative rest after a bay walk.

St-Valery was a busy port in the early Middle Ages, when there was much less sand in the Bay. Thanks to its tides and the encroachment of the sandbanks it has been declining for much of the time since, but, against the odds, has never quite gone the way of Montreuil and other ex-harbours along this shifting coastline. The building of the Somme Canal at the beginning of the 19th century gave it a further reprieve, but traffic still did not become exactly intense, and the only interlude of concentrated activity came during the 1914–18 war when the British Army, stuck for alternatives, decided to use little St-Valery as a transit base for landing men and supplies from England, on their way to the battlefields of the Somme.

At the eastern end of the quays, by the Somme Canal, stands the **Entrepôt des Sels**, a large 1736 salt warehouse built when salt was a royal monopoly. It sports a plaque indicating that William the Conqueror sailed from this spot on his way to Hastings in 1066. St-Valery was then in the midst of one of its greatest periods of activity. The rocky hill on which the old town stands was settled in the Neolithic era, and was used as a port by the Romans. In 611 an Irish monk called Walrick, Gualaric or Valerius (St Valery) came here, and founded an abbey that for centuries was one of the most prestigious in the region. The town also became a stronghold. As the Bayeux Tapestry vividly recounts, a few years before 1066, Harold of Wessex, sent on a mission to Normandy by Edward the Confessor, was shipwrecked on the coast of France and held to ransom by Count Guy de Ponthieu, until the Count's powerful neighbour William of Normandy demanded his release. This was the first step in Harold's supposed debt of honour to William, which is made so much of in the tapestry. St-Valery was a prime possession of the Counts of Ponthieu, and it is believed that Harold was held here; just past the western end of the quays there are the remains of an ancient tower, the **Tour Harold**, where in local legend the Saxon earl was imprisoned. The Conqueror himself returned here by accident, and this is one of three places on the French coast that have monuments claiming to be his point of departure for England: Barfleur, where William himself embarked, Dives-sur-Mer, where he met up with his main force, and St-Valery, where the Norman fleet was obliged to put in by bad weather.

The little old town of St-Valery, the **Ville-Haute**, is one of the most charming and atmospheric of French walled towns. On market days the port area can be vaguely busy; the old town scarcely ever. Its main entrance is the mostly-16th-century **Porte de Nevers** at the end of Quai du Romerel, named after a family of local lords, some of whom still lived in the house above the gate until quite recently. It was badly damaged the last time St-Valery became a battle zone, in May 1940, but has been finely restored. The steep cobbled street beyond the gate leads to the **Eglise St-Martin**, an impressive church that conforms to none of the architectural rules: it has two complete naves of almost equal size, having had to be rebuilt several times after wars, fires and other catastrophes. The exterior, mostly from the 1550s, has some great gargoyles, and is made of stone and black flint in an eye-catching chessboard pattern typical of the Picardy coast. In the narrow streets near the church there are several houses in the same style. Next to the church is **Place St-Martin**, with a sheer drop on one side down to the quays, and a wonderful view over the Bay.

Because St-Valery peaked so early as a military stronghold no one ever saw a need to undertake any systematic renovation of its fortifications, and parts of its medieval walls are among the oldest still standing. The rough-brick **Porte Guillaume**, the western entrance to the Ville-Haute, now with flowers growing out of its towers, is definitely old enough to have been here when Duke William paid his visits. Joan of Arc was brought through the gate as a prisoner in 1430, on her way to be handed over to the English in Rouen. Towards Porte Guillaume the town is delightfully rural. Chickens and other animals scratch about in the gardens of many houses, and roads that are ambitiously marked on the town map as 'rues' look more like plant-lined alleyways disappearing under wild flowers, or grassy country lanes that no one has quite got round to finishing off. In Rue Brandt, on the south side of the Ville-Haute, there is a special garden, the **Herbarium** (*open May–15 Nov daily 10–6; adm*), within the one-time garden of a convent-hospital, which seeks to preserve and revive the plants and medicinal herbs that would have been seen in a medieval monastery garden.

Activities

Local tourist offices can provide information on all the activities available around the Bay, plus walking and cycle guides, and tide tables.

Rides

Chemin de Fer de la Baie de la Somme, La Gare, St-Valery-sur-Somme, **t** 03 22 26 96 96, *www.chemin-fer-baie-somme.asso.fr*. This charming old railway runs between Le Crotoy and Cayeux, via St-Valery (the little station is at the Canal end of the quays). Timings vary: usually 3 trains each way each day, on every Sunday, most Saturdays and several other days, April–June and Sept–Oct, and daily in July–Aug. As well as standard services there are special trips, including evening trains with dinner served on board.

Commandant Charcot, 77 Place du Jeu du Battoir, St-Valery-sur-Somme, **t** 03 22 60 74 68. An open launch that sets out from St-Valery on a range of Bay trips, including seal-watching and evening 'sunset' sailings. Bookings can be made at the tourist office.

Walking, cycling and more

Walks into the Bay should never be attempted without a guide. Guided walks usually last about 3hrs and cover about 7km. Timings depend on tides and the weather, so check times with your guides as close as possible to when you want to go.

Au Vélocipède, 1 Rue du Puits Salé, St-Valery-sur-Somme, **t** 03 22 26 96 80. Bicycles of all kinds (including kids' bikes) for hire.

Centre Equestre Le Val de Selle, 5 Rue des Jardins, Le Crotoy, **t** 03 22 27 79 15. Horse and pony rides, with guide, through dunes and the beach from Le Crotoy.

Centre Permanent d'Initiatives pour l'Environnement (CPIE), 32 Route d'Amiens, Dury, **t** 03 22 34 24 27, *www.cpie80.com*. A respected conservation organization that runs a range of trips, including Bay walks, tours of Hable d'Ault bird reserve and seal-viewing. This is the main office, near Amiens; tours rendezvous in St-Valery.

No Shoes Club, 22 Allée de la Grève, Le Crotoy, **t** 03 22 27 11 50, *www.noshoes-club.com*. From his hut on Crotoy beach Damien Cornille offers a range of things to do: sand-yachts, kayaks and cycles for hire, guided Bay walks, and even a little beach bar. He speaks good English, and his trips can be recommended for non-French speakers looking for a relaxed tour. To find him, look for the 'no shoes' banner on the beach.

Promenade en Baie, 5 Chemin des Digues, Le Crotoy, **t** 03 22 27 47 36, *promenade.en.baie @wanadoo.fr*. Guided walks and other trips from the north side of the Bay.

Rando-Nature en Somme, Mairie, St-Valery-sur-Somme, **t** 03 22 26 92 30, *http://perso-wanadoo.fr/rando-nature*. Guided walks in the Bay.

From beside the Porte Guillaume Rue du Castel leads to the few remaining stones – many now incorporated into houses and gardens – of St-Valery's **castle**, which was begun as long ago as 900, and dismantled after the Revolution. Continuing outside the Porte Guillaume, a little way further on are the walls of the old **abbey**, also demolished after the Revolution. Within its walls there is now a luxurious private house. From there, a track leads through fields to the **Chapelle des Marins**, a 19th-century chapel in chessboard style built over the tomb of St Valery himself. Beneath it there is a spring associated with the saint called the **Source de la Fidelité**, although the water is now murky enough to deter all but the most desperate pilgrims.

St-Valery also has an engaging folk museum, the **Musée Picarvie** (*open April–May and Sept–mid-Nov Mon, Wed–Sun 2–6.30, closed Tues; June–Aug daily 2–6.30; adm*), on Quai du Romerel in the lower town. This is the work of an Abbeville builder, Paul Longuein, who over many years amassed a fascinating collection of over 6,000 items related to traditional crafts and every other aspect of life in the Picardy countryside, from tools, toys and cider presses to a whole schoolroom and shop interiors. One weekend in the middle of June each year, St-Valery also holds its **Fêtes Guillaume-le-Conquérant**, when locals celebrate their most famous visitor by dressing up in medieval outfits, and enjoying parades, mock battles, music and fireworks.

Beyond the appeal of St-Valery itself, few visitors come here without wanting to explore the Bay as well. Since the terrain is so flat, with such vast horizons, it's perfect for relaxing walking or cycling. Tourist offices have handy free booklets that show all the many foot- and cyclepaths. An easy and popular (if muddy) walk at low tide is simply to follow the well-marked path from the end of the quays, past the little holiday development at Cap Hornu and along the *digue* or dike beside the *mollières* (salt marshes) towards the mouth of the Bay. The full distance is nearly 10km. The patterns of the channels and swathes of grasses and marsh flowers are infinitely variable; at times, there's a strong sea wind; otherwise the stillness is impenetrable. Bird life includes virtually every kind of European wetland and wading bird, but especially oystercatchers, avocets, wild geese and ducks. Further out, the Bay contains large seal colonies, which can be seen from the shore, sometimes, or with boat trips.

There are also paths that cross the sandbanks and marshes, including the full *traversée de la Baie*, from St-Valery to Le Crotoy at low tide. However, walks **into** the Bay itself should **never be attempted without a guide**; there are dangerous patches of quicksand, and, while the sea may often be lost to view, the tide can also return with remarkable speed. Even if you only walk along the Bay shore, it's always advisable to have with you a current tide table, available from all tourist offices.

There are other possibilities too. Railway enthusiasts and many others drool over the **Chemin de Fer de la Baie de la Somme**, a genuine 1900s narrow-gauge steam railway that runs from Le Crotoy through Noyelles and St-Valery to Cayeux, and there are also boat trips. The Bay of the Somme is also popular for sailing, kayaking and, on the north side, where the sand is firmer, sand-yachting. For details and organizations that offer guided walks, cycle hire, kayaks, horse-riding and more, *see* left.

The path along the *digue* from St-Valery eventually comes to an end at **Le Hourdel**, a quite phenomenally calm and remote little fishing village with a lighthouse, a quay, a few boats and, for most of the day, no water. Past Le Hourdel the coast changes rapidly, from the marshy, placid bay to an endless bar of shingle and mounting waves along the open sea. If you have a car or bike, take the narrow coast route to Cayeux, the *Route Blanche*, a mysterious-looking road between heather-clad dunes of brilliant white sand that often seem to threaten to envelop it completely. Lost in the dunes is curious little **Brighton-les-Pins**, which once hoped to attract droves of English tourists with its name, and now looks a bit like a French town out of a Sam Shephard story.

Beyond it is **Cayeux**, famous as a fishing port since the Middle Ages, and which became a holiday resort in the 1900s. It has a long, rolling bank of shingle and sand beach, with an old-fashioned seafront alongside that except in August seems far too big for the town. Just south of Cayeux is another area of marsh that forms the bird reserve of **Hable d'Ault**, tours of which are offered by the CPIE (*see* left). Between Cayeux and St-Valery there is also the **Maison de l'Oiseau** (*open Jan–Mar and mid-Oct–Dec daily 11–5; April–mid-Oct daily 10–6; adm*), an ornithological study centre in an old Picard farmhouse, with (rather expensive) displays on the marsh birdlife.

Alternatively, take the road east from St-Valery, past Noyelles and more views over the *mollières* (salt marshes) to reach the north side of the Bay. Along the way, near Noyelles, a sign saying **Cimetière Chinois** points towards one of the area's strangest sites. When St-Valery was a British base during the First World War it was staffed, bizarrely, by Chinese labourers. In 1915 Britain began to recruit workers in China to make up for a labour shortage behind the lines, and by 1918 the 'Chinese Labour Corps' had over 90,000 men fetching and carrying for the army in France. Many died here, mostly due to disease, and are buried in the cemetery at Nolette, one of the strangest of the plots run by the Commonwealth War Graves Commission in France.

Le Crotoy is known in history as the place where Joan of Arc was first imprisoned after her capture by the Burgundians in 1430, but it also enjoyed a fashionable vogue at the end of the 19th century as a summer resort. Colette extolled the virtues of its light and giant skies, Seurat came to paint, Toulouse-Lautrec visited, and the Caudron brothers carried out some of the first experiments in French aviation on the sands. One of its most regular visitors was Jules Verne, who came here from Amiens virtually every summer, spending a lot of time with the experimenter in submarining Jacques-François Conseil, who provided much of the inspiration for *Twenty Thousand Leagues Under the Sea*. Thanks to its past Le Crotoy has more of an old seaside-town buzz than St-Valery, with elegant *Belle Epoque* houses, a proper promenade and a casino as well as a charming little fishing harbour and giant beach. This, like the equally windswept beaches of towns further north, is now a magnet for sand-yachters.

North of Le Crotoy the flat marsh fields – all land given up by the sea over several centuries – are occupied only by quiet villages like **Favières** or **St-Firmin**, and isolated farms next to clumps of trees. Inland the main centre is **Rue**, a very likeable place that has all the amiable placidity of a classic French country town. It was an important baronial seat in the early Middle Ages, when it had access to the sea, and so has some very fine architecture, especially the massive 15th-century **Belfry**, the **Chapelle de l'Hospice** and the superb 15th–16th-century Gothic **Chapelle du St-Esprit**.

From the D940 north of Rue a road cuts west to the sea and **Fort-Mahon-Plage**, one of those curious little isolated seaside resorts that crop up around the French coasts, with a traditional promenade, rows of second homes and a golf course half-hidden among the sand dunes. The similar but still smaller **Quend-Plage** is just to the south. Lively each summer, out of season both have a quirky, almost wistful remoteness.

Between Le Crotoy and Fort-Mahon is one of the Bay's foremost attractions, a must for anyone who wishes to see the local bird life. The wildlife reserve of **Marquenterre** (*t 03 22 25 66 99, www.parcdumarquenterre.com; open for admissions daily mid-Nov–Jan 10–3; Feb–Mar and Oct–mid-Nov 10–4; April–Sept 10–5; closing time 2hrs after last admission; adm*) occupies one of the most beautiful areas around the Bay, a 2,300-hectare stretch of marsh, lake and dunes. It's extremely well-organised for visitors with varying levels of birdwatching experience, with a clear *parcours d'initiation* path for beginners with good viewpoints from which you can see plenty of duck, geese, herons, waders and, with luck, polecats and wild boar. A walk around it takes about an hour. Those who wish to see more can follow longer paths into the reserve, to look for rarer species such as storks and spoonbill.

Shopping

The Baie de la Somme is no shopping centre, so for anyone looking for local products all attention focuses on the weekly **markets**. The Place des Pilotes market in **St-Valery** (*Sun am, smaller market Wed*) is one of the liveliest. **Le Crotoy** has a fine market (*Fri am, June–Sept also Tues*) that's especially good for fresh fish, and **Rue** has a real country market (*Sat am*), with wonderful fresh vegetables, breads, cakes, cheeses and every derivative of duck.

Where to Stay

St-Valery-sur-Somme ✉ 80230

L'Usage du Monde, 15 Rue du Puits-Salé, **t** 03 22 60 94 82, *usagedumonde@caramail.com* (*rooms €75–100 for two*). Not a standard B&B: the *sympa* owners Anne and Laurent Mancaux are artists and art restorers, and their fine Ville-Haute townhouse is also a gallery and contemporary art centre, often with artists in residence. The four rooms are quite luxurious, with décor that's a stylish mix of chic and bohemian. An original, engaging place.

Hôtel Picardia, 41 Quai du Romerel, **t** 03 22 60 32 30, *www.picardia.fr* (*double rooms €70, family rooms €90–110*). A historic old inn on St-Valery's quay imaginatively transformed into a charming new hotel, run with a fresh, original style by its young owners, both women, Marie-Françoise and Caroline. The 18 rooms, fully renovated with clever old-and-new décor, are bright and well-equipped, and 8 are 'duplexes' with exceptional facilities for families. There's a laidback *salon de thé*, and staff are very friendly and helpful.

La Gribane, 297 Quai Jeanne d'Arc, **t** 03 22 60 97 55 (*rooms/suites €68–82 for two, €130 for four*). A lovely B&B in one of the 1900s villas along the bayfront in St-Valery, which Michèle and Jean-Pierre Douchet have beautifully restored with a mix of modern style and maritime accessories (sea shells, sea pictures). The two 'studio' rooms in the main house fill with light, and looking out at the endless view is wonderful for clearing the head. One suite is a double with living room, the other also has a two-bed children's

room. Two smaller, cheaper but attractive rooms are in a separate building in the luxuriant garden. Delicious breakfasts are served in a big, bright room looking over the Bay.

Le Relais Guillaume de Normandy, 46 Quai du Romerel, **t** 03 22 60 82 36, *www.guillaumedenormandy.com* (*double rooms €56–65, family rooms €66–85*). St-Valery's most distinctive hotel, a large, elaborate house with garden in a style that's a mix of fairy-tale, neogothic, art-nouveau and Norman/ Picard traditional, topped off with roofs that in parts are almost pagoda-like. Local legend maintains the house was built in the 1890s for an English Lord who set up his French mistress here and kept trysts with her every weekend. The 14 rooms are not as spectacular, and a bit small – they could be called 'snugly comfortable' – but still have their characterful woodwork and ornate touches. Some rooms also have great Bay views. For the **restaurant**, *see* p.126.

M and Mme Deloison, 1 Quai du Romerel, **t/f** 03 22 26 92 17 (*rooms €45 for two*). Escapees from the city, the Deloisons make driftwood sculptures and have an antiques shop next to the market square. Their B&B rooms are next door, in a creaky 19th-century house. The rooms are a tad untidy, but have loads of engaging features, and the top-floor double has wonderful views. One room has a semi-separate child's room attached. They also have a superb self-contained apartment that's sometimes available, and is worth enquiring about.

Favières ✉ 80120

Les Garennes, 773 Rue de Romaine, **t/f** 03 22 27 21 07, *www.lesgarennes.com* (*rooms €55.60 for two*). Homely B&B on the eastern edge of Favières, with four bright, pretty rooms around a garden (with barbeque for guests' use). Well placed for anyone cycling the Bay.

La Vieille Forge, 930 Rue des Forges, **t** 03 22 27 75 58, *http://lavieilleforge.free.fr* (*rooms €54 for two*). Substantial *chambres-d'hôtes* in the former village blacksmiths, in the middle of Favières (and within walking distance of the Clé des Champs). The five rooms have been imaginatively decorated, and two adjacent rooms can be let as a family room. Excellent for walkers, or just for rural tranquillity.

Rue ✉ 80120

Le Lion d'Or, 5 Rue de la Barrière, t 03 22 25 74 18, *www.liondorrue.com* (*double rooms €45–77*). A pleasant, traditional *Logis de France* hotel, in a partly half-timbered inn on Rue's main street. Some of the 16 rooms are smallish, but they're well-equipped and distinctly cosy, and owners M and Mme Vandeville make everyone very welcome. The equally comfortable **restaurant** (*menus €14–35*) keeps to an unchanging small-town style, with bargain menus of local favourites.

Eating Alternatives

St-Valery-sur-Somme ✉ 80230

Relais Les Quatre Saisons, 2 Place Croix l'Abbé, t 03 22 60 51 01 (*menus €25–35*). This un-ostentatious little restaurant on the south side of the Ville-Haute is easy to miss, but has won great praise for its cuisine. Local dishes and produce, naturally, are high-lighted – *pré-salé* lamb *aux herbes*, *blanquette* of squid. The well-aged, rustic setting is offset by neat yellow linen, and the restaurant has plenty of St-Valery's soothing calm. *Closed Sun eve and Mon.*

Le Relais Guillaume de Normandy, 46 Quai du Romerel, t 03 22 60 82 36, *www.guillaumedenormandy.com* (*menus €17–42*). The appealingly ornate dining room matches the rest of the hotel (*see p.125*), but the most beautiful part of it is the conserva-tory overlooking the Bay, with misty views to accompany your lunch. Menus are a mix of local dishes and French standards: *assiette de fruits de mer* with prawns and Somme Bay shrimps, classic *ficelles picardes* and *pré-salé* lamb, a house speciality, prepared in several different ways. *Sept–June closed Tues.*

Le Nicol's, 15 Rue de la Ferté, t 03 22 26 82 96 (*menus €18.50–35*). In St-Valery's 'new town', near the tourist office, Le Nicol's has all the look of a French small-town restaurant – smart linen, flowers, neat table settings – but also presents some surprises. Local fish and seafood are mainstays, but the menus combine local classics – *moules, filets de sole aux crevettes*, rich meats – with unusual touches like fruit sauces, chorizo and other Spanish ingredients, and paella (*€14.50*).

Les Délices d'Elsa, 1 Rue de la Porte de Nevers, t 06 25 03 43 63 (*menus €15*). A tiny crêperie, *salon de thé* and ice-cream parlour up the cobbled street from the Porte de Nevers. The setting could scarcely be more olde worlde, and to match it there are all sorts of antique ornaments. As well as a good-value lunch menu, there are nice light dishes – crêpes, *galettes*, quiches, salads – and delicious ices.

Le Crotoy ✉ 80550

La Marinière, 27 Rue de la Porte du Pont, t 03 22 27 88 00 (*menus €24–38*). Small, brightly pretty and more discreet than most Le Crotoy restaurants, but this is the most respected eating house in town, above all for superb fresh Bay fish and seafood. The substantial menus allow you to eat a little, or go all-out for a real gourmet feast.

Chez Mado, 6 Quai Léonard, t 03 22 27 81 22 (*menus €15–46*). On the seafront and with a fabulous view from its *salle panoramique*, Chez Mado doesn't look like an average French seaside restaurant; built all of wood, it has big balconies along both floors, in a style that mixes French nautical and Wild West. Inside, tables fill up on summer week-ends with contented diners making their way through platters of quality fresh fish and seafood. The menus offer lots of choice, including an all-lobster menu (*€98 for two*).

Fort-Mahon ✉ 80790

Auberge de la Louvière, 27 Rue de Robinson, t 03 22 27 71 53 (*menus €18.50–39*). A charming family-run restaurant in a garden in the little resort of Fort-Mahon, offering few *haute-cuisine* frills but a warm welcome, and enjoyable classic dishes. From the central avenue of Fort-Mahon, signs direct you to it.

Quend-Plage ✉ 80120

Auberge Le Fiacre, Hameau de Routhiauville, t 03 22 23 47 30 (*menus €30–40*). In an isolated spot in the marsh country behind Fort-Mahon, this old farm has been very smartly renovated. The restaurant has a high reputation for its refined take on local clas-sics such as *ficelles picardes*, fish and seafood and Bay lamb. It also has 11 **guest rooms** (*€63–68 low season, €73–78 high season*), on the ground floor facing a large garden.

The Cathedral and the Canals: Amiens

13

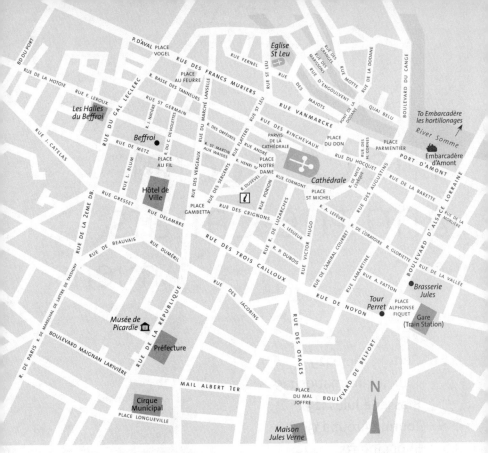

Amiens, capital of Picardy, is a historic city with a substantial modern sprawl and a charming and attractive heart. It was badly scarred in both World Wars, but in the middle of town there are still small, atmospheric streets and squares along the banks of the River Somme, where the Roman city was founded. It also has fine shops, a large student population, and a sparky street, café and night life; one of the best of France's regional museums; and a superb cathedral, France's largest, described by John Ruskin as the most perfect creation of medieval Christianity in northern Europe.

Amiens' natural setting, too, makes it a hugely engaging place to explore. In the 1470s, when it was one of the most important merchant cities in Europe, Louis XI of France called it 'my little Venice', and the reasons why are just as evident today. The Somme divides around a string of narrow islands, connected by footbridges and lined by old, steep-roofed houses with many-coloured façades that lean and bend. Just to the east the river runs through hundreds of man-made canals between drained marsh-gardens, the *Hortillonages*, which bring a stretch of silent, watery countryside right into the centre of the city. The produce from the dark, heavy soil of these allotments is a special feature of *Amienois* cooking. As a regional capital, Amiens has eating places from spectacular gourmet restaurants to laidback student bistros, but one of the best places to find a whole slice of local life and fine food is **Brasserie Jules**, a bustling, ultra-popular brasserie near the railway station.

Getting There

Amiens is about 1½hrs' drive from Calais on the A16 *autoroute*, two hours by other roads, and 1¼hrs from Paris (also by the A16). From the *autoroutes* follow signs for *Amiens-Centre* and *Centre-Ville* and aim for the ring of boulevards, which as usual run around the core of town. Traffic can be heavy, and parking in the centre is very restricted. There are pay-and-display ticket machines on most streets, and several well-signposted pay car parks. Outside the boulevards parking is free, so if possible it's a good idea to leave your car along or behind the boulevards on the south side, near the Mail Albert 1er

(the problem is, everyone in Amiens may be trying to do the same thing). From there, it's an easy walk up Rue de la République to the centre of town. In the train station area, where Brasserie Jules is located, parking is less of a problem.

Amiens has good **train** connections with Paris, Rouen, Calais, Lille and many other destinations. The station is beside the ring of boulevards, east of the city centre.

Tourist Information

Amiens: 6bis Rue Dusevel, t 03 22 71 60 50, *www.amiens.com/tourisme*. Open daily.

Brasserie Jules

18 Boulevard Alsace-Lorraine, t 03 22 71 18 40, www.brasserie-jules.fr. Open daily 10–4 and 6–midnight. Menus €15–24; carte average €35.

The French are attached to their traditions. This is an obvious fact: throughout France, people go on holiday in August, window boxes are neatly tended, singers try to look profound and, in food and catering, despite the arrival of international restaurants and a trend for slightly exotic ingredients, most eating places conform to one of a select set of Gallic restaurant types, whether in cuisine, *cadre bourgeois* décor, *Belle Epoque*-style woodwork or the professional mannerisms of waiters. It's an essential part of the national landscape. Some people find this instinctive French sense of tradition and of how things should be done annoying, and associate it with inflexibility and snootiness. And it's true, culinary traditionalism can be an excuse for complacency. It's also true, though, that French restaurant traditions provide an enormously rich range to choose from, and that when well handled these classic styles, with no need for any global innovations, can still be hugely enjoyable.

The cosy allure of the traditional – as well as fine food – must be a major element in the success of Brasserie Jules in Amiens. Occupying the ground floor of a modern block near the station, it's only a few years old, but inside the bright, cavernous space there are red-plush banquettes, giant potted palms, curving woodwork and elaborate chandeliers – all the elements that for any French person instantly evoke, just a tad ironically, the *Belle Epoque* and a *brasserie parisienne*. An extra local touch is that around the walls there are rather cranky 19th-century images of submarines, African animals and far-away places, in homage to Amiens' own *Belle Epoque* hero Jules Verne, who inspired the brasserie's name and whose face appears on the menu (after half a day in the city, he's easily recognizable). And it's enormously popular. As you settle in to one of the so-comfortable banquettes it can seem the whole of Amiens is coming in too: elderly couples who dine out once a week, business lunchers, family outings with plenty of kids, big men in jeans, students who've made no effort to dress at all and chic urbanites who never go out without radiating fashionable perfection. Briskly friendly waiters in requisite waistcoats and long aprons navigate skilfully between tables, and great efforts are made to accommodate unwieldy large groups. In marketing-speak, it's hard to imagine a restaurant with a more democratic demographic. It's a place where nobody could feel out of place, and it's great fun.

Classic décor wouldn't bring in notoriously picky French crowds, of course, if Brasserie Jules did not also provide great food and, all-important, an excellent *r-q-p* or *rapport qualité-prix*, the right value for money. Chefs Ludovic Neslin and Olivier Le Cam present *plats de toujours*, old favourites, but done with all the proper care associated with more intimate restaurants. In classic brasserie style, the menu is long and offers loads of choices, covering all the options from fresh mixed salads for a light lunch to giant towers of seafood for event dining, served with all the necessary panache. Set menus and the *carte* offer standards like duck terrines, grills, *daube* of beef, *confit de canard*, a richly buttery fish and seafood *choucroute* – the French equivalent of comfort food, to match the comfort of the setting. Every flavour is in its right place, especially (since we are in the Somme) in anything involving duck. Seafood is a highlight, again as brasserie tradition demands, from portions of prawns, lobsters or langoustines through several kinds of oysters to excellent mixed *assiettes* (€12–19.50) and magnificent *plateaux* – which can of course be shared – such as the *volcan d'or* (oysters, clams, langoustines, prawns, crab and plenty more, €37).

The wine list provides everything needed to go with the food, and to finish up there's a big list of suitably indulgent fruity and chocolatey desserts. Some might find Brasserie Jules's revival of old-style virtues a little odd these days, but after a while sitting at one of its tables it's possible to feel very much at home in Amiens.

Touring Around

If you begin a visit to Amiens by leaving your car on the southern boulevards, near Mail Albert 1er, you will immediately notice the **Cirque Municipal**, an odd drum-like building with ornate 19th-century details, which today is most often used for concerts. It is inseparably associated with one of Amiens' most celebrated residents, **Jules Verne**. He was actually born in Nantes, but in 1856 he came to Amiens for the wedding of a friend, and fell in love with the bride's sister, Honorine. They would be married for nearly 50 years. The couple lived here permanently from 1871, and Verne became an institution in the city. He was one of the first truly commercial authors – in 1862 he signed a contract with the publisher Hetzel to deliver three books a year – and by far the wealthiest writer in France, if not Europe, of his day. The inventor of science fiction was also not the kind of author who hid himself away in his study; instead, he busied himself with every aspect of Amiens life, served on the city council, and in 1875 even produced a book called *An Ideal City: Amiens in the Year 2000*, full of ideas (such as mechanized communal child-rearing) that so far have scarcely been taken up. Another of his many interests was the circus, and in 1889 he badgered his fellow-councillors into giving Amiens one of the world's few permanent circus halls.

In front of it there is a plaque that records that from the same spot, Place Longueville, the great man also made a flight in a balloon, in 1873. Just east of here at 44 Boulevard Jules Verne, parallel to the main boulevard, is the house where he died in 1905, although the **Maison Jules Verne** (*guided tours Tues–Fri 10–12 and 2–6, Sat, Sun and hols 2–6; adm*), where he actually lived most of the time, is just around the corner at 2 Rue Charles Dubois. It's now a very engaging museum – spruced up for the centenary of his death in 2005 – with several rooms much as they were in the Vernes' time, and models of flying machines, the *Nautilus* and other Vernian imaginings to take you into this remarkable man's very individual world.

From the Circus, cross the main boulevard and walk up Rue de la République (a route regularly taken by Verne on his constitutionals with his dog) to reach the **Musée de Picardie** (*open Tues–Sun 10–12.30 and 2–6; adm*). The grandest building in Amiens after the cathedral, it's a Second-Empire wedding cake of a museum, comparable to the Paris Opera, opened by Napoleon III in 1867 and with a large 'N' for Napoleon and 'E' for his empress Eugénie built into the front. Inside it is still more imposing, with a giant main staircase and a vast *Grand Salon* with murals by the Symbolist artist Puvis de Chavannes. They present a fanciful vision of the prehistoric Picards, but their monumental size, style and curious stillness are very impressive, and they influenced Gauguin and many later artists. And, even if you don't feel like a coffee, take a look at the cafeteria, a neogothic, neobyzantine extravaganza in red, blue and gold.

The museum collection is also highly impressive, and its greatest treasures are local. There are fine **Roman artefacts** from excavations of the first Amiens, *Samarobriva* or 'Bridge-over-the-Somme', which in the 2nd century AD was the most important city in northern Gaul. Other rooms contain wonderful **medieval sculptures** in wood and stone, mostly from Picardy and other parts of northern France; look out for the exquisite bas-reliefs on the Life of Christ, from around 1500. Most extraordinary, though, and unique, are the *Puys*, paintings offered to Amiens Cathedral in the 16th century by the Fraternity of Notre-Dame, an association of local merchants. It was the custom for each new master of the Fraternity to commission a painting, and together they present a panorama of Amiens and its burghers over more than a century. The artists were anonymous, but the paintings are superb – the *Vierge au Palmier* from 1520, for example, presents a vision of the city akin to Brueghel.

Beyond the *Puys* there are several fine works by more familiar, 'named' artists – El Greco, Salvator Rosa, Frans Hals and other Dutch masters, Fragonard and Boucher. The more modern sections are not so eye-catching, but the museum has one great contemporary addition in *Wall Drawing 711*, a rotunda on the ground floor painted in 1992 by the American artist Sol LeWitt in a whole spectrum of colours in complex, interacting geometrical patterns.

Opposite the museum there is an elegant Louis XV *hôtel particulier* that now houses the Prefecture of Picardy, but as you continue towards the city centre the architecture becomes more plainly modern and uniform. Amiens was a wealthy textile town from the early Middle Ages, and attained its greatest prestige around the time when the *Puys* were painted. Much of old Amiens, however, was destroyed in just two days, 18 and 19 May 1940, when German bombers rained incendiaries on the city. The cathedral and many larger stone buildings emerged remarkably undamaged – two contrasting architectural treasures that survived are the **Hôtel de Berny**, a 1630s *hôtel particulier* on Rue Victor Hugo that now houses a local history museum, and the **Hôtel Bouctot-Vagniez** near the boulevards on Rue des Otages, a spectacularly ornate art nouveau mansion built for a local textile millionaire in the 1900s. Most of the old wooden houses in the centre, however, went up like torches. Post-war, much of the city centre was rebuilt in a simple, unobtrusive modern style according to a plan by the architect Pierre Dufau.

Rue de la République ends when it meets the long street that, under different names, cuts across the city centre and forms its main commercial thoroughfare. Look to the right and away in the distance, where the street is called Rue de Noyon, you can see the busy area around the train station, with an odd-looking 1940s concrete skyscraper, the **Tour Perret**, built during post-war reconstruction. The central section, pedestrianized **Rue des Trois Cailloux**, is the heart of Amiens' main shopping zone. To the left, as Rue Delambre, the street leads to the very large **Hôtel de Ville**, rebuilt after the war. The square in front of it was remodelled in the 1990s to an innovative, locally controversial design by the Catalan architect Joan Roig, with some intriguing inclined fountains; across Rue des Trois Cailloux from Rue de la République there is also a still more recent modernistic space, triangular **Place Gambetta**, which however has in the middle of it the **Horloge Dewailly**, an extravagantly elaborate 1890s beaux-arts style clock that has been lavishly restored in all its green, red and gold glory.

Walk around the Hôtel de Ville and you come to a survivor of the 1940 fires, the solid 15th-century belfry, **Le Beffroi**, once, as it looks, a prison. Close by there is a glass-walled modern market hall, **Les Halles du Beffroi**. This is not the most atmospheric of French markets, but it's a great place to find high-quality foods and local produce.

From there, walk back past the *Beffroi* and across a few more streets to approach the cathedral. For the moment continue past it across the *parvis* or square, go down the steps on the other side and turn right down little Rue des Rinchevaux to reach the riverside district and **Place du Don**, an attractive cobbled square with 16th-century houses on three sides, some original and some restored, and the river on the other. Virtually every house contains an antique shop, restaurant or bar with pavement tables, and this is a major centre of evening- and night-life. Off the square at 67 Rue du Don is the tiny shop of Jean-Pierre Facquier, only remaining maker of the traditional Amiens puppets, the *Cabotans*, at the centre of which is always Lafleur, a roguish, Mr Punch figure in a red suit, considered the archetypal Amiens and Picard character.

The many renovations in Amiens in the last few years have included what seems to be almost the handing-over of whole parts of the riverside to the university, and large sections of Rue Vanmarcke and its continuations, running west from Place du Don, now contain shiny new but anonymous academic buildings. This college-spread has only increased the popularity of Place du Don and St-Leu across the river for student socializing, and there are plenty of buzzing bars, and a clutch of bigger discos mostly on Rue des Francs Mûriers. A more traditional note is struck in Place Parmentier, down the quayside from Place du Don, where on many Thursday and Saturday mornings vegetable and fruit growers from the *Hortillonages* tie up their boats packed with produce to sell direct (in June virtually all the growers take part in the *Fête des Hortillons* by the quay, one of France's most special markets). Look left from the quayside, towards Pont de la Dodane, and you see a man standing in mid-river, which never fails to entertain kids. This is actually a sculpture by the German artist Balkenhol, and if you look back from the bridge at Place du Don you'll see two more of his strangely life-like figures on either side of it, a man and a woman.

And across the river is Amiens' engaging little Venice, the canalside quarter of **St-Leu**, spread across islands in the Somme with little streets, alleys and bridges along and between the quiet waterways. This was formerly the weavers' and dyers' district, and the ne'er-do-well proletarian Lafleur is always seen as a native of St-Leu. It was less damaged than other areas in 1940, thanks to the river, but was run-down until restoration began in the 1980s, since when it has been newly fashionable. St-Leu's houses are endlessly varied: half-timbered, stucco or plain brick, and with woodwork painted in greens, blues, ochres and reds. One, 56 Rue des Marissons, looks only two metres wide. As you wander round – the only way to do it – you also find small craft and antique shops, especially on Rue Motte and in the arcade by Rue de la Dodane.

The great social focus of St-Leu is **Quai Bélu**, the picturesque stretch of quayside across from Place du Don, with restaurants, dance-bars and more peaceful cafés that all have terrace tables beside the river whenever the weather's favourable. It's an extremely pretty spot, and a very relaxing place to find in the middle of a city. Near the eastern end of the *quai* there is a recent addition, an unusually grand landing stage for local rowing clubs, the **Embarcadère d'Amont**. This is also the departure point for the *Bateau-Restaurant Le Picardie* (**t** 03 22 92 16 40), which offers cruises on the Somme with dinner included. Although only built in 1998, the *Embarcadère* has elaborate Victorian-looking balustrades, arches and other decorative touches, in a neo-Vernian style that has been taken up as the 'heritage style' of Amiens.

Immediately after lunch is the best time to visit the water gardens of the **Hortillonages**. To get to the landing point, follow the signs along the river bank to the right from Place du Don, cross the Boulevard de Beauvillé bridge, and the entrance is on the right. Tours (*April–Oct daily from 2pm on demand; the last tour may leave anytime between 3–7; tours last c. 1hr; adm*) of some of the over 50km of channels are run by the association of allotment holders in their traditional long, black, motorized punts.

Vegetable plots on land drained from the Somme were known here in Roman times, and have been extended ever since. As in the *Marais* of St-Omer, this wet, green maze has given rise to its own legends, and has been used as a place of refuge, most recently by Resistance fighters in the Second World War. At the beginning of the 20th century nearly a thousand people lived on the *Hortillonages*, a separate community. Only a handful do so now, but many people work the plots or use them as a weekend retreat. As you travel almost at water level around the apparently endless, silent canals, you see some plots that are neat gardens, with clipped hedges and even garden gnomes, and others that are more reminiscent of a mangrove swamp. Some contain whole swathes of parsley or celery, others rows of bright flowers. There are birds everywhere, and on some plots also goats, kept to keep down the fast-growing marsh grass. It's a different world of wonderful serenity, with its own fresh, still air.

This leaves till last the **cathedral**, up on its hill above Place du Don. For many it is the greatest of all Gothic cathedrals. Ruskin called the staggering **west front**, with its hundreds of figures of saints, apostles and biblical scenes, 'the Bible in stone'. It entranced him particularly because he saw in it the perfect example of the medieval unity of art and craft, and indeed in the small roundels around the bases of the three great portals, portraying virtues and vices or the course of the seasons, you can see every element of 13th-century life represented in fascinating detail. According to legend the central statue of Jesus, the *Beau Dieu*, was sculpted directly from a vision of Christ, and is extremely beautiful.

If you are disconcerted by the plain modern block at the foot of the cathedral, with its chocolate and souvenir shop, you are not alone. The 1999 plan of architect Bernard Huet for the renovation of the **cathedral square** was hugely controversial, and the new, incorrigibly bland buildings are loathed by most of Amiens. However, one other feature of the reconstruction work has been the comprehensive cleaning of the west façade, and the result of this is staggering. It's now probably cleaner than at any time since it was first built, and the details of its many levels are hypnotic. The façade and all its figures were once painted in bright colours, and new technology now allows the original colours to be projected back on to the façade in an astonishing son et lumière, an awe-inspiring, hugely effective spectacle (**La Cathédrale en Couleurs**, *mid-June–Sept and 15 Dec–6 Jan, times vary*). At Christmas, especially, it's truly magical.

When your neck can no longer stand craning up at the west front, walk around the outside of the cathedral to take in its buttresses and gargoyles before going inside. It has to be said that from the outside, especially from a distance, it can look odd: it seems too tall for its length, and has a strange, slender spire, the **Flèche**, from 1529. Inside, though, Amiens Cathedral soars like no other. Vaults and columns give the impression of reaching up forever, and the high windows give the nave a special luminosity. It was begun in 1220 after Amiens had acquired the head of John the Baptist, brought here in dubious circumstances after the Fourth Crusade (it can still be seen in the cathedral treasury). Most of it was built within 50 years, which gives it an unusual unity of style. Also, unusually for a medieval building, it has a known first architect, Robert de Luzarches, who died in about 1225, and whose name is written in the centre of the great 'Labyrinth' in the intricate tiled floor.

Amiens Cathedral has many treasures, and it is only possible to mention a few here. If the façade is the Bible in stone, the **choir stalls** are the Bible in wood, carved by Amiens craftsmen between 1508 and 1522. The outside walls of the choir, in the Ambulatory, are just as impressive, and have also been finely restored. Two series of scenes in polychrome painted stone from the early 16th century depict the life of John the Baptist, on one side, and St Firmin, credited with bringing Christianity to Amiens, on the other. The detail and colour of each scene are extraordinary, and, once again, they give a vivid picture of life at the time – look for example at the carving of the birth of St John, with the midwife bathing the baby. And, before you leave, look up to the three great **rose windows**. Much of their glass is no longer the original, but they are still breathtaking, more glass and light than stone. Afterwards, walk back down to Quai Bélu for a drink, and a great view of the cathedral from across the river.

Shopping

Amiens' culinary specialities are *macarons d'Amiens*, almond and fruit macaroons, known since at least 1855, and *pâté de canard d'Amiens*, first mentioned in 1643. Rue des Trois Cailloux and Rue Delambre – really the same street – form the shopping heart of Amiens, and Les Halles market has many fine stalls.

Amiens ✉ 80000

Le Fromathèque Picard-Gérard Quentin, Marché des Halles du Beffroi, **t** 03 22 91 96 22. The two giant stands of master cheese-merchant Gérard Quentin stand out vividly among the many others in the Halles: superb arrays of cheeses – local Picard Belval or Riceys, and others from the rest of France.

H. Martigny et Fils, 12 Rue Albert Dauphin, **t** 03 22 91 57 51. Founded in 1850, and one of the most attractive fine wine and spirits merchants you'll find, with bottle-racks set up like books for browsing. It has wonderful French wines, especially Bordeaux, plus 150 whiskies, superb selections of champagne, calvados and brandies, and over 180 beers. Many of the staff speak English, and they are charming and knowledgeable. The shop is in a street alongside the Hôtel de Ville.

Jean Trogneaux, Parvis de la Cathédrale, **t** 03 22 71 17 17. Run by the same family since 1872, Trogneaux is known above all for Amiens macaroons, but also has chocolates, gateaux, *tuiles* (chocolate-coated almond biscuits) and all sorts of chocolatey gifts. There are four shops in Amiens, the largest at 1 Rue Delambre, near the Hôtel de Ville.

Where to Stay

Amiens ✉ 80000

Hôtel Mercure Amiens Cathédrale, 17–19 Place au Feurre, **t** 03 22 22 00 20, *www.escalotel.com/relais.merc.amiens* (*double rooms €83–98*). Mercure hotels tend to be blandly functional, but when the chain took over this 18th-century former coaching inn it adapted the rambling building – partly out of necessity, for it's a listed historical monument – with taste and imagination. It combines something of the comforts and feel of a business hotel with the features of an old *hôtel particulier* – a grand Louis XV façade, a courtyard with Baroque fountain. There's a cocktail bar, 'Le Tour du Monde'.

Hôtel Le Saint-Louis, 24 Rue des Otages, **t** 03 22 91 76 03, *www.le-saintlouis.com* (*double rooms €52–62*). A likeable hotel in a convenient central location. It has recently been thoroughly renovated, with attractive modern touches to add to its traditional features, and the 12 bright rooms are of a high standard; the owners are amiably easy-going. There's a pleasant **restaurant** (*menus €12.50–28*), with varied menus of local dishes. *Restaurant closed Wed eves and Sun.*

Hôtel Alsace-Lorraine, 18 Rue de la Morlière, **t** 03 22 91 35 71, *alsace.lorraine@wanadoo.fr* (*double rooms €50–64*). In a district of 19th-century terraced houses just east of the boulevards – but still an easy walk from the cathedral and St-Leu – this hotel belies its surroundings with an all-white interior and lots of fresh flowers. The 13 rooms have their foibles – some bathrooms are a little elderly – but the owners are charming, breakfasts are ample, and it's very popular. The best rooms are the larger ones around a small courtyard at the rear of the hotel.

Hôtel Le Prieuré, 17 Rue Porion, **t** 03 22 71 16 71, **f** 03 22 92 46 16 (*double rooms €45–80*). Amiens' most distinctive hotel has been through the wars, and complete closure threatened when subsidence undermined the 17th-century former priory that forms its main building. Thankfully, it's now been restored, and remains a first-choice hotel in the city for an atmospheric stay. Pluses include its superb location, around a corner from the cathedral, the family-run feel, and an enjoyable eccentricity. Rooms (some in another building, no.6) run from plain and simple to quite luxurious. It no longer has a restaurant, but breakfast is served.

Hôtel au Spatial, 15 Rue Alexandre Fatton, **t** 03 22 91 53 23, *www.hotelspatial.com*. (*double rooms €35–52*). Not far from the train station, this is a modern hotel with rooms that vary in size, facilities and price, but are all straightforwardly comfortable. The hotel's plain lines are softened by bright flower displays, it has free parking, and staff are charming and helpful.

Creuse ✉ 80480

Mme Monique Lemaître, 26 Rue Principale, **t** 03 22 38 91 50, *monique.p.lemaitre @wanadoo.fr* (*rooms €45–65 for two, €90 for four*). A pleasant B&B in a village 14km west of Amiens, in a big old Picard farmhouse with red-tile roofs and single-storey wings around a garden. The three rooms and a suite are large and imaginatively decorated, and there's a delightful breakfast room. Mme Lemaître hosts walking weekends and courses in painting, French and English. *Open April–Oct.*

La Faloise ✉ 80250

Mme Serraz, 22 Rue de l'Eglise, **t** 03 22 41 41 88, *www.couleuretjardin.com* (*rooms €55 for two*). A delightful *chambres d'hôtes* in a restored farmhouse 26km south of Amiens, in an ultra-placid village. Quietly charming Mme Serraz is a painter and often hosts artists' workshops, and her own decorative ideas can be seen all around the five rooms. The village feels remarkably remote – there's no bar or restaurant – so guests have use of the kitchen. A very relaxing place to stay.

Eating Alternatives

Amiens ✉ 80000

Les Marissons, Pont de Dodane, **t** 03 22 92 96 66, *www.les-marissons.fr* (*menus €18.50 lunch only, €31–47*). Amiens' premier restaurant, a gourmet haven in an exquisite setting, a beautifully restored medieval boathouse next to St-Leu and the river. Antoine Benoît is one of France's finest chefs, with a total dedication to quality. Fresh local produce – sole, *coquilles St-Jacques*, eels, Somme Bay lamb – naturally forms the basis of his cooking, used in complex, delicate dishes such as turbot with a truly stunning leek sauce. Desserts, wines, cheeses and service are all impeccable. *Closed Sat midday and Sun.*

La Couronne, 64 Rue St-Leu, **t** 03 22 91 88 57, *http://la-couronne.picardieresto.com* (*menus €22–33*). A snug St-Leu restaurant that has long been known in Amiens as one of the best places to find classic *cuisine française* of unfailingly high quality. Recently under new management, it now has brighter décor, and

the kitchen is again setting standards with a few more international, global touches in its refined dishes, made with wonderfully fresh ingredients. *Closed Sat midday and Sun eve.*

Le Bouchon, 10 Rue Alexandre Fatton, **t** 03 22 91 14 32, *www.lebouchon.fr* (*menus €15–42*). Tucked away in a rather plain street, this little restaurant surprises with its imaginative, enjoyable cooking; specialities include pig's trotter with truffles and foie gras, and there are wonderfully subtle fish dishes. The atmosphere is comfortably relaxed.

Le Pot d'Etain, 15 Quai Bélu, **t** 03 22 72 10 80, *www.potdetain.com* (*menus €14–38*). One of the best of the clutch of restaurants with waterside *terrasses* along Quai Bélu. Mainstays of the menu are a *rôtisserie* range, including good steaks and a hearty *grande rôtisserie* or mixed grill, and quality seafood, such as ample *plateaux de fruits de mer*. Also cassoulet, varied salads, and good wines.

La Dent Creuse, 2 Rue Cormont, **t** 03 22 80 03 63, *www.ladentcreuse.com* (*menus €13 lunch only, €18–25*). A pretty restaurant beside the cathedral, with charming, old-fashioned service. Local classics come with luxurious touches: roast sea bass with courgettes in a *crème de champagne* sauce. There's a wide choice of *assiettes* combining salads with fish, duck, forest mushrooms and so on, and tables outside from which to admire the glorious architecture. *Closed Sun eve.*

Le T'chiot Zinc, 18 Rue de Noyon, **t** 03 22 91 43 79 (*menus €11.40–27.70*). A much-loved brasserie and *salon de thé* in an eccentric building near the station – it's much too tall for its width, and the façade is an extravaganza of neobaroque columns. Exceptional value set menus offer local standards such as *ficelles picardes*, rabbit terrines, grilled fish or duck; there's also a fine *assiette de fruits de mer* (*€16.20*). *Closed Sun and Mon midday.*

La Soupe à Cailloux, Place du Don, **t/f** 03 22 91 92 70 (*menus €13.20–19.50*). Amiens' most popular good-value bistro, in a great location by the river. Menus offer a wide choice: *tarte au maroilles* or a cassoulet of *moules*, and international creations like *lieu à la Thailandaise*. There are vegetarian choices on each menu. The house wine is pretty awful: this is somewhere where it's worth spending a little more. *Mid-Sept–May closed Mon.*

Normandy's Lost Frontier:
Eu

14

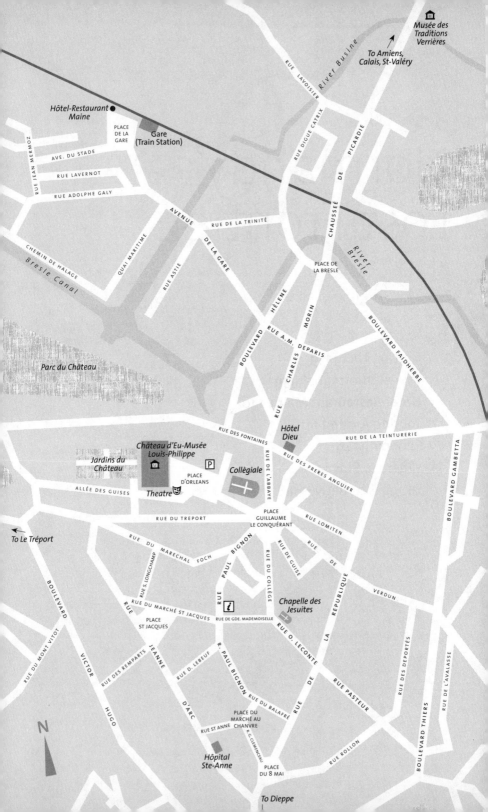

Getting There

Driving from the north, from the Calais roads (A16 or N1) via Abbeville on the D925 or from St-Valery on the D940, you arrive in Eu at a large roundabout, Place Albert I. Follow the sign for *Centre Ville* to another roundabout, Place de la Bresle. From there Rue Charles Morin, straight on, leads to the town centre. To go directly to the Hôtel-Restaurant Maine, take Bd Hélène, the next exit to the right, and after about 50m turn right onto Av de la Gare.

Coming from Dieppe on the D925, you also come to a large roundabout, Place Charles-de-Gaulle. Take the left exit, Bd Victor Hugo: at the next roundabout the right exit leads to Place Guillaume-le-Conquérant. To get to the Maine, go round the square and take the street down the hill to the right of the church, Rue de l'Abbaye, which leads into Rue Charles Morin. Second left is Rue Adjutant Deparis, which leads directly on to Av de la Gare.

Eu and Le Tréport have direct **train** services from Paris and Rouen, via Beauvais, and from Amiens via Abbeville, with 5–7 services daily on each route. Parisian day-trippers traditionally go only to Le Tréport, and ignore Eu.

Since the Paris trains all stop in Beauvais (1hr 40mins from Le Tréport), it's quite easy to get to this area from Beauvais airport.

Tourist Information

Eu: 41 Rue Paul Bignon, t 02 35 86 04 68, *www.ville-eu.fr*. Has information on the whole *Vallée de la Bresle*, and on tours, walks and visits to sites with limited access.

Criel-sur-Mer: 60 Rue de la Libération, t 02 35 86 56 91.

Mers-les-Bains: 43 Rue Jules Barni, t 02 27 28 06 46, *www.ville-merslesbains.fr*.

Le Tréport: Quai Sadi Carnot, t 02 35 86 05 69, *www.ville-le-treport.fr*.

The valley of the river Bresle marks the northeast border of Normandy, a long, straight cleft lined with stretches of thick woodland. It has not been a real frontier between states since the 13th century, but remains a significant dividing line: in food, in agriculture – between the grain fields of Picardy and the Norman pastures and orchards – and in the historical memory of the people. And, straddling the Bresle, there is the traditional main gateway to Normandy, the little town of Eu.

Today this town with its oddly monosyllabic name has a noticeably out-of-the-way feel, and is not very well known even in the rest of France. It's a relaxed, charming provincial town, its life centred on a main square that fills up with a market on some days and flocks of chattering *lycéens* on others. Eu has also cropped up in the history of both France and the British Isles a remarkable number of times and in a curious variety of circumstances, and hosted a whole gallery of heroes and villains. William the Conqueror was married here; later, it became a shrine to an Irish saint, and later still a summer residence of a French king, in which role it welcomed Queen Victoria.

This past has left Eu with a range of historic buildings, some hidden away, some of undeniable grandeur, exceptional for a small, ordinary town. Perhaps in part because they still receive relatively few visitors, the *Eudois* are also particularly welcoming. Inland there is the Forêt d'Eu, a swathe of wild, almost virgin forest, ideal for walking, that contains within it a still partially excavated Gallo-Roman city. Towards the sea are the *Belle Epoque* beach towns of Le Tréport and Mers-les-Bains, with giant cliffs, promenades, great seafood restaurants and a vigorously animated fishing harbour.

And Eu itself also has an exceptional restaurant, as unobtrusive and as idiosyncratic as the rest of town. The **Hôtel-Restaurant Maine**'s original style, food and hospitality make it worth a stopover in Eu all by itself.

Hôtel-Restaurant Maine

*20 Av de la Gare, t 02 35 86 16 64, www.hotel-maine.com. Open
Mon–Sat 12–2 and 7.30–9.30, Sun 12–2. Closed usually 2–3 weeks in Aug–Sept.
Menus €14.95 (Mon–Fri only), €24, carte €24 two courses, €40 three courses.*

A few trains still stop at Eu, even though most of the station has now been taken over by an insurance company. The Hôtel Maine, which until quite recently was still called the Hôtel de la Gare, is naturally enough alongside it, a plainish brick building with Mansart roof much like many other small station hotels put up around France at the end of the 19th century. Inside, the bar to the right of the entrance seems at first sight equally conventional, catering to a steady flow of locals. Look around, though, and you'll find a collection of modern designer lamps in the form of feet and other strange shapes, comic-strip pictures and some unusually comfortable furniture, indicating a quirky individuality you don't necessarily expect in a small-town restaurant. The distinctive tastes of Jean-Claude and Marie-Françoise Maine, owners since 1972, are just as present in the hotel upstairs (*see* p.146), which in parts has an almost radically stylish, post-modern look.

The dining room is entirely different again: large and ornate to the point of being baroque, in apple green, with classic bourgeois mouldings in the first section and a magnificent, sinuous Art Nouveau fireplace and window frames in the larger end room. It's also very comfortable, and around the walls there's plenty of odd bric-a-brac and an eccentric collection of paintings, especially old portraits of stolid local burghers, to add to the interest while you're thinking about your meal.

This cheerfully eclectic décor is only part of the place's originality and charm. Jean-Claude, tall, wiry and with an ample grey walrus moustache, often takes the orders, ambling from table to table and chatting with the clientele, many of them regulars. He does not cook himself but is clearly a very able master of ceremonies, for over many years and with different personnel the restaurant has maintained a distinctive style and quality of cooking that would not be out of place in a major metropolitan eating house. It's rooted in French and local tradition, with a refined use of butter to introduce you to Normandy. The pricing structure is original, and gives exceptional value: there are two main menus at €24, *du Pêcheur*, all fish and seafood, and *du Boucher*, all meat, with four courses in each. It's possible to have part of each menu for a lower price (€19.10, just first and main courses, €16.80, for a main and dessert), and the *carte* also follows a set-price formula, for three or two courses. Menus change completely with each season, providing a wonderfully varied and tempting choice.

The Maines and their team stress the importance of taste, rather than complexity for its own sake, and one outstanding feature of their meat dishes, especially, is the ideal combination of subtlety and full, rich, juicily enjoyable flavours. Ingredients are impeccable. A first course of chicken terrine with apple and calvados is perfectly matched, a great display of some of the basics of Norman cooking. To follow, a spring menu offers superb-quality chicken lightly marinated in lemon, and saddle of rabbit stuffed with camembert and mushrooms – the kind of thing that could be terrible if done crudely, but which here is smoothly, fragrantly delicate. On the carte, meanwhile, there might be a very satisfying beef fillet in an intricate spiced *croûte*, served with irresistible olive oil and tomato mash.

M Maine also takes good care of his wine list, and you can rely on his recommendations, such as supremely smooth Rhône labels that exactly complement the meats. The fish choices, which often highlight the local catch, might include a fine pâté of langoustines with ratatouille, and both surprising original creations and variants on classics such as fillet of sole served with tagliatelle and foie gras.

The same attention to detail is seen in the cheese course – including a fabulously flavoured local Neufchâtel – and desserts, such as a delightfully refreshing 'soup' of red berries and spices, or one of the regular specialities, iced nougat with a fresh fruit coulis. A meal here stays in the mind, with refined but flavoursome, enjoyable food that can appeal even to those who still suspect all French quality cooking of being over-fancified. Afterwards, if you don't have to drive anywhere, try one of Jean-Claude's great selection of calvados, especially the superbly fragrant *Hors d'Age*.

Touring Around

The first settlement of **Eu** appeared on a shelf of land above the Bresle, where the Château d'Eu and church of the *Collégiale* stand today. It was occupied under the Romans, but the town's history really begins in the 10th century, when the recently established dukes of Normandy built a castle here as the furthest defensive bastion of their new territories. It was also a port, with access to the sea along the Bresle. In 1050 William the Conqueror brought Matilda, daughter of the Count of Flanders, to the castle of Eu to marry him. Apparently she was none too keen on the match, and only submitted to it after William dragged her around her chambers by her hair. It is traditionally claimed that this was because he was so much in love he just couldn't take no for an answer, but it looks more like one more example of the Conqueror's usual thuggery. An abbey was founded near the castle, and the town grew up around the two. Eu has the oldest municipal charter of any town in Normandy, from 1151.

The town's central square, occupied by the wonderful market on Friday mornings, is **Place Guillaume-le-Conquérant**. It is dominated, however, by a great church dedicated to a more permanent resident of Eu, who was not Norman but Irish. This was **St Laurence O'Toole**, for centuries the only officially canonized Irish saint (since Saints Patrick, Kevin and many others had never been formally recognized by the Vatican). He was Archbishop of Dublin at the time of the first Anglo-Norman invasion of Ireland in 1169, and in 1180 was sent to England by the Irish lords to intercede with Henry II. The King all but ignored him, and went off to Normandy; Laurence, old and sick, followed after him, but only got as far as the Abbey at Eu, where he died, and the rest, as they say, is history. He had supposedly stopped the day before on the crest just north of Eu, where the 19th-century **Chapelle St-Laurent** now stands out against the sky, and, looking down, said, 'there I will take my rest'; he was also said to have raised seven people from the dead, and his canonization was begun very quickly, in part because of the papacy's own arguments with Henry II. Laurence's shrine at Eu immediately became an important pilgrimage centre, and remained so throughout the Middle Ages. More recently Eu has sought to revive its Irish links, and in a garden on the north side of the church there is now a Celtic cross in stone from St Laurence's birthplace in County Kildare, donated by a contemporary Dublin archbishop.

Laurence's church, officially Notre-Dame-et-St-Laurent but better known locally as the **Collégiale**, was begun as a pilgrimage church in 1186, replacing the much smaller earlier abbey church, and first completed a hundred years later. Like many French churches battered by the Revolution it was restored in the 19th century by the great Gothic revivalist Eugène Viollet-le-Duc, who said that he had seen churches that were bigger or taller, but none that were more beautiful. Most of the nave is the original from the late 12th century; the choir and the apse, in contrast, are an extravagant work of *Flamboyant* Gothic, built after a major fire in 1426. It is especially spectacular from the outside, with a tangle of buttresses to rival Notre-Dame in Paris. In spite of this contrast, the different styles harmonize, and the building is superbly light.

The *Collégiale* has very fine Baroque woodwork, especially the 1614 organ above the nave, and the statue of *Our Lady of Eu* in the Lady Chapel behind the choir. Its greatest treasure, though, is in a small chapel to the right of the choir, an exquisite 16th-century *Entombment of Christ* in polychrome stone. The modelling and colour of the eight figures around the dead Christ are superb: look only at their marvellously expressive hands. Like much else in Eu, it is oddly little-known; it is believed to have been made in Burgundy, and no one knows how it got here. The 13th-century **tomb of St Laurence**, meanwhile, is in the vaulted crypt, entered from one side of the nave. The crypt is massive, built to accommodate a steady flow of pilgrims; desecrated in the Revolution, it was restored in the 1820s by Louis-Philippe, Duke of Orléans and later King of France, who lined it with the tombs of his ancestors, counts of Eu and Artois.

In the later Middle Ages, Eu was another of the places where Joan of Arc was held on her way to her trial in Rouen, in 1430. Very little of the medieval town survives because, along with William the Conqueror's castle, it was burnt wholesale in 1475 on the orders of Louis XI of France, to prevent them falling into the hands of the English. Only the abbey and some churches remained intact. If, however, you walk from the south side of Place Guillaume up Eu's traditional main thoroughfare, **Rue Paul Bignon**, you enter an area of little winding streets built during a revival in the town's fortunes in the 16th and 17th centuries, with many fine Louis XIII-style merchants' houses in brick, occasionally with elaborate ornamental details. Rue Bignon, curving and narrow, also contains some great food shops, and the tourist office.

Overlooking a tiny square on Rue du Collège, which runs away from the main *place* just east of Rue Bignon, is the **Chapelle du Collège des Jésuites** (*open April–Nov Tues–Sat 10–12 and 2–6*). This was built following Eu's next intervention in history, in the French Wars of Religion (*c.* 1560–98). The title of Count of Eu had been passed around between several aristocratic dynasties, and in 1570 the then Countess, Catherine de Clèves, married Henri, Duc de Guise, known as *le Balafré* ('Scarface'), the foremost standard-bearer of intransigent Catholicism, and a perennial conspirator who played a significant part in the St Bartholomew's Day Massacre of Protestants in

Paris in 1572. Guise sought to make Eu a powerhouse of the Counter-Reformation, and founded a Jesuit college here (alongside the chapel, and now the main *lycée*) in 1582. His wife Catherine was notorious for her '*galanteries*' with a string of lovers, from servants to gentlemen, some of whom were murdered on Guise's orders; nevertheless, she shared his religious ideas and, after he himself was assassinated by agents of Henri III in 1588, developed something of a cult to his memory. Reconciled to the former-Protestant Bourbon King Henri IV, she lived to a great age, becoming known for her good works, and commissioned the chapel in Eu to be built in 1613.

As in many other Jesuit churches built around that time, its design is based on the mother church of the order, the Gesù in Rome, but in brick and stone instead of marble, and with decoration that's similarly a mix of Italian Renaissance and more local influences. The fine carving on the façade was the work of local sculptors, the Anguier brothers. Inside, the most prominent features by far are two giant, bombastic but very finely sculpted Baroque memorial tombs in marble, made for Catherine de Clèves in 1627, one for herself and one for her husband. Guise's is actually empty, since after his assassination Henri III had ordered that the Duke's remains be burnt and scattered in the Loire, to prevent them becoming a focus for his followers.

Thanks to the Guises and their successors there were once so many churches and religious foundations in Eu that in 1650 the Mayor complained that they blocked off many streets. Most were demolished after the Revolution. On Rue St-Anne there is still the **Hôpital Ste-Anne**, now the tax office, built in 1664 as an almshouse for orphan girls. On Rue de l'Abbaye, downhill beside the *Collégiale*, is the beautiful **Hôtel-Dieu**, a convent and hospital from 1654, built around a garden courtyard in a happy combination of Norman half-timbering and more august Louis XIII-style architecture. Today part of it is used to house finds from the Roman site at Bois-L'Abbé (*see* p.145).

The Guises were also responsible for the other building that, with the *Collégiale*, makes up the grand centrepiece of the town, facing the church across the stately Place d'Orléans, the French-Renaissance style **Château d'Eu**, begun on the site of the earlier castle in 1578. What we see today represents only a part of the vast palace, with four sides around a great courtyard, they had planned to create for themselves, for they were only able to complete part of one wing before *le Balafré* was murdered. In 1660 the château passed to Mademoiselle de Montpensier, known as *la Grande Mademoiselle*, cousin of Louis XIV, who was confined here by the Sun King to prevent her intriguing against him. It was she who first made it habitable, and added the elegant Le Nôtre-style French garden that forms the main part of the delightful park that sweeps away on its western side. The Château d'Eu is most associated, though, with Louis-Philippe of Orléans, who inherited it, with the title of Count of Eu, in 1821.

Louis-Philippe loved Eu; not only did he amply restore his château and the crypt of the *Collégiale*, he also had the **Bresle Canal** built, restoring the town's access to the sea for the first time in centuries, in part in order that he could sail up it in his yacht. Moreover, it continued to be his favourite residence after the revolution of July 1830 catapulted him into power as France's 'Citizen King', considered an archetype of respectable virtues, and famous for never going out without his umbrella. Eu became for a while the virtual summer capital of France, and a new, rather barracks-like

building, the **Pavillon des Ministres**, was put up next to the *Collégiale* to accommodate the members of the government who were obliged to decamp here for several
weeks each year. In September 1843 Queen Victoria and Prince Albert arrived at the
château for a week of picnics, parades, concerts and other entertainments. This was
the first time a British monarch had set foot in France since Henry VIII's meeting with
François I at the Field of the Cloth of Gold in 1520, a fact that enables Eu to claim the
title of 'Birthplace of the Entente Cordiale'. The visit had tremendous impact. Each
day's events were followed with rapt attention by the local population, and in the
following year every third girl born in Eu was named Victoria, Victoire or Victorine.

After Louis-Philippe was himself deposed by another revolution in 1848, Eu fell back
into obscurity, but in the 1870s the Republic returned the château to the King's
grandson the Comte de Paris, pretender to the French throne, who again restored the
house and gardens. Since 1964 it has belonged to the town, and part is now the
Mairie, while the rest is the **Château-Musée Louis-Philippe** (*open mid-Mar–early Nov
Mon, Wed, Thurs, Sat, Sun 10–12 and 2–6; Fri 2–6; closed Tues; adm*). Maintaining such a
large monument is a heavy burden for a small town, and restoration work has been
undertaken a bit at a time, almost as a community project, which rather adds to its
charm. One recently-restored room, the *Chambre Dorée*, still has the astonishingly
ornate 17th-century décor of the *Grande Mademoiselle*, while others were redecorated
in the 1870s for the Comte de Paris by Viollet-le-Duc, with fascinating, multicoloured
designs on the borderline between Gothic revival and Art Nouveau. Another highlight
is the *Galerie des Guises*, still only partially restored, with portraits of the Guise clan
that had been sold off in the 1900s and were only recovered thanks to the kindness of
a collector in Scotland. Most of the rooms, though, are as they were left by Louis-
Philippe. He was an undemonstrative king, and his palace is accordingly cosy. He was
also a man of his time, who installed in his château one of the earliest running-water
systems, driven by mill wheels on the canal, and one of the building's unmissable
features is its giant tangle of brass plumbing, There are many souvenirs of the British
visits, including paintings done at breakneck speed by Winterhalter and other artists
so that they could be shown to the royal couple before their departure.

In the 1850s a little municipal theatre, the **Théâtre du Château**, was created in one
of the pavillions on one side of the Place d'Orléans. This too has been restored, and its
red-and-gold interior can be visited whenever the box office is open (*Tues–Thur 2–6,
Fri and Sat 10–12 and 2–6*). Behind the château, the lush green park begins as a
tranquil, formal French garden, turning to beech woods the further you head into it.

Royal connections aside, the Bresle Valley is also known as the *Vallée de la Verre*, the
valley of glass. Glassmaking has been carried on here since the Middle Ages, and the
giant St-Gobain factory outside Mers-les-Bains now produces millions of Made-in-
France glasses to send around the globe; at the same time, along the Bresle there are
still small village glass workshops using semi-mechanized techniques. Eu now has a
Musée des Traditions Verrières (*open April–June and Oct Tues, Sat, Sun and hols 2.30–6;
July–Sept, Tues, Wed, Sat, Sun and hols 2.30–6; adm*) on Rue Sémichon, on the north
side of the town. The informative display on the history of glass is given a lively
personal touch by the retired glassworkers who act as guides (they predictably don't

know much English, but translated leaflets are provided, and English-speaking guides can sometimes be arranged via the tourist office). One speciality of the Bresle is fine bottle work, and one dazzling part of the museum is a room of delicately sculpted prototype flasks made for Givenchy, Chanel and all the grand names of *parfumerie*.

Glassmakers were first drawn to the Bresle Valley by its sandy soil and abundant supply of wood, from what is still today one of the most heavily wooded parts of northern France. For a change from sightseeing, escape the town into the **Forêt d'Eu**, a wild, atmospheric expanse of deciduous forest that's home to a range of wildlife that includes deer and wild boar. It's wonderful for walking, and there are easy paths into the woods from the Beaumont road, off the D49 south, and from near St-Pierre-en-Val, off the D1314 to Neufchâtel. For a guide to these and longer routes ask for a walking map at Eu tourist office, which also organizes walks led by foresters that end at a *carcachoux* or traditional woodcutters' hut deep in the woods, with a drink and maybe an opportunity to pick and cook the forest's prized wild mushrooms; riding is also popular, and the office has information on local riding centres. Further west, the roads alongside the forest drop down into the **Vallée de l'Yères**, a spectacularly pretty steep-sided, narrow valley possessed of an almost tangible, unmolested serenity, and which runs down to meet the sea at the little beach village of **Criel-sur-Mer**.

Just inside the Forêt d'Eu at **Bois-l'Abbé**, only 4km outside Eu itself, there is a major **Roman site** (*tours July–Sept Tues at 2pm; adm*) that is almost a new discovery. The existence of Roman remains in the area has been known since the 18th century, but thorough excavations have only been underway since the 1990s. They have already unearthed a mass of ceramics, a temple, an amphitheatre with a capacity of 4–6,000 and, most unusually, a women's public bath, indicating a Gallo-Roman city of considerable size and sophistication. Tours are run from Eu tourist office every week in summer, which also visit the Hôtel-Dieu, where the finds from the site are stored.

Alternatively, leave Eu in the opposite direction for the sea air of **Le Tréport**, where Prince Albert exercised daily by going swimming at seven in the morning. With an arching shingle beach beneath giant cliffs, it's a curious combination of a once quite genteel 19th-century resort and a busy, gritty fishing port, with dainty architecture on one side and giant cranes on the other. Fabulously fresh fish and shellfish are landed and sold every day at stalls along the Quai François I, and a near-unbroken line of seafood restaurants extends along the quay and round on to the beach front, nearly all offering the same, delicious range of lobsters, mussels, oysters, sole, and so on. Long a favourite escape for Parisians – the hoi-polloi, rather than the elite who make for Deauville – Le Tréport and its restaurant strip still draw in the crowds on summer weekends, and by the beach there's also a casino, *frites* stands and all the other essentials of the French seaside. **Mers-les-Bains**, on the Picardy side of the Bresle, is quieter and has a better beach, but its greatest distinction – in contrast to Le Tréport, which underwent much more 1960s reconstruction – is that it has kept its glorious circa-1900 beachfront architecture, a line of *Beaux-Arts* to Art Deco follies, with elaborate turrets, gables and balconies and elaborate patterns in brick and wood, painted pink, cream, orange and duck-egg blue, that look like so many candy-coloured castles beneath the wheeling seagulls.

Shopping

For anyone even vaguely interested in Norman foods and the best local specialities, the essential time to arrive in **Eu**, if at all possible, is on Friday morning, when the town centre is virtually taken over by one of the best **markets** in northern Normandy, which seems to draw in just about anyone within a 50km radius. Stalls offer excellent farmhouse terrines, ciders, breads, Neufchâtel cheeses and other fresh farm produce, plus everything else you might expect to find at an absolutely traditional country market.

There are also good morning markets in **Le Tréport** (*Tues and Sat*) and **Mers-les-Bains** (*Mon and Thurs*). Also – if you have the means to carry them away – fresh fish and shellfish are sold direct from the boats every day along Quai François I in Le Tréport.

Outside of market days, Rue Paul Bignon in Eu is the place to head for, with at least three irresistible *boulangeries-pâtisseries* and equally fine *charcuteries*.

Sept-Meules ✉ 76260

M and Mme Métel, 13 Rue de l'Yères, **t** 02 35 50 82 33. On their farm in Sept-Meules, south of St-Martin-le-Gaillard on the Pays de Bray road from Eu (D1314), the Métels makes fine farm cider and powerful *appellation contrôlée eau-de-vie de cidre*, a stronger variant on calvados, which is something of a speciality of the Vallée de l'Yères. Sept-Meules also puts on an annual apple festival, the *Croque-Pomme*, usually on a weekend in late October, with all the local producers presenting their wares for tasting.

Where to Stay

Eu ✉ 76260

Le Domaine de Joinville, Route du Tréport, **t** 02 35 50 52 52, *www.domainejoinville.com* (*rooms and suites €78–215*). The top-drawer option in the Vallée de la Bresle. This very luxurious country-house hotel is housed in one of the pavilions built around the Château d'Eu for Louis-Philippe in the 1830s, with its own beautifully-kept grounds. There are 24 large rooms and suites, and a suitably smart gourmet **restaurant** (*menus €38–50*). Styled with traditional opulence, the Domaine naturally offers every comfort – including a pool, tennis courts, a fitness centre and so on – in a rather self-consciously upscale atmosphere.

Mme Marie-Laure Riche, 64 Rue de la République, **t** 02 35 86 50 62 (*rooms €60 for two, €90 for four*). A distinguished 19th-century house in the old part of Eu, with two very spacious, very well appointed and very comfortable B&B rooms. One is a positively huge room/suite lined with modern wood panelling, with its own sitting area with fireplace, TV, Persian rugs and twin beds, with the option of extra beds if required. The other is not quite so big but still a very ample double. Bathrooms are also very well-equipped. Mme Riche is quietly welcoming, and breakfast can be served in a pretty dining room or in the garden at the back.

Mme Evelyne Duminil, 6 Rue Ste-Anne, **t** 02 35 50 75 56, *evelyneduminil@aol.com* (*rooms €50–60 for two*). Guests at this very charming B&B in the heart of Eu's old town get a chance to see much more than usual of the town's distinctive domestic architecture, as it is in a beautifully-maintained 17th-century town house with a lovely internal courtyard, ideal for sitting out after a day's exploring. The three spacious guest rooms combine comfort and character: two are doubles, and one can be let as a family room with space for up to four. Breakfast is served in a delightful wood-panelled dining room. Also, while it's in the middle of town and within walking distance of cafés and restaurants, Mme Duminil is also a keen cook, and *table d'hôte* meals can be arranged with advance notice.

Hôtel-Restaurant Maine, 20 Av de la Gare, **t** 02 35 86 16 64, *www.hotel-maine.com* (*double rooms €47.26–60.98*). A meal in the Maines' Art Nouveau dining room doesn't quite prepare you for the rooms above, which could almost qualify the Maine as the Bresle Valley's one and only style hotel. Room doors are orange, with big silver numbers reaching from top to bottom: each of the 18 rooms is different, and some have fairly traditional décor while others have more playful touches, and others sport a contemporary designer-ish look with iron-frame furniture. And all the rooms are very comfortable. A hotel, like the restaurant, with character, charm and flair.

Manoir de Beaumont, t 02 35 50 91 91, *www.demarquet.com* (*rooms €46 for two*). A beautifully renovated hunting lodge and manor house in a superb location on a wooded hill just south of Eu, surrounded by its own gardens and grounds and with wonderful views in several directions. Rooms are deliciously comfortable, with antique furniture, lots of light and many extras, and the breakfast room and lounge are especially pretty. Catherine Demarquet and her husband provide full information on every kind of activity available in the area, and there are bikes for guests' use.

Guerville ✉ 76340

Ferme de la Haye, t 03 22 26 14 26 (*rooms €40 for two, €58 for four*). A special *chambres d'hôtes* in an impressively big old farm, once a stud farm for racehorses, that stands entirely within the Forêt d'Eu – directions are given on how to find it, which are pretty necessary. M Jean Mairesse, who worked the farm before his retirement, is a craggy son of the Norman earth who in the evenings sits in traditional fashion on a stool beside the giant open fireplace to chew the fat (he knows some English); his wife Dominique is a sweet lady, and both – and their dog – are very welcoming. They have an eye for style, as seen in the attractive renovation of their one huge guest room. It's really a suite, with one giant double room, another with two singles, and an excellent bathroom, but is available for couples (the two rooms can't be let separately, as they lead off each other). It's a remarkable bargain. The location above all, surrounded by the forest, is wonderful, whether you want to go on long treks or just wander into the woods. Gamaches is 4km away, Eu about 16km.

Mers-les-Bains ✉ 80350

Hôtel Bellevue, 24 Esplanade du Général Leclerc, **t** 02 35 86 12 89, *www.aubellevue.com* (*double rooms €40 on landward side, €50 with sea view*). The Bellevue unquestionably has the best location of any hotel in Mers, presiding over the prom, and occupies a prime example of the endearingly grand mansions that line the seafront, so that it captures perfectly the Jacques Tati-esque charm that is a prime appeal of the town. Recently both the rooms and the wood-panelled lobby have also been done up a little, to make the most of their many *Belle Epoque* features. The bedrooms are bright and comfortable, and prices, even for the ones with the much sought-after sea view, are still remarkably low. A little cranky, it's a hotel that inspires affection, and it also has an equally enjoyable, equally classic-style restaurant, **Le Poissonnier** (*see* p.148).

Mesnil-Val ✉ 76910

Hostellerie de la Vieille Ferme, 23 Rue de la Mer, Criel-sur-Mer, **t** 02 35 86 72 18, **f** 02 35 86 12 67 (*double rooms €52–91*). This archetypically Norman half-timbered farmhouse from 1734 has been altered many times, and is now a classically picturesque country hotel. Most of its 33 rooms are in annexes that have been added behind the main house across and around a neat, flowery garden, and the most attractive, all at ground level, have their own garden terraces. Rooms are plainer in style than the rest of the hotel, but comfortable, and it's a short walk from the beach at Criel-Plage. Popular for years with British guests, it also has a restaurant, *see* p.148. *Closed Jan.*

Le Tréport ✉ 76470

Le Prieuré Ste-Croix, t 02 35 86 14 77 (*rooms €42–54 for two*). Although this magnificent *chambres d'hôtes* is officially in Le Tréport, it's closer to, and feels more a part of, Eu. The 'Priory' is the former manor farm of the royal estate of the Château d'Eu, behind the château itself (the entrance is a driveway off the main roundabout on the Le Tréport road, just as you leave Eu), with its own impressive courtyard and gardens. Parts of the house are medieval, others are 16th- or 19th-century; all the beautiful old rooms have antique furnishings and very good modern bathrooms. The ground floor 'double' is really a suite, with its own sitting room and access to a kitchenette.

Eating Alternatives

Eu ✉ 76260

La Bragance, Allée des Guises, Parc du Château, **t** 02 35 83 47 70 (*menus €13 lunch only; €18*). An attractive, unusual restaurant installed in the *glacière* or ice-house – a kind of giant brick igloo – and attached garden lodge built for Louis-Philippe beside the entrance to the park beside the Château d'Eu, with an especially pleasant summer terrace outside from which to view the park's beeches. The atmosphere is relaxed and *sympa* and the light, modern cooking takes full advantage of the giant old wood-burning grill that dominates one side of the dining room, with deliciously fresh meat and fish grills. There are also a few traditional local favourites, and, for a lighter meal, excellent mixed salads and single-course dishes. Great value, too. *Closed Mon.*

La Fringale, 40 Rue Charles Morin, **t** 02 35 50 75 55 (*dishes c. €5–8*). A popular daytime *crêperie* and café in Eu town centre with a relaxing feel and enjoyable light dishes that have a nice touch of home cooking. As well as varied crêpes there are sandwiches, salads, pasta dishes at lunchtime and moreish own-made cakes. *Open Mon–Sat 11–6, closed Sun.*

Mers-les-Bains ✉ 80350

Le Poissonnier, Hôtel Bellevue, 24 Esplanade du Général Leclerc, **t** 02 35 86 12 89, *www.aubellevue.com* (*menus €13–37*). Mers-les-Bains is something of a celebration of the eternal virtues of the French seaside, and the Hôtel Bellevue's restaurant suits it perfectly – a big seaside brasserie all in white and light blue, with lots of terrace tables under sunshades on the prom and extremely generous menus that offer fine fish and seafood in all sorts of classic combinations, from simple portions to exuberant mixed *plateaux*. Many other options are catered for too, with salads, snacks – including a *ficelle picarde*, since Mers is on the Picardy side of the Bresle – and meat grills. Settle into a platter of prawns, crab and lobster and a bottle of perfectly-chilled white wine, and watch the seafront-strollers go by.

Mesnil-Val ✉ 76910

Hostellerie de la Vieille Ferme, 23 Rue de la Mer, Criel-sur-Mer, **t** 02 35 86 72 18 (*menus €17–49*). The lovely dining room at the Vieille Ferme (*see p.147*) has the full ensemble of black-and-white timbering and stone door-ways to let you know you're in Normandy, plus neat table settings and lots of fresh flowers. The kitchen equally concentrates on Norman classics, with a *menu du terroir* that might include *marmite pêcheur* and *poulet fermier vallée d'auge*, and opulent *plateaux* of fresh local seafood. Very traditional, but satisfying. *Closed Sun eve and Mon, and Jan.*

St-Martin-le-Gaillard ✉ 76260

Le Moulin de Becquerel, **t** 02 35 86 74 94 (*carte average €26*). Between St Martin-le-Gaillard and St-Sulpice, a steep driveway turns off down to this riverside mill. The dining room is charming, and outside there are tables on a terrace. There's no set menu, only a *carte*, of good-value Norman favourites. At week-ends wedding parties and family outings may raise the volume a bit. *Closed June–Sept Sun eve and Mon; Oct–May Sun eve–Wed.*

Le Tréport ✉ 76470

La Matelote, 34 Quai François I, **t** 02 35 86 01 13 (*menus €12.05–38.10*). One of the biggest and most comfortable of the seafood specialists on Tréport quay, with first-floor *salle panoramique* with a view across to Mers-les-Bains. All the seafood classics – fish and seafood stews, *moules* – are nicely done, and for a feast you can tackle superb *plateaux de fruits de mer. Closed Tues eve.*

Le Riche Lieu, 50 Quai François I, **t** 02 35 86 26 55 (*menus €12.50–21.50*). A convivial seafood (of course) brasserie that's one of the best-value spots of the many on Tréport quay. Especially good are its exuberant platters with enough for two or more for around €24, ideal for a long, exploratory lunch.

Mon P'tit Bar, 3–5 Rue de la Rade, **t** 02 35 86 28 78 (*menus €10.80–15.80*). On the corner of a turning off Quai François I – but still with a harbour view from many tables – this big, bright brasserie has a friendly feel and serves food until late. Its seafood classics – *moules*, lobster, grilled fish – are not adventurous, but can't be beaten on price.

Pirates, Painters and Gardens:

Dieppe and the Caux Maritime

15

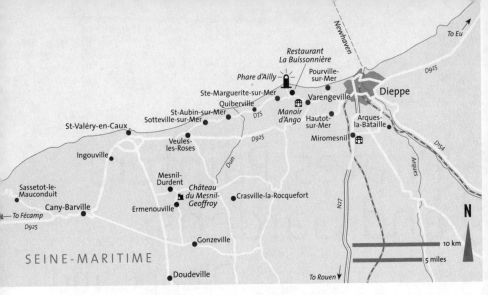

Dieppe is one of those Channel ports that are well worth exploring. It's a small city, with an old centre of narrow streets and little alleys, and still a busy, living port. Its name comes from the Old Norse for 'deep', and the deep-water harbour, the mouth of the River Arques, comes right into the middle of town, lined with cafés, restaurants and shops, so that, uniquely among Norman ports, it has something of the bustle and edge of a Mediterranean seaport town. Dieppe also has one of Normandy's very best town markets, eye-catching food shops and a buzzing café- and night-life.

The town has always lived, in different ways, from the sea: 17th-century Dieppe seamen sailed to Canada, while others brought back spices, ivory and other rarities from every point on the compass. Later, in the 1820s, Dieppe was the first town in France to follow Brighton and become a seaside resort. Its history has also been bound up with England. In the Middle Ages it was the chief port for English pilgrims on their way to Santiago or Rome, and post-Napoleon Dieppe had the first ever regular cross-Channel steam ferry service, in 1825. It was, too, an extraordinary focus of attraction for artists, British and French: Pissarro, Sickert and a long list of other painters all extolled the qualities of Dieppe's limpid, sea-coast light, and the town was a unique point of contact between the British and French art worlds.

The area stretching away to the west, with its distinctive small towns and villages, is known as the Caux Maritime. The shoreline consists of an almost continual line of cliffs, at the top of which you abruptly come to a massive, flat plateau, a land of giant, open horizons. Breaks in the cliff – of which Dieppe's own inlet is the largest – are like little oases, often remarkably lush, and each one is entirely different from any other. The Seine-Maritime is, too, the garden capital of France, and clustered around Dieppe are some of the most luxuriant, unusual and inventive examples in the country.

In food matters, Dieppe is predictably most famous for fish and seafood – especially served with the classic *dieppoise* sauce combining Norman cream with white wine and mushrooms. It also has a record of culinary variety, and in the beautiful village of Varengeville there is in **La Buissonnière**, a restaurant that for stylish originality and sophisticated, light, modern food stands out very much from the crowd.

Getting There

Ferries arrive at a terminal on the east side of Dieppe harbour; from there follow signs for *Centre Ville*. Parking is free on the fish quay and on the seafront, and cheap everywhere else. There are free courtesy buses for ferry foot passengers to the town centre. Driving from the north, leave the A16 *autoroute* near Abbeville and take the D925 via Eu.

To get to Varengeville, find the seafront Bd de Verdun and turn left, then left again by the castle to Place des Martyrs. A right turn following signs for Pourville and Varengeville leads to the Route de Pourville (D75), which runs along the cliffs through Varengeville. Look for a turning right signed to Cap d'Ailly and Phare d'Ailly lighthouse. La Buissonière is a little way up this road on the left.

There are several **trains** daily to Dieppe from Paris St-Lazare via Rouen. From Dieppe bus station (by the train station, just south of the harbour) local **bus 60/61** runs along the coast to Fécamp, via Varengeville, Veules, St-Valery and other points en route (*Mon–Sat only*).

For some **car hire** companies in Dieppe, *see* chapter 3. To phone for a **taxi** (which run to towns on the coast), call **t** 02 35 84 20 05.

Tourist Information

Dieppe: Pont Jehan Ango, **t** 02 32 14 40 60, *www.dieppetourisme.com*. The office is easy to find next to the Ango bridge, in the middle of the harbour.
Pourville-Varengeville: Rue des Verts Bois, Pourville, **t** 02 35 84 71 06.
St-Valéry-en-Caux: Maison Henri IV, **t** 02 35 97 00 63, *www.cauxmaritime.com*.
Veules-les-Roses: 12 Rue du Marché, **t** 02 35 97 63 05, *www.veules-les-roses.fr*.

La Buissonnière

Route du Phare d'Ailly, Varengeville-sur-Mer, **t/f** *02 35 83 17 13*.
Open Tues–Sat 12–2 and 7–9.30, Sun 12–2; closed Mon and Jan, Feb.
Menus €30–€44; carte *average €45*.

Varengeville-sur-Mer's fame as a beauty spot is due to a special combination of features: its location on top of giant cliffs, with superb views out to sea; a unique mix of fine architecture, from its Norman clifftop church to Edwin Lutyens' Bois des Moutiers house; an exceptional lushness; and the way in which the narrow lanes of the village wind up, down and along steep, snug little valleys full of densely packed woods, only to bring you out suddenly before sweeping views over the sea or the valleys to the south. Varengeville has attracted not only painters like Monet or Braque, but also plenty of well-heeled home-buyers, so that half-hidden among the trees there are some very grand and opulent houses and villas, often with elaborate *Belle Epoque* details. There are gardens everywhere, not just the publicized ones that are open to visitors. West of the village, towards Cap d'Ailly and its lighthouse, these woods give way to quite wild forest, which is much appreciated by walkers.

La Buissonnière, near the beginning of the Cap d'Ailly road, could just be the most ravishingly pretty restaurant imaginable. It occupies a neat 1930s villa surrounded by a luxuriant garden, shielded by tall hedges. Its owner Marijo Colombel is the kind of Frenchwoman who could be described as incorrigibly chic, but not at all in any icy way, for she has a charming smile and a warm generosity. Her house is the same. The dining room, in tasteful whites and pale greens and bathed in light through big windows, has a distinctive style – it has been featured in several design and décor magazines – but, again, is utterly comfortable rather than exhibiting any notion of design for its own sake. In summer the tables to have are the ones on shaded verandas around the sides of the house, ideal for a leisurely meal feeling the soft breeze through the trees and taking in all the colours of the garden, which for months at a time seems to explode with roses.

Mme Colombel used to work in marketing in Paris, but came to live here permanently a few years ago, in what had been a weekend home. She began the 'restaurant' on an informal basis, doing all the cooking herself. Word got around, and as the business grew she took on a chef, Ludovique Amart. They develop the menus together, combining her ideas and home cooking and his professional restaurant skills. She describes the Buissonnière's style as *cuisine de femme* – much lighter, more modern and more varied than the traditional local dishes, and with a touch of fantasy to reflect the style of the house, Varengeville and its gardens.

The menus are compact but still offer a wide choice. Dishes feature full, clear flavours, and local ingredients are expertly sourced. From the main menu, one of the restaurant's creations, a *mille-feuille* of aubergines with courgettes and a tomato fondue, makes a wonderfully refreshing summer starter, assembled from superbly fresh vegetables cooked with the exact balance of tenderness and crunch. To follow, the day's fish special, small turbot (*turbotin*) is beautifully cooked in an addictive, multi-layered mix of herbs, and served *aux petits légumes*, with more supremely fresh spring vegetables and ultra-delicate potato purée (in other words, the very finest mash). The menu is tilted towards fish and seafood, but also among the regulars are fine duck dishes, such as a clever *magret* of duck with apples, pepper and honey.

Mille-Feuille d'Aubergine à la Fondue de Tomate

Serves 4

2 large aubergines
1 courgette
6 large tomatoes
3 garlic cloves
100g/3½oz grated parmesan
1 bunch of basil
4 tablespoons olive oil

Cut the aubergines and the courgette lengthways into slices about 1 centimetre thick, and brown in about 1 spoonful of oil for 2 minutes.

Skin the tomatoes by first placing them in hot water, and then seed them and chop them finely. Finely chop the garlic and the basil. Cook the tomatoes in a frying pan with 3 spoonfuls of oil, salt and pepper, and the garlic and the basil.

Assemble the *mille-feuilles* on a greased baking tray. For each one, first place a slice of aubergine, pour onto it a tablespoon of the tomato fondue, add two slices of courgette, then sprinkle with parmesan. Repeat the same sequence for each *mille-feuille*. Then place them in the oven for 10 minutes at 220°C/425°F/Gas Mark 7.

Serve on a bed of lettuce, lightly dressed with olive oil, salt and pepper.

For the cheese course, the house speciality is roast Neufchâtel with toast, the cooking drawing out the cheese's punchy flavour. Desserts may be light, but this doesn't stop them being both intricate and luxurious, as in a house speciality, liquorice ice-cream with *pain d'épice*, or the utterly exquisite *croquant à la mousse chocolat et sorbet mandarine* – a mandarin sorbet that seems like the distilled essence of orange flavours, combined with just slightly bitter, slightly crunchy chocolate, and served so beautifully no one could avoid stopping to admire it before eating. And afterwards, since there's nothing here to weigh you down, you can take a walk through the woods by the lighthouse at the end of the road, to see more great views from the cliffs out to sea.

Touring Around

If you arrive in **Dieppe** on a Saturday morning, make straight for the centre of town and the ample Place Nationale, the adjacent Place St-Jacques around the church of the same name, and the Grande Rue, the now-pedestrianized main street that runs through the old town from the harbour quays. All three and many of the smaller streets in between are taken over by Dieppe's wonderful **market**, with a seemingly endless array of fruit, sausages, vegetables – particularly fine garlic and salad greens – fresh flowers, herbs, terrines, cheeses, cider and butter, as well as clothes, bargain-basement shoes and other miscellanea. It attracts farm producers from all over the surrounding region, and is one of the best places to find the highest quality, fresh Norman specialities – especially superb Neufchâtel and other cheeses – as well as produce from other parts of France, such as olives, oils and honeys. There is a smaller market on Tuesdays, Wednesdays and Thursdays, especially in summer.

The market thins out after about 1pm, but Dieppe's shops are also impressive, especially – unusually for a town of this size – for luxury foods. Dieppe is known for chocolate and sweets, and the Grande Rue contains several spectacular *chocolatiers*.

From the market squares, several short, narrow streets connect with the **port**, just to the east. This area had become run-down by the 1980s, but since then substantial renovation work has been set in motion. The tall brick or stone buildings that line the harbour side are distinctive, most of them built in the 18th century after a great part of the medieval town had been burnt down in an attack by an Anglo-Dutch fleet in 1694. Their stone-colonnaded arcades provide a special element in the harbour's atmosphere. The **Quai Henri IV**, the continuation of the Grande-Rue along the north side of the harbour, is now Dieppe's foremost visitor-magnet, lined nearly end-to-end by cafés and fish restaurants with the requisite quayside terrace tables.

Dieppe long had the most impressive approach of any of the Channel ports: from the 1850s until 1994 the Newhaven ferry sailed right into the harbour to dock (the new ferry terminal is just outside the main harbour, on the eastern side). In the absence of ferries, part of the outer harbour alongside Quai Henri IV, the **Avant-Port**, has become a yacht marina, but the business of the port – the movement of ships, cargoes and little boats – is still an integral feature of the town centre. If you carry on inland down Quai Duquesne or across to the Quai du Carénage, on the **Ile du Pollet** in the middle of the harbour, you can walk alongside the **fishing quays**, where most mornings you can see a dazzling array of superbly fresh fish and shellfish being unloaded, and equally dazzling stalls selling the day's catch, especially scallops.

Dieppe's 'deep inlet' was one of the first points on the French coast discovered by the Vikings as they raided southwards, but it really became an important port to the Normans after their conquest of England. It grew to a substantial size during the Middle Ages, both as a port on the road to Santiago and as a stronghold that was fought over several times during the Hundred Years' War. Its greatest expansion, however, came in the 16th and 17th centuries, when Dieppe seamen were among the first in northern Europe to join in the vogue for exploration and sail to other continents. In the 1520s, when they sought to join the trade with Africa and the East Indies, they found their way blocked by the Portuguese, who had arrived first. A Dieppe shipbuilder, Jean (or Jehan, in the old Norman spelling) Ango, was authorized by François I of France to raise a fleet of privateers, which battered the Portuguese into submission in a semi-private war. Ango died Dieppe's richest man and has been a local hero ever since, and his name still crops up all over town.

Its long prominence as a port is an essential part of Dieppe's individual character. In the 15th century, Venetian sailors on voyages between the Mediterranean and Flanders used Dieppe as a haven, and many are said to have settled in the district of Pollet and its island on the east side of the harbour, contributing Italian words to the local dialect. The Dieppois were associated with being unconventional, and a bit chippy and rebellious by comparison with their traditionalist neighbours inland. In the 16th and 17th centuries Dieppe had a large Protestant community, among them one of the town's greatest mariners, Abraham Duquesne, who became the effective head of Louis XIV's navy, even though as a Protestant he was not able to hold the post officially. More recently Dieppe's chippiness was expressed in growing frustration at the decline of the Newhaven-Dieppe ferry route. In the days when this provided the fastest rail-and-boat link between London and Paris it was the fashionable route of choice, but the expensive 1994 renovation of Dieppe's ferry port was not matched by any comparable investment on the other side. In 1999, following constant badgering from Dieppe, the Seine-Maritime *département* began the process of acquiring Newhaven ferry harbour to run it themselves and setting up the Transmanche Ferries service to run year-round, to add to the April to October Hoverspeed services.

Returning into town from the port, you will almost inevitably wander back to the market squares and Dieppe's largest church, **St-Jacques**, the pinnacles and buttresses of which loom up at the end of many streets and alleys. It's in need of restoration, but impressive nonetheless. The oldest part is the 13th-century nave, but its greatest feature is the 14th-century rose window on the west front, especially beautiful in the evening light. The line of chapels around the church were mostly built as donations by Dieppe shipowners in the 16th century, including one, the Sacré-Cœur, with very fine late-Gothic vaulting, and another with the tomb of Jehan Ango himself.

From the church, Rue St-Jacques leads off to meet up with the Grande-Rue in the intimate **Place du Puits-Salé**, the centre of Dieppe outside market hours. It is presided over by the **Café des Tribunaux**, one of the truly grand French traditional cafés. First built as a *cabaret* in the 18th century, it looks like something much more official, and did indeed serve as Dieppe's town hall at one time. As a café, it was an important place to be in the years when Dieppe acquired its artistic community. One of the first painters to come here was the English artist, long resident in France, Richard Bonington, who encouraged his friends Turner and Delacroix to visit Dieppe and paint its sea and sky in the 1820s. Later, Monet painted the church of St-Jacques, and Pissarro street scenes; other artists seen in Dieppe were Whistler, Renoir, Gauguin, William Nicholson, Degas and especially the latter's friend Walter Sickert, a near-fixture in the town over 40 years, who did much to introduce Impressionist ideas into English art (some, notably the author Patricia Cornwell, maintain that Sickert was actually Jack the Ripper and that his long stays in Dieppe cafés were really due to his need to avoid detection in England, but whether or not you follow this theory is a personal choice). In the 20th century, Braque, Miró and Barbara Hepworth were also drawn to Dieppe, and virtually all of them passed at some time or other through the Tribunaux. One figure most often associated with the place was Oscar Wilde. He first visited Dieppe in happier circumstances in 1878, invited by Sickert, and came back here, broken and depressed, immediately after his release from prison in 1897. He stayed for several months, spending long hours in cafés, and it is a matter of argument whether he wrote *The Ballad of Reading Gaol* in the Tribunaux or the competing Café Suisse by the port.

After an apéritif at the Tribunaux, it may be time to go out to Varengeville for lunch. Otherwise, or if you are coming back into town, continue west from Place du Puits-Salé to the end of Rue de la Barre or any of the old streets parallel to it, where all roads immediately begin to climb a steep hill, crowned by Dieppe's dramatic castle, which can be seen glowering down at you from many places in the town. It is now the **Château-Musée** (*open June–Sept daily 10–12 and 2–6; Oct–May Mon and Wed–Sat 10–12 and 2–5, Sun 10–12 and 2–6; closed Tues; adm*). Built mainly in the 14th and 15th centuries, the castle is a rambling medieval complex of ramparts, rooms, turrets and side-towers, with great views over the town and the sea.

The collection inside is an attractive mixture that, apart from a few nautical exhibits and an entertaining display on the history of sea bathing in Dieppe, mostly divides into two halves. One is made up of paintings, especially by artists associated with Dieppe; Renoirs, Boudins, Pissarros, Sickerts and an important collection of prints by Braque. Its greatest treasure, however, is its extraordinary collection of Dieppe ivories. When Dieppe was at its commercial height in the 17th century, its sailors wandered the coast of Africa trading for ivory tusks, which were brought back and worked on here by local carvers, renowned throughout Europe for their skill. They produced combs, fans, crucifixes, thimbles, pens, decorative scenes and all kinds of other articles in fine ivory; all are represented here, and, whatever you feel about the fate of the elephants, reveal a quite staggering level of painstaking, sensitive workmanship.

From the castle, take the steps down the seaward side of the hill to reach the sea front. At the foot of the hill is **Square du Canada**, which commemorates both the 'Canadian Martyrs' – Jesuit missionaries killed by Indians in Quebec in the 17th century – and the terrible military mess of the Dieppe Raid of 19 August 1942, when a predominantly Canadian force of 6,000 men paid an appalling price – three-quarters of them killed, wounded or captured – to demonstrate to the Allied commanders that a frontal assault on a Channel port was not a viable prospect. Dieppe's pretty and recently-restored 19th-century theatre on Rue du Commandant Fayolle, the **Petit Théâtre** (*open late May–mid Sept Mon and Wed–Sun 2–7, closed Tues; adm*) now houses a small museum on the events of 1942. Between there and the Square du Canada, next to the modern casino, there is a massive stone gateway, the **Porte des Tourelles**, which is the only remaining part of Dieppe's 14th-century walls.

In Dieppe the line of hotels and houses looking seawards along the promenade, Boulevard de Verdun, is a considerable distance from the actual sea front; the space between them is occupied by a mini-golf course, a *jardin d'enfants*, a swimming pool, tennis courts and the inevitable thalassotherapy centre. The beach is shingle, but is one of the closest to Paris, which was an important factor in prompting the Duchesse de Berry to introduce the English fad of sea-bathing into France here in 1824. Despite the rise of Deauville and the more ostentatious *Côte Fleurie*, Dieppe remained fashionable throughout the next century. Nowadays the seafront's grandeur seems a little faded, but like all old seaside resorts it still has plenty going on in summer. It also has a more modern attraction in the **Estran-Cité de la Mer** (*open daily 10–12 and 2–6; adm*), at the very eastern end of the front, an aquarium and exhibition on all things to do with the sea, with lots to do for kids.

Of the many attractions around Dieppe, one of the most distinguished is the **Château de Miromesnil** (*open May–Sept Mon and Wed–Sun 2–6; closed Tues; adm*), about 10km due south of the town near the N27 Rouen road . Begun in 1589, it's a very elegant example of a Henri IV-style, brick and stone château. The house had two famous residents: the Marquis de Miromesnil, one of the enlightened ministers of Louis XVI who attempted ineffectually to reform the *Ancien Régime* in the years leading up to the French Revolution, and Guy de Maupassant, who was born here in 1850. This happened rather by accident, since his father was given to living above his means and rented several châteaux and other residences around the region, and the family moved on from Miromesnil four years later. Particularly impressive, though, are the lush grounds and gardens outside, and especially the approach, an immensely long beech-lined avenue. In the woods of the park there is a lovely 12th-century chapel, with fine 16th-century wood panelling inside. The château can only be visited by taking the sometimes-eccentric guided tours.

Otherwise, follow the D75 coast road west from Dieppe. **Pourville** is a pleasant, relaxed little beach village, in a broader-than-usual gap in the cliffs, which is why it was chosen as one of the main landing beaches for the 1942 Dieppe Raid. In a more peaceful time it was particularly loved by Claude Monet, who rented a house and painted here with Alice Hoschedé in the 1880s before they made their definitive home in Giverny. In **Varengeville**, the next village along, the closest artistic associations are with Georges Braque, who lived here for 20 years until his death in 1963. He is buried in the little churchyard, the *Cimetière Marin*, along with a Napoleonic soldier who from his gravestone seems to have been present at an implausible number of battles. It is in an extraordinary location on top of one of the area's tallest cliffs, next to Varengeville's beautiful 12th-century church – now carefully shored up to prevent it sliding towards the sea. The church is marvellously peaceful, and has stained glass panels by Braque that combine wonderfully with the early-medieval structure. The view of the coast and the sea, with colours that shift continually from turquoise to grey, green or deep blue, is only one of Varengeville's celebrated features.

Now more of a smart residential community than a rural village, it also has two other special attractions. Just inland is the **Manoir d'Ango** (*open mid-Mar–mid-Nov daily 10–12.30 and 2–6.30; adm*), the grand and never-quite-finished palace that Dieppe's pirate-prince Jehan Ango had built with his ill-gotten gains, in another dramatic location atop a hill. It's a remarkable construction: a combination of Loire Valley-style French Renaissance château with finely worked Italian touches and a rustic Norman half-timbered manor house. In the great courtyard there's a giant drum that is France's largest pigeon loft (as symbols of wealth and status big pigeon lofts were the equivalent of a Mercedes and Rolex watches for 16th-century Norman aristocrats). Inside the house there is little to see (it is still a private residence), but next to it there is now a magnificently colourful hydrangea garden, oddly named **Shamrock** (*open mid-June–mid-Sept Mon, Wed–Sun 10–12 and 2.30–6, Tues 2.30–6; mid–end-June daily 2.30–6; adm*). It takes full advantage of the superb setting.

Varengeville's most renowned and unusual house and garden, though, is the **Bois des Moutiers** (*open 15 Mar–15 Nov; tickets sold 10–12 and 2–6, gardens open daily 10–7; adm; house tours by appointment*), a unique Anglo-French hybrid. It was built in 1898 for Guillaume Mallet, a wealthy Anglophile banker, by the subsequently distinguished English architect Edwin Lutyens and the garden designer Gertrude Jekyll. It is the only English Arts and Crafts house in France, and Jekyll's garden similarly flies in the face of formal French traditions. Architect and garden designer worked closely together, and each part is inseparable from the other. Both are fabulous. The house (*guided tours only*) is not simply a transplanted English building, but includes local Norman features – sometimes quite playfully – and remarkably combines a medievalist feel with a futuristic look, such as the wonderfully lofty and elegant music room. The garden, created from nothing and beatifully moulded to the contours of the hillsides, is ravishing, especially in May and June. Guillaume Mallet and his wife were also followers of the pan-religious movement the theosophists, and around house and garden there are occult touches, such as the circle of trees upon a knoll, probably created in imitation of a druidic circle. The house is still owned by the Mallet family, and the very affable Antoine Bouchayer-Mallet takes many of the guided tours.

Beyond Varengeville the road continues a little inland from the cliff tops. At **Sotteville**, about 15km further west, a turning seawards comes to an abrupt end above a steep gash in the rock, where a staircase of 230 steps provides the sole access to the beach, a magically atmospheric spot with crashing waves and fabulous views. A little further west again there is another of the area's special places, spectacularly pretty **Veules-les-Roses**, built along 'the smallest river in France', the Veules. This was another of the apparently endless number of places in France that was first brought to the attention of the world at large by Victor Hugo, and later was much appreciated by the Impressionists. Its little river runs for just one kilometre along a steep dip in the cliff, but picks up surprising force, which for centuries has been used to power a series of small mills, as well as to sustain the dainty watercress beds that are another characteristic of the town. Go past Veules along the main road and you may scarcely notice it: it's essential to stop and explore it on foot, along the '**Circuit de la Veules**' beside the river. The sheltered valley is extraordinarily lush, and the whole place is almost impossibly pretty, with thatched half-timbered mills and 19th-century villas forming an almost unreal, miniature town. The centre of the village is less *petite* but almost as attractive, and has a very unusual 16th-century Gothic church, **St-Martin**, with curious sculptures on its columns that do not represent any recognizable Christian imagery; one theory suggests they were influenced by pre-Columbian carvings seen by local mariners in the Americas. Veules also has a tiny beach.

St-Valery-en-Caux, capital of the Caux Maritime, was the site of bitter fighting in June 1940, when it was defended by French troops and the British 51st Highland Division, cut off from the main British force which had retreated to Dunkirk – which is why the town is now twinned with Inverness. Much of it had to be completely rebuilt post-war, but the old **Quartier des Pénitents** by the west bank of the harbour survived, a little knot of narrow alleys with a Gothic church and, by the quay, the giant 1540 half-timbered **Maison Henri IV**, which now houses the tourist office and a small museum. Otherwise, modern St-Valery is a likeable, busy fishing and yachting port, with plenty of movement in the harbour and a pebble beach at the foot of its cliffs.

Inland from Veules and St-Valery, the Valley of the Dun and the Caux plateau can appear superficially bleak, but anyone wishing to lose themselves in a rural world can easily spend an entertaining afternoon wandering in no particular direction between the villages, past half-timbered cottages, solid grey sandstone churches and village ponds and greens. It's a land of isolated villages glimpsed between clumps of trees in the misty flatness, with its own distinctive traditions, an area that provided much of the material for the rural tales of Maupassant. And in virtually every village there is the glimpse of a Baroque château in isolated grandeur at the end of its *allée* of trees, for the Caux seems to have the highest concentration of baronial residences anywhere in Normandy. Villages with striking châteaux or manors include **Gonzeville**, **Crasville-le-Rocquefort** and especially **Ermenouville**, built almost entirely around its giant 18th-century château (*only open for France's national heritage weekend, in Sept*). And near Mesnil-Durdent – around 10km from St-Valery and the smallest municipality in the Seine-Maritime, with just 27 inhabitants – there is one of the grandest of the region's mansions, the **Château de Mesnil-Geoffroy** (*open May–Sept Fri–Sun and hols 2.30–6; park and rose garden only open June–mid-July Mon, Fri–Sun and hols 2.30–6; adm*). It was built in the 17th century in Louis XIII style and greatly extended in the 18th, when it was the residence of one of Louis XV's ministers. The current owners, Prince and Princesse Kayali, have taken great pains to restore both the décor the house wore in its grandest incarnation and the huge Le Nôtre-style gardens, with maze, aviary and a very celebrated rose garden. Visitors can see the house with a tour, and wander freely around the park. What's more, you can also stay as guests, for Mesnil-Geoffroy is one of France's most opulent *chambres d'hôtes* (*see* right).

Shopping

The Saturday **market** is the great target for shoppers in **Dieppe**, but there are some stalls in the town centre mid-week as well. The best shopping streets are the Grande-Rue, Rue St-Jacques and Rue d'Ecosse. Other attractive markets are in **Veules-les-Roses** (*Wed*), and **St-Valery-en-Caux** (*Fri, and Sun in summer*).

For convenience shopping, the big centre in Dieppe is the **Belvédère shopping mall**, beside a roundabout on the Rouen road out of town, with a well-stocked Auchan. Two more hypermarkets, Intermarché and Leclerc, are nearby.

Dieppe ✉ 76200

La Centrale des Vins, 56 Route de l'Ancien Port, Etran-Martin-Eglise, **t** 02 35 84 28 71. One of Dieppe's best large-scale wine and drinks outlets, with over 300 wines and helpful staff. It's in a suburb just south of town, but signs lead you to it.

Divernet, 138 Grande-Rue, **t** 02 35 84 13 87. The most opulent of Dieppe's chocolate specialists, with a magnetic display of handmade chocolates, biscuits and pastries, and also a brasserie, *traiteur* and *salon de thé*.

L'Epicier Olivier, 18 Rue St-Jacques, **t** 02 35 84 22 55. Claude Olivier is brother to Philippe, the near-legendary Boulogne master cheese-merchant, but his marvellous old shop is not as specialized: as well as the fine cheeses maturing in the *caves* beneath the shop – including the best local Neufchâtel – there's a great range of coffees, fine wines, ciders, preserves and many other delicacies.

Le Sommelier, 27 Rue des Maillots, **t** 02 35 06 05 20. In a narrow street off Rue St-Jacques, this attractive wine merchant has a wide-ranging stock of French wines, brandies and liqueurs, and regularly offers tastings.

Where to Stay

Dieppe ✉ 76200

Villa des Capucins, 11 Rue des Capucins, **t** 02 35 82 16 52, *www.mediazoom.com/capucins* (*rooms €59 for two, €95 for four*). On a workaday street in the old fishing quarter of Le Pollet, Mme Ghislaine Boré's *chambres d'hôtes* gives little away from the outside. Inside the gate, though, is a big enclosed garden, with a turreted 19th-century house at the end. It was formerly a Capuchin convent, and the comfortable, cleverly decorated guest rooms are in former outbuildings beside the garden. Breakfast is served in the antique-filled main house, and Mme Boré takes great care of her guests.

Hôtel-Restaurant Au Grand Duquesne, 15 Place St-Jacques, **t** 02 32 14 61 10, *www.augrandduquesne.fr* (*double rooms €29–43*). A classic *Logis* hotel in the heart of old Dieppe, near St-Jacques, renovated after being damaged by a fire in 2004. Excellent for getting an instant shot of French town life, and the street outside isn't usually noisy at night. Rooms are cosy and comfortable, and there's a good **restaurant** (*see* p.160).

Bar-Hôtel l'Entracte, 39 Rue du Commandant Fayolle, **t** 02 35 84 26 45 (*double rooms €28–32*). Dieppe's favourite budget choice, by the castle and the casino, is equally popular with travelling students and Canadian war veterans, whose insignia decorates the bar. All rooms have some sort of sea view, and are plain but comfortable. Owners Michel and Jocelyne are very *sympa*, and breakfast is served in the bar downstairs, a real neighbourhood café.

Ermenouville ✉ 76740

Château du Mesnil-Geoffroy, **t** 02 35 57 12 77, *www.chateau-mesnil-geoffroy.com* (*rooms €65–110 for two, breakfast extra, €9.20 per person*). For a taste of the *Ancien Régime*, try some of France's most sumptuous *chambres d'hôtes*, in a remarkable private château (*see* left). The five rooms combine magnificent Louis XVI décor with fine modern bathrooms and other necessities, and have exquisite views of the rose garden. Princesse Kayali is a gracious hostess, and gourmet dinners based on 18th-century recipes can be arranged. A special experience.

Ingouville-sur-Mer ✉ 76119

Mer et Campagne, 49 Grande Rue, **t** 02 35 57 26 45 *http://site.voila.fr/meretcampagne* (*rooms €40 for two*). A modernized Caux farmhouse in a tranquil location about 3km west of St-Valéry. There are four bright B&B rooms with double or twin beds, and extra beds can be added. Nathalie and Christian Ouin and their young family set a relaxed atmosphere, there are lots of animals around, and it's very popular with families.

Pourville-sur-Mer ✉ 76550

Les Hauts de Pourville, Mme Colette Marchand, t 02 35 84 14 29, www.gite-pourville.com (rooms €41–45 for two). Mme Marchand has three B&B rooms in her modern house on the cliffs above Pourville, with fabulous views and – a rare extra – a heated indoor pool. The rooms, decorated with her paintings, are very spacious and comfortable.

Varengeville-sur-Mer ✉ 76119

Les Catamurons, Route de l'Eglise, t 02 35 85 14 34, www.catamurons.com (rooms €43–60 for two). Two very pretty, light B&B rooms in an old chaumière cottage with garden in one of the leafy lanes of Varengeville. The ground-floor double has a kitchenette; the upstairs room can sleep 2–4. Owners Jean-Jacques and Emma Verchère are very helpful.

Veules-les-Roses ✉ 76780

Relais Douce France, 13 Rue du Docteur Girard, t 02 35 57 85 30, www.doucefrance.fr (suites €85–150 for two, €190 for four). In the middle of Veules, beside the babbling river, this imposing old coaching inn with fortified gateway has been attractively restored to become a non-conventional hotel. It's made up of large, very comfortable suites and apartments, sleeping 2–4, several with kitchenettes. There's no full restaurant, but a lovely salon de thé (dishes c. €10) with light meals, and tables on a flower-filled terrace.

Eating Alternatives

Dieppe ✉ 76200

A la Marmite Dieppoise, 8 Rue St-Jean, t 02 35 84 24 26 (menus €27–40). An unchanging old-fashioned restaurant near the port, known as the place to try Dieppe's classic dish the eponymous marmite dieppoise – a powerful stew of fish, scallops and other seafood in a Norman cream sauce. It can sound like overkill, but done well it's delicious. Closed Sun eve and Mon.

Restaurant du Port, 99 Quai Henri IV, t 02 35 84 36 64 (menus €16–29). Near the end of Quai Henri IV – restaurant row – the bright little restaurant of award-winning chef Michel Mouny serves imaginative food that's a cut above the harbourside norm. Fish and seafood are of course highlights, but there's a range of other alternatives. Excellent value.

Hôtel-Restaurant Au Grand Duquesne, 15 Place St-Jacques, t 02 32 14 61 10, www.augrand-duquesne.fr (menus €12–28). The Grand Duquesne's popular restaurant serves excellent seafood – including a celebrated marmite dieppoise – and offers a range of menus at amenable prices. Great for taking in the atmosphere on market day.

Le Bistrôt du Pollet, 23 Rue Tête de Bœuf, t 02 35 84 68 57 (carte average €23). A pretty, unassuming little bistro on the Ile du Pollet that's very highly regarded by locals. There's no set menu, only a chalked-up carte, but prices are a bargain. Skilfully-prepared fish and seafood is the bistro's forte, plus a few meat mains. Very popular, so get there early or book. Closed Sun and Mon.

Café Suisse, 19 Arcades de la Bourse, t 02 35 84 10 69 (lunch menu €13). Dieppe's 'other' historic café, in the arcades by the corner of the Grande-Rue, now has little in it that Oscar Wilde would recognize. The current owners have opened it up to a few global influences with vegetarian dishes as well as brasserie classics, organic foods and drinks, and even English breakfasts.

Café des Tribunaux, 1 Place Puits-Salé, t 02 32 14 44 65 (dishes c. €6–15). The legendary Tribunaux (see p.155) has a brasserie menu plus a few seafood dishes and snacks. Its outside tables are a great vantage point on Dieppe's street life; inside, there's plenty of animated chatter in the dark-wood booths, despite all the ghosts that linger there.

Veules-les-Roses ✉ 76780

Les Galets, 3 Rue Victor Hugo, t 02 35 97 61 33 (menus €30–70). A much-admired restaurant near the sea where chef Gilbert Plaisance produces imaginative modern variants on Norman cuisine. Being in Veules, it's extremely pretty, with a distinctly romantic garden. Closed Tues and Wed.

Benedictine Luxuries:
Fécamp and Etretat

16

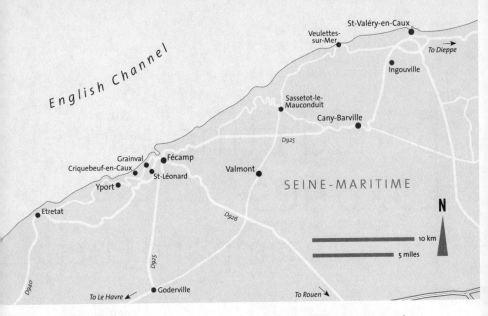

Some towns are conventionally pretty, all scenery and fine architecture, or have distinctive museums or cultural monuments; some may be no beauties but are strong on life and atmosphere. Others manage to combine a little of all these qualities in different measures. One such is Fécamp. Like Dieppe and the other ports of northern Normandy it sits in a gash in the long chalk cliff that lines this coast, dubbed the *Côte d'Albâtre* (Alabaster). At Fécamp the break in the cliffs is especially narrow, so that they stand huge, white and impressive above the town, squeezing most of it into a snug valley running inland. Its harbour is similarly an inlet much longer than it is wide, still very much a working port with a fishing fleet, but now shared by an increasing number of yachts. At the end of the harbour, beneath the cliffs, is the giant shingle bank of the beach, backed by a traditional French seaside prom, where if you don't fancy windsurfing you can stroll and watch the gulls soaring against the wind.

In the year 1001 Duke Richard II of Normandy established one of the largest Benedictine abbeys in France in Fécamp, and during the Middle Ages it was among the most important pilgrimage centres in Europe, thanks to its shrine of the Precious Blood of Christ, believed to have been deposited here by Joseph of Arimathea. Fécamp was also one of the favoured capitals of the Norman dukes, and William the Conqueror threw lavish revels here at Easter 1067 to celebrate his conquest of England. Much later, it became a gritty deep-sea fishing port, whose men sailed off for months at a time to search for cod on the other side of the Atlantic. From the 1830s on it also followed in the footsteps of Brighton and Dieppe and became one of the first seaside resorts, but Fécamp is marked out from all other towns along this coast by one unique, slightly mad feature, the result of the epic fancy of one man: the neo-Renaissance-Gothic-Baroque palace, museum and distillery that is the home of Bénédictine liqueur.

Getting There

Fécamp is about a 40min drive from Le Havre on the D925 via Goderville (or longer on the more attractive D940 coast road through Etretat), slightly further from Dieppe (also on the D925). From Calais and the north on the A16 and A29 *autoroutes*, turn off at exit 8, just west of Yvetot, on to the D926.

The Auberge de la Rouge is in St-Léonard, about 2km south of Fécamp town. From the town centre follow signs for the Le Havre road (D925), which begins as Rue Charles Leborgne. Climb the hill and after a few bends you will arrive in St-Léonard, where the Auberge is unmissable on the left, with its own car park. Coming from Le Havre, the Auberge will be on your right before you reach Fécamp.

Fécamp has **train** connections in two directions, from Le Havre and from Paris (St-Lazare) and Rouen. From the station, near the harbour, the best way to get to St-Léonard is by cab.

Tourist Information

Fécamp: Maison du Tourisme, 113 Rue Alexandre Le Grand, **t** 02 35 28 51 01, *www.fecamptourisme.com*. In summer there's also an information kiosk on the seafront, by the Musée des Terre-Neuvas (*May–June Sat, Sun; July–Aug daily*).

Etretat: Place Maurice Guillard, **t** 02 35 27 05 21, *www.etretat.net*.

Yport: 18 Place JP Laurens, **t** 02 35 29 77 31, *www.yport.net*.

The coast west of Fécamp is also the most celebratedly beautiful part of the whole Côte d'Albâtre, above all Etretat, 20km away along the shore. Of all the many places on the north Normandy coast associated with the Impressionists, none was perhaps more important for painters like Monet and Boudin than this little oasis-town and its cliffs, with their ravishing light and spectacular rock formations. In the same era it also became a singular and raffish resort for the upper crusts of France and Europe. This combination has left little Etretat with a very individual, delicately cranky atmosphere – part of which is a very special range of eccentrically luxurious accommodation and dining places – that can still be seen today.

When the *Fécampois* wish to celebrate or tackle Sunday lunch in style, they commonly head for the **Auberge de la Rouge**, just outside town. It's an impressive, half-timbered Norman inn, a century old and supposedly named after the first owner and her red hair. In the last few years a young chef has added culinary innovations to the Auberge's established repertoire of superior variations on classic Norman and French cuisine. If you're feeling a desire to be pleasantly pampered, La Rouge is ideal.

Auberge de la Rouge

Route du Havre, St-Léonard, t 02 35 28 07 59, www.auberge-rouge.com. Open Tues–Sat 12–2.30 and 7–9.30, Sun 12–2.30; closed Mon and two weeks Feb–Mar. Menus €17–49, carte average €55.

You enter the Auberge via a large gateway and an especially pretty leafy garden, with a pond, a fountain and loungers, chairs and tables where you can sit outside to eat or drink in summer. The eight attractive hotel rooms are around the garden, behind flowers and greenery. The same comfortable degree of luxury is continued in the main building. The old inn has been elegantly renovated throughout: in the dining room, there are model boats and nautical prints that recall Fécamp's maritime traditions, fine silver and enough carpeting to create a satisfying hush. The waist-coated waiters exude traditional professionalism, but the atmosphere is friendly and charming, and few restaurants at this level have better facilities for families with small children, from highchairs and toys to a flexible children's menu (€10).

All French towns tend to have one restaurant that is generally considered the best in the area, and in Fécamp for many years this accolade has gone to the Auberge de la Rouge. For just as long the restaurant was inseparable from the figure of its ebullient chef-proprietor Claude Guyot who, as well as preparing superb Norman cuisine, ran marathons, gave cookery courses, held special lunches for Fécamp's football club and contributed in many other ways to local life. In 2000, however, M Guyot finally decided to retire, and after careful thought passed on his inheritance to a new young chef, Thierry Enderlin, and his wife Anneke.

Claude Guyot was a hard act to follow, a supreme expert in traditional, buttery Norman sauces without a trace of heaviness. A faithful clientele like that of La Rouge also has high expectations, and their favourites. Thierry Enderlin is from the south of France and has his own, more modern style, with more use of olive oil and reductions rather than butter and *roux*. He has retained lynchpins of the menu, such as the delicious ocean-fish dishes, and, naturally, the use of the finest local ingredients, but also introduced his own imprint. His approach is experimental and inquisitive, open to incorporating new, globally-influenced ingredients and flavours – as is currently very fashionable in France, so long as they're combined with the essentials of French tradition. Another innovation is that the *carte* offers a choice of vegetarian dishes, such as an assortment of vegetable pâtés with pasta and *morilles* mushrooms.

His dishes are light and intricate, and often feature radical combinations of foods and flavours (meat and fish, sweet and savoury) in Pacific-rim style, but still using entirely locally-sourced ingredients. Brochette of prawns with salad and fresh herbs sounds fairly conventional, but arrives with a highly original, oriental-influenced soya-based dressing that beautifully, and surprisingly, sets off the main ingredients. *Pièce de boeuf de Normandie grillé, beurre noisette au thym brûlé* is essentially, as it should be, a superbly juicy steak, cooked absolutely exactly and with delicately woody tones from the wood-fired grill, but again it comes with other, subtle flavours and textures from the mix of fabulously fresh herbs. Fish-based main offerings might include pollack (*lieu*) sautéd in marsala with a *croquant* of tomatoes and fennel, or some of Fécamp's superb turbot roasted with Bayonne ham.

To go with these luxurious dishes there's an equally luxurious wine cellar, with a particularly good choice of fine rosés, and one tradition of the Rouge that has not been challenged is that of the *trou normand*, the sybaritic little bowl of apple sorbet in calvados that comes between first and main courses (except on the €17 menu). The cheese course is a showcase of Normandy cheeses, but save some room for the Auberge's wonderful, rich desserts. A *moelleux au chocolat* is an extravagantly rich and smooth chocolate sponge pudding, offset against a suavely refreshing portion of honey ice-cream; on the *carte*, meanwhile, there might be ravioli stuffed with exotic fruits and mint, with an apricot and mango coulis. As a final touch, the *petits-fours* served with coffee might be little tarts of woodland fruits, in fine, crumbly pastry.

Touring Around

In Fécamp, visitors' eyes tend to be drawn towards the town's most spectacular attraction. The **Palais Bénédictine** (*t 02 35 10 26 10, www.benedictine.fr; 1½hr guided tours Feb–Mar and Nov–Dec daily 10.30–11.45 and 2–5; April–early July and Sept–Oct daily 10–12 and 2–5.30; early July–Aug daily 10–6; closed Jan; adm*) has pinnacle towers, baronial staircases and fine stained glass, and has to be the world's grandest distillery. It was built for the founder of the company, Alexandre Le Grand, and stands comparison with William Randolph Hearst's San Simeon as one of the most extravagant creations of the pirate-prince era of capitalism.

The recipe for Bénédictine liqueur was invented by an Italian monk at Fécamp Abbey in about 1510, and for centuries it was made only by the monks, for medicinal purposes. The Le Grands were a local family of beer and wine merchants, and when the abbey was dissolved during the French Revolution an erudite Le Grand forebear bought up many relics and monastic documents, to prevent them being destroyed. In 1863 Alexandre, then aged 33, was browsing through these old papers when he came across the recipe, and a new life opened up before him. Not content just to tinker with the liqueur a little and put it on sale in the family shop, he chose to advertise his product aggressively, using some of the best poster artists of the great age of French graphic art, and to aim for exports. The French had only a certain capacity for a sweet liqueur, and right from the start Bénédictine's market was the world.

The results were immediate. Le Grand also sought very deliberately to create a prestigious image for his brand, and to root it in history; providing a palace for his distillery naturally added to the mystique around the liqueur, and suggested a continuity with the ancient abbey. There was a shrewd commercial element in his plan, but looking at the Palais it's impossible not to think that Le Grand's personal ambition, romantic fantasy and obsessive antiquarianism played a major part as well. No expense was spared; then, in January 1892, the recently finished Palais burnt down. Undismayed, Le Grand rebuilt it on an even bigger scale. He did not live to see it all completed, dying in 1898, two years before its final inauguration.

The Palais Bénédictine has often been dismissed as pure kitsch, but recent opinion has been more generous. Le Grand employed an otherwise obscure local architect, Camille Albert, who was thought to be influenced mainly by Viollet-le-Duc, godfather of the Gothic revival in France. So eclectic is the Palais, though, that Albert's imagination seems as close to that of Charles Garnier, creator of the Paris Opera and prime exponent of pure extravagance in French architecture. In stone and brick, the Palais appears neo-gothic from a distance, but has windows and arches that would suit a Loire Valley Renaissance château; inside, there are rooms in operatic Baroque. The standard of workmanship in details such as the glass and ironwork is extremely high.

The grandest parts of the Palais were built as a **museum** to house the collection of artefacts, mostly medieval and Renaissance, amassed by Le Grand – religious statuary, paintings, carved wooden chests, English alabaster altarpieces, Limoges enamels, furniture and magnificent 15th-century illuminated manuscripts. As a private collection it's hugely opulent, but also engagingly quirky and personal; there is a whole room, for example, full of 16th–18th-century doorknobs, locks, keys and door-knockers. After the museum rooms the tour takes in the distillery and cellars, with an imaginative display on the many herbs used in Bénédictine, although the famous recipe is of course not divulged. There is also a gallery that hosts shows of contemporary art. Free tastings are offered in the stylish bar, before the tour ends in the shop. Bénédictine is now part of the Bacardi empire, which, conscious that it has not exactly been a hip tipple in recent years, is promoting it as a cocktail mixer in concoctions such as the Rainbow (Bénédictine, rum, orange juice, peach nectar and grenadine).

Opposite the main entrance is the tourist office; from there, take the street downhill beside the Palais, Rue du Domaine, to reach Rue de la Mer, and turn right for the centre of town. Early Fécamp and the abbey that once exercised control over much of the surrounding area grew up on higher ground some way inland, and the fishing community by the port was almost a separate village until the 19th century. Rue de la Mer – once the path between the two – becomes Rue St-Etienne and then runs out into Fécamp's two main squares, **Place St-Etienne** to the left, dominated by the fine 16th-century church of St-Etienne, and the larger **Place Charles-de-Gaulle** on the right, which, if it's Saturday, will be filled by the market. The main shopping streets are also close by, around Rues Jacques Huet and Alexandre Legros. The **Musée des Arts et de l'Enfance** (*21 Rue A-Legros; open Sept–June Mon and Wed–Sun 2–5.30, closed Tues; July and Aug daily 2–6; adm; same ticket also admits to Musée des Terre-Neuvas*) is a very charming museum in an 18th-century *hôtel* with an original display of local ceramics, carved ivories, painting, furniture, archaeological finds and especially items related to childhood, including a rare and remarkable collection of antique babies' bottles.

From the landward end of Rue A-Legros, Rue Leroux leads into the oldest part of Fécamp, and to the **abbey**. The main surviving monastic buildings, rebuilt in the 17th and 18th centuries and Classical-Baroque in style, now form the **Hôtel de Ville**. Alongside them is the abbey church, the **Abbatiale de la Trinité**, which is larger than many cathedrals. Like the rest of the abbey it was given a rather jarring 18th-century façade, but behind it the church is a beautiful example of early Gothic in plain, light-coloured stone, an interesting contrast to the Bénédictine's decorative overkill.

Its visual impact stems especially from it being unusually long (127m) for its width. This is the fourth church on this site. The legend that some of the **Precious Blood** had made its way to Fécamp was known in the 7th century, and a small women's convent and chapel grew up at the shrine. At the end of the 10th century, to mark the first millennium and in fulfilment of a vow to his father, Richard I of Normandy, Duke Richard II built a far grander church and attracted the Benedictines here to found a men's abbey. The tombs of both Richards are in the south transept. So many pilgrims came to Fécamp that this church too became inadequate, and it was entirely rebuilt in Romanesque style in 1106. This third church was then destroyed by fire in 1168, and replaced by the present Gothic church, most of which was completed by 1220.

The Precious Blood is still there, in a reliquary on the marble altar from 1510, by the Italian Renaissance sculptor Viscardo. More striking, though, and in front of the altar is a rare Romanesque reliquary chest, believed to have been used for the transfer of the remains of Richards I and II. Elsewhere in the church there is a delicate

Renaissance carved chancel screen, behind which, in the side chapels, are superb medieval carved tombs and stained glass. In the south transept there is an exquisite, vivid carving of the *Entombment of the Virgin* in polychrome stone (1495), but most remarkable is the giant 1667 clock in the north transept, which indicates the time, months, seasons and even the tides. Outside, opposite the church's main entrance, some ruins remain of the **Palais Ducal**, the palace of the dukes of Normandy; in the streets off to the left, such as Rue Arquaise, there are still several medieval houses.

From the abbey a walk seawards, veering to the right through Rue Jacques-Huet and the shopping streets around the market, will bring you eventually to Quai Bérigny and the **harbour**. Commercial and fishing traffic is now largely confined to the inner basin; the outer harbour is mainly a *port de plaisance* for yachts. The break-waters of the outer harbour are lined with wooden walkways, called *estacades*, on wooden piers above the water, and a stroll along them is a very pleasant way to see the port. Alternatively, in **Place Nicolas Selle**, where Quai Bérigny meets Rue de la Mer, there are several outdoor cafés and brasseries in which to have a drink while engaging in the time-honoured custom of watching boats go up and down.

It was the building of the port in the 19th century that made old Fécamp and the fishing community into one town. Fécamp had a high-seas fishing fleet, especially dedicated to fishing for cod on the Newfoundland (*Terre-Neuve*) Banks, and for decades a large proportion of the town's menfolk disappeared for months each year on these perilous Atlantic voyages, in sailing ships known as *Terre-Neuvas*, while others worked in shipyards and fish-smokers. This was the town known to Maupassant, 'ever pervaded by the smell of fish'. The streets alongside the port and, oddly, around the Palais Bénédictine still have some of the look of a 19th-century industrial town, with rows of small terraced houses. At the end of the harbour, just around the corner on the sea front (or Boulevard Albert Ier), there's an imaginative modern museum, the **Musée des Terre-Neuvas et de la Pêche** (*open Sept–June Mon and Wed–Sun 10–12 and 2–5.30, closed Tues; July and Aug daily 10–7; adm; same ticket also admits to Musée des Arts et de l'Enfance*), dedicated to Fécamp's maritime traditions. Of great interest to anyone with nautical leanings, it also has entertaining displays on local social history, and the development of Fécamp as a seaside resort.

The **seafront** was the other major 19th-century addition to the town, running along the beach to end at the casino and a footpath up to the cliffs. The beach is all pebbles and not much good for swimming, but fine for windsurfing or a paddle. Alternatively, if you're feeling energetic, make your way back across the quays to the north side of the port, from where there is a steep but enjoyable climb up the giant cliff via a historic pilgrims' path, the **Côte de la Vierge**, to the chapel of **Notre-Dame-de-Salut**, where Fécamp fishermen traditionally gave thanks for a safe return. There are also old German blockhouses, and wonderful views over the town and out to sea.

West of Fécamp the D940 to Etretat curves slightly inland, but several turnings head back to the sea, and the narrow winding lane of the D211 – and the GR21 long-distance footpath – stay close to the cliff edge. About 8km from Fécamp is **Yport**, one of the coast's curiosities. It's like Fécamp, Dieppe or other breaks in the cliff along this coast, only in miniature: in a deep little valley that almost seems hidden from the world by its sea cliffs, with a small beach, small casino and a village instead of a town. Its curious remoteness began to attract visitors in the 19th century, and Boudin, Maupassant, Corot and André Gide all visited at different times. Today, it has some curiously elegant shops for such a small place, and a very placid atmosphere. **Grainval**, between Yport and Fécamp, is an even smaller, very peaceful beach village.

One of the most distinctive features that make up Yport and Etretat is their special climatic conditions. The steep valleys in which they sit are sheltered from the Atlantic winds, creating lush, almost subtropical microclimates that contrast strikingly with the flat plateau just above them. **Etretat** also has the most dramatic **cliffs** on the whole coast, standing like massive gateways to the beach and battered by the sea into giant arches that look eerily as if they must have been the product of human intervention, with a solitary pinnacle of rock, **L'Aiguille** or The Needle, just offshore. Monet did a whole series of paintings of these cliffs at different times of day, and Boudin, Corot, Courbet and innumerable other artists were drawn to them as well. At about the same time, Etretat's combination of sea air, famously clear light and balmy temperatures led to it being recommended as an especially healthy place to stay, and it became a fashionable resort favoured by high society and minor royalty. Offenbach took a villa here, when he was the most popular composer in France. It was this combination of artists and aristocracy that led to the sides of the valley being taken over by dottily grand villas, in a style that could be called Second Empire-fairytale.

Etretat's collection of the French equivalent of over-the-top Victoriana – turrets, pinnacles, curving balconies, hidden gardens – is an essential part of its whimsical individuality. One writer associated with the town was Maurice Leblanc, whose stories of the 'gentleman burglar' Arsène Lupin rivalled Sherlock Holmes in popularity in France. Leblanc's own fantasy cottage, **Le Clos Lupin** (*open April–Sept daily 10–7; Oct–Mar Mon and Fri–Sun 11–5; adm*), now hosts a kind of 'performance-museum' that makes the most of the house's mysteriousness, and can be enjoyed even if you're not familiar with the Lupin stories. One of the most astonishing of Etretat's houses is the **Château Les Aygües** (*guided tours July and Aug Mon and Wed–Sun 2–6, closed Tues; adm*), towering up by the road from Fécamp. It was once owned by a Russian prince, and in the 1860s was used as a summer home by scandalous Queen Isabel II of Spain. Nowaday, as well as being Etretat's wildest B&B (*see* right), it can be visited on tours with the owners, who are devoted to their house and its antique contents.

There is much that is 'mock' in Etretat (as well as some drab 1960s buildings by the beach, put up when the 19th century was less appreciated). In the centre of the town there is an imposing timber-frame Norman **market hall** which, despite appearances, was only built in 1926, albeit using the very best-quality timbers from the Eure, from where the style was copied. Today, the hall houses knick-knack shops. As a renowned beauty spot, without the workaday concerns of Fécamp, Etretat fills up on summer weekends, but it retains a great deal of quirky charm. And no one can take anything away from the cliffs. There are superb walks along the clifftops to the west (the **Falaise d'Aval**) and to the east (**Falaise d'Amont**); the tourist office has free maps, but the paths are also well marked-out. The view from the east back across to the *Falaise d'Aval* at sunset is one of the Côte d'Albâtre's greatest pleasures.

Shopping

Fécamp's large **market** fills the town centre on Saturdays; the most attractive shops are in the same area, especially Rue Jacques-Huet. In **Etretat** market day is on Thursday, and **Yport** has a market on Wednesday.

Fécamp ✉ 76400

Brûlerie Fécampoise, 26 Rue Jacques-Huet, t 02 35 27 68 21. A delightful little shop specializing in fine coffees (and teas), roasted and ground to your order. There's also a little *café-salon*, for tasting on-site.

Caves Bérigny, 91 Quai Bérigny, t/f 02 35 27 19 79. A compact wine merchant on the harbour quay. The all-French stock is varied and expertly selected; prices are competitive, and the staff are helpful. *Open Tues–Sat and 10am–1pm Sun; closed Mon.*

Etretat ✉ 76790

Fromagerie Le Valaine, Manoir du Cateuil, Route du Havre, t 02 35 27 14 02. A goat farm just west of Etretat, well-signposted on the D940, that produces fine *chèvre*, as well as home-made ice-cream, chocolates, goat pâté with calvados, and farm cider. *Shop open Easter–Nov daily, closed 12.30–2. Guided tours in French, English and German, Sun 11am; July–Aug also Mon–Wed and Sat 11am.*

Maison Tranchard, 10 Av George V, t 02 35 27 01 56, and 2 Rue Alphonse Karr. A French town with an upper-crust history like Etretat naturally has its places to find the best Gallic foodstuffs, and the unchallenged first-choice purveyors of gourmet goodies are the two Tranchard shops, founded 1886. The George V shop is the main *épicerie*, with wonderful honeys, terrines, chocolates, coffees and foie gras, and a superior choice of wines, Normandy ciders and calvados; around the corner on Rue Alphonse Karr is the equally superb *fromagerie*. Fabulous.

Yport ✉ 76111

Epicerie Fine Daniel, 66 Rue Emmanuel Foy, t 02 35 27 35 45. A very pleasant small *épicerie* that has all the French corner-shop necessities, excellent fruit and veg and a very attractive selection of locally-made terrines, calvados and other products.

Where to Stay

Fécamp ✉ 76400

Auberge de la Rouge, Route du Havre, St-Léonard, t 02 35 28 07 59, *www.auberge-rouge.com* (*double rooms €60*). Most of the Auberge's eight compact guest rooms have a bathroom and single bed on a lower level, and a double bed on a platform above. They open on to the lovely garden behind the inn.

Hôtel d'Angleterre, 91–93 Rue de la Plage, t 02 35 28 01 60, *www.hotelangleterre.com* (*double rooms €30–54 low season, €38–60 high season*). One street back from the beach, this looks like an archetypical French 19th-century hotel, but has a youthful feel (it has a laid-back '*Pub Anglais*'). The 27 rooms are bright and airy; prices vary by size. Its **Restaurant de la Manche** has bargain menus (*€12–15*).

Les Cirrus, 9 Rue de la Mer, t 02 35 28 82 65 (*room €46 for two*). One suite-sized B&B room in a venerable townhouse in the heart of Fécamp, with a flower-filled courtyard garden invisible from the street. The room can easily be adapted to sleep up to four.

Criquebeuf-en-Caux ✉ 76111

Le Bout de la Ville, t/f 02 35 28 01 32 (*rooms €42 for two, €70 for four*). A Caux-style brick farmhouse with two cosy B&B rooms. M and Mme Basille are warm and welcoming, and outside there's a pleasant garden, and the activity of the farm. *Table-d'hôte* dinners (*€18*) can be arranged on request.

Etretat ✉ 76790

Château Les Aygües, Route de Fécamp, t 02 35 28 92 77 (*Oriental Room €122; Suite de la Reine €212*). One of Etretat's rare attractions: an extraordinary 19th-century fantasy house, with grand staircases, turrets and ornamental brickwork. The current owners have lovingly restored it and filled it with a dazzling collection of antiques (in summer they take tours, *see* left). The two guest rooms are astonishing: the 'Oriental Room' has Chinese fittings, twin beds and a circular shower room in a tower; the *Suite de la Reine* is Napoleon III-style with two double beds and ornate bathroom. The breakfast room is equally camp-palatial,

with views of the wooded garden. There's a no-children rule (too many antiques), and it's not for everyone, but if you like it, you'll love it. *Rooms available Easter–1 Nov only.*
Domaine St-Clair-Le Donjon, Chemin de St-Clair, t 02 35 27 08 23, *www.ledonjon-etretat.fr (double rooms €90–190 low season, €160–250 high season).* A luxury hotel in one of Etretat's most extravagant old residences, an ivy-clad 1860s mock-château in a superb location amid cedars on the heights behind the town, with soaring views. It's undeniably touristy but extremely comfortable, with many extras such as a heated pool in the gardens. Its 11 rooms differ in size, décor and view. There's a fine restaurant (*see right*).
Hôtel La Résidence, Manoir de la Salamandre, 4 Bd René Coty, t 02 35 27 02 87, *www.etretat.net/residence (double rooms €31–106).* With massive gables and carved balconies this building looks the very essence of ancient Norman half-timbering, but is in fact a reconstruction of two 15th–16th-century houses from Lisieux, brought here in the 1920s. Never mind: the interior has a cranky charm, with wonderful timber staircase, and the 15 rooms are pretty and comfortable. They vary in size and price. It also has an original restaurant (*see right*).

Sassetot-Le-Mauconduit ✉ 76540
Château de Sassetot-Le-Mauconduit, t 02 35 28 00 11, *www.chateau-de-sassetot.com (double rooms €78–129 low season, €87–158 high season; suites €164–314).* This elegant 18th-century château, in its own park 15km east of Fécamp, is now a sumptuous country-house hotel. Empress Elizabeth of Austria, known as Sissi, stayed here in the 1870s, and the regal 'Sissi Suite' is the star accommodation (and has to be booked well ahead). Standard rooms are a little small, so if you're here for a splurge it's worth going for a *chambre charme* or junior suite.

Yport ✉ 76111
Le Petit Navire, 26 Rue Emmanuel Foy, t 02 35 28 00 94, *www.lepetitnavire.com (rooms €48 for two).* A charming B&B a few metres from Yport's little beach, with a lovely breakfast room. The four rooms are bright and pretty, and all have sea views. One sleeps up to four.

Eating Alternatives

Fécamp ✉ 76400
Le Maritime, 2 Place Nicolas Selles, t 02 35 28 21 71 *(menus €15.50–35.50).* A bustling quayside brasserie, with a *salle panoramique* with a great view over the harbour, and good-value seafood favourites: *sole normande*, *moules*, grills, platters of *fruits de mer*, oysters, lobster and fish-and-seafood stews.

Etretat ✉ 76790
Domaine St-Clair-Le Donjon, Chemin de St-Clair, t 02 35 27 08 23, *www.ledonjon-etretat.fr (menus €39–49).* Le Donjon's restaurant is pretty and ultra-comfortable, with seasonal menus of opulent dishes that often combine local traditions and produce – wild mushrooms, lamb, duck, seafood, cheeses– with a few globetrotting touches.
Manoir de la Salamandre, 4 Bd René Coty, t 02 35 27 02 87, *www.etretat.net/residence (menus €14.75–29).* The restaurant in the Manoir (*see left*) has a lovely timbered dining room, and a street-side terrace. Its food departs from the local norm: fish is a speciality, but much use is made of organic ingredients, and there are always vegetarian dishes on offer, and an organic wine list.

Grainval ✉ 76400
Auberge Les Tonnelles, t 02 35 28 77 18, *www.aubergelestonnelles.com (menus €14–23).* Bright, airy, relaxed little restaurant run by an Anglo-French couple on the way down to the tiny inlet of Grainval. Great-value menus offer local dishes made with fresh farm ingredients, plus salads, snacks and delicious homemade cakes. It's also a hotel *(double rooms €40)*, with six light, pretty rooms, one a family room.

Sassetot-Le-Mauconduit ✉ 76540
Château de Sassetot-Le-Mauconduit, t 02 35 28 00 11, *www.chateau-de-sassetot.com (menus €19 Mon–Fri lunch only, €26–58).* Sassetot's dining room has 18th-century panelling, big fireplaces and plenty of fresh flowers; in good weather there are tables on the terrace. The menu is refined and good value; save room for decadent desserts such as *nougat glacé à la Bénédictine*.

Deep in France:
the Pays de Bray

17

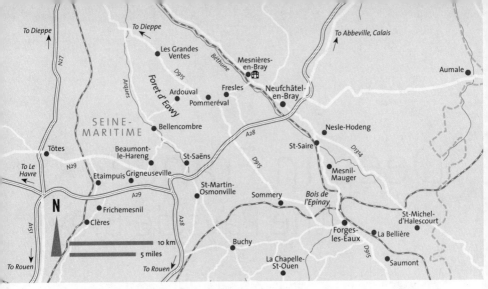

Long, rolling ridges rise and fall between steep-sided valleys in the Pays de Bray, the long rift that runs from just below Dieppe diagonally southeast towards Beauvais and Paris. It's a geological oddity, known as the *Boutonnière* or 'Buttonhole' – a cleft of clay and sandstone between two great slabs of chalk which has created a pocket of hilly, often lush landscape, small rivers and long stretches of woodland in between the flat and monotonous plateaux of Caux and Picardy.

The clay soil makes excellent pasture, and the region's sheep and brown-and-white dairy cattle are often its most visible inhabitants. This is the home of Neufchâtel cheese, by far the oldest of the classic Normandy cheeses, already known before William the Conqueror first set foot in England. Since the coming of railways in the 1850s the fortunes of the Pays de Bray have been tied to the markets of Paris, as one of the capital's favourite sources of butter, cheese and every other kind of dairy product. In Gournay-en-Bray in 1850 Charles Gervais, an enterprising local businessman with a shop in Paris, began to manufacture the *Petit-Suisse*, supposedly invented in a happy collaboration between an itinerant Swiss farmhand and a Norman milkmaid. Today, Gervais produce huge quantities of *Petits-Suisses*, yogurts and cheeses. The Bray valleys are also known for their duck, geese and the products made from them, and, not surprisingly, for their apples and ciders.

And yet the overall impression given by the Pays de Bray, especially in the north, is not one of an area given over to large-scale agribusiness. Instead the farms are small and discreet, often built in a distinctive brick-chalet style with low-hanging roofs. Nor, despite its range of traditional produce, is this a part of Normandy where agri-tourism is intensively developed. It has its special destinations – including three of the most spectacular gardens in France's most garden-conscious region – but the local tourist authorities have adopted the slogan of *Normand tout simplement*, 'Simply Norman', perhaps a shy way of admitting that its villages, local museums and many speciality food producers are engagingly low-key rather than postcard-pretty. It's a genuine piece of rural France, one of the most attractive, characterful and peaceful stretches of countryside between Paris and the Channel coast.

Getting There

The main road into the Pays de Bray is the A28 Abbeville–Rouen *autoroute*, which cuts off the A16 from Calais and runs just south of Neufchâtel-en-Bray, parallel to the old N28/ D928. Calais–Neufchâtel is about a 2hr drive. From Dieppe two tranquil roads lead into the Pays de Bray, the D1 to Neufchâtel and D915 to Forges-les-Eaux, and take *c.* 45mins or less.

In Forges all roads converge on the main square, Place de la République, and the smaller Place Brévière to one side. The Hôtel de la Paix nearly overlooks the latter. If you come in from Neufchâtel on the D1314, you see the hotel on the right just before entering the square. Entering from Dieppe or Rouen on the D915 you arrive at Place Brévière; turn left and the hotel is on the left. The Amiens and Paris roads enter the same square, on the eastern side.

Neufchâtel and Forges no longer have **train** services but from Forges SNCF **buses** run to Serqueux, 3km north, from where there are trains to Paris via Gisors. SNCF buses also run between Forges, Neufchâtel and Dieppe.

Tourist Information

Forges-les-Eaux: Rue Albert Bochet, t 02 35 90 52 10, *www.ville-forges-les-eaux.fr*. The office is just off Place de la République.
Neufchâtel-en-Bray: 6 Place Notre-Dame, t 02 35 93 22 96, *otsi.neufchatel-en-bray@wanadoo.fr*.
St-Saëns–Forêt d'Eawy: Place Maintenon, St-Saëns, t 02 35 34 57 75, *ville.de.saint.saens.si@wanadoo.fr*.

Activities

The Pays de Bray offers a great range of possibilities for walking, cycling, riding and otherwise exploring. Tourist offices have free guides to all the many paths, and can advise on current local facilities; for renting bikes, the best places are Neufchâtel and Forges. One especially interesting initiative is the **Avenue Verte**, a foot, cycle and bridal path that runs all the way along the now-disused railway line from Beaubec-La Rosière, just north of Forges, to Dieppe (40km). It is planned to continue it southwards all the way to Paris.

The Pays de Bray was also once a border area, the eastern frontier of the independent Duchy of Normandy. It was settled relatively late, much of it in the 12th century, and many of the villages have small, plain Romanesque churches from that time. The towns, similarly small-scale, grew up as markets for the surrounding farms. An exception is Forges-les-Eaux, which has a rather grander past as a spa, 'discovered' in the 17th century. And at the centre of Forges is the **Hôtel de la Paix**, a classic small-town *Logis* hotel, where M Rémy Michel has won an enviable reputation throughout the valleys with his satisfying, traditional Norman cooking.

Hôtel de la Paix

15 Rue de Neufchâtel, Forges-les-Eaux, t 02 35 90 51 22, www.hotellapaix.fr.
Open Mon 7.15–9.30, Tues–Sat 12–2 and 7.15–9.30, Sun 12–2; June–Sept also open midday Mon public hols. Menus €11.55 Tues–Sat lunch only, €15.50–33.50; vegetarian menu €14.50; carte average €35.

Come into the restaurant at the Hôtel de la Paix, especially at the weekend, and you feel you are entering *la France profonde*, the 'deep France' that many French politicians claim to communicate with regularly. M Michel reckons – and this is a considered observation, not a casual remark – that in the more than 27 years since he took over the hotel 80 per cent of the inhabitants of Forges-les-Eaux and the vicinity have eaten there at some point; many return at least once a month. Around the tables you will see

Poulet au Cidre Fermier

Serves 4

1 free-range chicken, about 1.8kg/3lb
1 carrot, finely diced
1 onion, finely diced
1 tablespoon plain flour, plus more for dusting
1 tablespoon tomato purée
1 garlic clove, crushed or chopped
bouquet garni (thyme, bay leaf and parsley stems, tied)
40g/1½oz butter
100g/3½oz lardons, blanched
250g/9oz mushrooms, sliced
1 shallot, finely chopped
2–3 tablespoons calvados
250ml/9fl oz dry cider
3 tablespoons double cream or crème fraîche
salt and pepper

Joint the chicken and keep in the fridge until required.

Roughly chop the carcass and brown it in a little butter in a heavy casserole with the carrot and onion, either in a hot oven or on the hob. Sprinkle with flour, stir to blend and continue cooking until the mixture is lightly browned, stirring occasionally. Cover with cold water and add the tomato purée, the garlic and bouquet garni. Bring to a boil, reduce the heat and simmer gently for 30 minutes, skimming off the foam as necessary. Strain the stock, discarding the solids, and reserve.

Dust the chicken pieces lightly with flour; season with salt and pepper. Heat the butter in a pan over a medium heat until foaming. Add the chicken, skin-side down, and sauté until lightly browned. Turn over, and brown the other side.

Add the lardons, mushrooms and shallot, reduce the heat, cover and cook for about 30 minutes, stirring occasionally, until the chicken is just cooked through. Remove the chicken, mushrooms and lardons and skim off the fat from the pan.

Add the calvados to the pan and flame. Add the cider and boil until it is almost all evaporated. Add the reserved stock and boil 2–3 minutes until slightly reduced, stir in the cream and return the chicken to the pan to reheat. Taste for seasoning. Serve the chicken surrounded by lardons and mushrooms, and pour the sauce over evenly.

family groups, young couples, big men in denims and sweaters, ladies with dogs, men in suits and every other element of local society, plus a few British blow-ins.

As usual in the French countryside, the décor is not self-consciously rustic: the dining room is bright and comfortable, substantially renovated like the hotel, and decorated with local painted ceramics. In the last few years M Michel has taken more of a back seat in the kitchen, where his long-serving assistant Nicolas Bruynsteen is often in charge, and been more visible front-of-house, overseeing the well-schooled young staff. La Paix's cooking is firmly based in the classic Norman repertoire – plenty of duck, ham, chicken and steaks, fish such as cod, sole and salmon, and cream, cheese and cider sauces. This does not mean that it is not creative, and dishes such as the *suprème de barbue* (brill) *au cidre* – a menu regular – are skilful variations on local styles and ingredients. A meal here is a demonstration of the virtues of traditional French cooking at its best, with all the basics – quality ingredients, freshness, care in preparation and skill – in the right balance.

The hotel always has four exceptional set menus, handily labelled A to D. They change a little from time to time, but each offers a generous choice of quality Norman cooking at very reasonable prices. The B menu (€18.60) includes a delicious savoury salad with chicken livers, apple and Neufchâtel cheese; mains include *poulet au cidre* and lamb with a tarragon sauce. The most truly local dishes are on C, the *menu du terroir*, such as the richly meaty duck terrine *à la Rouennaise*, an ideal version of a local classic served with irresistible homemade pickled gherkins, maybe followed by a wonderfully subtly-flavoured sea bass with a sorrel cream sauce.

All but the A menu include a cheese course, which includes not just all the Norman favourites but also a rare and magnificently knotty-looking *Vieux Neufchâtel*, a must for lovers of strong cheeses. For dessert, to stay with a theme, you might go for another archetypical local standard, a mouthwateringly fresh *tarte aux pommes*.

The excellent cellar is well above the norm for a small-town hotel. There's nothing on the wine list that isn't French – the very idea – but there is a fine representation of classic French regions, and especially Bordeaux. You can venture into some very *grand cru* bottles indeed, should you wish, but even if you stay at the more accessible end you'll find that wines have been carefully selected, with individual attention.

Touring Around

Neufchâtel-en-Bray, at the junction of the roads from Dieppe and Abbeville, is the traditional capital of the Pays de Bray, although no longer its largest town. It's also one of the best places to buy Neufchâtel cheese, most of all at the **market**, which every Saturday fills both the square around the church of Notre-Dame, halfway up the hill of the Grande-Rue, and Place 11 Novembre further up. This being a country market it's best to get there in good time, for many stalls start packing up soon after midday; the best cheese displays are generally inside the covered market in Place 11 Novembre. In addition to the local cheese you can find fine *chèvre*, as well as the usual stalls offering excellent terrines, spit-roasted chickens, wonderful fresh vegetables and a huge number of leather jackets. Around them you can watch what seems like nearly half the population of the Pays de Bray, chatting and mingling.

Neufchâtel cheese is mentioned in a document from 1035, and some was already being shipped to England in its current form in the 16th century, but it was not given an *appellation contrôlée* until 1977. It still comes entirely from local farms, for there are no large-scale producers. The cheese is made in a variety of shapes: cylinders (*bondes*), rectangles (*briquettes* and *carrés*) and, most distinctively, hearts (*cœurs*). This doesn't affect the flavour, which depends on whether it's *jeune* (up to twelve days old), *demi-affiné* (one to three weeks) or *affiné* (one to three months), the last of which has a pretty gnarled appearance. The story goes that the heart shape was first made by Norman milkmaids during the Hundred Years' War, in an effort to 'soften the hearts' of the depraved English soldiery.

When the market is not in session, Neufchâtel is a quiet country town, where the sound of the occasional passing van echoes in the clean valley air. Several buildings along the Grande Rue have the functional lines of 1940s reconstruction architecture, an indication that Neufchâtel was badly damaged during the Second World War, in 1940. The church of **Notre-Dame**, at the hub of one of the market squares, was begun in 1126 and has a fine 13th-century Gothic choir. It too was severely hit by German bombing in 1940, and a good deal of the present building is a reconstruction. Remarkably unharmed, however, was its most beautiful possession, a delicate 16th-century carved *Entombment of Christ*, in one of the side chapels. At the foot of the hill of the Grande-Rue, in a pretty 16th-century merchants' house, there is a charming local museum of rural traditions and crafts, the **Musée Mathon-Durand** (*open April–mid-June and mid-Sept–Oct Sun 3–6; mid-June–mid-Sept Tues–Sun 3–6; adm*), with a collection of local glass and pottery and a monumental 1837 cider press.

South of Neufchâtel the D1314 road passes under the A28 *autoroute* to immediately re-enter open downland. Modern regulations have made it more complicated to visit farms to see cheese being made, but an increasing number of farms have adapted to these bureaucratic hoops and now open for direct sales, and often farm tours. Local tourist offices have an abundance of literature on Neufchâtel – including books of recipes for using it in cooking – and all the places that offer farm sales. The actual foods aside, searching out farm food producers – not just of cheese but of ciders, terrines, honey and more – is one of the most enjoyable ways of exploring the area, meandering away from the main routes through tiny lanes and villages such as **Mesnil-Mauger**, where massive old farmhouses and a tumbledown château stand between much smaller cottages, all with a pleasant air of quaint remoteness.

The D1314 brings you into **Forges-les-Eaux** on the north side, from where it looks like another straightforward country town, with a few cafés and the Hôtel de la Paix around the central squares. A walk down Rue de la République after lunch will reveal its smarter aspect. The town's hot springs, the *Eaux*, were discovered in the 16th century, but were not widely known until 1633, when Louis XIII, his queen Anne of Austria and Cardinal Richelieu arrived here together to try the waters. Forges was quickly transformed into a fashionable spa, and remained so throughout the *Ancien Régime*, numbering Voltaire and many other distinguished names among its visitors. In the 19th century, however, when Europe's greatest watering holes were doing their best business, the town was largely forgotten. The spa was redeveloped in the 1950s, when the bulky modern **Grand Casino** was built amid neat gardens on the western side of town by the Andelle river, fronted by a neoclassical gate from a convent in Gisors destroyed in the war. More recently casino and spa were taken over by Club Med, which has made them into one of France's premier health-and-leisure farms.

The casino stands beside **Avenue des Sources**, a broad and elegant stretch of the Rue de la République–Dieppe road that seems strikingly out of sorts with the humble main part of town just to the east. On the north side of the avenue the river widens into two pretty lakes with pedalos for hire, and in between them there is a formal French-style park originally laid out in the spa's most fashionable era in the 18th century. Walk through this park and you will come to the **Bois d'Epinay**, an unspoilt forest with well-marked paths where you can wander for miles.

While the spa was declining in the 19th century, one business that was doing well in Forges was the manufacture of painted earthenware using local clay, introduced by an Englishman, George Wood, in 1797. The town has a good collection of the simple but decorative Forges earthenware, the **Collection de Faïences** (*admission Tues–Fri, ask at tourist office; adm*). It's currently housed in the Hôtel de Ville awaiting a permanent home, but can still be visited via a visit to the tourist office. This industry too fell into decline in the 20th century, but recently attempts have been made to revive it.

The area's most interesting museum is a wonderful 'farm-museum', the **Ferme de Bray** (*open Easter–June and Sept–Nov Sat, Sun and public hols 2–7; July and Aug daily 2–7; adm*), well-signposted on the D915, 7km north of Forges near Sommery. Its owner Patrice Perrier, an engaging combination of Norman farmer and middle-aged hippy, has a document that shows that his family have been on this property since 1452. He ran it as a dairy farm until the 1980s, when he realized that in the age of quotas the farm itself was more of an asset than anything it could produce. The main farmhouse is 16th-century, and nearby there's a 15th-century watermill, a *laiterie* (dairy) built and altered from 1400 to 1800, and a 15th-century brick bread oven and 17th-century horse-driven cider press, both still regularly in use. Running through the middle of the farm is what was for centuries the main road between Dieppe and Paris, until the line of the modern D915 was laid out in Napoleon's time. It all seems implausibly ancient, especially since no conscious effort has ever been made to bring it all together.

The farm also has lovely *chambres d'hôtes* (*see* p.180), a large trout-fishing pond, a picnic area, meals (for groups) and courses in such things as cider-making and restoring the local wattle-and-daub style buildings, cleverly orientated towards urbanites who buy up old properties and find them to be crumbling away. An explanatory leaflet is provided in English. This is not a synthetic heritage site, but a fascinating repository of rural traditions, and very amiably run. A series of special events is held at the farm through the year, and it also hosts farmers' markets.

From Sommery, anyone going on south should backtrack to Forges-les-Eaux for the roads to Rouen or Paris; otherwise, continue the circuit northwards on the D915. Back to the north of Neufchâtel is the Pays de Bray's grandest monument, the Renaissance **Château de Mesnières-en-Bray** (*guided tours Mar–mid-June and mid-Sept–Oct Sat, Sun and hols 2.30–6.30; mid-June–mid-Sept daily 2.30–6.30; adm*), built between 1520 and 1550 for the De Boissay family. The white and grey exterior is dramatic and imposing, especially if you approach it as once intended, head-on to the main façade on the little road from the D915 via Fresles, rather than on the D1 from Neufchâtel. It has massive round drum towers with pinnacle tops on either side, and steeply raked roofs and ornamented windows in the central building; between the towers is a superb peacock-tail-shaped staircase, added in the 18th century and designed to be ridden up on horseback. It's rather like a smaller version of the contemporary châteaux in the

Loire Valley, a connection explained by the close connections between the De Boissays and the Amboises, lords of Chaumont, one of the grandest Loire mansions.

The interior, on the other hand, is a mixed bag. Mesnières' last aristocratic owners, the De Biencourts, reclaimed it after the Revolution but ruined themselves restoring it, and in 1835 they sold it to a Catholic order as an orphanage. Today, most of it is an agricultural college, still run by the same order. Parts of it are beautiful, especially the **Galerie des Cerfs** (Stags), with seven life-sized statues of stags installed by a hunting-mad *seigneur* in 1660, and the superb original chapel, with magnificent Renaissance stained glass and Baroque woodwork. Other rooms have the shabby look of an under-heated boarding school, and there is a huge, gloomy neogothic additional **chapel**, built for the orphanage in the 1860s. The guided tours, given by students, take you indiscriminately round all of them (in French only, with a leaflet in English).

The western flank of the Pays de Bray contains its most lushly wooded, densely green landscapes. To the left along the D915 going north is the **Forêt d'Eawy**, 20km of dense and beautiful beech forest. Several roads run into the forest, and tourist offices have maps of the foot- and bridle paths such as the *Allée des Limousins*, a renowned 14km track that's a riders' favourite. A number of riding centres around the area have horses for hire, and generally offer guided trekking trips as well. The villages in and around the forest are some of the loveliest in all the Bray valleys, notably **Ardouval**, **Bellencombre** and **St-Saëns**, ancestral home of the composer. St-Saëns also has a particularly luxuriant golf course, with a genuine château for a clubhouse.

A little further west again is a remarkable 'triangle' of three of the Seine-Maritime's, and France's, most impressive recently-created private gardens. In Grigneuseville, about 6km from St-Saëns south of the N29 Tôtes road, is **Agapanthe** (*open April–Oct Mon, Tues, Thurs–Sun 2–7, closed Wed; adm*), an exquisite, intimate garden dedicated above all, as the name suggests, to agapanthus. A couple of kilometres west in Etaimpuis is the **Clos du Coudray** (*open April–Oct daily 10–7; adm*), a much bigger and more luxuriant organic garden with over 7,000 species from around the world, especially poppies, dahlias and flowering maples. Other highlights include areas arranged by colour (a yellow garden, a white garden), a giant rock garden of alpine plants and a rose garden that is fabulously colourful in June and July.

Most spectacular of all are the **Jardins de Bellevue** (*open daily 10–6; adm*), in Beaumont-le-Hareng, back towards St-Saëns. Created from nothing since the 1980s by Martine Lemonnier and her family, this extraordinary hillside shangri-la is as much a botanical reserve as a conventional garden. Around the six-hectare estate there are hundreds of rare and strange trees and plants from across the world, especially Asia, particularly high-altitude species: Himalayan plums, Japanese maples, pure-white trees from China, giant lilies, and Europe's largest collection of Christmas roses. Colours are superbly combined, and there is something in flower every month of the year – hence, unusually, it is open all year round as well. Also, while admissions end at 6pm, once inside you can stay at your leisure until sunset. There is a small café, and a delightful B&B alongside the garden (*see* right). You can wander around independently, or book a tour (in English) with one of the Lemonniers, whose enthusiasm for their creation carries you with it as much as the delicate colours of the plants.

Shopping

Saturday's **market** in **Neufchâtel** is the best place to find fine Pays de Bray specialities all in one go. Other good markets are in **Forges-les-Eaux** (*Thurs and Sun*), **St-Saëns** (*Thurs*) and **Bellencombre** (*Tues*). *Bray Fermier* farmers' markets that showcase local farm producers are held in several towns and villages through the year, and each year in June there is a *Brayonnade* weekend in Neufchâtel for the whole district. Dates and locations for all these events vary, but local tourist offices have current details, as well as leaflets listing the growing number of farms open for direct sales of cheeses and other fresh produce.

La Chapelle-St-Ouen ✉ 76780
Ferme-Brasserie La Chapelle, t 02 35 09 21 54, *www.northmaen.com*. Not so traditional, but imaginative: a 'farm-brewery' where Dominique Camus produces very good, wheaty beers, with very 'Norman' names like his *Northmaen* light and dark beers.

Nesle-Hodeng ✉ 76270
La Ferme des Fontaines, t 02 32 97 06 46. Alex and Françoise Brianchon make *appellation contrôlée* Neufchâtel cheese and sell it direct. Mme Brianchon also gives tours of the *caves*, with a demonstration of cheese-making (*by reservation, Mar–Nov*). The farm is about 6km south of Neufchâtel, just north of the turn off the D1314 for Nesle-Hodeng.

St-Michel-d'Halescourt ✉ 76440
M and Mme Fougeray-Duclos, t/f 02 35 90 61 39. Denise and Hervé Fougeray-Duclos raise sheep and produce high-quality cider, calvados, *pommeau* and apple juice on their spectacular farm in one of the most beautiful parts of the Pays de Bray, 5km east of Forges-les-Eaux. It's best to phone ahead.

St-Saire ✉ 76270
Le Clos du Bourg, t/f 02 32 97 10 74. This farm co-op produces some of the most highly regarded ciders in the Seine-Maritime – used by many chefs – as well as fine calvados, *pommeau* and fresh apple juice. *Shop open Mon–Sat 9–12 and 2–6; July and Aug also open Sun; farm tours available.*

Au Panier Fermier, t 02 35 94 12 30. A farm shop that's a shared outlet for a number of local *terroir* food producers – with farmhouse cheeses, terrines, fresh veg, jams and more. It's well signposted in St-Saire. *Open Wed–Fri 2.30–6.30, Sat 10–6.30, Sun 10–12.*

Where to Stay

Forges-les-Eaux ✉ 76440
La Folie du Bois des Fontaines, Av des Sources, **t** 02 32 89 50 68, **f** 02 32 89 50 67 (*rooms and suites €99–278 low season, €104–304 high season*). The luxury option in the Pays de Bray. In a former château by the avenue through the smart side of Forges-les-Eaux, it's aimed squarely at the romantic hideaway market, with ten emphatically opulent rooms with things like two-seater jacuzzis with gold taps and classical statuary, and coy names like *fou d'amour*. For real palace-boudoir glitz, take one of the two *suites royales*. The Folie no longer has a gourmet restaurant, only breakfast and room service for guests, but it may regain one in future.

Hôtel de la Paix, 15 Rue de Neufchâtel, **t** 02 35 90 51 22, *www.hotellapaix.fr* (*double rooms €53–70*). La Paix's 18 rooms are comfortable, with good bathrooms and other facilities. The décor is simple; character is provided by the hotel's relaxed feel, and there are very good deals for half- or full *pension*. Very popular: book ahead, especially at weekends.

Ardouval ✉ 76680
M and Mme Grain, 14 Rue des Cèdres, **t** 02 35 93 14 48 (*room €50 for two*). The house is modern, but the setting is wonderful: the Forêt d'Eawy comes right up to the edge of the lovely garden, so that it couldn't be better for walking or cycling. M and Mme Grain have just one very comfortable room, a double with space for extra beds.

Beaumont-le-Hareng ✉ 76850
La Cour Cormont, 20 Chemin de l'Eglise, **t** 02 35 33 31 74, *rmc.lemmonier@wanadoo.fr* (*rooms €55 for two, €85 for four*). Special B&B rooms next to the spectacular Jardins de Bellevue (*see left*), and run by the same Lemonnier family. Two are in a wonderful old thatched

cottage, both with a double and a single bed and a kitchenette; two more rooms are in a converted stable, with no kitchens but space for up to four people. The location is genuinely magical.

Neufchâtel-en-Bray ✉ 76270

Hôtel du Grand Cerf, 9 Grande-Rue-Fausse-Porte, **t** 02 35 93 00 02, *grand-cerf.hotel@wanadoo.fr* (*double rooms €43–48*). The traditional 'main hotel' of Neufchâtel, a *Logis* right on the main street. Stay here and you're in the middle of country-town life; the 12 rooms are plain but comfortable and well-maintained.

Le Cellier du Val Boury, **t** 02 35 93 26 95, *www.cellier-val-boury.com* (*rooms €43 for two, €70 for four*). A beautiful B&B in a giant farm on the edge of Neufchâtel. Breakfast is served in the main house; the four rooms (three doubles and a family room, all with excellent facilities) are across the courtyard in a spectacular 17th-century wine store. In the courtyard there are tables and a play area, and there are also two self-contained *gîtes*. The centre of Neufchâtel is in easy walking distance, but it feels very rural.

St-Saëns ✉ 76680

Le Logis d'Eawy, 1 Rue du 31 Août 1944, **t** 06 19 15 52 04, *www.logisdeawy.com* (*rooms €50–65 for two, €80–85 for four*). A superb half-timbered coaching inn in the middle of this lovely forest village, magnificently restored by Françoise and Bernard Benkovsky, respecting all its original details. There's a courtyard and garden, a living room and a breakfast room with 18th-century panelling. The four B&B rooms cover a range of options: two romantic doubles, two exceptional suites – kids can have a separate room as good as their parents' one.

Sommery ✉ 76440

La Ferme de Bray, **t** 02 35 90 57 27, *http://ferme-de-bray.free.fr* (*rooms €42 for two, €61 for four*). The extraordinary Ferme de Bray (*see p.177*) also contains five delightful B&B rooms, in one of the many outhouses – cosy showcases of Norman country style, with hefty carved-wood furniture. A special place to stay.

Eating Alternatives

Forges-les-Eaux ✉ 76440

Crêperie aux Trois Pommes, 9 Place Brévière, **t** 02 35 09 87 86 (*dishes c. €5–15*). Enjoyable *crêperie* and grill on Forges' main square, offering light meals: salads, *galettes*, sweet crêpes and a few larger things like steaks. Several dishes feature local cider and cheese.

Frichemesnil ✉ 76690

Au Souper Fin, Place de l'Eglise, **t** 02 35 33 33 38, *eric.buisset@free.fr* (*menus €16 lunch only, €28–42*). It's a great surprise in a tiny village to find this delightful little restaurant, with impressively sophisticated cuisine: *pavé* of venison with bilberry sauce, plenty of duck, and other imaginative dishes. Set menus are great value. It's also a **hotel** (*double rooms €50*), but since it has just two bright, pretty rooms it feels more like a B&B. *Oct–April restaurant closed Wed and Thurs*

Neufchâtel-en-Bray ✉ 76270

Hôtel du Grand Cerf, 9 Grande-Rue-Fausse-Porte, **t** 02 35 93 00 02 (*menus €14–30*). Even more a local institution than the hotel (*see left*), the kind of place to see all human life go by after the Saturday market. The hearty Norman cooking is very satisfying – homemade terrines, *lapin au cidre* – and it's renowned for big portions and great value.

St-Martin-Osmonville ✉ 76680

Auberge de la Varenne, 2 Route de la Libération, **t** 02 35 34 13 80 (*menus €19.10–33.55*). Pleasant roadside inn in a great hilltop location, with beautiful views. Good-value menus are strong on traditional Norman cooking: homemade rabbit pâté, local cheeses and calvados-rich desserts. *Closed Sun eve, Mon and Wed eve.*

St-Saëns ✉ 76680

Le Relais Normand, Place Maintenon, **t** 02 35 34 38 93 (*menus €11.50–26*). On St-Saëns' main square, this likeable little restaurant provides local produce and local dishes cooked with a light, imaginative touch, as well as a range of single-course options. As often in the Pays de Bray, it's excellent value. *Closed Sun eves and Wed.*

The Half-timbered City:
Rouen

18

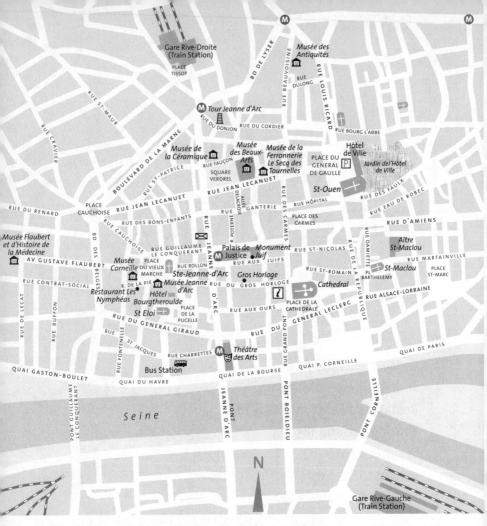

Rouen, historic capital of Normandy, is a city characterized by a dense intertwining of old and new. It is a thriving city: an industrial hub, a business and transport centre and, despite being so far from the sea, a major port. It was terribly ravaged in the Second World War, and large parts of it have had to be rebuilt, but throughout the centre of Rouen there are medieval streets and squares, delicate Renaissance carvings and grand 18th-century monuments – to such an extent that it has been labelled *la ville-musée*. Most of all, there are whole rows and alleys of half-timbering, for old Rouen was one of the largest communities ever built in this style, more often associated with cottages and quiet country towns.

Rouen is also a Gothic city. The period of its greatest wealth and energy at the end of the Middle Ages coincided with the apogee of French *Flamboyant* Gothic, favouring the most elaborate lace-work carvings and the most intricate decoration. The great cathedral painted so many times by Monet is one of a trinity of magnificent major Gothic religious buildings in Rouen, with the abbey of St-Ouen and the church of St-Maclou. Around them there are many more Gothic churches with superb stained glass – for which the city is renowned – civic buildings and merchant palaces, even a Gothic half-timbered cemetery, giving Rouen at night, especially, a distinct air of mystery. The city of Flaubert and Marcel Duchamp also has a vibrant contemporary life, and one of the best French regional art museums. And running through the middle of Rouen – along the attractive pedestrianized streets – are all the shops, cafés, restaurants and street life characteristic of a modern French city.

Rouen is also long-established as one of the gastronomic capitals of France. Its distinctive style has been characterized by a combination of loyalty to certain local, Norman traditions – especially the near-addiction to duck – with a very urbane refinement. The city's diners have always had some of France's finest restaurants to choose from, and today one of the most admired chefs in Rouen is Patrice Kukurudz, whose restaurant **Les Nymphéas** is unobtrusively located just off the Place du Vieux Marché, the old market square.

Getting There

Driving into Rouen is slightly complicated by the fact that it does not have a ring road to filter the traffic, which can be atrocious. All three main routes into the city – the A28 *autoroute* from Calais and the north, the A29 and A15 from Le Havre, and the Avenue de Caen which leads in from the A13 from Caen or Paris – tend to bring you via *Centre Ville* signs to the long quays along the north bank of the Seine. The best way to get off them and into town is to turn up Rue de la République, which runs through the east side of the city centre. Then it's best to leave your car for the day: there are useful **car parks** at Vieille Tour, off Rue du Général Leclerc, and beneath the square in front of the Hôtel de Ville and St-Ouen. On-street parking is very restricted. There are pay-and-display parking spaces in many streets, but it is generally easier to use an underground car park.

Rouen is major hub of **train** services with frequent connections to Paris (Gare St-Lazare, 1hr 15mins), Le Havre, Dieppe, Caen and many other parts of France. All passenger trains run from the **Gare Rive-Droite** station, at the north end of Rue Jeanne d'Arc. The **bus station** (*Gare Routière*) is near the opposite end of the same street, on Rue des Charettes, by the river. Buses run from there to all the surrounding region.

Rouen's Boos **airport**, 10km to the east, has French domestic and European flights, but so far none from the UK.

Getting Around

Central Rouen is easily walkable, but there are plenty of local **buses**, and a *Carte Découverte* ticket can be bought at the tourist office that gives unlimited travel on public transport for from one to three days. The **Métrobus** line that goes up and down Rue Jeanne d'Arc (actually a modern tram) is not usually of much use to visitors unless you wish to get to areas outside the centre or to somewhere south of the river, such as the Place des Emmurées flea market.

Taxis are also plentiful; if you need to phone for a cab, call **t** 02 35 88 50 50.

Les Nymphéas restaurant can best be located by first finding Place du Vieux Marché, on the west side of the city centre (which also has an underground car park). Although its address is officially in Rue de la Pie, the entrance is on the south side of the square.

Tourist Information

Rouen: Hôtel des Finances, 25 Place de la Cathédrale, **t** 02 32 08 32 40, *www.rouentourisme.com. Open daily.*
Internet Access: Progress Multimedia, 44–46 Allée Delacroix, **t** 02 35 07 70 89, *www.progress-multimedia.com.* Since public Net access remains so oddly scarce in France, this helpful shop can be very handy when you need to check your mail. *Open Mon–Sat until 8.30pm.*

Les Nymphéas

7–9 Rue de la Pie, **t** *02 35 89 26 69,* **f** *02 35 70 98 81.*
Open Tues–Sat 12–1.45 and 8–9.30, Sun 12–1.45. Book always.
Menus €27.50 Tues–Thur and Fri lunch only, €36–63; carte *average €65.*

The Place du Vieux Marché has been one of Rouen's busiest, most bustling squares since the early Middle Ages. Pass through the discreet entrance to Les Nymphéas, however, just off the square in a beautifully restored half-timbered building, and you enter a snug little haven of luxury: opulent curtaining, abundant flowers and, visible beyond the main dining room, a ravishingly pretty neoimpressionist garden, where you can eat surrounded by flowers in summer. It's a place to find all the classic French culinary arts: the perfect place settings, the quietly charming staff, the sommelier's flick of his crisp white napkin. The wine list which he administers is encyclopaedic.

Presiding over the restaurant is M Patrice Kukurudz. He has been a chef for nearly 30 years, and took over Les Nymphéas in 1991. His personal explanation of his craft is rather like a declaration of principles of a certain classic French approach. He believes that in cooking you need to be aware of traditions – which in Rouen means Norman tradition – and to preserve the roots of a cuisine, because you need to have a base upon which you can create and experiment, so that you don't end up trying to run before you can walk. He also thinks that it's quite acceptable, and maybe increasingly necessary, for restaurants to act slightly as 'temples of tradition', holding up ideals of good practice so people at least know what they are, and how this or that traditional dish should be done. This shouldn't be any justification for inflexibility, however, because a chef also needs to use his imagination. In his own cooking he makes great use of local staples such as duck and turbot – one of his specialities is *canard sauvageon à la Rouennaise* (with wild instead of farmed duck) – but each of them is used in original ways. Nor does he want his restaurant to be solemn or over-formal. As well as being seductively pretty, Les Nymphéas is a very comfortable place to be, although you will fit in better with other diners if you're at least a little dressed up.

The dominant impression given by Patrice Kukurudz' cooking is of a tremendous refinement. It begins with the *mises-en-bouche*, perhaps a portion of roast Neufchâtel cheese *aux fines herbes*, a tiny but wonderfully deep-flavoured introduction. Of the first courses, a salad of grilled langoustines with avocado and gazpacho is ideally summery, with every ingredient fabulously fresh, the little cup of gazpacho a rich mix of almost mysterious tones to offset against the superb seafood. Between courses you have the option of an exquisite sorbet and calvados *trou normand*. Main courses might include a *carré de veau escalopé, ris en fricassée, jus parfumé aux morilles* – the *parfumé* a reminder of another feature of the cooking here, that ingredients, flavours and seasonings are so subtly handled they often seem more like elusive presences or aromas than conventional tastes. In this case, the earthy tone of the *morilles* mushrooms spectacularly manages to be both fragrant and richly satisfying at the same time. Fine use is naturally made of seasonal produce, as in turbot with an assortment of forest mushrooms in autumn, but one of

M Kukurudz' most celebrated specialities is permanent – his superbly textured *civet de homard* (lobster stew), made with fine sauternes.

The cheese course is innovative, served with fruit breads, while desserts continue the delicate style, as in a *biscuit* with caramelized apples and a lovely, vibrantly fresh caramel ice-cream. This is not grandstanding cooking, throwing together radical combinations for effect, but a style that knows exactly what it's doing, making use of very refined skills. Everything is subtle, so that seekers after hearty flavours might be disappointed. Once in a while, though, it's luxuriously pleasurable.

Touring Around

Claude Monet painted the west front of **Rouen Cathedral** over 30 times, forever trying to capture the changing play of light over its complex surfaces. He did so from three different vantage points, all of them indoors, convincing shopkeepers to let him use their upstairs rooms. His final location was above a drapers' shop in the south-west corner of the cathedral square, from where he painted his most famous series of the great west portal. In a moment of inspiration the local tourist authorities, as part of their 'Impressionist Itineraries' (leaflets on which are available at the tourist office), have placed a plaque as near as possible to the site of the room, to allow you to compare image and reality. The actual building was destroyed in the Second World War, which left the square a good deal larger than it was in Monet's time.

The Cathedral is the kind of medieval building that really should have no unity at all, but which somehow works. William the Conqueror presided over the consecration of the first Rouen Cathedral in 1063. This plain Norman building was severely damaged by fire at the beginning of the 13th century, which conveniently provided an opportunity for comprehensive rebuilding in Gothic style. The west façade itself is almost a display case of medieval architecture. The relatively simple tower to the left, the north side, the **Tour St-Romain**, is a 12th-century survivor from the Norman cathedral, although topped by a much more elaborate upper level and roof added in the 1470s; on the other, south side is the *Flamboyant* **Tour de Beurre** (Butter Tower), built at the end of the 15th century – paid for with a special tax to avoid having to give up butter for Lent. Between them, the two smaller portals, one on the left with scenes of the life of St John the Baptist and the other of St Stephen, are from the first, 13th-century Gothic reconstruction; the soaring screens above them were added in the 14th century, while the extraordinary central portal, rising up to a 'Tree of Jesse', was built by the greatest of Rouen's *Flamboyant* Gothic architects Roulland le Roux in 1509–21. If you walk all the way around the outside of the cathedral you can see many more of the *Flamboyant* details added around the same period, especially the rhythmic lines of triangular gables along the sides, the remarkable portals of the transepts, and the magnificent gateway to 'Bookseller's Court', the passageway by the north transept.

Inside, the main structure of the cathedral is much simpler, with an exquisitely lofty, plain 13th-century early Gothic nave. The interior is very dark, which makes all the more breathtaking the cathedral's superb glass, a great deal of which dates from around 1230. Much of the stained glass had fortunately been stored away at the beginning of the Second World War and so escaped later bombing, but it is interspersed with many windows of plain clear glass, which gives the building a strangely ghostly feel. Most fascinating of all the glass windows is the one that tells with poetic detail the story of St Julian the Hospitaller and his attempts to avoid a prediction that he would murder his parents, on the north side of the chapel. The Choir is fabulous, both for its glass and the elegance of its early-Gothic arches. Around it are the tombs of several Norman dukes and other members of their dynasty, including the great founder of the clan, Rollo, and Richard the Lionheart. Their effigies are dwarfed by two massive 16th-century tombs in the Lady Chapel at the very far end, that of Rouen's great patrons the two Cardinals d'Amboise, designed by Roulland le Roux in a style similar to that of his *Flamboyant* buildings, and the equally ornate 1535 tomb of the Seneschal of Normandy Louis de Brézé.

Another feature of the cathedral is that it is visibly battered, many of its carvings pitted by bomb damage. It used to be much more so, for restoration work has been going on more or less since the Second World War, when Rouen was probably more ravaged than any other city in France. It was devastated by German attacks in 1940 – which set off instant fires in a city with so much wood – and again by Allied bombing in 1944, including one misconceived British night raid on 19 April when many aircraft, targeted to hit the railway yards south of the river, got lost and dropped their bombs on the city instead. The restoration effort has been extraordinary, to the extent that it is genuinely difficult to distinguish between real survivors and restored buildings. However, some parts – like the quays and much of the area between the cathedral and the Seine – were rebuilt in the usual functional post-war reconstruction style.

Performing Duck: *Caneton Rouennais*

Caneton Rouennais or *canard à la presse*, Rouennais duck, is a dish from the days when French *haute cuisine* was the only proper cuisine there was, and was served at banquets to whiskered gentlemen with expansive waistcoats and gold watch chains. It was a particular favourite of King Edward VII, not a man you would associate with a light lunch. Drawn at some point from Norman country cooking, it's really a very theatrical, purely restaurant dish. The most renowned modern recipe is that of the *Caneton Rouennais Félix Faure* as defined by the patriarch of the Hôtel de Dieppe in Rouen, Michel Guéret, who based it on that of Louis Convert, one-time personal chef to Edward VII, under whom he did his apprenticeship. The Dieppe (*see* p.192) is the great temple of traditional *caneton*, and the Guérets have founded an international *Ordre des Canardiers*, 'master duck-preparers', to ensure its survival. Order *caneton* at the hotel and it will be prepared at your table with all the right theatricality, by a *maître-canardier* with medal of office on a blue ribbon around his neck.

Essential to *caneton rouennais* is that the duck should be suffocated or strangled and not have its throat cut, so that the meat is unbled. Before you see it, the carcass is cleaned and the heart, liver and other giblets are minced and combined with a stock of beef, shallots, thyme, spices and red wine to make a *fond rouennais*, the

Immediately opposite the cathedral in Place de la Cathédrale, the tourist office enjoys a very grand setting inside the 1509 **Hôtel des Finances**, so-called because it was built for the chief tax collector of the time. It was also designed by Roulland le Roux, and is one of his most interesting buildings, with fine proportions combined with his usual ornate decoration reflecting a move from pure *Flamboyant* Gothic to a more restrained approach influenced by the Italian Renaissance. The cathedral square also makes a natural starting point for exploring Rouen. To the north, Rue des Carmes leads to the main shopping area and the museums; beside the tourist office, Rue du Gros Horloge leads to the famous 'great clock' and the old market area; while to the left of the cathedral, Rue St-Romain, half-timbered from end to end and full of idiosyncratic shops, takes you into one of the most characterful areas of old Rouen.

Rouen began life as a Roman city called *Rotomagus*, but its development really gathered pace after 911, when the Norse chieftain Rollo made it his capital. After King Philippe-Auguste of France took Normandy from King John in 1204, he built a large new castle in Rouen, in the north of the city. Like the rest of Normandy it had a major role in the Hundred Years' War, and was besieged and taken by Henry V of England in 1418. It was because the city was the hub of English power in France that the captured Joan of Arc was brought here, to be tried in the abbey of St-Ouen before she was burnt at the stake in Place du Vieux Marché on 30 May 1431. Once French power revived, however – driving out the English in 1449 – the city entered a virtual golden age. Trade expanded rapidly, and Rouen enjoyed power and wealth. It was especially favoured by Cardinal d'Amboise, first of France's great Cardinal-Ministers and Archbishop of Rouen, who at the beginning of the 16th century sponsored all kinds of buildings around the city, many by his favourite architect Roulland le Roux.

special stock. The duck carcass is also spit-roast for 17 minutes. At this point these ingredients and other equipment are brought to your table, on a special trolley. The duck carcass is then intricately carved with a great deal of flamboyant movement, and the sliced breasts are put to one side while the wings are taken off to the kitchen to be breaded and grilled. Then comes the most theatrical part of the operation, the use of the duck press, the bizarre apparatus that towers up in the middle of the trolley. There are very few true duck presses in existence: even the Dieppe only has three, the finest an extraordinary piece by the famed Parisian silversmiths Christofle. The now carved and meatless carcass is cut into pieces and sealed inside the press, where it is compacted by turning the great wheel on top of the devilish machine, all to produce a little silver gravy boat-full of concentrated, bloody duck-juice. This is used in the last great performance, the making of the sauce, combining together the blood, the *fond rouennais*, butter, lemon, port and flambéd calvados or cognac, before it is finally served together with the breast meat and the breaded wings.

The result is extraordinary, an intensely powerful, deep, textured flavour, quite unique and with scarcely any similarity to conventional roast duck. It's also about the richest dish ever fed to man, with nothing at all to do with contemporary fashions in light food, so afterwards a leisurely afternoon, or port and cigars, is in order.

Rue St-Romain ends at the modern Rue de la République. Just across it is Place Barthélemy, a gem of a half-timbered square around the church of **St-Maclou**, the second point in Rouen's Gothic church triangle. Dedicated to the same Welsh/Breton saint as the city of St-Malo, it's much smaller than the cathedral, and much more abruptly vertical, but still awe-inspiring. Instead of an architectural mishmash, it's an integral work of *Flamboyant* Gothic, built between 1437 and 1517. The west portal, facing you, is astonishing, as much like a Gothic fantasy as a real Gothic structure, with stone carvings of the *Last Judgment* and massive carved timber doors that have remarkably survived from the 16th century. It's a sombre, blackened church; it was severely damaged in 1944, and the effects of bombing are still plain to see: there are many windows that are now clear as well as some marvellous stained glass.

From the back of the church, head a little way up Rue Martainville and look out for a tiny (signposted) entry to the left. This will take you via a low-ceilinged passageway into the **Aître St-Maclou** (*open daily 8am–8pm*), a large, complete 16th-century half-timbered courtyard, with precariously sloping upper galleries and erratically angled timbers, carved with death's-heads, crossed bones and skeletons. The Aître was first created as a cemetery for plague victims during the Black Death, in 1348; later, it became a general cemetery for the poor of Rouen, and the current buildings were erected in the 1520s, as ossuaries to contain the bones from re-used graves. Today it houses Rouen's School of Fine Arts, which only makes it more bizarre: there are fashion workshops in some of the old bone-halls, and the students seem oblivious to the strangeness of their surroundings.

If you're in this area on a Sunday, continue along Rue Martainville to Place St-Marc, site of the weekly flea market. Otherwise, cut back to St-Maclou and turn right up Rue Damiette, another of this area's fascinating old alleys. This will lead you to Place De Gaulle and Rouen's third great Gothic temple, the **Abbatiale St-Ouen** (*open mid-Mar–Oct Tues–Sat 10–12.15 and 2–6, Sun 9–12.15 and 2–6, closed Mon; mid-Jan–mid-Mar and Nov–mid-Dec Tues, Sat and Sun 10–12 and 2–5; closed mid-Dec–mid-Jan; adm*), now rivalled by the huge 19th-century Hôtel de Ville, built on former abbey land next to it.

Enter the abbey church through the spectacular Gothic portal on the south side, known as the 'Porch of the Marmosets' because some of the strange little figures in its intricate carvings were long thought to represent monkeys. The abbey dates from the pre-Norman era, for it was founded in about 750, in commemoration of the local saint Ouen who had been Bishop of Rouen for over 40 years in the previous century. At the beginning of the 14th century, however, Abbot Jean Roussel announced his attention to build a new 'Celestial Jerusalem' and commissioned the great church we can see today, built in the simpler, mid-Gothic style known in French as *Rayonnant*. Inside, the overriding impression given by the great nave is of soaring immensity. It is much lighter and appears much larger than the cathedral, because it is less cluttered but also because of the beautiful purity of its lines. It also has dazzling stained glass, which has survived better than that in any other of the Rouen churches, some of it from the 14th-century rebuilding of the abbey but most added in a more Renaissance style between 1500 and 1550. Among the most astonishing is the 15th-century rose window in the north transept, in an almost modern-looking star pattern.

From Place Général de Gaulle busy Rue Jean Lecanuet runs directly to Rouen's 'museum quarter'. The august-looking **Musée des Beaux Arts** (*open Mon and Wed–Sun 10–6; closed Tues and most public hols; adm*) has one of the liveliest French regional museum collections, with far more variety and fewer dull local painters than can be the case. It has its great masterpieces, above all Caravaggio's *Flagellation of Christ on the Cross*, with just three figures emerging out of darkness and a quite astonishing figure of Christ, and *Demócrito*, one of Velázquez' immensely penetrating portraits of Spanish court jesters. There are also very fine works by Perugino and Gérard David, and a whole room of giant canvases by Veronese, originally painted for the church of San Rocco in Rome. From closer to home there are dramatic small paintings by the Rouen-born Géricault, and a good Impressionist collection, including (of course) a Monet of Rouen Cathedral. Later attractions include several excellent Sickerts and a room dedicated to the region's great contribution to modern art Marcel Duchamp, born at Blainville-Crevon, near Ry (*see* p.198), in 1887. His creations are shown together with those of his less well-known sister and brothers, all fellow avant-garde artists. The museum also has its engaging surprises: eccentric Symbolists like Alfred Agache, and a rare piece of 17th-century English Catholic art, *Lord Arundel of Wardour and his wife Cecily at the Foot of the Cross* by John Michael Wright, painted for the Convent of the English Poor Clares in Rouen, which was endowed by the Arundel family. The Beaux-Arts also hosts a dynamic series of temporary shows.

The other museums nearby follow more specific interests. The **Musée de la Céramique** (*open Mon and Wed–Sun 10–1 and 2–6; closed Tues and most public hols; adm*), in a distinguished 1650s *hôtel particulier* across the square, is dedicated primarily to the distinctive style of decorated porcelain produced in Rouen from the 16th to the 18th centuries, but also has Italian and Delftware, with many beautiful pieces; the **Musée de la Ferronerie-Le Secq des Tournelles** (*open Mon and Wed–Sun 10–1 and 2–6; closed Tues and most public hols; adm*), in the former church of St-Laurent behind the Beaux-Arts, contains an often bizarre collection of historic ironwork – keys, lamps, ornaments, remarkably fine gates and so on. A few streets further north is the **Tour Jeanne d'Arc** (*open April–Sept Mon and Wed–Sat 10–12.30 and 2–6, Sun 2–6.30; Oct–April Mon and Wed–Sat 10–12.30 and 2–5, Sun 2–5.30; closed Tues; adm*), so-called because it has been traditionally been believed that Joan of Arc was imprisoned and tortured there, although this is probably untrue. The massive tower is the only remaining part of Philippe-Auguste's 13th-century castle, and is more interesting than its contents, a small exhibition on the history of Rouen.

From the Beaux-Arts, cross Rue Lecanuet and go down the wide Allée Delacroix to Rue Ganterie, Rouen's most attractive shopping street. Wander back towards the cathedral along Rue des Carmes; just to the east in pretty Place des Carmes is Rouen's statue of Flaubert. At the tourist office, turn up Rue du Gros Horloge. Looming up ever larger in front of you is one of the city's most celebrated monuments, the **Gros Horloge**, an extraordinarily lavish, gilt-detailed Renaissance clock built over the street in the 1520s. As impressive as the actual clock are the exuberant carvings beneath the arch, and a matchingly ornate water fountain built under Louis XV in the 1730s. One of the oldest streets in the city, Rue du Gros Horloge is still busy, full of shops and bars. Turn right (north) up one of the alleys either side of the clock and you will see the magnificent courtyard and façade of the **Palais de Justice**, the greatest *Flamboyant* Gothic civil building in Rouen. Its restoration was one of the most painstaking tasks undertaken after 1945. The palace was built from 1499 to 1526 to house the *Parlement* and Exchequer of Normandy, and the most intricate sections were by Roulland le Roux. After the Revolution, it was taken over by Rouen's law courts. The street on which it stands, Rue aux Juifs, was at the centre of one of the oldest Jewish communities in France before their expulsion by royal dictat in 1306. During the restoration a room was discovered beneath part of the Palais, now called the **Monument Juif**, that had been built around 1100 and is believed to have been part of a synagogue – the oldest relic of Jewish life in France. Sadly, after a time during which it could be visited, it has now been closed again for security reasons.

At the west end of Rue aux Juifs, cross noisy Rue Jeanne d'Arc and continue in the same direction to reach **Place du Vieux Marché**, ringed by exquisite restaurants (like Les Nymphéas) and budget cafés. Its old church of St-Vincent was destroyed in 1944, and in its place is the striking 1970s church of **Ste-Jeanne-d'Arc**, with a swooping, bird-like roof. Imaginatively integrated into the church's structure are the brilliantly coloured glass from St-Vincent, which had been protected during the war, and France's largest monument to the Maid of Orléans. The tacky **Musée Jeanne d'Arc** (*open daily mid-April–Sept 9.30–7; Oct–mid-April 10–12 and 2–6; adm*) on the south side of the square, on the other hand, does its heroine no favours; the waxwork tableau of Joan at the stake, especially, is a hoot. From the southeast corner of the market square, to the left of the museum, walk down Rue Panneret to enter Place de la Pucelle, another lovely, small medieval square. On it there stands the 16th-century mansion the **Hôtel de Bourgtheroulde** (*courtyard open Mon–Fri 8.30–5, Sat, Sun and hols 2.30–5.30*), a fascinatingly transitional building: the initial structure is pure *Flamboyant* Gothic, with characteristic lace-work carvings and decoration, but the later stages were built more spaciously under Renaissance influence.

Boulevard des Belges more or less marks the western limit of central Rouen, but carry on across it down Avenue Flaubert to one of France's most intriguing museums, the **Musée Flaubert et d'Histoire de la Médicine** (*open Tues 10–6, Wed–Sat 10–12 and 2–6; closed Sun, Mon and hols; adm*), next to the large hospital of the Hôtel-Dieu. It is, first of all, the birthplace of France's greatest novelist, born here in 1821 when his father was the hospital's Chief Surgeon – the size of the house gives an indication of how important Flaubert *père* was in the life of Rouen at that time. The Flaubert exhibits – the bright room where he was born, the medical books he consulted in researching his novels – are fascinating. They share the house, though, with the historical collection of one of France's oldest and most distinguished public hospitals. There's a hospital bed that slept six, an altarpiece from a plague chapel, the 'cabinet of curiosities' of the renowned Dr Le Cat, an 18th-century predecessor of Dr Flaubert, including mummified bodies, and an astonishing collection on childbirth. And in one room there's also Flaubert's parrot, the stuffed parakeet borrowed by Flaubert, never returned, and made famous by Julian Barnes' novel. Nearly 200 years after it was stuffed it's still a perky little bird, perhaps because so many people come to see it.

Shopping

Rue des Carmes, Rue Beauvoisine, Rue St-Lô and Rue Ganterie are the window-shoppers' target, with the most chic fashion shops. There's a clutch of fine food shops near the Vieux Marché, especially on Rue Rollon. Many are open on Sunday mornings, like the market.

The main **market** is in Place du Vieux Marché (*Tues–Sun am*). Flea markets are held in Place St-Marc (*Sun am*) and Place des Emmurées (*Thurs all day*). It's south of the river; take a tram from Rue Jeanne d'Arc to Place Joffre.

Rouen ✉ 76000

Caves Berigny, 7 Rue Rollon, t 02 35 07 57 54. An attractive fine wine merchant near the Vieux Marché, with a carefully chosen stock of modern French wines, and fine calvados and Normandy ciders. *Open Sun am.*

Fayencerie Augy, 26 Rue St-Romain, t 02 35 88 77 47. Dedicated to maintaining Rouen's own tradition of decorated porcelain: Augy also create original designs, and can make personalized pieces. It's possible to visit the workshop, by appointment. *Closed Mon.*

Fromagerie François Olivier, 40 Rue de l'Hôpital, t 02 35 71 10 40. François Olivier is the son of the current owner of Olivier in Dieppe and nephew of Philippe Olivier of Boulogne, so his credentials are impressive. He's also very friendly, and keen to guide customers through his superb, varied cheese stock.

Fromagerie du Vieux Marché, 18 Rue Rollon, t 02 35 71 11 00. Busy cheese merchant with a complete range of fine Norman cheeses, and a few other temptations such as fine apple preserves. *Open Sun am.*

Where to Stay

Rouen ✉ 76000

Villa Bertha, 4 Rue Dieutre, t 02 35 07 53 60, *www.villa-bertha.com* (*suites €111–149*). A stylish 1930s Art Deco mansion on one of the hills just north of the city centre, lovingly restored by owner Sylvie de Boulatsel. The three *chambres d'hôtes* suites are magnificently luxurious: other special features include a tiled *hammam* or Arab bath, and a pergola above the beautiful garden terrace.

Hôtel de Dieppe, Place Bernard Tissot, t 02 35 71 96 00, *www.bestwestern.fr* (*double rooms €88–110*). This classic hotel is now affiliated to Best Western, but it has been run by one branch or another of the Guéret-Le Grand family ever since it opened opposite the railway station in the 1880s. The very professional staff seem as much part of the place too, and it's run with a distinctive charm and brio. The 41 rooms are large, well-equipped and very comfortable. It has a smart cocktail bar, and the restaurant (*see p.192*) is a temple of traditional Rouen cuisine.

Hôtel de la Cathédrale, 12 Rue St-Romain, t 02 35 71 57 95, *www.hotel-de-la-cathedrale.fr* (*double rooms €59–85*). An imposing 17th-century half-timbered townhouse in one of old Rouen's most characterful streets that has only recently fully recovered from bomb damage, and become this very attractive hotel. The 26 pretty rooms have all-new facilities but make the most of their original features; breakfast is served in a manorial chamber with grand stone fireplace or in the lovely garden courtyard, a real city oasis.

Hôtel Le Vieux Carré, 34 Rue Ganterie, t 02 35 71 67 70, *www.vieux-carre.fr* (*double rooms €55–57*). One of the most successful of Rouen's new-style, informal hotels, run by Patrick Beaumont, who also had a hand in the Hôtel des Carmes (*see below*). Staff are young and relaxed, and modern, comfortable rooms have been combined with the historic half-timbered building with style and flair. There's an equally successful restaurant (*see p.192*), and breakfast is served in the courtyard in summer. There is, though, no lift. Very popular: book ahead.

Hôtel Le Cardinal, 1 Place de la Cathédrale, t 02 35 70 24 42, f 02 35 89 75 14 (*double rooms €45–66*). The hotel with the best location in Rouen. Some three-quarters of its 18 rooms have views of the cathedral; the very best on the top floors have balconies. The rooms are comfortable but functional; character is provided by the owner and her staff, who are friendly in a slightly cranky way.

M Philippe Aunay, 45 Rue aux Ours, t 02 35 70 99 68 (*rooms €52 for two*). This lofty half-timbered townhouse is an amazing survivor: despite being in one of the narrow streets near the cathedral it was miraculously little damaged in the 1944 bombing. It is entered via a stone passageway dating from 1424; Philippe Aunay's family have lived in the house ever since his great-grandfather had a fabric shop on the ground floor. Inside, it's packed with a collection of antiques and curios that outdoes many museums. There are three B&B rooms, with huge character and very comfortable. One can be adapted as a family room. M Aunay speaks English, and is a fountain of local knowledge.

Hôtel des Carmes, 33 Place des Carmes, **t** 02 35 71 92 31, *www.hoteldescarmes.fr.st* (*double rooms €42–58*). A venerable hotel with great Art Nouveau façade that was thoroughly done up in 1996 with bright, modern colours in its 12 rooms and a pretty breakfast room on the ground floor – setting a new, fresh, unstuffy style for Rouen hotels that has been much copied. Rooms at the front are the best, with views over the square. Note: there are a lot of stairs, and no lift.

Hôtel des Arcades, 52 Rue des Carmes, **t** 02 35 70 10 30, *hotel-des-arcades@wanadoo.fr* (*double rooms €30–47*). A simple hotel in one of the 1960s blocks in the town centre that makes a decent budget option. The rooms are light and well-kept, and there's a charming little breakfast bar.

Eating Alternatives

Rouen ✉ 76000

Restaurant Les Quatre Saisons – Hôtel de Dieppe, Place Bernard Tissot, **t** 02 35 71 96 00, *www.bestwestern.fr* (*menus €19–35*). The smart, pampering restaurant in the Dieppe hotel has full and varied menus of Norman-based cuisine, but the thing to have here is traditional Rouennais duck (*for a minimum of two, see* p.186), of which the Guéret family are prime exponents. Other dishes feature uninhibited modern cuisine with a luxurious touch, as in the richly chocolaty desserts.

Pascaline, 5 Rue de la Poterne, **t** 02 35 89 67 44 (*menus €10.90–21.70*). Run by the same family that owns the Hôtel de Dieppe, Pascaline is a less formal, popular brasserie, but which still uses best-quality ingredients. It offers lots of options – brasserie staples like steaks, classic fish dishes and St-Vaast

oysters, excellent-value set menus, and, very unusually in France, well-stocked self-service salad and dessert bars. There's also a good, flexible kids' menu. *Open daily till 11.30pm.*

Le Vieux Carré, 34 Rue Ganterie, **t** 02 35 71 67 70, *www.vieux-carre.fr* (*lunch menu €12*). In the ground floor and courtyard of the hotel (see p.191), this pretty, relaxing place has a look that stylishly combines old and new, with leather armchairs and cool music in the background. It's called a *Gourmet Salon de Thé*, and it specializes in the kind of light, fresh lunches popular with young French urban diners. The excellent-value lunch offers a main course, starter or dessert and a glass of wine: other options include one-course *assiettes* such as mixed salads and pastas, and vegetarian choices such as a delicious omelette with *girolles* mushrooms. It's open for teas, coffees and snacks in the afternoon, and at weekends there's a brunch menu. *Open Tues–Sun 11.30am–6.30pm.*

Le Petit Zinc, 20 Place du Vieux Marché, **t** 02 35 89 39 69 (*dishes c. €4–18*). A busy, lively bar-bistro with retro-style décor and tables on the Vieux Marché square, popular with a youth-ish crowd. Chalked-up lists offer plenty of choices from *tartine* open sandwiches to seafood, salads, and grills, and there's an ample wine range. *Closed Sun.*

Le Socrate, 46–48 Rue Ganterie, **t** 02 35 70 32 03 (*menus €10.50–13*). Stylishly sleek modern bar-brasserie with a big outside terrace in a great people-watching spot. Prices are ultra-competitive: set menus are less the main event than one-course dishes, such as very imaginative salads and pasta dishes. Moreish cakes and desserts, too.

Brasserie Paul, 1 Place de la Cathédrale, **t** 02 35 71 86 07 (*menus €10.50–17.10*). A classic brasserie opposite the cathedral that opens every day from bright and early till 2am (*full menu available only to 11pm*), for breakfast, coffee, excellent lunches, quick snacks, late-night drinks or warmers of French onion soup. The terrace outside offers about the nearest seat you'll get to Monet's view of the cathedral. Apollinaire ate here, Marcel Duchamp came here often during a time when he gave up art for chess, and Simone de Beauvoir came in for breakfast every day when she taught in Rouen during the 1930s.

Bovaryland:
Ry and the
Forêt de Lyons

19

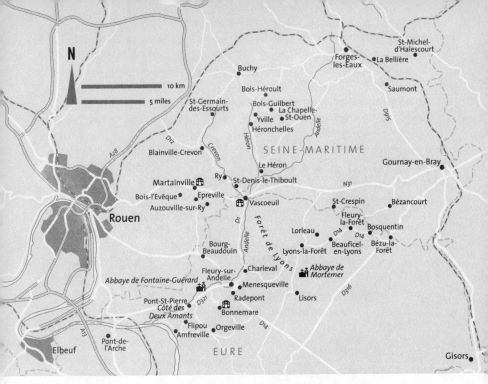

Seeking out the real settings that featured in or inspired novels, films or any other kind of fiction is perhaps a special taste, like Marmite. If you share it, when a book has created a world in your head there is great fascination in relating it to actual places on the ground. It is all the more so when a book can be so peculiarly, and surprisingly, associated with specific locations as can that monument of French literature, often considered the first true modern novel, Flaubert's *Madame Bovary*.

Flaubert never admitted that his fictional town of 'Yonville-l'Abbaye' was related to any one place in particular, but a great deal of the action and geography of the book can be identified with the country town of Ry, some 20km east of Rouen, and Ry was moreover the scene of the incident that inspired *Madame Bovary* in the first place. Today, Ry is pervaded by imaginary memories of Yonville, and an exploration of the town and its surrounding villages allows anyone to try a little of the kind of literary reconstruction undertaken by Julian Barnes in *Flaubert's Parrot*.

Away from its Flaubertian associations, and without the aura of autumnal gloom with which Flaubert surrounded it, the countryside north of Ry that tourist leaflets now pertly refer to as the *Pays d'Emma* has other attractions: it runs up the valleys of two fast-flowing, gleaming rivers, the Crevon and the Héron, with beautifully individual villages with crumbling châteaux and historic churches towering up above the trees. And to the south is the Forêt de Lyons, one of the largest beech woods in Europe, a superb stretch of dense woodland crisscrossed by paths and with wonderful vistas from its many hills. At its centre is Lyons-la-Forêt, one of the most extravagantly pretty half-timbered towns in Normandy. Just to the west, minor rivers, roads and forest all meet up in the narrow valley of the Andelle, another quick,

Getting There

From Calais and the north or Dieppe, the most direct route into this region is the A28 *autoroute* south; leave it at exit 12, near Buchy, and cut across minor lanes to Ry, or follow the A28 to its end just outside Rouen and look for a turning east onto the N31 for Beauvais, which passes just south of Ry. From Le Havre, cut across on the A29 to meet the A28 and loop around Rouen, or leave the A29 at Yvetot to cross the Seine by the Pont de Brotonne and get on the A13 *autoroute*.

To get to Pont-St-Pierre, leave the A13 at exit 20, Pont de l'Arche, cross the Seine to the east bank and take the D321 to Pont-St-Pierre. The Bonne Marmite is easy to find on the main street. To reach Pont-St-Pierre or the Forêt de Lyons from the north via Ry, follow the road signposted to Vascœuil and Fleury-sur-Andelle, a slow but pretty route.

The only **train** line in this area is from Rouen to Gisors via Fleury-sur-Andelle. **Buses** run from Rouen to Ry and Lyons-la-Forêt, and from Fleury to Lyons.

Tourist Information

Lyons-la-Forêt: Office de Tourisme du Pays de Lyons-Andelle, 20 Rue de l'Hôtel de Ville, **t** 02 32 49 31 65, *otsi-pays-lyons-andelle @wanadoo.fr*. The main information office for the whole Forêt de Lyons. Has good free walking guides, and will point you towards riding and cycle hire facilities.

Charleval: 77bis Grande Rue, **t** 02 32 48 19 59, *www.charleval.fr*.

La Feuillie: Mairie, **t** 02 35 09 68 03.

Pont-St-Pierre: Piscine Intercommunale, **t** 02 32 49 70 90.

Ry: Maison de l'Abreuvoir, **t** 02 35 23 19 90.

lively river, lined by lush forest and snug villages as it runs down to meet the Seine. Scattered through this area is a remarkable collection of châteaux – it can look like one in every village – from France's golden era between the 16th and 18th centuries.

In its restaurants, this area offers a mixture of Norman country tradition and the more refined, contemporary cuisine you might expect in a region not too far from a city like Rouen, or even Paris. Both these elements – and a superlative wine selection – can be found under one roof at the **Hostellerie La Bonne Marmite**, a magnificent old inn in Pont-St-Pierre, at the southern end of the Andelle valley.

Hostellerie La Bonne Marmite

*10 Rue René Raban, Pont-St-Pierre, **t** 02 32 49 70 24, www.la-bonne-marmite.com. Open Tues 7.30–9, Wed–Sat 12–2.30 and 7.30–9, Sun 12–2.30. Closed Mon and two weeks Feb–Mar, two weeks July–Aug. Menus €17 Wed–Sat lunch only, €25–79.50; carte average €55.*

Pont-St-Pierre is a sizeable little town that gets quite bustling at times, at least on some days of the week. It is centred on the much-reduced remains of its old Norman motte-and-bailey castle, but the most striking building in town has to be its historic inn, the Bonne Marmite, presiding over a curve in the main road as it runs down to the Andelle. It has one of the most imposing of Norman half-timbered façades, eight windows long; through the coach-and-four-sized gateway is a lovely flower-and-ivy-clad courtyard. Enter the main building and you find a little island of old-world comfort, far away from the traffic outside. Like many similar old auberges and *hostelleries* it began life as an 18th-century *relais de poste* or coaching inn. Since 1966 it has been tended with devotion by M Maurice Amiot and his wife Denise. Their very personal care is visible in all kinds of details: the elegantly manorial décor in the timber-ceilinged dining room, the wonderfully snug and comfortable bar; they also designed the whimsical 'coat of arms' on the baronial-looking plates, combining the lions of Normandy, the keys of St Peter, Bacchus and a little *marmite* or cooking pot.

In his time at the Bonne Marmite Maurice Amiot has also won a string of awards for his cooking. Although he has been at his craft many years, he is the kind of chef who can always teach young contemporary cooks new tricks: his style combines a sense of tradition with inventiveness, a timeless use of strong, unmasked flavours and superb ingredients with original combinations and a light touch. A first course of *boudins de langoustines* – finely-chopped 'puddings' – with a lobster sauce is magnificently enjoyable, the very essence of fine fresh seafood imaginatively prepared. To follow, an *entrecôte vigneronne* is equally a showcase example of a classic French way of cooking steak, with first-quality meat and a deeply satisfying richly-textured sauce. The house specialities include several dishes based on lobster, such as lobster ravioli or M Amiot's award-winning *civet de homard* (lobster stew). His menus also cover a whole range of options, from a (relatively) light good-value lunch to unreserved indulgent luxury with specialities such as beef with ceps and *girolles* mushrooms and opulent top-range lists like the €53 *menu découverte* or €79.50 *menu dégustation*.

The cheese course also gives you a choice, between a traditional Norman cheese-board and a more modern mix of warm *chèvre* with salad or seasonal fruit. This provides a suitable pause before another highlight, the desserts, above all those that include fruit, from original inventions such as *galettes* with woodland berries or the perfect versions of local classics like *tarte aux pommes*. Everything is beautifully done, right down to the melt-in-your-mouth shortbread *petits-fours* and superior coffee.

M and Mme Amiot are warm, attentive and charming hosts, which, with the comfort of the setting and the satisfying food (and the smart guest rooms, *see* p.204), gives the Bonne Marmite a distinctly cosy-but-sybaritic feel. This is rounded off by one other major feature, the wine cellar, which is as much the Amiots' pride and joy as the products of the kitchen. It too has won many awards, and is one of the finest in Normandy: there are over 600 reds on the list, and around 270 whites. Among them there is a magnificent selection of French *grands crus* and rare bottles dating back to 1858, but the Amiots are also – rare in France – open-minded oenophiles, and have included in their cellars a variety of New World wines.

Touring Around

In *Madame Bovary* Flaubert describes 'Yonville-l'Abbaye' as a market town about 20 miles from Rouen, 'on the borders of Normandy, Picardy and the Ile-de-France, a bastard region where the language is without accentuation', and where 'they make the worst Neufchâtel cheeses in the whole district'. Having insulted the local cheese, he goes on to present the town as a symbol of banality and small-town tedium. The novel being a story of everyday tragedy, imbued with sadness, you might think that anywhere would back away from being identified with such an image, but such is the power of *Madame Bovary* as a French cultural icon that people have long come to **Ry** looking for a scent of Emma, ever since the scandal caused by its first publication. The town for its part has embraced its fate, so that reality and its literary identity seem constantly to blend into one another.

Some of the details given by Flaubert in his description of Yonville don't quite fit with Ry, and some could suggest Forges-les-Eaux, but there is no doubt that in its fundamentals Yonville is based on Ry. For one thing, Ry provided the storyline of *Madame Bovary*. In 1848 the attention of Rouen and its region was seized by a scandal in which Delphine Delamare (or Couturier, her maiden name), the young wife of a country doctor in Ry called Eugène Delamare, poisoned herself; it quickly emerged that she had run up huge debts, and had had a lover, or lovers. Eugène Delamare, destroyed by despair, poisoned himself in turn the following year. The story was suggested to Flaubert as a basis for a novel in 1851 by his friend Louis Bouilhet, who had known Eugène Delamare in Rouen, 'a poor devil of an *officier de santé*', like Charles Bovary, not even a fully-qualified doctor. Flaubert knew Delamare too, for he had studied under Flaubert's father at the hospital in Rouen, and Flaubert's mother had helped Delamare's mother after her son's death. Another of his friends, Maxime du Camp, wrote that he had also met Delphine, and recalled that she had a soft voice 'dishonoured' by a strong Norman country accent. Flaubert initially rejected the idea of writing about the events in Ry: in his earlier writings he had tried to deal with grander subjects, and he thought the Delamare case was too banal; oddly for a writer considered so provocative he also didn't like the idea of offending the Delamares and other people in Rouen. However, Bouilhet convinced him.

When you arrive in Ry today the most remarkable thing is the precision with which Flaubert followed its layout in creating Yonville, almost as if having got over his reservations he set out to reconstruct the incident, in a Truman Capote-Norman Mailer factoid style. This is what makes Ry and Yonville so difficult to tell apart. The main street or Grande Rue, 'about a gunshot in length, with a few shops on each side', is still there, so short and stubby that, if you imagine it without the few cars and trucks that pass by, you can still get a wistful sense of the claustrophobia that is so palpable in the book. The Crédit Agricole savings bank occupies the (much altered) building that in Flaubert's day was the Hôtel de Rouen, or the Hôtel Lion d'Or in the book; the curious half-timbered building that is now the Bovary restaurant was in the 1840s the Hôtel de France, which features in *Madame Bovary* as the Café Français, the Lion d'Or's new-fangled rival. Next to it, the old timber *Halles* or market is now the *Mairie*; across the street at no.32, the souvenir shop now just called *Emma* was long ago the Pharmacie Jouanne, the precise model for the shop of legendary busybody M Homais. The two houses that were lived in successively by the Delamares were the big half-timbered house on the corner of the D12 to Blainville (which did not exist at that time) and the smaller no.60, above the modern pharmacy. All around there are touristy references: even the local *épicerie* is called *Au Marché d'Emma*, and on some of the local literature the Delamares are referred to as the Delamare-Bovarys, as if any idea that Delphine had an identity of her own has disappeared into the woods.

A turn off the Grande Rue will take you to the **church**, where Eugène Delamare and his daughter, also called Delphine, are buried. The church dates from the 12th to the 17th centuries, and is fronted by a superb Renaissance portico in carved wood that's a remarkably elaborate feature to find in such a small and insignificant place. The old farm next to the church was the home of the wet nurse employed by Delphine Delamare for her child, the model for Emma Bovary's nurse Mère Rollet. Right at the other end of the Grande Rue, by the River Crevon and the tourist office, elevated literary thoughts are given a tweek in the cheeks by Ry's main 'attraction', the **Galerie Bovary** (*open Easter–June, Sept and Oct Mon, Sat, Sun and hols 11–12 and 2–7; July and Aug Mon, Sat, Sun and hols 11–12 and 2–7, Tues–Fri 3–6; adm*), installed in an old cider press, in which scenes from the book are brought to life by … automated puppets. Flaubert would presumably have taken a hammer to it, or roared with laughter. By a strange piece of serendipity, opposite the *Galerie* there is a sombre 19th-century brick building with an old-fashioned brass plaque with the words *Médecin de Garde* and the names of the two men currently in charge, which looks more like a part of *Madame Bovary* than most of the specifically Bovarian sites. Being a local doctor in Ry must be a heavy burden to bear, forever wondering whether you're always trying your best like poor Charles Bovary without actually getting anything right, and when your wife is going to start becoming chronically dissatisfied.

Outside of Ry, the ***Circuit Bovary*** signposted on the lanes and indicated on leaflets available at local tourist offices is, like the *Routes du Cidre* and similar routes worked out by French tourist offices elsewhere, an interesting means of getting to know the countryside, Bovary connections aside. South of Ry, a lovely road leads over a crest to the village of **St-Denis-le-Thiboult**, southwest of which is the hamlet of **Villers**, where there is an essential reference point for those most in love with our tragic heroine, the little manor house where she had her meetings with her aristocratic lover Rodolphe. It's not open to visitors, but is clearly visible from the N31 Rouen road, set back among trees. Again, Flaubert didn't make much up: this was the house where Delphine Delamare went to meet her lover Louis Campion, a spendthrift local gentleman who had retreated to his estate here to avoid the debts he had incurred in Paris and Rouen. In a further confusion of realities, the house is now near-universally known as La Huchette, as it is in the book, instead of by its real name of Gratianville.

In the opposite direction, following the D12 north from Ry along the green valley of the Crevon will take you to **Blainville-Crevon**, a very attractive, large village with the moodily impressive ruins of a medieval castle and a fine *Flamboyant* Gothic **church**, commissioned in 1488 by a local lord, Jean d'Estouteville. Eugène and Delphine Delamare were married here in 1839; inside, there is some very refined 15th-century carving in wood. Blainville was also the birthplace in 1887 of Marcel Duchamp. The Dadaist's dadda had the very respectable occupation of local notary, and served several times as Blainville's mayor. From there, a still smaller lane leads alongside the vivid little Crevon to **St-Germain-des-Essourts**, the birthplace of Delphine Couturier-Delamare. It's also an exceptionally pretty place: the name 'des-Essourts' comes from its large number of small springs, which are used to support the growing of water-cress, in little beds alongside the river.

The main *Circuit Bovary* reaches its northernmost point at the old Pays de Bray town of Buchy – with a spectacular timber-roofed market hall – but there are many roads that cut across between the Crevon and the still prettier, narrower valley of the Héronchelles, a name that originated in the number of herons seen along it. **Bois-Héroult**, on the open plateau above the valley, is a village around a small château, built for a gentleman of Buchy in 1721, and its huge manor farm. This is an area with many horses, and **Bois-Guilbert** is known for its *ferme-equestre* and riding centre (information, **t** 02 35 34 42 51). It occupies the elegant 17th-century château of the Domaine de Bois-Guilbert, once home to the early economist and savant Pierre le Pesant de Boisguilbert, a friend of the dramatist Corneille, who stayed here several times. Back down in the valley, **Héronchelles** village and tiny **Yville** are two of the loveliest places in the area, at a point where the little river is at its liveliest and clearest. Héronchelles also contains an august 16th-century Renaissance manor, and the villages all along the valley present an impressive array of churches, mostly with grey-slate spires like giant pots. At **Le Héron** the ivy-clad ruins of the medieval church stand by the roadside, with geese and ducks scrabbling beneath them, like a romantic folly; it was destroyed by fire in 1879. Le Héron also has a Flaubert connection as the site of the château of the Marquis de Pomereu, where the future writer attended a ball when aged 15 that gave him one of his first tastes of aristocratic living; he is said to have used it as a model for the ball at the château of La Vaubyessard, which so feeds the fantasies of Emma Bovary. The château of Le Héron was destroyed during the Second World War, but much of its Le Nôtre-style formal gardens still exists.

Nearby there are some more intact châteaux to visit. A short way west of Ry is the **Château de Martainville**. Begun in 1485 for a powerful Rouen merchant, Jacques Le Pelletier, it is one of the earliest creations of the French Renaissance style, in brick with soaring slate roofs and massive pepperpot towers, and of a very different order of comfort and opulence from the medieval castles that preceded it. It now houses the **Musée des Traditions et Arts Normands** (*open April–Sept Mon and Wed–Sat 10–12.30 and 2–6, Sun 2–6.30; Oct–Mar Mon and Wed–Sat 10–12.30 and 2–5, Sun 2–5.30; closed Tues; adm*), an illuminating folk museum with traditional costume, lace, embroideries, carved furniture and other artefacts of everyday life from around Upper Normandy, which combines well with surviving sections of the château interiors like the massive 15th-century kitchen. Some 6km southeast of here is the **Château de Vascœuil** (*open early April, late Oct–mid-Nov daily 2.30–5.30, late April–June, Sept–mid-Oct daily 2.30–6.30, July and Aug daily 11–7; closed mid-Nov–Mar; adm*). This is less distinguished as a building, a much more rugged stone pile built and altered many times from the 12th to the 16th centuries, with a great drum-like 16th-century pigeon loft in the garden alongside. It is known, though, as the home of the 19th-century historian Jules Michelet, and has a museum dedicated to him. Probably of more interest to most visitors is the arts centre that Vascœuil also contains, with a **sculpture garden** that includes work by famous names like Dalí and Braque as well as more off-the-wall creations by French contemporary artists. A lively series of concerts and exhibitions is held in the château and gardens each summer – Léger, Delvaux and Cocteau have all featured. Vascœuil also has an unusually lovely riverside café.

To the east of the River Andelle and the parallel D1 as they run south from Vascœuil is the **Forêt de Lyons**, extending for over 10,000 hectares, or 40 square miles. This was one of the favourite hunting grounds of the Anglo-Norman dukes, and later other kings and aristocrats, which is a major reason why it has survived. The forest has been reduced from its medieval extent, and there are large gaps and clearings around the villages within it, but it remains one of the largest stretches of native deciduous forest in northern Europe, a giant wild woodland of towering beeches with, in many sections, only limited human interruptions between the rolling crests and deep little valleys. It's especially lovely to come here in autumn, when the trees are red and gold in the clear light. The forest is still very dense in parts, and the shelter it provided made it a major focus of Maquis Resistance activity during the Second World War. There are many routes and paths into the woods, but the best way to begin is to head to its main village, **Lyons-la-Forêt**, and pick up a map at the tourist office.

Ry may have the 'real' Flaubert connections but the two French film adaptations of *Madame Bovary*, by Jean Renoir in 1934 and Claude Chabrol in 1991, both used Lyons-la-Forêt as a location, perhaps because poor Ry just didn't look 'historic' enough. Lyons is also one of that select bunch of communities accoladed as being one of the *Plus Beaux Villages de France*. And it's true: Lyons is ravishingly pretty, almost entirely made up of half-timbered houses built from the 16th to the 18th centuries. Genuinely modern structures can be counted on the fingers of one hand. Lyons predictably draws the crowds on summer weekends, but in spring and autumn, especially during the week, it's often surprisingly left to itself, and the atmosphere in the cafés around its superb main square is unfussy and relaxed.

Lyons is unusual in that the Norman castle around which the village grew up has almost entirely disappeared. The castle reached its greatest size under Henry I, King of England and Duke of Normandy and youngest son of William the Conqueror. It was one of his favourite residences, and he died here in 1135. In the 16th century, as the old castle crumbled into disuse, the current village was built on top of its remains, thus covering most traces of it. If, however, you walk from the foot of Rue de l'Hôtel de Ville across the D32 and down the path toward the River Lieure and the 'Trois Moulins', an idyllically pretty set of three tiny water mills next to small ponds, and then look back at Lyons you can see clearly the way in which the 1652 **Benedictine Convent**, to the left, was built on the base of the old Norman masonry. The convent was one of several religious houses established in Lyons in the 17th century; all of them closed with the Revolution. Because of Lyons' curious growth, the village church of **St-Denis** is oddly isolated outside the village, a five-minute walk to the west, as it was founded outside the castle walls in the 12th century. It was given a Gothic transformation in the 15th–16th centuries, and has fine carvings of figures of saints, in wood from the forest.

The steep **Rue d'Enfer** or 'Hell Street', half-timbered from end to end, is the most attractive way up from the main road to the centre of the village. On the left at no.4 is the little house, now with a plaque, where Maurice Ravel stayed several times in the 1920s, when he came here to compose amid the rural calm. The main square at the top is the heart of Lyons and an astonishing Norman monument, especially the south side, facing you, an array of different patterns in half-timbering. With its bars and local shops as well as antique emporia, it's also pleasantly alive. One of the most timeworn-looking houses on the square was the birthplace, in 1612, of the poet of Jewish descent Isaac de Benserade, an important figure at the court of Louis XIV, after whom the square is officially named. Dominating the middle of the square is the **Halles**, the tiled-roofed, open-sided market hall, built in the 18th century for the powerful *Ancien Régime* aristocrat and local benefactor the Duke of Penthièvre, who also commissioned the surprisingly plain Hôtel de Ville around the corner.

From Lyons paths lead off into the woods in all directions (one of the best easy walks is just to carry on along the path beyond the Trois Moulins, into the woods across the river). Other paths are indicated on maps available from the tourist office (next to the Hôtel de Ville), which also organizes **guided walks** (*weekends April–Sept, usually in French only*). There are many more places to explore in the forest around Lyons, especially along the lane to the north-east through **Lorleau**. Directly eastwards, the little D14 road runs through **Beauficel**, which has a magnificent church with giant wooden porch, to **Fleury-la-Forêt**, a village with a curiously remote feel dispersed around its grand Louis XIII-style **château**, which now provides memorable B&B rooms (*see* p.203). Fleury château can also be visited (*open Feb–mid-June and mid-Sept–Nov Sat, Sun and hols 2–6; mid-June–mid-Sept daily 2–6; adm*); guided tours take you around the main rooms with their scarcely altered 18th-century décor, and a small but engaging doll museum, and you are free to wander around the rambling park. For something more rustic, just to the east **Bézu-la-Forêt** contains a homely but charming locally-run farm museum, with all sorts of artefacts relating to the tradi-tional life of the forest villages, **La Ferme de Rome** (*open May, June, Sept and Oct Sat, Sun and hols 2–6; July and Aug daily 2–6; adm*). It also has a shop with local produce for sale. Directly south of Lyons-la-Forêt near Lisors are the remains of the Cistercian **Abbaye de Mortemer**, another institution that in the 12th century was greatly favoured by Henry I and his daughter Matilda (*park open daily 1.30–6; abbey and museum open May–Sept daily 2–6; Oct–April Sat, Sun and hols 2–5.30; adm*). It is surrounded by a huge forested park, with three small lakes and St Catherine's Spring, where the young women of the region once went to pray for a husband. Still visible from the medieval abbey are the castle-like 12th-century walls, part of the solid Norman chapterhouse and the 15th-century pigeon loft. Mortemer is now a well-developed tourist attraction: the main abbey buildings, rebuilt in the 17th century, contain as well as some more religious relics a **Musée de Légendes et Fantômes**, legends and ghosts, designed to evoke things that go bump in the night, and medieval pageants are staged in the ruins every Saturday night during August.

Outside the forest to the west is the **Valley of the Andelle**, one of the most attractive of the valleys that run down to join the Seine. **Fleury-sur-Andelle** is a straightforward country town. The valley below it is delightful: the division, found in all the Seine-Maritime valleys, is particularly marked between the sombre plateaux on either side of brown, open fields and huge horizons and the soft valley of woods and meadows below, where everything is greenness and running water. A good way of avoiding whatever traffic you might find on the D321 down the left bank is to cross over on to the parallel D149 down the right, a very quiet country road.

About 3km southwest of Fleury-sur-Andelle at **Radepont** you have a choice of monuments. A turn southwards up a very narrow lane will take you to the very grand and slightly mysterious **Château de Bonnemare** (*park usually open mid-April–mid-Oct Sun 2.30–6; guided tours of house mid-April–mid-Oct one Sun each month; timings variable, check with local tourist offices*), built in 1570 in late French-Renaissance style for Nicolas Leconte de Daqueville, President of the *Parlement* of Rouen. Its glowering perimeter walls completely dominate the tiny hamlet of Bonnemare; to get the full effect of the château go around it to the south side, intended as the main approach, where the giant slate-roofed *châtelet* or gatehouse stares down an extraordinarily long, straight *allée* of lime trees. Inside the walls are large gardens, a manor farm with bakery and 17th-century cider press and, in the house itself, several rooms with their original decoration. Its private owners only open it up infrequently, so ask at tourist offices about current possibilities. In contrast, a short journey back across the river and down the right bank leads to the ruins of the Cistercian **Abbaye de Fontaine-Guérard** (*open April–June and Sept–Oct Tues–Sun 2–6; July and Aug Tues–Sun 2–6.30; adm*), nestling in the woods. A nuns' convent, it was founded in the 12th century, and the now-ruined abbey church was completed in 1281. The nuns' parlour, a dormitory with massive timber roof, a Gothic work chamber and a chapel are all fairly intact, and the superb vaulted chapterhouse is one of the finest surviving works of Norman monastic architecture. Above all, it's a wonderfully serene place, with the river alongside and the white stone chapterhouse sheltered by trees as if in its own bower.

Little more than a kilometre further south along the D149 another still larger set of towers rises up above the trees, a monument not from the Middle Ages but from the Industrial Revolution. These are the extraordinary remains of the **Anciennes Filatures Levavasseur**, a textile mill built in the 1850s by an ambitious local landowner to make use of the current of the Andelle. As a 'cathedral of industry' it was built in the English neogothic style, with a scale and lavishness that seems completely out of proportion to its purpose; moreover, most of it burnt down only 20 years later, although parts of the factory were still in use until the Second World War. Today, its ruins loom up through the woods as atmospherically as those of any ruined medieval cathedral.

The roads either side of the river meet up at **Pont-St-Pierre**. In the centre of the town there are the ruins of another medieval fortress, and a fine 12th-century church, **St-Nicholas**, which has an exceptional wealth of medieval wooden carvings and some relics saved from Fontaine-Guérard. To the south a road winds round via **Amfreville** to the top of the **Côte des Deux Amants**, a massive rock escarpment overlooking the point where the Andelle joins the Seine. Its name refers to a medieval legend in which a jealous king, not wishing to relinquish his daughter Caliste, declared that no man could marry her unless he could run non-stop to the top of the great rock with her in his arms. Her noble beloved Raoul duly undertook to do it, but collapsed and died just as he reached the summit, whereupon she died as well in sympathy. Caliste and Raoul, the 'two lovers', are said to be buried at the top (to which there's also a footpath from Pont-St-Pierre, for anyone wishing to follow their route). Below at Amfreville are the last set of locks on the Seine going seawards, and from the top of the Côte there are fabulous views over the Andelle and up and down the Seine valley.

Shopping

The largest market in this area is in **Buchy** on Mondays; other country markets are in **Ry** (*Sat*), **Lyons-la-Forêt** (*Thurs*) and **Pont-St-Pierre** (*Sat*). The *Halles* in Lyons-la-Forêt also hosts exhibitions and antiques fairs in summer.

Lisors ✉ 27440

La Ferme des Acacias, Rue de l'Eglise, **t** 02 32 49 11 23. The Ouine family make traditional *charcuterie* and sell it from their farm, near the Abbaye de Mortemer. *Open Fri and Sat.*

Lyons-la-Forêt ✉ 27480

Boutique des 4 Fermières, 22bis Rue de l'Hôtel de Ville, **t** 02 32 49 19 73. An attractive little cooperative shop next to Lyons tourist office that sells produce from several local farms – cheeses, cider, *charcuterie*, homemade biscuits and more. *Open Thurs–Sun.*

Orgeville-Flipou ✉ 27380

Les Vergers d'Orgeville, 5 Chemin des Prés, **t** 02 32 49 72 3. A big cider farm about 3km south of Pont-St-Pierre, selling high-quality cider – no calvados – apples, in season, and honey.

Where to Stay

Bézancourt ✉ 76220

Château du Landel, **t** 02 35 90 16 01, *www.chateau-du-landel.fr* (*double rooms €77–153*). An elegant 18th-century château that is now a country-house hotel. The best of its 17 rooms are in period style, others are more contemporary and a bit plainer. There's a fine **restaurant** (*menus €25–40*), and in the grounds there are tennis courts and a pool. *Closed mid-Nov–mid-Mar.*

Bourg-Beaudouin ✉ 27380

Ferme du Coquetot, 46 Rue du Coq, **t/f** 02 32 49 09 91 (*rooms €37–52 for two, €50–60 for three*). This big old Norman manor farm is owned by a friendly young couple, Bénédicte and Jean-Luc Delavoye. Their four B&B rooms are lovely, and there's a big family room, a sitting room and access to a kitchenette. They also have a wonderful *gîte* in a converted dovecot, with room for up to four.

Fleury-la-Forêt ✉ 27480

Château de Fleury-la-Forêt, **t** 02 32 49 63 91, *www.chateau-fleury-la-foret.com* (*rooms €65 for two, €110 for four*). Of all the Norman châteaux that now have *chambres d'hôtes*, Fleury offers one of the most special experiences. It's not that it's the most luxurious: it's just that in few other places do you get such a sense that you've walked into a scene from the *Ancien Régime* (with plumbing). The largest suite is a marvellous place for a dangerous liaison; breakfast is served in an astonishing 18th-century kitchen. Guests have free access to the rest of the château and doll museum (*see p.201*). Don't worry: the guided tours don't enter your bedroom.

Lorleau ✉ 27480

Mme Marie-Christine Paris, 3 Hameau St-Crespin, **t/f** 02 32 49 62 22 (*rooms €43 for two, €65–70 for four*). M and Mme Paris' modernized farm is in a wonderful location surrounded by fields and the Forêt de Lyons. Two very comfortable, suite-sized B&B rooms are in a converted stables: one has a superb view. Mme Paris serves up fine breakfasts, and can point you to the best walks nearby, and has bikes for rent. St-Crespin is a tiny collection of farms off the lane northeast from Lyons, beyond Lorleau village.

Lyons-la-Forêt ✉ 27480

Hôtel de la Licorne, 27 Place Isaac de Bensérade, **t** 02 32 49 62 02, *www.licorne-hotel.com* (*double rooms €68–95, suites €100–133*). The Licorne (unicorn) has been an inn since 1610, and has one of the best half-timbered frontages on Lyons' main square. Recently, however, the creaky old inn has been expensively done up. Rooms are now pretty plush, and there are luxurious suite-style *'appartements'*. Other features – the superb old carved staircase, the garden courtyard – are still there. It no longer has a restaurant, but breakfast is served for guests.

Les Lions de Beauclerc, 7 Rue de l'Hôtel de Ville, **t** 02 32 49 18 90, *http://leslionsdebeauclerc.free.fr* (*rooms €54–69 for two, €89 for four*). The owners of this large 19th-century building in the middle of Lyons began with an antique shop, then opened a *crêperie* (*see p.204*) and in

2004 added a hotel *de charme*. There are five rooms (one a family room), each individually and sumptuously decorated with antiques. The garden terrace is lovely for summer breakfasts; service is very attentive. A bargain.

Le Pré aux Biches, 11 Rue de l'Essart-Mador, Les Taisnières, **t** 02 32 49 85 52, *lepreauxbiches@free.fr* (*rooms €43 for two*). This well-modernized *longère* farmhouse in tiny Les Taisnières – just west of Lyons – is surrounded by a delightful wooded garden. The three big B&B rooms have lots of light; each has its own entrance, but they can also connect with each other. Hosts Franck and Natalie Langlois have a welcoming approach, and *table d'hôte* meals can be arranged (€20), with all sorts of homemade goodies.

Martainville-Epreville ✉ 76116

M and Mme Aucreterre, 534 Rue des Marronniers, Epreville, **t** 02 35 23 76 05, *http://jy.aucreterre.free.fr* (*rooms €43–57 for two*). Note: this neat house with garden is in Epreville, not Martainville. There are four bright and pretty B&B rooms, all different, from mid-sized to very large. M and Mme Aucreterre are hugely welcoming, provide all sorts of information and will make any effort for their guests. Breakfasts include homemade cakes and abundant fresh fruit.

Pont-St-Pierre ✉ 27360

Hostellerie La Bonne Marmite, 10 Rue René Raban, **t** 02 32 49 70 24, *www.la-bonne-marmite.com* (*double rooms €60–90*). The Bonne Marmite's nine spacious guest rooms are a cut above the country-hotel norm, and decorated in more-or-less Louis XIII or Louis XVI styles (with modern fittings). The largest are very grand, and some have four-poster beds. Service is exceptional. *Closed two weeks Feb–Mar and two weeks July–Aug.*

Eating Alternatives

Lyons-la-Forêt ✉ 27480

Restaurant de La Halle, 6 Place Isaac de Benserade, **t** 02 32 49 49 92 (*menus €17.50–26*). A great little country-bistro style restaurant in an ideal situation on Lyons' ravishing main square. With half-timbering

inside and out and masses of geraniums beneath the windows, it has all the trad local features, but the friendly young staff give it a likeably fresh feel. Excellent-value menus feature fresh-flavoured dishes such as a tangy seafood tagliatelle, and varied salads, omelettes and light dishes. In front, there are terrace tables most of the year.

Les Lions de Beauclerc, 7 Rue de l'Hôtel de Ville, **t** 02 32 49 18 90, *http://leslionsdebeauclerc.free.fr* (*menus €14–26*). An attractive mix of dishes is served in the Lions' (*see* p.203) charming *crêperie-salon de thé*: savoury *galettes*, *crêpes*, great mixed salads and one-course dishes, good-value set menus. Very friendly, and great for a light meal after a walk. *Closed Tues.*

Ménesqueville ✉ 27850

Le Relais de la Lieure, 1 Rue Général de Gaulle, **t** 02 32 49 60 44 (*menus €10 lunch only, €14–35*). This cosy inn next to the River Lieure has a real French-countryside feel, with pullovered farmers coming in looking for satisfying food. Menus keep pretty much to local favourites, with plenty of meat with cheesy and mushroomy sauces. It's also a *Logis* hotel, with 16 pleasant rooms (*double rooms €50–66*), some facing a bright garden.

Ry ✉ 76116

Le Bovary, Grande Rue, **t** 02 35 23 61 46 (*menus €9.50–30*). This restaurant occupies the former Hôtel de France – the Café Français, in *Madame Bovary* – one of the most charming half-timbered buildings on Ry's main street. It naturally has its touristy side, but it's also a decent-value local. Local classics – terrines, duck dishes – feature strongly, together with fish and seafood, and salads and snacks. *Closed Mon eve and Tues.*

L'Hirondelle, Grande Rue, **t** 02 35 02 01 46 (*menus €8.50–25.50*). A bit of a radical alternative in Ry, but one of the village's most attractive places to eat, with a nice outside terrace and semi-contemporary décor. The menu highlights not Normandy but the food of southwest France, with Bayonne ham, *cassoulet* and even a few Spanish things like paella. There's also a choice of salads, crêpes, omelettes and one-course dishes. *Closed Sun eve and Mon.*

Monet's Paradise:

Giverny and the Seine Valley

20

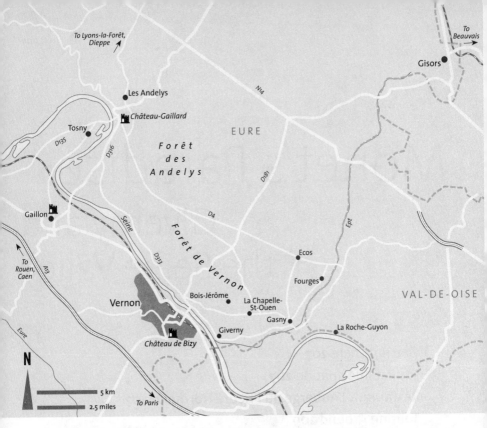

Light. Water. Colour. Fields with swathes of poppies and irises. Bright dresses and dappled sunlight through trees above tranquil, dusty paths and green-banked rivers. The Impressionists left images of France that still have their power to seduce despite all their arch-familiarity. Normandy has an often-repeated claim to have been the birthplace of Impressionism, which has a good deal to it: Boudin, one of the precursors of the movement, rarely strayed far from Honfleur, Monet was raised in Le Havre, and towns along the Norman coast such as Trouville and Etretat inspired whole schools of artists. The Seine Valley, too, was the subject of innumerable river scenes. Nowhere, though, has become more closely associated with a particular painter than Giverny, beside the Seine just inside the borders of Normandy, where Claude Monet lived from 1883 until his death in 1926.

Monet discovered Giverny by accident from the window of a train, but it isn't difficult to see why the Seine between Paris and Rouen was such an attraction to artists seeking light and nature. The river wanders quietly through bends and long meanders. In midstream there is a line of small islands, with the odd boathouse and thickets of weeping willows and poplars that are matched by the woods scattered along the banks on either side, often climbing up steep hills and cliffs that at times make the valley almost like a gorge. It is not that the river isn't used, for even today a few well-laden barges still chug upstream towards Paris. This, though, only adds to the river's character, without detracting from its beauty.

Getting There

This part of the Seine Valley is easily accessible from Caen, Le Havre or Paris via the A13 *autoroute*: exit at junction 18 (Louviers) and take the D135 east for Les Andelys, or from junction 16 for the most direct route to Vernon (D181) and Giverny.

From Dieppe, the quickest route is usually the D915 through Forges-les-Eaux to Gournay, and then the D316 to Les Andelys (*c. 1½hrs*). Driving from Calais and the north, stay on the A16 Paris *autoroute* as far as Beauvais (exit 15), and then take the D981 for Gisors and Vernon (*c. 3hrs*).

To get to Gasny and the Auberge du Prieuré Normand from Giverny (*c. 7km*), follow the D5 below the Fondation Monet eastwards. The restaurant is in the middle of the village.

Several **trains** each day on the Paris (St-Lazare)–Rouen line stop at Vernon, and slower trains also stop at Gaillon, the nearest station to Les Andelys. During the Fondation Monet season (*April–Oct*) there are frequent buses to Giverny from Vernon train station. Timings are linked to train times, with about 10 buses each way daily Mon–Sat, about five Sun and hols.

Giverny is included in any number of **tour** programmes from Paris, but the limitations of these are that you will almost certainly see the gardens at the most crowded times of day, and that your time there may well be limited.

Tourist Information

Very little is open in Giverny when the Fondation Monet is closed (*Nov–Mar*).
Les Andelys: Rue Philippe Auguste, Le Petit-Andely, **t** 02 32 54 41 93, *www.ville-andelys.fr. Open Feb–Nov.*
Gaillon: 4 Place Aristide Briand, **t/f** 02 32 53 08 25. *Open Mar–Oct.*
Giverny: Musée d'Art Américain car park. An 'information point' run by the Vernon office. *Open April–Oct.*
Vernon: 36 Rue Carnot, **t** 02 32 51 39 60, *ot.vernon27@wanadoo.fr.*

History has been marching along the Seine Valley since Roman times. Along the river are towns such as Les Andelys and Vernon, with Romanesque and Gothic churches, and Renaissance and neoclassical châteaux. This was also the route chosen at the end of the 12th century by Philippe Auguste of France when he began his drive to subdue his over-mighty vassals, the dukes of Normandy and kings of England. To resist him, Richard the Lionheart built a massive castle, Château-Gaillard, on a crag above Les Andelys, now one of the most atmospheric of medieval ruins.

The combination of a world-famous attraction like Monet's house and garden and so many beauty spots naturally means this area has plenty of places to eat, with the also-predictable downside that they can get crowded. Some also justify their billing better than others. To get away from high-pressure tourism and find excellent, imaginative food, seek out the **Auberge du Prieuré Normand**, an appealingly un-assuming restaurant in Gasny, a few kilometres east of Giverny along the River Epte.

L'Auberge du Prieuré Normand

1 Place de la République, Gasny, **t** *02 32 52 10 01, prieure.normand@wanadoo.fr.*
Open Mon and Thurs–Sun 12–2 and 7–9, Tues 12–2.
Closed Wed and three weeks Aug. Menus €22.50–40; carte average €40.

The Epte is one of the smaller, faster-flowing tributaries of the Seine. Gasny sits just above and alongside it, a quiet, straightforwardly attractive, working country village that's often unnoticed by those who only aim for the Seine Valley's A-list destinations and then move on. The Auberge du Prieuré Normand is in the middle of the village and has a similarly unostentatious style, a neat, traditionally pretty Norman inn with long tiled roof, modern conservatory, just a bit of half-timbering and plenty of flowers around doors and windows. As already hinted, this part of the Seine Valley has a sizeable crop of celebrated, grand and grand-ish restaurants that seduce their largely Parisian and foreign clientele with elaborate menus, gift-shop exquisite décor and explosively flowery garden terraces – at corresponding prices. Ask around among people who know the district, however, and many will tell you with little hesitation that, for consistently high-quality cuisine put together with all the care and attention to detail that the best French cooking demands, the best chef in the area by some way is M Philippe Robert, chef-proprietor of the Prieuré Normand.

His skills are certainly appreciated by local diners – and not just because the restaurant is also excellent value. For anyone who visits Giverny and complains about being trapped in a tourist bubble, a visit to the Prieuré Normand is a must: on a weekday lunchtime the auberge fills up with all the human variety needed in a proper French country restaurant, elderly couples, families, the local bohemians and the local businessmen, plus a few foreigners who have wandered up the road from the Seine. The most attractive tables are in the bright, airy conservatory facing the village street, but the inside dining rooms are also comfortable and pleasant, lemon-painted and all with their essential fresh flowers. M Robert is a personal presence in the dining room, taking orders and reappearing during the meal to check everything is as it should be. The wine list does everything it needs to, and the quality of extras and details – bread, coffee, *pain d'épices* with dessert – is outstanding.

Philippe Robert's cooking is a nice combination of refinement and generosity. This is immediately apparent in the *mises-en-bouches*, which instead of the usual tiny appetizers might be a substantial – but perfectly refreshing – piece of *fromage blanc* served with a lovely shallot-based *pistou*, followed by a little cup of cucumber soup. Of first courses-proper, the summer menu might include *tomate farcie printanière et asperges en surprise* – beef tomatoes stuffed with salmon and mixed vegetables (the 'surprise') and served with both fresh and white asparagus – a beautifully summery starter, light but deeply satisfying at the same time, made with absolutely fresh ingredients and with an intricately herby dressing around the salmon. A main course of roast breast of guinea fowl *et lard paysan*, with country bacon, is equally both strong and subtle, with a deliciously delicate woodland flavour in the meat and a superbly rich, mushroomy sauce. Every ingredient stands out, including the bacon: French *lard* can often be a bit anonymous, but this is nothing of the sort, with a full, powerful flavour like high-quality gammon.

Even though Gasny is only about two kilometres into Normandy the cheese course highlights Norman cheeses, with the option of camembert and a goats' cheese *au calvados* with salad and *pain d'épice*. Desserts might include an engaging *cannelloni glacé au praliné* – not so much anything to do with pasta as a tightly-rolled, crunchy praline crêpe, and very moreish. And if you decide to stay for coffee, the auberge often has a few little café tables outside, from where you can admire the trees that give even plain and simple Gasny its Impressionist colour.

Marbré de Foie Gras aux Pommes, Petite Salade et Pain de Campagne Grillé

Serves 8
800g/1lb 12oz foie gras
50ml/2fl oz calvados
300g/11oz apples
1 tablespoon powdered gelatine
paprika
salt

Bake the apples in their skins in an oven at 200°C/400°F/Gas Mark 6 for around 50 minutes, until they are well cooked through. Peel and core them, then mash into a coarse purée with a fork, mixing in the calvados.

Dissolve the gelatine in 100ml/3½fl oz of water.

Cut the foie gras into fairly thick slices, season with salt and paprika and sear by pan-frying quickly over a high heat. Then arrange the slices in a terrine, starting with a slice of foie gras, then a layer of the apple mixture and then some of the gelatine. Repeat the layers in the same order until all the ingredients have been used up. Leave to chill, under a suitable weight.

Remove the *marbré* from the terrine and cut into slices. Serve accompanied by a salad with balsamic vinegar dressing and slices of toasted *pain de campagne* or similar country-style bread.

Touring Around

Les Andelys make up the most attractive of the riverside towns between Paris and Rouen. The Andelys are plural because there are two of them: Le Petit-Andely, built next to the river to provide supplies for Richard the Lionheart's castle, and the much older Le Grand-Andely, founded by the Romans, and a little way from the Seine up a narrow valley. Since the 19th century they have been joined into one town by a long, straight main street, which changes its name as it goes along. For an overview of the town and for magnificent views over the Seine Valley and the surrounding countryside, go immediately up to Château-Gaillard. From Le Petit-Andely there's an invigoratingly steep walk up to the castle, beginning by the tourist office; by car, you must follow a well-signposted one-way system all the way through Le Grand-Andely and round to the right via a fairly precipitous winding lane to come upon the château and its crag from behind.

When Richard the Lionheart returned from his famous imprisonment in Austria after the Third Crusade, he found that his former childhood friend, fellow-Crusader and (it has always been rumoured) lover King Philippe Auguste of France was planning to end the effective independence of the Duchy of Normandy and bring it under the control of the French crown. To stop him, Richard resolved to build the most advanced fortification yet seen in Europe, incorporating all the lessons he had learned from Crusader and Arab castles in Palestine.

In a prodigious effort **Château-Gaillard** was built in only one year, from 1196 to 1197. Richard was hugely proud of his creation. Philippe was deterred for a few years, but after the Lionheart's death his hapless brother John seemed an easier adversary, and in 1203 a French army besieged the castle. It resisted them as it was supposed to do for several months, until some of Philippe's troops gained entry by stealth – it has long been said that they did so by clambering up through the latrines, but it now seems almost certain that they came through a window in the chapel. The castle fell in March 1204, and with it the dual Anglo-Norman monarchy came to an end. Château-Gaillard, though, continued to be an important stronghold through the wars of the later Middle Ages and into the French Wars of Religion of the 1560s to the 1590s, so much so that in the 17th century Henri IV and later Richelieu ordered that it be progressively demolished so that it could never bother them again.

Their demolition work and centuries of pilfering by local builders have taken their toll on the castle, but the sections that remain – the keep, part of an outer bastion, parts of the walls – are still massive and awe-inspiring. The keep's giant, bullish, 16ft-thick walls seem to grow out of the rock, and, visible for miles, look as if they could still at least partly fulfil their original purpose. In the last few years the local authorities have installed a totally unnecessary concrete viewing platform (in the market in Les Andelys you can sometimes sign a petition asking for this eyesore to be removed), and in future it is possible that access to the whole castle may only be possible during official opening times. For the moment, though, they only apply to the **Keep** (*open 15 Mar–15 Nov Mon and Wed–Sun 10–1 and 2–6, tours at 10, 11, 12, 2, 3, 4, 5pm; closed Tues; adm*), around which there are guided tours. You are free at all times to wander around the other parts of what so far is still a very wild ruin, and enjoy the views over the river, its islands and the plains beyond. They are especially spectacular at sunset.

Le Petit-Andely is an attractive quarter of little narrow lanes with some half-timbered old buildings, a lovely riverside walk, the delightful terraces of restaurants like the Chaîne d'Or and the Normandie (*see pp.215, 216*) and, in summer, boat-trips across to the **Ile du Château** island in mid-Seine and an open-air swimming pool by the river. **Le Grand-Andely** is appropriately larger, with an ample central square where the market is held on Saturdays. Not far away is the Collegiate Church of **Notre-Dame**, standing on the site of a monastery founded in the 6th century by Saint Clothilde, wife of Clovis, first of France's Frankish kings. The present church is a classic assemblage of architectural periods: the main nave is plain, 13th-century Gothic, but on either side there are transepts in elaborate, 15th-century *Flamboyant* and later Renaissance styles, with finely worked rose windows. Inside, there is some beautiful 16th-century stained glass, and, in the chapels, two fine altar paintings by a local painter of some renown, Quentin Varin. He was the first teacher of Les Andelys' most famous son, Nicolas Poussin, the greatest of all French Baroque painters, born just outside the two towns in 1594. Unusually, Poussin seems to have felt very little devotion to his *terroir*; he scarcely returned after leaving to study in Paris in his twenties, and did most of his major work in Rome. However, there is a small **Musée Nicolas Poussin** (*open Mon and Wed–Sun 2–6; closed Tues; adm*), not far from the market square (actually Place Nicolas Poussin). It has one of his major paintings, *Coriolanus answering the tears of his mother*, together with a few articles associated with him and an eccentric collection of unrelated artefacts and pictures by other local artists.

From Les Andelys avoid the main D316 road and cross the Seine by the town's bridge on the D135, signposted towards Louviers. Shortly after crossing the river turn off to the left (south) onto the still smaller D176 road through **Tosny** – a charming village that's the site of a micro-micro-brewery (*see* p.214) – to follow the river south along the west bank, past delightful views and through clumps of woodland, to **Gaillon**, a little half-timbered town with the finest Renaissance château in Normandy, **Château-Gaillon**. The massive crag on which it stands, with the town's streets winding up towards it, had been the site of a castle throughout the Middle Ages, but beginning in 1497 this was comprehensively demolished and replaced by the all-new present château on the orders of Cardinal d'Amboise, Archbishop of Rouen and great minister of the Kings of France (*see* p.187). His ideas for his new château were inspired by Renaissance mansions he had seen in Italy, and it had a huge influence on later French Renaissance architecture. The interior was severely damaged during the Revolution, but the elegantly ornate exterior, one of the first examples of Italianate influence in France, is by far its most important feature. Château-Gaillon is currently undergoing a long-delayed restoration programme, and it is expected that at some point it will be regularly open to visitors, but this is unfortunately the kind of project that can drag on for years. From Gaillon, the N15 runs down the river bank to Vernon.

Today **Vernon** is a busy place, one of the main centres of France's high-tech industries. At its heart there is still the old riverside town, and the knot of narrow streets around the giant Gothic church of the **Collégiale** has a Victor Hugo-esque air, all wild gables, sloping roofs and leaning half-timbering. The local tourist office is installed in the most spectacular building in town, the **Maison du Temps Jadis** or 'House of Time Gone By' next to the church, the kind of huge Norman timber building that seems to be permanently sliding sideways. The church itself has a superb 15th-century façade with a spectacular rose window, while inside there is a rare 17th-century organ. There is a pleasant walk along the river bank to the south of the town centre, while just across on the east bank, to the left of the modern bridge, is the **Vieux Moulin**, a half-timbered mill-cottage on top of the last three surviving arches of the medieval bridge that carried traffic across the Seine from the time of Philippe Auguste to the 18th century. As an important river crossing Vernon also acquired all sorts of fortifications: next to the Vieux Moulin is the **Château des Tourelles**, a dramatic 12th-century keep built to protect the bridge, while in the middle of the old town is a massive round tower from the same era, the **Tour des Archives**.

Vernon's most grandiose monument, though, is the **Château de Bizy** (*open April–Oct Tues–Sun 10–12 and 2–6, closed Mon; Mar Sat and Sun 2–5; guided tours only; adm*), in its own large park on the hill on the western side of the town. In contrast to Renaissance Gaillon, Bizy – sometimes called the 'Little Versailles' – is pure *Ancien Régime*, built in 1741 by the fashionable architect Constant d'Ivry for the Duc de Belle-Isle, one of the most important figures of the reign of Louis XV. Its most impressive feature is the remarkably intricate visual coordination between rooms, windows, archways, gates and the paths in the grounds, to create surprise vistas that run from room to room and out into the courtyards and the park. The château's contents are a bit of a mixture, reflecting its complicated history. It passed to another aristocratic family before the Revolution, and then to Louis-Philippe; since the 1900s it has been owned by the Dukes of Albufera, descendants of Marshal Suchet, one of the generals who rose with Napoleon. It has uniforms, portraits and other memorabilia associated with the founder of the clan, and the guided tours deal with the Napoleonic era with patriotic reverence, even though Suchet was one of the Marshals who dumped the Emperor and went over to the restored Louis XVIII in 1814.

Cross the Seine by the new bridge in Vernon and turn right to reach **Giverny**, where all eyes naturally turn to the **Fondation Claude Monet** (*open April–Oct Tues–Sun 9.30–6; closed Mon; adm*). Here you are only about 70km from Paris, and Monet's house and gardens are fixtures on all the city coach tour programmes. They are therefore very often full of people, especially in mid-summer, so it's worth trying to visit towards the beginning or the end of the season, and on a weekday – as so often with ultra-popular sites, it's surprising how much of it you can have to yourself just by straying a little from the conventional schedule. Equally, Monet's images of his garden are as widely commercialized as the *Mona Lisa*, reproduced on thousands of birthday cards and tea towels. Some people say, therefore, that the house and gardens are now spoilt, too well-known, and no longer worth seeing. However, these gardens are so beautiful they are impossible to spoil.

Monet moved here in 1883 with Alice Hoschedé, a friend of his first wife who had been abandoned by her husband, and their several children by their respective first marriages. They later married. When he first arrived Monet, then 43, rented the house and its main garden, called the **Clos Normand**. As he became more successful he was able to buy them and remodel the garden exactly to his liking, and beginning in 1890 he added an additional plot in which to create, from nothing, his **Japanese Water Garden** and lily pond. At that time the Water Garden was separated from the main plot by a railway line and a dusty track. This track is now a main road, but access from one side to the other is made easy by a pedestrian underpass paid for by the Texan millionaire and sometime diplomat Walter Annenberg. The restoration carried out since the 1960s and the current immaculate condition of the house and gardens, in fact, are due in great part to American benefactors.

Each of the gardens has a different character. The Clos Normand was originally a traditional French garden with neat, formal paths, but Monet's love for colours soon overcame these limitations. These are not gardens for those obsessed with precisely-defined flowerbeds and straight lines: they are all about abundance, exuberance and explosions of colour. There are great flashes of azaleas, foxgloves, crocuses and – Monet's particular favourite – irises; begonias and roses climb over frames and metal arches, and the alley carpeted with dazzling orange nasturtiums is an astonishing natural image in itself. Each season, each month, produces its special colours. The Water Garden meanwhile is leafy and focused on the pond, often surrounded by white wisteria. This naturally attracts the biggest crowds, especially the Japanese bridge, but one of the best features of Giverny is that you are free to wander as you like, and maybe do just what the old man did: sit in silence for hours watching the changes in the light. Have patience, and even the most crazed video freak will move out of the way at some point.

The **house** is almost as pretty as the gardens, beautifully light and, remarkably, still possessed of a cosy and almost lived-in feel. Most striking and surprising in a house of that time are the colours: summery yellows in the dining room, blue tiles and duck-egg woodwork in the kitchen, where Monet himself used to cook up elaborate dinners and cakes for his many guests. Decorating virtually every wall is one of the world's finest collections of **Japanese prints**, including superb works by Hokusai, Utamaro and others. They are the original examples acquired by Monet, arranged exactly as he hung them; in his spacious, comfortable studio, however, there are only reproductions of the paintings he owned and some of his own works, the originals of most of which are in the Musée Marmottan in Paris and other museums. The last stage in the visit to the house is the warehouse-like **studio** Monet had built in order to work on his giant near-abstract water-lily paintings, the *Nymphéas*, in the years before his death. Today, it contains reproductions of them and a large and fairly overpowering souvenir shop, with Monet lilies on every imaginable item.

Outside, along Giverny's main street – Rue Claude Monet – several of the pretty old houses are now occupied by painters offering Monet-like flower paintings, a little neo-Impressionist industry. On the other side of the road is the lavishly appointed **Musée d'Art Américain** (*open April–Oct Tues–Sun 10–6, closed Mon; adm*). In the 1890s several young painters, mostly Americans, arrived in Giverny to follow the master's example, and this museum, founded by a former US Ambassador to France and his wife, is intended to showcase their work and that of other American artists living in France around that time. Monet's reactions to his fan club were mixed; some became his friends and one, Theodore Butler, married his stepdaughter and is buried in the Monet family grave in Giverny; others he just found irritating. Much of the work in the museum prompts a similar response. With some the thought occurs that they might have done better by trying to be more original instead of sitting at Monet's feet, but there are some very fine pictures by artists such as Mary Cassatt. Also, the museum hosts a very lively series of temporary exhibitions each year, often of 20th-century and contemporary American art, and has a fine restaurant (*see* p.216).

The best time to see Giverny village is after about five in the evening, when the tour buses have gone back to Paris. It can to an extraordinary extent still look much as it must have first appeared to Monet, as a tranquil, pretty Norman village strung out along its long main street, with just a few boys idling on bicycles amid lengthening shadows while the sun glances softly off the rooftops. Some way past the Musée d'Art Américain is the old **Hôtel Baudy**, where most of the young Americans, and more familiar figures such as Renoir and Pissarro, stayed during their visits here, and which is now a likeable 'museum-café-restaurant' (*see* p.216). The 'museum' part comes not from any exhibit but from the fact that the dining room is a museum in itself, lined with pictures and near-exactly as it was in Monet's time, and at the back there's a wonderful old studio-hut once rented by Cézanne. Further on is the simple village **church**, where Claude Monet is buried, with the rest of his family.

Shopping

The best traditional market in this area is in **Les Andelys** (*Sat*). **Vernon** has an open-air market (*Sun*), and a covered market (*Mon–Fri*).

Bois-Jérôme ✉ 27620

Les Vergers de Giverny, 1 Rue Ste Geneviève, La Chapelle St-Ouen, **t** 02 32 51 29 36. La Chapelle St-Ouen is on the flat plateau above Giverny, separate from Bois-Jérôme (follow the road uphill from Giverny, from Rue Hoschedé-Monet). This beautiful old cider farm in the centre of the village produces an exceptional dry cider and fine fresh apple juice, and there are other attractions: the shop sells *chèvre*, terrines, honey, jams and fruit tarts from nearby farms, and in the massive barn there is a charming **café**, with salads and *collations* (light dishes) of farm produce. *Shop open Tues–Sun; café open April–Oct Thurs–Sun and hols.*

Ecos ✉ 27630

Ferme du Val Corbon, **t** 02 32 52 19 82. A big farm by the road between Gasny and Ecos, where the Durdan family sell their own *chèvre* cheeses, cider, fresh apple juice, honey and preserves. *Open Mar–Nov, closed Wed.*

Tosny ✉ 27700

Brasserie Duplessi, 13 Rue aux Moines, **t** 02 32 51 55 75. What must be one of the world's smallest breweries, in an ancient stone courtyard. The main product is the malty *Richard Cœur de Lion* dark beer. *Open daily, brewery tours July Sat and Sun at 3.30pm.*

Vernon ✉ 27200

La Fromagerie, 14 Rue St-Jacques, **t** 02 32 51 99 00. Part of a chain of fine *fromageries* that began here and has shops around France, with carefully matured cheeses from France, Italy and elsewhere.
Guérard & Floc'h, 2 and 7 Rue Ste-Geneviève, **t** 02 32 21 50 16. Vernon's leading combination wine shop, *fruiterie* and *épicerie*, with a range worthy of a major city. Fine wines and liqueurs, *charcuterie*, preserves and other delicacies are at no.2; superb fruit, salad vegetables, more liqueurs and *limonades artesanales* are across the street at no.7.

Where to Stay

Giverny ✉ 27620

Note that in Giverny itself most hotels and restaurants are closed from November to March. During the season – above all in mid-summer – rooms there are in great demand, so book well ahead. It's easier to find rooms a few kilometres away.
Le Moulin des Chennevières, 34 Chemin du Roy, **t** 06 81 13 77 72, *givernymoulin@aol.com* (*rooms €100–120 for two; €160 for four*). An extraordinary old mill just outside Giverny converted by Stéphanie and Gérard Guillemard in 2004 into a special *chambres d'hôtes*. Prices are above B&B average but so are the rooms: they're in a medieval tower, one lovely double at the top and two that form a suite for up to four, sharing a bathroom and a terrace balcony with wonderful views. Breakfast is served in a magnificently baronial salon or in a fine garden. Bikes are provided for guests. *Usually open April–Oct; check at other times.*
La Réserve, **t/f** 02 32 21 99 09 (*rooms €95–154*). Luxurious *chambres d'hôtes* in a house that looks like a grand old manor – though it was built only a few years ago – and is furnished throughout with antiques. The rooms are huge, and positively palatial. The owners, Didier and Marie-Lorraine Brunet, have been described as 'the best hosts imaginable': they're especially charming and attentive, speak excellent English and provide an ample list of local information. The house is on the plateau above Giverny to the east; follow the uphill turn from Giverny village towards Chapelle-St-Ouen and look for discreet white signs. *Usually open April–Nov.*
Le Clos Fleuri, 5 Rue de la Dime, **t** 02 32 21 36 51, *danielle-claude-fouche@wanadoo.fr* (*room €70 for two*). M and Mme Fouche – who lived in Australia for many years – have one large, smart B&B room in their elegant house. It's in the middle of Giverny, with a delightful garden. *Open April–Oct.*
La Musardière, 123 Rue Claude Monet, **t** 02 31 21 03 18, *http://giverny.org/hotels/musarde* (*double rooms €54–71*). This big, utterly French 19th-century house seems all of a piece with Giverny's period flavour. Rooms are a bit pricey, this being Giverny, but have

red plush décor and metal bedsteads that add to the hotel's *Belle Epoque*-fantasy flavour. Several have pretty views. There's a garden terrace, and a **restaurant-crêperie** (*menus €26–36*) with crêpes and full menu. *Hotel open all year; restaurant April–Oct.*

Le Bon Maréchal, 1 Rue du Colombier, **t/f** 02 32 51 39 70, (*rooms €50–65 for two*). 'Ivy-clad' may be a cliché, but it's hard to avoid it with this fine old house off Giverny's main street, as it's almost buried in green foliage. Beside it there's a lovely walled courtyard-garden. Marie-Claire and Michel Boscher have three bright and attractive B&B rooms, one with space for up to four, and the atmosphere is likeably relaxed. Also, they are open all year.

Le Coin des Artistes, 65 Rue Claude Monet, **t** 02 32 21 36 77, http://giverny.org/hotels/pain (*rooms €50 for two, €80 for two*). A charming B&B on Giverny's main street with an art gallery in the bar-breakfast room. Above, Mme Laurence Pain has four bright rooms, one a family room. All are decorated in suitably Monet-esque style, and have high-standard bathrooms. It's open all year round.

Les Andelys ✉ 27700

La Chaîne d'Or, 25–27 Rue Grande, Le Petit-Andely, **t** 02 32 54 00 31, chaineor@wanadoo.fr (*double rooms and suites €85–122*). This much admired luxury hotel, in an inn that has been welcoming guests since 1751, is famed for its ravishing terrace by the Seine and wonderful river views – on a sunny day, the glittering light off the water seems present in every corner of the building. The traditionally-styled rooms are all impressive, but take a plush suite or a room with river view for a really pampering stay. Staff are charming, and it has a celebrated restaurant (*see p.216*).

Hôtel de Normandie, 1 Rue Grande, Le Petit-Andely, **t** 02 32 54 10 52, www.hotel-normandie-andelys.com (*double rooms €52–60*). An alternative to the Chaîne d'Or in Les Andelys: another historic half-timbered inn with lovely riverside garden, but with a simpler style and lower prices. Run for years by the Bourguignon family, it has the warm, cosy atmosphere of a well-run small-town hotel, and its old-fashioned comforts include a high-standard restaurant (*see p216*).

La Haye-Gaillard, Route de Clery, **t** 02 32 51 66 23, hamot.christophe@wanadoo.fr (*rooms €46 for two*). A giant farm on the plateau above Les Andelys, just a short walk from Château-Gaillard and with great, open horizons. Christophe Hamot has two quite different B&B rooms: one is a pleasant but straightforward double, the other is in a converted dovecote, and much more special (it also has space for a child's bed). There are bikes available for hire.

Gaillon ✉ 27600

Chez Claudine, 2 Chemin de Ste-Barbe, **t** 02 32 52 96 67, c.lions@wanadoo.fr (*rooms €45 for two*). Claudine Lions' house is in a magnificent location, on a hill far above Gaillon town and a short walk from Château-Gaillon. A former journalist, she runs her house with a distinctive friendliness and really does make you feel like a house guest rather than just a customer. The three B&B rooms are spacious and have lots of creature comforts, and breakfast is served in her kitchen or in the huge garden, looking out over a fabulous view. Exceptional value.

Vernon ✉ 27200

Hôtel d'Evreux-Restaurant Le Relais Normand, 11 Place d'Evreux, **t** 02 32 21 16 12, hotel.evreux@wanadoo.fr (*double rooms €33–45 low season, €38–49 high season*). A popular hotel with Art-Nouveau sign and Norman-*Belle Epoque* façade. The 12 rooms are reliably comfortable, and there's a pretty interior courtyard. The restaurant (*see p.216*) is a local favourite. It's in the middle of town, but the rooms are quiet at night.

Eating Alternatives

Giverny ✉ 27620

Les Jardins de Giverny, Rue du Roy, **t** 02 32 21 60 80, **f** 02 32 51 93 77 (*menus €15–26*). The smartest option in Giverny itself, popular with older Monet-lovers, set in a *Belle Epoque* house with tables in a rose garden, and a rather old-fashioned, formal style. The cuisine of chef Serge Pirault is refined and quite ambitious: game terrine and *fruits de mer*, or a *croustillant* of cod garnished with seaweed. There's also a highly regarded wine list. It's aimed squarely at Fondation Monet visitors, so opening times are especially brief. *Open April–Oct; daily midday only, exc Sat open lunch and dinner.*

Terra Café, Musée d'Art Américain, 92 Rue Claude Monet, **t** 02 32 51 94 61 *(menu €14.50, dishes c. €10–16)*. The Museum of American Art *(see p.213)* has brought a new style to eating in Giverny with its smart, bright café-brasserie, with minimalist but comfortable modern décor and an attractive garden terrace. The good-value menus feature light, internationally-influenced food, in a seasonal set menu and excellent salads, quiches and single-course dishes. It's open when the museum is, but the full menu is only served until 3pm, from when it's a *salon de thé* with smaller dishes and snacks. *Open April–Oct Tues–Sun 10–6, closed Mon.*

Musée-Hôtel Baudy, 81 Rue Claude Monet, **t** 02 32 21 10 03 *(menu €18.50, dishes €7–10.50)*. No longer a hotel, but the place where Cézanne, Sisley and Monet's American friends stayed in Giverny is now a laid-back café-restaurant that retains a decently bohemian feel and serves Giverny's best-value food: a daily *plat du jour*, a varied set menu, good mixed salads and *assiettes*, and of course coffee served all day. The dining room is lined with pictures, and there are occasional art shows and painting courses. There are also great fresh juices, and sipping a *citron pressé* in the Baudy is a fine way to take stock after the Monet-seeking crowds have gone back to Paris. *Open April–Oct; Tues–Sat all day, Sun till 4pm, closed Mon.*

Les Andelys ✉ 27700

La Chaîne d'Or, 25–27 Rue Grande, Le Petit-Andely, **t** 02 32 54 00 31, *chaineor@wanadoo.fr (menus €27–85.50)*. The Chaîne d'Or is as established as a gourmet destination as it is as a hotel. The style is opulent (like the prices): refined dishes include roast guinea fowl with a red pepper coulis and fresh pasta, or red mullet with an anchovy butter and celery fondue, and exquisite desserts. Service is as classically correct as the décor, and there are much sought-after terrace tables by the Seine. *Closed Sun eve and Mon.*

Hôtel de Normandie, 1 Rue Grande, Le Petit-Andely, **t** 02 32 54 10 52, *www.hotel-normandie-andelys.com (menus €16.50–45)*. The restaurant in the Normandie *(see p.215)* does what it has done for a long time – classic French and Norman cuisine – and does it very well: homemade terrines, seafood salads, excellent lamb and traditional desserts. To get a table on the terrace with a good view of the Ile du Château, the island in the middle of the Seine, be sure to ask when booking; even if you do not, though, the dining room is very pretty.

Fourges ✉ 27630

Le Moulin de Fourges, 38 Rue du Moulin, **t** 02 32 52 12 12, *www.moulin-de-fourges.com (menus €25–35)*. The number-one restaurant *de charme* around Giverny. This 18th-century mill with gingerbread-house roofs is so exaggeratedly pretty you think it must be artificial (it isn't), and the shady gardens beside the Epte are utterly delightful. There is only a *menu-carte*, giving a choice from the *carte* for a set price: the modern cuisine is luxurious and inventive. The downside is that it's hugely popular, above all on summer weekends (when it's in big demand for wedding receptions, held in a separate building). Book well ahead or go mid-week. *Closed Nov–late Mar; in season, closed Sun eves and Mon, exc July and Aug open daily.*

Vernon ✉ 27200

Hôtel d'Evreux-Restaurant Le Relais Normand, 11 Place d'Evreux, **t** 02 32 21 16 12, *hotel.evreux@wanadoo.fr (menus €21–27)*. The comfortable restaurant at the hotel *(see p.215)* is known as one of the best in the area for satisfying Norman staples, with lots of duck and apples, alongside more unusual specialities such as a homemade sausage of pigs' trotters with truffles. *Closed Sun eve.*

Le Bistro des Fleurs, 73 Rue Carnot, **t** 02 32 21 29 19 *(menu €15)*. A popular, easygoing bistro in the middle of Vernon with bargain *plats du jour (€10)* and straightforward dishes: ham in cider, grilled fish, salads and quiches. The same owners also have a more formal restaurant next door at no.71, **Les Fleurs** *(menus €21–42)*, with more refined Norman cuisine. *Closed Sun and Mon eve.*

Explorers and Eccentrics:
Honfleur

21

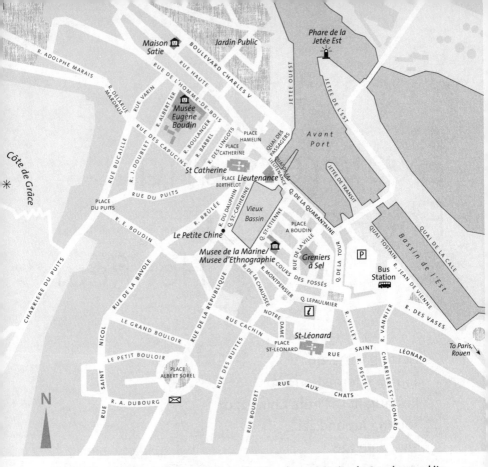

Honfleur is a town unlike any other on the French coast. It sits clustered around its little harbour, ringed by an erratic line of 17th-century grey slate and timber-fronted skyscrapers that the more you look at them seem as strange as the ancient tower-cities of the Yemen or Tibet. Around it there is the idyllic Norman rural heartland of the Pays d'Auge, Deauville, Trouville and the other resorts of the Côte Fleurie, and the very visible industries of Le Havre, but Honfleur doesn't seem to have that much to do with any of them. It stands on its own within its curious little circle of hills, apparently tied more to the sea than to the land.

Honfleur has played a part in French maritime, military, economic and cultural life, and produced a range of famous offspring, out of all proportion to its size (it still has fewer than 9,000 inhabitants). It was fought over many times in the Hundred Years' War, when there were times that Honfleur appeared to carry on the fight more or less on its own while the rest of France was occupied with other things. Honfleur disputes with St-Malo the paternity of French Canada (the *Malouin* Cartier discovered the St Lawrence river, but it was from Honfleur that Champlain set out to found the Quebec colony in 1608). As well as shiploads of hardy mariners, Honfleur has also been home to Frédéric Le Play, one of the founders of modern sociology and economics, and the historian Albert Sorel. Eugène Boudin, the painter often

Getting There

The closest entry port to Honfleur from Britain is Le Havre, about 30 minutes' drive away via the A29 *autoroute* and the Pont de Normandie (toll bridge). From Caen-Ouistreham, take the A13 *autoroute* east past Pont-l'Evêque and then the A29 north, which will take about an hour; a more leisurely alternative is the D513 coast road via Cabourg and Deauville. From Calais, the Tunnel or Dieppe, the best route is to take the A16, A28 and A29 *autoroutes* towards Le Havre and cross the Pont de Normandie, avoiding Rouen. From Paris, follow the A13 and then the A29.

Inside Honfleur parking is restricted, especially in summer; the most convenient car parks are around the east side of the harbour. From there, walk back to the Vieux Bassin. The entrance to Rue du Dauphin is a few steps down Rue de la République, on the right, from the harbour. Walk up the hill of Rue du Dauphin and the Petite Chine is on the right.

The nearest **train** station is at Deauville (*see* p.231), from where Calvados Bus Verts' **no. 20 bus** (Caen–Le Havre) runs to Honfleur.

Tourist Information

Honfleur: Quai Lepaulmier, **t** 02 31 89 23 30, *www.ot-honfleur.fr*. The tourist office is on the main street around the south side of the Enclos. Among other service, it offers a Pass-Musées, giving discounts on admission to all the local museums. It also organizes guided tours, some available in English.

Internet Access: **Cyberpub Honfleur**, 55 Rue de la République, **t** 02 31 89 95 83, *www.honfleur.com/cyberpub*. A rare facility, open in the evenings.

considered the forefather of Impressionism, was born in Honfleur in 1824 and founded a whole school of 'Seine estuary' painters, teaching the young Monet and inspiring many of his friends such as Renoir and Bazille. Honfleur also produced two of France's greatest eccentrics, the wonderfully off-the-wall humorist Alphonse Allais and the completely unique mind of Erik Satie.

Within its small space Honfleur is a place of enormous charm. The old port or Vieux Bassin is still alive with yachts and old sailing ships, and behind its towering façades Honfleur is a town of narrow lanes, unexpected architecture and tiny alleys. Beautiful in summer, it's also a wonderfully atmospheric place to wander around on a dark, damp evening, mistily quiet, full of strange shadows and surprising corners, and with a sense of having as many accumulated memories as places twenty times its size. Distributed between the old streets is a unique collection of museums. Because of its fame Honfleur is also one of those places that one tends to visit along with crowds of other people, above all on summer weekends; to avoid the hordes, it's best to go outside of July or August, and during the week. However, its visitor numbers do not mean that it feels swamped or tacky. Perhaps it just has too much character for that: outside the old harbour there's still a well-functioning fishing port, and for all the many prettied-up places its bars and cafés and even many of the galleries and antique shops still have a strong tang of real life.

Honfleur also has about one restaurant for every 80 permanent residents. It's a place that people go to for lunch, especially on summer Sundays, descending upon the Vieux Bassin from Paris and all over Normandy and beyond. In this food-lover's haven, choice is not a problem. One of the most distinctive places to eat among the many is **La Petite Chine**, a very stylish little *salon de thé*.

La Petite Chine

14–16 Rue du Dauphin, t 02 31 89 36 52, f 02 31 89 18 94.
Open Tues–Fri 11–7, Sat and Sun 10–7. Closed Mon, and usually two weeks
in June, and two weeks from 11 Nov. Carte *average €15–20.*

Honfleur may be best known for seafood restaurants, but La Petite Chine offers a radical contrast. It occupies one of the old town's most idiosyncratic buildings, one of the tall thin towers on Quai Ste-Catherine: the entrance is actually on the bend of Rue du Dauphin, but the building is so narrow that, as you soon realize, the other side of each main room is several floors above the quay. As you climb the winding staircases to the upper floors, you get more light, and better and better views over the old harbour. Some of the best views of all are actually from the toilet right on the top floor. The décor throughout is extremely pretty, in a very neat, very French kind of way: yellow walls and cushions in carefully coordinated colours, little wooden tables, lots of modern bric-a-brac – ceramic dogs and elephants, all kinds of unusual tea services, bowls of artificial fruit, and plenty of fresh flowers. It's undoubtedly twee, but also rather chic, in a very French sort of way.

La Petite Chine is a *salon de thé*, which can mean various things. It does, of course, serve teas – a very superior list of over 100 varieties. It very often also means, as here, a place that presents light, single-course lunches as alternatives to the traditional full restaurant menu, in a way that's ever-more fashionable in France. *Salons de thé* tend to be more feminine spaces than restaurants, both in terms of who runs them and who uses them. La Petite Chine is very popular with Honfleur's 'ladies who lunch', and with a generally fairly fashionable crowd. The atmosphere is calm and easygoing. Sophie Marceau and a few other famous faces drop in quite regularly, but it wouldn't do to make a fuss about it and start rubbernecking.

The owner, Fan, is a character: vibrant and friendly, with close-cropped, bright yellow hair and a penchant for wearing strong colours. She first opened La Petite Chine as a shop selling gifts and curios – hence the unusual ceramics – and only preparing food as a sideline, but it gradually took over. She and her kitchen crew are responsible for most of the savoury dishes, while partner Jean-Claude is in charge of the *salon*'s renowned cakes and ice-creams. La Petite Chine opens for leisurely weekend breakfasts and brunches, with excellent freshly squeezed orange juice; during the week, the lunch menu might feature five or six options, as well as a few fixtures such as homemade vegetable *potage*. Among them might be a leek and smoked salmon tart with salad, a choice of savoury *crêpes*, or mixed salad and meat-or-cheese *assiettes*, and there are always a few all-vegetarian choices. Ingredients are deliciously fresh: a *flan de chèvre* has a nice oniony tang combined with the goats' cheese and ideally crumbly pastry, and comes with a generous, perfectly fresh salad and some very original, intriguingly herby homemade chutney; a *tarte de thon* – really a tuna quiche – has with it more fine fresh salad with a delicate vinaigrette that perfectly complements the flavour of the fish. To drink, as alternatives to teas and water there are beers, local cider and a fine range of fresh fruit juices and fruit cocktails.

While considering their choice of teas, few people manage to resist Jean-Claude's cakes and desserts, especially the tarts, small pies and crumbles oozing with spectacularly fresh fruit, maybe with a ball of his ice-cream on the side, or the equally homemade pistachio nougat. Afterwards, take a look around the shop, where you will see some of Jean-Claude's fine photographs of Honfleur.

Touring Around

The **Vieux Bassin**, the inner harbour, is the natural centre of Honfleur and one of France's most special ports. All around it there are café and restaurant terraces from which to take in the scene. It still usually contains a few fishing boats, although the greater part of its moorings are taken up by yachts, and an assortment of historic sailing boats such as the old *chalutière* sailing boats once typical of the Seine estuary, which are given special facilities in Honfleur. The main business of fishing has shifted to the much larger Avant-Port outside the Vieux Bassin, although on most evenings you can see some fishing boats come up to the **Quai de la Lieutenance**, the quay and bridge across the mouth of the old harbour, to unload their catch – especially Honfleur's prized *crevettes* or prawns, which can only be sold direct there by fishermen's wives, a historic right that is jealously guarded. This is not any tradition that's kept up just to charm the tourists, for if you stand there a while you can see many locals nip down rapidly to pick up some fresh *crevettes* for their dinner.

The landmark on this quay is the **Lieutenance** itself, the four-square stone 16th-century former residence of the Lieutenant-Governors of Honfleur. Attached to it is the **Porte de Caen**, the last remaining part of the town ramparts built in the same period, inside which there is a plaque commemorating Champlain's departure for Quebec from this same spot. If you look back from the Lieutenance across the Vieux Bassin you see an emphatic contrast between the two sides of the harbour. The **Quai St-Etienne**, to the left along the southeast side, contains a charming but fairly normal line of old French three-to-four-storey harbour-side houses, some half-timbered and some in stucco. The really extraordinary sight is along the **Quai Ste-Catherine** to the right, Honfleur's sheer curtain wall of slate and timber blocks, seven, eight or even ten storeys high, sometimes inexplicably narrow for their height, none of them with a roof at the same level as its neighbour and looking a little as if at any moment they might all knock each other over like a pack of cards.

The two sides of the Vieux Bassin correspond to the two parts of historic Honfleur. The area behind the Quai St-Etienne, known as *L'Enclos* or 'The Enclosure', is the very oldest part – once the original, tiny walled town. First heard of in the 11th century, it became increasingly important after the French takeover of Normandy in 1204, as the primary maritime stronghold at the mouth of the Seine. The Faubourg Ste-Catherine to the northwest grew up outside the initial fortified area, separated from the Enclos by streams and a large pool, where the Vieux Bassin is today. Honfleur naturally attracted the attention of the English in the Hundred Years' War, during which many of its early-medieval buildings were destroyed. The French recapture of Honfleur in

1466 is often held to signify the end of that endless war, and the years that followed were some of the most dynamic in the town's history. In the early 1500s Honfleur sailors explored the coasts of Brazil and Canada, and traded around the coasts of Europe. A new set of fortifications was built around the Enclos and the port, and in 1608 Samuel Champlain used Honfleur as his base for the foundation of Quebec.

A major transformation came in the 1660s, when Louis XIV's great minister Colbert ordered the demolition of virtually all of the town's walls and the building of one of France's first all-weather harbours, giving the Vieux Bassin the solid form it has today. The tower-houses of Quai Ste-Catherine were mostly built in the years immediately afterwards, their unique form dictated by the need to adapt to the steep incline west of the harbour and to maximize space. Colbert also set out to ensure that Quebec became a proper colony rather than a military outpost, and Honfleur was the main departure port for migrants to Canada, who were drawn predominantly from the Norman countryside. Among them were several thousand young women, labelled the *filles du roi*, the king's daughters. The colony was very short of women, and so poor and unattached girls from around Normandy were gathered up and given little option but to be shipped off to Canada, where the men were ordered to select one and marry her within two weeks of the women's arrival. Later, Honfleur ships took part in the slave trade (something that's rarely mentioned nowadays). In the 19th century, fishing took over from trade and exploration as the town's major occupation.

L'Enclos is a charming area, a little knot of low, partly medieval buildings, neatly square in shape, and arranged between tiny streets, alleys and even smaller courtyards, with the historic main throughfare, Rue de la Ville, running through its centre. Quai de la Quarantaine is Honfleur's cheap restaurant row, with a line of boisterous bistros with big outdoor terraces, virtually all specializing in seafood. Rue de la Ville has several attractive small shops, but is dominated by the giant **Greniers à Sel**, the royal salt warehouses, built on the orders of Colbert in 1670. Royal control over the sale and supply of salt was one of the most characteristic and rigorously enforced features of *Ancien Régime* France (and one of the most widely hated, which contributed directly to the Revolution of 1789). Honfleur was a major importer of salt, and needed a great deal of it for the preparation of salt cod, so its warehouses were some of the largest in the country. The *Greniers* are massive stone halls, with spectacular timber roofs that have recently been restored; they are now used for exhibitions, concerts and various other events.

The Enclos also contains Honfleur's two most traditional museums. On Quai St-Etienne itself is the **Musée de la Marine** (*open mid-Feb–Mar and Oct–mid-Nov Tues–Fri 2–5.30, Sat and Sun 10–12 and 2–5.30; April–Sept Tues–Sun 10–12 and 2–6.30; closed Mon and mid-Nov–mid-Feb; adm, joint ticket with Musée d'Ethnographie*). It occupies the stout little former church of Saint-Etienne, on a site where a church has stood since 1050, although the present Gothic structure was begun in 1369. The museum display is a quaint collection of relics of the days of sail – shipbuilders' models, figure-heads, charts, sea chests, and intriguing instructions to 17th-century boat-builders.

The **Musée d'Ethnographie et d'Art Populaire Normand** (*joint ticket with Musée de la Marine*), around the corner up tiny Rue de la Prison, is more eccentric. It is entered by what looks like a centuries-old courtyard, but is actually a mixture of buildings that really have stood here through the epochs with others brought from elsewhere – an manor from Lisieux, an old stone farm well. At the far end of the right-hand side of the courtyard, on the other hand, is the only remaining part of the 14th-century wall of the *Enclos*, while next to it is the prison of the 16th-century Vicomte de Rocheville, who enjoyed the aristocratic privilege of keeping a personal lock-up for those who defied his authority. Inside there's a suitably dark dungeon, and part of Honfleur's old town pillory. The main museum is a real mishmash. There are religious images, and pictures of famous Honfleurians, but its main exhibits are reconstructions of Norman interiors from the 17th to the 19th centuries – a 'weavers' room' from the Pay de Caux, a 'young ladies bedroom' with magnificent 18th-century carved furniture.

The Enclos comes to an end at Quai Lepaulmier. Across it to the south is the **Faubourg St-Léonard**, whose main monument is the church of **St-Léonard**, built at the end of the 15th century, with a fine *Flamboyant* Gothic portal and an octagonal bell tower added in 1760 that is completely out of style with the rest of the building. An organic food market is now held in front of the church every Wednesday morning.

From Quai Lepaulmier a walk around the landward end of the Vieux Bassin will take you toward the **Faubourg Ste-Catherine**. The district's big, sloping twin main squares, Place Berthelot and Place Ste-Catherine, are another of the town's highlights, the site of the main market every Saturday, and lined by a lively mix of cafés and restaurants. In the middle, theoretically dividing the two squares from each other, is the church of **Ste-Catherine**, Honfleur's extraordinary half-timbered wooden 'cathedral'. An early stone church on this site was destroyed, along with many other buildings nearby, during the English occupation. To celebrate their departure at the end of the 1460s it was decided to rebuild Ste-Catherine, but all available stone was earmarked for restoring the town's fortifications. However, Honfleur's master shipbuilders offered to build a new church themselves, using their own skills. Structurally it is quite extraordinary: the two parallel naves are in effect giant, upturned ship's hulls, and it is believed they were built entirely separately, one in about 1468 and the other in 1496, since it was impossible using these methods to construct one roof to cover the whole area. Inside, the effect is astonishing, with a wonderful sense of space and loftiness. Just as impressive is the staggering quality of the carving in innumerable details, many added over the following two centuries: look out particularly for the fascinating series showing 16th-century musical instruments along the balustrade of the organ loft, interrupted by blank panels where the coats of arms of local aristocrats were sliced off during the Revolution. Another of Ste-Catherine's special features is its **bell tower**, also of wood on a stone base, which for structural reasons was built separately from the church beside one end of it.

The Ste-Catherine district was the classic fishing quarter of Honfleur, and is endlessly fascinating to explore. It's made up of long streets running along the hillside, linked by passages and stairways that appear in tiny gaps in the main streets. Rue Haute, Upper Street, the district's main thoroughfare, is, with suitable Honfleur eccentricity, near the bottom. All along these streets there's a fascinating jumble of half-timbering, slate-fronting and other styles – no.30 Rue Haute is a great example, its timbers apparently sinking into the street; elsewhere, there are glimpses of half-timbered courtyards decked in brilliant arrays of flowers. This area – especially the lower end of Rue de l'Homme-de-Bois – is also one of the best places in Honfleur for finding original art and craft galleries. On the inland side of the district is **La Forge** (25 *Rue de la Foulerie; open Fri–Sun 3–7*), an extraordinary sculpture garden made up of the multicoloured, bizarre, dream-like creations of artist Florence Marie.

Rue de l'Homme-de-Bois and Rue Haute meet near the harbour in **Place Hamelin**, an attractive small square lined with yet more restaurants. Its name comes not from any connection with pied pipers but from Rear-Admiral Hamelin, one of the commanders of Napoleon's navy, born here in 1768. Above no.6 there is a plaque recording that this was also the birthplace in 1854 of **Alphonse Allais**, France's greatest comic writer. His marvellously loopy imagination produced, among many other things, the world's first entirely abstract art show, with paintings such as an all-red canvas titled *Apoplectic Cardinals Harvesting Tomatoes by the Red Sea*; he also came up with the great French philosophical aphorism 'I think, therefore I forget'. His only foray into English was in a sadly now out-of-print anthology translated by Miles Kington in the 1970s, but his writings, precursors of 20th-century surreal humour, deserve much wider recognition.

A walk up Rue de l'Homme-de-Bois will take you to the **Musée Eugène Boudin** (*open mid-Mar–Sept Mon and Wed–Sun 10–12 and 2–6; Oct–mid-Mar Mon and Wed–Fri 2.30–5, Sat and Sun 10–12 and 2.30–5; closed Tues; adm*), which was established by Boudin himself in 1868, together with another Honfleur-born painter, Louis-Alexandre Dubourg. The interior is modern, but the museum stays true to its founders' intentions as a showcase for the 'Seine estuary' or 'Honfleur school' of painters. The area's special light had drawn painters to it ever since the 1820s, but it was the locally-born Boudin with his free-flowing brush strokes who first established a distinctive 'Seine estuary' style. He also took on the young Claude Monet, then only 15, as his pupil in 1855, and encouraged other young painters such as Renoir, Sisley and Pissarro. The museum is naturally very strong in works by Boudin himself, with seascapes and beach and harbour scenes of Honfleur, Trouville and other places along the coast, and fascinating cabinets of his sketches and pastel roughs. Other artists represented include Jongkind, Courbet and Monet, and there are fine 20th-century paintings by Vallotin, Hebdo and above all Raoul Dufy, born in Le Havre like Monet, and represented by vibrantly colourful Seine estuary scenes. The museum also has an 'ethnographic' collection of popular arts, mostly of lace, embroidery and traditional costumes.

From the Boudin museum, head further up Rue de l'Homme-de-Bois and go down any of the suitably surreal-looking stairways to the right to descend to Rue Haute and Honfleur's newest but most must-see museum, the **Maisons Satie** (*open June–Sept Mon and Wed–Sun 10–7; Oct–Dec and mid-Feb–May Mon and Wed–Sun 11–6; closed Tues and Jan–mid-Feb; adm*), in the rambling old half-timbered house where the town's greatest eccentric of all, Erik Satie, was born in 1866. Satie – who was a friend of Alphonse Allais – left this house when he was 12, and it subsequently went through many owners before it was left to the town and opened as a museum in 1998, so that there was little in it directly connected to him. Rather than just open up empty rooms with a few scarcely related artefacts, the adventurous decision was taken to fill the house with inventively designed scenes evoking the many aspects of the very unique world of Satie, supported by videos and interactive effects. You go around the museum with earphones and a tape – the English version is excellent – which moves to the right place automatically as you enter different rooms, so that you can go back and forth if you wish. It works wonderfully well in opening up the Satie universe: his appointment as 'Chapel Master' to the esoteric cult of the Rosicrucians while simultaneously working as a cabaret pianist, his (now fashionable) insistence on wearing only black clothes and eating only white food. And above all there is music, far more than in most museums dedicated to musicians: not only delightful well-known pieces like *Gymnopédies* and *Gnossiennes* but a huge variety of other work, from awesome oratorios and bizarre religious works to 'Furniture Music', designed to be as bland as possible, and *Bonjour Biqui*, a 25-second piece commemorating Satie's very short love affair with the painter Suzanne Valadon, known as Biqui. At the end of the tour you can ride on the 'pedalo quaver', a mad music machine on which you pedal round a kind of merry-go-round generating different sounds as you go. It's a 'museum' that suits its subject exactly: illuminating, enjoyable and with a great sense of unpredictable Satie-esque humour. The shop sells Satie CDs, including a great anthology of music heard on the tour that is only available here.

One other aspect of the museum has nothing directly to do with Satie, but seems to fit in curiously well. During the restoration of the house the discovery was made behind the plaster of a wall of ancient graffiti, with one scene dated 1543 and several from the 15th century. Most are of ships and boats – sometimes well-drawn – and one can well imagine bored youths sitting on the stairs, dreaming of sailing away.

As you leave the Maisons Satie, a walk across Boulevard Charles V will take you to Honfleur's main park, the **Jardin Public**, and eventually the town's pretty shabby and unused beach. A better brief excursion out of town is the climb – very steep, if you're walking – to the top of the giant cliff-escarpment of the **Côte-de-Grâce**, at the back of the Faubourg Ste-Catherine. Its summit above the sea has been a lookout point and local pilgrimage centre for over a thousand years. A chapel was built here by Duke Richard II of Normandy in 1023, but it collapsed in the 1530s due to erosion of the cliff. The current chapel of **Notre-Dame-de-Grâce**, nestling between lofty trees, was built in 1600–1615 in a plain early Baroque style. For a similar number of centuries it has been traditional for Honfleur's mariners to pray at Notre-Dame-de-Grâce before and after voyages and to give thanks here for the saving of lives at sea, and the interior is lined with *ex voto* plaques of thanks to Our Lady of Mercy, which add to the atmospheric darkness of the chapel and a notable atmosphere of religious intensity.

The limitless view from the Côte-de-Grâce was one of those that most inspired Boudin and the young Impressionists. However, certain things have happened since then. Le Havre has been rebuilt and extended, stretching along the north bank of the river with oil refineries, factories, a huge Renault export depot. East of old Honfleur is the town's new industrial area, looming above which is the awesome stretch of the Pont de Normandie, the longest single-span suspension bridge in Europe. Between them sits historic Honfleur, apparently blithely unaware of the changes that have taken place all around it.

Shopping

Honfleur is full of art and antique shops and artists' studios. Some trade on old glories for the sake of the tourist trade, but in among them there are livelier, more enterprising spaces. Imaginative galleries that showcase good new painting and decorative arts are found especially on or around Rue Haute and Rue de l'Homme de Bois. Honfleur also hosts an **antiques market** in Place St-Léonard and Rue Cachin (*2nd Sun of each month*).

Honfleur's regular **market** is in Place Ste-Catherine (*Sat am*), and is one of the region's best, with wonderful produce from the Pays d'Auge and the rest of Normandy. A smaller *bio* (organic) market is held every week in Place St-Léonard (*Wed am*).

Honfleur ✉ 14600

Compagnie des Calvados, 19 Rue de la Ville, t 02 31 89 57 56. A wonderful place to find the best of Normandy's distinctive drinks – cider, *pommeau*, *poiré* – under one roof, instead of having to search out farms all over the region. The array of calvados is fabulous, with bottles from over 80 different makers, and there are almost as many ciders. The young, English-speaking staff can be a big help in orienting your buying.

Goutte de Pluie, 18 Rue de l'Homme-de-Bois, t 02 31 89 09 08. One of the more individual art spaces, a striking contemporary glass and jewellery gallery that frequently features elegant, understated modern work. *Usually open Sat, Sun and hols, or by appointment.*

Gribouille, 16 Rue de l'Homme-de-Bois, t 02 31 89 29 54. A delightful little grocery shop specializing in *produits régionaux*: an excellent range of fine calvados, *pommeau* and ciders, an unusually wide choice of cider vinegars – including matured and aromatic varieties – jams, biscuits, terrines and cheeses. Service is personal and very friendly.

Gris Pomme, 32 Rue de la Ville, t 02 31 89 39 99. At the landward end of Rue de la Ville, this attractive little craft and household-items shop has, among many other things, very attractive and usable original ceramics at accessible prices, and similarly eye-catching cushions and textiles. There's also a small *café-salon de thé*, with a nice line in cakes.

Les Marianiks, 35 Rue du Dauphin, t 02 31 89 98 00, *www.marianiks.com*. Queues often snake into the street from this little shop, attracted by its magnificent cabinets of superb handmade chocolates. Other specialities are *paniers de pommes*, little marzipan apples, with or without calvados. Service is very charming, presentation impeccable.

L'Oeil du Chat, 13 Rue Rue de l'Homme de Bois, t 02 31 89 42 70. This disorderly emporium stands out among the more *comme-il-faut* shops on this street. Second-hand books are its main business, but with them there are stacks of anything collectable – old advertising, stylish miniature mannequins from shop displays, games and all sorts of junk.

Le Temps des Cerises, 46 Rue des Lingots/ 8 Rue des Capucins, t 02 31 89 77 79. An old curiosity shop packed full of all kinds of things from odd knick-knacks to valuable antiques: old toys, furniture, porcelain, lots of glassware. Great for idle browsing.

Where to Stay

Honfleur has long had a sizeable choice of both luxury and mid-range hotels. Recently they have been joined by a clutch of small modern 'boutique' hotels, put together with very individual care and style, which provide a fresh alternative to the traditional standards.

Honfleur ✉ 14600

Ferme St-Siméon, Rue Adolphe Marais, t 02 31 81 78 00, *www.fermesaintsimeon.fr* (*rooms €150–550, suites €750–850*). The undoubted top of the tree in Honfleur, the 'Farm' sits in its own grounds on a lofty ridge overlooking the Seine just west of the town. It's famed for its associations with the Impressionists, who stayed and painted here in the days when it was a much more humble establishment. Today this Relais-et-Châteaux hotel is devil-may-care expensive, and a stay is a true entry into French luxury (except that its clientele is made up very much of the internationally wealthy). As well as opulent rooms and vast suites there is a gourmet restaurant, a garden terrace, a stunning indoor pool and an especially lavish range of health and beauty facilities, to hone one's look to perfection. One drawback is that the expense doesn't get the hotel a better view of Le Havre across the river, which has got a lot more industrial since Monet's day.

La Maison de Lucie, 44 Rue des Capucins, **t** 02 31 14 40 40, *www.lamaisondelucie.com* (*double rooms €110–190, suite €285, cottage €315*). In a grand 19th-century house with courtyard – the name refers to the poet Lucie Delarue-Mardrus, born here in 1874 – this is less a hotel than a unique B&B. It has just four magnificent rooms and two still-more magnificent suites, decorated with an extravagant, sexy mix of the house's original features, antiques, contemporary design and a touch of pure Orientalist fantasy. In the cellar, guests can use a neo-Moorish jacuzzi. Like Honfleur's other style hotels, it gives the option of an (also very impressive) self-contained *petite maison* or cottage, across the courtyard. The owners are both hip and charming. A place for a really special stay.

L'Absinthe, 1 Rue de la Ville, **t** 02 31 89 23 23, *www.absinthe.fr* (*double rooms €98–129, suite €220*). One of Honfleur's special hotels, in a 16th-century former presbytery at the top of the main street of L'Enclos. Owner Antoine Ceffrey has restored it with real flair, respecting the charm and structure of the building while adding elegant, stylish modern details. Near the entrance there's a delightful lounge with giant fireplace; above, the six rooms have a distinct touch of luxury, and the suite is fabulous. Service is very attentive, and rooms are in great demand. The equally striking Absinthe restaurant (*see* p.228) is across the street.

Les Maisons de Léa, Place Ste-Catherine, **t** 02 31 14 49 49, *www.lesmaisonsdelea.com* (*double rooms €95–165, suite €220*). A romantic, sumptuous hotel *de charme* in a wonderful location, with views of Ste-Catherine from many rooms. The whole hotel has been made over in the rather chichi but unquestionably pretty style beloved of French design magazines: rooms come in one of four themes and sets of colours, *Romance* (flowery), *Capitaine* (nautical blues and whites), *Campagne* (mellow yellows) and *Baltimore* (American Shaker, but without austerity). They vary in size and price, but all are charming. The hotel has a self-contained

cottage, with room for five (*€260 per night, €1,200 per week*). There's an equally lovely *salon de thé*, and service is very welcoming.

Hôtel des Loges, 18 Rue Brûlée, **t** 02 31 89 38 26, *www.hoteldesloges.com* (*double rooms €90–115, €145 for three*). A set of old-Honfleur houses now contains the most stylish of the new hotels, a model combination of contemporary design with a historic setting. Owner Catherine Chouridis – who used to work in cinema – has an emphatically modern approach, with clean lines and grey, yellow and deep red colours, but there's no sense of minimalist chill, for the atmosphere is fresh, comfortable and relaxed. The 14 rooms are very well-equipped – wide-screen TVs, DVDs in each – and at the back there's a complete cottage in the same style, with kitchen and space for up to five, a superior town *gîte* (*€250 per weekend, €550 per week*). Fresh-produce breakfasts are served (until noon) in a similarly-stylish dining room, and service is specially obliging. So many guests ask where they can get things seen in the hotel (fine sheets, lamps...) that you can now buy them in a shop alongside, with fresh preserves and other produce.

Hôtel Le Cheval Blanc, 2 Quai des Passagers, **t** 02 31 81 65 00, *www.hotel-honfleur.com* (*double rooms €70–180, studio and suites €230–425*). The great asset of this hotel is its matchless location on the port, with fine sea or harbour views from nearly all its rooms. The building has been a hotel for centuries, through many renovations: it's accordingly traditional in style, but the 31 rooms are very comfortable. They vary a lot in size: some are larger de luxe rooms, and there's an apartment-like 'studio' and spacious suites, with jacuzzis and other extras.

Hôtel du Dauphin, 10 Place Berthelot, **t** 02 31 89 15 53, *www.hotel-du-dauphin.com* (*double rooms €66–92, family rooms and suites €92–151*). Popular hotel with 34 comfortable rooms and a suite between two buildings, the grey-slate fronted house that contains the reception and a half-timbered building on Place Berthelot itself. They combine old-world style with good modern fittings, and vary in size: the best are in the older 'annexe', several of which have superb views of the church of Ste-Catherine.

Eating Alternatives

Honfleur ✉ 14600

L'Absinthe, 10 Quai de la Quarantaine, **t** 02 31 89 39 00 (menus €30–60). This attractive restaurant stands out amid the bargain seafood bistros on Quai de la Quarantaine, for its elegant style, for its combination of an old Honfleur heavy-timbered building and chic modern design, and for the innovative, unconventional menu, featuring interesting dishes with international, even oriental touches. A sister to L'Absinthe hotel (see p.227), it's run with similar zip and flair, and the food is consistently among Honfleur's best. For summer, there's a pretty, plant-clad terrace. For a less opulent meal, the group also have their own, also-stylish brasserie, **La Grenouille**, at 16 Quai de la Quarantaine (**t** 02 31 89 04 24; menus €16–23).

Au Vieux Honfleur, 13 Quai St-Etienne, **t** 02 31 89 15 31 (menus €29–48.50). A classic Honfleur restaurant, with terrace tables on the Enclos side of the Vieux Bassin that are ideally placed for surveying the remarkable architecture along Quai Ste-Catherine. The 'Old Honfleur' is indeed old-fashioned in its unchanging style, but is consistently highly regarded, and one of the best of the harbourside restaurants. There's an ample carte, but for a big bouffe try the terroir menu, with grilled lobster and langoustines with tarragon, or the platters of fruits de mer.

La Terrasse de l'Assiette, 8 Place Ste-Catherine, **t** 02 31 89 31 33 (menus €25–45). One of Honfleur's premier gourmet restaurants, and Michelin-starred. Chef Gérard Bonnefoy is known as a master of classic French sauces, but he also likes to experiment: try lobster gazpacho or poitrine de pigeon rôti avec son jus aux arômes de cacao. Other specialities include fabulous sea-fresh fish, cooked many different ways. Plus, it has a delicious location, with a terrasse facing the church of Ste-Catherine. Sept–June closed Mon and Tues; July and Aug closed Mon.

Le Bréard, 7 Rue du Puits, **t** 02 31 89 53 40 (menus €18–32). Representative of Honfleur's more modern side, this bright, fresh-looking restaurant has not been going long, but many consider its young chef Fabrice Sebire one of the most able in town. His style is innovative and open-minded, skilfully combining superb local produce – especially fish – with a global range of ingredients in intricate dishes like prétexte autour du thon – tuna cooked several different ways – with Japanese mustard. The main menus, too, are fine value. Service is contemporary, like the décor, and likeably relaxed.

Entre Terre et Mer, 12 Place Hamelin, **t** 02 31 89 70 60 (menus €23–29). Fish and seafood tend to be pre-eminent in Honfleur restaurants, but 'Between Land and Sea' offers a completely meat-based menu as well as a list of fish and fruits de mer, including superb specials using the day's catch. Both are varied and of high quality (and you can of course mix the two). The décor is a clever blend of traditional and chic, and it also has tables outside on Place Hamelin whenever the weather allows.

Le Bistrot du Port, 14 Quai de la Quarantaine, **t** 02 31 89 21 84 (menus €16–25). A little rough and ready, but perennially popular and a great place for bargain seafood lunches – moules-frites, local crevettes, plateaux de fruits de mer or just a snack. Waiters weaving skilfully between the tables of its giant terrace keep everyone supplied, and you couldn't do better for Gallic atmosphere.

Au Gars Normand, 8 Quai des Passagers, **t** 02 31 89 05 28 (menus €15–20). With its battered old sign, and location by the port, the 'Norman Lad' looks the part of a classic fishermen's inn. Inside, there's a friendly atmosphere, and beneath the venerable timbers the restaurant is neater and more comfortable than the rustic exterior might lead you to expect. The set menus are exceptional value: fruits de mer as usual are the speciality, but there are also fine Norman fish and meat dishes, such as poulet vallée d'auge or turbot in a sauce normande.

La Tortue, 36 Rue de l'Homme-de-Bois, **t** 02 31 89 04 93 (menu €12–30). A pretty, small bistro-style restaurant near the Musée Boudin with, very unusually, a full vegetarian menu (€12) as well as more conventional dishes such as cod in cider, or a fine salade paysanne with cold meats. The main menus offer a generous choice, and several include a trou normand. Closed Tues (Oct–May), and Jan.

Moules, Movers and Shakers:
Trouville and Deauville

22

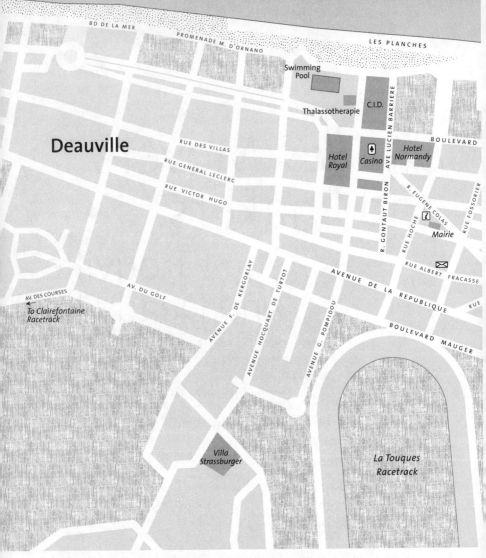

Fleeting glimpses of French actresses and Euro-celebrities, sharply preserved matrons promenading with little dogs, *Belle Epoque* roués staggering ruined from the casino, men and women with flawless skin lolling in unbelievably comfortable chairs at beach-front cafés, a precise sense of chic and luxury: these are the images and ideas conjured up by Deauville, legendary capital of the *Côte Fleurie*. This stretch of coast at the mouth of the Seine has been the seaside of affluent Paris since the mid-19th century, when Deauville, above all, became the capital's self-styled 21st *arrondissement*, and in the 1900s anyone who was anyone could be found at some time each summer on parade along its neatly clipped seafront. More recently, its position has been challenged by the more reliable weather of other resorts further south, but Deauville has fought to maintain its status, promoting its overall ritziness and its role as a venue for prestige events.

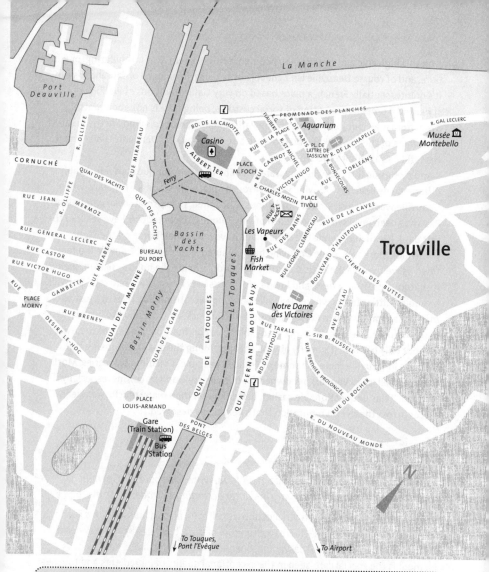

La Manche

Port
Deauville

CORNUCHÉ

R. OLLIFFE

QUAI DES YACHTS

RUE MIRABEAU

BD. DE LA CAHOTTE

PROMENADE DES PLANCHES

Aquarium

R. GAL LECLERC

*Musée
Montebello*

Casino

Q. ALBERT 1ER

Ferry

RUE JEAN

R. OLLIFFE

MERMOZ

QUAI DES YACHTS

BUREAU
DU PORT

*Bassin
des
Yachts*

RUE GENERAL LECLERC

RUE CASTOR

RUE VICTOR HUGO

RUE MIRABEAU

QUAI DE LA MARINE

Bassin Morny

GAMBETTA

RUE BRENEY

PLACE
MORNY

DÉSIRE LE-HOC

QUAI DE LA GARE

QUAI DE LA TOUQUES

La Touques

QUAI FERNAND MOUREAUX

RUE DE LA PLAGE

RUE DE PARIS

R. FLAUBERT

R. ST MICHEL

RUE CARNOT

VICTOR HUGO

R. CHARLES MOZIN

RUE DU MARCHÉ

Les Vapeurs

RUE DES BAINS

*Fish
Market*

RUE GEORGE CLEMENCEAU

PLACE
M. FOCH

PLACE
TIVOLI

PL. DE
LATTRE DE
TASSIGNY

R. DE LA CHAPELLE

R. D'ORLEANS

R. BONSECOURS

RUE DE LA CAVEE

BOULEVARD D'HAUTPOUL

CHEMIN DES BUTTES

Trouville

*Notre Dame
des Victoires*

RUE TARALE

BD D'HAUTPOUL

R. SIR B. RUSSELL

AVE D'EYLAU

RUE BERTHIER PROLONGEE

RUE DU ROCHER

R. DU NOUVEAU MONDE

PLACE
LOUIS-ARMAND

Gare
(Train Station)

Bus
Station

PONT
DES BELGES

To Touques,
Pont l'Evêque

To Airport

N

Getting There

Approach Deauville/Trouville on the N177 in from Caen, Rouen and the A13 *autoroute* and you come up the Deauville side of the River Touques, and shortly come to Pont des Belges, the only bridge between them. Cross the bridge, and Quai Fernand Moureaux runs off towards the sea on the left. Les Vapeurs is about halfway up. If you are coming from the east and Honfleur on the D513, you arrive at the Trouville end of the bridge, in which case turn right along the quay.

There are frequent **trains** to Deauville from Gare St-Lazare in Paris, via Lisieux. There is also a local line from Deauville to Cabourg (*services daily late-June–early Sept, weekends only at other times*). Buses run along the coast all year.

Tourist Information

Deauville: Place de la Mairie, t 02 31 14 40 00, *www.deauville.org*.
Trouville: 32 Quai Fernand Moureaux, t 02 31 14 60 70, *www.trouvillesurmer.org*.

All this high chic and *trés distingué* opulence might seem a bit intimidating, or a bore, and of course Deauville isn't cheap, but take it with a pinch of salt and it's fun. It's quintessentially French, a place based on very Gallic traditions of wellbeing, style, and a proper observation of social customs; being here is not about getting away from it all, but getting into it. The Parisian *haut-bourgeois* who are the greatest sustainers of the town like to do things in a certain way, and Deauville is one resort that still has a definite social Season.

And alongside it is Trouville, separated only by the River Touques but remarkably different. The beach at Trouville was a favourite place of escape for Parisians when Deauville was still a stretch of sand dunes. Since then, the normal social geography of Paris has been reversed at the mouth of the Touques: the *bourgeois* have secured the Left Bank (Deauville), while the bohemians have made their home on the Right (Trouville). Moreover, while Deauville has remained a pure resort, Trouville is a real town as well, with a life of its own that carries on outside the holiday season, seen in its harbour, its fishing fleet, and in one of France's very finest town markets. Trouville has quirky little streets where Deauville has long, well-trimmed drives; it's just as much of an immersion in *la vie française*, but laid-back, amiable and hip in a way its neighbour can rarely be. It's more enjoyable to eat on the Trouville side of the river, and not only because it's nearly always cheaper. Along the quay overlooking the Touques in Trouville there are some of France's best, most bustling brasseries. Most famous of all is **Les Vapeurs**, renowned for both its style and its cuisine, especially seafood. It has unquestionable cachet, better known than many much swankier places across the river, a reputation that's very richly deserved.

Les Vapeurs

160 Quai Fernand Moureaux, t 02 31 88 15 24, www.lesvapeurs.fr. Open daily 8am–1am, closing time may vary in winter according to trade. Carte *average €25.*

When restaurant owners in other countries call their place a brasserie, this is what they are hoping to achieve – this same mixture of buzz, bustle, light, unfussy décor, fine but accessible food and easygoing, open-all-hours atmosphere. An added element is the special care, seen in the exceptional quality of ingredients and touches such as the plentiful fresh flowers, that is needed to sustain a place like this over many years. There has been a change in ownership since it opened in 1927, as the Bazire family who founded Les Vapeurs signed it over to Gilbert and Ghislaine Meslin in 1997, but the new owners have scarcely changed a thing, probably because neither the regulars nor the staff would ever allow them to. Throughout, it has retained the same Art Deco fittings, with curious 1930s accessories and mirrors that are now adorned with an accumulation of souvenirs and signed photographs. It seems quite small from the entrance, long and narrow with tables intimately packed down each side (and note: the clientele tend to smoke), but it's labyrinthine inside, with several rooms upstairs. One change has been the over-the-top flashing sign installed outside for the 70th anniversary in 1997, but this only adds to the brasserie's vibrant style.

Moules à la Crème Normande

Serves 4

2.25kg/5lbs mussels
500ml/17fl oz dry white wine
2 onions, finely chopped
500ml/17fl oz crème fraîche
2 tablespoons chopped fresh parsley
salt and pepper

Discard any broken mussels and those with open shells that refuse to close when tapped. Under cold running water, scrape the mussel shells with a knife to remove any barnacles and pull out any stringy beards.

In a large heavy flameproof casserole, combine the wine, onions and a little pepper. Bring to the boil over a medium heat and cook for 2 minutes. Add the mussels and cook, tightly covered, for 5 minutes, or until the mussels open, shaking and tossing the pan occasionally. Remove mussels to a bowl and cover to keep warm.

Pour off the cooking liquor into a large saucepan, leaving behind the gritty bit at the bottom, add the cream, and boil to reduce by half, about 7–10 minutes. Add the mussels and parsley. Cook for about a minute more to reheat the mussels. Divide the mussels and the creamy liquor among warm soup plates, and serve.

Gérard Depardieu pops in when he's in town, and over the years every French entertainment star anyone has ever heard of and many Hollywood and international names – in town for the Film Festival – have signed the *Livre d'Or*, among them the director of *Diner* and much else besides Barry Levinson, who wrote that you can eat here better than in any diner. In high season there are also fashion types, and people who work in French TV, vying for the best tables alongside the zinc bar or on the pavement outside. But despite all this celebrity hubbub, the place still manages to generate a comfortable warmth, with locals coming in just to eat a quick lunch alone, and plenty of ordinary punters among the poseurs.

Mutterings have been made about the service at Les Vapeurs. The squad of men in white shirts and black bow ties are certainly the kind of Frenchmen for whom going 'bof!' and shrugging their shoulders is second nature, but my own experience is that, once they've got over showing you their smattering of English, the waiters here are genuinely friendly in a quick-fire way. Les Vapeurs gets busy, and they don't hang about – the zippiness of the staff and their agility in negotiating the tables are essential to the ambience – but requests for changes or extras are met with professional aplomb, and they'll never harass you to hurry your coffee.

Since this is a brasserie, there is only a *carte* menu, and eating a full meal can be expensive, but it's perfectly acceptable to have just one or two plainer dishes. Starters are straightforward, with a sizeable selection of simple, fresh salads. There's also plenty of food for people who like to use their fingers, such as one of the great specialities, *crevettes grises* – shrimps, swiftly boiled with salt and pepper. Eat them in their shells, minus only heads and tails. Real aficionados eat the tails too.

Main courses include steaks, and above all many varieties of superbly fresh fish, all landed right in Trouville. Some are fixtures on the menu, like sole, while others are seasonal market specials such as sea bream, plainly grilled or served in a classic sauce. What many people around you will be dealing with, however, are the mussels. Les Vapeurs is above all home to what is probably the definitive *moules marinières*, a superlative concatenation of subtle flavours that contrives to explode and melt in the mouth simultaneously. If you want your mussels with more traditional Norman richness, try them *à la crème normande*, an equally delicious combination of seafood, wine and cream. The chips are excellent too, and the brasserie's steady supply of perfectly chilled muscadet is an ideal accompaniment.

Don't pass on the classic desserts. A *crêpe suzette* with Grand Marnier is wonderfully boozy, and the pear *Belle Helène* and *tarte tatin* are beautifully made and packed with fresh fruit – and with them appears a whole earthenware tub of crème fraîche. The mere sight of it must cause fainting fits in any self-respecting Californian movie executive; follow it up with a shot of Calvados, and you're truly set up for the day.

The Meslins also offer an attractive alternative next door, **Les Voiles, t** 02 31 88 45 85, which has shorter, more conventional French restaurant hours, and is cheaper, rather more spacious and has set menus (*menus €11.80–19.90*).

Touring Around

Dieppe may have beaten it as France's first seaside resort, but thanks to a better beach and its good connections with Paris **Trouville** quickly became more popular. The first beach huts appeared in the 1840s, and when Napoleon III began to bring his court here in the following decade its popularity was assured. The great forerunner of Impressionism Eugène Boudin, and later Monet and Renoir, all painted here, and the view along the wooden boardwalk or *planches*, with flags fluttering in the wind, must be one of the most familiar images in 19th-century French painting. After the elite had transferred their allegiance to Deauville, Trouville continued to draw in the crowds. Maupassant, in his 1888 novel *Pierre et Jean*, described the beach as looking like 'a long garden full of brilliantly coloured flowers', covered in 'sunshades of all colours, hats of all shapes, dresses of all shades'.

Trouville's **beach** has been its fortune, a sweep of soft sand running away to the cliffs in the far distance to the east, fine for frolicking in the waves even though it can be a hike to reach the water at low tide, and backed by the *planches* for all its length. It's a relaxing, old-style seafront, with bars, ice-cream stands and grand old beach villas, and still fills up on summer weekends. Part-way along it is the **Natur'Aquarium** (*open daily Easter–June and Sept–Oct 10–12 and 2–6.30; July and Aug 10–7; Nov–Easter 2–6; adm*), for a rainy day, with displays of all sorts of marine life. Trouville's casino, at the point where the seafront meets the Touques, has recently been done up by the same Barrière organization that dominates entertainment in Deauville.

Away from the beach, Trouville is an engaging, idiosyncratic town, with little narrow streets intersecting and winding up suddenly steep hillsides, and a good deal of bizarre Norman holiday-town architecture combining half-timbering and pebble dash: 19th-century churches sport neo-Byzantine flourishes, and even prosaic public buildings like the post office have a certain mad seaside grandeur about them. The town's bohemian aura is reflected in its bar and bistro life, with a string of suitably relaxed hang-outs along the charming Rue des Bains, and in its interesting antique, fashion and curio shops. On Rue du Général Leclerc, the long street that runs parallel to the beach, there is the **Musée Montebello** (*open April–Sept Mon and Wed–Sun 2–6.30; closed Tues; adm*), with an engaging display on varied aspects of local life: charming works by Boudin and other Trouville painters, designs by the poster artist and long-term Trouvillite Raymond Savignac (who also drew the menu at Les Vapeurs) and an endearing exhibit on the early history of French seaside holidays.

Trouville has another major focus of activity, the long quay along the Touques, where fishing boats are moored in line to unload their catch, and the location of Les Vapeurs and other good bars and restaurants. The best times to come here are on Wednesday and Sunday mornings, when the tree-shaded space along the quays is the site of Trouville's wonderful **market** (from July to September, some stalls are also there every day). It's a fascinating combination of luxury food display and jumble sale. Because Trouville and Deauville together offer a large number of generally free-spending customers, many of Normandy's finest producers of traditional foods bring their wares here: farmhouse cheeses, terrines, pâtés and *confits* of duck, *andouilles* and other gutsy products, ciders and calvados, honey, cakes and traditional breads. The only permanent building is the **fish market**, where the day's catch is put on sale a few feet from where it is landed. The displays of *tourteaux*, sea bass, mussels, prawns, *bigorneaux* and other less familiar sea creatures are utterly spectacular, and the lack of any fishy odours is a vivid testament to their freshness. This is also a market that thoroughly demonstrates Trouville's quirky, small-town identity, for as you wander around you'll find alongside the gourmet delicacies stalls selling anything from scarves featuring Johnny Halliday or Eminem, unidentified stretches of elastic, bargain overcoats or trilby hats to American quilts, fire extinguishers, rare books and vaguely baroque furniture. It's wonderfully vibrant and rough-and-ready, and nothing to do with the supposed stuffiness of the Côte Fleurie.

The market ends at the bridge across the river, called **Pont des Belges** because of the curious fact that Deauville and Trouville were liberated in August 1944 by a Belgian Brigade operating with the Canadian Army. On the other side, you can walk down a neat, shaded path along the Touques, or stroll into the broad avenues of **Deauville**. The town is a product of the decadent Second Empire. In 1860 Napoleon III's half-brother the Duc de Morny strayed across from Trouville and decided to develop the empty dunes on the left bank of the river, as a much more exclusive, and so more profitable, resort. Another major contributor to its development was a speculator called Eugène Cornuché, who at the turn of the 20th century built the current seafront and casino. Deauville's two great heydays were either side of the First World War, and in the Jazz Age flappers danced the night away at parties in the town's extravagant villas, and entertainers such as Mistinguett and Maurice Chevalier were obligatorily snapped in photo opportunities on the seafront every year.

Since Deauville is an artificial town, its promoters were able to control building and impose particular styles, and above all the one known locally as 'Anglo-Normand', with much use of mock-traditional half-timbering in giant mansions several storeys high, giving the impression of a Pays d'Auge manor house after a severe dose of steroids. Walk around the neatly-kept streets of the town and you find a fascinating variety of such creations, with pepperpot towers, turrets, Swiss-chalet roofs, gingerbread-house windows, pagoda cornices and all kinds of other fanciful details, all within smart gardens surrounded by tightly clipped hedges. It's the presence of so much mock architecture in Deauville that gives the place its distinctly Beverly Hills, slightly dotty look. There are relatively few shops, and as many *esthéticiennes* as food stores. Most of the town's grand residences remain strictly private, but one that can be visited (if only very briefly) is the **Villa Strassburger** (*guided tours Aug only Wed and Thur 3pm, 4pm; adm*), a vast half-timbered palace near La Touques racetrack. Built in 1907 for Baron Henri de Rothschild, it was acquired in the 1920s by American millionaire, playboy and racing fanatic Ralph Strassburger, who used it to host famously wild parties.

Right next to Pont des Belges is one of the most engagingly silly of the Anglo-Normand edifices, the half-timbered **railway station**. Carry on past it and veer to the right, and you come to the heart of town. At the centre of Deauville is the shiny white casino, overlooking the beach, looking a bit like the White House with the upper floors missing. On either side of it are two of the three Empress-Dowagers of Deauville hotels, the Normandy and the Royal. The third, the Hôtel du Golf, perhaps the largest half-timbered cottage ever built, is on Mont Canisy at the back of the town, next to its golf holes, one of the finest courses in France.

The casino and the grand hotels are separated from the beach-front by a flat, open area, lined with flowerbeds, that now contains such services as tennis courts, an indoor pool and the esplanade of the **Centre International de Deauville** (CID), the venue for exhibitions, festivals and conferences. Beyond that, finally, is the beach, lined with more wooden *Planches* that form Deauville's historic promenade. The bars along it – Le Ciro's, the Bar du Soleil, the Bar de la Mer – are perhaps the original beach cafés; they still draw in the visiting glamour today, busily air-kissing across the tables. You also see Deauville's more regular clientele along the promenade, participating in their daily rituals. The French middle classes have a persistent fondness for little dogs, and parts of Deauville could be considered a preserve where all the poodles and pekinese that have disappeared from the rest of the world have been taken for safety. There are clusters of the kind of wealthy young French people best identified by their complete domination of the art of wearing a pullover, and every so often pretty girls and boys appear on roller blades and push a piece of paper towards you, promoting something. After the bars come to an end there are lines of well-kept beach cabins, the little fences between them painted in imitation Hollywood Boulevard-style with the names of international film figures who presumably have passed through.

Next to the esplanade by the casino there is a large centre for **thalassotherapy**: bombardment with sea water through a high-pressure hose. *Le thalasso* fits all the requirements of a French middle-class health fad: you don't have to do anything, it's all done to you, and it's as much about looking good as it is about health. It's also supposed to be very good for *le stress*. There are *thalasso* centres all round the French coast, but the Deauville establishment is naturally one of the most luxurious.

Deauville's Season runs essentially from late June to early September. In the last 30 years, though, the town has had to work much harder to keep up its prestige, so this has been increasingly extended on either side. Programmes listing all the events organized each year are available from the tourist office. One major thing to do in Deauville is to go to the **races**, for this is one of the most important centres of the French (and European) horse world. There are two tracks, **La Touques** for flat racing and the more casual **Clairefontaine**, mainly used for steeplechases and trotting. Both have beautifully maintained buildings in *Anglo-Normand* manor house-style, and hold meetings through the summer season, with additional races and thoroughbred sales – attracting buyers from around the world – at La Touques in October. Clairefontaine also offers free guided tours, every day in season at 10.30am.

Some Deauville events are definitely the kind of occasions where you would not want to turn up wearing the wrong hat – notably the *Grand Prix de Deauville*, the traditional end to the racing season at La Touques at the end of August. Others are much less sniffy, and Deauville most lets its hair down during the *Festival du Cinéma Américain* in early September, which generally previews American movies before their European release dates, and always ensures that major Hollywood figures such as Steven Spielberg or Robert de Niro put in an appearance.

From November to mid-spring, while Trouville stays alive, Deauville largely closes down. A few people still come up for weekends to catch the sea air, but many of the grand houses are tightly shuttered, the lines of beach umbrellas are tied up like so many coloured pillars, and the streets are oddly but atmospherically quiet. Note, too, that this is also the town from which Jean-Louis Trintignant drove Anouk Aimée back to Paris in *Un Homme et une Femme*, so on a rainy day you could always drive around looking moonily at the wipers and going *Yaba-daba-da, Yaba-daba-da* ad infinitum.

If you've had enough of Deauville, follow the D513 road westwards, through the neat little seaside towns that make up the rest of the Côte Fleurie. **Villers-sur-Mer** is more Trouville than Deauville, an unfussy little beach town with a laid-back air, and great views at sunset. Just to the west are the celebrated cliffs known as the **Vaches Noires**, beneath which there's a great walk at low tide. They are known above all for fossils, and so Villers has a rather lovable-looking giant dinosaur effigy in the middle of its prom. Almost hidden in among the resorts is the ancient town of **Dives-sur-Mer**, from where William the Conqueror's main fleet set sail for Hastings. Its port has since largely silted up, but it still has a fine Romanesque and Gothic church and a superb 15th-century covered market hall, which hosts another vibrant market on Saturdays.

Deauville may have reinvented itself a little for the modern era, but the *Belle Epoque* lives on in **Cabourg**, just west of Dives, where Marcel Proust came for his adolescent holidays, and which he immortalized as 'Balbec' in *A la Recherche du Temps Perdu*. All roads in Cabourg lead to the Grand Hotel, around which the town was created. It looks exactly like the kind of hotel that would have been patronized by the Margaret Dumont character in the Marx Brothers movies, but now trades shamelessly on its Proustian associations by offering wildly expensive teas in its *salon de thé*.

Shopping

Shopping is especially easy in **Trouville**: the market fills the quays along the Touques every Wednesday and Sunday, and the fish market, in the centre of the quay, is open every day; the town's most interesting shops, meanwhile, are all concentrated on Quai Fernand Moureaux, the pedestrianized alley of Rue des Bains that runs off it, or on Rue d'Orléans, which runs on from the end of Rue des Bains.

Deauville's main area for luxury shopping is around the flower-decked Place Morny, with the tourist office nearby; for foods, Rue Désiré-le-Hoc, between Place Morny and the station, is Deauville's street of gourmet goodies.

Trouville ✉ 14360

La Cave Trouvillaise, 34–36 Rue des Bains, t 02 31 88 87 49. A fine wine merchant in a characterful old 19th-century shop in the heart of Trouville, looking like a piece of the Impressionist era itself, with an excellently varied wine stock and a superb collection of fine calvados and local ciders.

Aux Ducs de Normandie, 85 Rue des Bains, t 02 31 88 96 10. An eye-catching *confiserie artisanale*, with delicious homemade chocolates, little fancy cakes and other goodies.

Dupont avec un Thé, 134–136 Quai Fernand Moureaux, t 02 31 88 13 82. From the staff of life to complete indulgence – the renowned Dupont shops (also in Dives, Cabourg and Houlgate) include a *boulangerie* with fabulous fresh breads, a *pâtisserie* with great cakes and a *chocolaterie* with handmade chocolates and ice creams. Plus there's a (very popular) *salon de thé*, so you can try some of the goods before buying.

Le Fromager, 50 Rue des Bains, t 02 31 98 24 14. As well as an excellent selection of local cheeses – wonderful Pont-l'Evêque, Livarot and fresh Camembert – this little shop also stocks farmhouse ciders, meaty and mushroomy terrines, and other Norman produce.

Ma Pomme, 65 Rue des Bains, t 02 31 87 93 13. This pretty little shop takes the Norman apple obsession to its limits: everything that's local and apple-based is here – cider, calvados, *pommeau*, apple cakes, apple sweets, apple jams and more. Is there anything you *can't* do with apples?

Deauville ✉ 14800

Charcuterie Bernard, 31 Rue Désiré-le-Hoc, t 02 31 88 22 30. One of the more discreet of Deauville's luxury food outlets, Bernard has fine sausages, hams, cheeses and other delicacies. Staff are unfussily charming.

Au Duc de Morny, 59a Rue Désiré-le-Hoc, t 02 31 88 20 34. A kind of shop that France invented: a gleaming combination of *pâtisserie*, *confiserie* and *boulangerie*, with delectable cakes, exquisite sculptures in chocolate, and fine breads, all beautifully presented *comme il faut*. Even if you can't decide what to buy, the display is magnetic.

La Halle aux Vins, 10 Quai de la Touques, t 02 31 98 33 85. On the quay facing across the river to Trouville, this huge warehouse-wine store has an un-Deauville-like casual style. *Closed Mon; open Sun am.*

Where to Stay

On the Côte Fleurie prices, and availability, vary enormously by season (and often from weekdays to weekends). Many Deauville hotels close entirely from November to March.

Trouville ✉ 14360

La Maison Jul, 5 Rue Bonsecours, t 02 31 88 12 23/**mob** 06 83 45 77 98, *lydiejouan@hotmail.com* (*rooms €80 for two*). A chic modern B&B in an old Trouville townhouse with a mellow tranquility that reflects the personality of owner Lydie Jouan. The four bedrooms and *tour-de-force* lounge and breakfast room have been designed with a special, zen-influenced elegance, in whites and subtle colours: the atmosphere is individual and welcoming. Fine breakfasts feature organic produce.

Hôtel Le Central, 158 Quai Fernand Moureaux, t 02 31 88 80 84, *www.adeauville.com/lecentral.htm* (*double rooms €63–82, suites €110–120*). One of Trouville's most popular hotels, in a stately building fronted by 1930s-style signs rising out of the quayside beside Les Vapeurs. Truth to tell its rooms are more functional than characterful, but the location, with harbour views from many rooms, is the best in town, and the hotel has an enjoyable brio. The brasserie below is open late (*see* p.240). Note to drivers: the garage soon fills up, and its entrance is very narrow, so you might prefer just to park in the street.

Hôtel-Restaurant Carmen, 24 Rue Carnot, **t** 02 31 88 35 43, *lb.carmen@wanadoo.fr* (*double rooms €58–86*). A long-running family-run *Logis de France* hotel. The stairs (with no lift) creak a little, but the 16 rooms have been renovated in the last few years. Although it's not far from the beach and the port, the rooms don't actually have a view of either, but the hotel is extra cosy, and staff give a warm welcome. Its **restaurant** (*menus €12–32*) offers reliable Norman cuisine. *Closed two weeks Nov–Dec, three weeks Jan.*

Hôtel La Maison Normande, 4 Place du Maréchal de Lattre de Tassigny, **t** 02 31 88 12 25, *www.maisonnormande.com* (*double rooms €37–64*). A big old Anglo-Norman hotel that's one of the area's best near-budget options. The 17 rooms are simple but well-kept, and vary in size, facilities and prices. The owners are laidback and friendly, and there's a cool little breakfast room.

Deauville ✉ 14800

Hôtel Le Normandy Barrière, 38 Rue Jean Mermoz, **t** 02 31 98 66 22, *www.lucienbarriere.com* (*double rooms €302–602; various packages available*). Once in a while, driven by an itch for an all-out splurge, you may want to take the Deauville experience head-on. If so, you need to stay in one of the town's extraordinary grand hotels. All three – the Normandy, Royal and Golf – are owned, with the casino, by the same Lucien Barrière organization. The Normandy, a mad half-timbered fantasy mansion from 1912, is the largest of them all, with 258 rooms and suites, and the only one open year-round; the 176-room **Golf** next to its superb golf course is only open in-season (*Christmas and Mar–Oct*). The comforts and service offered by all three are of course fabulous: at the Normandy they include a choice of gourmet restaurants, an indoor pool, tennis courts, live entertainment and a health and beauty centre worthy of a health farm. Package deals including show and casino admissions, golf, beauty treatments and so on, with a minimum two- or four-night stay, soften the prices a little.

Hôtel de la Côte Fleurie, 55 Av de la République, **t** 02 31 98 47 47, **f** 02 31 98 47 46 (*double rooms €61–115*). A charming small hotel in a quiet part of Deauville, with attentive owners and a very pretty garden terrace. The 15 rooms all have décor *de charme*, and are brightly comfortable; if you don't feel like the garden, generous breakfasts are also served in an antique-lined dining room.

Hôtel Le Trophée, 81 Rue du Général Leclerc, **t** 02 31 88 45 86, *www.letrophee.com* (*double rooms €59–144*). A good option for those who wish to try out Deauville without paying top prices, a smart, comfortable hotel in the centre of town, with 24 rooms and two suites, and the nice extra of a courtyard swimming pool. The traditionally elegant restaurant, **Le Flambée** (*menus €24–45*), has smartly presented Norman cuisine.

Cabourg ✉ 14390

L'Argentine, 3 Jardins du Casino, **t** 02 31 91 14 25, *www.argentine-cabourg.com* (*rooms for two €50–120 low season, €70–162 high season*). Cabourg's Grand Hôtel might seem too much, but a dip into the town's Proustian ambience is more fun at this extravagant B&B, in a huge Art Nouveau mansion – opposite the hotel – built for a Mayor of Cabourg in 1895. The five lavish rooms, all decorated with antiques, have Proustian names like 'Guermantes', and there's an equally over-the-top *salon de thé*. Prices vary even more than usual through the year, and off-season are a real bargain.

Villers-sur-Mer ✉ 14640

Hôtel Outre-Mer, 1 Rue du Maréchal Leclerc, **t** 02 31 87 04 64, *www.hoteloutremer.com* (*double rooms €92–115*). France's new-model chic hotels tend to use understated shades, but Elizabeth Leray and Jean-Yves Lefrançois have taken a radical tack by making over this venerable seafront hotel in a riot of colour, with a different set in each room, often using English Designers' Guild fabrics. The results are dazzling, and the orange-tinged rooms that catch Villers' celebrated sunsets are ravishing. Several rooms have balconies, and there are two very large family rooms. There's an equally colourful bar-café, and the hotel has a great laidback, friendly feel.

Eating Alternatives

Trouville ✉ 14360

La Petite Auberge, 7 Rue Carnot, **t** 02 31 88 11 07 (*menus €21–44*). In contrast to the usual brasserie-and-bistro style of Trouville's eating places, the Petite Auberge is a neat, intimate restaurant with pretty décor and sophisticated classic cuisine. Menus highlight market-fresh ingredients – listed simply as 'the rabbit', 'the cod', 'the beef' and so on – which the chef prepares in one of many inventive styles. *Closed Tues and Wed.*

Brasserie Le Central, 158 Quai Fernand Moureaux, **t** 02 31 88 13 68 (carte *average €25*). Although it's alongside Les Vapeurs (so that it's not easy to see where the outdoor tables of one end and those of the other begin), the big brasserie in the Hôtel Central (*see p.238*) is condemned never to have the history or quite the cachet of its neighbour. However, it too is a classic of sorts, with 1930s décor, and it's a fine alternative when Les Vapeurs is full, or if you need to stretch out (the Central is by some way the less cramped of the two). The menu features all the brasserie classics, naturally highlighting *moules* and grilled fish, but with a huge choice of other dishes, served through the day and late into the night.

Tivoli Bistro, 27 Rue Charles Mozin, **t** 02 31 98 43 44 (*menus €16.50–24*). This little bistro is greatly praised by many Trouville visitors for its satisfying food and especially warm, hospitable atmosphere.There are no adventures in the food, which sticks to local classics like *canard au cidre* and a great *cassolette de poissons*, but it's always well put together, enjoyable and excellent value.

Bistrot Les Quatre Chats, 8 Rue d'Orléans, **t** 02 31 88 94 94 (*dishes c. €8–20*). An intimate Trouville-bohemian bistro with a circa-1900 look provided by heavy wooden tables, old prints, books, posters and a spectacular antique coffee machine. Food and drink includes fine wines, cocktails, homebaked bread and small dishes described as 'tapas': there's no set menu (so prices can mount up). Options might include light salads and *tarte aux légumes confits* or local classics like *daube de bœuf. Closed Wed, Thurs exc July and Aug, and Jan.*

Cocotte Café, 58 Rue des Bains, **t** 02 31 88 89 69 (*menus €11.50–15.50*). A convivial little bistro much appreciated by locals and regular visitors to the coast for its neighbourhood-café atmosphere and excellent quality at very reasonable prices. Amiable chef-host Hervé prepares his menus with an admirable eye to whatever's best in the market that day, and they might include such things as seafood tagliatelle, a traditional *poulet vallée d'auge* or great fish and seafood brochettes. *Closed Mon and Tues.*

La Maison, 66 Rue des Bains, **t** 02 31 81 43 10, (*dishes c.€6–10*). This is the proper name of this wine-bar and bistro, but you're likely first to notice 'Du Coq Hardi' on the window, from the brewery near Lille whose products are among the quality beers the Maison has in stock. It's a hip, dark little bar, run by a friendly crew and with décor that's a mix of mock-old and stylish new. As well as beers, it has an imaginative list of fine wines; to eat, there are mixed *assiettes*, salads, soups, desserts and *tartines*, open sandwiches.

Deauville ✉ 14800

Le Ciro's, Bd de la Mer, **t** 02 31 14 31 31 (*menu €39*). If you're doing Deauville properly you have at least to call in at Ciro's, for years the number-one place to see and be seen, and one of France's definitive beach-front bar-restaurants. Its mainly-seafood cuisine has an august reputation, with refined options such as *moules au safran* and tournedos of salmon in calvados. The set menu is high-quality, but it's best known for its *carte* of such star dishes as lobster *à l'armoricaine* (flambéd in cognac and with a cream and wine sauce). If you're concerned about the price, then you probably shouldn't be here: for a sampler, have a lighter dish or an *apéritif* on the terrace. Dress: smart casual, and be sure to pay equal attention to both.

Chez Miocque, 81 Rue Eugène Colas, **t** 02 31 88 09 52 (*dishes c.€12–30*). The classic Deauville restaurants are the *haute gamme* establishments in the *grands hôtels*, but the Miocque is a more easygoing bar-brasserie, with seafood, grills and lighter dishes such as assorted salads, at a wide range of prices. The terrace tables make a good place from which to watch the Deauville world go by.

Cider and Flowers:
the Northern Pays d'Auge

23

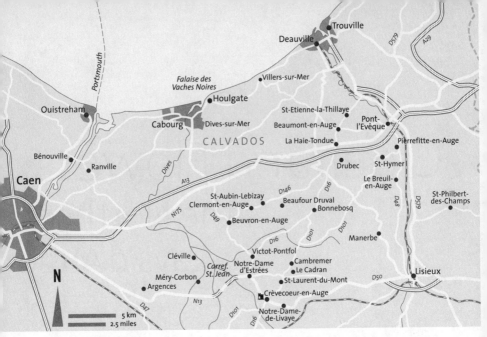

Three of the four classic Norman cheeses – Camembert, Livarot and Pont-l'Evêque – and the ciders traditionally considered the best in all Normandy all come from the Pays d'Auge, the vaguely defined area of rambling, intertwined valleys that spreads roughly from east of Caen across towards the River Risle, and from near the coast at Honfleur down beyond Vimoutiers in the south. Known as a region of agricultural abundance since the early Middle Ages, it also provides the classic image of the Normandy countryside: half-timbered, thatched-roofed farms and manor houses with roses climbing up the walls, scattered between apple orchards, woods and open fields across green valleys. At times the landscape seems almost impossibly lush, with a perfect prettiness that can be hard to credit.

This is also the best area in the region in which to search out and sample the local specialities. Meander along the narrow lanes, some of them almost tunnel-like between ranks of giant, wildly beautiful beeches, and there are any number of farms to be discovered that sell their own cider, calvados, fresh apple juice and other delicacies, while fine cheeses and other dairy produce and rich farmhouse terrines can be found at the spectacular local town markets.

The Pays d'Auge divides more or less in two halves, north and south, very roughly along the line of the N13 Caen–Lisieux road (for the southern half, see Chapter 24). To the north is the most important area for ciders – and the home of the most celebrated calvados – while in the south, cheese is king. The northern Pays d'Auge also has the leafiest, most intimate and sheltered valleys, the narrowest and most intriguingly tortuous lanes, the prettiest villages apparently hidden away up green hillsides. There are relatively few major monuments, but the landscape itself is a monument, making this little Arcadia a delightful place to experience with no fixed destination, wandering up the deserted little roads that crisscross each other through the valleys to find more magnificent old farms.

Getting There

The fast road through this area is the A13 Paris–Caen *autoroute*, which passes close to Pont-l'Evêque, and meets the A28 from Calais and the north near Rouen. Parallel to the A13, if you want to take things more gently and/or not pay *autoroute* tolls, there is the old N175. Caen/Ouistreham to Pont-l'Evêque takes about 45mins on the A13, 1hr by the N175. Le Havre is about 1hr from Pont-l'Evêque via the A29 and the Pont de Normandie (toll bridge).

St-Hymer is a few kilometres south of Pont-l'Evêque: from the A13, take the Pont-l'Evêque exit to meet the N175 in the middle of town, and turn left towards Caen. If you approach Pont-l'Evêque from the north, from Deauville, Honfleur or the Pont de Normandie, turn right at the same crossroads. On the west side of Pont-l'Evêque there is a turn south off the N175 on to the D48, signposted to Lisieux; a short way down this road, past the *autoroute*, there is a right turn for the D280A to Pierrefitte-en-Auge and St-Hymer.

Pont-l'Evêque has **train** services on the Paris–Lisieux–Deauville line; many journeys involve a change in Lisieux. Calvados **Bus Verts** run from beside the station to many villages, but for exploring, a car or bike is essential.

Tourist Information

Beuvron-en-Auge: Les Halles, Place du Village, t/f 02 31 39 59 14. *Open June–Sept only.*
Cambremer: Rue Pasteur, t 02 31 63 08 87, *www.cambremer.fr.*
Pont-l'Evêque: 16 bis Rue St-Michel, t 02 31 64 12 77, *www.pontleveque.com.*

Follow your nose – sometimes literally, for the air often carries a fragrant but noticeable scent of apples. If the fragrance brings on hunger pangs, an ideal place in which to slow up for a few hours and get further immersed in the atmosphere of rural calm is the **Auberge du Prieuré** in St-Hymer, a little half-timbered inn beside a bubbling river in a luscious sheltered valley, with cider from the barrel and light, simple meals that make the most of ideally fresh local produce.

L'Auberge du Prieuré

Le Bourg, St-Hymer, t 02 31 64 07 82. Open Wed 12–2.30, light meals available 2.30–6, Thurs–Sun 12–2.30, 7–8.30, light meals available 2.30–6.
Closed Mon and Tues except public holidays. Menu €18.50; carte average €15.

St-Hymer is not that far from the *autoroute* and the busy N175, and yet seems utterly oblivious of them in its tranquillity. As soon as you pass under the *autoroute* heading south on the D48 the road becomes quiet, green and rural, between orchards and hedges, with an open view eastwards across the lush expanse of the Touques valley. A few kilometres further on, a small sign points to the right towards Pierrefitte-en-Auge and St-Hymer. This will immediately take you still further from the routine racing of the traffic, leading you via a surprisingly sharp turn onto a narrow lane that bends and winds steeply up a giant, humpbacked ridge to Pierrefitte-en-Auge, a superb old village with a fine church and another of Normandy's finest half-timbered inns, the Auberge des Deux Tonneaux (*see* p.250). Keep climbing through Pierrefitte, over the top of the next big crest, and then suddenly you drop down into a tiny, thickly wooded, hidden valley, with at the middle of it a fast-flowing little river and the dazzlingly pretty village of St-Hymer.

It obviously can't be true, but it's only natural to have the thought for at least a moment that maybe the rest of the world has forgotten it's there. St-Hymer grew up around a Benedictine priory, founded by one Hugues de Montfort in this snug but remote spot in 1066. Much of the priory still exists, including the very impressive village church, built in the 14th century and with beautiful stained glass and 17th-century woodwork. Around it, the village's multi-varied half-timbered houses are scattered around the hillsides and into the woods. St-Hymer may not usually receive much road traffic, but the village and its valley are a favourite destination for walkers and riders. An ample range of footpaths and bridle-paths runs through and around St-Hymer, with a great mix of landscapes, from silent, closely-wooded dells and hollows to windswept crests with sweeping vistas over the surrounding valleys.

The Auberge du Prieuré, as its name suggests, was also once part of the priory. It sits next to St-Hymer's babbling brook of a river, a classic Pays d'Auge half-timbered inn with black and white walls overhung by a drooping roof that almost seems to roll up and down like a wave. From a distance it's part-hidden by a cluster of broad-leaf trees, which shade the Auberge's lovely little riverside terrace. Inside the inn, there's a warren of small, intimate rooms with wood panelling, low ceilings and dark timbers.

The setting may be timeless, but recently the old Auberge has seen some changes. The young chef now in charge, Ludovic Valenski, has recognized that many of his clientele are walkers, who would probably greatly appreciate a drink and some light food as a reward for getting all the way up to St-Hymer, but might not be sure of when this is likely to happen. In response, he has challenged the apparently sacred rule that in rural Normandy food cannot be served between two and seven pm. The full set menu is still only available for lunch and dinner, but the Auberge stays open in the afternoons for drinks and *goûters*, light and/or cold snacks. The main menu sticks close to classic Norman *terroir* dishes – *lapin grand-mère* (rabbit braised in cider and *pommeau* with mushrooms, onions and herbs), chicken *vallée d'Auge*, terrines, grills. The *goûters* include wonderful omelettes, platters of mixed cheeses, a gutsy *assiette de cochonnailles* with *andouillettes*, ham and other things made from a pig, sweet crepes and a fine *tarte aux pommes*. As often in Norman country cooking, quality comes not from any great refinement but from the sheer goodness of the local ingredients, from the cheeses to the herbs and deep-yellow eggs used in the omelettes.

Cider is served in jugs or *pichets*, from a quarter-litre to a litre, or there are beers, soft drinks and a few wines. Once you're done with watching the river, if you don't feel like a long hike, there are plenty of pathways offering leisurely walks into the woods.

Touring Around

Together with greenness and the thick leaf-coverage from the beech trees, the third great abiding image of the northern Pays d'Auge is half-timbering. Once you get away from the main trunk routes virtually every small town and village is made up predominantly of **maisons de colombage**, half-timbered houses. Norman half-timbering uses more and thinner uprights than its English equivalent, giving a more stripey look; the three basic elements of the technique – the *poteaux* (structural timbers), *écharpes* (diagonals) and *colombages* (the thinner pieces between the main timbers) – provide an endless variety of design possibilities, with intricate zig-zags, buttresses and counterposed panels creating a fascinating diversity. The steep, fairy-tale roofs are sometimes of thatch, but more often of moss-covered tile. The farms tend to sprawl into several equally impressive buildings, for it has been the practice for the original house to become a barn or cowshed once a larger one could be built.

Apples, cider and calvados are the Auge farms' most inescapable products. Farmers in the Bessin and the Cotentin *bocage* might not agree, but the Pays d'Auge ciders have traditionally been the most highly regarded in the whole of Normandy, and this is the only area with the hallowed accolade of an *appellation d'origine contrôlée* for its ciders (as opposed to calvados, which has always been subject to more official controls). Normandy ciders are infinitely variable (from place to place and year to year, much more even than wines), but Auge ciders are often slightly fruitier than those from other areas, with a round, full-ish, warm body and a denser, golden colour: lovers of dry ciders may prefer those from stonier soils further west. Auge calvados, similarly, is relatively full-bodied, but marvellously subtle. Locating good cider farms is made very easy by the official **Route du Cidre**, which is well signposted along the roads. Farms that meet the exacting demands of the *appellation contrôlée* for Auge ciders and offer direct sales to the public are indicated by small signs with an apple and the words *Cru de Cambremer* by their gates. The local cider authorities also set a recommended price for direct-sale ciders. All local tourist offices have leaflets on the *Route* and cider producers in the area, and on the special farm open days that are often held between spring and autumn. Food and drink aside, this is also naturally a wonderful area for walking and horse riding, and tourist offices equally have walking maps and information on local riding centres.

Pont-l'Evêque is the most important town in the northern Pays d'Auge and is immortalized in the name of one of its finest cheeses, first produced some time in the 13th century. The town, unfortunately, is a little disappointing: it suffered greatly in the Second World War, and suffers today from its role as a major road junction. At its centre, though, there is still a characterful old heart that's interesting to stroll around, especially the Rue de Vaucelles and the streets around it, with several 15th–17th-century half-timbered houses. The church of **St-Michel**, begun in the 13th century and rebuilt in *Flamboyant* Gothic style in the 15th, is grandly impressive, with a very odd square tower. Just west of Pont-l'Evêque, a detour of a few kilometres down a quiet road will take you to **Beaumont-en-Auge**. A large, placid village, it's a place of homage for scientists as the birthplace of the 18th-century mathematician Laplace, but its most remarkable feature is its wonderful location at the top of a precipitous escarpment, with hypnotic views down to Deauville and even out to sea.

Head south from Pont-l'Evêque, towards **Pierrefitte-en-Auge** and **St-Hymer**, and you really enter the Pays d'Auge landscape. From St-Hymer, if you continue along the meandering lane of the D280A, it will eventually lead you via hills and gulleys to **Drubec**, where it meets the main 'artery' of the northern Pays d'Auge, the D16. Turn left (south), and about 5km further on, a little to the north of the village of

Bonnebosq, you will see signs off to the left for the **Manoir du Champ Versant** (*guided tours July and Aug Wed–Sun 3–6, closed Mon and Tues; adm*), a classic 16th-century Pays d'Auge manor house. As with many Norman manors, one of its most engaging features is its combination of rusticity (the half-timbered façade, the drooping tile roof) with more ornate touches to fit the status of the country gentry for whom it was built, such as the fine ornamental brickwork supporting the chimneys. Inside, there is a small museum of traditional furniture and ceramics of the Pays d'Auge, and visitors also see the other parts of the rambling manor – the stables, barns, cider press, bakery, calvados distillery and more. There are also rooms available as *chambres d'hôtes*, open for other months as well as July and August (*see p.249*).

From Bonnebosq, carry on south along the D16, ignoring other turnings, until you see a turn right on to the D49 for **Victot-Pontfol** and **Beuvron**, to enter perhaps the very prettiest part of the entire Pays d'Auge. Very shortly the countryside begins to resemble a small-scale Kentucky. As well as apple country, this is also prime horse-breeding territory, generally for *le Trot* – trotting races – rather than flat racing, and between the orchards there are plenty of lushly carpeted meadows containing some very sleek, elegant horses behind white-painted fences.

Beuvron-en-Auge proudly announces its listing as one of the *plus beaux villages de France*, and few people would argue. It's a remarkable ensemble of Norman houses, mostly built between the 16th and 18th centuries. The delightful main square, where the timbers form crosses, arrowheads and other intricate patterns against a gentle background of clay wash, is a wonderful demonstration of the ingenuity and imagination of the region's anonymous builders. One of the highlights is the 16th-century **Vieux Manoir**, on the south side of the *place*, with its gargoyle-like carvings, but really the whole village is the attraction. As one of the most beautiful of all the Auge's many beauty spots, Beuvron inevitably gets congested on summer Sundays, but it's very hard to take away its charm. The little timber market hall in the middle of the square now contains a restaurant and shops, and the village also has plenty of craft and souvenir shops and others selling local delicacies. Most are a bit expensive, but seek out the **Ferme de Beuvron**, a farm cooperative that takes over one of the few brick buildings on the north road out of the village with a farmers' market of fine produce (*most weekends all year, some other days in July and Aug*).

Leaving Beuvron to the north, turn right on to the tiny D146 for Clermont, one of the leafiest of country lanes. Don't miss the sign to the left for the **Chapelle de Clermont**. A footpath leads through a canopy of dense beeches to the chapel, on a precipitous crag where you suddenly emerge to find soaring views over the Dives valley to the west, and sometimes a strong, gusting wind to wake you up. Believed to have been founded in the 12th century or even earlier, and then rebuilt in the 15th, the chapel is wonderfully simple: it is whitewashed inside, with some fine locally carved statues of saints around the walls, including an oddly cute *Virgin and Child*.

Clermont is also a good place to pick up the *Route du Cidre* and begin cider hunting. Even if you've already bought enough cider to last you a year, following the route through the maze of lanes east of Beuvron is one of the most enjoyable ways of exploring the area and getting to know its idiosyncrasies. The back roads of the Pays d'Auge can often seem deliberately confusing, and sometimes look like they're taking you into a solid green wall, but – just when you think all hope is lost – a *Route du Cidre* sign will turn up to help out.

The **apple harvest** runs from late September to November, and the dryness of the cider depends on how long it is left to ferment in the barrel. Once bottled, cider, unlike calvados, does not change significantly with age. A few farms produce some very sweet *cidre nouveau* by Christmas, but more normal *demi* and *brut* (dry) ciders do not become available until February or March, and so the best time for tasting and buying is from spring to summer. By October, while the large producers will still have ciders on sale, the smallest farms may have sold their production for the year. The cider producers of the Pays d'Auge cover both of the two main 'categories' found in Normandy. Some are basic farms where, having been attracted in by the apple sign and *'Cidre-Calvados-Vente Directe-OUVERTE'*, you can start to wonder whether you're being had on, as not even the dog takes much notice of you until someone finally appears and with very few words unbolts the large half-timbered sheds where the cider is kept. Others are much more sophisticated operations, often around large manor houses, and with separate farm shops. Whether producers are of one or the other kind (or somewhere in the middle) has no relevance to quality. Some farmers will also show you around their cider sheds, but in all cases it's advisable not to call during the sacred hours of lunch (*12.30–2*) or too late in the evening.

As you wander around the countryside, through lovely, leaf-shrouded villages like **Beaufour-Druval**, you periodically emerge back on to the D16, which serves as a handy reference point (another is the Carrefour St-Jean, the wide crossroads where the D16 meets the N13 Caen–Lisieux road). East of the D16 the lanes tend to converge on **Cambremer**, the other main town (or larger village) in the area. It's a pleasant, likeable place, not as postcard-pretty as Beuvron and therefore less touristy. Cambremer also has a very attractive main square, with enjoyable cafés and restaurants, built on a steep hill, so that you get different perspectives from one side or the other.

The road continues south to **St-Laurent-du-Mont**, from where it's not far down a lovely road to the crossroads village of **Crèvecœur-en-Auge** with, just to the west, its **château** (*open April–June and Sept daily 11–6; July and Aug daily 11–7; Oct Sun 2–6; closed Nov–Mar; adm*). Crèvecœur immediately suggests a picture-book illustration of a Norman motte-and-bailey castle; its oldest ramparts were built before its lord joined Duke William in invading England, while the other, half-timbered buildings around the grassed-over courtyard were built and rebuilt over subsequent centuries. Most impressive is the giant dovecote – built shortly after the castle was sacked by an English army in 1449 – an indication of the status of Crèvecœur's owners, since only the aristocracy were allowed such buildings in medieval Normandy. Curiously, Crèvecoeur has since the 1970s been owned by a foundation created by the Alsatian Schlumberger engineering family, who have restored it to house a museum on oil exploration, the interest of which is a matter of taste. However, the castle also contains exhibits of more direct Norman interest on traditional building techniques, medieval music, local customs and so on, which are often fascinating, and in July and August it hosts early music performances, pageants and similar medieval-ish events.

Shopping

The Pays d'Auge not only has some of Normandy's best traditional produce but also many of its best country **markets**. There are weekly markets all year in **Pont-l'Evêque** (*Mon*), **Bonnebosq** (*Wed*), **Cambremer** (*Fri*) and **Beuvron** (*Sat*). Not to be missed in summer are the additional *Marchés à l'Ancienne* in Pont-l'Evêque and Cambremer (*both Easter Sun, Whit Sun, July and Aug every Sun am*), where many of the area's best farm producers set up stalls. Many farms host markets on different weekends; tourist offices will have details.

The Pays d'Auge equally has the largest concentration of small farm producers who sell direct to the public. Tourist offices' *Route du Cidre* and *Goûtez le Pays d'Auge* leaflets are very helpful, and more places can be found by looking for signs along the roads. Many farms have open days and tours, mostly in summer; in Oct–Nov, during the apple harvest, many cider farms offer *weekends au pressoir*, when you help out with collecting the crop in return for a convivial look at the cider- and calvados-making process and, naturally, as much cider as you can drink. Cambremer tourist office is the best source of details for each year.

Cambremer ✉ 14340

Calvados Pierre Huet, Manoir La Brière des Fontaines, **t** 02 31 63 01 09, *www.calvados-huet.com*. One of the grand names in the world of calvados, based in a magnificent Auge manor house on the road towards Crèvecœur. As well as supremely fragrant calvados, the Huet family produce delicious ciders, *pommeau* and other apple products. Staff are charming, and the guided tours (*in English as required*) are entertaining and informative. *Shop open Mon–Sat and Sun am; guided tours daily; adm, refunded on any purchases.*

Ferme de la Mimarnel, **t/f** 02 31 63 00 50. For once, not a cider farm: Jacques-Antoine Motte produces superb *chèvre* – plain or with herbs – and gives tours of his farm and *fromagerie* (*by reservation, daily exc Thurs*). It's south of Cambremer, on the D50 road, east of the crossroads with the D101; there's usually a sign, but it can be hard to see. *Open for sales daily exc Sat am and Thurs.*

Méry-Corbon ✉ 14370

Mme Odile Gasson, **t** 02 31 23 66 21. A dairy farm in the Dives valley west of Carrefour St-Jean, where Mme Gasson makes and sells delicious farm butter, crème fraîche and *confiture de lait*, a kind of light toffee spread. *Open daily exc Thurs am and Sun; farm tours July–Aug Thurs pm, adm.*

St-Aubin-Lebizay ✉ 14340

Mme Denis, **t/f** 02 31 65 13 39. A low-key little cider farm. Unusually, while Mme Denis produces good ciders and calvados, her speciality is *poiré*, perry.

Gerard Desvoyé, Le Lieu Gris, **t/f** 02 31 65 11 94. M Desvoyé's farm is as genuinely rural as you could wish for, but his award-winning *demi-sec* and *brut* ciders are supplied to smart wine and spirits merchants in Rouen and Paris. Bought from his own shed, they're a real bargain, and he also has fine calvados, *pommeau*, jams and truly exceptional cider vinegar. There are also two basic, cosy *gîtes*.

Where to Stay

Beuvron-en-Auge ✉ 14430

Manoir de Sens, **t** 02 31 79 23 05. *www.manoirdesens.com* (*rooms €65–110 for two*). A grand black-and-white-timbered Auge mansion in beautifully-kept grounds beside the road north of Beuvron. The five rooms of different sizes have a fine old-fashioned French-manorial touch (and good bathrooms). The estate is also a stud and cider farm, and owners the David family are more down-to-earth than the house might suggest. Riding (of course) and all sorts of other activities are available nearby.

Aux Trois Damoiselles, Place Michel Vermughen, **t** 02 31 39 61 38. *www.auxtroisdamoiselles.com* (*rooms €70–86 for two, €120 for four*). This grey-timbered inn fits in perfectly with the old structures around it, but in fact was begun – using all-traditional materials – in 2000, to fill an unsightly concreted gap in Beuvron's otherwise-perfect half-timbered main square. It's the creation of M Philippe David, owner of the Manoir de Sens. The five rooms are simpler than at the Manoir, and some-

times the mix of new and old styles doesn't quite work (bathrooms are small), but it has charm, and the location is lovely. The family room, in the eaves, is the best. There's a *salon de thé*, and a shop with local produce.
Mme Monique Hamelin, La Place de Beuvron, **t/f** 02 31 39 00 62 (*rooms €47–49 for two*). A perfect black-and-white half-timbered Auge house, around a flower-filled courtyard in the middle of Beuvron. Mme Hamelin has two B&B rooms, and breakfast is served in a room as charming as the rest of the house. *Closed Nov– Easter.*

Bonnebosq ✉ 14340
Manoir du Champ Versant, **t/f** 02 31 65 11 07 (*rooms €47–50 for two*). The great attraction here is the chance to stay in one of the Pays d'Auge's most historic half-timbered manors (*see p.246*). The two *chambres d'hôtes* are relatively simple, but pretty, and breakfast is served in a superbly baronial chamber. Despite its fame, owners the Letresor family are likeably laidback. *Closed Nov–Easter.*

Cambremer ✉ 14340
Château Les Bruyères, Route du Cadran, **t** 02 31 32 22 45, *www.chateaulesbruyeres.com* (*double rooms €75–155 low season, €75–195 high season*). Not the most historic of châteaux, since most of the house is 19th-century, but Les Bruyères, in a lovely setting north of Cambremer, is now a comfortable country-house hotel. Its 13 rooms vary in size and price, but all are plushly pretty, and around the house there's a well tended garden, with the special asset of a swimming pool. It also has an elegant **restaurant** (*menus €40–55*), with refined, individually prepared cuisine, open by reservation only.
Manoir de Cantepie, Le Cadran, **t/f** 02 31 62 87 27 (*rooms €45–55 for two*). Distinctly grand *chambres d'hôtes* in an extraordinary 16th-century manor – the kind of Pays d'Auge house that looks as if it couldn't possibly be real, but must have been cooked up in Hollywood around 1935 for Errol Flynn to leap out of one of the windows. Inside, there are dark wood panels, mock-medieval paintings and elaborate carving. The three lavish guest rooms are each in a different colour, and the breakfast room and gardens are

magnificent. Owner M. Gherrak and his wife are attentive hosts. The house is by the D50, a few kilometres east of Cambremer. *Closed mid-Nov–Feb.*

Notre-Dame-de-Livaye ✉ 14340
Aux Pommiers de Livaye, **t** 02 31 63 01 28, *http://bandb.normandy.free.fr* (*rooms €76–89 for two, €145 for four*). A lovely half-timbered house by the N13 east of Crèvecœur. There are five double rooms, with space for extra beds, in a cottage by the garden, and a 'family suite' in the main house. All are pretty twee, but very comfy, and wonderfully well cared for. Madame offers *table d'hôte* **dinners** (*€24*), and there are pots and pots of homemade jam for sale.

St-Aubin-Lebizay ✉ 14340
Cour l'Epée, **t/f** 02 31 65 13 45, **e** *aj.tesniere@wanadoo.fr* (*rooms €60–65 for two, €86 for four*). This big modernized house has a superb location on a height between St-Aubin and Cambremer, looking down over fields, woods and its own lush gardens. The three B&B rooms are all large and comfortable, and all enjoy breathtaking views, but the one to go for is the family-sized suite. *Closed mid-Nov–mid-Feb.*

St-Etienne-la-Thillaye ✉ 14950
La Maison de Sophie, Le Presbytère, **t** 02 31 65 69 97, *www.lamaisondesophie.fr* (*rooms €130 for two, children €30 per child*). Sophie Dudemaine may not mean much to English-speakers, but in France she's a top TV cook, and her books sell a million copies. Recently she has turned this 18th-century presbytery into an exceptional *chambres d'hôtes*. She hosts cookery weekends there, guests for which have priority, but most of the time it's open to anybody. The five rooms, each different, are very chic, and exquisite; facilities for kids in the *chambre pitchoun* are amazing – based in the idea that they can be entertained while *les parents* are in the (fabulous) kitchen. The lady herself is not usually at the house, but her staff are very *charmant*. Residents can also enjoy gourmet *table d'hôte* meals (*€35–50*). There's a lovely garden, and a shop with modern kitchenware, and Sophie's books. Foodie heaven.

St-Laurent-du-Mont ✉ 14340

La Vignerie, t/f 02 31 63 08 65,
e *mfhuet@club-internet.fr* (*rooms €37 for two, €46 for three*). An imposing old stone farm where Mme Huet – a member of the Cambremer calvados family (see p.248) – has six B&B rooms, alongside a remarkable old cider press. They're straightforward but cosy, and one large family room has a lovely balcony for taking in the countryside. It's off the D50 road, west of St-Laurent village.

Eating Alternatives

Beaufour-Druval ✉ 14340

Les Puces Gourmandes, Route de Dozulé, t 02 31 65 12 91 (*menus €10–17*). Another Pays d'Auge restaurant that seems to have got lost in the woods: this curious little restaurant and *salon de thé* stands part-shrouded in foliage in a tiny village. To add to the surprise it doesn't serve up hearty Norman feasts but a bohemian mix of salads, pâtés, cheeses and other light dishes, at bargain prices; there's also a lunch menu, and aromatic teas. Evening meals can be served by reservation. *Open Easter–Sept noon–8pm, Easter–June and Sept Sat, Sun and hols, July and Aug daily.*

Beaumont-en-Auge ✉ 14950

Auberge de l'Abbaye, 2 Rue de la Libération, t 02 31 64 82 31, *http://aubergelabbaye.com* (*menus €28–50*). A snug, comfortable restaurant with smart traditional décor in the centre of Beaumont where chef Christian Girault has earned a high reputation for his sophisticated versions of Norman cuisine. Inventive desserts and dishes using local cheeses are particular specialities. *Closed (Sept–June) Tues and Wed.*

Beuvron-en-Auge ✉ 14430

Le Pavé d'Auge, Place du Village, t 02 31 79 26 71 (*menus €29–52*). The gourmet option in Beuvron, occupying part of the old half-timbered market hall in the main square. Inside, the décor is smartly comfortable and very pretty; the food takes some inspiration from local cooking but is distinctly refined, making succulent use of Norman hams,

mushrooms, fresh fruit and other produce. *Closed Mon and (exc July and Aug) Tues; also Dec and one week early July.*

Auberge de la Boule d'Or, t 02 31 79 78 78 (*menus €22–29*). In a bulging half-timbered house on Beuvron's square, the Boule d'Or has all the right features – an intimate dining room with up-and-down oak beams to duck under. The restaurant maintains a high standard, with quite sophisticated versions of local classics – *andouilles*, rabbit in cider – along with French standards like *sole meunière. Closed Tues eve and Wed.*

La Forge, t 02 31 79 29 74 (*menus €19.50–35*). A cheaper alternative in Beuvron, with a pretty dining room and atmospheric little bar. The food runs from straightforward lunches to sizeable menus, with good meat-and-cider Norman specialities, and a brasserie range of lighter dishes, snacks and sweet *crêpes* (but not savoury *galettes*). *Closed Wed.*

Cambremer ✉ 14340

Au P'tit Normand, Place de l'Eglise, t 02 31 32 03 20 (*menus €13.72–21*). A bright little restaurant and *saladerie* on Cambremer's main square. Its style is fresh and friendly, and it keeps longer hours than many restaurants nearby (great for anyone not quite used to rigid Norman meal times). The food covers a range of options: set menus are great value – with very good steaks – and there are excellent omelettes, snacks and salads, and tangy country desserts.

Pierrefitte-en-Auge ✉ 14130

L'Auberge des Deux Tonneaux, t 02 31 64 31 00 (*menus €20–36*). Almost an unmissable sight of the Pays d'Auge in itself. Dating from the 17th century, it looks very much a place where a musketeer might have met a serving wench: black-and-white timbered and shrouded in thatch and geraniums, with bench tables outside on a green terrace surrounded by apple trees and with a fabulous view over the Touques valley. To eat, there are suitably traditional Norman *terroir* dishes – *lapin grand-mère*, gutsy sausages, omelettes, appley desserts – made with deliciously fresh produce. To drink, in a place like this, try cider from the barrel. *Closed Mon exc July and Aug, and mid-Nov–Jan.*

Camembert and *Grands Châteaux*:
the Southern Pays d'Auge and Falaise

24

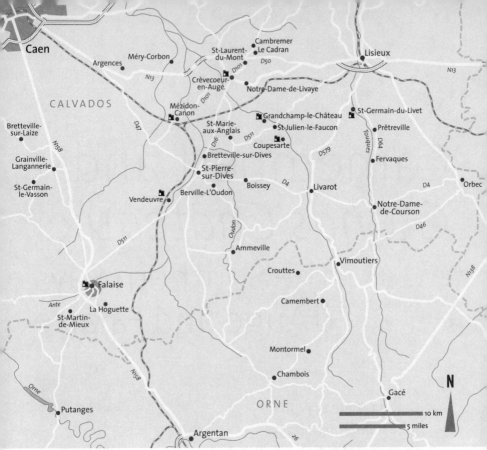

In the southern half of the Pays d'Auge, roughly below Crèvecœur and the N13, the fields are larger, the landscape a bit more open, than to the north, and villages tend to sprawl more rather than stay confined between woods in intimate valleys. To the southwest the Auge fields blend into the still more open countryside of the *Pays de Falaise*, a more windswept, glowering landscape of rolling plains. Falaise is also a significant point of transition within Normandy, from the brick, wood, and half-timbered houses of the east to the four-square stone cottages, manors and farms that increasingly predominate as you head west towards the Cotentin.

With famous names like Camembert, Livarot and Pont-l'Evêque, and lesser-known varieties like Petit-Lisieux and Pavé d'Auge, the southern Pays d'Auge is one of the foremost cheese-producing regions in France (and the world). Most of it is still produced on small family farms dotted across the very tranquil countryside. This is still one of the most genuinely rural areas of France, a place where the traditions of the *terroir* retain a strength that is hard to credit in industrial northern Europe.

As in the north, this is an area where it's as enjoyable just to wander around as to head for any point on the map. There are early Norman churches, and a spectacular range of historic houses: from battered medieval castles to opulent *Ancien Régime* châteaux. Falaise, as well as being the site of the bloody climax of the 1944 battle for Normandy, was the first home of William the Conqueror.

Getting There

From Ouistreham and the Caen ring road, two main roads lead into this area: the N13 to Lisieux, and the N158 for Falaise. From Paris, Le Havre or the north on the A13 *autoroute*; exit at Pont-l'Evêque, head due south on the D579, and cut westwards at Le Breuil-en-Auge to Manerbe, to head for the N13 and so avoid the traffic bottleneck of Lisieux.

St-Julien-le-Faucon sits across the D511 Lisieux–St-Pierre-sur-Dives road, connected to the N13 by winding lanes. The Auberge de la Levrette is beside the main square.

The Caen–Alençon **train** line runs through this area, with stations at Mézidon-Canon, St-Pierre-sur-Dives and Coulibœuf (for Falaise).

Calvados **Bus Verts** run to many larger villages, especially from Caen and Lisieux.

Tourist Information

Falaise: Bd de la Libération, **t** 02 31 90 17 26, *www.otsifalaise.com*.
Livarot: 1 Place Georges Bisson, **t** 02 31 63 47 39, *www.ot-livarot.org*.
Orbec: 6 Rue Grande, **t** 02 31 32 56 68, *www.mairie.orbec.fr*.
St-Pierre-sur-Dives: 23 Rue St-Benoît, **t** 02 31 20 97 90, *www.mairie.saint.pierre. sur.dives.fr*.
Vimoutiers: 10 Av du Général de Gaulle, **t** 02 33 39 30 29, *ot.vimoutiers@wanadoo.fr*.

The basis of the region's food is, naturally, the superb, fresh produce of its farms. Its presentation combines the pure and hearty Norman cream-and-cider tradition with those spectacular little shoots of culinary invention and refinement that in France turn up even in the most out-of-the-way places – such as the **Auberge de la Levrette** in St-Julien-le-Faucon, a relaxed village inn serving very subtle creative cooking.

L'Auberge de la Levrette

St-Julien-le-Faucon, **t** *02 31 63 81 20,* **f** *02 31 63 97 05.*
Open Wed–Sat 12–2.30 and 7.30–9, Sun 12–2.30. Closed Mon and Tues, one week Oct and Christmas. Menus €22–30; carte average €38.

The current chef-proprietor of the *auberge*, Georges Fayet, has a copy of a document indicating that its building was begun in 1752, as a *relais de chasse* (hunting lodge) for the Marquis de Grandchamp, lord of the château of Grandchamp just to the north and much else nearby. He was particularly fond of hunting hares, hence the name, *La Levrette*. After the Revolution it became a *relais de poste*, a coaching inn. The *auberge* and a house across the road are the oldest buildings in the village after the church.

It is a classic Pays d'Auge inn, with half-timbering for most of its length and a brick extension casually added at one end. At the back there's an unusually large hall, which was used as a barracks in the Second World War by German soldiers, who left the marks of their target practice in the old coaching yard alongside. In the 1950s the hall served as a village cinema, and today it's used for weddings and other feasts. Inside the main *auberge*, the lovely dining room has low ceilings, a mass of heavy old timbers and magnificent 1750s fireplaces. There's nothing deliberately rustic here, though: it's also extremely comfortable, with the proper little vases of flowers on pink tablecloths and other modestly pretty details. La Levrette is phenomenally good value, even in an area where dining is scarcely ever expensive. It's also usually as tranquil as the countryside around it, and other diners will mostly be local.

M and Mme Fayet are from Clermont-Ferrand, but have worked in Normandy for some 20 years, so that he has become thoroughly immersed in Norman cooking and Norman ingredients. However, rather than strictly traditional dishes he tends to present his own creative variations on local produce, put together with great skill. A terrine of chicken, duck and goose livers is both magnificently gutsy and surprisingly subtle, and served with a great, refreshing *grenadine d'oignons*, onion chutney. As a main course, *bœuf longuement braisé sur un jus à l'oseille* features absolutely first-quality beef infused with a wonderfully deep, satisfying flavour from the sorrel gravy – and comes with equally impressive fresh veg. Meat dishes take pride of place here, but fish choices might include locally-caught perch with a creamy potato *brandade*.

This is one place where it would seem perverse to pass on the cheese course, which is perfect, with cheeses from the renowned Fromagerie de la Houssaye in Boissey (*see* p.259). Space must also be left, however, for desserts: Georges Fayet is a superb *pâtissier*, and this is a serious dessert-lovers' restaurant. He often creates an off-menu *dessert du jour*, and new flavours of homemade ice-cream. It's possible to think that too much is made of apples in Normandy, but all such notions are forgotten in the face of his apple creations, bringing out apple essences and apple flavours you didn't even know existed. After that, a fragrant calvados is the natural way to end your meal, along with some chocolatey, homemade petit fours.

Sablé façon Tatin, quenelle à la cannelle

Serves 4

best-quality round sablé biscuits, 2 per person
7 fairly sharp-flavoured apples (Granny Smith's or similar)
200g/7oz sugar
100g/3½oz salted butter
50ml/2fl oz calvados
4 scoops cinnamon ice-cream (1 per person)

Put the sugar in a pan with 1 tablespoon of water and heat gently until the sugar has dissolved; increase the heat and boil until the caramel is golden, and then remove from the heat, add the butter cut into pieces and stir it in until it is fully melted and blended in with the rest of the caramel. Peel, core and dice 6 of the apples, add to the caramel and cook gently, stirring regularly, until they are tender but not too brown, for about 20 minutes. Remove the apple cubes with a slotted spoon and set aside. Add the calvados to the caramel in the pan, and stir to blend.

When the diced apple is nearly cooked, core the remaining apple (without peeling), and slice as thinly as possible (vertically or horizontally, as preferred). Sprinkle with a little lemon juice to prevent browning, if you prepare any further in advance.

To serve, place two sablé biscuits on each plate, and top one with a scoop of cinnamon ice cream, and the other with a portion of diced apple. Drizzle the calvados-flavoured caramel over both. Finally, arrange the sliced apple around the edge of the plates, as a garnish.

Touring Around

If you can be in this area on a Monday, make every effort to get to the Pays d'Auge's largest market, in **St-Pierre-sur-Dives**. It has been held here virtually every Monday morning since the early Middle Ages, and the town largely grew up around it. The *Halles*, the giant covered market hall at its centre, was first built in the 11th century, and has been altered and faithfully rebuilt several times since then after fires and other disasters, the last in 1944. The Monday market is a powerful reminder that the Pays d'Auge remains very much a rural, small-farm area: inside the *Halles* there are geese, ducks, chickens, rabbits and any other small farmyard animal you can think of, and all of them alive. It's as basic as can be, but in among the craggy farmers buying and selling there are also obviously more urban folk discussing the merits of this or that live bird, which can be a shock, but is also an indication of the strength of the French dedication to fresh food. To buy food that isn't still animate, look outside, where the market also sprawls over two very large, open squares. Close to the *Halles*, there are stalls with superb local meat and *charcuterie*, great fruit and vegetables, and some of the very best Camembert, Livarot and other local cheeses. At others you can buy fresh flowers, all-weather jackets, toys, machinery and leather bags. The market, very traditionally, begins to pack up around half past twelve. A more sedate antiques market is also held in the *Halles*, on the first Sunday of each month.

Once the market crowds have gone back to their villages, St-Pierre is a slow-moving, peaceful town, spread out along a long, straight street, called **Route de Falaise** for most of its length, which runs roughly north-south. With its huge market squares, the town seems a little too big for its permanent population. Next to the *Mairie* just off Route de Falaise is the church of the **Abbatiale** (*open daily 9.30–12 and 2.30–6*), the chief surviving part of what was once one of the largest abbeys in Normandy. Converted into St-Pierre's parish church after the dissolution of the abbey during the Revolution, it's one of the most impressive and calmly atmospheric of Norman town churches, with a delicate 14th-century Gothic façade added to the massively solid 12th–13th-century nave, transepts and main tower. Beside it are part of the abbey's **cloister** and a beautiful 13th-century *Salle Capitulaire* or chapterhouse. It is used to present a range of exhibitions, and in July and August the cloister also hosts *Les Animations du Cloître* every Friday, a series of craft shows, markets and other events.

St-Pierre also contains, above the very helpful tourist office one street south of the church, the most important of the Pays d'Auge's cheese museums: the **Musée des Techniques Fromagères** (*open mid-April–mid-Oct Mon–Fri 9.30–12.30 and 1.30–6, Sat 10–12 and 2–5; mid-Oct–mid-April Mon–Fri 9.30–12.30 and 1.30–5.30; adm*), which tells you a vast amount about cheese-making in true French didactic style (afterwards, unwind by quizzing each other about how much you remember). Opposite it there is a more relaxing attraction, the **Jardin-Conservatoire des Fleurs et Légumes du Pays d'Auge** (*open May–Sept*), a charming little garden with examples of all the great many plants, flowers and herbs found in the region. It's also called the *Jardin des Femmes*, on the basis that country kitchen gardens – whether of culinary or medicinal plants – were always a woman's responsibility. It's run with a delightfully informal style: to see it, and for a guided tour, just ask in the tourist office, and one of the gardeners (some of whom speak English) will be found to take you around.

The southern Pays d'Auge is, for obvious reasons, well blessed with cheese museums. More engaging than the St-Pierre museum (and more accessible to English-speakers) are the museum at the **Fromagerie de Livarot** (*open April–Sept Mon–Sat 9–5.30*), and the **Musée du Camembert** in Vimoutiers (*open April–Oct Mon 2–6, Tues–Sat 9–12 and 2–6, Sun and hols 10–12 and 2.30–6; Nov–Mar Mon 2–5.30, Tues–Sat 10–12 and 2–5.30; adm*). Both museums have oddly fascinating (no, really) collections of cheese labels, and of course also have shops. Vimoutiers' best-known monument is a statue, in the main square, of **Marie Harel**, the milkmaid credited with the 'invention' of Camembert. As the legend goes, in the years after the Revolution Marie gave shelter to a fugitive priest, who in return gave her a special cheese recipe, and so a new *grand fromage* was born. Her home village of **Camembert** itself is a few kilometres south. Spread over a crest in a hilly valley, it's an idyllic place – despite the tacky souvenir-overkill that surrounds the **Maison du Camembert** museum, shop and visitor centre (*open May–Sept daily 10–12 and 2–6, Oct–April Wed–Sun 10–12 and 2–5; adm*).

If you've seen enough of cheese, it could be time to explore some of the Auge region's country manors. About two kilometres north of St-Julien-le-Faucon is the **Château of Grandchamp**. It's closed to visitors, but from the road it's possible to see, beyond the half-timbered gatehouse, the brick and stone façade of the house, built in two stages in the 16th and 17th centuries, with four strangely oriental-looking turrets. South of St-Julien there is the remarkable 15th-century **Manoir de Coupesarte** – also not open to visitors – one of the loveliest of the area's half-timbered manors, with a placid moat on three sides and half-timbered turrets on all four corners. A little to the west is the village of **Ste-Marie-aux-Anglais**, which has a remarkable, tiny 11th-century church, one of the oldest in Normandy never to have been substantially altered since it was built. It is often closed, but it's worth trying to visit on a Sunday to see the rare ceiling paintings inside; visible outside are its beautiful early medieval carvings.

Some 15km to the east is the grandest 16th-century French-Renaissance style château in the Pays d'Auge, at **St-Germain-de-Livet** (*guided tours Feb–Sept and mid-Oct–mid-Nov daily 11–6; closed early Oct and mid-Nov–Jan; last admission 1hr before closing; adm*), nestling at the bottom of a valley and fronted by a garden ablaze with dahlias. Romantically baronial, it is renowned above all for its façade, with giant pepperpot turrets and walls in an almost playful checkerboard pattern of stone and differently coloured bricks, combined with an earlier, half-timbered house at one side. Inside, the castle has stone-walled rooms giving way to others with plain, dark décor added in the 1900s. There are still many original details, such as the beautiful tiling, and rare 16th-century frescoes of biblical scenes in the guardroom.

For a complete contrast in style and era, cut back west of the D511 to the **Château de Canon** at Mézidon-Canon (*gardens open Easter–30 June Sat, Sun and hols 2–6; July–Sept Mon and Wed–Sun 2–7; adm*). The house was begun in the 1720s, but greatly altered and extended from the 1770s to the 1780s for Jean-Baptiste Elie de Beaumont, a noted lawyer, friend of Voltaire and follower of the advanced ideas of his day. The château itself is closed to visitors, but Canon is most famous for its remarkable gardens, laid out by Elie de Beaumont and his wife Anne-Louise in line with Enlightenment philosophical ideas. They are full of little follies, sculptures, artificial groves and other curious features: highlights are a Chinese summerhouse, an exquisite pond, the Greek-style 'Temple of the Weeping Woman', erected by the grief-stricken Elie de Beaumont after the death of his wife in 1783, and above all the **Chartreuses**, a series of interconnected walled gardens and orchards that fill with luminous arrays of flowers each summer. A hall in the grounds was home to the *Fêtes des Bonnes Gens*, the 'Feasts of Good People', begun by the Elie de Beaumonts in 1775, in which deserving local villagers were given prizes for services to the community, as a democratic celebration of fraternity. There is also an estate shop (*see* p.259).

A less high-minded and more extravagant side of 18th-century France is on view just south of St-Pierre-sur-Dives in the **Château de Vendeuvre** (*open Easter week daily 2–6; April and Oct–11 Nov Sun and hols 2–6; May–June and Sept daily 11–6; July and Aug daily 11–6.30; closed 11 Nov–Easter; adm*), a Louis-Quinze *bon-bon* of a stately home that is a revelation to anyone who thought the French aristocracy had been on hard times since 1789. Gutted in 1944, it has been lavishly and beautifully restored by the Comtes de Vendeuvre with all of its original, pastel-shaded décor, plus a remarkable collection of furniture and bric-a-brac. In each room there are also life-size automata, which start up as you come in: especially entertaining is the kitchen, where the automaton talks manically as it shows off the different pots and pans. In the *Orangerie* the Comtesse has the world's largest collection of miniature furniture – some made as toys, others as curiosities, others as demonstration pieces by craftsmen – a whimsical display of extraordinary skills. Outside are the *Jardins d'Eau-Surprises*, a fanciful water garden with elaborate concealed fountains set off by electric sensors as you walk by. It's all pretty twee, but very entertaining.

South of Vendeuvre the D511 leads across a flat plain to **Falaise**. Virtually nowhere in Normandy was completely unscathed by the Second World War, but Falaise formed one of the great anvils of the battle. In August 1944, as the British and Canadian armies pushed southwards from Caen, the Americans broke out from the Normandy bridgehead at Avranches, cut across Brittany to Nantes and swung east to Alençon and Argentan, almost encircling the German armies in Normandy in the 'Falaise Pocket', the only exit from which was the 'Falaise Gap' between Falaise and Argentan. The German defence of Falaise against Allied efforts to close the Gap was the final deciding battle of the Normandy campaign, as the German generals struggled to extricate their armies (in the face of increasingly deranged orders from Hitler). Falaise and its surrounding villages were pounded into rubble before the Gap was finally shut, when Polish and US troops met at Chambois, to the southeast, on 19–20 August.

Post-war, much of Falaise was rebuilt in straightforward reconstruction style, which rather fails to match its spectacular location on a gorge in a valley of the River Ante, still dominated by one of the grandest of Norman castles, built like all good Norman strongholds on the highest point for miles around and with massive masonry that resisted 20th-century bombs and artillery better than anything else in the area. It is a likeable, untouristy town – with a good market – which still has some characterful old corners, especially in the steep, narrow streets along the gorge. Its war museum, the

Musée Août 44 (*open April–11 Nov daily 10–12 and 2–6; adm*), gives full information about the battle of the Pocket. Locals, though, are less given to recalling the painful events of 1944 than to commemorating Falaise's role as the birthplace of William the Conqueror, and still more as the home of his mother, Arlette, a livelier local heroine than saintly Marie the cheese girl. As the legend goes: one day in 1027 Robert, younger son of the Duke of Normandy, was returning to Falaise castle after a day's hunting when he caught sight of the humble tanner's daughter Arlette, just sweet 17 and doing the family wash in the river, and was smitten. He tried to exercise his *droit de seigneur*, but the feisty Arlette refused to accept any furtive affair and insisted on entering the castle by the main gate. Later, Robert succeeded his brother to become Robert 'the Magnificent', Duke of Normandy. Their son grew up in Falaise castle, but, never formally legitimized, would be known as William the Bastard until he became King of England and acquired the rather more dignified title of 'Conqueror'.

A very belligerent 19th-century statue of William dominates the square, predictably Place Guillaume-le-Conquérant, leading up to the **Château Guillaume-le-Conquérant** (*open April–June and Sept daily 10–6, July and Aug daily 10–7; Oct–Dec and mid-Feb–Mar Mon and Thurs–Sun 10–6; closed Jan–mid-Feb; adm*). Its current name is a bit misleading, for not much of the castle William knew survives: the massive **Great Keep** was rebuilt for his youngest son, Henry I, in the 1120s, a smaller keep was added by Henry II in the 1150s and the round **Talbot Tower** was actually built for Philippe Auguste of France, after he had successfully ended the independence of William's descendants in Normandy in 1204. It remains one of the most dramatic of Norman castles, with its keeps and towers standing out on rocky crags, surrounded by a vast walled bailey courtyard. Visitors to the castle today, however, may appreciate a little advance warning. Besieged by Henry V of England in 1417, Falaise castle was last used in war in the 16th century and was already a ruin by the 19th, when some restoration work was done, which was largely undone in 1944. Since the 1980s, the castle has been the object of a radical renovation programme led by Bruno Decaris, chief architect of France's Department of Historic Monuments: a leaflet explains, perhaps to pacify those whose jaws drop when they see it, that it has been conceived in line with recent international practice that in restoring a monument there should be no confusion between the remnants of the original and the restoration work – in other words, that new additions are better than fake-old. Whole floors have been added within previously empty walls: in parts it looks as if the new sections are there to make it easier to appreciate the original structure, in others it appears more that the medieval masonry has just been used as a base for a striking contemporary building, including lifts from a sci-fi film alongside the Great Keep. The new rooms are used to host interesting exhibitions, concerts of early music and other events each summer. And, one great plus, the restoration of the towers allows you to get right to the top, from where there are wonderful views over the town, the gorge and the plain.

You can also look down to the **Fontaine d'Arlette**, the place where the tanner's daughter first flirted with the Duke's son. A pleasant path leads down the grassy flanks of the castle to this little spring by the river, now surrounded by a monument, where the seeds of the English monarchy, as it were, were sown.

Shopping

The Monday **market** in **St-Pierre-sur-Dives** is far the most important in the area, but there are more in **Orbec** (*Wed*), **Livarot** (*Thurs*), **Falaise** (*Sat*), **Vimoutiers** (*Mon, Fri*) and **Mézidon-Canon** (*Sun*). In July and August St-Pierre-sur-Dives hosts an extra farmers' market every Friday (*4.30–7.30pm*). Food aside, St-Pierre has an antiques market in the *Halles* on the first Sunday of each month all year.

To find more food producers, get the *Goûtez le Pays d'Auge* leaflet, from tourist offices.

Boissey ✉ 14170
Fromagerie de la Houssaye, t 02 31 20 64 00. Even in a region of fine cheesemakers this *fromagerie* – by the D4 road east of St-Pierre – has a lofty reputation. Livarot and Pont-l'Evêque are specialities. *Open Mon–Fri only.*

Fervaques ✉ 14140
Ferme de la Moissonière, t 02 31 32 32 13. The Lallier family produces fine Pont-l'Evêque and Pavé d'Auge cheeses on their farm on the south side of Fervaques, on the D64. *Open every afternoon (exc Sun) until c. 4pm.*

Mézidon-Canon ✉ 14270
Ferme du Château, t 02 31 20 71 50. The shop in the Château de Canon (*see* p.257) has the estate's own ciders, calvados, *poiré*, apple juice and organic produce. *Open Easter–May Sat and Sun 3–7; June–Sept daily 3–7.*

Prêtreville ✉ 14140
Manoir de Querville, t 02 31 32 31 88. M Hubert Courtemanche makes ciders and refined calvados on this extraordinary old farm in deep country south of Lisieux. Seeking it out is a real experience: first find Prêtreville village, and keep going past the church.

St-Germain-le-Vasson ✉ 14190
Ferme des Massinots, t 02 31 90 54 22, *tocheport@wanadoo.fr.* As well as running their *ferme-auberge* (*see* p.260) the Tocheports produce prize-winning foie gras, *rillettes* and other duck and goose products and fine ciders, *pommeau* and calvados, all available from the farm shop. *Farm tours, by reservation.*

Where to Stay

Berville-L'Oudon ✉ 14170
Ferme de l'Oudon, t 02 31 20 77 96, *www.fermedeloudon.com* (*rooms €55–70 for two, €70–85 for three*). A big stone farm with three modernized B&B rooms, two with space for three beds. It has a nice garden for summer breakfasts, and **evening meals** (*€28*) can be provided.

Bretteville-sur-Dives ✉ 14170
Le Pressoir de Glatigny, t 02 31 20 68 93 (*rooms €40 for two, €62 for four*). A peaceful B&B in an 18th-century farm with rambling outbuildings and old cider press (*pressoir*). There are three pretty rooms (one a family room), a lounge, and access to a kitchen.

Bretteville-sur-Laize ✉ 14680
Château des Riffets, t 02 31 23 53 21, *www.jeanluc.de/riffets* (*rooms €90–145*). A small château in 15 hectares of wooded grounds south of Caen. The four rooms combine old château character – gilt mirrors and antiques – with modern extras like jacuzzis and power showers, and there's a pool in the garden. M and Mme Cantel are very affable, and can provide expansive **evening meals** with advance notice (*€40*).

Crouttes ✉ 61120
Le Prieuré St-Michel, t 02 33 39 15 15, *leprieuresaintmichel@wanadoo.fr* (*rooms €95–125 for two*). This 13th–14th-century Benedictine priory was the home of the painter Edgar Chahine, and is now a centre hosting concerts, exhibitions and courses. Around it there's an exquisite park, with superb rose and herb gardens, and five lovely guest rooms in half-timbered cottages. **Dinner** (*€30*) is available by reservation.

Falaise ✉ 14700
Bed & Breakfast Falaise,
1 Rue du Sergent Goubin, **t** 02 31 40 95 86, *www.bandbfalaise.com* (*rooms from €85 for two*). Paul de Rooij – who is Dutch, and speaks excellent English – has restored this 18th-century town mansion as a special *chambres d'hôtes*. The five high-ceilinged rooms are beautiful, and there are loads of

extras – a library-sitting room, a pool, and gardens with a terrace on top of a medieval tower in the town ramparts. A star.

Hôtel de la Poste,
38 Rue Georges Clemenceau, **t** 02 31 90 13 14, *hotel.delaposte@wanadoo.fr* (*double rooms €48–95*). A pleasant, reliably comfortable *Logis* hotel in the middle of town, with 15 well-equipped rooms. The **restaurant** (*menus €15–37*) serves enjoyable Norman fare. *Restaurant closed Sun eve and Mon.*

Hameau Vaston, **t/f** 02 31 90 10 10 (*rooms €38 for two, €48 for three*). A massive-walled old *falaisien* stone farm 1km north of Falaise town, with two straightforward, cosy rooms. Atmospheric, and very good value.

Notre-Dame-de-Courson ✉ 14140

Manoir de Courson, **t/f** 02 31 32 30 69, *www.manoirdecourson.com* (*suites €125–180 for two*). A grand Norman manor – a listed monument – that Gérard and Sopheakna Goy have made into a luxurious B&B. Mme Goy is Cambodian, and her origins are reflected in the décor of its three seductive suites. There's also a pool, in a lovely garden.

St-Pierre-sur-Dives ✉ 14170

Château des Roches, 37 Rue du Bosq, **t/f** 02 31 20 60 80, *www.chateaudesroches.com* (*rooms €65–70 for two, €113 for four*). A special *chambres d'hôtes* in a 19th-century mansion, with garden, on the outskirts of St-Pierre – but still a short walk from the centre. The three huge guest rooms are furnished with antiques, and one is a spectacular suite with space for up to five. **Evening meals** (*€22*) can be provided. It's very good value; rates are lower for longer stays.

Eating Alternatives

Falaise ✉ 14700

L'Attache, Route de Caen, **t** 02 31 90 05 38 (*menus €17–33*). One on its own in Norman cuisine – chef Alain Hastain uses wild herbs, woodland mushrooms and edible flowers that he collects himself, combined with fine local meats and fresh seafood in hugely inventive, light dishes. Booking is essential. *Closed Mon and late Sept–early Oct.*

La Fine Fourchette, 52 Rue Georges Clemenceau, **t** 02 31 90 08 59 (*menus €13.90–36*). A popular, comfortable restaurant in the town centre. Chef Gilbert Costil keeps up with culinary trends, and his menus feature light, subtle touches, as in his fine fish and pasta dishes. Excellent value. *Closed Tues eve and early Feb.*

St-Germain-le-Vasson ✉ 14190

Ferme-Auberge des Massinots, **t** 02 31 90 54 22, *tocheport@wanadoo.fr.* (*menus €13.50–30*). A giant old courtyard farm where Anne-Marie Tocheport and her family prepare fine meals using their own produce. Dishes might include a copious *salade normande*, roast chicken in *pommeau* and fruit tarts; to drink, there's the farm's own cider and calvados, and wines and liqueurs. Meals are served in a convivial dining room, with a wood fire when the weather turns. Always book. There's also a farm shop (*see p.259*). *Closed Sun eve and mid-Dec–mid-Jan.*

St-Pierre-sur-Dives ✉ 14170

Hôtel Les Agriculteurs, 118 Rue de Falaise, **t** 02 31 20 72 78, *http://perso.wanadoo. fr/lesagriculteurs* (*menus €11–25*). As irreplacable a part of local life as the market. The giant restaurant provides no-nonsense Norman cooking – *jambon au cidre*, chicken *vallée d'Auge*, apple desserts – made with superb local ingredients. It's also a *Logis* **hotel** (*double rooms €29–39*), with 10 light, good-value rooms. *Restaurant closed Sun eve.*

Ste-Marie-aux-Anglais ✉ 14270

L'Auberge du Doux Marais, **t** 02 31 63 82 81 (*menus €20–40*). A farm inn deep in the countryside (head east from the tiny village of Ste-Marie-aux-Anglais, then more or less south looking for signs to Doux Marais) which is very popular with locals. Owners Bernard and Marinette offer spectacularly good-value menus of inventive Norman country cooking: *galettes* with Camembert sauce, meats grilled over a wood fire, guinea fowl in *pommeau*, *teurgoules* and apple desserts. A very friendly, relaxing place. Booking is essential, as they only cook to order. *Closed Sun eve and (Sept–June) Mon.*

Long Memories:
Normandy Beaches

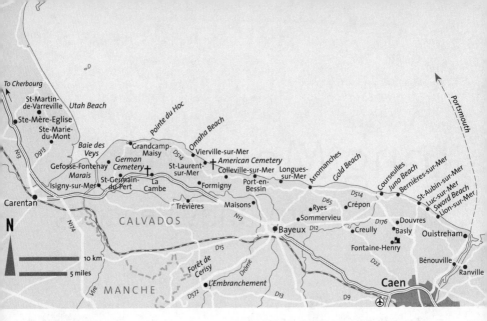

The wide arc of the Lower Normandy coast, stretching west from the Bay of the Seine and the River Orne to the Cotentin Peninsula, is a fine, open coastline, gentle in parts and more rocky and abrupt in others. Today it's hard to disassociate this coast from the events of summer 1944. Even on French maps the area is now marked as the *Plages du Débarquement*, and following the commemorations of the 50th and 60th anniversaries in 1994 and 2004 every point of historical significance has been smartly signposted, with an abundance of information provided for anyone wishing to retrace any part of the Normandy campaign.

Surprising, perhaps, to first-time visitors is the sheer length of the stretch of coast covered by the D-Day invasion beaches, close to 60 miles from end to end. The eastern section from Ouistreham to Arromanches, corresponding to the British and Canadian beaches of Gold, Juno and Sword, is otherwise known as the *Côte de Nacre* or 'Mother of Pearl Coast', a near-continuous, quite narrow beach fronted by a line of old-fashioned French seaside towns. Obviously, nowhere chooses to be a battlefield, but for the machine guns to have sliced up the sand and the flail tanks to have crashed ashore here seems particularly bizarre. Further west the towns fade away, and the lush farmland of the Bessin plain comes down almost to the sea's edge. The coastline is broken up by sandstone cliffs, punctuated by wide, open beaches, the largest of them Omaha, where the main US invasion force so nearly came to disaster. Finally, Utah Beach is further west again, on the Cotentin peninsula.

The D-Day sites and museums may be an obvious centre of attention, but this area's more conventional attractions shouldn't be ignored. The Bessin is actually one of the best farming areas in Normandy, the tranquil home of *crème fraîche*. Its old stone villages are truly rural, with massive Norman churches, and the region's most distinctive feature of all is its extraordinarily grand medieval farms – several of which contain unforgettable places to stay – which stand out like great stone towers across the countryside. The Bessin also has some very distinguished full-blown châteaux.

Getting There

The direct route to this area from Britain is by the Portsmouth–Caen ferry, the harbour for which is actually in Ouistreham: from the ferry terminal, turn immediately right to get onto the coast road. Ouistreham is about 1hr from Le Havre, via the Pont de Normandie (toll bridge) and the A13 *autoroute*, which is also the main road from Paris. Paris–Caen takes about 2½–3hrs by car. Utah Beach is *c.* 45mins from Cherbourg on the N13.

Crépon village is a crossroads of several country lanes. From Arromanches, take the Ouistreham road, and at the back of the town take a sharp right turn on to the D65, signposted for Creully. From Bayeux, take the D12 for Douvres, and in Sommervieu continue on to the D112. From Caen, take the D22, signposted to Creully and Arromanches.

The Paris–Cherbourg **train** line runs inland from the coast, with main stops at Caen, Bayeux and Carentan. Calvados *département* has a good **bus** service, **Les Bus Verts**, with connecting services that can take you all the way from Ouistreham to Isigny (information, *www.busverts14.fr*). In the Manche (around Utah Beach), services are less frequent, but there are buses from Carentan to Ste-Mère-Eglise. Several small companies also offer minibus tours of the beaches (*see* right).

Tourist Information

Many of the small towns along the *Côte de Nacre* also have local information offices.
Arromanches: 2 Rue du Maréchal Joffre, **t** 02 31 21 47 56, *www.arromanches.com*.
Courseulles-sur-Mer:
5 Rue du 11 Novembre, **t** 02 31 37 46 80, *tourisme.courseulles@wanadoo.fr*
Grandcamp-Maisy: 118 Rue Aristide Briand, **t** 02 31 22 62 44, *ot-grandcamp-maisy@wanadoo.fr*.
Ouistreham-Riva Bella: Jardins du Casino, **t** 02 31 97 18 63, *www.ville-ouistreham.fr*. There is also a smaller information point in Place Général de Gaulle, by the ferry terminal.
Port-en-Bessin: Quai Baron Gérard, **t** 02 31 22 45 80, *www.bayeux-tourism.com*.
Ste-Mère-Eglise: 6 Rue Eisenhower, **t** 02 33 21 00 33, *www.sainte-mere-eglise.info*.

Beach and Battlefield Tours

All these companies offer minibus tours, with guides, of the Normandy battlefields.
Battlebus, 16 Rue de la Maîtrise, 14400 Bayeux, **t** 02 31 22 28 82, *www.battlebus.fr*.
D-Day Tours, Bayeux, **t** 02 31 51 70 52, *www.d-daybeaches.com*.
Normandy Tours, 26 Place de la Gare, Bayeux, **t** 02 31 92 10 70, *www.d-day-beachestours.com*.

A few kilometres inland from the beaches, its few streets normally patrolled only by tractors, is Crépon, population 203. It has some of the finest fortified manors and farms of any of the Bessin villages, and in one of them, **La Rançonnière**, there is a hotel-restaurant offering some of the most sophisticated food in the area, based on superbly fresh local produce.

Ferme de la Rançonnière

Route d'Arromanches, Crépon, **t** *02 31 22 21 73, www.ranconniere.com.*
Open daily 12–1.30 and 7–9. Closed two weeks Jan.
Menus €15 (Mon–Fri and Sat midday only), €25–40.

The oldest part of La Rançonnière, a tower on one side of the courtyard, dates from the 15th century, and the farm buildings shelter within a massive sandstone outer wall, the watchtowers, crenellations and other fortifications of which were still being added to until the 1760s, such was the fear in these parts of the English and other marauders. Today, the courtyard contains lawns, flowerbeds and some café-style

Terrine de Pavé d'Isigny, douceur au calvados

Serves 8

750g/1lb 10 oz Pavé d'Isigny, or similar dry, soft, fairly salty cows' milk cheese
3 slices smoked ham (ideally *jambon de pays*, a strongly flavoured, gammony ham)
250ml/8fl oz single cream
3 apples
5 eggs
3 egg yolks
50g/2 oz clarified butter
500ml/1 pint chicken stock
salt and pepper

For the sauce and salad:
25g/1 oz unsalted butter
2–4 tablespoons flour
125ml/4fl oz calvados
400g/1lb mixed salad greens (*mesclun*)
For a vinaigrette: olive oil
cider vinegar
salt and pepper

The terrine needs to be prepared at least a day before you wish to serve it.

Cut up and grate the cheese. Mix the whole eggs, the extra egg yolks, the cream and the chicken stock together well, and season with salt and pepper. Core and peel the apples, and cut them into quarters.

Line a suitably-sized terrine with the slices of ham. Cover the base of the terrine with grated cheese, and top with apple quarters, repeating each layer as many times as necessary until the terrine is full. Then pour over the egg, cream and stock mixture, which should, again, come up to the rim of the dish. Place the terrine in a roasting tin or *bain-marie* (double boiler), add enough water to come halfway up the dish and bake in a preheated oven at 140°C/275°F/Gas Mark 1 for 1 hour 20 minutes. Afterwards, leave to set in a cool place for at least 24 hours before using.

Before serving, make a light roux with the unsalted butter and enough flour to give the desired consistency, and stir in the calvados. Pour a circle of this sauce onto each plate, and in the middle place some salad greens, dressed with the cider vinaigrette.

Slice the terrine and pan-fry each slice quickly on each side in the clarified butter. Place on top of the salad greens, and serve warm.

tables. The father of Mme Agnès Vereecke, the present owner, bought the farm after the Second World War, and the family opened it as a hotel in the 1970s. It's now mainly run by Mme Vereecke's daughter, Isabelle Sileghem, and her husband. The superb hotel rooms (*see* p.272) occupy the magnificent 17th-century main house, while the dining room is in a former stable. Big and barn-like, with thick stone walls, a giant fireplace, oak beams and long white-linen-clad tables with bouquets of pinks on each one, it fills up at weekends, but is generally much quieter at other times.

Whichever day you arrive, your fellow-diners will very likely be tucking into some form of poultry or similar winged game, which is spectacularly good here. In a *magret de canard* with a *pommeau* sauce the meat is superbly strongly-flavoured, almost ham-like; *suprême de volaille aux parfums de Normandie* features chicken breasts cooked in an intricate mix of local herbs and served with a fabulous potato gratin with a hint of liquorice. The freshness of all the fowl is quite tangible on the tongue, and all have so much taste they make the standard supermarket chicken seem a different creature altogether. The Rançonnière's chef Bruno Champion has a notably inventive touch: sauces are rich, often fruity but perfectly suited to the meats, and in his seasonings he makes great use of ingredients that are scarcely common in standard Norman cooking – liquorice, nutmeg, allspice, pine kernels, hazelnuts – as well as the classic flavours of apples and calvados.

There is a reason why the poultry is so good here. Until a few years ago La Rançonnière took in quality poultry and fowl from farms around the district for slaughtering and dressing on-site. This has now ended, but even so all the poultry used in the restaurant still comes from nearby farms, and so could scarcely be any closer to source unless you went and bought the bird yourself.

There are of course alternatives to poultry: a meatless starter of *millefeuilles de légumes* is an invigorating mix of beautifully fresh spring veg – aubergines, courgettes, fennel, onions and more – with a tangy dressing with *espelette* pepper; a menu fixture and house speciality is a terrine of *pavé d'Isigny* cheese (similar to pavé d'Auge) with a calvados sauce, the kind of Norman cream, egg and meat combination that can sound like all too much, but is deliciously smooth and satisfying when done well. There's also a daily main-course fresh fish special. The wine list is ample, and between courses the main menus both offer a very healthy *trou Normand*, with a lovely scoop of apple ice-cream and a hefty shot of calvados, a true taste of the land of William the Conqueror. Cheese is another house speciality, with an all-local selection; particularly enjoyable are the *chèvres* and *pavés* from nearby farms.

Desserts similarly combine country traditions and more urbane delights – from *teurgoules*, the crusty Norman rice pudding, to lighter patisserie pleasures like a *bavarois* of explosively fresh red berries with an irresistible, intriguingly herby coulis. After that, and maybe a calvados to accompany coffee and petits fours, a wander into the field of clover at the back of the farm is in order, to round out the contentment.

Touring Around

Crépon is an attractive, peaceful, little place, with a traditional *bar-tabac* as well as its noble ensemble of yellow sandstone Bessin manors. At the centre of the village is the 12th-century Romanesque **church**, with a huge, typically solid Norman tower, and in its dark interior some exceptional 17th- and 18th-century Baroque woodwork. About 4km south of Crépon is the dramatic romantic pile that is the **Château de Creully** (*guided tours July–mid-Sept Tues–Fri 10.30–12.30 and 2.30–5.30; adm*), a remarkable mix of medieval base, looming 16th-century towers and Louis XIII additions. In 1944 Creully had the distinction of housing the first BBC radio station in Normandy, and inside there is a small radio museum. Creully village is another that has a very fine 12th–15th-century **church**, within which is the tomb of Antoine de Sillans (*d.* 1641), the *Seigneur* of Creully responsible for many alterations to the castle.

Another 6km or so east of Creully is the grandest of all Bessin mansions, the spectacular 16th-century **Château de Fontaine-Henry** (*guided tours Easter–mid-June and mid-Sept–Oct Sat, Sun and hols 2.30–6.30; mid-June–mid-Sept Mon and Wed–Sun 2.30–6.30; adm*). Surrounded by lush gardens, it is still privately owned, by descendants of the family for whom it was built. Above the ornate carved façade is one of the tallest French Renaissance-style roofs, a magnificent slate peak that's the same height as the building below it; other parts are much older, and there is a beautiful 13th-century chapel. Inside, as well as very elegant rooms mostly in 19th-century style, there are some fine paintings, by Rigaud, Géricault and Correggio. In July and August, the château reopens for magical night-time tours on Friday evenings (*details from tourist offices*), and also hosts concerts of early and Baroque music.

For most visitors to this area, though, the Bessin's historic châteaux come second in interest to the war sites along the coast. There are war museums of all sizes and for all tastes in Normandy – for a full list, get *The D-Day Landings and the Battle of Normandy* booklet, free from all tourist offices – and there is a scheme by which, if you buy a full-price ticket at any of the publicly-owned 1944 museums, you have discounts on entry to all the others for the next 30 days. To make a start it's worth getting an overview, which can be provided by either of the two largest museums.

The **Caen Mémorial–Musée pour la Paix** (*open daily mid-Jan–late Feb and Nov–Dec 9–6, late Feb–early July and Sept–Oct 9–7; early July–Aug 9–8; last admission 1hr 45mins before closing; closed two weeks Jan and some public hols; adm, free for under-10s and Second World War veterans*) is a state-of-the-art facility opened in 1988, a sculptural slab of a building with a gash for an entrance to recall the violence of war, in a landscaped park on the north side of the Caen *Périphérique* ring road (so that it's not necessary to go into the city to visit it). Its different sections are imaginative, strongly visual mixed-media displays as much as traditional museum exhibits, with a strong sense of drama – there is a powerfully emotional room on the Holocaust – and the visit culminates with an hour-long, three-screen film centred on the Normandy battles. The Mémorial also seeks to present a global picture of the causes of the war from 1918, the political and social background and life at the time, and, since this is a peace not a war museum, there is a separate exhibit on the Nobel Peace Prize. There are also more museum-like exhibits, such as wartime aircraft hanging from the roof, and what must be the most comprehensive D-Day book and souvenir shop in existence. A full visit to the Mémorial including the film requires over two hours.

Militaria enthusiasts and those with a more immediate interest in the Normandy campaign itself tend to prefer the **Musée-Mémorial de la Bataille de Normandie** (*open daily May–mid-Sept 9.30–6.30; mid-Sept–April 10–12.30 and 2–6; closed two weeks Jan; adm*), opposite the largest British war cemetery in Normandy at Bayeux. This one has tanks, trucks, artillery, aeroplanes, all kinds of other equipment and any number of uniforms, arranged on sometimes slightly wobbly shop dummies, plus a

hugely comprehensive display of press cuttings and other material that, if you take
time to read it all, enables you to follow the campaign almost day-by-day, or to home
in on particular incidents. As in many similarly traditional smaller museums, all these
military accessories can fade into a blur to the uninitiated, but in amongst it all there
are still personal details and items that cut through to the quick, such as the various
pieces of paper that informed the family of Canadian airman James Lanfranchi that
he wouldn't be coming home. Again, a visit to the museum easily takes two hours.

To see the D-Day coast itself, maybe after visiting one of the main museums, it's
best to start at one end. Just off the Caen-Ouistreham road at Bénouville is the
Pegasus Bridge over the Caen Canal, taken by the British 6th Airborne Division at
midnight on 5 June 1944. Like many Normandy sites it all seems very peaceful, especially with a gentle breeze across the water and the canal dredger quietly chugging
away. In a brambly field at the Ranville end of the bridge the places where the para-
troops' gliders landed, remarkably close to the target, are precisely marked; across the
bridge is the **Café Gondrée**, the 'First House Liberated in France', where the Gondrée
family have been dispensing hospitality to British veterans ever since, and which is
now itself almost as much a museum as a bar. Next to the bridge on the eastern,
Ranville, bank there is a glossy museum, the **Mémorial Pegasus** (*open daily May–Aug
9.30–6.30; Feb–April and Sept–Nov 10–1 and 2–5; closed Dec and Jan; adm*). Opened in
2000 to replace the modest museum that for years stood on the Bénouville side, it's
suitably state-of-the-art, with a film and loads of information. The bridge that
currently spans the canal is not actually the one that was fought over in 1944, but a
wider model installed a few years ago; the otherwise very similar old bridge now sits
in a field alongside the Mémorial, 'beached' and surrounded by artillery. In summer a
son et lumière is presented at the Bénouville Bridge (*May–Sept every night exc Mon*).

Ouistreham is a pleasant harbour and seaside town that has gained many more
restaurants, cafés and so on since it acquired the Portsmouth ferry route. A few
streets inland, and ignored by most visitors, it also has one of the finest of all classic
Norman **churches**, from the 12th century. From Ouistreham the road turns west along
the beaches of the *Côte de Nacre*, now popular with windsurfers and lined with
holiday homes, some quite grand, others much more modest, between the centres of
the small seaside towns. In summer, sand spreads inland along the sides of the
streets, kids pad around barefoot, and there are plenty of bars and snack stands with
moules-frites and shops offering freshly caught *tourteaux* and *homards*. Every so
often the seafront is interrupted by a tank set in concrete, with a plaque.

This area has a history of other things as well as warfare. The eastern end of the
Côte de Nacre is exceptionally rich in fossils, and **Lion-sur-Mer** has an engaging private
museum and shop, the **Maison du Fossile** (*open May and Oct Mon and Wed–Sun 2–6;
June–Sept Mon and Wed–Sun 10–12 and 2–6; Nov–April Sat, Sun and hols 2–6; adm*), an
astonishing collection assembled entirely by local fossil-hunters. **Luc-sur-Mer** is a bit
more substantial than most of the other towns, with a glossy modernized casino
dominating the front, and a big thalassotherapy centre; at **St-Aubin-sur-Mer** the
casino is more modest, but has a striking Art Deco mosaic façade, perhaps a sign of
former glory. **Courseulles** is a larger, more modern resort, with a pretty yacht marina

surrounded by recently-built holiday apartments. Monuments record that this was the place where both Churchill and De Gaulle came ashore on their visits to the beachhead after D-Day. Courseulles was also the centre of the Canadian D-Day beach, Juno, and its seafront now hosts the very impressive **Juno Beach Centre** (*open daily April–Sept 9–7, Feb–Mar and Oct–Dec 10–1 and 2–6, closed Jan; adm*), the Canadian national D-Day memorial. Canadians justifiably resent that their contribution is often ignored, and this elegantly-designed centre should put everyone right: it's one of the most enterprising Normandy museums, with a much wider scope than D-Day itself. Exhibits also tell you a great deal about Canada in the 1930s, Canadian attitudes to the war and every other campaign Canadians took part in as well as Normandy; techniques are equally varied, with films and vivid, very moving audio and video testimony by veterans as well as things to see and read. There's a fine multimedia library, if you want to look further into any topic, and a shop. A visit takes one to two hours.

Beyond Courseulles the holiday cottages thin out, and lush meadows with quietly grazing brown-and-white Normandy cows come down to meet the beaches. A few kilometres further on, though, is one of the most visited points on the coast, **Arromanches**, still ringed, like so many giant, peculiarly angular beached whales, by several of the huge concrete-and-iron blocks of the Mulberry harbour, the entirely artificial port created here to supply the landing forces. For a few weeks the busiest port in the world, Arromanches is otherwise an attractive small beach town, with two main war-related exhibits, the **Musée du Débarquement** (*open daily Mar and Oct 9.30–12.30 and 1.30–5.30; April 9–12.30 and 1.30–6; May–Aug 9–7; Sept 9–6; Nov–Dec and Feb 10–12.30 and 1.30–5; closed Jan; adm*), with an interesting film on the immense engineering effort the Mulberry represented; and **Arromanches 360**, a high-impact film show using a 360° wrap-around screen (*shows daily Feb–April and Oct–Dec 10.10–4.40; May and Sept 10.10–5.40; June–Aug 9.10–6.40; closed Jan; adm*).

To the west the cliffs rise rapidly, while the main coast road cuts inland through hedgerows and small, sheltered villages, although for walkers the GR261 footpath keeps mainly to the cliff edge. Atop the cliffs at **Longues-sur-Mer** are the bunkers of the last of the German batteries along this coast that still has its guns in place, battered and rusting and pointing impotently into the sky. It's also a beautiful place, with paths surrounded by heather and blackberries, and superb views out to sea and along the shoreline. **Port-en-Bessin** is, unlike most towns in this area, a busy working fishing port, with a charming harbour, great seafood restaurants and a good market on Sundays; it's also the location of one of the oddest Normandy museums, the private **Musée des Epaves Sous-marines du Débarquement** (*open May Sat, Sun and hols 10–12 and 2–6; June–Sept daily 10–12 and 2–6; closed Oct–April; adm*). Since 1968 owner Jacques Lemonchois has had the sole concession from the French government to salvage all the various kinds of scrap metal sunk off the Normandy coast, and the 'Museum of Wrecks from the Landings' is in effect his yard. There are whole tanks, ships' turbines, guns, plates and all kinds of smaller items such as coat hooks, razors and old pennies from sunken ships, all rusted a uniform brown. It has a strangely ghoulish feel, more than the other museums; in answer to persistent demand from visitors, there are also cartridges, old engine parts and other bits and pieces for sale.

Beyond Port-en-Bessin the road reaches **Colleville**, **St-Laurent** and **Vierville** (all 'sur-Mer'), now signposted to the world as **Omaha Beach**. The US invasion force lost over 1,000 men here, a far worse casualty rate than on any of the other beaches. It's actually a fine, open stretch of sand, lined with just a few bars and beach houses, and a few people still use it as such. Omaha has all of three D-Day museums, all privately run by militaria collectors and so with a crankiness not found in the more rigorous public museums. Longest-running is the **Musée-Mémorial d'Omaha Beach** (*open daily mid-Feb–mid-Mar 10–12.30 and 2.30–6; mid-Mar–mid-May and mid-Sept–mid-Nov 9.30–6.30; mid-May–June and early Sept 9.30–7; July and Aug 9.30–7.30; closed mid-Nov–mid-Feb; adm*) in St-Laurent, assembled by a local enthusiast over decades. It's a little tatty, but gains in intimacy with details such as toothbrushes, pay books, letters, Army-issue condoms and the *US Soldier's Guide to France*, totalling all of 40 pages. The **Musée D-Day Omaha** (*open daily April–May and Oct–11 Nov 10–12.30 and 2–6; June–Sept 9.30–7.30; closed 12 Nov–Mar; adm*) in Vierville is still more of a mishmash, with all sorts of 1944 relics – weapons, helmets, every kind of uniform, bits of shot-down aircraft and, in front of the building, some landing craft. Lastly there's the recently created **Big Red One Assault Museum** (*open daily Mar–May and Sept–Nov 9–12 and 2–6, June–Aug 9–7; closed Dec–Feb; adm*), above the beach at the Colleville end, dedicated to the US 1st Infantry Division, which landed at this point on D-Day.

Also on the cliffs above the beach at Colleville is the **American Cemetery** (*open daily 9–5; closed 25 Dec and 1 Jan*), a transplanted piece of American monumental architecture, finely landscaped and with some of the most sharply trimmed lawns and flowerbeds you'll ever see. Nearly 10,000 of the US dead from France and Belgium were brought together in this one huge plot: the precisely aligned white crosses and stars of David carry only a minimum of information, demonstrating the depth of loss by sheer scale. There are marked differences between the war cemeteries of different countries. The British and Canadian dead are divided following Commonwealth War Graves Commission practice between several smaller, more intimate cemeteries; particularly tranquil is the British cemetery at **Ryes-Bazenville**, between Crépon and Bayeux. The other difference stems from the work of the Commission in enabling families to place personal messages on gravestones, small, simple epitaphs that make each man a missed individual, a painstaking task of enormous kindness. The huge **German cemeteries**, such as at La Cambe south of Omaha, are different again: sombre, devoid of any military insignia and imbued with an immense sadness.

A little further west from Omaha is **Pointe-du-Hoc**, where Colonel James Rudder and his US 2nd Ranger Battalion scaled the cliffs in a few minutes flat on the morning of D-Day in an attempt to silence a German battery on top. This is now American territory, ceded as a memorial (to the extent that even the fencing is Made in USA, perhaps brought here out of distrust for any comparable French product). Although grassed over by time, the land behind the point has been left pitted and cratered, a torn-up landscape that gives a clear idea of the ferocity of the fighting. This is nevertheless another beautiful, tranquil place, with the grassy, yellow sandstone cliffs the Rangers improbably climbed above a small rocky beach where gulls and waders pick for shellfish. And, in the early evening, you can watch a fine sunset over the Cotentin.

About 3km from the point is **Grandcamp-Maisy**, another attractive small fishing port, with good cafés along the harbour-side, and the **Musée des Rangers** (*open April–Oct Mon 3–6, Tues–Sun 10–1 and 3–6, closed Nov–Mar; adm*), which tells the full story of Pointe-du-Hoc. At Grandcamp the main D514 coast road turns south, for Utah Beach is separated from the rest of the landing beaches by the *marais* or marshland at the mouths of the Rivers Vire and Douve, which is now a nature reserve. The narrow lanes that lead off westwards from the D514, through the beautifully tranquil village of **Géfosse-Fontenay**, peter out on the shores of the **Baie des Veys**, an atmospheric expanse of giant mud flats and oyster beds. The wetlands contain an abundance of bird life, including rare white storks, buzzards and the red-breasted merganser. There is a particularly good, accessible walk through part of the inland wetlands from **St-Germain-du-Pert**, with a well-marked path; tourist offices have good free maps.

The D514 meanwhile leads down to meet the main N13 and carry on west through **Isigny**, a town dedicated 250 per cent and more to the production of *crème fraîche*, and **Carentan**, a plainish market town. Just beyond, the D913 turns off back towards the coast and the village of **Ste-Marie-du-Mont** and **Utah Beach**. Utah is a long, windswept stretch of dunes, with a big tidal reach and open horizons backed by flat marsh fields, and so none of the steep terrain that caused so many problems at Omaha. Its fine museum, the **Musée du Débarquement-Utah Beach** (*open Feb–Mar and early Nov daily 10–12.30 and 2–5.30; April and May daily 10–6; June–Sept daily 9.30–7; Oct daily 10–12.30 and 2–6; mid-Nov–Dec Sat, Sun and hols 10–12.30 and 2–5.30; closed Jan; adm*), has a panoramic viewing room overlooking the beach. About 10km inland is one of the most popular of the Normandy Invasion sites, **Ste-Mère-Eglise**, the little town at the centre of the US paratroop drops on the night of 5–6 June. It has one of the most-visited museums, the **Musée Airborne** (*open daily Feb–Mar and Oct–Nov 10–12 and 2–6; April–May and Sept 9–12 and 2–6.45; June–Aug 9–6.45; closed Dec and Jan; adm*), with a genuine Douglas C47 Dakota in the yard. Around the town there are also information boards with photos taken of the same streets during the battle, which give a fascinating, step-by-step image of what happened here.

Ste-Mère has other attractions too. It is the site of Normandy's largest livestock market, and a beautiful old farm on the edge of the town – one of the granite manors that are as characteristic of the Cotentin peninsula as sandstone farms are of the Bessin – is now the **Ferme-Musée du Cotentin** (*open daily April, May and hols 2–6, June and Sept 11–6; July and Aug 11–7; closed Oct–Mar; adm*), a country-life centre that makes full use of the farm's magnificent kitchens, bread oven and cider press. It also has excellent B&B rooms (*see p.273*). And Ste-Mère also has perhaps the oddest of Normandy war memorials. Hanging down one side of the 13th-century Norman **church tower** in the middle of town is a dummy dressed as a US soldier, dangling from a parachute. This commemorates the exploit of paratrooper John Steele, who, as anyone who has seen the 1960s film *The Longest Day* knows, was caught by his parachute on the tower as he fell and hung there throughout the night and much of the next day, ignored by the Germans around the church who assumed he was dead. Mr Steele died a few years ago but used to revisit Ste-Mère quite regularly, and now looks likely to stay there in effigy forever.

Shopping

The best traditional **markets** along this coast are in **Arromanches** (*Wed*), **Port-en-Bessin** (*Sun*), **Isigny-sur-Mer** (*Wed and Sat*) and **Ste-Mère-Eglise** (*Thurs*) but all the towns have a street-sale of some kind one day a week.

The Bessin produces very fine ciders and calvados, with a distinctive style: quite dry and astringent, less fruity and full-bodied than the Auge ciders but with a greater freshness than the driest ciders of the Cotentin. Because of the semi-flatness of the Bessin plain the cider farms are relatively large and easy to find, and are often well-organized to receive visitors. As usual, tourist offices have leaflets listing local farms that open for direct sales and/or tours.

Colleville-sur-Mer ✉ 14710

Ferme du Clos Tassin, t 02 31 22 41 51. This cider farm is relatively small for the Bessin, but still has a well-organized farm shop with apple jam and vinegars as well as calvados, *pommeau* and ciders. The Picquenard family also have five simple B&B **rooms** (*rooms €38–40 for two*). The farm is on the east side of Colleville on the road towards Port-en-Bessin, not far from Omaha Beach.

Formigny ✉ 14710

Les Jardins, t/f 02 31 22 48 99. A dairy farm just inland from Omaha Beach, on the road towards Trevières, where the Gaullier family sell their own *crème fraîche*, butter, goats' and cow's milk cheeses and *confiture du lait*. Call ahead and you can order a fresh farm chicken. *Open Mon–Sat afternoons only.*

Isigny-sur-Mer ✉ 14230

UCL Isigny, 2 Rue du Dr Boutrois, **t** 02 31 51 33 88, *www.isigny-ste-mere.com* (*guided tours July and Aug Mon–Sat 10, 11, 2, 3 and 4; Sept–June tours available by reservation*). With its *appellation d'origine contrôlée*, Isigny (an area which for culinary purposes runs up to Ste-Mère-Eglise) is the capital of *crème fraîche* for the entire known universe, and this is the cooperative's official visitor centre. There's also a shop, open all year round, where you can stock up on AOC butter, Camembert, Pont-l'Evêque and other cheeses, as well as the essential *crème cru*.

St-Germain-du-Pert ✉ 14230

Les Vergers de Romilly, t 02 31 22 71 77 (*guided tours Wed 2.30pm; reservation advisable*). A large cider farm of beautiful orchards around a majestic Bessin stone farmhouse. One of the best producers in the area, it has dry and sweet ciders, *pommeau*, cider vinegar, wonderful fresh apple juice and a complete range of superior calvados. The charming Mme Renaud, who speaks good English, takes the entertaining tours every Wednesday; they are much better than many cider visits, giving a very good idea of the work of the farm and how both cider and calvados are made. The farm is just south of the N13, and well signposted.

St-Laurent-sur-Mer ✉ 14710

Ferme de la Sapinière, t 02 31 22 40 51. An impressively large and manorial-looking cider farm in the middle of the village behind Omaha Beach. The range of products for sale includes ciders, *pommeau*, a select variety of calvados of different ages, and pure apple juice. Free farm tours are available by reservation.

Where to Stay

This coast has a particularly ample supply of attractive and exceptional-value *chambres d'hôtes* (B&B) rooms. Tourist offices and the various *chambres d'hôtes* organizations (*see* chapter 3) have full listings.

Arromanches ✉ 14117

Hôtel de la Marine, Quai du Canada, **t** 02 31 22 34 19, *www.hotel-de-la-marine.fr* (*double rooms €61–76; €106–140 for four*). This classic *Logis de France* hotel has been welcoming British veterans, their families and friends virtually ever since 1945. It has the best location in town, dominating the middle of the seafront and with a 180° view of the beach and the Mulberry harbour. The Marine has also returned its customers' loyalty by keeping up a high level of comfort and personal service, and the 28 rooms have recently been attractively done up. The hotel also has a popular restaurant (*see* p273). *Closed Nov–mid-Feb.*

Crépon ✉ 14480

Ferme de la Rançonnière, Route d'Arromanches, **t** 02 31 22 21 73, *www.ranconniere.com* (*double rooms €45–128, suites €138–178*). The rooms at the Rançonnière (*see p.263*) are perhaps still more impressive than the rest of the grand old farm. There are 34 in the main house and 12 in a smaller manor house, the **Ferme de Mathan**, a few hundred metres away. No two are the same: all have a wonderfully baronial style, with giant carved wardrobes, grand oak chairs, massive beams even in the (modern) bathrooms and an amazing double-decker family room with a room-within-a-room reached by spiral staircase that's ideal for kids with ideas of haunted castles. The rooms in the Ferme de Mathan are a little less distinctive, but still attractive, and might be preferred by those who like a lot of light and space. Prices vary according to the size and facilities of each room. A memorable place to spend a few nights.

Manoir de Crépon, Route d'Arromanches, **t** 02 31 22 21 27, *manoirdecrepon@wanadoo.fr* (*rooms €70 for two, €100 for four*). Not medieval like so many Bessin houses, but an elegant manor house from the 1760s, amid a lovely French-style garden. Mme Anne-Marie Poisson has two double B&B rooms and two suites: like the house, they're very light and spacious, with high ceilings and creaking wooden floors, and decorated with antiques (some added, some just part of the house). Her two suites are made up of two rooms each, sharing a bathroom. The breakfast room, with massive timber table, is especially delightful. Mme Poisson is very charming, and also has an antiques shop in another part of the house.

Géfosse-Fontenay ✉ 14230

Manoir de la Rivière, **t** 02 31 22 64 45, *www.chez.com/manoirdelariviere* (*rooms €50 for two, €90 for four*). A stunning B&B in a massive medieval fortress-farmhouse amid quiet fields on the edge of the Marais at the mouth of the Vire, between Omaha and Utah beaches. The three guest rooms have high ceilings, antique country furniture, modern bathrooms and views over the fields; one is an atmospheric double, the others each have a double and an extra bed. Breakfast is served in a lordly room with giant fireplace, and **evening meals** can be provided with prior notice (*€20, minimum four persons*). The farm also has two equally special self-contained *gîtes* (*€130–200 for two nights, €230–390 per week*). In the main house there is a four-room apartment, while the other is an extraordinary double in a 13th-century watchtower in the garden – one of the star rural-romantic retreats of all time. M and Mme Leharivel, who still run La Rivière as a dairy farm, are charm itself.

Maisons and Sully ✉ 14400

Château de Sully, Route de Port-en-Bessin, Sully, **t** 02 31 22 29 48, *www.chateauxhotels.com/sully* (*double rooms €100–137, suites and apartments €165–280*). A 22-room château-hotel prominently located by the road from Bayeux to Port-en-Bessin, in 6 hectares of grounds. The rather austere 18th-century mansion is approached along a neat drive between ample lawns, alongside which there are two 16th-century towers. Inside things are plainer, but the traditionally-styled rooms have all the requisite country-house comforts. The larger 'Superior' rooms and the suites are notably more attractive than standard rooms. Lounges and public areas are smartly cosy, and the very plush **restaurant** (menus €33–70) overlooks the flower-filled garden. One very impressive feature is the conservatory-style swimming pool, which can be indoor or almost open-air according to the weather. *Closed Dec–Feb.*

Manoir du Carel, Maisons, **t** 02 31 22 37 00, *www.bienvenue-au-chateau.com* (*rooms €120–130 for two*). One of the largest of the Bessin's fortified manors, with a castle-like tower at its centre, this remarkable farm dominates the view in the tiny village of Maisons, half-way between Bayeux and Port-en-Bessin. As well as being a working farm (with some very fine horses), it contains three equally manorial B&B rooms, combining stone floors, antique furniture and tasteful renovation with luxury comforts. There is also a self-contained *gîte* (*€150 for up to four*) in a separate house in the grounds, with its own small garden.

Ouistreham ✉ 14150
Hôtel-Restaurant Le Normandie,
71 Av Michel Cabieu, **t** 02 31 97 19 57,
www.lenormandie.com (*double rooms*
€58–60). Very conveniently located near the
ferry port, the Normandie is best-known as a
restaurant (*see* p.274), but also has 22 hotel
rooms. Thanks to the hotel's 19th-century
design, they're not spacious – some are of a
size that some people would see as snug,
but others would just call small – but have
been well renovated, and are comfortably
equipped. *Closed mid-Dec–mid-Jan.*

St-Laurent-sur-Mer ✉ 14710
La Sapinière, 100 Rue de la 2ème Division
d'Infanterie US, **t** 02 31 92 71 72,
www.chez.com/lasapiniere (*double rooms*
€60–75, €99 for four). For once, not a hotel
with venerable Norman timbering or
stonework – this original modern beach
hotel consists of 15 rooms in individual
wooden cabins, in the dunes just behind
Omaha Beach. They're bright, comfortably
equipped and very spacious, and each has its
own terrace on the garden at the back, and
views of the beach at the front. It's just a
two-minute walk from the beach, and the
friendly staff can also direct you to facilities
for golf, riding, sand-yachting and many
other activities available nearby. Plus, it has
Omaha Beach's best restaurant (*see* p.274).
Closed Nov–Mar.

St-Martin-de-Varreville ✉ 50480
Manoir de Juganville, 39 Les Mezières, **t** 02 33
95 01 97, *www.juganville.com* (*rooms €54–90*
for two, €100 for four). An impressively
baronial 16th-century stone manor in the
countryside behind Utah Beach, with giant
pepperpot tower attached, which has been
restored and decorated by Pascal and
Chantal Jean with great care and taste. They
have four large, atmospheric B&B rooms,
each with its own mix of antiques and
stylish, subtly inventive colour schemes, and
with very high-standard bathrooms with
massage showers. Two rooms (one double,
one twin) make up a suite sharing a bathroom, which would be equally good for a
family or a group. Downstairs, there's a very
comfortable lounge and a library, and the

Jeans can advise on all sorts of activities
available nearby. A very relaxing base for
seeing the coast and the Cotentin.

Ste-Mère-Eglise ✉ 50480
Ferme-Musée du Cotentin,
Chemin de Beauvais, **t** 02 33 95 40 20,
musee.sainte-mere@cg50.fr (*rooms €36 for*
two, €50 for four). This magnificent
17th–18th-century granite farm on the north
side of Ste-Mère, as well as being a museum
of Cotentin country life (*see* p.270), has four
characterful, cosy *chambres d'hôtes* rooms.
They're very spacious – and so excellent for
families – and combine antique fittings that
are literally museum pieces with modern
comforts (TVs in every room). Guests have
use of a kitchen, and free access to the
museum; staff are charming, and low prices
make it extraordinary value. *Closed Dec–Jan.*

Eating Alternatives

Arromanches ✉ 14117
Hôtel de la Marine, Quai du Canada, **t** 02 31 22
34 19, *www.hotel-de-la-marine.fr* (*menus*
€19–49). The restaurant at La Marine (*see*
p.271) has the best view in Arromanches of
the bay and the Mulberry harbour from the
panoramique windows of the dining room
and the big, comfortable bar. It has also kept
a loyal following among visitors and locals
for its reliably enjoyable food, and especially
its seafood specialities: lobster, *moules*
marinières, grilled sea bass and so on. Meat
dishes and Norman comfort-food desserts
are good value, too. *Closed Nov-mid-Feb.*

Bernières-sur-Mer ✉ 14490
L'As de Trèfle, 420 Rue Léopold Hettier, **t** 02 31
97 22 60 (*menus €17 Mon–Fri only, €26–36*).
An attractive restaurant in a small house
that its young owners, Gilles and Sandrine
Poudras, renovated themselves a few streets
inland from Bernières seafront and Juno
Beach. They have won great praise for their
commitment to quality and fresh approach
to Norman cooking: ingredients – lobster,
andouille sausages, duck and cheeses – are
painstakingly selected; dishes, whether
innovations like a *gratin* of fish and seafood

in Neufchâtel cheese or classics like a *tarte tatin*, are packed with flavour. Prices are very reasonable, the dining room is pretty and there are a few tables on a terrace. *Closed Sun eve (Oct–May) and Mon.*

Ouistreham ✉ 14150
Hôtel-Restaurant Le Normandie,
71 Av Michel Cabieu, **t** 02 31 97 19 57, *www.lenormandie.com (menus €18–54)*. Ouistreham's highly regarded *Belle Epoque* hotel-restaurant (*see* p.273) has been thoroughly renovated in recent years, and the dining room has a comfortably smart look; the food of chef Christian Maudouit – a well-known local figure – is also refined, with sophisticated Norman dishes such as seafood quiches, lobster with lentils and other vegetables, and excellent classics like chicken in cider. *Closed Nov–Mar Sun eve and Mon, and mid-Dec–mid-Jan.*

Port-en-Bessin ✉ 14520
L'Ecailler, 2 Rue de Bayeux, **t** 02 31 22 92 16, *lecailler@msn.com (menus €25–67)*. An attractive restaurant near the quayside in Port-en-Bessin with rather smart, contemporary styling in dark wood instead of the customary French seaside brasserie décor. Its food is innovative too, and has a high reputation: fish and seafood are still the mainstays, but in subtle combinations such as one of the specialities, red mullet marinated with a touch of citrus. There are generous main set menus and an attractive *carte*, but for a really opulent feast you can go for the *menu autour du homard* (€67), with every course (bar the dessert) based on lobster. *Closed Sun eve and Mon.*
Le Bistrot d'à Côté, 18 Rue Michel Lefournier, **t/f** 02 31 51 79 12 *(menus €14.50–23.50)*. This bright and suitably nautical-looking seafood restaurant just off the harbour is very popular with locals. The menu features all the classics, from *moules* several different ways to exceptional platters of *fruits de mer*, and the fish and seafood are as fresh as they could be. The set menus are wonderful value, with refined choices even in the more economical lists. Staff are friendly, and well-used to foreign visitors. *Closed Tues and Wed exc July and Aug.*

St-Laurent-sur-Mer ✉ 14710
La Sapinière, 100 Rue de la 2ème Division d'Infanterie US, **t** 02 31 92 71 72, *www.chez.com/lasapiniere (dishes c. €5–16.50)*. The laidback Sapinière hotel behind Omaha Beach (*see* p.273) has a big, bright wooden-cabin dining room, surrounded by wooden decking with terrace tables. The open kitchen and wood-fired grill offer a range of good-value food suited to the beach-side location: crepes, salads, *moules* different ways (with the essential *frites*), generous *plats du jour* and larger options such as *magret de canard*. *Open April–Oct daily 8am–9pm; closed Nov–Mar.*

Ste-Marie-du-Mont ✉ 50480
Restaurant L'Estaminet,
44 Place de l'Eglise, **t** 02 33 71 57 01, *www.restaurant-estaminet.com (menus €10.50–28)*. A popular, pretty little restaurant in the middle of Ste-Marie, with stone walls, traditional furniture and enjoyable classic Norman cooking – oysters, mussels, duck, a hearty *marmite du pecheur* fish and seafood stew, and fruity desserts. They also have five basic **rooms** (*double rooms €26–37*). *Closed (Sept–June only) Tues eve and Wed.*
Restaurant Le Roosevelt, Utah Beach, **t** 02 33 71 53 47, *www.le-roosevelt.com (dishes c. €9–18)*. One part of this mid-Atlantic-looking place among the dunes on Utah Beach is a cluttered ad hoc information centre and souvenir shop. The rest of it is the nearest French equivalent to a roadside diner, with decent snacks and salads, a few seafood standards like *moules-frites* and the occasional larger *plat du jour*.

Ste-Mère-Eglise ✉ 50480
Auberge Le John Steele, 4 Rue Cap de Laine, **t** 02 33 41 41 16 *(menus €12.35–23.75)*. As much an institution behind Utah as the Marine is in Arromanches, the *auberge*, named after the US paratrooper caught on Ste-Mère's church tower, has a well-maintained popularity for its warm atmosphere and quality Norman *terroir* cooking, using excellent fresh ingredients. It has seven simple hotel **rooms** (*double rooms €35–39*). The restaurant can get very busy in midsummer. *Closed (Oct–June only) Sun eve and Mon.*

Bishop Odo's Town:
Bayeux

26

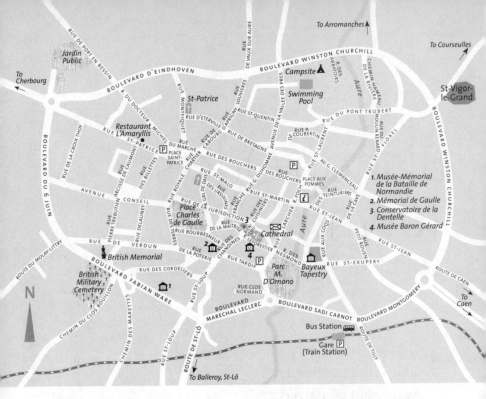

Bayeux is a small town where everything fits together. Its great treasure the Bayeux Tapestry, recounting with wonderful vividness the story of the Norman conquest of England, is complemented perfectly by the magnificent cathedral for which it was made. Around them there are winding streets, medieval stone courtyards, elegant *Ancien Régime* townhouses and quiet gardens. The town owes its completeness to a remarkable piece of good fortune. Bayeux was taken by British troops on the morning of 7 June 1944, only one day after the great invasion, as the first substantial town in France to be liberated and probably the one taken with the least serious fighting. It was thus spared the terrible devastation that swept over the towns and villages to the south, east and west, and so stands today as a remarkably intact survivor of pre-war Normandy.

It's not just its major monuments and historic houses that make Bayeux such a charming place to wander around, but also the simple, archetypically French 19th-century houses with their grey fronts and shuttered windows, the irregular jumble of roofs, the contrast between its bustling market and the placidity of old squares just a few steps away. It also makes an excellent base for visiting all the areas around it.

The capital of the Bessin, a lush green plain of cattle, cheese, cider, massive fortified farmhouses and superb Norman churches, Bayeux has a curious feel somewhere between a town and a big village. In food, it's a stronghold of Norman tradition: apples, *crème fraîche*, fine beef, cider, meaty terrines, excellent seafood fresh from the coast nearby. One of the best places to find very enjoyable and imaginative local cuisine is an unassuming little restaurant, **L'Amaryllis**, off Bayeux's market square.

Getting There

The main road from Caen or Cherbourg (the N13), and all other roads into Bayeux meet the *périphérique* ring of boulevards that, under different names, runs all the way around the town. A good place to leave the boulevards is the roundabout at the meeting point of Bd Sadi Carnot and Bd Maréchal Leclerc, just east of the railway station on the south side. A turn north from here leads quickly to the centre via Rue Larcher, passing a free car park. Parking in Bayeux, in any case, is not expensive.

The town's central axis is the crossroads at the end of Rue Larcher (where the main streets, east–west and north–south, change names). Rue St-Jean leads off to the east, with the tourist office the first building on the left. L'Amaryllis restaurant is towards the western end of Bayeux's long main street, just west of the market square, Place St-Patrice, at which point the street is called Rue St-Patrice.

Bayeux has good **train** links on the Paris (St-Lazare)–Caen–Cherbourg line. The station is on the south side of the boulevards, from where it's an easy walk into town. Calvados **Bus Verts'** station, with services to Port-en-Bessin, Arromanches, Courseulles and towns on the coast, is next to the train station. Buses are frequent Mon–Sat, but very scarce Sun.

Tourist Information

Bayeux: Pont St-Jean, **t** 02 31 51 28 28, *www.bayeux-tourism.com*. The Bayeux office is one of the biggest tourist offices in the region, and provides a wide range of services. For some private agencies based in Bayeux that offer minibus **tours** of the Normandy battlefields, *see* p.263.

Internet Access: Micro Sim Plus, 67 Rue des Bouchers, **t** 02 31 22 06 02, *www.microsimplus.com*. A handy facility.

L'Amaryllis

*32 Rue St-Patrice, **t** 02 31 22 47 94, **f** 02 31 22 50 03.*
Open Sept–June Tues–Sat 12–2 and 7–9.30, Sun 12–2, closed Mon; July and Aug daily 12–2 and 7–9.30. Closed mid-Dec–Jan. Menus €15–32; carte average €40.

If French cooking retains its traditional standing nowadays, when it's supposedly possible to find sophisticated restaurants serving far more varied, innovative, Italian-influenced-Pacific-Rim-global-fusion food in every city of the world, it's because of the depth of France's *culture gastronomique* – a phrase that never sits happily in English – the habitual level of interest in, knowledge of and concern for fine fresh food throughout the country. And one essential aspect of this is not the scattering of multi-starred famous eating-houses, but the number of skilled cooks in quite modest restaurants in relatively out-of-the-way places around France who, without any wish to grab the headlines or get their own TV series, are still prepared to work to the highest standards. It's not that every Frenchman in a restaurant is a great cook, or that there aren't bad restaurants in France. It is the case, though, that in every part of the country there will be at least a few chefs who, maybe with just a purely local reputation, work dedicatedly away at their craft, developing their skills, seeking out the very best ingredients and producing intricate, time-intensive dishes. And this dedication, this willingness to take the trouble, is the basis of quality.

Such a chef is Pascal Marie, of L'Amaryllis in Bayeux. His restaurant, at the quieter western end of Bayeux's main street near the market square, is small, neat and pretty, with décor in fresh pale blues and white, comfortable seating, a bar on one side and the essential fresh flowers on each table. He worked in several places before he and his wife opened L'Amaryllis in 1990, but always stayed close to his west-Norman roots – Courseulles, Villers Bocage, the Lion d'Or here in Bayeux, the prestigious Absinthe in Honfleur (*see* p.228). His refined, Norman-based dishes, though, would not be out of place in a far more high-profile city location – except that there the fabulously fresh country ingredients would be far harder to come by.

Even the supposedly basic, €15 set menu offers a wide choice of pleasures. Of the first courses on a late-summer menu, *millefeuille de pommes confites et d'andouille de Vire* features a lovely contrast between slightly bitter-sweet apple and the deliciously smokey, rich flavour of authentically gutsy Norman sausage; an all-vegetarian starter, a *poêlée de légumes de moment*, is a warm seasonal salad that's both refreshing and substantial, and full of good things – green beans, broccoli, artichokes, tomatoes, mushrooms and quite a bit more. Among the main courses might be *jambonette de canard*, duck that has been boned and preserved in its own fat before cooking, producing extraordinary tender meat with an especially delicate flavour. Fish options could include fillet of red mullet with vegetables in a cider sauce – a perfect presentation of traditional Norman cooking – or skate offset by a subtle *confit* of shallots. With the basic menu you have to choose between a cheese course or dessert, but if you push the boat a little further out there's naturally a well-picked choice of Norman cheeses. Desserts run from fine fresh sorbets and a sophisticated 'soup' of red berries with wine and spices to a juicy version of an all-time local classic, *tarte aux pommes et calvados*, with or without *crème fraîche*.

A meal at L'Amaryllis is a demonstration of the virtues of the French cult of fresh ingredients and closeness to source at its most effective. All the birds used in the many duck dishes come from a farm just outside Bayeux, all the vegetables equally come from just down the road – and it shows. And, as you sit at one of the restaurant's snug little tables, watching the number of passers-by dwindle after the market on a Saturday afternoon, a meal here is a very pleasant experience too. Service is by the quietly charming Mme Marie. She also runs a small hotel alongside, **Hôtel Le Continental** (*30–32 Rue St-Patrice*, **t** *02 31 92 69 30*), which offers very good *demi-pension* deals with the restaurant (*double rooms with dinner for two €73–78*). Even if you don't take a room, one other not-unimportant thing to note is that for €15 at L'Amaryllis you can have a meal that would (for example) cost three times as much just about anywhere in Britain.

Touring Around

The origins of Bayeux fade off into prehistory. It was the capital of a Gaulish tribe called the *Bajocasses*, and became a significant Roman town. It was still a sizeable community in the 9th century, and attracted the attention of the raiding Vikings. The near-legendary Viking chieftain and founder of Normandy Rollo (or *Rollon*, in French) married Popa, the daughter of the Frankish Count of Bayeux, and their son, the future William Longsword, second Duke of Normandy, was born here in 905. Bayeux can thus claim to be the true home of the remarkable dynasty of Norman Dukes. It was also one of the last towns in Normandy where Norse was regularly spoken, into the 11th century. Bayeux reached its greatest importance around the time of the Norman conquest of England, when it was the main power base of Odo de Conteville, Bishop of Bayeux but also William the Conqueror's half-brother, comrade-in-arms (despite being a priest) and turbulent and often troublesome minister. In the same period, however, William – partly because of his quarrel with the disloyal Odo, whom he imprisoned in 1082 – decisively shifted the focus of the Norman state to his own favourite town, Caen, a move that would eventually lead to Bayeux's decline. The town and the Bessin would still be fought over at many stages of the Hundred Years' War, which is when their fortified townhouses, manors and farms were built. Later, though, Bayeux would settle back into being a much quieter provincial market town.

The spine of Bayeux is the long, more-or-less straight street that runs northwest to southeast, with different names in different sections (which happens a lot in Bayeux): from the west, Rue St-Patrice, Rue St-Malo, Rue St-Martin and Rue St-Jean. Bayeux also has a very noticeable central axis, the crossroads where the main street changes from Rue St-Martin to Rue St-Jean, and is crossed by a street called Rue Foch to the north and Rue Larcher to the south. The main street is the only one in Bayeux that's often quite busy, with a fair amount of traffic and crowds of shoppers on Saturday afternoons; walk up any of the side streets, and very soon stillness prevails.

Walk along the main route and around the surrounding little streets and you can discover a fascinating mixture of timeworn old houses. From the 16th to 18th centuries Bayeux was a prosperous little town, and its merchants and gentlemen were able to build themselves many *hôtels particuliers* or town mansions. On the corner of Rue St-Martin and **Rue des Cuisiniers** is the oldest completely intact house in Bayeux, a wonderfully massive 14th-century house, a mix of Bessin stone and half-timbering, that rises up to its erratic roof line thorugh three tiers and in different sections, with a fascinating combination of the vertical and the horizontal. At 4 Rue St-Malo is the **Grand Hôtel d'Argouges**, a 15th–16th-century mansion mainly in stone, much altered in its upper floors, but which still possesses an imposing courtyard. King François I of France is said to have slept here, in 1532. Remnants of Viking Bayeux are, naturally, a matter of archaeology, but poking up all over the old town, often half-unnoticed behind much later houses and yards, are soaring 14th-century stone watchtowers, built to warn of the approach of the English or other troublemakers. **Rue Franche**, the turning to the south where Rue St-Martin becomes Rue St-Malo, contains almost a compendium of the history of Bayeux since about 1300. The **Hôtel de Rubercy**, at no.5, has a plainish 19th-century façade, but if you stand back and look above it you can see a turreted 15th-century watchtower; no.7, the **Hôtel de la Crespillière**, is a classically elegant French 18th-century townhouse; no.13, the **Manoir de St-Manvieu**, is a 16th-century residence concealed behind another simple 19th-century front; while no.18 is the 15th-century **Manoir Gilles Buhot**, where you can still pick out the medieval structure despite all the later alterations.

Across Rues St-Martin/St-Malo from Rue Franche in Rue Genas Duhomme, even the Méliès cinema is housed behind the columns of an 18th-century *hôtel*. This street is crossed by **Rue des Bouchers**, a long, charming old street with many more *hôtels* from the same era, some a little battered at the edges, and some sheltering behind gardens. To the left Rue des Bouchers runs up parallel to Rue St-Malo to **Place St-Patrice**, Bayeux's main market square (also known just as *Place du Marché*), a big, 19th-century space with several pleasant, untouristy bars and restaurants around it or nearby, including L'Amaryllis. The market fills the square every Saturday.

Back at the central crossroads, the main street continues eastwards via the **Pont St-Jean** (with the tourist office on top of it) over the Aure, a lovely, lively little river that's lined by buildings from all sorts of eras. Behind the tourist office is the courtyard-like **Place aux Pommes**, with a few craft shops. **Rue St-Jean** across the bridge is pedestrianized and forms one of the most picturesque parts of old Bayeux, with a line of cafés and brasseries with pavement terraces. At 51 Rue St-Jean a passageway leads to the 16th-century **Hôtel du Croissant**, a superb stone house on an intimate courtyard with a rocket-like six-storey watchtower. **Rue des Teinturiers** – the 'street of dyers', who needed to have their pretty noxious workshops alongside the river – turns off Rue St-Jean to the north. This now-quiet little street contains, at no.45, Bayeux's smallest house, a truly tiny little structure that looks like an insert put in to prop up the two houses either side of it, so that it's hard to think it was ever really a separate building. Balzac also lived in this street for a few months in 1822.

Bayeux's main monuments are in the compact little knot of streets south of St-Malo–St-Martin–St-Jean. A short walk down Rue des Cuisiniers (which turns into **Rue Bienvenu**) takes you to the spectacular west front and main entrance of the **cathedral**. Begun in the mid-11th century, it was completed rapidly under the patronage of Odo de Conteville, and consecrated in 1077. At around the same time Odo also commissioned the Bayeux Tapestry, to hang inside it. The building was damaged by a fire in the next century – which the tapestry remarkably escaped – and was subsequently rebuilt and altered at several different times, and so, like so many medieval cathedrals, is a mixture of eras and styles. Foremost among them are its original Norman Romanesque, and 13th-century Gothic.

The essential basis of the west front is in the two immense towers on either side, survivors from Odo's cathedral, with Gothic details all around them in the portal in between and the spires on top. If you walk all the way around the back of the cathedral you can also see the dramatic 13th-century Gothic flying buttresses around the apse. One of the last major sections added to the cathedral was the 15th-century central tower, on top of which there is a rather odd 19th-century dome, which is about the only part of the whole building that doesn't really fit. Inside, the nave is all tremendous Norman simplicity, a superbly serene space. The majestic main arches and giant pillars of the transept are largely unchanged since Odo's time, while the upper levels and parts of the vaults were added in a harmonious, unelaborate Norman Gothic style in the 13th century. The nave is celebrated for its Norman-Romanesque carving, which is wonderfully simple, including long friezes of intertwined foliage and leaf designs running above the arches. The apse and chancel are a more intricate example of fine Norman Gothic, and contain some restored wall paintings of early Bishops of Bayeux and some beautiful 16th-century glass. The woodwork, in contrast – the high altar, the choir stalls, the giant pulpit – is high

Baroque and mostly from the 18th century. One of the most atmospheric parts of the cathedral is the beautifully plain 11th-century crypt, with some curious 15th-century frescoes of angels and the delicately sculpted tomb of a canon from the same era.

As you leave the cathedral, look across Rue Bienvenu at the superb old 16th-century half-timbered house at no.6, known as the **Maison d'Adam et Eve**. It is so-named because of the wonderful carvings on its upper storeys, including a very coy-looking Adam and a more provocative Eve either side of the Serpent entwined around a tree. It is now home to the **Conservatoire de la Dentelle de Bayeux** (open Mon–Sat 10–12.30 and 2–6, closed Sun), the Lacemaking Conservatory, dedicated to maintaining one of the town's most historic crafts, the making of bobbin lace, in the traditional manner by passing it on from one lacemaker to another. The art – traditionally 100 per cent female – had in fact virtually died out, but has been revived by studying antique lace and initiatives such as the conservatoire. Open to all, the centre provides a range of long- and shorter-term courses, and visitors can watch lacemakers at work, hunched over their tiny pieces surrounded by pins, bobbins and threads. There's an exhibition on the history and techniques of lace and a permanent display of superb, exquisite pieces, both antique lace and sometimes radically innovative modern lace work, and a shop, with equally beautiful work by students at the conservatoire for sale.

On the north side of the cathedral is the tiny Rue de la Chaîne, which contains the 18th-century former Bishop's Palace, which is normally meant to house Bayeux's art museum, the Musée Baron Gérard. This, though, has fallen foul of one of France's interminable museum-renovation schemes, which is not due for completion until 2008, and until then the museum has been partly transferred to the Hôtel du Doyen a couple of streets away (see below). Do not miss, though, the lovely courtyard between the palace and the cathedral, shaded by a magnificent plane tree that began life as Bayeux's 'Tree of Liberty', provocatively planted outside the old Bishops' Palace by Revolutionaries in 1797.

The **Hôtel du Doyen** on Rue Leforestier was also once one of Bayeux's many ecclesiastical buildings, an impressive 18th-century complex that once housed a convent, a seminary and diocesan offices. Currently it is serving as a 'temporary home' ('temporary' here meaning several years) for the **Musée Baron Gérard** (open Sept–June daily 10–12.30 and 2–6; July and Aug daily 10–12.30 and 2–7; adm; joint ticket with Bayeux Tapestry). This is one of the oldest of France's local museums, and, like many, is a curious, often engaging mixture. The temporary exhibition in the hôtel concentrates on keeping on show the museum's large painting and porcelain collections, with a few items and oddities in other fields. The Baron Gérard's paintings include some minor Renaissance Italian works and a surprising portrait of Sir Thomas More from the school of (but not by) Holbein, but the greater part of them are by lesser-known French, and especially local, painters from the 17th to the 19th centuries. A bit more familiar are the works from the Impressionist era, including a lovely group portrait by Gustave Caillebotte, some nature paintings by the local artist Albert de Balleroy (see p.291), a few Boudins and a very small Corot (all French local museums have a Corot). The porcelain collection showcases the work of the factory that produced porcelain in Bayeux from 1812 until 1951, in attractively simple designs that would sell well today, had the company not gone bankrupt in the crisis after the Second World War. The museum's other possessions include marquetry furniture, Gallo-Roman artefacts excavated nearby, Bayeux lace and historical curiosities like a cabinet on the introduction of the metric system by Revolutionary France, but how many will be viewable while the renovation continues is unpredictable.

Another museum is on Rue des Bourbesnour, a little to the west, the **Mémorial Général de Gaulle** (*open mid-Mar–mid-Nov daily 9.30–12.30 and 2–6.30; adm*). De Gaulle came to Bayeux a few days after it was freed from the Germans and made his first speech on liberated French soil here on 14 June 1944, speaking to an ecstatic crowd from the Sous-Préfecture in the large, park-like square just to the west. Now **Place Charles de Gaulle**, it marks the site of Bayeux's castle, and so was previously Place du Château. The General returned here two years later, to make another speech in which he put forward his ideas for the Constitution of the post-war Republic. All these events and others associated with De Gaulle are recorded with due reverence in his Bayeux museum, but for non-Gaullists its main interest is usually that it is housed in the **Hôtel du Gouverneur**, the residence of the royal governors of Bayeux under the *Ancien Régime*. Built in the 15th and 16th centuries, it is one of the most baronial of all the town's old stone mansions, with a truly spectacular watchtower that is wider – due to strange little 'annexes' having been added – at the top than it is at the bottom. From the *Mémorial* or Place de Gaulle a short walk through the streets to the south will take you to Bayeux's main 1944 war museum, the **Musée-Mémorial de la Bataille de Normandie** and the British war memorial and cemetery (*see* pp.266–7).

This leaves till last the town's great jewel, the **Bayeux Tapestry** (*open daily mid-Mar–April and Sept–Oct 9–6.30; May–Aug 9–7; Nov–mid-Mar 9.30–12.30 and 2–6; closed 25 Dec, 1 Jan and one week Jan; last admission 45mins before closing time; adm; joint ticket with Musée Baron Gérard*). Nowadays it is excellently presented in the **Centre Guillaume-le-Conquérant**, in a former seminary, just east of Rue Larcher and the river. A decent visit to the tapestry will require at least two and a half hours, and can easily take more. It includes an audiovisual display, a film, shown alternately in French and English, and an extensive exhibition on the historical background, which you can visit before you enter the tapestry room itself. It can seem a lot, but the presentation is very imaginatively done, and in fact is pretty much a model of how to illustrate a historical artefact and make it as accessible as possible without trivialising it; only the film, with its sentimental account of William the Conqueror's illegitimate birth and his mother Arlette the tanner's daughter (*see* p.258), is a little silly. The exhibition, based on a timeline, leaves you fully informed by the time you actually reach the tapestry, where an excellent audio guide (available in English and several other languages) will take you through it scene-by-scene. It is kept in dim light for its own preservation, but its colours are still remarkably vivid.

The Bayeux Tapestry is the kind of historical artefact that can seem very familiar, but becomes all the more impressive when seen close up. Strictly speaking it is an embroidery, not a tapestry. It was commissioned by Bishop Odo for his new cathedral at some time between 1066 and his imprisonment in 1082, and is mentioned in cathedral inventories from the 15th century as still hanging around the nave, above the main arches. In France it has often been referred to as *La Tapisserie de la Reine Mathilde*, because of a belief that it had been commissioned by William the Conqueror's queen Matilda, but this is no longer given any credit. Little is known with certainty about exactly where and how it was made, but because of similarities in style between the tapestry and Saxon embroideries it is now believed that it was made by nuns in England and then brought to Bayeux.

Odo commissioned the tapestry to flatter his half-brother William and as a monumental piece of propaganda, presenting the Normans' justification for their invasion of England. Functioning like an early comic strip, it tells its story with great narrative drive, and a remarkable visual rhythm. The central thrust of the first half is to justify William's claim to the throne of England, by putting forward emphatically the Normans' claim that his rival Harold of Wessex had previously agreed to support William's rights himself. The childless old king Edward the Confessor is shown sending Harold as an ambassador to Normandy; his ship is blown off course and lands somewhere near Saint-Valery-sur-Somme, where he is taken prisoner by the Count of Ponthieu, but William ransoms Harold and welcomes him to the Norman court. Harold then accompanies the Duke on a campaign in Brittany, where he fights bravely, saving Norman soldiers from drowning in the Bay of Mont Saint-Michel. The two become friends, and – according to the Tapestry, although Harold would certainly have denied it – Harold swears an oath on holy relics in Bayeux to become William's vassal and support him as King of England when Edward dies; thus, the Tapestry states, by subsequently claiming the throne for himself Harold was in 11th-century terms breaking a sacred bond and committing a heinous blasphemy. By standing up for his own rights against this devil William was even doing God's work for him. Having made clear William's claim, the tapestry gets on with recounting the story of the invasion preparations, the voyage and the landing at Pevensey, leading up to the final scenes of the Battle of Hastings, depicted with enormous energy and realism, right down to the peasants stripping the bodies of the dead.

Perhaps the greatest fascination of the tapestry, however, is in all the incidental details of 11th-century life that appear along the way – the way that ships are built, or the sailors hitching up their tunics as they jump on to the beach. The main narrative panel that runs along the middle of the long cloth strip is flanked at top and bottom by separate lines of panels, which become cleverly intertwined with the main story towards the end as the conflict becomes more and more intense. In them there are mythological scenes, real and imaginary animals, scenes of peasant life and farming in the different seasons, and all kinds of other details that make it vividly human. The Saxon English are shown with long red moustaches, just as they still are in Astérix cartoons. There are just four women in the Bayeux Tapestry: one is Eve, naturally shown with Adam and the Serpent, another may be a servant, dimly glimpsed at the foot of the bed of the dying King Edward, while another is a Saxon woman seen fleeing her house as it is burnt by Norman soldiers, an eternal image of war. The fourth is the mysterious *Aelfgyva*, in scene 15, who some claim was William's daughter, promised in marriage to Harold, although others say she's a purely incidental figure involved in some sort of illicit behaviour with a priest.

Shopping

Bayeux's main weekly **market**, in Place St-Patrice (*Sat*), is an excellent place to pick up local produce. There is also a smaller market on Rue St-Jean (*Wed*). Bayeux also has an assortment of antique shops, most of them along Rue St-Jean or Rue St-Martin.

Bayeux ✉ 14400

Cave St-Jean, 65 Rue St-Jean, **t/f** 02 31 10 16 69. This sizeable traditional wine and drinks shop has a well-varied selection of fine French wines at decent prices, and more Norman specialities such as ciders, calvados and *pommeau*. *Open Sun am; closed (Oct–Easter) Mon.*

Cidre et Calvados Les Remparts, 4 Rue Bourbesneur, **t/f** 02 31 92 50 40, *cidrelecornu@wanadoo.fr*. Proof that Bayeux is a very, very tranquil town is that it contains Normandy's only urban cider *caves*. The orchards are actually on the edge of town, but M François Lecornu's cellars are in the centre, in a big 17th-century stone house in one corner of the Place de Gaulle. Inside, great barrels of calvados are gently maturing, and he also produces fine ciders and apéritifs. Tastings are free, and you can tour of the cellars (they are very used to English-speakers). The Lecornus also have a very attractive B&B, **Logis Les Remparts** (*see* p.285). *Caves open April–mid-Oct Tues–Sun 10–8, mid-Oct–Mar 10–1 and 5–8.*

Au Comptoir des Saveurs, 45 Rue St-Martin, **t/f** 02 31 21 57 99. A delightful little shop with the complete range of Norman delicacies and specialities, beautifully displayed – cider, calvados, *pommeau*, liqueurs, jams and preserves, pâtés, handmade chocolates, biscuits and more. Exquisite gift baskets can be made up to order, with your personal selection. *Closed four weeks in Jan–Feb.*

Naphtaline, 16 Parvis de la Cathédrale, **t** 02 31 21 50 03, *www.naphtaline-bayeux.com*. Opposite the cathedral, this pretty if twee shop specializes in high-quality reproductions of Bayeux's most traditional crafts – tapestries, embroidery, porcelain and lace, in many different designs. Tapestry cushions and lace-trimmed table linen are especially popular. *Closed Jan and Feb.*

Where to Stay

Bayeux ✉ 14400

Grand Hôtel de Luxembourg-Hôtel de Brunville, 25 Rue des Bouchers, **t** 02 31 92 00 04, *www.bestwestern.fr* (*rooms and suites €99–230*). Bayeux's historic premier hotel, in an elegant 18th-century *hôtel particulier*, has since the 1990s been affiliated to the Best Western chain, and has expanded to incorporate the almost as distinguished **Hôtel de Brunville**, 9 Rue Genas Duhomme, **t** 02 31 21 18 00 (*rooms and suites €68–220*), around the corner. There are 61 rooms between the two buildings; those in the Luxembourg are pretty opulent, those in the Brunville are smaller and a bit plainer. Both buildings have been refurbished and while some of the resulting renovation is fairly bland, facilities are luxury standard. Both hotels have large, smart restaurants (*menus €13–34*). *Closed three weeks Jan.*

Hôtel Churchill, 14–16 Rue St-Jean, **t** 02 31 21 31 80, *www.hotel-churchill.com* (*double rooms €60–122*). Standing four-square in the middle of Bayeux, this popular former coaching inn has been catering to visitors to the town and the Normandy beaches for many years. Recently, new owners Rima and François Hébert have set about renovating the old place, bringing a fresh approach and spruced-up rooms to add to the hotel's character. The 31 rooms vary in size, but all are attractive and comfortably equipped, and several at the back have great views of the cathedral. Staff are very helpful to their (many) English-speaking guests. It couldn't be more central, but there's also ample free parking, in the square at the back of the hotel. *Closed Jan.*

Hôtel d'Argouges, 21 Rue St-Patrice, **t** 02 31 92 88 86, *dargouges@aol.com* (*double rooms €51–130*). A strikingly elegant, very comfortable hotel in the 18th-century former mansion of the Argouges family, in its own large garden on the west side of Bayeux, near the market square. The 28 rooms are divided between the main house, and an also-18th-century but less grand house behind it in the garden. They combine modern comforts with old château style and many period features, and have great charm, the best rooms have views of the lovely walled garden. The lounges and breakfast room are quite palatial, and the staff are very charming, too. There's no restaurant.

Le Petit Matin, 2bis Rue de Quincangrogne, **t/f** 02 31 10 09 27, *www.fleurs-soleil.tm.fr* (*rooms €60 for two*). A very charming B&B in a venerable townhouse in the middle of Bayeux (Rue Quincangrogne is a tiny alley off Rue de la Jurisdiction). Owner Pascal Lebret has three guest rooms, all very comfortable, and individually decorated with style. The lounge, breakfast room and little walled garden are just as pretty. Convivial **evening meals** (*€20*) can be arranged as well. M Lebret makes everyone feel at home, and it's a very relaxing place to come back to after a day's sightseeing.

Logis Les Remparts, 4 Rue Bourbesnour, **t/f** 02 31 92 50 40, *www.bayeux-bandb.com* (*rooms €50 for two, €80–100 for four*). Christèle Lecornu, wife of Bayeux's cider-maker François (*see* p.284), is in charge of this enjoyable B&B, very central but overlooking the green expanse of Place Charles de Gaulle. They have three very comfortable rooms, with excellent bathrooms, in an old townhouse above their cider caves. Each has a different, attractive colour scheme; two have a double and a single bed in each, one is a 'family suite' with space for up to four. Breakfasts are generous, and, of course, there's always plenty of cider available. It's very good value, and very popular, so book well ahead.

Relais de la Liberté, 22 Rue des Bouchers, **t** 02 31 92 67 72, *anthony.voidie@wanadoo.fr* (*rooms €30–38 for two, €70 for four, breakfast extra*). This pleasant little guest house is only a short way north of Bayeux's main street, but quaint old Rue des Bouchers is very tranquil. Its four rooms are a real bargain: three are doubles, one is a family room with space for up to four. There's a little garden at the back of the house, and the owners are charmingly easygoing.

Family Home, 39 Rue Général de Dais, **t** 02 31 92 15 22, *www.fuaj.org* (*dormitory beds €18–20 per person, double rooms €30, breakfast included*). A curious combination, in a lovely old 17th-century house just off Place de Gaulle. It is an official youth hostel, but its 31 rooms come in all kinds of sizes, with from one to seven beds, and with varying facilities, from shared showers to private bathrooms. Some of the double rooms (notably nos. 17 and 18) are characterful old rooms with bathrooms and furnished with antiques, and an extraordinary bargain; others are much plainer, but they're still bright, well-cared for and good value. There's no difference in price, and Mme Lefèvre usually allocates them on a first-come, first-served basis. Everyone tends to be drawn a little into the hostel atmosphere, especially if you have **evening meals** (*€12*), served at a long communal table. Its fans, though, love the place, and M and Mme Lefèvre also organize a range of bargain minibus tours around the region for budget travellers.

St-Vigor-le-Grand ✉ 14400

Le Hameau Caugy, 2 Rue Bienvenu, **t/f** 02 31 92 09 39 (*room €35 for two, €55 for four*). A typically big, imposing Bessin stone farmhouse, with a tranquil, rural atmosphere, but only just outside Bayeux's boulevards off the road to Courseulles. There's just one B&B room, but it's huge, with space for four and a lovely sitting area (with TV); it gets light from two sides, with an independent entrance and French doors onto a delightful garden. The décor is brightly imaginative and makes the most of the building's time-worn features, and the bathroom is high-standard. Ideal as a family room, it can be booked just as a double, and is remarkable value. Owners M and Mme Suzanne are quietly friendly, and can babysit for guests.

Subles ✉ 14400

Moulin de Hard, **t** 02 31 21 37 17 (*rooms €70 for two*). Three beautiful B&B rooms in a wonderful 18th-century stone mill, which has been carefully and imaginatively restored by owners M and Mme Porcher using natural materials. Two are doubles, one has twin beds, and each room has its individual character. Alongside the mill there's a rushing water-race and a bright little private river – where guests can fish – and there's an equally lovely, very colourful garden. Subles is about 6km south of Bayeux, off the D572 St-Lô road.

Eating Alternatives

There is a string of cheapish brasseries, crêperies and bistros, some of which open relatively late, spread out along Rue St-Jean and Rue St-Martin.

Bayeux ✉ 14400

Le Coline d'Enzo, 2–4 Rue des Bouchers, t 02 31 92 03 01 (*menus €21.50–41.50*). A recent addition to Bayeux, this neat restaurant has quickly become established as the town's foremost gourmet eating spot, at suitable prices. There's nothing Italian about chef Nicolas Marie's cooking – the restaurant's name is actually a combination of the names of his daughter and his brother; rather, he combines Norman traditions, *haute cuisine* and modern global influences. Many of his dishes are especially intricate, particularly in the top-range menus, with creations such as a *millefeuille* of sea bream *compôtée façon bouillabaisse* with onions and fennel and served with aïoli; even simpler dishes are impressively distinctive. Décor is modern and understatedly elegant. *Closed Sun and Mon.*

Le Petit Bistrot, 2 Rue Bienvenu, t 02 31 51 85 40 (*menus €15–25*). Right opposite the cathedral, this atmospheric little restaurant has an unusually varied range of Norman dishes, and particularly good fish and seafood. The chef describes himself as an *artisan cuisinier*, and dishes are prepared with care: first courses might include a rich fish soup or a delicious mixed *salade gourmande*, followed by fillets of sea bream or *magret* of duck. It's truly tiny, so book. *Closed (Sept–June) Sun and Mon.*

L'Assiette Normande, 5 Rue des Chanoînes, t/f 02 31 22 04 61 (*menus €11–29.50*). A popular, moderately touristy restaurant a short walk from the cathedral and the tapestry, with a generous, good-value range of food that covers plenty of options, from excellent, very big mixed salads with lots of good ingredients to meaty Norman classics like chicken in a cider sauce, more refined dishes like sea bass roast with cider and theatrical favourites such as baked apples flambéd in calvados. Service is charming. *Closed Mon and (Sept–June) Tues.*

Le Petit Normand, 35 Rue Larcher, t 02 31 22 88 66 (*menus €17.50–24.50*). A straightforward bistro that's hard to beat on value: there's a big range of satisfying one-course dishes such as omelettes with a variety of fillings, different mixed salads and steaks (*from c. €6*), and generous set menus. The basic menu might include *entrecôte au poivre* or salmon in a fruity wine-based sauce; to drink, there's local cider as well as a practical range of wines. *Open daily; June–Sept open continuously noon–11pm.*

Lowenbrau-La Taverne des Ducs, 41 Rue St-Patrice, t 02 31 92 09 88 (*menus €14.50–31*). A big and busy brasserie overlooking Bayeux's market square, a fine place to call in for Saturday lunch. It's bright and a bit brash, but at its booth tables you can sample a full range of brasserie staples like *moules* several different ways, onion soup, or meat and fish grills, and there's a big choice of beers.

La Fringale, 43 Rue St-Jean, t/f 02 31 21 34 40 (*menus €12.90–25*). Of the many restaurants, brasseries and other eating-places along Rue St-Jean, the Fringale is most recommended by locals. The set menus and sizeable *carte* offer a mix of Norman classics – *magret de canard au cidre*, *moules à la crème* – with brasserie staples like meat and seafood grills and a good range of snacks and salads. It's bright – the lighting could not be called subtle – and comfortable, and at the front there's a popular terrace for watching locals and all the tourists go by. *Closed Wed and mid-Dec–mid-Feb.*

Le Pommier, 38–40 Rue des Cuisiniers, t 02 31 21 52 10 (*menus €10.50–25.50*). This pretty little place by the cathedral is quite touristy (there's a *menu D-Day*), but offers an interesting variety of truly Norman dishes using all-local produce. It's well used to catering to non-local tastes, and has plenty for kids and a short vegetarian menu (*€15.75*). *Closed (Sept–June) Tues and Wed.*

La Cassonade, 35 Rue Bienvenu, t 02 31 92 47 32 (*dishes c. €8–15*). A popular, enjoyable *crêperie* on a corner next to the cathedral, with all the standards – sweet crêpes with fruit, ice-cream and chocolaty fillings, a good range of savoury *galettes* – and some nicely varied salads and larger dishes. *Closed Mon eve and Tues.*

Norman Heartland:
Balleroy and the *Pré-Bocage*

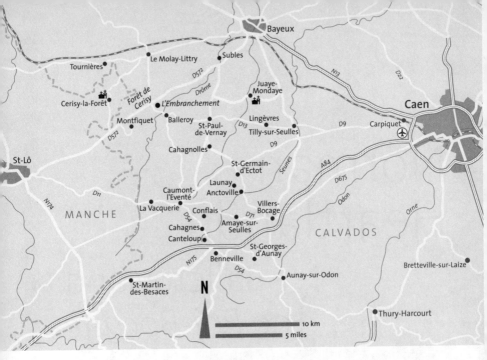

France is a country of villages, French politicians used to say with a rhetorical flourish, of villages and small towns. This isn't nearly as true as it used to be, but a glance at any map will show that there are still enormous areas of the country with no major cities, holes between the main highways occupied by lace-works of lanes and tiny places with curious names. Some are famous as places of beauty, while others have few associations and can come as a complete discovery; and in between the lanes and villages there are patches of almost untouched countryside.

The 50-mile-wide stretch of land between Bayeux, Caen and St-Lô is one such region, with no great centre but a string of engaging small towns and innumerable old Norman villages. In landscape it's a transitional area with plenty of contrasts, from forest and the rolling plain of the Bessin in the north to twisting valleys, hedges and ever-steeper inclines further south. The fields are larger, the hedgerows usually less all-enclosing and the vistas more open than in the true Normandy *bocage* country to the west, and so this area is known as the *Pré-Bocage*. Even so, there are still many villages and farms that seem near-completely hidden and lost amid its dips and bends, and a great deal of gentle beauty.

To the north there is a broad stretch of natural beech forest, the Forêt de Cerisy, which is wonderful for walks, next to one of the most impressive but least-known of early Norman abbeys, at Cerisy-la-Forêt. As one of the more lush and garden-like parts of Normandy, the area just north of the *Pré-Bocage* was also deemed a suitable place for the aristocracy of the *Ancien Régime* to build their country residences, and at Balleroy there is one of the most elegant of French 17th-century mansions, now owned by the American Forbes family. In 1944 the *Pré-Bocage* was one of the areas that saw the most bitter fighting in Normandy, and places like Tilly-sur-Seulles and Villers-Bocage still carry powerful resonances from that time.

Getting There

From the Caen ring road – meeting point for the road from Ouistreham and all roads from Paris and further east – the A84 *autoroute* runs southwest, passing just south of Villers-Bocage. A more direct and more placid route to Balleroy itself is to take the Carpiquet airport turn off the ring road, onto the D9-D13 via Tilly-sur-Seulles. From Bayeux, the D572 St-Lô road passes north of Balleroy. A familiar landmark in this area is the *Embranchement*, the crossroads (with no village) in the Forêt de Cerisy where the D572 and roads to Balleroy, Le Molay-Littry and Cerisy-la-Forêt all meet.

To get to the Manoir de la Drôme from Bayeux, turn left at the Embranchement, and as you drop into the dip at the entrance to Balleroy the restaurant is on the left. From

Caen and Tilly you enter the village on the opposite side, by the main approach: turn right at the castle and the Manoir is at the bottom of the dip on the right.

The nearest mainline **train** station is Bayeux. A few trains on the Bayeux–Cherbourg line still stop at Le Molay-Littry. Calvados **Bus Verts** buses run from Bayeux or Caen, but to explore any further you really need a car or bike.

Tourist Information

Aunay-sur-Odon: Place de l'Hôtel de Ville, **t** 02 31 77 60 32, *otpb@tiscali.fr*.
Caumont-l'Eventé: Place St-Clair, **t** 02 31 77 50 29, *otpb@tiscali.fr*.
Villers-Bocage: Place Général de Gaulle, **t** 02 31 77 16 14, *otpb@tiscali.fr*.

As a truly rural place the *Pré-Bocage* is naturally an excellent area for discovering food products of the Norman *terroir*. Before beginning any exploration, get one of various leaflets from tourist offices indicating the *Route des Traditions*. Their purpose is ostensibly to guide people to local farm producers, but the real object seems to be to take you down some of the narrowest, most winding and most cavernous lanes in Normandy, and get you utterly lost. The *route* winds its way with no obvious rhyme or reason between villages that sometimes seem to be properly named, and sometimes do not, and other places where there are names but no villages. But, at the end of the roads you discover wonderful ciders, breads and honeys.

The modest restaurants of the *Pré-Bocage* tend to serve straightforward, enjoyable, traditional Norman cooking. This is France, though, where refined cuisine also turns up even among the woods and fields. And in Balleroy, suitably close to the château, there is one of the premier restaurants in the whole of Normandy, M Denis Leclerc's **Manoir de la Drôme**, in a pretty old stone house in a garden beside the River Drôme.

Manoir de la Drôme

129 Rue des Forges, Balleroy, **t** *02 31 21 60 94, denisleclerc@wanadoo.fr. Open Tues and Thurs–Sat 12.15–2 and 7.15–8.30, Sun 12.15–2; closed Mon, Wed and two weeks Jan–Feb, one week late Oct–Nov. Menus €45 and €60; carte average €65.*

The northern arm of the 'T' that is François Mansart's design for Balleroy village runs away from the château down a long incline towards the River Drôme. The Manoir de la Drôme is to the right just before the river, shrouded by trees and down a short driveway. It isn't really a *manoir*, and looks as much like a large, well done-up country cottage as a restaurant. Around it there is a very pretty, flower-filled garden, with a lawn where some tables are set up in summer. Inside, the dining room has a certain air of being in somebody's house, together with other touches that are very much those of a first-class restaurant, such as the smooth welcome provided by Mme Leclerc and her waiting staff. With a view of the garden through French windows, it's tranquillity itself, and extremely comfortable; combined with the luxurious food that you're about to enjoy, it all adds up to a little bathe in well-being.

Your eating experience begins with the little bowl of appetizers on the table as you sit down: at first it's quite hard to make out what they are, but they're actually cloves of garlic, blanched and marinated for a long time in balsamic vinegar to give a new, fabulously delicate flavour (a house speciality, they're pretty addictive, but little pots of them can be bought on the way out to take away). The pleasures continue with two sets of *mises-en-bouche*-proper, which immediately let you know that Denis Leclerc is not a chef hesitant about vigorous flavours: perhaps some little biscuits with dates, cheeses and pickles perfectly matched by a slice of strong, wood-smoked Norman ham, and then poached quails' eggs with a tiny but delicious *emincé* of courgettes with surprising tones of garlic and turmeric. At around the same time, the waiter arrives to present the refined wine list – including an unusually good choice of *fine-cru* half bottles – with a suitably devoted hush.

The menu itself is highly sophisticated, describing a range of intricate dishes: subtle creations with local fish and seafood are particular specialities, as in langoustines sautéd with spices and cocoa liqueur, or a fricassee of sole with foie gras and shallots. However, M Leclerc is the kind of French chef whose dedication to fresh ingredients knows no bounds, and so he also seems to make up much of his menu on the hop, according to what's fresh that day. A big, expansive man, he emerges at some point to take the orders himself, which is when he'll tell you about all the day's specials. And it seems only sensible to follow his recommendations.

A first course might be lobster removed from its shell, cooked in a sauce of its own *corail* or roe and then returned to the shell and finished with a light gratin, a rich, creamy dish that's also superbly subtle, imbued with a powerful underlying flavour from the *corail*. Main courses include wonderful fresh-fish-of-the-day specials, such as roast John Dory with *girolles*, *trompettes* and other forest mushrooms and served with a little cake of potato purée and bacon, perfectly combining the ideally fresh fish, a light, buttery sauce and the woodland earthiness of the mushrooms. Throughout, dishes have a marvellous depth of flavour, with contrasting tastes and tones often hinted at rather than simply appearing up-front.

The opulent subtleties continue to the end. After the model cheeseboard, which includes two beautifully smooth local *chèvres* and an interesting Camembert marinated in-house in cider and calvados, there arrives the *pré-dessert*, maybe a very refreshing little bowl of two kinds of plums with cinnamon. The wait for the main dessert is worth it, for this is maybe the *coup de grâce* of the whole meal. If there's anything similar to a *gratin* of berries, don't miss it: this is one of the great fruit desserts, with explosively fresh hot berries set against a perfectly light, elusively citrussy gratin, and sometimes served together with extraordinary strawberry and lime sorbets. This is truly sybaritic, special occasion food. If there are some butterflies to watch in the garden as well, then your feeling of euphoria should be complete.

Touring Around

Balleroy is different from all the other villages around it. Most Norman villages date back to the early Middle Ages, and coexist with their châteaux with no great sense of organization or design. Balleroy, on the other hand, was built or rather rebuilt in the 17th century entirely around its grand château, almost like a model village. If you approach it in the intended way, from Caen and the east, you first see the neat, tall façade of the château away in the distance, facing you at the end of a dead-straight road. On either side of this road are two long lines of stone cottages, set back behind lawns interrupted by a few precisely spaced trees, like extras announcing the arrival of the major player. The road continues on between the houses to descend into a steep dip, where it ends at a T-junction with a broad square and, on the opposite side, the ornate gates of the château-proper. It's a remarkable *coup de théâtre*, an eloquent demonstration of the château-builder's wealth and power; enter the village from the north or south and you feel almost as if you're arriving backstage.

The château was built in 1631 by the great François Mansart, one of the most celebrated architects of the era and credited with the invention of the Mansard roof, for Jean de Choisy, Chancellor to Gaston d'Orléans, brother of Louis XIII. Mansart's reconstruction of Balleroy village, a classically French exercise in the remodelling of the world along symmetrical lines, was highly influential in the design of many later projects, including Versailles (much of which was built by his nephew, Jules Hardouin-Mansart). The Choisys retained the estate for the rest of the century despite a few eccentricities, which reached a peak with the transvestite Abbé de Choisy, an author, reluctant priest and notorious figure at the French court, who always wore women's clothing and only agreed to dress as a man when sent off on an embassy to Siam by Louis XIV. The château meanwhile passed to his niece and then by marriage to the Balleroy family, who managed to hold on to it, with the title Marquis de Balleroy, through the Revolution and right up until 1970. Their most notable offshoot was Albert de Balleroy, a 19th-century painter who was a friend of Manet and other Impressionists. He seems condemned to be dismissed as a rich young man who dabbled in painting and could be relied on to bail out his less well-heeled friends rather than be accepted as an original artist, an impression his favourite subjects, animals and hunting scenes painted around his home, have done little to dispel.

So much for history. Balleroy's fortunes took a different turn in 1970, when it was bought by megabucks millionaire Malcolm Forbes, owner of *Forbes Magazine* and many other things, as one of his several homes around the world. He spent millions on restoring the house, and made it a showcase for one of his obsessions, ballooning, with a balloon museum and international balloon-meets. Malcolm Forbes was also a legendary networker – photos at the château show him pressing flesh with every US President from Truman to Bush senior, Henry Kissinger, Elizabeth Taylor and all sorts of other famous faces – and he brought many of his friends and contacts to see his French château. He died in 1990, but his sons Christopher and ex-Presidential hopeful Steve Forbes and the rest of the family still use the house and periodically entertain here lavishly, which gives it a buzz uncommon in more rustic Norman châteaux.

The **Château de Balleroy** (*open mid-Mar–June and Sept–mid-Oct Mon and Wed–Sun 10–6, closed Tues; July and Aug daily 10–6; closed mid-Oct–mid-Mar; adm, last tours 45mins before closing; joint ticket for château and museum, separate tickets also available*) is approached via a precise Le Nôtre-style garden that leads via a small bridge to a courtyard in front of the mansion itself. The house is a pure piece of Louis XIII early French Baroque in brick and stone, with a three-storey central block flanked by lower wings, all beneath Mansard roofs. In a manner that seems exaggerated even for a Baroque creation, the elegant visual effects are all directed to the approach and the façade, as in a theatre set: look at the château from the side and it appears far less well-proportioned, and too tall for its depth. Inside, there's a mixture of rooms that have been very carefully restored and touches of pure ostentation, as if Mr Forbes wasn't quite sure whether he really cared for the house or just wanted to play with it.

The entrance salon has the genuine look of an old château, with animal paintings by Albert de Balleroy. The smoking room is dedicated to him, with more paintings that show him to have been an able, sensuous painter despite his unadventurous themes. The room itself seems very comprehensively restored with Second Empire décor, until you look up and see that the ceiling was painted for Forbes with bright toy-packaging paintings of ... balloons. The ultra-opulent dining room has ornate wooden panelling that originally came from a Parisian *hôtel particulier*, while three bedrooms have been decorated by Christopher Forbes, apparently a great Victorian enthusiast, with a collection of 19th-century artefacts including a bust of the Duke of Wellington. The spectacular **Salon d'Honneur**, on the other hand, has been superbly restored with its original 17th-century Italianate decoration. It has a very fine high-baroque painted ceiling, by Charles de la Fausse, of the *Four Seasons*, while around the walls there is a majestic series of portraits by the Flemish painter Juste d'Egmont of *Gaston d'Orléans*, *Louis XIII* and other members of the Bourbon royal family in the 1630s.

The Balloon Museum, the **Musée des Ballons**, is in a stable block beside the garden, and deals engagingly with every aspect of ballooning from the Montgolfier brothers onwards. The spectacular biannual Balleroy **International Balloon Meets**, when 20 or more brilliantly-coloured balloons float serenely over the château, are held in odd-numbered years, nearly always in June, and one is due in 2005. Behind the château is the large, green **park**, with 3km of pathways that visitors are free to explore, and the peaceful 1651 **chapel**, also by François Mansart, but in a plainer, more traditional style. Balleroy **village** is a tranquil, relaxed, characterful little place, apparently unconcerned with any happenings at the big house, and with pleasant cafés on its grand square.

The road that leaves Balleroy to the north soon enters the **Forêt de Cerisy**, an over-2,000 hectare (5,000 acre) stretch of native deciduous forest (mostly beech) of the kind that's ever harder to find in northern Europe. Within it there are deer and wild boar as well as foxes, badgers and rabbits, and woodcocks, buzzards and various other birds of prey. The forest is not the most organized attraction, as the only information centre is a small hut with some map-boards near the *Embranchement* crossroads on the D572, so for long hikes it's best to get maps in advance. However, there are sign-boards at all the turnings off the forest roads, and the paths are well maintained and clearly marked. A good place to use as a jumping-off point for a walk is the **Maison**

Forestière du Rond-Point, about 2km northwest of the *Embranchement* on the road to Cerisy, a meeting point of several tracks and footpaths, with a parking area. From there, you can walk as far as you like along deliciously quiet, leaf-shrouded paths.

The same road emerges out of the forest into **Cerisy-la-Forêt**, a quiet village with a broad main street where one vehicle seems to pass about every half an hour. A sign points towards one of the least-known but most beautiful sights in Normandy, the **Abbaye de Cerisy-la-Forêt** (*open Easter–Oct daily 9–6.30; guided tours Easter–Sept daily 10.30–12.30 and 2.30–6.30, Oct Sat, Sun and hols 10.30–12.30 and 2.30–6.30; adm*). It is very nearly 1,000 years old: it was founded in 1032 by William the Conqueror's father, Duke Robert the Magnificent, and most of the abbey church had been built by the time William invaded England. It stands in a supremely peaceful location on the edge of the village, with cows and horses grazing in fields around it and grassy slopes on one side that run down to the lovely *étang* or pond that supplied the monks with water and fresh fish. The abbey has had its troubles: it was ransacked by Protestants in 1562, and in the long centuries of decline from its early-medieval peak it suffered many alterations and demolitions, including the destruction of part of the church in the 19th century. The most important parts of it, though, are extraordinarily intact.

Cerisy receives relatively few visitors, so outside of summer weekends you can often have it to yourself. Most of the monastery buildings – the cloister, the refectories, the monks' parlours - were knocked down in the Napoleonic era, but pieces of them and their outline can still be seen in the fields alongside, between the horses. The existing remains consist mainly of the church or **Abbatiale** itself, the **Salle de Justice** or court-room, and the Gothic **Chapelle de l'Abbé**, added in 1260. If you go around by yourself you can only enter the main church, but with the guided tours you also see the other rooms and the chapel, via its curiously romantic little colonnaded staircase. Nearby is an enormous grinding wheel, once used by the monks to prepare their corn. An essential part of any visit is to wander around the outside, on to the green slope, from where you can best appreciate the church's massive perpendicularity and the skill with which its yellow stone walls are buttressed into the hill.

The interior of the Abbatiale represents something close to the quintessence of Norman Romanesque architecture, in all its superb simplicity. It is currently covered in a cream wash, which adds to its rather ghostly tranquillity (recordings of Gregorian chant also play semi-permanently). The nave now has only three of its original seven bays, as the others were demolished as unsafe in the 19th century, but what remains is sufficiently impressive. It rises through three tiers of columns; look out for some Scandinavian-looking carved heads on the capitals of the middle tier. The brilliantly light apse, beyond the Gothic carved wood choir stalls, is unique in Norman architecture in consisting of three levels of windows, leading up to an exquisite vaulted roof.

The church also contains an exhibition on Norman architecture, in Normandy and England, and the *étang*, which has been beautifully landscaped, is now surrounded by a modern sculpture garden with work drawn from all over the world, a surprising juxtaposition with the old abbey that works perfectly. From across the pond you also get a matchless view of the abbey looming up above you, its grand pepper-pot spire pointing skywards, a magical image of millennial serenity.

Both Cerisy and Balleroy were fortunate in that their serenity was relatively little disturbed in 1944, as both were taken by the Allies quite early in the Normandy campaign. The *Pré-Bocage* further south saw intense fighting, as the British army sought to break out of its initial beachhead. Nowhere suffered more than **Tilly-sur-Seulles**. Between 7 and 26 June this little crossroads village was taken and retaken by the British and Germans 23 times, sometimes changing hands more than once in the same day. The local population took shelter wherever they could; some 10 per cent of them died. Finally, British bulldozers flattened its remaining ruins, to prevent them being used as cover in any more German counterattacks and to stop them blocking advancing traffic, and so Tilly became the only place in Normandy to be all-but obliterated in the conflict. Post-war, the only major structure to be rebuilt was the simple little 12th-century chapel of Notre-Dame-du-Val, which now houses the **Musée de la Bataille de Tilly** (*open May and Sept Sat, Sun and hols 10–12 and 1.30–5.30; June–Aug daily 10–12 and 1.30–5.30; closed Oct–April; adm*). This is one of the most affecting of Normandy's war museums, put together mainly by local people and British veterans, and concentrating on individual experiences rather than strategies. Beside the Balleroy road out of Tilly there is a **British war cemetery**, among the 1,224 graves of which is that of the poet Keith Douglas.

South of Tilly the *Pré-Bocage* extends between and over a series of long, roughly southwest-running ridges, the tops of which contain the main towns – none of them really much more than big villages – and are followed by the main roads. **Villers-Bocage** was the scene of one of the most dramatic incidents in the battle on 13 June 1944, when a single German tank across a sunken *bocage* road turned back an entire British Division, a spectacular demonstration of the superiority of Porsche technology. Villers-Bocage was also reconstructed after 1945. It hosts the area's most important market, but apart from that there's no big reason to go there, other than to take a gulp of its small-town Frenchness. **Caumont-l'Eventé** has retained more of its 19th-century architecture and occupies a spectacular location on top of an especially steep ridge, with wonderful views from its small squares. Caumont has a visitor attraction in the **Souterroscope des Ardoisières** (*open Oct–Dec and mid-Feb–April Tues–Sun 10–5; May, June and Sept Mon–Sat 10–5; July and Aug daily 10–6; adm*), a deep limestone cave where guided tours are provided. Southwest in **St-Martin-des-Besaces** there's another small military museum, the **Musée de la Percée du Bocage** (*open May Sat, Sun and hols 10–12 and 2–6, June–mid-Sept Mon and Wed–Sun 10–12 and 2–6; closed mid-Sept–April; adm*), dedicated to the heavy fighting that took place around the village at the end of July 1944 as British troops broke through the *bocage*.

The biggest attraction in this area, though, has to be the countryside between the towns and major roads, and the way it goes on and on and feels so distant from any urban centre. In among its lost cold-comfort farms are many small food producers, including those on the *Route des Traditions*; particularly beautiful among the villages are **Anctoville**, **Cahagnes** and **St-Georges-d'Aunay**, the latter two on the way south towards the third 'big town' of the *Pré-Bocage*, **Aunay-sur-Odon**. It's especially lovely to wander around this area towards evening, when as you top the ridges you're often rewarded with delicious golden sunsets over the woods and hedges.

Shopping

The biggest **market** in the *Pré-Bocage* is in **Villers-Bocage** (*Wed*); others are in **Caumont-l'Eventé** (*Thurs*) and **Aunay-sur-Odon** (*Sat*), and **Balleroy** has a small market (*Tues*). In summer look out for farmers' markets at the **Ferme de Canteloup** and **Le Clos d'Orval** (*see* below). Many farm producers have stalls at one or all of these markets; otherwise, the *Route des Traditions* and other leaflets from tourist offices will help you track them down.

Amayé-sur-Seulles ✉ 14310

Le Clos d'Orval, t 02 31 77 02 87. A beautiful big old farm, reached via several twists and turns off the D71, producing a superb range of ciders, *pommeau*, very refined calvados, cider vinegar, apple juice and jams, that has won many awards. Visitors can sample the product, and look around the extensive *caves* and a fascinating little museum of cider making. The Clos d'Orval also hosts occasional **farmers' markets** (*marchés à la ferme*) in July and August. *Open daily.*

Cahagnes ✉ 14240

Ferme de Canteloup, Village de Canteloup, t 02 31 77 99 47. Buy home-made *rillettes*, terrines, and other poultry products, plus fresh farm chickens, duck or guinea fowl from the Butet family's farm shop, in a tiny hamlet just south of Cahagnes. They also offer farm tours, and host a **farmers' market** for the whole *Route des Traditions* one Sunday in late July. *Open Thurs and Sat 2–6; Fri 1–4.30.*

Ferme du Loterot, Village de Conflais, t 02 31 77 54 08, *www.loterot.com*. As a change from the usual Norman apple drinks, Georges and Claire-France Leveque make their own entirely original calvados-based liqueurs, with names like *crème de calvados* and *Drakking*. As well as being open for tastings and sales they offer tours, by appointment.

La Vacquerie ✉ 14240

Miel Charozé, Le Haut Hamel, t 02 31 77 40 79. Just west of La Vacquerie on the north side of the D11, a sign guides you down a lane that leads, eventually, to the beautiful farm of beekeepers Odile and Roger Charozé, producers of prizewinning honey. Belying its apparent backwoods remoteness it's a stylish operation, and the farm shop has every kind of honey and bee-related product: pollen, beauty products, homemade biscuits and cakes, royal jelly, mead and even honey-based wood polish. Visitors can tour the farm and hives (*free exc large groups*), with a talk by M Charozé (in English if needed), and there's an exhibition on beekeeping, and a picnic spot. *Closed Sun and hols.*

Angora Brigitte Monroty, Route de St-Lô (D71-D11), t 02 31 77 46 85, *http://angoramonroty.free.fr*. A farm dedicated to raising and working with angora rabbits and their wool. Visitors can tour the farm, see an exhibition, and buy raw wool or a big range of angora clothing, from kids' hats and scarves to elegant tops and cardigans. Angora clothes can also be made to measure, and ordered online. *Closed Sun.*

Where to Stay

Cahagnes ✉ 14240

Ferme de Benneville, Benneville, t 02 31 77 58 05, *ferme.benneville@wanadoo.fr* (*rooms €37 for two, €54 for four*). A pretty, convivial farm B&B between Caumont and Aunay. You can just take a room, but generous *table-d'hôte* meals are a speciality (*€15*). M and Mme Guilbert's hospitality is renowned, and they can show you where to walk, ride, fish or play golf nearby. There are four rooms, three with space for up to four. The house is off the N175, east of the junction with the D54 south of Cahagnes; despite the addition of the *autoroute*, it's still very peaceful.

Cahagnolles ✉ 14490

Ferme du Château, t 02 31 22 75 61 (*rooms €38 for two, €60 for four*). A magnificent stone farm in deep countryside – north of Cahagnolles village, on the D99 road – where Francis and Nathalie Simon have two B&B rooms in one of the former farm buildings. Across an ample courtyard from the main house, they've been renovated in a simple, modern style, but are comfortable and very spacious, and each has space for up to four. There's a cosy breakfast room, and a delightful garden. A very tranquil spot.

Montfiquet-Balleroy ✉ 14490

Le Relais de la Forêt, L'Embranchement (D572), t 02 31 21 39 78, *www.relais-de-la-foret.com* (*double rooms €42.90*). The only sizeable building near the *Embranchement* in the Forêt de Cerisy is impossible to miss – a big, curiously motel-like place with stags' heads on the walls, and huge function rooms for the ceremonies of French country life. The rooms are bright and functional, but decent value, and the restaurant (*see* right) is enjoyable. And, it's right on the edge of the forest.

St-Paul-du-Vernay ✉ 14490

La Ferme du Bois, t/f 02 31 21 42 01, *ferme.du.bois@wanadoo.fr* (*rooms €43–46 for two, €65 for four*). Even in a region full of extraordinary old stone farms this one is spectacular, arranged around a beautifully kept courtyard. The *chambres d'hôtes*, both very attractively decorated, consist of one double and a two-room suite. **Evening meals** (*€18*) are served with prior notice. Its setting between St-Paul and Juaye-Mondaye is beautiful, very rural but well-placed for Bayeux and the coast. *Closed Nov–Easter.*

Tournières ✉ 14330

La Ferme de Marcelet, t/f 02 31 22 90 86 (*rooms €36 for two, €56 for four*). A very pleasant B&B in a massive stone dairy farm just outside Tournières, north of Cerisy, with its own signpost down a lane on the south side of the D15. It was originally a fortified manor, parts of which date from the 12th century. The five rooms are extremely cosy, and one big family room is especially lovely. Breakfast is served in the farmhouse kitchen, using lots of the farm's own produce; Mme Isidor also cooks ample **evening meals** (*€18*), with prior notice.

Villers-Bocage ✉ 14310

Hôtel Les Trois Rois, 2 Place Jeanne d'Arc, t 02 31 77 00 32, *www.les-trois-rois.com* (*double rooms €35.50–58*). Villers' classic *Logis* hotel has one of the *Pré-Bocage*'s most renowned restaurants (*see* right), and nine rooms, recently renovated but still with traditional, rather opulent décor. Service is personal, and the hotel has a nicely cosy, old-fashioned feel. *Closed Jan and last week June.*

Eating Alternatives

Montfiquet-Balleroy ✉ 14490

Le Relais de la Forêt, L'Embranchement (D572), t 02 31 21 39 78, *www.relais-de-la-foret.com* (*menus €10.37–24.60*). The big, cheerful dining room at the Relais (*see* left) has the same motel-and-forest-lodge style as the exterior, and is fronted by a sunny terrace (with garden gnomes). It's a friendly, buzzy place, and offers a wide, good-quality choice at modest prices: *flambéd* prawns, *magret* of duck in *pommeau*, or an ample range of brasserie-style dishes and mixed salads.

St-Georges-d'Aunay ✉ 14260

Ferme-Auberge des Saulques, Les Saulques, t 02 31 77 03 51 (*menus €15–27*). In a huge farm that's easy to find on the west side of the D54, a little south of the A13, not far past the turning for St-Georges-d'Aunay, Mme Claudine Louis' *ferme-auberge* offers ample menus of classic local dishes using wonderful fresh produce from the farm itself: *rillettes*, foie gras (a speciality), chicken, guinea fowl or duck *au cidre*, salads, *feuilletés* of *chèvre* or Camembert, and hefty desserts like *teurgoules* and Norman fruit tarts. Booking is essential. *Closed Sun eve and Mon, and two weeks Jan.*

Tilly-sur-Seulles ✉ 14250

Hôtel Jeanne d'Arc, 2 Rue de Bayeux, t 02 31 80 80 13, f 02 31 80 81 19 (*menus €14–€25*). The dining room has big, curving windows overlooking Tilly's crossroads, and there's a little garden alongside. It's a comfortable, lively place, a town meeting-point, and to eat there's traditional local fare – chicken *vallée d'auge*, grilled fish, excellent cheeses. It also has 12 plain **rooms** (*double rooms €57*).

Villers-Bocage ✉ 14310

Hôtel Les Trois Rois, 2 Place Jeanne d'Arc, t 02 31 77 00 32, *www.les-trois-rois.com* (*menus €18.50–48.50*). The restaurant at the Trois Rois has long been renowned as one of the region's best for classic Norman cuisine, from good-value lunches to grand gourmet menus. With traditional décor to match, it has an enjoyably relaxed, small-town feel, and service is charming.

Seafood
on the Rocks:
Barfleur, St-Vaast
and the Val de Saire

28

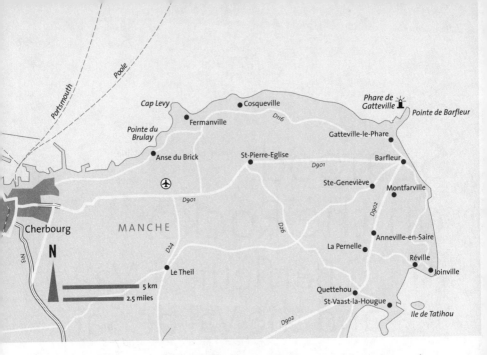

Oysters, mussels, prawns, clams and lobster, and fish such as sole, sea bass and monkfish are the most renowned produce of the northeast Cotentin, the rugged coastline that winds round from Cherbourg to meet the flatlands and beaches of the central Normandy coast. The little harbours around this coast have traditionally had their special assets: lobsters at Barfleur, or oysters, renowned for their unique, vaguely nutty flavour, at St-Vaast-la-Hougue.

The northeast corner of the Cotentin is often known as the *Val de Saire*, after the little river valley that runs through the middle of it, but this soft green valley is not necessarily its most prominent feature. The old fishing harbours of the area are built of granite like the rest of the tip of the Cotentin, grey and severe when the weather sets in, lighter and brighter when the sun appears. Small and full of character, they have an airy tranquillity and relaxed pace that belies their proximity to Cherbourg. They were once centres of much greater activity, closely associated with England: after 1066 Barfleur was the main port linking the two halves of the Anglo-Norman empire, and this coast later saw major battles during the centuries of Anglo-French warfare. Today its harbours are favourite ports of call for cross-Channel yachters.

Between the villages, the shoreline is a succession of rocky headlands, cliffs and crags, interrupted by beautiful little coves and some fine beaches, with great walks and views along the way. Inland, the countryside – in abrupt contrast to the windswept west side of the Cotentin – is surprisingly leafy and lush, with rich pastures and pockets of thick woodland that produce excellent vegetables, beef and hams, which are almost as highly regarded as the local fish and seafood. For a really memorable display of local produce, find your way to **Au Bouquet de Cosqueville** on the north coast, a charming hotel-restaurant above a beach where Eric Pouhier presents food that's a fine blend of first-rate ingredients, skill and inventive flair.

Getting There

The main Val de Saire road from Cherbourg is the D901 straight across to Barfleur (27km), but a more scenic route is the D116 around the coast; to get into it, take the coastal boulevard from Cherbourg harbour and follow signs for *Barfleur par la Côte*. This road runs through Cosqueville, where a sign to *Plage de Vicq* leads to the Bouquet de Cosqueville. From the D901, turn north in St-Pierre-Eglise.

The nearest **train** stations are in Cherbourg, end of the line from Paris (St-Lazare) via Caen, and Valognes. Local **buses** run from Cherbourg to Barfleur and St-Vaast (*Mon–Sat only*).

Tourist Information

Barfleur: 2 Rond-Point Guillaume-le-Conquérant, **t** 02 33 54 02 48, *www.ville-barfleur.fr*.
Fermanville: Place Marie Ravenel, **t** 02 33 54 61 12, *otsi.fermanville@dial.oleane.com*.
Quettehou: Place de la Mairie, **t/f** 02 33 43 63 21.
St-Pierre-Eglise: 23 Place Abbé St-Pierre, **t** 02 33 54 37 20, *tourisme.saint-pierre-eglise@wanadoo.fr*.
St-Vaast-la-Hougue: 1 Place Général de Gaulle, **t/f** 02 33 23 19 32, *www.saint-vaast-reville.com*.

Au Bouquet de Cosqueville

Hameau Remond (Plage de Vicq), **t** 02 33 54 32 81, *www.bouquetdecosqueville.com*. *Open Sept–June Mon and Thurs–Sun 12–2 and 7–8.30, closed Tues and Wed; July and Aug daily 12–2 and 7–8.30. Menus (P'tit Gastro) €13–17, (main restaurant) €19–68; carte average €60.*

The village of Cosqueville sits snugly around the coast road on a rise a little way back from the sea, partly shrouded in hedgerows like most of the Cotentin villages. Partway through the village, a sign points seawards towards the *Plage de Vicq*. Follow it, and about halfway down the hill you will see in front of you a large, well-maintained granite house, with awnings over the windows and a few tables in front, the Bouquet de Cosqueville. Beyond it, the Plage de Vicq is one of the best sandy beaches in the whole of the Cotentin, for walks, paddling or even swimming.

Eric Pouhier grew up only a few kilometres away, and he and his wife Mylène took over the 'Bouquet' in 1987, when they were both in their early 20s. It was then just a basic village bar-*épicerie*, and they have built it up ever since, with a remarkable display of sustained enterprise – adding on the comfortable hotel rooms (*see* p.304), diversifying with cheaper *P'tit Gastro* menus of brasserie-style seafood classics and a *traiteur* catering service for private events. Eric Pouhier is to some extent one of France's self-taught chefs, one who, after his initial training, has largely learnt on the job. This doesn't mean there's anything remotely basic or amateurish about the Bouquet de Cosqueville. The dining room is neat, bright, pretty and easy to settle into, in traditional French style. There's a very large and refined wine list (all French, of course). And the food is outstanding, winning him an ever-growing reputation.

The several main-restaurant menus all begin very properly with an *amuse-bouche*, maybe a roll of *magret de canard séché*, almost a duck concentrate, subtly sweetened with a caramel of *pommeau*. To follow that powerful introduction – given where you are – it really seems you have to go for the *assiette de fruits de mer*. The tool box of hooks, tongs and other implements that's impeccably laid out in front of you lets you know that this is going to be a considerable operation. The *assiette* is a magnificent assembly of half a crab, prawns, shrimps, whelks, periwinkles and St-Vaast oysters, with a superb tang of the sea and all of such fabulous quality that you really don't want to let any part of them get away. It's an ideal dish for a leisurely afternoon, as you make your way through it, taking all the time that's needed, experimenting with this or that piece of cutlery to try and get at that last enticing flake of crab. As the last shells are cleared away, the palate is readied for the next stage with a superior sorbet *trou normand*, an essence of fresh apples combined with very refined calvados.

Main courses might include tuna very precisely pan-fried and served with a classic ratatouille, the kind of dish that can only work with the very best fresh ingredients – the tuna is of course not local, but still of exceptional quality. The menus are tilted towards fish and seafood, but there are also fine meat options, such as boned quails cooked in cider with foie gras, with a strongly robust – but still subtle – country flavour. For cheese, you can choose between a conventional board or a *croustillant* of camembert, with a beautifully delicate crust. Desserts meanwhile demonstrate that Eric Pouhier is not just a fish or meat specialist, with such things as an extraordinary lemon and basil ice cream. This is a meal that's richly and intricately flavoured, but never heavy. And if it's a sunny day, a walk down to the beach makes a perfect sequel.

Touring Around

The D116 coast road runs east out of Cherbourg through a string of little towns, each with their own *plage*, where people take to the sands on hot July weekends. After the houses have thinned out a bit more you reach **Anse du Brick**, a little seaside resort in its own right, where the coast opens up to leave a well-sized beach that's popular with surfers, and which often gets packed in summer. Perched on the cliffs above there's a selection of bars and restaurants, all with the same great view. Sheltering Anse du Brick is **Pointe du Brulay**, the first of several rocky points along this coast, from where there are sweeping views back across the whole of Cherbourg Bay.

At **Fermanville**, the next village east, a road turns off to the left for **Cap Lévy**, with another fine lighthouse and **Fort Lévi**, a Napoleonic-era fortress converted into a special B&B (*see* p.304), above a minute beach and harbour. The cape is another great place for a windswept walk, with a choice of views in two directions, into Cherbourg Bay or back to Barfleur. Like Anse du Brick it's a good jumping off point for the **GR223 coastal footpath**, which can take you – via perhaps a bus ride through Cherbourg – all the way around the Cotentin from Utah Beach to Avranches. From Fermanville it's 4km to **Cosqueville**, where a steeply dipping lane leads down to one of the Cotentin's best restaurants (*see* above) and to one of its best beaches, the **Plage du Vicq**, in a broad inlet, sheltered and windswept by turns, that catches the sun wonderfully on summer evenings. From Cosqueville you can cut back to St-Pierre-Eglise and the D901 and be in Barfleur in about 20 minutes, but if you're not in any hurry it's much more entertaining to continue on the winding D116. The road runs a little inland, through tiny, close-clustered villages between hedges and still-narrower side lanes that run down to the sea, with every so often beautiful views of rocky inlets between cliffs.

Barfleur is a charming little granite fishing port, nowadays with a fair number of yachts and dinghies sharing space with fishing boats in the harbour. There's rarely much traffic to disturb the people chatting in the middle of the street, but partway round the apparently unnecessarily wide arc of the waterfront there's an attractive quayside café, the **Café de France**, where you can grab a table to take in the pre-lunch activity. A squat 17th-century church dominates the vista at the harbour's end, next to a tiny beach amid the rocks where some brave souls occasionally take to the waters.

The population of Barfleur is now around 600. There is little here to indicate that 900 years ago it was well over ten times that number, and that this was then one of the busiest harbours in Europe. William the Conqueror himself first set out from here on his voyage towards Hastings, in his Barfleur-built ship the *Mora*, and it became the Norman monarchs' principal port for communications with their new possessions in England, with constant traffic in both directions. The main street is now named after Thomas à Becket, another frequent traveller, and Richard the Lionheart passed through here in 1194 on his journey back to reclaim his throne after the Third Crusade. Earlier, Barfleur was the site of a famous nautical disaster, in 1120, when the *Blanche Nef* (the White Ship) sank just outside the harbour, taking with it William Aetheling, only son of Henry I, together with several royal bastards and many of the élite of the Anglo-Norman court, church and aristocracy. This was an early incident of Hooray-Henryism: according to the only survivor, a Rouen butcher, passengers and crew were all very drunk, and tried to overtake ships that had left ahead of them, thus straying out of the channel and on to the Barfleur rocks. The death of the King's heir would lead to civil war between Henry's daughter, Matilda, and a rival claimant, Stephen.

The Anglo-Norman empire was the making of Barfleur's brief fortune, and when Normandy was absorbed into France in 1204 its trade and prestige suffered a rapid downturn. Barfleur remained sufficiently significant, however, for it still to be a target for the English in the Hundred Years' War. In 1346 Edward III's son, the Black Prince, landed at St-Vaast and sacked and burnt Barfleur. A few years later came the Black Death, and Barfleur never recovered its stride. By the 16th century it was only a village of some 150 people. More recently, the development of Cherbourg, heavily promoted by Napoleon, definitively consigned both Barfleur and St-Vaast to peaceful obscurity.

Owing to its treacherous rocks, however, Barfleur does have the distinction of possessing France's oldest lifeboat station, opened in 1865, and one of its tallest light-houses, on **Pointe de Barfleur**. A footpath runs all the way to the point (4km) from beside the church on Barfleur harbour. By road or footpath you also pass through the unusual old village of **Gatteville-le-Phare**, with a huge open square alongside one of the most remarkable of Norman churches. Much of it was rebuilt in the 18th century, but it still has its near-unique 12th-century tower, ringed by a strange balustrade, which from a distance can look as much like a fortress or even a mosque as a church. Across the square there is also a tiny sailors' chapel, the **Chapelle des Marins**, built in the reign of Henry I. The **Phare de Gatteville** (*open daily Mar and Oct 10–12 and 2–5; April and Sept 10–12 and 2–6; May–Aug 10–12 and 2–7; Nov–Dec and Feb 10–12 and 2–4; closed Jan; adm*), the lighthouse, is an impressively stark monument, extraordinarily tall and thin, in a wind-blasted spot where the air can clear most headaches. It may be closed, for safety, when gales are up. There is one step up for each day of the year, and those who reach the top are rewarded with wonderful seascapes and views, on a good day, from La Hague in the west round to Grandcamp at the mouth of the Vire.

A short way south of Barfleur is **Montfarville**, one of the most beautifully tranquil of the Val de Saire villages, with leafy, winding little streets that are only just car-width. It too has a very unusual church, built in the 1760s to replace an earlier medieval one, with details in carved stone and wood that seem very grand for a small village. Its great surprise is inside on its vaulted ceiling, decorated in 1879 with vividly coloured paintings on the *Life of Christ* by the locally-born artist Guillaume Fouace. There are lovely walks between Montfarville and the neighbouring villages of **Anneville** and **Ste-Geneviève**. Nearby, a pretty road runs southwards more-or-less along the shore to the **Pointe de Saire**. Once around the point, facing into the Bay of St-Vaast, there are some more good beaches around **Jonville** and **Réville**, with a delicious combination of quiet green countryside, placid mud flats and long, misty views at low tide.

A little inland, across the D902 about halfway between St-Vaast and Barfleur, there is one of the Cotentin's most renowned beauty spots, the remarkable village of **La Pernelle**. Its main street improbably runs almost straight up a near sheer-sided ridge to a little granite church at the top, from alongside which there are limitless views that have been eulogized by a host of literati, over the Cotentin, down the coast and out to sea. This is an ancient pilgrimage site, and in a grotto below the crest there is an image of the Virgin of Lourdes, installed in the 1920s. In the Second World War the heights of La Pernelle also attracted the attention of the Germans, who installed an observation post, which is still there, and a long-dismantled gun battery that in June 1944 caused trouble to the US troops landing at Utah Beach, 30km south. This drew down massive bombardment, and ownership of the hill was fiercely contested. Of the church only the unbreakable 14th-century stone tower really survived, and much of the present building is a reconstruction; in the entrance there's a watercolour, painted by a German prisoner-of-war, showing what the restorers had to work with. There's also a bar-restaurant on the crest (*see* p.306), for studying the view at a leisured pace.

St-Vaast-la-Hougue, largest of the northeast Cotentin ports, is a broad, attractive harbour, quite a lot busier than Barfleur, with plenty of bars and restaurants around the waterfront, and in the centre of the view an eccentric 19th-century **Mariners' Chapel** and imposing granite lighthouse. There's still a sizeable fishing trade, and an unmissable market on Saturdays. The famous **oyster beds** are just south of town, and some open for visits and tastings (*Ets. Lefèvre, 6 Rue des Parcs; guided tours Mon–Fri 8–12 and 2–6; adm*). Almost as prominent a part of modern St-Vaast is the well-equipped marina, well patronized by the French and British yachting communities. South of the port a narrow spit of land runs down to La Hougue point and the dramatic pile of **Fort de la Hougue**, looking as if it rises straight out of the sea, and still a military installation (*open for guided tours only, July–Aug usually Wed, for details contact tourist office*). On either side of the spit there are sheltered coves and beaches.

The seas offshore were the scene of a famous naval encounter, the battle of La Hougue, a clash that saw France's own nautical Charge of the Light Brigade. In 1692 Louis XIV hatched a plan for his greatest admiral, Tourville, to sail with a squadron from Brest, rendezvous with reinforcements from the Mediterranean, pick up 30,000 mostly Irish soldiers encamped at St-Vaast, and carry them across the Channel before the English and Dutch fleets could join together to oppose him. Once there, helped by English Jacobite plotters, they would restore James II to the British throne. However, bad weather prevented the French Mediterranean fleet from making its way up the coast; Tourville pointed out that the same winds would make it easier for the Anglo-Dutch fleet to join forces, but was told not to question the King's orders. Once the Admiral had set sail, Louis received news that, as predicted, the Allied fleet had made their rendezvous, and that the Jacobite conspiracy in England was no more than a damp squib. A boat was sent to call Tourville back, but failed to find him in the bad weather. On 29 May 1692, Tourville with his 44 ships rounded Barfleur point, to find an Anglo-Dutch fleet of 100 ships in front of him. In a scene from romantic literature, the French commanders all agreed the only sensible course was to turn back; however, Tourville read the King's orders to engage the enemy, they accepted they had no choice, and continued to sail onwards, to the amazement of their opponents. To everyone's greater astonishment, in the day's fighting the French actually came off slightly the better. During the night and the next day, though, part of the French fleet was scattered by winds, while the rest took refuge in the unprotected harbours of the Cotentin. The English fleet was able to sail into St-Vaast and set fire to many of Tourville's ships, ending any possibility of a French invasion in support of James II.

Following the battle, somewhat after the horse had bolted, a team of Marshal Vauban's engineers was sent to build defences at Fort de la Hougue and on the low green island of **Tatihou**, which looms in the background of St-Vaast harbour and adds much to the interest of the view. It stayed a military base into the 20th century, but since 1992 has been open to the public. You normally get there by amphibious vehicle, tickets for which are sold at **Accueil Tatihou** on the quay in St-Vaast (*open April–Sept; crossings every 30mins daily 10–5.30, last return from Tatihou 6pm; adm, return boat tickets only and tickets including museum and tower available*). It's advisable to book in summer – there's a limit to the numbers allowed each day – and to arrive early.

As well as a chance to wander around one of the most complete of France's many Vauban-style fortifications, Tatihou offers many other things to do. There's a **maritime museum**, centred around artefacts, from weapons to plates, recovered from ships sunk in the 1692 battle, and a workshop that builds and restores traditional Norman fishing craft. There's a pleasant restaurant (*see p.306*), and free historical and birding tours are available in July and August. Each summer, too, the island hosts a series of exhibitions, theatre shows, concerts and events, especially the **Traversées du Tatihou-Musiques du Large** music festival in August, centred on folk, world and 'maritime' music (*information: www.tatihou.com*). One of the most popular parts of the festival is the *Traversée*, the walk across to the island at low tide (with guides), although you can also get the boat in the normal way. One of Tatihou's primary attractions, though, is just that, since it was kept isolated by the military for centuries, most of it is a pristine expanse of grassy moorland, rocks and dunes, great for walking and a conservation area especially rich in sea birds such as cormorants, terns and gulls. If you stay on the island (*see p.305*), you can see them at sunset and sunrise.

Shopping

The Saturday **market** in **St-Vaast** is by far the best in the area, and for food is one of the best in Normandy. The presence of the holiday and yacht clientele attracts fine food producers from a wide area: particularly excellent, apart from the seafood, are the vegetables, hams and charcuterie, and fresh *brioches* and breads. The fresh flower stalls are beautiful too. **Barfleur**'s market is a more modest affair (*Tues, Sat and Sun*), and there's a country market in **St-Pierre-Eglise** (*Wed*).

St-Vaast-la-Hougue ✉ 50550

Maison Gosselin, 25–27 Rue de Verrüe, t 02 33 54 40 06, *www.maison-gosselin.fr*. Just about anything you can't find at the market you can get in this St-Vaast institution, founded in 1889. Belying its small-town location, this classic *épicerie* has every kind of luxury foodstuff, from many that are exclusive to the shop – pâtés, terrines, coffees, jams, cheeses, chocolates – to others from around the world. There's a renowned wine selection, and a whole room dedicated to calvados and whiskies. And, as a sign in English tells you, they also deliver to boats in the harbour. *Closed (Sept–June) Mon; open Sun am all year.*

Poissonnerie Le Barbenchon, 4 Rue de Verrüe, t 02 33 22 21 00. Some other things you can't find *chez Gosselin* are on sale here, at this multi-prize-winning fishmonger. Even if you don't have a convenient means to take away superbly fresh oysters, lobsters, sea bass or mussels, it's a spectacular display just to see. If you do have a large freezer box, they make up fabulous *plâteaux de fruits de mer*.

Le Theil ✉ 50330

Ferme du Moulin des Corvées, 9 Route de Digosville, t/f 02 33 20 05 46. A large farm deep in the Val de Saire countryside – north of Le Theil village – where Christine and Samuel Brostin produce distinctive fine Camembert, *fromage blanc*, cream and butter. As well as selling direct from the farm, they also have stalls at several local markets. *Open for sales Oct–Mar Mon–Wed, Fri and Sat 2–6, April–June and Sept daily 2–6, July and Aug daily 2-6 and 7.30–9pm.*

Where to Stay

For a beautiful B&B near central Cherbourg (in the suburb of Equeurdreville), *see p.315.*

Barfleur ✉ 50760

Hôtel le Conquérant, 18 Rue St-Thomas-Becket, t 02 33 54 00 82, f 02 33 54 65 25 (*double rooms €34–79.50*). A pleasant hotel in a big, four-square granite mansion, the main parts of which are 17th-century, on Barfleur's tranquil main thoroughfare. There's a beautiful garden at the back, where breakfast can be served in summer. The 13 traditionally-styled rooms offer a good range of comforts, and some have great views over the garden. They vary in size, facilities and price, and the largest, all with garden view, have quite an opulent feel. The Conquérant no longer has a full restaurant, but good-value, light **evening meals** (*menus €13.90–23.50*) are available to residents only, served in a cosy dining room. *Closed mid-Nov–mid-Mar.*

Cosqueville ✉ 50330

Au Bouquet de Cosqueville, Hameau Remond (Plage de Vicq), t 02 33 54 32 81, *www.bouquetdecosqueville.com* (*double rooms €29–50*). The six rooms above the restaurant (*see p.299*) are snugly comfortable, with bright décor. Some are quite small, but the best – with recently-refurbished bathrooms – have wonderful sea views, over one of the Val de Saire's most attractive beaches. It's deliciously peaceful at night, with the waves the only sound.

Fermanville ✉ 50840

Fort du Cap Lévi, 7 Le Cap Lévi, t 02 33 23 68 68, *chambre.fermanville@cg50.fr* (*rooms €60–65 for two*). The fortress at the end of Cap Lévi, built on Napoleon's orders to defend Cherbourg against British attack, has been turned into a very unusual *chambres d'hôtes*, with five guest rooms. Their décor is surprisingly fresh and modern, and they're well equipped and comfortable; those with a (fabulous) sea view cost a little more. Apart from the romantic oddity of the old fort itself, the great draw is the extraordinary location, above all of its breakfast room, in a veranda high on the walls, with truly fabulous 180° views out to sea, just in the right place to catch the sunset. *Closed Jan.*

Gatteville-le-Phare ✉ 50760

La Maison de Fourmi, Village de Roville, **t** 02 33 43 78 74, *http://raymonde.rouland.free.fr* (*rooms €65 for two, €90 for four*). A delightful B&B run with flair by Raymonde Roulland (known as Fourmi) and her husband Joseph, in the minute hamlet of Roville, near the road to Gatteville light-house. Their house, a typical Val de Saire 18th-century granite farmhouse, has been very originally restored: both the Roullands have travelled a great deal, and the four guest rooms, with names like *Indochine* and *Océane*, are decorated with photographs and artefacts from their trips, in a mixture of the local and the exotic. *Indochine* can be rented as a two-room suite, ample for four. There's also a big, pretty garden, where guests can have breakfast in summer.

Montfarville ✉ 50760

Le Manoir, **t/f** 02 33 23 14 21 (*rooms €65 for two; €85 for three*). This sombre-fronted 16th-century granite manor house is beautifully maintained by M and Mme Gabroy, with individual décor, antiques and personal mementos to complement its giant fire-places, and a real air of comfort. The two rooms (one double, one with a side room with extra bed) are large and full of light, and the breakfast room has a sea view; outside, there's a luxuriantly flowery garden. It's about 2km south of Barfleur, and a short walk from the centre of Montfarville village.

Réville ✉ 50760

La Villa Gervaiserie, La Pré St-Martin, **t** 02 33 54 54 64, *www.lagervaiserie.com* (*double rooms €85–109*). For once, not remotely a historic building, but a distinctive all-modern hotel. Instead of looking for venerable walls Gisèle and Alain Travert have made the most of their superb location, right on the shore in Réville, looking across to Tatihou and St-Vaast. All the 10 rooms face the sea and have floor-to-ceiling windows and balconies; in some rooms in this area you get a glimpse of a sea view, but here it seems to invade the whole room. The décor is equally modern,

but comfortable, and facilities are excellent. One room is a very large family room. There's no restaurant, but all rooms are provided with minibar, a corkscrew and glasses, for picnics on the balcony. Mme Travert is very charming and helpful: the area is very popular for riding, and she can direct you towards riding facilities and all other local amenities.

Manoir de Cabourg, **t/f** 02 33 54 48 42 (*rooms €40–45 for two*). One gets used to dramatic old manor houses in Normandy, but this one could almost take a prize for atmosphere. Parts of it are 15th-century, and the entrance to the huge courtyard is via a fortress-like stone archway. The Marie family's main business is breeding horses, and it still feels very much a working farm. There are three *chambres d'hôtes* rooms, all doubles; two are attractive but relatively simple, but one, the *chambre du sire*, is magnificently baronial, with its own giant stone fireplace. Although the farm feels lost in the countryside, it's still just a walk away from the sea.

St-Vaast-la-Hougue ✉ 50550

Hôtel de France–Restaurant des Fuchsias, 20 Rue Maréchal Foch, **t** 02 33 54 42 26, *www.france-fuchsias.com* (*double rooms €29–98*). St-Vaast's classic hotel is snugly tucked into a street running away from the harbour, and offers unchanging comfort. Beyond the pretty entrance patio lies its greatest asset, a delightfully leafy garden, with the eponymous giant fuchsias. Chamber music concerts take place in the garden in August. The rooms are similarly traditional and slightly chintzy, and vary in standard (and price): some of the oldest are a bit cramped, while newer, more spacious rooms in a garden annexe are very airy and comfortable. The restaurant is equally popular (*see p.306*). *Closed Jan and Feb.*

Tatihou, Accueil Tatihou, Quai Vauban, St-Vaast-la-Hougue, **t** 02 33 54 33 33/02 33 23 19 92, *www.tatihou.com* (*rooms €37–46 per person half-board, €47–64 per person full-board*). Tatihou has 34 guest rooms in a former barracks, built in 1818. They're orientated towards groups, but are available to anyone. Full- or half-board is obligatory – logically, as there's nowhere else to eat on the island, and you can't leave after the last boat. Rooms are functional but comfortable, and the great thing is of course the location, location, location. *Closed Oct–Mar*.

Ste-Geneviève ✉ 50760

Manoir de la Fèvrerie, t 02 33 54 33 53, **f** 02 33 22 12 50 (*rooms €55–67 for two*). A hugely impressive old granite 16th-17th century manor house, surrounded by a broad court-yard and gardens, in a quiet village 3km from Barfleur. Mme Marie-France Caillet has three B&B rooms (two doubles, one twin), reached via grand stone staircases. Each of them has been individually and beautifully decorated, with a delightful mix of colours, and every detail taken care of. Mme and M Caillet are very hospitable, and breakfast is served in a magnificent old room with a monumental stone fireplace. A special place to stay, it's very popular, so book well ahead.

Eating Alternatives

Barfleur ✉ 50760

Hôtel Moderne, 1 Place Charles de Gaulle, **t** 02 33 23 12 44 (*menus €18–55*). Long-established as Barfleur's best, the Moderne has picked up new verve in the last few years with the arrival of an adventurous young chef, Frédéric Cauchemez. Menus run from excellent-value lunches to sumptuous gourmet feasts, and his star dishes are notably intricate, combining superb local seafood and produce with innovative seasonings in such things as stuffed squid with wine *aux fines herbes*. Scrumptious desserts are another speciality. Le Moderne is also a tiny **hotel**, with just three comfy, old-fashioned rooms (*double rooms €40–54*).

Montfarville ✉ 50760

Restaurant T'Cheu Suzanne, Rue de la Poste, **t** 02 33 54 04 54 (*menus €11.50–21*). A friendly village bistro-bar-*tabac* in the centre of Montfarville, near the church. The owners speak English, and the bargain menus cater to a wide range of needs – from hearty Norman classics such as oysters, mussels, local smoked ham, fish grills and *jambon au cidre* to light crepes, *galettes* and salads.

La Pernelle ✉ 50630

Le Panoramique, t 02 33 54 13 79, *www.le-panoramique.fr* (*menus €13.90–29.90*). Right next to the church – and the old German bunkers – at the very top of La Pernelle hill, 123m up, this big, modern restaurant natu-rally has giant panoramic windows and an ample outside terrace from which to admire the fabulous, endless view. While you're contemplating infinity you can also choose from a wide range of good-value food – from light brasserie staples like *moules*, crepes, *galettes* and salads to quite elaborate multi-course *menus gastronomiques*.

St-Vaast-la-Hougue ✉ 50550

Restaurant des Fuchsias, 20 Rue Maréchal Foch, **t** 02 33 54 42 26, *www.france-fuchsias.com* (*menus €17–42*). Like the rest of the Hôtel de France (*see* p.305), the restaurant, which extends into the garden, is extremely pretty. The menu is, of course, strong on seafood – local oysters, monkfish, sea bass, turbot in imaginatively light sauces – but fruity desserts are also among the highlights. White-jacketed waiters ensure that everyone leaves feeling comfortably cosseted, and it has a great many devoted British regulars. *Closed Jan and Feb; Mar–June and Sept–Dec Mon.*

Le Débarcadère, Place de Gaulle, **t** 02 33 54 43 45 (*dishes c. €5–12*). A bright harbour-side restaurant-brasserie with a big terrace by the quay, a laidback, buzzy atmosphere and a largely local clientele. Inside, there's a neat little dining area on one side, and a big screen for watching sports on the other. The menu offers plenty of choice, and is a real bargain, including pizzas, a wide range of mixed salads and big plates of *moules-frites*.

Restaurant du Fort-Tatihou, Accueil Tatihou, Quai Vauban, St-Vaast-la-Hougue, **t** 02 33 54 33 33/02 33 23 19 92, *www.tatihou.com*. The café-restaurant on Tatihou has been expanded in the last few years, and offers an enjoyable range of mixed salads, omelettes, crepes and other light meals that go down well after a walk around the island. Evening meals are only provided for people staying in the island's guest rooms (*see* p.305). *Open April–Sept daily 12–3*.

The End
of the World:
the Cap de la Hague

29

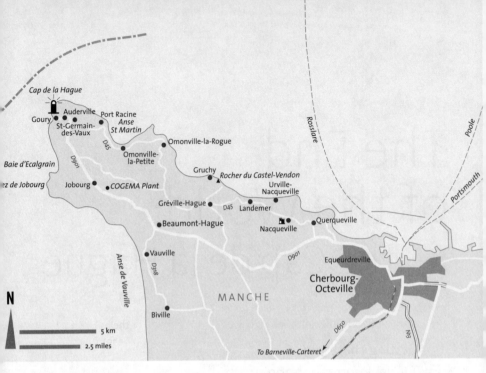

La Hague peninsula is a 15-mile arm of granite reaching out into the sea west of Cherbourg. From the very edge of the city's harbour, you enter a world of increasingly narrow lanes, sometimes virtually enclosed by towering hedgerows, which then opens up into bog and moorland running right to the rim of the massive cliffs that fall away into the surf. Intermittently you come across little huddled grey-stone villages, built to withstand severe weather, that look as if they might house communities of Cornish or Welsh Methodists were it not for the stout old Norman Catholic churches in the middle of each of them.

Another key feature of this landscape is its remarkable and surprising variety, for towards the centre of the peninsula, wherever there are valleys and corners sheltered from the wind, there are microclimates that are often astonishingly lush, soft and leafy. La Hague is exceptionally beautiful when the sun shines, when the wild flowers are out along the cliffs, the light picks up the redness of the heather and you can watch the changing colours of the sea below; it's also a great and wild place to visit even if the weather is less favourable, when giant waves crash against the rocks and the Atlantic blasters are enough to clear anyone's head.

At the very end of the peninsula, where the landscape is at its most rugged, there is a little rocky inlet, long a refuge for endangered mariners, with a lighthouse that looks exactly how a lighthouse ought to look. This is Goury. There is a lifeboat station, a shingle beach, a few boats, about six or seven houses and, sometimes, a van selling sandwiches. There's also a surprisingly large tourist office, for the Cape attracts its share of visitors in summer. Still, it is the sense of isolation that predominates, and this seems an unlikely location for a fine restaurant.

Getting There

There is a relatively quick route from Cherbourg to the end of La Hague, along the D901 road, which runs along the south side of the peninsula and will take you there in about 30–45mins. To make a trip of it, though, it's far better to take the much smaller D45, via a right turn off the D901 on the way out of Cherbourg in Hameau-de-la-Mer (signposted to Querqueville), and then maybe return by the south route. For most of its length the D45 winds along the north side of La Hague, with a few hairpin bends along the way. Most people will want to stop at a few points along the road, but if you drive straight down you should reach the Cape in a little under an hour. Both roads meet in Auderville, the last real village on the peninsula where, on one side of the widening of the roads that could be called the village square, there is a narrow lane signposted to Goury.

Alternatively the energetic can take the **GR223 long-distance footpath** which runs all the way round La Hague peninsula, keeping to the coast. It's clearly marked and easy to find.

The nearest **train** station is in Cherbourg, from where **buses** run a few times daily to Beaumont-Hague, and less frequently to Auderville.

Tourist Information

Beaumont-Hague: Office de Tourisme de la Hague, 45 Rue Jallot, **t** 02 33 52 74 94, *www.lahague.org*
Goury: t 02 33 04 50 26. *Open April–Oct and French school hols.*

Nevertheless, at the centre of the clutch of grey granite cottages is the **Auberge de Goury**, where owner Pascal Retout has presided since the end of the 1970s with amiable hyperactivity, throwing out rapid snatches of conversation to regulars in between attending to some of the cooking and much else. The style is casual and straightforward, but devotees often make their way here all the way from Cherbourg and beyond just for midweek lunch. When the weather's fine you can sit outside and watch the waves; at other times, when the wind is up, stout stone walls and the smell of the log fire on which the grilled fish is prepared, make you feel snug and sheltered, in a place once considered one of the ends of the known world.

L'Auberge de Goury

Port de Goury, **t** *02 33 52 77 01. Open Tues–Sun 12–2 and 7–9.30.*
Closed Mon and three weeks Jan. Menus €15.50–52; carte average €30.

The menu at Goury now carries a poetic note that thanks everyone for coming, whoever they are and however they got here – by car, boat, through fog and Atlantic gales or by trekking along the footpath. This is of course a literary flourish, but once you're inside it does feel a little as if you've reached a refuge on some distant shore. All of which only encourages you to settle in, get comfortable and take your time, which is all to the good, since to be enjoyed properly a meal here can take a while. This is not due to any breakdown in organization, but a reflection of the fact that this kind of food often takes some time to eat, and also that the goodness of the food stems above all from the sheer freshness and quality of the basic ingredients, and the care and attention shown in the individual preparation of each dish. So, if there is any delay, it's as well to accept the offer of, maybe, a glass of champagne or kir and a plate of *crevettes grises*, and sit back at your table or stand at the little wooden bar for a few minutes while examining the décor, the delightful view through the windows, your fellow diners and the lobsters and crabs manoeuvring in their tank.

The existence of an *auberge* in this lonely spot is a story in itself. It was built in 1857 by one Thomas Anquétil and his wife Emélie. At that time, one of the essential means of getting by for the people of La Hague was smuggling goods from the Channel Islands, particularly tobacco, and the Anquétils clearly reckoned – Thomas himself was a farmer by day and a smuggler by night – that smugglers, too, might need a warming meal and a drink. This smugglers' den, though, naturally attracted the attention of the *douaniers*, the customs officers. In winter 1864 Thomas was bringing in a shipment from Alderney when he was ambushed by a customs patrol, and pursued down the coast to Vauville. To escape capture he hid for a whole night on the beach, but caught a severe chill, and died on New Year's Day 1865. Emélie kept on the *auberge*, and a few years later married her nearest neighbour, the lighthouse keeper.

Today the restaurant wears its history lightly. Parts that are genuinely old, such as the main dining room with its plain stone walls and open fireplace, are clearly visible, while alongside them other parts are simple and modern, like the bright extension. Instead of smugglers the clientele are a broad mix – a few foreigners, local couples and families, and groups of workmates who have converged from miles around.

If you eat just one course here it has to be the grilled fish (sea bass, sole, red mullet, turbot, john dory, monkfish, according to what's best that day), cooked by Pascal Retout himself on the wood fire in the main dining room. Tinged with subtle flavours from the wood smoke, it's a revelation of how good simply but perfectly cooked fresh food can be. He uses mainly chestnut and hazel for the fire, and complains that it's increasingly difficult to find wood of sufficient quality, but fortunately seems to be sure of a supply for some time to come. There's always grilled fish (often sea bream) even in the simplest set menu, but this is one restaurant where it's worth making a day of it and going for one of the longer lists – which are still fantastic value.

There are several choices for first course, but the star must be the *assiette du pêcheur*, a giant pile made up of oysters, langoustines, half a large crab, clams, superlative prawns, *bulots* (large whelks), *bigorneaux* (winkles) and other things you may never have seen before, with crustily fresh bread and a bowl of fabulous fresh mayonnaise on the side. This brings you into the meal gradually by forcing you to take

Douillon aux Pommes

The *Douillon Normand* is one of the simplest of the region's many classic fruit desserts, which can equally be made with pears (as a *douillon aux poires*). For each person, take a large green apple, core it, and wrap it entirely in puff pastry; brush with beaten egg, place on a baking sheet and put in a hot oven, at 200°C/400°F/ Gas Mark 6. Cook for 30 minutes or until the pastry is golden and the apples are tender (test with a skewer). Once cooked, serve them quickly on top of *crème fraîche* sprinkled with sugar, and, just before serving, add some apple compote on top of each *douillon* and flambé them with a dash of calvados (or if preferred, just add the calvados to the apple compote).

your time and get to grips with your food, literally. Other options to start with might be a homemade duck terrine, a selection of smoked fish, oysters and a superb bowl of *moules à la crème*, the sauce of which is easily good enough to be offered separately as a soup. The style is essentially Norman-traditional, but the *auberge* is not averse to catching you out with entirely new creations like a *surprise du chef* that combines home-smoked salmon, beef mince, raisins, pistachios and juniper berries, a radically un-Norman culinary adventure that's beautifully done.

Five-course meals used to be almost a speciality at Goury, but things have got a little more moderate, so that unless you go for the *carte* or one of the top-line menus – which also highlight succulent variations on lobster – you must choose between fish or meat for a main course. Given the emphasis on fish, meat dishes might be expected to be a bit of an afterthought, but the grilled lamb – a menu fixture, cooked on the other side of the fire from the fish – is of the highest quality, and the dish of the day might be an excellent version of a local classic such as *magret de canard* in a *pommeau* sauce, with vegetables and tasty *frites*. To drink, there's a reasonably-priced wine list, with plenty of refreshing whites that go excellently with the fish.

The final courses are as fine as the openers. In a region where competition is not exactly lacking, Pascal Retout has an exceptional cheese selection, which recently included a whole range of real farmhouse cheeses – Vieux Lisieux (rather like Pont l'Evêque, washed in calvados and spices), Cabourg, fine *chèvres*, superb Neufchâtel. And there's still one more house favourite to come, one of the range of often boozy Norman apple or pear desserts, or maybe a sorbet, or a rich, pure chocolate mousse, before you finish things off, well into the afternoon, with a good strong coffee.

Touring Around

The greatest glory of La Hague is its scenery. As you travel west along its northern flank you begin to get dramatic views over the sea from the fern- and heather-covered cliffs, while in between the road snakes inland around abrupt narrow bends encased by dense hedgerows. One of the most beautiful routes around the Cape is the **GR223 footpath**, which is also known here as the *Sentier des Douaniers*, the Customs Officers' Path, since it originated as a track used to keep a check on smuggling among the rocks. It stays close to the shore and cliff edge all the way around the peninsula from Querqueville, just outside Cherbourg, and only turns a little inland as it leaves La Hague beyond Vauville, in the south. Even if you don't take on the whole footpath, it's still easy to walk along it for a kilometre or so, as access to it is well indicated at several points along the D45 with the sign *Sentier Littoral*.

La Hague was also one of the areas of strongest Viking settlement in Normandy, and most of the place names ending in -*ville* indicate villages founded by Norse chieftains (Querqueville, 'Koki's ville', Auderville, 'Odern's ville', and so on). In **Querqueville**, almost before you have properly left Cherbourg, and with a lovely view back across the harbour, there is the tiny 10th-century, pre-Romanesque **Chapelle de St-Germain**, possibly the oldest church or chapel in Normandy and almost certainly the oldest still in use. It's a beautifully simple little building with bare rough-stone walls, almost hidden in the shadow of a much larger later village church. Many other villages on the peninsula – Gréville-Hague, Auderville, Jobourg and others – have churches dating back to the era of William the Conqueror and his immediate descendants.

A little west of Querqueville is the turning for the **Château de Nacqueville** (*guided tours only; Easter–Sept Mon, Wed, Thurs, Sat and Sun every hour 2–5; closed Tues and Fri except public hols; adm*). An elegant combination of French Renaissance château and local granite, it was built for the Grimouville family between 1510 and 1570, and later passed via various marriages to the brother of the great 19th-century political writer and essayist Alexis de Tocqueville, author of *Democracy in America*, who wrote many of his works during summers spent here. It stands in one of the peninsula's sheltered valleys, and is surrounded by a luxuriant 'English-style' garden, created for the anglophile de Tocquevilles by an English landscape artist in the 1830s. With broad lawns, artificial streams and ponds, and great beds of azaleas and rhodedendrons, it explodes into flower in May (note: some of the staff do not share the garden's charm, and while there is no official minimum limit for the tours, if fewer than ten people turn up on a weekday or at the end of the day they may find a tour is cancelled).

Below the château, **Urville-Nacqueville** is a plain little village, but has a broad and breezy stone and pebble beach, interrupted by a few remains of Second World War German blockhouses, that's very popular with kite flyers. Further west again, near the old hotel and viewpoint at **Landemer** (*see* p.315), there looms beside the D45 the much older manor of **Dur-Ecu** ('Strong Shield'; *open early July–early Sept daily, manor 3–7, gardens and maze 11–1 and 2–7; adm, combined tickets for manor and gardens or separate tickets available*), a massive, turreted granite pile that looks as if it could easily have been designed for a movie of a Poe story starring Vincent Price. A few years ago it was a closed-up, romantic semi-ruin, but it has been restored and the exterior and courtyards – but still not the interior – can be visited in summer. Its giant upper walls are 16th-century, but parts of the foundations date back to a 9th-century Viking stronghold; as well as the fortified manor itself and its attached manor farm there are watermills, a grand dovecote and a thickly wooded park. Dur-Ecu's most unusual and popular feature, though, is a recent addition, the **Labyrinthe** or 'Maize Maze' created in maize (corn) by British specialist maze designer Adrian Fisher, which is carefully replanted each year to keep it as intriguing and difficult to escape from as possible.

The Hague peninsula may feel remote even today, but it has nevertheless played its part in *la vie française*. **Gréville-Hague**, in a loop in the D45, was the birthplace of Jean-François Millet, and he painted its squat, typically Norman stone church and other parts of the village many times both before and after moving on to his more familiar themes of peasant life in the Seine valley. The house where he was born in 1814, a short way back towards the sea in the beautiful little hamlet of **Gruchy**, has been restored as the **Maison Natale de Jean-François Millet** (*open daily April, May and public hols in Oct–Mar 2–6, June and Sept 11–6; July and Aug 11–7; closed Oct–Mar exc hols; adm*). It's an atmospheric old cottage and an imaginative museum, centred on the one big room that was home to Millet, his parents, his eight brothers and sisters and their grandmother. Given that they were among the more prosperous inhabitants of Gruchy this is an eloquent indication of the simplicity of life on La Hague at that time. In other rooms there are paintings by him of scenes around the village, and exhibits on his moves to Paris and Barbizon, and the enormous influence he had on other painters, especially Van Gogh. Millet is much more than just one more artist in France: for decades his work was more frequently reproduced than that of any other French painter, and it used to be said that there was a print of his *Angelus* (a peasant couple praying in the fields) in every home in the country. There's a room showing some of the many uses made of his most familiar images, from plates, pepper pots and kitsch gifts to packaging and beer labels. From the house there's a fine short walk downhill along the narrow lane to a footpath and then a viewpoint above the sea, with a dramatic vista of **Castel-Vendon**, the huge, glowering mountain of rock just to the east. This was one of Millet's favourite walks, and he must have come here time and time again as a boy – he later did several paintings of the rock from this same spot, as you'll instantly recognize from the reproductions in the museum.

Omonville-la-Petite is further along the peninsula and inland, almost lost in another steep, sheltered valley. The contrast with the bleak and windblown moorland by the sea cliffs is extraordinary: the village and its little hollows are exceptionally quaint and lush, and are covered in bright flowers in summer. Omonville was the last home of a great figure of more contemporary French culture, the poet Jacques Prévert, author of *Paroles* and of the scripts for many classics of the golden age of French cinema such as *Le crime de Monsieur Lange*, *Le jour se lève* and *Les enfants du paradis*. He died here in 1977, and his widow Janine stayed on in their house, a stunningly pretty cottage with exuberant garden, until her own death in 1993, since when it has been opened as the **Maison Jacques Prévert** (*open daily April, May and public hols in Oct–Mar 2–6, June and Sept 11–6; July and Aug 11–7; closed Oct–Mar exc hols; adm*). Visitors must park next to the village churchyard, where both Préverts and their daughter Michelle are buried, and then walk up a quiet lane.

Rather than a display of Prévert effects, much of the house has been made into an exhibition space that each year hosts a single exhibition devoted to a Prévert-related theme of one or other of his activities or acquaintances – painters such as Miró and Max Ernst, photographers like Robert Doisneau, other poets and his cinema work. There are also videos and photographs of Prévert, which allow us to conclude that he shared with Jean Gabin the distinction of perfecting the famous French technique of talking, eating and generally living with a cigarette clamped permanently in one side of the mouth at a 45-degree angle. Still intact on the upstairs floor is his airy, comfortable living- and writing-room, which looks as if he might walk in at any moment; sometimes a tape is played – maybe of Juliette Gréco, or of Yves Montand singing another Prévert creation, *Les Feuilles d'Automne*, for which he wrote the lyrics – and the evocation of a certain period of French life couldn't be more complete.

Omonville-la-Rogue is an attractive little fishing port, the existence of which was first recorded in 1026. Just outside it is **Le Tourp** (*open Tues–Sat Jan–June and Sept–Dec 10–1 and 2–5.30; July and Aug 10–1 and 2–6.30; closed Mon and late Dec–early Jan; last admission 1hr before closing; adm*), another massively baronial stone manor, which has been converted into a modern arts and exhibition centre. Permanent features include a lovely sculpture garden, an exhibit on the natural world of La Hague (informative, but often heavy going) and a rather chic café, and each year there are new temporary shows. West of Omonville the terrain loses much of its leafiness and becomes much more wind-blasted and moor-like. A little further on the road comes upon tiny **Port Racine**, an inlet of grey shingle with a few boats tied up, which a sign proclaims to be '*le port le plus petit de France*'. Since there are only two reasonably substantial buildings in the whole place nobody's likely to argue. There is also a special **garden** (*open Easter–Sept*) created in homage to Jacques Prévert by his friend Gérard Fasberti. Beyond Port Racine, the road climbs up sharply to **St-Germain-des-Vaux**, before dropping down again to **Auderville**, an engaging little place with very fresh air and a main street that serves as a relaxed village square. From one side of the village, on a bright day, British territory (Alderney) seems extraordinarily close, the other side of Goury lighthouse, but when the weather changes it disappears from view.

The coastline on the south side of La Hague is less inhabited and more open than the north, with sweeping bays of giant cliffs above empty, sandy beaches. Coming from Goury, a sharp turn off the D901 in Auderville, signposted to Ecalgrain and Jobourg, will take you to the viewpoint overlooking the **Baie d'Ecalgrain**, a magnificent arc of sand and surf, and then to the **Nez de Jobourg**, at 128m often described as the tallest cliffs in Europe. From both points you can examine Alderney on a clear day, although at other times the wind may be enough to knock you straight back inland instead. Again, there are plenty of opportunities for walking on the GR223 footpath.

After you rejoin the main road at Jobourg village it soon becomes surprisingly wide. This indicates that you are about to pass the truly vast bulk of the Beaumont-La Hague **nuclear reprocessing plant**, also known as **COGEMA**, a symbol of official France's notorious modern love affair with all things nuclear. It's hard to know what to say about this giant carbuncle, which looms into view at certain points around the peninsula; local opinion, in line with a traditional French gung-ho attitude towards technology, was for years accepting of it, but lately has become much more critical, and there's a permanent protesters' camp at the entrance. The administration was once very keen to invite the public in to have a look around, but since September 2001 the full plant tours have had to be abandoned, although interested visitors can still take a look around the outside of the building (*details from tourist offices*).

From Beaumont you can continue on the D901 back to Cherbourg, or turn south on to the D318, a precipitously steep road that runs down a deep heather-lined valley to reach another wonderful, open bay, the **Anse de Vauville**, where there are miles of cliffs, an immense sandy beach, a campsite in summer, a pizzeria and a bird reserve (*contact tourist offices for details*). **Vauville** itself is another of the more extraordinary villages of La Hague, with centuries-old stone houses, a Neolithic dolmen and an 11th-century priory, and a feel of being far from the world amid its giant landscape. Around the old stone manor of the **Château de Vauville** (*guided tours only; May–June and Sept Tues, Fri, Sat and Sun 2–6; July and Aug daily 2–6; adm*) there's a very unusual, semitropical botanical garden, which is rich in southern hemisphere plants. And, at the south end of the bay, there are stretches of beach where – unusually – it's actually suggested you can swim or windsurf as well as just watch the breakers.

Where to Stay

Auderville ✉ 50440

Hôtel du Cap, t 02 33 52 73 46, **f** 02 33 01 56 30 (*double rooms €41–48*). Occupying a very solid old Norman farmhouse with farmyard on one side – now a pretty garden – and fields falling away to the sea on the other, this relaxed little hotel has eight big, quite modern, comfortable rooms. Several have great sea views through the eaves, and there's a very pleasant, airy breakfast room.

Ferme de Coulon, t 02 33 01 56 39, **f** 02 33 01 56 30 (*rooms €38 for two*). Next door to the Hôtel du Cap, this old farm is run by the same Lecouvey family but is not a hotel but a *chambres d'hôtes*, with five simple, decent-value B&B rooms. Its big plus is the location, with stunning views from some rooms.

Equeurdreville (Cherbourg) ✉ 50120

La Maison Duchevreuil, t 02 33 01 33 10, *http://perso.wanadoo.fr/maison-duchevreuil* (*rooms €90 for two, €105 for four*). While officially distinct, Equeurdreville is effectively part of Cherbourg, just west of the city. This house, with an 18th-century main mansion in a medieval walled courtyard, was the local manor when it was just a village, and the suburb grew up around it. Sophie and Bruno Draber have restored the house as a labour of love, creating a magnificent garden – which Mme Draber is happy to show you around – that's a haven of peace within the town. They currently have one B&B suite (but plan to add at least one more), in a building beside the courtyard. It's a stylishly-decorated suite, with very large studio-style double bedroom and sitting area, a bathroom to match and smaller room with single bed; it has its own entrance, with a table, fridge and microwave. Breakfast is served in the lovely main house, with plenty of fresh fruit from the garden. M and Mme Draber are very hospitable, and it's a great introduction to France after arriving in Cherbourg.

Gréville-Hague ✉ 50440

Hameau aux Fèvres, t 02 33 52 75 80, **f** 02 33 94 20 54 (*room €35 for two, €60 for four*). The spectacular location is the great draw of this very peaceful B&B. It's one of a tiny cluster of houses above the main village of Gréville-Hague, reached via a very steep, winding lane that turns off the coast road near Landemer. Once at the top, you'll find a few granite cottages scattered among trees and gardens, of which this farm is the largest; turn around, and laid out far below you is the sea, and an almost infinite horizon. The one guest room is more like a suite, with one double room and a possible annexe room with twin beds; it's simply and comfortably decorated, and gets loads of light. The hamlet is great for walking, although getting there without a car is very difficult.

Omonville-la-Petite ✉ 50440

Hôtel La Fossardière, Hameau de la Fosse, **t** 02 33 52 19 83, **f** 02 33 52 73 49 (*double rooms €40–63*). One of La Hague's most comfortable options, in another delicious location. The tiny hamlet of La Fosse seems like a micro-climate within the micro-climate of Omonville-la-Petite, a snug dip in the ground where plants and flowers almost leap out of the granite walls. The hotel's ten rooms are distributed between two cottages: the conversion is ingenious, but some rooms are a bit dark. All though are attractively decorated, with good bathrooms and other comforts. Breakfast is served in the former village bakery, which also serves as a bar. The English-speaking owner, Gilles Fossard, runs the hotel with flair, and extras include a small sauna. *Closed 15 Nov–15 Mar.*

Hôtel St-Martin des Grèves, t 02 33 01 87 87, *www.hotel-st-martin.fr.st* (*double rooms €36–48*). In a big granite house by the D45 west of Omonville-la-Petite, overlooking Anse St-Martin bay and Port Racine, the St-Martin has 22 rooms between a main house and a garden annexe. They are not hugely individual but all pleasantly comfortable, and five at the front benefit from a superb ocean view. There's a large, bright garden, and staff are charmingly hospitable.

Urville-Nacqueville ✉ 50460

Hôtel-Restaurant Le Landemer, Landemer, **t** 02 33 03 43 00, *http://le-landemer.com* (*double rooms €30–60*). The oldest hotel on La Hague, opened in 1851, secured one of the best imaginable locations, on a bend in the coast road jutting out above cliffs and a lovely beach. Millet painted from its terrace, which has a famously beautiful view along the red-green flanks of the coast. Today it's a rather eccentric old hotel that makes up for its old-fashioned rooms with loads of character, the very friendly, laidback charm of owner M Leroy and his staff, low prices and that fabulous setting. There are nine cosy rooms, of which six have sea views; top floor rooms are the most attractive, while those on the first floor are very simple (but among the cheapest around). The restaurant (*see right*) has the same quirkiness as the hotel. Landemer is about halfway between Urville-Nacqueville and Gréville-Hague.

La Blanche Maison, 874 Rue St-Laurent, **t** 02 33 03 48 79, *http://blanchemaison.chez.tiscali.fr* (*room €40 for two*). A very pretty B&B in a converted farm on the coast road between Urville-Nacqueville and Dur-Ecu manor. Thick hedges on the land side of the road make the entrance hard to find: once you make the sharp turn into the steep driveway you enter one of La Hague's little pockets of lushness, with an exceptionally dense, varied, leafy garden. As you climb up the crest you also get a fabulous view of the sea. There's only one guest room, almost a self-contained *gîte* in a separate part of the ancient granite farm, with access to a kitchenette, and reached by a stone staircase. An extra bed can be arranged. Though only 10km from Cherbourg, it feels very hidden and peaceful, and is close both to the GR223 footpath and to Urville-Nacqueville beach.

Eating Alternatives

Auderville ✉ 50440

La Malle aux Epices, **t** 02 33 52 77 44 (*menus €10.50–22*). Auderville's bar-brasserie-*tabac* took on a radical new style in 2004 when it was taken over by a couple who worked for years in the West Indies, and introduced La Hague to Thai and Caribbean dishes (as well as offering classic crepes, oysters, steaks and so on, to keep everybody happy). It's naturally a great innovation for anyone in need of a change from strictly local cuisine, and also has fairly flexible hours. The décor

features bamboo furniture and other 'exotic' touches, there's occasional live music, and its owners, the Barjettas, keep up a very welcoming atmosphere. In good weather there's a pretty terrace by the village street.

St-Germain-des-Vaux ✉ 50440

Le Moulin à Vent, Hameau Danneville, **t** 02 33 52 75 20 (*menus €15–45*). One of La Hague's most highly regarded restaurants, in another remarkable location high up above Port Racine on the road inland to St-Germain-des-Vaux, with a ruined stone windmill beside it. The view and freshness of the air are fabulous, and there's a very pretty garden and summer terrace for making the most of them (look south, sadly, and you see the Beaumont-Hague nuclear facility, but this can be avoided). The food is as renowned as the setting. Fish and seafood are chef Michel Briens' main specialities, especially lobster grilled over a wood fire and served in various different ways, platters of oysters and mussels, and superbly fresh fish, maybe red mullet or John Dory. He also highlights organic produce, and makes fine use of local meats like Cotentin ham. The wood-baked bread, Norman cheeses and rich desserts are as impressive as the main delicacies. *Closed Sun eve and Mon.*

Urville-Nacqueville ✉ 50460

Hôtel-Restaurant Le Landemer, Landemer, **t** 02 33 03 43 00, *http://le-landemer.com* (*menus €15 Mon–Sat only, €22–29*). The popular restaurant at the Landemer (see p.315) has the same amiable, old-style local feel as the hotel. On the menu are generous classic Norman and seafood dishes, including some more elaborate options with langoustines and St-Vaast oysters. A superb extra is the view from its dining room and terrace, as enjoyed by Millet in the 1870s.

Vauville ✉ 50440

Les Tamarins, Belle Rive, **t** 02 33 04 74 04 (*dishes c. €9–18*). A handy and welcoming pizzeria-grill near the beach in Vauville, in an old Cotentin stone cottage with a pleasant outside terrace. It offers enjoyable pizzas, salads, sandwiches, drinks and occasional fish or meat grills.

Castles and Dunes:
the Western Cotentin Coast

30

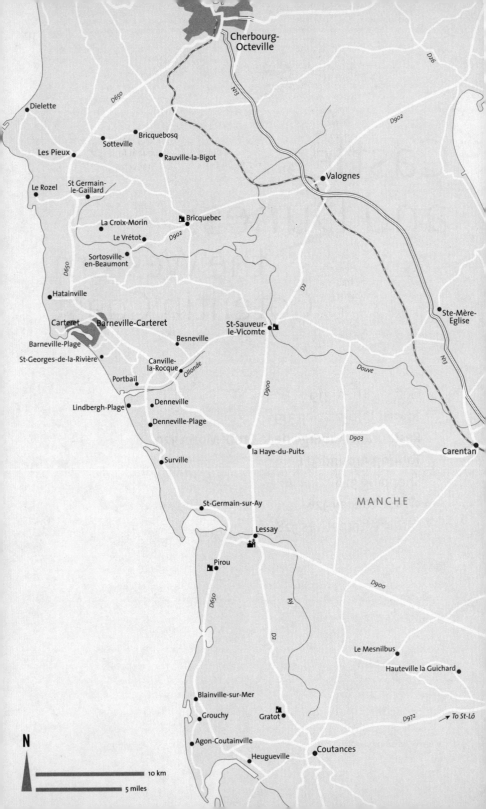

Getting There

From Cherbourg the D650 (follow signs for Barneville-Carteret) leads to the coast. From Caen and the east, leave the N13 at Carentan for the D903 west via La Haye-du-Puits.

To get to La Croix Morin from Barneville-Carteret, take the D902 towards Bricquebec and after about 10km look for a sharp turn left for Le Vretot; instead of going into Le Vretot village, look for a sign on the left for La Croix Morin. From Cherbourg on the D650 look for a lane signposted to Bricquebec, opposite a turn off coastwards to Surtainville, which meets the road from Le Vretot at La Croix Morin crossroads. Don't be put off if either road seems to be going nowhere: they do.

The nearest mainline **train** station is in Valognes, but a *Train Touristique* (an old 1930s narrow-gauge line) runs between Carteret and Portbail (*April–June and Sept–Oct Sat and Sun, July–Aug daily*). Coutances has train connections with Avranches, Caen and Paris (Gare Montparnasse). **Buses** run from Cherbourg to Barneville and Coutances.

Ferries to the **Channel Islands** are run by **Hugo Express** (Gare Maritime, Carteret, t 02 33 01 10 11, *www.hugoexpress.com*). Boats take passengers only, and run from Carteret and Portbail to Jersey and Guernsey, and from tiny Diélette, north of Les Pieux, to Guernsey and Alderney. Services have operated April–Sept only, but may run all year in future. Jersey ferries also sail from Granville (*see* p.331).

Tourist Information

Barneville-Carteret: 10 Rue des Ecoles, Barneville, t 02 33 04 90 58, *www.barneville-carteret.net*. Also in Place Flandres-Dunkerque, Carteret, t 02 33 04 94 54.
Bricquebec: 13 Place Ste-Anne, t 02 33 52 21 65, *www.ville-bricquebec.fr*.
Coutances: Place Georges Leclerc, t 02 33 19 08 10, *tourisme-coutances@wanadoo.fr*.
Les Pieux: 6 Rue Centrale, t 02 33 52 81 60, *www.tourisme-lespieux.com*.
Portbail: 26 Rue Philippe Lebel, t 02 33 04 03 07, *www.portbail.org*.

France stands out for its combination of affluent modernity and an apparently contradictory attachment to tradition. The west coast of the Cotentin peninsula – sometimes called the *Côte des Iles* because it faces, and has a good deal of contact with, the Channel Islands – contains a whole collection of French contrasts and characteristics, a distinctive mix of cragginess and gentility. Its shore is one of the wildest on France's Atlantic coast – a long line of windswept, grassy dunes beside immense sandy beaches and crashing surf, with fierce currents that often make swimming hazardous. Every so often there are inlets leading to old fishing villages, and little islands of good behaviour in the shape of small family seaside resorts. Scattered among the dunes are clutches of *Belle Epoque* villas, or modern holiday cottages. A short way inland, however, there are some of the most undisturbedly rustic villages and least modernized countryside you'll find anywhere in France.

The Western Cotentin's role in world affairs peaked a long time ago. It was one of the most important areas of early Viking settlement in Normandy, and men from here travelled with William the Conqueror to England, and set out on the still greater adventure that saw a Norman kingdom established in 11th-century Sicily. Since this flurry of activity nearly a thousand years ago, apart from a few more bursts of warfare, the region has generally kept to itself. Its early prominence is reflected in the presence of some of the finest works of Norman Romanesque architecture, whether great monuments such as the abbey at Lessay and Coutances Cathedral, or fortified village churches. There are also many castles – not elegant châteaux, but real early-medieval warrior castles, with battlements, turrets and crumbling walls.

In food the Western Cotentin shows as many contrasts as in anything else. In the resorts on the coast there are simple creperies, and restaurants that serve freshly-caught fish and seafood with all the niceties associated with French metropolitan catering. Inland, restaurants are surprisingly thin on the ground, and the fare tends to stay close to its straightforward Norman roots. For anyone who really wants to get in touch with the rural side of the area, a rare experience awaits at the **Auberge de la Croix Morin**, a little inn at a lonely road junction between Bricquebec and the coast.

Auberge de la Croix Morin

La Croix Morin, Le Vrétot, t 02 33 52 22 64. Open Mon–Fri and Sun 8am–8pm; Nov–Mar also open Fri, Sat from 8pm by reservation; always book evening and Sunday meals (opening hours can be eccentric). Menus €12 Mon–Fri, €13.50 Sun, other menus by reservation €14–23.50; dishes c. €9–11; soirées normandes €12.

Many people still travel to France with a Stella Artois or Jean de Florette fantasy at the back of their minds. That is, the hope of walking into an utterly basic village inn with stone walls, stone flags, gnarled wooden tables, plain but goodness-packed country cooking and the local brew slammed down in jugs, places filled with grizzled *paysans*, costing next to nothing and soaked in authenticity. This is actually quite hard to find, for the French tend not to mythologize roughing it much and many country restaurant owners, in particular, seem unable to see a bare stone wall without wanting to cover it in imitation Louis XVI wallpaper and put in tables with white linen and dainty bowls of flowers. The Croix Morin may not entirely fit the bill – there's paint and wallpaper instead of bare stone, and no one can be relied on to be entirely grizzled these days – but it's a place so un-madeover that even locals speak of it with a certain awe, as if they're surprised to find it still exists.

The 'Croix Morin' itself is an isolated crossroads in one of the wilder parts of the Cotentin countryside, and the restaurant is a small, whitewashed old inn beside it. Beyond the low doorway there's an old-fashioned country dining room, with benches and communal tables topped with plastic cloths running away from the fireplace, where Mme Lefey, a charming woman in a matter-of-fact, Norman country way, tends the day's grilled meats. There's also a larger but less atmospheric room that's mainly used on Sundays. At the back of the *auberge* is a luxuriant produce garden, the source of all the vegetables and herbs used in the cooking, of which Mme Lefey is very proud.

The basic lunch menu usually begins with an '*hors-d'œuvre* of the day', maybe a bowl of chunks of smoked herring (i.e. kippers) with boiled potatoes in a vinaigrette. To follow, there's grilled meats, the speciality: smoked ham, *andouillettes, côte de porc*, lamb chops and more, all beautifully cooked over the wood fire, and served with *frites*, mixed veg or a bowl of garden peas. The Sunday lunch menu is a bit longer, and might include *jambon au pommeau*, as well as a still wider range of grilled meat. Off the menu there are a few light dishes, such as omelettes, salads or platters of charcuterie, and you can also order ahead more extensive menus with more elaborate dishes, including another speciality, *gigot* or leg of lamb, slow-roasted over the fire.

These are followed by Camembert, Livarot and other classic Norman cheeses, served on a big slab of wood. For dessert there might be a classic *tarte aux pommes*, or often *riz au lait* (rice pudding). The choice of drinks runs between wine and – naturally the one to go for – a generous bottle of dry local cider, drawn from the barrel.

La Croix Morin's most renowned speciality of all, though, is its kippers. Fat, flavour-rich herrings are available from November to March, and are freshly smoked over the fire and served up with *frites* and a few veg in *soirées normandes*, evening sessions that have something of a legend about them. To make up the rest of the menu there's a hearty Norman soup as a starter, and then cheeses and comfort-food desserts. It's essential to book for these winter kipper-feasts: they're normally only held at weekends, but may be happening on other nights of the week, so it's worth checking.

Touring Around

The D650 road that cuts across the top of the Cotentin turns south to follow more or less the line of the coast at **Les Pieux**, a business-like little country town. All along it narrow lanes run off between the hedgerows toward the sea; for walkers, the **GR223 long-distance footpath** stays close to the shore all the way down the Cotentin coast (except for a cut inland from Lessay to Coutances, but an older path still follows the coast). At **Le Rozel** there is a majestic rocky crag, the **Pointe du Rozel**, which looms over the sands on either side. Immediately to the south, **Surtainville** has one of this coast's most beautiful beaches, almost 3km long, an immense, empty space of open dunes, full of birds, and limitless skies framed on one side by the red cliffs of the Pointe du Rozel. It's a superb beach for evening walks, watching the sunset as the wind whips through the coarse grass. **Hatainville**, further south, is another great, wild beach, and has a semi-official nudist section at its southern end. Note, though, that these beaches are unsupervised by life guards, and strong currents and shifting sands mean you should not attempt to swim here, nor go out of your depth. Also, neither has much in the way of shops or bars, so you need to take everything with you.

Inland the countryside is as impressive in a different way. To the north, around **Bricqueboscq** and Rauville-la-Bigot – only a few kilometres outside Cherbourg – there is one of the densest patches of *bocage* country in Normandy (for an explanation of *bocage*, see p.330), a world of steep hills, huge hedges and lanes so narrow they barely let tractors pass. Further south, this gives way to stretches of unbroken forest or moorland. Villages pop up unexpectedly, making it an intriguing area to explore, especially if you're looking for cider and other traditional produce from small-farm producers.

The market hub of this part of the *bocage* is **Bricquebec**, an engaging country town with a pleasantly relaxed pace. The centre of town is still very much its Norman motte-and-bailey castle, the *Vieux Château*, the giant keep or *donjon* of which, begun in the 11th century and last rebuilt in the 14th, dominates the view from miles around, while the walled courtyard forms the town's most attractive square. In the clock tower next to the main keep is the **Musée du Vieux Château** (*open July and Aug Mon and Wed–Sun 2–4; closed Tues; adm*), which mainly deals with Cotentin folk traditions and rural life, although you can also climb up part of the *donjon* and descend into a 13th-century crypt. Another part of the castle is occupied by the Hostellerie du Château hotel (*see* p.327). Bricquebec has attractive small shops, and hosts the largest market in the northern Cotentin, each Monday, and its biggest festival, the *Fête de Ste-Anne* (*last weekend in July*). Just to the north is the **Abbaye de Notre-Dame-de-Grâce**, a Cistercian monastery 'refounded' after the Revolution in 1824. It has a retreat centre, and a visitor centre with a video-exhibit on the life of the community (*open daily 2–5*).

Southeast of Bricquebec, a lovely wooded road leads to **St-Sauveur-le-Vicomte**, another sleepy old country town centred on a still more impressive castle, also called the **Vieux Château** (*guided tours July and Aug Mon–Sat 3, 4, 5pm; adm*). Begun around the year 1000, it was extended by the English in the 14th century, during the Hundred Years' War, when it was a major stronghold that was fought over several times; today, the castle's massive grey and yellow stone towers seem to dwarf the rest of the town.

Barneville-Carteret, back on the coast, is the main resort centre of the *Côte des Iles*, although it's still a modest place by the standards of Trouville or of resorts further south. It consists of three parts, united in one municipality since 1965: **Barneville**, a historic old village on a hill overlooking the narrow estuary of the River Gerfleur; **Carteret**, a fishing port on the north side of the estuary that's now at least half-used by yachts; and **Barneville-Plage**, to the south, a seaside suburb of neat holiday villas in lines parallel to the beach. Any expectations of a really chic resort are dashed by Barneville, which still has very much a casual, country-village feel. It also has a fine Norman-Romanesque church, **St-Germain**, built in around 1140 but altered many times, most strikingly with a castle-like battlemented tower from the 15th century. This would have served as a watch-tower against English marauders during the Hundred Years' War; similar battlements can be seen all along the peninsula.

Barneville-Carteret is a low-key little resort, with two good beaches that are sheltered and have lifeguards: Barneville-Plage is the larger, the family beach, while the one beyond the end of the harbour in Carteret is prettier. Carteret is the main focus of animation in town, with its yachting marina and port-side promenade, but only one street that's a little chic, the **Rue de Paris**, with the local gourmets' favourite, the Hôtel de la Marine, and a few smartish shops. Above the harbour, roads lead past balconied *Belle Epoque* villas to peter out by the lighthouse at the top of Cap de Carteret, a magnificent rocky point from where you get superb views over the coast to the north and south, and of cormorants on the rocks below. North of the cape you can walk down to another beach, which joins up with the dunes at Hatainville.

St-Georges-de-la-Rivière, a summer seaside village just below Barneville-Plage, has some of the most impressive dunes along the whole coast, and contains the **Maison de la Dune information centre** (*usually open June–Sept only; closed Sun*), which has information on local birdlife. A couple of kilometres further south is one of the loveliest of the Cotentin harbours, **Portbail**, on another small inlet, the mouth of the River Ollonde. Each side of the bay is very flat, and the quality of the light is as striking as the crisp air. On a spit of land at the mouth of the inlet are the quay for the Jersey ferries and the beach, a great bank of sand and shingle; they are joined by a long, low causeway to the original village on the mainland, a classic Norman fishing village with a few restaurants around the harbour. Unmissable from every angle is the pyramid-topped monolithic tower of the church of **Notre-Dame**, one of the oldest Norman churches, begun in the early 11th century but with fortifications added in the 15th. Alongside it are the remains of a 4th-century AD **Gallo-Roman baptistry** (*baptistry open permanently; guided tours of church July–Aug Tues–Sat 10.30–12 and 3.30–7.30, Sun 3.30–7.30; adm*), the only one of its kind in France north of the Loire.

Still on the trail of unusual historic churches, a detour inland, up the D15 towards St-Sauveur-le-Vicomte, will lead you very quickly to the delightful *bocage* village of **Canville-la-Rocque**, with an impressively solid 12th-century church. Its greatest treasures are some rare early 16th-century naive frescoes – only discovered in the 1980s – that evidently date from the time when this was a stop on the pilgrim route to Santiago de Compostela. They tell in fascinating and moralistic detail the legend of a pilgrim who was distracted from his goal by a deceitful woman.

South of Portbail, along the coast, beaches vary between the atmospherically empty (where, as before, you need to be very careful when going into the water) and those that are a little more occupied. **Lindbergh-Plage** is a very open, deserted spot, so named because this is where Charles Lindbergh crossed the French coast on his solo Atlantic flight in 1927; **Denneville** is a little more built up. **Surville** is one of the most beautiful spots on this part of the coast, with miles of empty dunes and rocks – with a small creperie at one end in summer – and, just inland, a lovely old stone village. A little further south the road bends inland around the estuary of the River Ay, and the old village of **St-Germain-sur-Ay**, with its dark, remote-feeling church founded in 1190. South of the Ay, **Pirou-Plage** is almost a little seaside town, with seafront restaurants; **Anneville** and **Blainville** are two more of the largely-undisturbed points on this stretch of coast; while **Agon-Coutainville** is a mini-resort of holiday homes.

A road cuts off the coast road near St-Germain-sur-Ay to **Lessay**, just inland, an important centre for the processing of the products of the Cotentin's farms, with some interesting traditional food producers. Its greatest attraction, though, is the **Abbatiale de la Ste-Trinité** (*church open daily 9–7; abbey buildings open for guided tours only July–Aug daily 10–12 and 2.30–6.30; adm for tours*) soaring up with massive strength in the middle of town. The abbey's current state of completeness is somewhat deceptive, for Lessay saw some of the heaviest fighting in Normandy in 1944, and the abbey was devastated; after the war, it underwent a remarkable 12-year restoration programme, making use as much as possible of stone from the same sources as the original. This only allows us to appreciate its qualities all the better. With its immensely long nave, Lessay's abbey church must be among the finest creations of Norman architecture for sheer awe-inspiring beauty. Founded in 1056, it was the first ever Norman building to have Gothic-transition ogival vaults, but what the visitor is first aware of is its plain, soaring simplicity. Reconstruction or not, the effect is completely timeless. The other abbey buildings are closed to visitors most of the year, but are in any case mostly from the 18th century, and far less interesting.

To the south is the **Lande de Lessay**, a flat plain with a mixture of *bocage*, moorland and marsh. Still half-unnoticed within it are two unmissable castles. There are castles and there are castles, but some can be disappointingly comfortable and distant from knights-in-armour fantasies: not these two. Because the Cotentin was left poor and unfashionable throughout France's golden era from the 16th to the 18th centuries, few fundamental alterations were ever made to them, and they remain as extraordinarily intact monuments to the Middle Ages.

The castle of **Pirou** (*open Oct–Dec, Feb–Mar Mon, Wed–Sun 10–12 and 2–5, closed Tues; Mar–Oct Mon, Wed–Sun 10–12 and 2–6.30; closed Tues exc July and Aug; adm; joint ticket available with Abbaye de La Lucerne, see p.335*), reached via a winding lane off the D650 coast road south of Lessay, was entirely forgotten until the 1960s, overgrown amid the fields. Since then it has been cleaned and opened up, but still retains an extraordinary sense of ancientness. In its origins Pirou is the oldest of all the castles in Normandy, for there was almost certainly a stronghold here that resisted Viking attacks in the 9th century. By the 11th century it had passed by marriage to the Norman lord Serlon, son of Tancrède de Hauteville, founding patriarch of the Norman conquerors of Sicily. As the eldest son Serlon remained in Normandy when his father and brothers went off to Italy (*see* right). The castle saw action throughout the Middle Ages, and particularly in the Hundred Years' War. Subsequently it was inhabited by various families of minor nobles, but by the 19th century it was semi-abandoned, supposedly full of ghosts, and used as a hide-out by smugglers from Jersey.

The main structure of the castle is 12th-century, upon an older base. As you approach it along a leafy farm track, there is a remarkable perspective through three successive entrance gates, beyond which you have to do almost a complete circuit of the moat before reaching the bridge to the castle itself – all so that the defenders could get a clear look and maybe arrow-shot at you before deciding to let you in. Within its duck-pond moat Pirou looks exactly like a child's drawing of a castle, with its giant slate and granite walls, turrets and battlements. Around the courtyard outside the moat are the beautifully plain chapel, the bakery and the former manorial courthouse, which contains a (recently-made) tapestry recounting the story of the Normans in Sicily. The guardhouse, the first room inside the keep, is one of the oldest parts of Pirou, with a huge fireplace with one-piece stone lintel. Beyond it there is a cramped inner courtyard, with on either side tumbledown houses built onto the old walls in the 17th and 18th centuries. From one corner of the courtyard you can climb to the battlements, up precipitous staircases and through narrow walkways. From the very top of the tower you can clearly appreciate that Pirou dominates the plain, with wonderful views out to sea, and easily imagine Norman sentries on this same spot.

The other castle, **Gratot** (*open daily 10–7; adm*), is 15km south towards Coutances. If Pirou looks like a kid's drawing of a castle, Gratot, with pepper-pot turrets and a moat that in places is wide enough to be a small lake, looks just like a picture-book, fairy-tale idea of one, and comes with its very own fairy story attached. The main part of it is 14th-century, although additions continued to be made until the 18th. It was the stronghold of the Argouges clan, the most celebrated of which was the maverick *Chevalier* Jean d'Argouges, who played a double game in the Hundred Years' War and won eternal opprobrium in France by handing over Granville to the English for hard cash. The story refers to a local fairy who supposedly agreed to become mortal and marry an Argouges, on condition that he never mentioned death in her presence. They lived together blissfully happily for ten years, until one night she was taking an inordinately long time getting ready for a banquet, whereupon the flat-footed *chevalier* stumped upstairs and asked if she was waiting until they were all dead: his fairy wife then slipped out the window, and this Argouges was left to weep away his life alone. Sceptics may be unimpressed, but the castle's 'Fairy Tower' (*Tour à la Fée*), with one rectangular room atop an almost round tower, is the ideal site for such a tale.

The last scion of the Argouges, a humble artillery captain, sold his château in 1777. Gratot then passed through various owners, but was still occupied, as a farm, at the turn of the 20th century. A wedding was due to be held there in 1914, when part of the roof fell in on the banqueting tables, fortunately before the guests had arrived. This convinced the last owner to give it up as a bad job. It was entirely derelict by 1968, when restoration was begun by local volunteers. Today Gratot is used as a venue for a range of summer festivals. On other days, when you may well have it to yourself except for stray cats and the ducks in the moat, it has a mistily romantic aura.

East of Gratot is a beautiful stretch of sometimes almost impenetrably dense *bocage* countryside. The pretty village of **Le Mesnilbus** has an enjoyable country *auberge* (*see* p.328) and is a good place to find footpaths or go pony trekking through the woods. It has a very odd war memorial, the tail and engine of a US Thunderbolt aircraft that crashed nearby in July 1944. A little to the east is **Hauteville-la-Guichard**. Equally tiny, it would go unnoticed on the map were it not for the fact that this was once the seat of Tancrède de Hauteville, the instigator of the Normans' adventure in Italy. The Norman lords of the Cotentin were always a troublesome bunch, reluctant to accept the authority of their Dukes in Rouen and Caen, and in 1036 Tancrède and three of his sons, among them the fearsome Guillaume *Bras-de-Fer* ('Iron-Arm'), set out for the Mediterranean, supposedly on a pilgrimage to the Holy Land. They got no further than Italy, where they took work as mercenaries, agreeing to return briefly to the Cotentin to recruit Norman soldiers to serve in the era's endless wars. Within a few years they had tired of fighting for others and set themselves up on their own. 'Iron-Arm' made himself King of Apulia, but he was surpassed by his younger brother Roger, who established a Norman kingdom of Sicily that, belying the Hautevilles' brutish reputation, would be one of the most sophisticated states in Europe and last for over 150 years. In honour of this astonishing dynasty little Hauteville now has the **Musée Tancrède de Hauteville** (*normally open mid-June–mid-Sept Tues–Fri 2–6.30, Sat and Sun 10–12 and 2–6.30, closed Mon; adm*), recounting their epic story.

Coutances, capital of the central Cotentin, is a quiet town built, like Avranches, on one of the tallest hills the Normans could find. It's a town of fine churches, above all its wonderful **cathedral**, whose enormously tall twin spires dominate all approaches to the town – and can be seen from Jersey on a good day. First built in plain Norman style in the 11th century, it was rebuilt in the 13th, but its Gothic façade is unlike any other – an entirely unique Norman combination of elaborate traceries and strangely modern, almost rocket-like false towers. Around the outside there are great gargoyles, of smiling sheep and growling dogs. Another of the sights of Coutances is the Second-Empire **Jardin Public**, which stands out among the many French formal parks for its superb view and the dazzling colours of its lush and intricate flower beds.

Shopping

The largest Cotentin country market is in Bricquebec (*Mon*): others are in **Coutances** (*Thurs*), **Barneville** village (*Sat*) and **Carteret** (*Thurs*) and in July–Aug there's also one in **Barneville-Plage** (*Sun*). Several food and craft establishments in the Cotentin form part of a *Route de la Table* (*details from tourist offices*).

Bricquebec ✉ 50260

Charcuterie Artisanale Guilbert, 18 Rue Armand Levéel, **t** 02 33 52 20 65. A tiny shop near the château, selling traditional Norman pork products – *boudin noir* (black pudding), *andouilles*, terrines, *rillettes*, superb smoked hams and sausages. *Closed Tues.*

Bricqueboscq ✉ 50340

M Emile Mahieu, Hameau Les Mesles, **t** 02 33 04 41 19. A small-farm cider producer in a knot of dense *bocage* north of Bricqueboscq; only 15km from Cherbourg, it feels as if it's in the middle of a green, brambly nowhere. The fresh apple juice, *pommeau* and ciders are crisp and fresh, and the fragrant calvados is superb. There's also apple jam and *confiture de lait* (toffee spread). *Open Mar–June and Sept–Dec Thurs–Sat; July–Aug Mon–Sat.*

Lessay ✉ 50430

Laiterie du Val d'Ay, 1 Rue des Planquettes, **t** 02 33 46 41 33, *www.reaux.fr*. Better-known as Réo, from its most-used label, this small dairy produces high-quality Camembert, butter and *crème fraîche*. Tours with tastings July–mid-Sept Mon–Fri 10–12.30 and 2–4; shop open April–Sept Mon–Fri.

Le Rozel ✉ 50340

La Mielle, **t** 02 33 52 41 62. Near the dunes by Le Rozel, M and Mme Connefroy's farm produces award-winning *crème fraîche*, cottage cheese, butter and yogurt, and asparagus in summer. *Closed Sat and Sun.*

Sortosville-en-Beaumont ✉ 50270

Maison du Biscuit, **t** 02 33 04 09 04, *www.maisonbiscuit.fr*. Dedicated to craft biscuit-making, with a big shop and a pretty *salon de thé*. Their own range includes handmade *palets* and *galettes normandes*, ladies' fingers, petits fours, *pains d'epice* and more, and they also sell jams, vinegars, gourmet foods and natural soaps. Great for last-minute gifts. *Closed Mon, and Jan.*

Sotteville ✉ 50340

Cidrerie Théo Capelle, **t** 02 33 04 41 17. The Cotentin's largest cider producer, M Capelle produces ciders, calvados, *pommeau*, apple juice and fruit liqueurs of his own creation. Trying ciders here is a more conventional experience than searching out small farms: the well-organized tours include a video, and there's a farm shop and tasting area. The farm is well-signposted from the D650.

Where to Stay

Barneville-Carteret ✉ 50270

Hôtel de la Marine, 11 Rue de Paris, **t** 02 33 53 83 31, **f** 02 33 53 39 60 (*double rooms €78–138*). Plush comforts and a great location, beside Carteret quay: at high tide, the harbour-side rooms – some with balconies – are right above the water. Rooms are quiet and comfortable, with mellow décor; the atmosphere is (according to taste) a bit formal, but guests feel suitably pampered, and the restaurant (*see p.328*) is renowned. *Closed mid-Nov–Mar.*

Hôtel des Ormes, Quay Barbey d'Aurevilly, **t** 02 33 52 23 50, *www.hoteldesormes.fr* (*double rooms €85–98, €113 for three*). Recently comprehensively renovated, the Ormes now has a much more youthful, fresher style than most Barneville hotels. It's in a fine old house in a quiet part of Carteret quayside; five of the ten rooms have great harbour views (and cost a bit more), the rest face a lovely garden. Décor in the rooms is a mix of trad-plush and more modern colourings. Staff are friendly and relaxed, and there's a very likeable bar-*salon de thé* for taking stock when you come back from seeing the area. For 2005 the hotel is due to open a restaurant, with light modern dishes.

La Tourelle, 5 Rue du Pic Mallet, **t** 02 33 04 90 22 (*rooms €40 for two, €65 for four*). A charming B&B in an old cottage on the main square of Barneville village. There are four rooms, three doubles and a suite with two extra beds in a separate room. Breakfast is served in a lovely old room with giant fireplace. Owner Gérard Lebourgeois is very helpful and knowledgeable about the area, and his house has a nicely relaxed feel.

Besneville ✉ 50390

M and Mme Langrène, 7 Route de la Forêt, Hameau d'Auxais, t/f 02 33 41 72 61, *plangrene@wanadoo.fr (room €62 for two, €70 for three)*. Some *chambres d'hôtes* just stand out from the norm. Like many Cotentin villages Besneville is a sprawling place made up of several tiny *hameaux*, up winding green lanes. In Auxais, one of the furthest-flung, is the 19th-century house of Pierre and Béatrice Langrène, a charming couple who seem to have set up a B&B as much as an interest as a business. Their one 'room' is a complete suite, with a double and a single bed, and entirely decorated in a remarkable collection of antiques. Guests have the run of a magnificent garden, and breakfasts, with organic produce, are superb.

Bricquebec ✉ 50260

L'Hostellerie du Château, 4 Cours du Château, t 02 33 52 24 49, *lhostellerie.chateau@wanadoo.fr (double rooms €60–90)*. The setting is hard to top: the hotel is inside the massive Norman keep of Bricquebec, in the manor house built onto the castle in the late Middle Ages. It has lots of charm, and what's more Queen Victoria slept here, on a visit to France in 1857, for this was one of the first of Normandy's 'château-hotels'. The grand room where a plaque recalls her stay is the best; some rooms are small and plain, but those overlooking the courtyard are attractive. The **restaurant** *(menus €20–34)* is in the former Knights' Hall, between stone pillars and baronial fireplaces. The food – Norman classics like *moules a la crème* or roast lamb – is not as impressive as the setting, but enjoyable.

Canville-la-Rocque ✉ 50580

La Rue, t 02 33 53 03 06 *(rooms €50 for two, €75 for four)*. A *chambres d'hôtes* in a fine old granite farmhouse, restored and filled with an impressive antiques collection. The two rooms are quite special – one a double, the

other a suite, with two singles and a double Norman box-bed in carved wood (with doors for you to shut yourself in at night). The breakfast room is lovely, and M and Mme Frugier are very friendly, pleasant hosts.

Portbail ✉ 50580

M and Mme Vasselin, 16 Rue Gilles Poërier, Hameau de Gouey, t 02 33 04 80 27 *(rooms €40–70 for two, €75 for four)*. The Vasselins are real Norman country people, bluff on first acquaintance, but friendly underneath. Their big stone farmhouse – restored by themselves – has four B&B rooms, one standard double and three very large rooms on an upper floor, one of which could easily take five people. They're plainly decorated, but very well-kept. Guests have the use of a big lounge, and a huge garden behind the house. On the landward side of Portbail but an easy walk from the sea, it's very peaceful.

Surville ✉ 50250

Le Clos du Puits, La Rue, t 02 33 07 06 52, *www.closdupuits.com (rooms €60–70 for two, €85 for three)*. Another exceptional B&B, in Surville village 2km inland from the beach. The imposing stone house is actually quite modern, but it's hard to believe, as it was built using entirely traditional Cotentin techniques and materials. The two stylish rooms are both suites, one with a double main bedroom and one single bed, one with a double and two singles, and the extra beds are in entirely separate rooms. Owner Martine Ferey is a charming host – and speaks excellent English – and sets the calm, mellow tone for her house. Generous, unhurried breakfasts, served in her huge kitchen, feature organic produce.

Le Vrétot ✉ 50260

Manoir du Val Jouet, t 02 33 52 24 42 *(rooms €40 for two)*. A beautiful 15th–16th-century manor just off the D902 road below Le Vrétot, surrounded by an equally lovely, deliciously peaceful garden. M and Mme Davenet have just one, suite-style B&B room, a double with two single beds in a side room and its own sitting room. It's extremely pretty and comfortable and the owners have many return customers.

Eating Alternatives

Barneville-Carteret ✉ 50270

Hôtel de la Marine, 11 Rue de Paris, **t** 02 33 53 83 31 (*menus €28–50*). The established premier restaurant on the *Côte des Iles* has a wonderful location on the harbour's edge, and an opulent style like the hotel (*see p.326*). Chef Laurent Cesne makes the most of local seafood, often in elaborate combinations, and his lobster and scallop dishes are renowned. *Closed mid-Nov–Mar, and Sun eve and Mon midday exc July and Aug.*

Au Paradis du Gourmet, Rue du Lait, Hameau de Bas, **t** 02 33 04 95 33 (*menus €18–50*). The name set out young chef Anthony Gerbeau's ambitions, and lets you know that this former creperie, in a lovely setting between Barneville and Barneville-Plage, is no longer a place for a simple snack. His menus are notably elaborate even for France, and include a special menu of variations on truffles (*€95, must be ordered ahead*). He's won a high reputation, and the Paradis is now a reference point for local food-lovers.

Gratot ✉ 50200

Le Tournebride, **t** 02 33 45 11 00 (*menus €16–40*). A comfortable, pretty traditional restaurant – in, of course, a big granite house – near the entrance to Gratot castle. Good-value menus at several price levels offer lots to choose from, highlighting – also of course – Norman meat, fish and seafood classics, and it's a firm local favourite.

Heugueville-sur-Sienne ✉ 50200

Le Mascaret, 16 Route de la Sienne, **t** 02 33 45 86 09 (*menus €29–60*). Chef Philippe Hardy and his Bulgarian wife Nadia have caused something of a stir with this original restaurant between Coutances and Agon-Coutainville, using local produce in internationally-influenced cuisine pretty much of their own creation. Innovative combinations of vegetables, spices and particularly edible flowers are specialities, in distinctly luxurious dishes. The décor is just as distinctive: outside it's a traditional Cotentin granite house, inside it's magnificently colourful. *Closed Mon and eves Wed, Sun, all Jan and two weeks Nov.*

Le Mesnilbus ✉ 50490

Auberge des Bonnes Gens, **t** 02 33 07 66 85 (*menus €13.74–22.90*). Very popular *auberge du terroir* in a giant old granite inn deep in the *bocage*. Local produce and seafood are used in hearty feasts of Norman classics – especially *jambon braisé au cidre* – followed by slab-loads of cheese and apple desserts, with cider, calvados or a decent choice of beers and wines. The *auberge* also has four simple **rooms** (*€31.25 for two*). *Closed (Oct–Easter) Sun eve and Mon.*

Portbail ✉ 50580

Le Cabestan, 3 La Caillourie, **t** 02 33 04 35 30 (*menus €16–33*). This bright restaurant in nautical blue and white stands right beside Portbail's pebble-spit beach, so the specialities are naturally ultra-fresh fish seafood, finely presented. It's friendly, great value and very popular, and eating while looking out over the harbour and beach and into the mist is a real pleasure. *Closed Mon and Tues.*

St-Germain-le-Gaillard ✉ 50340

Ferme-Auberge de Bunehou, **t** 02 33 52 80 69 (*menus €13.72–18.29*). A popular *ferme-auberge* on a big manor-farm, inland from Les Pieux. Meals are served in two large, no-frills dining rooms, and outside there are ponds, and a kids' play area. Bargain menus feature classic Norman country cooking using produce straight from the farm – trout mousse, chicken *au cidre* or roast duck, local cheeses, *teurgoules*, homemade ice cream. In theory bookings are taken only for groups on weekdays except in August, but since the definition of a group seems to be flexible it's worth checking when you call. *Open for individual bookings mid-Mar–July and Sept–Jan Sat and Sun midday only, Aug daily; Group bookings taken at other times.*

Sortosville-en-Beaumont ✉ 50270

Le Berlingot, **t** 02 33 53 87 16 (*menus €10–21*). This unassuming restaurant-creperie, off the D650, is very popular for its quality food at low prices: steaks and other meats grilled on an open fire, salads, crêpes and *galettes* (*under €8*). The décor is pretty and rustic, service is charming; it's often necessary to book. *Closed Tues, Wed and mid-Nov–Mar.*

Far Away among the Hedgerows:
The Cotentin *Bocage*

31

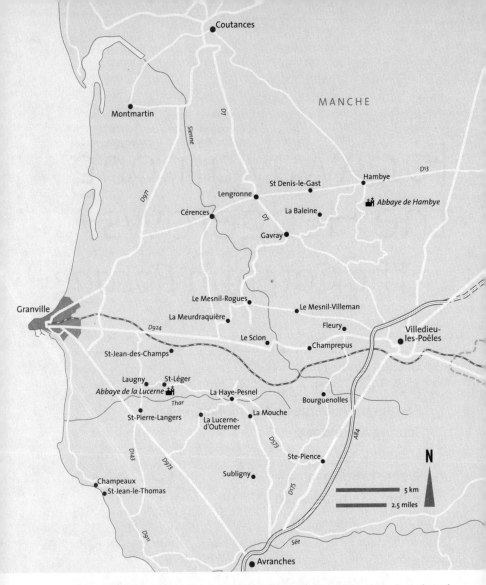

The *bocage* country of Normandy stretches across the Cotentin peninsula and much of western Calvados and the Orne, a countryside of innumerable villages, solid stone houses, small, scattered farms, and fields separated by giant, stone-bottomed hedgerows, all spread over rolling hills between patches of thick woodland. The fields are rarely more than a hundred yards wide, and at times so small their grass becomes almost invisible between the hedges. The word *bocage* is best known in English in connection with the Second World War, for this is also the countryside that caused such misery to the Allied armies after D-Day, when the region's trademark hedgerows gave the Germans ready-made defences that had to be taken one by one. It's a real leap of the imagination to conceive of these horrors here today, when the hedges are picturesque instead of threatening and an absolute calm pervades the countryside.

Getting There

The main roads from Cherbourg meet at Coutances, to divide again south of the town; take the road to the left, the D7 inland, signposted to Gavray and Villedieu. From Caen and the east, leave the A84 *autoroute* at exit 37 (Villedieu), and take the D9 north to Gavray. At Gavray, the D7 veers southwest. After about 5km, look out for the turn for Le Mesnil-Rogues to the left – a sharp, narrow turn. Coming from the south, the turn off the D7 is less abrupt.

Granville and Villedieu-les-Poêles have **trains** to Avranches and Paris (Gare Montparnasse). Local **bus** services are pretty infrequent.

Passenger-only ferries between Granville and **Jersey** are operated by **Hugo Express** (Gare Maritime, Granville, **t** 02 33 61 08 88,

www.hugoexpress.com), with sailings daily, April–Sept (possibly all year in future); more Channel Islands ferries sail from Barneville-Carteret (*see* p.319). Ferries also run April–Sept to the **Iles Chausey**, the tiny French islands off the coast; ferry operators include **Corsaire**, **t** 08 25 16 80 50, www.compagniecorsaire.com.

Tourist Information

Gavray: Place de la Bascule, **t/f** 02 33 50 10 10.
Granville: 4 Cours Jonville, **t** 02 33 91 30 03, www.ville-granville.fr.
Hambye: Rue Louis d'Estouteville (*July–Aug*).
La Haye-Pesnel: Rue de la Libération, **t** 02 33 90 75 02.
Villedieu-les-Poêles: Place Costils, **t/f** 02 33 61 05 69, www.ot-villedieu.fr

---

The southern Cotentin, inland from Coutances and Avranches, is one of the most beautiful parts of the *bocage*. The beech woods are denser and more extensive, and the broader hills further north give way to steep inclines along lush, neat little valleys, spanned by a web of tiny, winding lanes. In the early Middle Ages, when most of the region was still covered by forest, several monasteries were founded here, their monks attracted by its very remoteness and isolation.

This is also one of the best areas in Normandy to sample farm ciders and other traditional foods and crafts. Cheese, for once, is not foremost among the region's products, but there are plenty of small cider producers that welcome visitors, and the Cotentin's ham, duck, lamb, beef and their derivatives are renowned. And, when it comes to exploring the very French concept that food is always better at source, where better than an *auberge du terroir*, officially recognized as serving only local produce. The welcoming **Auberge du Mesnil-Rogues** occupies a granite building in a tiny village in the heart of the *bocage*. Presided over by the aptly named Joseph Cotentin, it's dedicated to presenting country produce at its best.

L'Auberge du Mesnil-Rogues

Le Mesnil-Rogues, t 02 33 61 37 12, joseph.cotentin@wanadoo.fr.
Open Oct–early Jan Wed and Sun 12–3, Thurs–Sat 12–3 and 7–9; early Feb–Sept Wed–Sun 12–3 and 7–9. Closed Mon and Tues, four weeks Jan–Feb, and three weeks late Sept–mid-Oct. Menus €18.50–30.40; carte average €30.

The centrepiece of the main dining room at the Auberge is the massive, old and distinctly manorial stone fireplace, which Mme Cotentin visits every so often to check on the meat grilling over beech logs – every Friday a whole ham is slowly spit-roasted there, ready for the night's special of *jambon façon York cuit à la broche*. There's no deliberate rusticity here, though, for this is something to which few French restaurants aspire; the rest of the room is neat and smart, with striped and flowery wallpaper, pretty tablecloths and flowers on the tables. Of the three additional dining rooms, one is positively ornate, with plush and gold fittings. All four regularly fill up with the big, noisy family groups that home in on the *Auberge* from miles around for Sunday lunch. This is a family restaurant in more ways than one – outside, across a small garden, there's a well-equipped play area, with slides and climbing frames, and requests for highchairs and other infant accessories are happily answered.

An *auberge du terroir* this may be, but this doesn't mean the food is unsophisticated. M. Cotentin worked for several years in the Paris region before returning to his own *terroir* and, as well as Norman tradition, there are well-developed skills evident in his cooking. Like any good French chef he experiments, and, while superb grilled meats remain his most renowned forte, he has also developed a variety of *terre et mer* mixed meat and seafood dishes. His menus, moreover, provide an opportunity to sample a range of dishes for an exceptionally reasonable outlay; for anyone who only wants a smaller meal, there's an excellent choice of one-course *assiettes du terroir*, local classics such as braised ham *à la normande* (in cream and cider sauce), *andouilles* on a bed of potatoes (with balsamic vinegar), *poule au pot* or assorted Normandy cheeses with farm-fresh salad (*all around €7.60–10*). The wine list is compact but satisfying, with several good classic reds that make an excellent match for the meats.

Among the starters, there are salads and local river fish, as well as home-made terrines and foie gras; recently there's also been a *marbré* terrine of *lieu* (pollack) and *andouille*, a memorable blend of strong and subtle flavours. From June to September, when langoustines are available in Granville, the waitresses may take up position behind many diners to tie on rather cute little pink bibs in preparation for slurpy dishes such as *langoustines à la crème de calvados*. With a sweet and richly buttery-and-boozy, finger-licking sauce, they're hugely enjoyable, and unquestionably a luxury (from autumn into spring, similar dishes may be made with *coquilles St-Jacques*). Main courses include variations on duck, lamb and ham, many with Norman cider, cream or cheese sauces, and fish dishes such as sea bream in *pommeau*, or distinctive *terre et mer* combinations like roast sea bass with *andouille*. Serious carnivores, though, will want to try the grilled meats, such as brochette of lamb, *cochon de lait* (suckling pig) or the various cuts of beef that are fixtures on the menu, all served with discreet, nicely subtle mixes of ideally fresh veg. The English have long had a reputation in French restaurants for liking meat well- (meaning over-) done. In this case, overcome any prejudices and ask for it *saignant* or even *bleu*. Meat of this quality scarcely needs any cooking at all.

After some Livarot from the fine cheeseboard, desserts present a tough choice. If you're looking for stout comfort food, there's an excellent *teurgoule*, the Norman rice pudding, with fine cinnamon flavours and a thick, crispy crust; but, it's hard not to choose the homemade patisserie of the day, which might be a fabulously fresh, juicy apple tart or, for a contrast of apple flavours, a delicate *sabayon de pommes*. At the end of the meal, M Cotentin himself emerges from his kitchen, to tour the tables with a very genuine beaming smile.

Magret de Canard au Pommeau

Serves 4

2 duck breasts

150ml/5fl oz *pommeau*

150ml/5fl oz chicken stock

150ml/5fl oz double cream

salt and pepper

3 apples

Dress the duck breasts: cut away the excess fat on either side, and remove the nerve along one side of each breast. With a small knife, lightly score the skin in a crisscross pattern. Just before cooking, season with salt and pepper.

Take a cast-iron casserole dish, or a very heavy frying pan, and preheat it dry. When it's very hot, lay the duck breasts in it, skin side downwards. The heat immediately melts the fat; lift the breasts gently from time to time so that it can penetrate underneath. Cook this side for 6–7 minutes, making sure that the skin doesn't get too brown. Then turn the breasts over and cook on the other side for 4–5 mins. Transfer the breasts to a plate, skin side downwards, and keep warm.

To make the sauce, pour off the fat from the pan, and then deglaze with the *pommeau*, stirring to incorporate the sediment from the base of the pan. Add the chicken stock, return to the heat and then reduce a little before adding the cream. Reduce the whole mixture to the desired consistency. Taste, and season if required.

Serve the duck breasts in slices, with the sauce poured over them. Around them, add the apples, previously peeled, thinly sliced and fried in a little butter.

Touring Around

About 15km south of Coutances the D7 enters the Valley of the Sienne. At Lengronne, on the north side of the valley, a turn to the left onto the D13 leads to the large village of **Hambye**, from where another turn south will take you to one of the region's best-known monuments, the ruins of the Benedictine **Abbaye de Hambye** (*open April–Oct daily 10–12 and 2–6, 45mins guided tours Mon and Wed–Sun 10–11.30 and 2–5.30; July and Aug special detailed tours Mon 2pm; adm*), looming lichen-clad above the trees. Founded in 1145 by Guillaume de Paynel, Lord of Hambye, and much-favoured by Henry II of England and Normandy, it was still occupied until the Revolution, after which it rapidly fell into dereliction, thanks mostly to its being used by locals as a stone quarry. It is the largest complex of medieval monastic buildings in Normandy after Mont St-Michel. Though battered and roofless, the abbey church still stands as one of the finest examples of Norman Gothic, for the soaring simplicity of its unusually tall, narrow arches and its massive tower, still improbably perched almost intact on top of the giant arches, a full 100ft above the nave.

Some of the monastic buildings are still more intact, and extensive restoration work has been undertaken in recent years, particularly in the kitchens, the cider press and the *scriptorium*, or room for the copying of manuscripts. The Monks' Parlour has a remarkable 13th-century decorated ceiling, painted very simply with flowers, while the kitchen has a truly magnificent giant fireplace; the Chapterhouse, virtually undamaged, is similar in shape and vaulting to that in Norwich, with which Hambye had close links during the Middle Ages. On show in some rooms are a few rare pieces of medieval furniture, liturgical ornaments dating back to the early centuries of the abbey and some 17th-century tapestries, and there are also occasional temporary exhibitions. The normal guided tours of Hambye are in French only, and non-French speakers must tag along with an information sheet in English or other languages; you can wander around on your own, but note that unless you join the tour you will not have access to many interesting parts of the abbey, such as the Chapterhouse and the Parlour (this is not made clear at the entrance, and the admission ticket is the same). One compromise is to go round with the tour and then stay behind afterwards to get a better look at the church and cloister, which are open to all.

The setting of Hambye, next to the Sienne in a flat bend in the valley surrounded by woods, is as beautiful as the ruins themselves. Within walking distance is one of the *bocage*'s most popular hotel-restaurants, the Auberge de l'Abbaye (*see* pp.339, 340). From Hambye a string of lanes lead westwards up hill and down dale towards **Gavray** and **Le Mesnil-Rogues**. The *bocage* countryside can seem like a dense green web, in which the towering foliage of trees and unkempt hedges could be gently closing in around you – especially if you wander up any of the narrower lanes that follow the most apparently incomprehensible twists and turns. This overpowering greenness all adds to the area's fascination, and to its noticeable feeling of remoteness. This is a man-made landscape – in the shape of the hedgerows, built up over centuries – but it's one in which nature seems very much the most powerful factor. The most beautiful places in the *bocage* come when a road emerges from the green womb to meet one of the rivers like the Sienne, a flashing stream of brilliantly clear water.

Around you there are also plenty of opportunities for cider-tasting and investigating other local specialities. One of the most spectacularly pretty of all the *bocage* villages is **La Baleine**, a little cluster of houses on a particularly narrow and steep-sided bend in the Sienne valley, with an old humpbacked bridge across the river. It has one of France's smallest *mairies*, next to a much larger, four-square stone *auberge*. Right beside the bridge on the north side is the **Andouillerie de la Vallée de la Sienne**, which produces high-quality Norman versions of *andouilles* and *andouillettes*, gut and offal sausages, using traditional craft methods, smoking them over forest woods. Charcuterie enthusiasts can go on tours of the *Andouillerie* (*see* p.338).

After lunch, perhaps, turn back from the Auberge du Mesnil-Rogues towards the main D7 and go straight across it onto the narrow road downhill to **La Meurdraquière**, site of two impressive old farms, their driveways either side of a crossroads like book-ends, Bruno Vastel's Ferme de la Granterie, which offers *chambres d'hôtes* rooms and occasionally cider, and Roland Venisse's La Butte, with rooms, cider and calvados at all times (*see* pp.338, 339). The Cotentin ciders, though still nothing like rough cider, are in general a little drier and not quite so smooth as those from the Pays d'Auge. The best time to try them is from April to September, for the region's cider farmers are small producers, and may have sold much of their stock by October – although most will keep some bottles back for sale at least until Christmas, and calvados is available at all times. Also in La Meurdraquière is another farm, La Percehaye, which specialises in beekeeping, and offers farmhouse honeys. A little further southwest, off the D924 Granville road near **St-Jean-des-Champs**, is the Ferme de la Hermitière, one of the area's larger cider farms, where, as well as offering ciders and calvados for sale, owner Jean-Luc Colombier gives tours of his centuries-old farm, its orchards, still and cider presses, with a video on cider-making and a year in the life of the farm (*see p.338*).

From La Hermitière, if you've had enough cider-tasting for a while, look for the road, a little way east towards Villedieu on the south side of the main road, signed for St-Jean-des-Champs and the Abbaye de la Lucerne. This can seem almost deliberately deceptive, for, despite a recent signing-offensive, having got you on to this leaf-shrouded lane the authorities then omit to place many more signs to the abbey. It's best to accept the occasional false turning, appreciate the scenery, and more or less follow signs towards **St-Léger**. Then, just when you think you're totally lost, you roll around a hill and there, nestling in a wood-clad valley like a medieval vision, is the **Abbaye de la Lucerne d'Outremer** (*open mid-Feb–Mar and Dec Mon, Wed–Sun 10–12 and 2–5.30, closed Tues; April–Sept daily 10–12 and 2–6.30; Oct and Nov daily 10–12 and 2–5.30; closed Jan–mid-Feb; adm; joint ticket available with castle of Pirou, see p.324*).

La Lucerne is less well-known than Hambye (possibly because it's harder to find), but, if you visit only one of the Cotentin's ruined abbeys, this should be it. It's more atmospheric, and you're left to wander around it on your own; it's also less of a ruin, both because it survived post-Revolutionary destruction better, and because La Lucerne is the centre of a remarkable project. The abbey is not just being restored in certain details or shored up against collapse, it is being rebuilt. Since 1959 it has been in the care of a private foundation, the ultimate goal of which is to rebuild the abbey and re-establish a monastic community here. This was little more than a pious hope until the mid-1990s, but since then work has proceeded at a steadier pace. The nave of the great abbey church, half of which had collapsed, has now been substantially rebuilt, and the garden leading in from the gatehouse has been relaid following as much as possible its original lines. This 'reconstruction' of a monument from an utterly different era is disconcerting, going against normal expectations; however, it's hard not to be engaged by the completely non-21st century ambition of the project.

La Lucerne's sub-title 'd'Outremer' stems from its persistent loyalty during the Middle Ages 'across the sea', to England. Its site was chosen in 1161 by the Blessed Achard, then Bishop of Avranches, a major figure in the Anglo-Norman church who had also been Canon of Bridlington in County Durham. In 1204, when Philippe Auguste of France seized control of the Duchy of Normandy, the monks of La Lucerne remained stubbornly loyal to their former Duke, King John, in opposition to the French ecclesiastical stronghold of Mont St-Michel. Moreover, when the English reappeared in the area during the Hundred Years' War, the abbey again offered them its allegiance, providing a chaplain for Edward III. However, this did not prevent it becoming one of the largest religious houses in France, up until dissolution in 1791.

The main **church** was built between 1164 and 1178. Given that by this time Notre-Dame in Paris and other great works of early French Gothic were under construction to the east, the style – which has been respected in the current restoration – is remarkably simple and conservative, an unadorned Norman Romanesque little changed since the Conqueror's time. The building's very plainness gives it strength; alongside the church there is the even simpler **Chapel of the Blessed Achard**, a beautifully plain space that is one of the oldest parts of the abbey. Towards the back of the church a door leads through to the slightly later, more Gothic **Chapterhouse** and **Cloister**, still in ruins but earmarked for work at some point in the future. Clearly visible and in much less need of restoration is the **Lavatorium**, the monks' washing area, with classic Norman-style carving. Another door off the cloister leads to the giant 18th-century **refectory**, built on top of an impressive 12th-century vaulted cellar. Only recently opened to visitors, the refectory has as its centrepiece a spectacular, worm-eaten but still intact original timber staircase.

Another feature of La Lucerne is that, in its valley, the abbey always seems close to water: at the back of the church there is a small aqueduct, and alongside there is an almost lake-sized pond, separating the main buildings from the 18th-century Bishops' Palace. This is now a private house, and visitors are asked not to go too close, but there doesn't seem to be a problem in sitting by the pond for a while on a sunny afternoon. The restored church already contains a superb 1780s organ – originally built for the cathedral in Chambéry, near the Alps, and brought here in the 1970s – and Mass is said every Sunday at 11.15am. During July and August there are performances of organ music, Gregorian chant and other religious music in the church, and exhibitions on related themes are presented in the abbey buildings.

Behind the abbey to the east is a substantial stretch of the **Forêt de la Lucerne**, the thick deciduous wood that once covered most of the valley of the Thar, one of the Cotentin's fast-flowing rivers. Through the forest and beside the abbey there runs the **GR226 long-distance footpath**, which follows the line of one of the **Chemins aux Anglais**, the old tracks used by medieval English pilgrims on their way to Mont St-Michel and Santiago de Compostela, and which to the west runs to St-Pierre-Langers and then down to the Bay of Mont St-Michel. Using the footpath and side-tracks off to the south (free maps are available at the abbey) it's an easy 3km walk to the pretty village of **La Lucerne d'Outremer**, where there is an enjoyable *auberge* (*see* p.340).

East of La Lucerne is the capital of the southern *bocage*, **Villedieu-les-Poêles**. The 'City-of-God-of-the-Cooking-Pots' is so-called because since the 12th century the town has been single-mindedly dedicated to the working of copper, pewter and other metals. It became so because in the 1100s Henry I of England gave the town to the Knights of St John, with trading privileges that encouraged industry; the surrounding *bocage* was for centuries poor and overpopulated, and unemployed farm boys flocked into Villedieu to work in the metal trades and other crafts that developed.

The stone and slate medieval town is classically pretty, with a special architectural style of its own. It is centred on one long main street along a ridge, called **Place de la République** at the lower end, narrowing into **Rue Général Huard**, on either side of which narrow alleyways run away into courtyards of grey stone houses, the old copperworkers' homes and workshops. It's also much visited, with shops selling copper, kitchenware and other crafts almost end to end along the main street.

The town also has several museums and open workshops to showcase its trades, notably the **Fonderie des Cloches** (*tours Feb–June and Sept–Nov Tues–Sat 10–12.30 and 2–5.30; July and Aug daily 9–6; adm*), in Rue du Pont Chignon, one of the last entirely traditional bell-foundries in Europe; the **Atelier du Cuivre** (*54 Rue Général Huard; open Mon–Fri 9–12 and 1.30–6, Sat 9–12 and 2.30–5.30; adm*); and, in a fine 18th-century copperworkers' courtyard, the **Musée de la Poeslerie et de la Dentelle** (*25 Rue Général Huard; open April–mid-Nov Mon and Wed–Sun 10–12.30 and 2–6.30, Tues 2–6.30; adm*), the Museum of Copperworking and Lacemaking – the latter was formerly carried on by the town's women, while men worked the metal. And, if you know anyone who likes copper pots, this is the perfect place for gift buying. To help you, the town has actually introduced an *appellation contrôlée* for genuine Villedieu copperware.

A radical contrast is offered by the other substantial town in this area, **Granville**. The largest and one of the most characterful of the harbour towns on the Cotentin coast, it's a place of contrasting atmospheres. It was actually founded by the English, in the 15th century, as a base from which to attack the French in Mont St-Michel, and the old town, the **Haute-Ville**, reflects its military origins in its spectacular location, on a giant spit of rock jutting into the Atlantic, a natural fortress. There's a great walk around the line of the old ramparts encircling the Haute-Ville, with limitless sea views. Within its tight space old Granville is an atmospheric town of verticals, with steep cobbled streets between strangely tall, thin 16th- and 17th-century buildings perched on the hillsides, and impressive interconnecting squares. In the middle of the old town there is a massive 15th-century church, **Notre-Dame**, and the main shopping street, Rue des Juifs. The Haute-Ville also has two attractive museums, the **Musée du Vieux Granville** (*open April–June Mon and Wed–Sun 10–12 and 2–6; July–Sept Mon and Wed–Sun 10–12 and 2–6.30; Oct–Mar Wed, Sat and Sun 2–6; adm*), mainly on maritime history; and the **Musée d'Art Moderne Richard Anacréon** (*open July–Sept Mon and Wed–Sun 11–6; Oct–June Mon and Wed–Sat 2–6; adm*), an intriguingly personal museum containing the collections of a Paris bookseller, born in Granville, who was a friend of, and collected pictures by, many great names in 20th-century art – Derain, Dufy, Vlaminck, Picasso and more. It also hosts temporary shows of modern and contemporary art.

Granville's lower town, the **Basse-Ville**, is very different, a much more modern, workaday place, centred on the lively fishing port. It also contains the **Gare Maritime**, for ferries to Jersey, and a line of renowned seafood restaurants on the harbour side below the Haute-Ville. Across on the other flank of the Haute-Ville spit to the north, you can find a third side to Granville, its seaside town, with a casino, and a long, narrow beach that's still popular in summer. In the late 19th century Granville became one of the many fashionable places around the French coasts for respectable people to spend their summers, and on the heights above the beach there are neat lanes of *Belle Epoque* bourgeois villas, most still in very good shape. One of the grandest is the **Musée et Jardin Christian Dior** (*open mid-May–mid-Sept daily 10–12.30 and 2–6.30; adm*), the pink mansion that was the summer home of the great couturier's family when he was a child. Surrounded by perfectly trimmed (even chic) gardens, it contains designs and memorabilia mainly drawn from Dior's early years, as complete a contrast with the blue-overalled world of the *bocage* as you're likely to get.

Shopping

The largest **market** in this area is in **Villedieu** (*Tues*). There's also a good market in **Granville** (*Sat, smaller market Wed*) and an interesting little market in **Gavray** (*Sat*). Several traditional food and craft establishments in the Cotentin form part of a *Route de la Table*; visit four or more and you qualify for a *cadeau-surprise* of goodies (*details from tourist offices*). Among those taking part are the Laitiere du Val d'Ay (*see* p.326), the Andouillerie de la Vallée de la Sienne and the Ferme de l'Hermitière.

La Baleine (St-Denis-le-Gast) ✉ 50450

L'Andouillerie de la Vallée de la Sienne, Pont de la Baleine, **t** 02 33 61 44 20, *www.andouillerie.fr*. Deep in the forest something stirs, this workshop, in a fairytale site next to the humpbacked bridge in tiny La Baleine (so it's easy to miss, if you're concentrating on the winding bends). Inside it are M Bernard Boscher and his staff, dedicated to making the finest *andouilles* – Norman smoked gut sausages – using only traditional techniques, and with carefully chosen ingredients. As well as *andouilles* and *andouillettes* you can buy *rillettes*, bacon and other smoked meats, and locally-made fruit liqueurs; whole sausages or slices are available vacuum-packed for travelling purchasers. *Shop open Tues–Sun, closed Mon. Guided tours July and Aug daily 11am and 2.30–5.30; other times by appointment.*

Cérences ✉ 50510

Le Manoir de Guelle, t 02 33 51 99 06. Products, of the duck: terrines, *rillettes, confits de canard*, smoked duck breasts, foie gras and also some beef products, all made right on the farm, the same specialities that are used in the *ferme-auberge* (*see* p.340). *Open daily.*

Champrepus ✉ 50800

Au Fournil d'Antan, Village de l'Eglise, **t** 02 33 90 01 86. Best identified by a board outside offering *Pain Levain*, this traditional village bakery – on the D924, opposite Champrepus church – is renowned for its superb country breads, baked in an historic wood-fired oven. As well as breads from *baguettes* to *pains de campagne* it offers delicious *teurgoules* (Norman crusty rice puddings), a traditional by-product of Norman country baking, cooked in the bread oven as it cools down. *Open Tues–Sat 8–8.*

Le Mesnil-Rogues ✉ 50450

La Pinotière, t 02 33 61 38 98. Amid the *bocage* cider farms, Mme Legallais' farm is dedicated to raising goats, and produces a fine *chèvre*. Her shop has other local produce (preserves and ciders) and the farm has four B&B rooms (*€32 for two*). To find it follow *Fromages de Chèvres* signs from the centre of the village.

La Meurdraquière ✉ 50510

Ferme de la Butte, t 02 33 61 31 52. Wander into La Butte and Roland Venisse will bluffly leave his apple-crusher to open up his shed and sit at a massive log table with you while you try out his very fine *brut* cider and powerful calvados. They have won many awards, but he and his wife sell directly from the farm or to local *auberges*, not through shops. They also have B&B **rooms** (*see* p.339). *Closed Sun.*

St-Jean-des-Champs ✉ 50320

Ferme de l'Hermitière, t 02 33 61 31 51, *www.ferme-hermitiere.com*. Jean-Luc Colombier's guided tours (*c. 1½hrs*) of his big farm outside St-Jean-des-Champs give a very good idea of the processes used in making cider, *pommeau* and calvados. Included is the *eco-musée* farm museum, and all tours end with a tasting. At the shop you can buy fine sweet and dry ciders, fresh apple juice, *pommeau*, not overly-sweet *poiré* (perry) and a superior range of calvados. *Tours Easter–June Mon–Fri 2–6; July and Aug Mon–Sat 10–12 and 1.30–6; Sept Mon–Fri 10–12 and 1.30–6; adm. Shop open daily exc Sun.*

Villedieu-les-Poêles ✉ 50800

La Cour du Paradis, 40–44 Rue Dr Havard, **t** 02 33 50 54 66. Intended as a showcase for the products of the local *terroir*, this little shop in an old Villedieu house has an appealingly chaotic style – as well as all sorts of products from the Manche – both foods and craftwork – there are stacks of foods from all over France, and even an *épicerie anglaise* corner where expats can find English tea and HP sauce. Great for browsing. *Sept–June closed Wed and Mon am; July and Aug open daily.*

Where to Stay

Hambye ✉ 50450

Auberge de l'Abbaye, Route de l'Abbaye, **t** 02 33 61 42 19, *aubergedelabbaye@wanadoo.fr* (*double rooms €50–53*). A much-loved *Logis* hotel in a delightful location, next to the River Sienne and very near Hambye abbey. The seven rooms are comfortable, and there's a very pretty, well-kept garden from where you can see the abbey tower poking out above the trees. What wins most praise, though, is the warmth and enthusiasm of the Allain family. Equally popular is their excellent restaurant (*see* p.340). *Closed two weeks late-Feb and late-Sept–Oct.*

Le Mesnil-Villeman ✉ 50450

L'Orail, **t** 02 33 61 75 96 (*room €34 for two*). A lovely old farm in very peaceful countryside just east of Le Mesnil-Rogues. M and Mme Fauçon are exceptionally sweet, warm and welcoming: when they retired from working the farm a few years ago they set about doing up the house and creating a magnificent garden, which they will proudly show you. Their one B&B room (a double, with space for extra beds) is really a gîte, with its own entrance and kitchen – making it amazing value. Even though you have a kitchen, Mme will still bring you your breakfast. A lovely place for a relaxing stay, and seeing the best of the countryside.

La Meurdraquière ✉ 50510

La Granterie, 10 Route de St-Martin, **t** 02 33 90 26 45, **f** 02 33 91 96 32 (*rooms €45 for two*). A giant 17th-century farmhouse, like something out of Balzac, on a similarly rambling farm. Bruno and Delphine Vastel have two comfortable B&B rooms, with plenty of character and good bathrooms, and guests have the use of a living room and kitchen. The farm's magnificent cider shed, dating from 1689, is still sometimes put to use.
Ferme de la Butte, **t** 02 33 61 31 52, **f** 02 33 61 17 64 (*rooms €33–37 for two, €42 for four*). M and Mme Venisse, as well as being fine cider producers (*see* p.338), have three well-equipped *chambres d'hôtes* in a converted barn alongside their main farm. One is fully adapted for disabled access; the large, family room has ample space for four, and all the rooms have the use of a living room and well fitted-out, shared kitchen. It's deep in the middle of the countryside, and there's excellent cider available at any time.

Ste-Pience ✉ 50870

Manoir de la Porte, **t** 02 33 68 13 61, *www.manoir-de-la-porte.com* (*rooms €60–70 for two, €75 for three*). One of the *bocage*'s exceptional B&Bs, in a 16th-century priory with pepperpot turrets, surrounded by a lovely wooded park with pond that makes it deliciously peaceful. The owners, M and Mme Lagadec, are a retired couple who are very proud of their house. The two spacious guest rooms each have a double and a single bed, and are decorated with a mix of antiques and modern touches. Guests have use of a kitchen, and in the grounds there's a large *gîte*, with room for as many as 12. The house is a little north of Ste-Pience but quite hard to find, so ask for directions; note also that the Lagadecs will collect guests from train stations for no extra charge. *Closed Nov.*

Subligny ✉ 50870

La Grande Coquerie, **t** 02 33 61 50 23, *www.coquerie.com* (*rooms €45 for two*). A superior B&B in a very large farm amid lawns and beautiful gardens. Its main business is as a stud farm, so the house is surrounded by horses (which are, though, much too valuable for guests to be allowed to ride them). The two rooms are extremely pretty, each with its own colour scheme and antique furnishings; breakfast is served in a fabulous old room with fireplace, timber table and lots of flowers. M and Mme Dulin also have self-contained *gîtes*. The farm is some way north of Subligny, off the D573.

Villedieu-les-Poêles ✉ 50800

Hôtel St-Pierre et St-Michel, 12 Place de la République, **t** 02 33 61 00 11, *www.st-pierre-hotel.com* (*double rooms €40–43*). A traditional *Logis* hotel-restaurant on Villedieu's main square, with a typical country-town-hotel three-storey frontage and flower boxes beneath its windows. The 22 rooms have simple, pretty décor and good bathrooms; those at the front can be a little noisy, especially during the Tuesday market. The **restaurant** is one of the town's most popular, serving enjoyable Norman fare (*menus €19–31*). *Closed mid-Jan–mid-Feb.*

Eating Alternatives

La Baleine (St-Denis-le-Gast) ✉ 50450
Auberge de la Baleine, t 02 33 90 92 74 (*menus €13–30*). A big, plain old inn in a superb location in La Baleine, near the Sienne and with terrace tables outside on sunny days. Its *terroir*-based traditional cooking features the superb sausages from the *andouillerie* across the bridge (*see* p.338), but a wide range of other local produce – and Granville seafood – is used too. There are also four very simple, budget guest **rooms** (*€29–37*).

Cérences ✉ 50510
Le Manoir de Guelle, t 02 33 51 99 06 (*menus €21–28*). A *ferme-auberge*, using produce from the farm itself, in an 18th-century manor farm by the Sienne near Cérences. Duck in its many forms is a speciality, particularly *magret* grilled on a wood fire in the grand old fireplace, but there's also fine lamb, and delicious fruity and creamy farmhouse desserts. Plus there's the farm shop (*see* p.338). *Open Sat eve and Sun midday; group bookings possible on other days.*

Fleury ✉ 50800
La Clef des Champs, Route de Granville, t 02 33 59 31 36 (*menus €9.50–25*). A likeable little café-*tabac*-restaurant beside the Granville road through Fleury, west of Villedieu. Bargain menus include grilled meats, pâtés, salads or other local favourites, made with no frills but good fresh ingredients. A very handily-placed call-in for a snack or a light meal. *Closed Sept–May Sun.*

Granville ✉ 50400
Le Phare, Rue du Port, t 02 33 50 12 94 (*menus €10.52–24.39*). Of all the seafood restaurants on the harbour side in Granville, the Phare has the most return visitors. Granville is a working harbour and this is a bustling, straightforward restaurant, with a first-floor *salle panoramique* for taking a leisurely view of the port. The fish and seafood, naturally,

couldn't be fresher. It's by the very end of the quay on the right of the harbour, looking seawards; if you can't get in, there are more good seafood brasseries along the same quay. *Closed (Dec–Jan) Tues and Wed.*

Hambye ✉ 50450
Auberge de l'Abbaye, Route de l'Abbaye, t 02 33 61 42 19, *aubergedelabbaye@wanadoo.fr* (*menus €20–54*). The restaurant at Hambye's Auberge (*see* p.339) has an international fan club, both for Jean Allain's imaginative and enjoyable food and for the friendly, personal style with which it is served. He presents dishes from other parts of France – a change from all-Norman cooking – all prepared with care and using excellent ingredients. The wine list is similarly impressive, and wide-ranging. *Closed Sun eve and Mon, and two weeks late-Feb and late-Sept–Oct.*

La Lucerne d'Outremer ✉ 50320
Le Courtil de la Lucerne, t 02 33 61 22 02 (*menus €14–27*). This imposing 18th-century granite Presbytery, surrounded by a well-tended garden, is – after the church – about the largest building in La Lucerne, a few kilometres east of the abbey. It's one of the smarter *auberges du terroir*, with neat dining room and extensive menus. Dishes may have sophisticated touches, but the style is still hearty, with lots of cheese and calvados, and meals finish with indulgent desserts like a speciality calvados ice-cream soufflé. *Closed Tues (Oct–April only) and Wed, and Feb.*

Villedieu-les-Poêles ✉ 50800
La Ferme de Malte, 11 Rue Jules Tétrel, t 02 33 91 35 91, *www.lafermedemalte.fr* (*menus €16–52*). An original venture in a distinguished 18th-century house, with garden, just outside central Villedieu near the Granville road. The dining rooms are especially pretty, providing a suitable setting for chef Alain Duval's refined, creative cooking, strongly based on market freshness. It's also an unusually pampering **hotel**. There are just two elegant, suite-like rooms and a two-bedroom gîte (*double rooms €120–150; gîte €500 per week*), but guests enjoy all sorts of comforts including a well-sized garden pool with its own great view.

Mystic Mountain:
Mont St-Michel
and its Bay

32

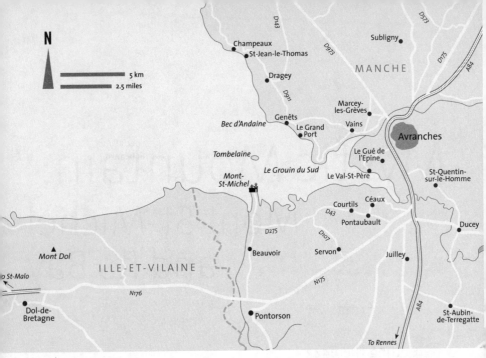

In southwestern Normandy, all routes and eyes seem to converge on the giant pinnacle of Mont St-Michel. Like a natural extension of the tiny rock on which it stands, the abbey can be seen from all angles towering above the surrounding empty wastes of sand and water, whether first seen sharply outlined from miles away on a clear day, or dimly glimpsed in silhouette through mists and the not-infrequent rain. First built to embody a particularly intense ideal of Christianity, it can still suggest a celestial vision against the sky. Even the giant arc of the bay itself seems to have been created as a great amphitheatre for the glory of the abbey.

The *Merveille de l'Occident*, the 'Wonder of the Western World', as it has often been called, is also France's greatest tourist attraction outside Paris. Pilgrims have been flocking here for over a thousand years, and since the first tourists began to travel for pleasure in the 19th century it has been one the obligatory stops. Consequently, as with the Vatican, St Mark's in Venice or any other site that's beyond mere fame, to see Mont St-Michel is usually to see it together with hundreds of other people. This can be disheartening, and to avoid the biggest crowds it's best to visit in spring, autumn or winter. However, even with the crowds the holy mountain is still extraordinary. The abbey looks astonishing from a distance, and is truly staggering from close up. If it were not so well-known, perhaps no one would quite believe it was there.

And all around it is the Bay, a mysterious expanse of constantly shifting sands, channels and salt marshes every bit as strange and enigmatic as the Mount, known for its unpredictable weather, and where the horizon sometimes seems infinitely far away to the west and at other moments is impossible to make out in the mist. It has the longest, deepest tides in Europe, with the sea a full 15 kilometres away at low tide. This immense flatness contains an abundance of birds and shellfish, while the marshes around its edge are used to graze much-prized *pré-salé* or salt-marsh lamb.

Getting There

All roads from Cherbourg, Caen and Paris converge at Avranches to form the N175, which sweeps around the Bay of Mont St-Michel into Brittany (where it become the N176). South of Avranches an exit signposted Mont St-Michel leads to the D75, the most attractive route to the Mount, which skirts the south side of the Bay. To go direct to Servon, stay on the N175 for 5km and look for a right turn.

Coming from Mont St-Michel, turn left onto the D275-D75 road at the south end of the causeway, and right again at sign for Servon.

Trains run to Avranches and Pontorson from Cherbourg and Paris (Gare Montparnasse). **Buses** run to Mont St-Michel from both towns.

Tourist Information

A great deal of information on the Bay is on *www.manchetourisme.com*.
Avranches: 2 Rue du Général de Gaulle, t 02 33 58 00 22, *www.ot-avranches.com*.
Mont St-Michel: t 02 33 60 14 30, *www.ot-montsaintmichel.com*.

Pontorson: Place de l'Hôtel de Ville, t 02 33 60 20 65, *www.mont-saint-michel-baie.com*.
St-Jean-le-Thomas: 21 Place Lejaudet, t 02 33 70 90 71.

Maisons de la Baie

The four Maisons are special information and exhibition centres, in beautiful locations round the Bay shore. They are the best sources for information on walks, nature- and wildlife-related activities and the ecology of the Bay in general. The Vains and Courtils centres also have interesting interactive exhibits on the formation and history of the Bay. All are open April–Sept, and in French school holidays.
Maison de la Baie de Courtils, Route de la Roche Torin, t 02 33 89 66 00, *musee.courtils@cg50.fr*.
Maison de la Baie de Genêts, 4 Place des Halles, t 02 33 89 64 00, *info@maisonbaie.com*.
Maison de la Baie de Vains, St-Léonard, Route du Grouin du Sud, t 02 33 89 06 06, *musee.vains-saint-leonard@cg50.fr*.
Maison de la Baie de Vivier-sur-Mer, t 02 99 48 84 38, *www.maison-baie.com*.

A century ago visitors to Mont St-Michel always ate and slept there too. You can eat there today, for a price, but meals on the Mount now rarely justify the restaurants' inflated charges. For a meal that doesn't disappoint it's better to eat away from the rock, and one of the best options is the simply named **Auberge du Terroir** in Servon, 10km away in the countryside south of the Bay, an exceptional village restaurant with sophisticated cuisine based entirely on wonderfully fresh local produce.

L'Auberge du Terroir

Le Bourg, Servon, t 02 33 60 17 92, aubergeduterroir@wanadoo.fr.
Open mid-June–mid-Sept daily 12–2.30 and 7–8.30; mid-Sept–mid-June Mon, Tues, Thurs, Fri and Sun 12–2.30 and 7–8.30, Sat 7–8.30, closed Wed.
Closed mid-Nov–mid-Dec and late Feb. Menus €17–39; carte average €40.

The label *auberge du terroir* tends to suggest sturdy country cooking, and around Normandy there are many such *auberges* that always have on the menu things like farmhouse terrines, *jambon au cidre* and *tarte tatin* with lashings of *crème fraîche*. The name in fact simply means that all the ingredients used are from the local *terroir*, and, French chefs being French chefs, it's hard for them to be left alone with even the most traditional local products without trying out their own ideas on how to cook them. In Servon, anyone expecting old-fashioned rustic fare will be very surprised.

First, the setting. It looks rural enough, in a large house in a calmly peaceful granite village typical of those on the solid ground around the south of the bay, with beautifully fresh, clean air. Inside, the dining room has pale colours, lots of light, crisp linen, tasteful flower arrangements and an air of serenity. Mme Annie Lefort, in charge of front-of-house, sees that every detail is attended to with quiet charm. As you wait to order, superbly crusty homemade bread arrives, along with a notably refined wine list.

Neither chef Thierry Lefort nor his wife are actually from this area, but came here in the early 1990s from Limoges. He is, though, an enthusiast for the produce of the Bay of Mont St-Michel, and especially its *agneau de pré-salé*, salt-marsh lamb, available only from May to September. Mont St-Michel lamb is often considered the finest of the similar meats from around France (inhabitants of the Baie de la Somme would of course not agree). M Lefort also maintains a wonderful herb garden, which gives him access to a constantly changing range of seasonings, used with great inventiveness.

A starter of foie gras with fig *confiture* is a superbly balanced, sweet-and-savoury mix. Thierry Lefort's approach to cooking is infinitely painstaking: his foie gras takes three days to make, as do several other specialities. And while his dishes are always very delicately done, their subtle flavours often go together with a no-holds-barred tendency, a confident, unrestrained use of wholesome ingredients. In fillet of pork *confit aux pommes* with dried tomatoes, supremely tender meat is enhanced by sweet tomatoes, a fabulous potato purée – Thierry Lefort has a real way with mash – and a deep-textured sauce with an almost bitter apple flavour that lingers in the mind.

Local seafood is another regular feature, whether oysters, sea bass or the catch of the day. To finish, after fine cheeses, there are lighter choices like sorbets, or, usually, M Lefort's extraordinary, light-and-rich-together saffron *crème brûlée*. Take a mouthful of it while sniffing the sprig of lavender from the garden, on the side of the plate. But note: it's more than ever essential to book, above all for weekends.

Crèmes Brûlées

Serves 4–8

14 egg yolks
350g/12oz caster sugar
1½ litres/3 pints *crème fleurette*
    (liquid *crème fraîche*; single cream is the closest equivalent)
500ml/1 pint milk
1 strand of saffron

This recipe produces an exceptionally rich *crème brûlée*. In a large saucepan, mix together the cream, milk and saffron and warm on a low heat for 20 minutes. While this is cooking, beat the egg yolks together with 300g of the sugar until fluffy. Allow each mixture to sit for 15 minutes. Then blend them evenly together in a food processor, for 3 minutes at speed 2. Leave this mixture to chill in the fridge overnight.

The next morning preheat the oven to 100°C/175°F/Gas Mark 1. Pour the cream mix into ramekins and place in the oven for 1 hour. Before serving, sprinkle an even layer of sugar on top of each ramekin and caramelize under the grill or with a chef's torch.

Touring Around

Avranches sits atop a clutch of giant granite hills that on one side fall away almost precipitously down to the great flat plain of the Bay of Mont St-Michel. Its history is inextricably bound up with that of the Mount. According to medieval manuscripts, in the year 708 the Archangel Michael appeared to St Aubert, Bishop of Avranches, and commanded him to build a shrine on what was then just a rocky outcrop covered in trees in the middle of the bay. Aubert, evidently an early rationalist despite his saintly status, dismissed this as a dream, and even did so again when Michael came a second time. The third time the angry Archangel gave him a sharp prod in the side of the head, and so the Bishop, duly called to attention, built the first small oratory on the Mount. The 19th-century church of **St-Gervais** in Avranches contains as its greatest relic the skull of St Aubert, with a small hole supposedly left by the Archangel's finger.

Also in Avranches is the **Plate-forme**, the small square where in 1172, at the instigation of Robert de Torigni, Bishop of Avranches and abbot of Mont St-Michel, Henry II of England and Normandy knelt for a whole day dressed only in his shirt in penance for the murder of Thomas à Becket. This is also a vantage point from which, coming from the east, you have the first great views across the Bay, and of Mont St-Michel at its centre. Henry knelt in front of Avranches Cathedral, which was then being built to De Torigni's own design; however, like much of the same abbot's building work on Mont St-Michel, it was overambitious, and collapsed in the 18th century.

A few streets away is Avranches' **Hôtel de Ville**, which contains a matchless treasure, the surviving books and documents from the library of Mont St-Michel, saved during the Revolution. A spectacular selection of these **Manuscrits du Mont St-Michel** is on display each summer (*open June and Sept daily 10–12 and 2–6; July and Aug daily 10–6; adm*). Nearby, the **Musée Municipal** (*open June–Sept daily 10–12.30 and 2–6; adm*) has a reconstruction of a medieval manuscript workshop and displays on more recent local traditions. More recently still, Avranches was the jumping-off point for General Patton's breakout from Normandy in 1944, and just south of town there is a war museum, the **Musée de la Seconde Guerre Mondiale** (*open April–June and Sept–11 Nov daily 9.30–12.30 and 2–6; July and Aug daily 9.30–6.30; 12 Nov–Mar Sun 9.30–12.30 and 2–6; adm*), an eccentric private collection of the dummies-in-old-uniforms kind.

Avranches is a good point from which to explore the **north side of the Bay**. Traditionally, pilgrims from England and the north got their first, extraordinary sight of Mont St-Michel from one of the most spectacular places of all, the towering cliffs at **Champeaux**, dubbed the '*plus beau kilomètre de France*' because of the lush stretch of coastal forest that lines its lower slopes. All along the narrow road that follows the Bay shore you get astonishing views, in snatches or long stretches, as you seem to circle the Mount, as if it were an object of worship in itself. A contemplation of the ever-present silhouette of Mont St-Michel is as much a part of any visit as a tour of the abbey buildings, above all at sunset, when you can well imagine medieval pilgrims thinking they had come within the presence of the divine. When the weather closes in (as often happens) you see a different but equally awesome sight, for even when little else is distinguishable, the misty spire rises up out of the murk.

Genêts is a distinctive village, with more superb views, which like Avranches is inseparable from the Mount. It grew up as a departure point for pilgrims walking to the abbey, in the centuries when there was no causeway from the mainland. It is still the main centre today for anyone seeking the unforgettable experience of getting to Mont St-Michel on foot across the sands, from the nearby **Bec d'Andaine** point (*see* p.347). **On no account should anyone attempt this without a guide.** Legends abound about the giant tides and quicksands of the bay, and in the Middle Ages thousands of unwary pilgrims were lost to the sands, mists and the sudden arrival of the sea.

Between the villages tracks and paths run to the shoreline, to beautifully peaceful, often deserted spots, with sheep grazing in the salt marshes, and the Mount and the shifting Bay horizons away in the distance – **Le Grouin du Sud** and **Le Gué de l'Epine** are two of the most atmospheric. Near the former is Vains' **Maison de la Baie**, with a vivid display on the ecology of the Bay. It is a unique area of unstable, shifting territory, neither sea nor land, between the granite solids of the Cotentin and Brittany. Scattered in the sands, like three pebbles, are three immovable granite rocks: Mont St-Michel, little **Tombelaine** to its north and **Mont-Dol**, long swallowed by land to become a curious mountain near Dol-de-Bretagne, on the Breton side of the Bay.

The **south side of the Bay** has been notoriously volatile, and much of the land here has been reclaimed from the sea. The Couesnon river, the frontier between Normandy and Brittany, was for centuries seen as the region's curse because of its flooding and erratic course, until Dutch engineers set its present banks and drained 'polders' west of the river in the 1860s. This drainage work, however, and the causeway added in 1877 greatly aggravated the problem of silting up in the Bay. After long argument, a plan is in motion for the causeway to be removed, so that Mont St-Michel will be an island again. It will be linked to the mainland only by an elegant metal footbridge, with a light tramway for rapid access, which will allow the movement of the tides. This is due for completion in 2009, but access to the Mount will remain open throughout.

South of Avranches the main road runs down to **Pontorson**, a pleasant town that makes a good base for visiting the Mount. On the way it may be a good time to stop at Servon for lunch. Afterwards, head back to Pontaubault to get back to the coast road for Mont St-Michel, now the D43. As the road winds across the flat, marshy fields, the abbey appears once again like a lodestar, sometimes hidden from view, at others re-emerging suddenly around a bend in the hedgerows. Along the way is **Courtils**, a lovely village on the very edge of the salt flats, with another **Maison de la Baie**.

As you finally come to the **causeway** to the Mount you're reminded with a thump that you are entering one of the world's great tourist sites, as its base is decorated with garish lines of shiny hotels, petrol stations and fast-throughput restaurants. Beyond them you come on to the causeway proper, one of the greatest approaches in the world, with the Mount towering ever larger at the far end. For as long as the causeway continues to exist, if you are driving try to continue to car park 1, nearest the entrance. From there a narrow walkway leads to the first gate in the 15th-century ramparts, and the tourist office. Carry on through the massive **Porte du Roi**, the model of a medieval citadel, into Mont St-Michel's only real street, the **Grande Rue**, which winds anti-clockwise around the rock. Local tourist literature optimistically refers to

Walking to the Mount

Walking across the sands at low tide is the most historic, and magical, route to Mont St-Michel. But – no one should attempt any Bay walk without an experienced guide. Several organizations run guided walks, with fully qualified guides; the main season is April–Oct, but some walks run all year. The main departure point is the old pilgrims' starting place of the Bec d'Andaine, just north of Genêts, but walks also leave from the Grouin du Sud, near Vains. The Bec has been a victim of its own popularity, with thousands passing through in high season, and a conservation scheme has begun involving moving the parking area back from the shore. To miss the crowds, don't go in July and August, especially weekends.

The walk (barefoot, and in shorts) is 7km in each direction, and takes 1hr 45mins one way, 4hrs 30mins return, with an hour on the Mount in between. English-speaking guides can be arranged; check too if other tours in English are running. As well as the basic route, others are available that include uninhabited Tombelaine or old pilgrims' paths, and for the adventurous there are sunset and night walks. Several guides offer crossings on horseback.

Bay Guides and Tours

Listed here are some of the licensed guides' groups. More information on activities around Mont St-Michel can be found at tourist offices and the Maisons de la Baie (*see* p.343).

Chemins de la Baie, 34 Rue de l'Ortillon, Genêts, t 02 33 89 80 88, *www.cheminsdelabaie.fr*. Tours all year.

Découverte de la Baie, La Maison du Guide, 1 Rue Montoise, Genêts, t 02 33 70 83 49, *www.decouvertebaie.com*. A varied programme including horseback crossings.

Didier Lavadoux, 36 Grande Rue, Genêts, t/f 02 33 70 84 19, e *didier.lavadoux@wanadoo.fr*. An independent guide specializing in small groups, and an expert on Bay birdlife.

Sport-Evasion, 1 Rue de Tombelaine, Le Val-St-Père, t 02 33 68 10 00, *www.sport-evasion-fr.com*. Also cycle tours.

its shopkeepers 'maintaining a tradition born in catering to pilgrims in the Middle Ages'. This means they have been peddling junk for centuries. However, with their St-Michael thermometers, model boats, daft T-shirts, *crêpes* and Breton biscuits, you could say the Grande Rue traders reinforce the original imagery of the Mount, in which the climb up is supposed to lead out of the dross of worldly life towards God.

As well as the abbey Mont St-Michel has other museums and exhibits, none of them especially impressive. The **Musée de la Mer et de l'Ecologie** has boat models and exhibits on the development of the Bay; the **Archéoscope** is a multi-media show on the history and legends of Mont St-Michel; the **Logis Tiphaine** is a 14th-century house that belonged to the wife of Bertrand du Guesclin, French hero of the Hundred Years' War; and the **Musée Historique** tells the Mount's history through waxworks (*all open mid-Feb–11 Nov daily 9.30–5.30, Christmas week daily 10–5; adm, joint ticket for all four museums*). More interesting is the town itself. The Grande Rue can seem Disneyfied, but it's still an extraordinary image of a medieval street – a few feet wide for much of its length, with remarkably tall half-timbered gables that appear impossibly close together. The rest of the town is a labyrinth of passages, stairways and ramparts.

The Grande Rue winds up and round into the **Grand Degré** or great staircase up to the abbey. Maupassant wrote that from different angles Mont St-Michel can look like a cathedral, or a fortress. It has similarities to the Potala Palace in Tibet. Vast quantities of granite were brought from the Chausey Islands to build it, in an astonishing feat of early engineering. No one knows how many of its builders died at their work. Neglected after the 16th century, the Mount was rediscovered by Romantics such as Chateaubriand and Hugo, and from there entered the universal Gothic imagination.

Particularly striking are its proportions – some walls and windows are enormous beyond expectations, other rooms are quite intimate. One of the most imposing sections is the Grand Degré itself, rising steeply between awesomely high walls.

The **Abbey** (*open daily May–Aug 9–7, Sept–April 9–6, last entry 1hr before closing; closed some hols; adm*) is a complex building in which rooms and wings from different periods are all intertwined, so that it is impossible to see it in chronological order. St Aubert's oratory was succeeded by the first church on the rock in the early 10th century, but building really accelerated after the Benedictines took over the Mount in 966. The main church was begun in 1017 by Abbot Hildebert, and the most important parts of it were completed in 1058, under William the Conqueror. One of the abbey's greatest periods was the late 12th century, under Robert de Torigni, who made it a major centre for manuscript production, and built in a Gothic-Transition style.

Part of the legend of Mont St-Michel is that it has never been captured in war. This really applies to strictly non-French armies, for in 1204, when Philippe Auguste of France was struggling to wrest Normandy from King John, Breton soldiers allied to the French king took the Mount and severely damaged it in a fire. In atonement the king commissioned an entire new wing on the north side of the Mount, the masterpiece of high Gothic called the **Merveille** or Marvel. In return, Mont St-Michel became a bastion of French power in Normandy, and later resisted the English throughout the Hundred Years' War. Alterations were still being made to its buildings until the 18th century, but the abbey was closed during the Revolution. It was made into a prison, remaining so until it became one of France's first national monuments in 1874.

It is theoretically possible to visit without a guide, but if you do you will find many sections closed to you. Mont St-Michel is, in any case, difficult for first-time visitors to find their way round alone, so it's worth taking the official tours (*for no extra charge, in various languages*). The basic tour lasts about an hour, but still does not visit all the abbey; extended tours are also available, for an extra charge. Since 1966, the abbey's millennium, there has again been a religious presence of a few monks and nuns on the Mount. Mass is celebrated every day at 12.15pm, and they also hold retreats.

When you finally reach the top of the Grand Degré, you emerge on to the **Western Platform**, with a fine view of the Bay across to Cancale, and where the guides begin their tours. Surprisingly, the abbey church has a plain neoclassical façade, from the 1770s. It once had a massive Gothic-Transition frontage designed by Robert de Torigni, but like his cathedral in Avranches this was not structurally all it should have been, and when it finally fell down in the 18th century it took with it three of the seven arches of Abbot Hildebert's 11th-century nave. **Inside** the church, you are immediately made aware of the extraordinary, mystical ambition of the abbey's builders. It was not built *against* the Mount, but *on top* of it, with the peak of the rock precisely beneath the centre of the church's cross, so that the whole thing is actually a cathedral suspended in midair. Around the centre are Hildebert's original four massive columns, the basis of the whole structure, in classic, severe Norman Romanesque.

The choir, on the other hand, is in a light, graceful *Flamboyant* Gothic style, completed only in 1521, and built after the original choir had also given way, in the 15th century. The church thus contains both the first and final phases of medieval architecture.

The tour route runs in a rough spiral downwards, in a way that broadly mirrors the way the abbey was conceived, with the church at its apex, monastic and official apartments below, and rooms for the reception of poor pilgrims at the bottom. On the same level as the church is one of the most famous parts of the *Merveille*, the superb **Cloister** (1218–28), suspended in space with sheer walls beneath it on two sides. It leads to the **Refectory**, famed for the complex diffusion of light through its windows. Today, like the church, it can appear austere and granite-grey, but colour is the one feature of the abbey that's now most missing: its halls were so large because the abbots entertained exalted guests frequently, and they would have been decorated throughout with frescoes, tiles and tapestries. Today, the only way to get an idea of the colours of Mont St-Michel is through the manuscripts kept at Avranches.

As you descend, the intricacy with which rooms lead into each other is constantly surprising. Beneath the Cloister is the rib-vaulted **Promenoir** from 1115. It was built as a place for monks to take exercise, but also served as a refectory before the building of the one above, and Robert de Torigni entertained Henry II, Eleanor of Aquitaine and their court here in 1158. Nearby there is a human treadmill, used to haul supplies up an extraordinarily tall chute, which was installed as part of the prison in the 19th century. Beyond is the mysteriously atmospheric crypt of the **Gros Piliers** or 'Great Pillars', a thicket of giant granite columns. Look up through a little hole in the centre of the ceiling and you suddenly realize you are underneath the choir of the church.

The most elegant room in the abbey is the **Guests' Hall**, part of the *Merveille*, with one row of slim columns down the centre. French Kings were received here on their visits to the Mount. The **Knights' Hall** is much larger. Despite its name it was actually the main workroom of the abbey, where monks copied manuscripts, with two huge fireplaces to keep them warm. The last room on the main tour is the 12th–13th-century **Almonry**, where charity was given to poor pilgrims, and now the bookshop.

After leaving the buildings, walk around the windblown **gardens** on the north side of the Mount, a great place from which to admire the truly giant outside walls of the abbey, on buttresses that seem to soar up out of the rock. You can also see the **spire**, only completed in the 1890s in the post-prison restoration of the Mount. Another thing to look out for from the gardens or the ramparts is the incoming tide. The speed of tides in the Bay, which so terrified medieval pilgrims, is often compared to a galloping horse; it's more like a remorseless, fast trot, but is spectacular, especially during spring and autumn high tides. Tide tables are provided at the tourist office.

In summer, try to come back to the abbey at night for the son et lumière, currently titled **Méditations** (*open June Fri, Sat and hols 6–11pm, July and Aug Mon–Sat 6–11pm; first two weeks Sept 5–10pm; last entry 1hr before closing; adm*). The exact programmes (and possibly the title) change each year. Their great attraction – on top of the fact that the abbey is much less crowded than by day – is that you are free to wander at will, or stay and examine the shadows in one room if you wish. You also see parts of the abbey not visited on the main tour, notably **Notre-Dame-sous-Terre**, the wonderfully simple 10th-century first church of Mont St-Michel, which actually supports the nave of Hildebert's church. It's a superb way of experiencing the atmospheres of Mont St-Michel, despite all the exploitation down below, in all their mystical power.

Shopping

The best **markets** around the Bay are in Pontorson (*Wed*) and Avranches (*Sat*). In summer there's also a market in Genêts (*Sun*).

Courtils ✉ 50220

Brasserie de la Baie, 6 Route de la Roche Torin, t 02 33 60 37 65, *clesenechal@mail.cpod.fr*. A tiny brewery near the very edge of the Bay in Courtils where Christophe Lesenechal makes a fine range of beers with entirely traditional methods. He also gives tours. *Open Thurs–Sat 3–9.*

St-Aubin-de-Terregatte ✉ 50240

Cave de Mirande, t 02 33 48 42 18, *www.cave-de-mirande.fr*. Although this farm is more organized than many – with website and *ferme-auberge* restaurant (*see* p.352) – it still feels utterly rural, with a huge rambling courtyard. Jacques Daunay produces a full range of fine ciders, calvados and *pommeau*, and a unique strong apéritif, *Mirandel*. On most Thursdays in July and August the farm hosts *marchés à la ferme* bringing together local food producers.

Where to Stay

Céaux ✉ 50220

Le Mée Provost, t 02 33 60 49 03 (*rooms €40 for two, €58 for four*). A real farm B&B right in the 'corner' of the Bay, outside the village of Céaux. The Delaunay family have five guest rooms (two family rooms and three doubles): comfortably equipped, with old-fashioned décor, they're cosy, and wonderful value. Guests have access to a kitchen, but this would mean missing out on Mme Delaunay's breakfasts, served in a beautiful old room in the main house. The Delaunays are very friendly, and the farm is only about a 1km walk from the Bay shore.

Champeaux ✉ 50530

Hôtel les Hermelles-Au Marquis de Tombelaine, 25 Route des Falaises, t 02 33 61 85 94, *claude.giard@wanadoo.fr* (*double rooms €46–52*). The very popular Marquis de Tombelaine restaurant (*see* p.352) has a six-room hotel above it. Rooms are light and comfortable, but their greatest draw is that in those at the front you wake up to a superb view across to Mont St-Michel. Check on the view when booking. *Closed Jan.*

Courtils ✉ 50220

Manoir de la Roche Torin, t 02 33 70 96 55, *www.manoir-rochetorin.com* (*double rooms €78–198*). One of the most luxurious options around the Bay, in a grand, rather English-looking ivy-clad 19th-century house in a superb location right on the edge of the marshes north of Courtils village. Of the 15 elegant rooms the ones really to go for are those that actually have views of the Mont, two of which have garden terraces. Other luxury-standard rooms and a suite have larger terraces, but less view, but you can get the same wonderful view by walking a few steps beyond the end of the lush garden. Public rooms are plushly comfortable, and there's a fine restaurant (*see* p.352).

Dragey ✉ 50530

Le Clos St-Jean, 8 Route des Cognets, t 02 33 48 78 09, *maussion.virginie@wanadoo.fr* (*rooms €45–55 for two*). The great draw of this modern house is its location, on a hillside west of Dragey village, with stupendous views of the Bay and Mont St-Michel from the breakfast room, garden and the luminous main guest room. It's a very large double; the other room, a twin, is smaller and doesn't have the view, but is still comfortable. Owner Virginie Maussion has a likeably relaxed charm.

Ducey ✉ 50220

Auberge de la Selune, 2 Rue St-Germain, t 02 33 48 53 62, *www.selune.com* (*double rooms €52–55*). A four-square country hotel in an attractive town south of Avranches, which has been thoroughly renovated with the bright modern-traditional mix much favoured in French hotels. Beyond the reception desk there is a lovely garden beside the fast-flowing River Selune (winner of awards as the best-kept hotel garden in Normandy). The 19 rooms are brightly comfortable, and the restaurant is one of the area's best (*see* p.352). *Closed late-Nov–mid-Dec.*

Juilley ✉ 50220

Les Blotteries, t/f 02 33 60 84 95, *www.les-blotteries.com* (*rooms €57–61 for two, €73–79 for three*). A lovely B&B on a fine old farm (with goats), run with style by the especially friendly Jean-Malo and Laurence Tizon. The three rooms are each in a different part of the farm: one in the main house is a very large double, with fabulous timber floor and space for another bed; in the former bakery is a huge family room with space for five, and the stables room is an intimate retreat for two. Breakfasts are served in a baronial room in the main house, and the Tizons provide every kind of information for their guests. It's south of Juilley village, on the way to St-James.

Marcey-les-Grèves ✉ 50300

Hôtel La Ramade, 2 Rue de la Côte, t 02 33 58 27 40, *www.laramade.fr* (*double rooms €58–108*). An unusual, intimate hotel recently opened in a large 18th-century house just northwest of Avranches. Marcey is not the most interesting town around the Bay, but once inside La Ramade's garden you're in a snug island of discreet luxury. The nine rooms have been carefully and individually decorated in delicate light colours, in a very French style that's chichi or stunningly pretty, depending on your own taste. They're utterly comfortable, and Verónique Morvan and her staff are also especially attentive. The breakfast room-*salon de thé* is equally enticing and outside in the lovely garden there's a one-room *gîte* (*€250–380 per week*), in the same style. Prices vary by season.

Pontorson ✉ 50170

Hôtel Montgomery, 13 Rue Couesnon, t 02 33 60 00 09, *www.hotel-montgomery.com* (*double rooms €55–145*). The official name of this hotel is 'Best Western Montgomery', but it's still one of the most historic, characterful places to stay around the Bay. It occupies the 500-year-old former mansion of the Counts of Montgomery, distant relatives of the British Field Marshal, and the original 1550s main staircase, carved wood, fireplaces and rambling corridors are spectacular: lovers of historic houses adore it. Some of the 32 rooms are in the same style, with four-poster beds and dark-beamed ceilings, others are more conventional, but all are comfortable. Prices vary by the size and character of the room. There's also a pretty garden terrace, and a restaurant (*not open to non-residents*). Staff are charming. *Closed two weeks Feb and two weeks Nov.*

Hôtel de Bretagne, 59 Rue Couesnon, t 02 33 60 10 55, *www.lebretagnepontorson.com* (*double rooms €39–64*). Pontorson's 'other' star hotel isn't as historic as the Montgomery – it was built in 1903, squarely in the *Belle Epoque* – but lacks for nothing in character and quirky charm, from the décor to the welcoming way it's run. Some of the 15 rooms are rather plain, while others are larger and better-equipped, but all are pleasantly comfortable, and the hotel has an enjoyable feel. There's an excellent restaurant (*see* p.352), and a great little lounge bar.

Servon ✉ 50170

Auberge du Terroir, t 02 33 60 17 92, *aubergeduterroir@wanadoo.fr* (*double rooms €48–64*). The Auberge has six very attractive guest rooms, between the main house and an adjacent annexe. Very comfortable, they vary in size: all have been thoroughly renovated recently and are decorated in a colourful, neatly flowery style, each with different colours and details. Servon is very peaceful and, of course, you have the restaurant right at hand (*see* p.343).

Vains ✉ 50300

Le Coin à la Carelle, t 02 33 48 50 34 (*rooms €48 for two, €65 for three*). A place to experience the peace of the Bay, on the edge of the marshes; it doesn't actually have a view of the Mount (it's just around a corner), but plenty of misty horizons. Evelyne Bourée's old house has been thoroughly modernized, and her two B&B rooms, both with picture windows, are ultra-comfortable. One is a family room, and there's also a lovely guests' lounge. M Bourée is hugely enthusiastic and helpful, and as well as great organic breakfasts provides bikes for guests' use. The house is great for walkers, with the coastal footpath right by the garden. To get to it, find the Vains *Maison de la Baie*, and keep going on the Bayside road.

Eating Alternatives

Champeaux ✉ 50530

Au Marquis de Tombelaine,
25 Route des Falaises, **t** 02 33 61 85 94,
claude.giard@wanadoo.fr (*menus €19.90–59.60*). One of the best eating stops on the north side of the Bay, in a fabulous location on the cliffs north of Champeaux. Chef Claude Giard offers classic French cuisine with Norman touches – lobster is a speciality, but just as fine are sea bass, Bay lamb, and creamy desserts. It's also a hotel (*see p.350*). *Closed Tues eve, Wed, and Jan.*

Courtils ✉ 50220

Manoir de la Roche Torin, **t** 02 33 70 96 55, *www.manoir-rochetorin.com* (*menus €20–49*). The big, pretty dining room at the hotel (*see p.350*) has a superb outlook, across gardens and salt marshes to the Mount. On the inland side, there are tables in a garden. Its cooking has a high reputation: mainstays of the menu are *pré-salé* lamb, and opulent seafood dishes. A great plus is the chance of a post-lunch stroll along the Bay's edge.

Ducey ✉ 50220

Auberge de la Selune, 2 Rue St-Germain, **t** 02 33 48 53 62, *www.selune.com* (*menus €15–36*). Like the rest of the hotel (*see p.350*), the Auberge's dining room has a feel of classic comfort. The impressive cooking of Jean-Pierre Girres offers imaginative surprises: specialities include a fragrant *truite soufflé* and a vegetarian aubergine gateau with red pepper coulis. *Closed (Oct–Mar) Mon, and late Nov–mid-Dec.*

Genêts ✉ 50530

Chez François, Rue Jérémie, **t** 02 33 70 83 98 (*dishes c. €7–18*). A bit like a brick-and-stone cave, this is a great village café-bistro with a speciality of grilled meats – pork chops, *andouillette* sausages, lamb – and some fish, cooked on a wood fire in a massive old fireplace. To go with them there are fresh salads, shellfish and rich desserts. It's as simple as they come, but very enjoyable, and a favourite place to finish up after the Bay walk to Mont St-Michel. As it's so popular, get there early for lunch. *Closed Thurs.*

Mont St-Michel ✉ 50116

La Mère Poulard, Grande Rue, **t** 02 33 89 68 68, *www.mere-poulard.com* (*menus €35–75*). The historic inn of Mont St-Michel, visited by a host of famous names since it opened in the 1870s. It had been sitting on its overpriced laurels for years, but in 2003, to general surprise, Michel Bruneau, winner of two Michelin stars at his restaurant La Bourride in Caen, took over as head chef, so it now has ambitious, very refined cuisine (to go with the same high prices). A cheaper alternative is next door, **Les Terrasses Poulard** (*menus €15–29*). The Poulard group also has four hotels on or near the Mount.

Auberge St-Pierre, Grande Rue, **t** 02 33 60 14 03, *www.auberge-saint-pierre.fr* (*menus €22–32*). One of the more attractive places to eat on Mont St-Michel, thanks to a location in one of the tall, thin 15th-century houses on the Grande Rue, and its decent Norman food at decent prices. At the back, there's a pretty and tranquil flowery terrace. It's also a *Logis* **hotel** (*double rooms €75–150*), with 21 snug rooms.

Pontorson ✉ 50170

Hôtel de Bretagne, 59 Rue Couesnon, **t** 02 33 60 10 55, *www.lebretagnepontorson.com* (*menus €14.50–38*). The restaurant at the Bretagne (*see p.351*) is as individual as the hotel, with an Art Nouveau dining room at the front, and an almost country-courtyard-like space within. The enjoyable food includes plenty of local classics – chicken braised in cider, Bay lamb, oysters in a Camembert *gratin*, fruity desserts – and is great value. *Closed Mon (Oct–Mar) and Jan.*

St-Aubin-de-Terregatte ✉ 50240

Ferme-Auberge de Mirande, **t** 02 33 60 05 46, *www.cave-de-mirande.fr* (*menus €14–25*). This impressive cider farm (*see p.350*) contains a very enjoyable *ferme-auberge*, with a huge dining room for big groups and a smaller, far cosier one for more casual diners. Farm-fresh produce is used in a delicious range of dishes – duck in different ways, leek tarts, trout fillet. The owners are very charming country people, and it's a great place for a leisurely, satisfying meal. *Closed Sun eve and Mon.*

A Fortress on the Ocean:
St-Malo

33

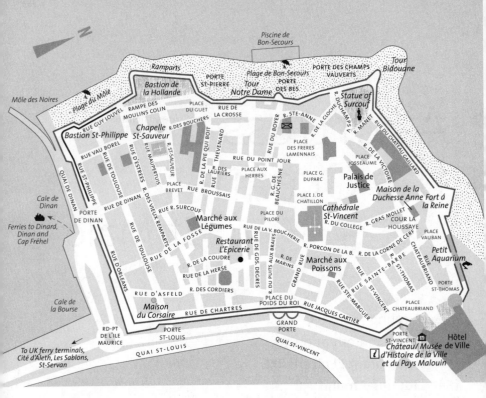

Piscine de
Bon-Secours

Ramparts

Plage de Bon-Secours

PORTE DES CHAMPS
VAUVERTS

Tour
Bidouane

Môle des Noires

Plage du Môle

Bastion de
la Hollande

PORTE
ST-PIERRE
Tour
Notre Dame

PORTE
DES BES

R. STE-ANNE

Statue of
Surcouf

PLACE
DU GUET

RUE DE
LA CROSSE

R. DU BOYER

R. DE LA CLOCHE

R. DES CHAMPS V.

R. MANET

RUE DU CHATEAUGAILLARD

Bastion St-Philippe

RUE GUY LOUVEL

RAMPE DES
MOULINS COLIN

Chapelle
St-Sauveur

R.DES BOUCHERS

RUE ST-SAUVEUR

RUE DE LA PIE QUI BOIT

RUE THEVENARD

RUE DU POINT JOUR

PLACE
DES FRERES
LAMENNAIS

PLACE DE LA VICTOIRE

PLACE
JOSSEAUME

RUE VAU BOREL

RUE ST-PHILIPPE

RUE DE TOULOUSE

RUE MAUPERTUIS

RUE D'ESTREES

R. DES
LAURIERS

PLACE AUX
HERBES

R.G. DE BEAUCHESNE

PLACE G.
DUPARC

Palais de
Justice

PLACE
BREVET

RUE DE DINAN

R. DES VIEUX REMPARTS

RUE BROUSSAIS

PLACE AUX
BRAIES

PLACE J. DE
CHATILLON

Cathédrale
St-Vincent

Maison de la
Duchesse Anne Fort á
la Reine

QUAI DE DINAN

Cale de
Dinan

Ferries to Dinard,
Dinan and
Cap Fréhel

PORTE
DE DINAN

RUE R. SURCOUF

PLACE DU
PILORI

R. GRAS MOLLET

COUR LA
HOUSSAYE

RUE DE TOULOUSE

Marché aux
Légumes

RUE DE LA V. BOUCHERIE

R. DU COLLEGE

R. DE LA CORNE DE CERF

PLACE
VAUBAN

RUE D'ORLEANS

RUE DE LA FOSSE

Restaurant
L'Epicerie

RUE DE GDS. DEGRES

R. DE
MARINS

R. PORCON DE LA B.

R. DE LA CORNE DE CERF

Petit
Aquarium

R. DE LA COUDRE

RUE DE LA HERSE

RUE DU PUITS AUX BRAIES

GRAND RUE

Marché aux
Poissons

RUE STE-BARBE

RUE CHATEAUBRIAND

PORTE
ST-THOMAS

Cale de
la Bourse

RUE D'ASFELD

R. DES CORDIERS

PLACE DU
POIDS DU ROI

RUE STE-MARGUER.

RUE ST-VINCENT

RUE ST-THOMAS

Maison
du Corsaire

RUE DE CHARTRES

RUE JACQUES CARTIER

PLACE
CHATEAUBRIAND

RD-PT
DE L'ÎLE
MAURICE

PORTE
ST-LOUIS

GRAND
PORTE

PORTE
ST-VINCENT

Hôtel
de Ville

To UK ferry terminals,
Cité d'Aleth, Les Sablons,
St-Servan

QUAI ST-LOUIS

QUAI ST-VINCENT

Château/ Musée
d'Histoire de la Ville
et du Pays Malouin

St-Malo, with a walled city still at its centre, has the most spectacular location of
any of the ports along France's north coast. The old city looks almost as much a part
of the sea as the land, its spires and giant ramparts filling up completely a spit of
earth jutting out into the Atlantic at the mouth of the River Rance. Around it, the eye
follows surf breaking over a scattering of tiny rocky islands, across to the green banks
on the other side of the estuary. Its life has inevitably been tied to the sea. Mariners
from St-Malo, called *Malouins*, sailed to every corner of the earth: to Canada, the
Indian Ocean, and Polynesia, and the French and Spanish names for the Falkland
Islands, the *Malouïnes* or *Malvinas*, stem from the fact that they were first discovered
by men from here. This was the home port of many of France's greatest explorers.

The *Malouins* were also known for their bellicose independence. When the Duchy of
Brittany was still independent in the Middle Ages, St-Malo appealed to the authority
of the kings of France against their duke; at other times, they did the same thing in
reverse, and at one point in the 16th century announced that they were 'neither
Frenchmen, nor Bretons' and declared an independent republic. The city was already
notorious in the 13th century for its pirates, who demanded tribute from ships in the
channel, and from the 17th century for close on 200 years St-Malo carried on
worldwide wars virtually all of its own against England, Holland, Portugal and any
other challengers, through its legendary privateers or *Corsairs*, whose names –
Duguay-Trouin, Surcouf – crop up all over the city today as favourite sons.

Getting There

The **ferry terminal** used by Brittany Ferries (*from Portsmouth*), Condor (*from Poole, Jersey, Guernsey*) and Emeraude (*from Jersey*) is just south of the walled city of St-Malo, between the old town and the Aleth peninsula. The old city (*Intra-Muros*) is within walking distance: from the terminal, turn left to get to it, or right for Cité d'Aleth and St-Servan. Coming into St-Malo from anywhere inland, follow signs for *Centre Ville* and *Intra-Muros*. They (and the *quai* from the ferries) will bring you to Porte St-Vincent, the main entry for vehicles into the walled city. Just outside it is the tourist office, and large free or pay-and-display car parks; it's best to use them, as parking inside the walls can be difficult and expensive, while nowhere within the old city is very far to reach by foot.

Walk through the gate and you come straight into Place Châteaubriand. To get to L'Epicerie restaurant, turn left and follow the ramparts to Place du Poids du Roi, then take a right fork down Rue des Cordiers. A turn up any of the little streets on the right will take you to Rue de la Herse, and the restaurant.

Ferries across the River Rance to Dinard leave from the Cale de Dinan, on the south side of the old city. A range of boat trips on the Rance and along the Brittany coast is also available; tourist offices have details.

Train services to St-Malo from Paris (Gare Montparnasse) and the rest of France run via Rennes, and some routes involve changing there. The station (Gare Centrale) is on the landward side of the harbour, at the opposite end of Av Louis Martin from the tourist office. It's a fair walk from the old city, but buses run up and down the avenue frequently.

Dinard **airport**, used by Ryanair, is 10km west of St-Malo across the Rance estuary. Special buses leave the airport 30 minutes after the arrival of each flight, and run to Gare Centrale train station in St-Malo; in the other direction, buses leave Gare Centrale two hours before each departing flight. There are also plenty of taxis. Airport information, t 02 99 46 71 24.

For some local **car hire** offices, *see* chapter 3. To call a local **taxi**, phone t 02 99 81 30 30.

Tourist Information

St-Malo: Esplanade St-Vincent, t 02 99 56 64 48, *www.saint-malo-tourisme.com*. St-Malo's particularly well-equipped tourist office is very easy to find just outside the old city, by Porte St-Vincent.

This privateering led to retaliation, and St-Malo was attacked many times by British and Dutch fleets. To resist them, small forts were built on the islands offshore.

Today, these forts and the old city ramparts still give St-Malo the air of a bristling naval stronghold, but inside, the atmosphere is now entirely peaceful. Within the walls of the old city, known as *Intra-Muros*, chasm-like streets between tall granite houses open up into ample squares, lined with cafés for watching the town go by. Outside, at the very foot of the ramparts, there are beaches that fill up with modern *Malouins* and visitors each summer. Miraculously restored after the Second World War, it's a city that has retained its old character but has a vigorous modern life as well, visible in its shops, markets, cafés, theatres and festivals. Away from the walled city, there are the basins of the port and the broad streets of modern St-Malo, but also small, wooded promontories and sheltered rocky coves that are ideal for sailing.

In culinary matters, St Malo, as might be expected, has always relied heavily on fish and seafood, and also shown an open-minded willingness to mix Breton tradition – *galettes*, lobster, mussels – with elements from Normandy, the rest of France and further afield. A superb example of local originality is **L'Epicerie**, a little restaurant in a cobbled street *Intra-Muros*, where a very able young chef offers deliciously imaginative dishes assembled with a distinctly contemporary, eclectic approach.

L'Epicerie

18 Rue de la Herse, t *02 23 18 34 55. Open Tues–Sat 12–2 and 7.30–10.*
Closed Sun and Mon; winter holiday periods vary. Carte *average €28.*

A quick walk around *Intra-Muros* St-Malo lets you know that this is not a place
where you're going to be short of places to eat. The old city is in the midst of a real
restaurant boom, most visible beneath the ramparts along Rue Jacques Cartier and
Rue de Chartres, which now host an unbroken line of bistros, brasseries and – of
course – crêperies with terrace tables, and plastic canopies for all-weather protection.
Crêpes aside, most of these eating spots stick fairly safely to the French-Breton
coastal classics, with seafood menus offering mussels different ways, lots of sole,
out-to-dazzle *plateaux de fruits de mer* and so on. Which is all well and good, and can
be very enjoyable, if done well – although in St-Malo's rash of new *touristique*
restaurants this can't be guaranteed. St-Malo, though, is known for being an
adventurers' city, and the old town also has far more adventurous food to offer.

L'Epicerie sits on one of the prettiest old streets within the labyrinth of *Intra-Muros*,
a little way back from the main rampart drag. It's a bit of a locals' secret, and has just
24 covers (so booking is very important). Inside, there are none of the old ships' wheels
and sailing-boat pictures beloved of seafood brasseries, but an understatedly stylish
contemporary interior in terracotta reds, with a strikingly original centrepiece-array of
fresh flowers and an open kitchen at the back. The friendly young waiting staff,
similarly, do not sport a single crisp white shirt, bow tie or little black skirt but wear
their own, casual, clothes. There are no set menus, only three options daily for each
course, so that the compact kitchen can give their full care and attention to each dish.
And the choices listed, chalked up on big green boards, are enticingly unfamiliar.

Despite this apparently radically un-French style, young chef Mickaël Saiget, who
opened L'Epicerie with a group of friends in 2004, insists his starting point is still that
holy grail of modern French cooking, *les meilleurs produits* – the rigorous sourcing of
first-quality fresh ingredients. Whenever possible everything he uses is local or
locally-landed, mostly from small-scale and organic producers, and he has built up
close and personal collaborative relationships with all his suppliers – even the
providers of more 'distant' produce, such as tuna – to ensure he gets just what he
wants. Having secured the best, he makes them his own, with a very individual touch.
The results are often out of this world.

As well as the vibrant freshness of every ingredient – so that everything has its full
and proper flavour – subtly original contrasts and layers of tastes and textures are
another Epicerie hallmark. Mickaël Saiget's range of complements and culinary minor
notes is exceptionally broad – including rare herbs, a global mix of mushrooms, and
an especially original use of local seasonal nuts – and many dishes here leave you
playing guessing games as to just what that delicious new flavour-mix might be. A
first course of a *mi-cuit* tuna with aubergine caviar features perfectly cooked, almost
sweet tuna, and with it comes, unannounced, one of the best spring rolls ever made,
with an ideally crusty case and a mysterious filling that includes ginger, garlic, carrots,

Saumon Mariné aux Herbes Fraîches et Fenouil, avec Mesclun des Salades

Serves 4–6

1kg/2lb 4oz fresh salmon, in fillets
500g/1lb 2oz fine salt
500g/1lb 2oz caster sugar
25g/1oz mixed pepper (*cinq poivres*)
25g/1oz ground fennel
50g/2oz fresh herbs – coriander, fennel leaves and chives
mixed salad greens, to taste

Mix the salt and the sugar well together, and then stir in the pepper and the ground fennel. Finely chop the herbs, and then add them to the mixture. Stir it thoroughly to ensure that it is evenly blended.

Take a sealable plastic container, large enough to hold all the salmon (or one smaller container for each 1–2 fillets). Cover the bottom of the container with a layer of the marinade mixture. Place the salmon on top of it, skin side down. Then spread more of the marinade on top of the salmon, so that it is completely covered. Close the container and place it in the fridge for 36 hours.

At the end of this time, take out the salmon and rinse it well in cold water. Carefully pat dry with kitchen paper, and coat each fillet lightly in olive oil.

To serve, finely slice the salmon and arrange the slices on each plate. To go with them, arrange a *mesclun* of salad greens – rocket, lamb's lettuce, endive, and so on, according to taste. Sprinkle the salad with a little olive oil, pepper and chopped chives. In summer, add some diced tomato or an avocado purée.

courgettes, coriander and other things. A pumpkin *velouté* with a sprinkling of *lardons* (diced bacon) at first seems a fairly straightforward soup, but roll it round the tongue a little more and you pick up exquisitely nutty hints of chestnut. Monkfish wrapped in bacon, a relatively conventional main course, stands out thanks to the beautiful handling of its perfectly matched, finely flavoured main ingredients; another main, farm-fresh guinea fowl *rôtie et pochée* – roast and poached – features both dark and white meat in another superbly clever blend, and is served with a selection of autumn vegetables that throws up a whole array of wonderfully herby, nutty tastes and aromas, and includes a fabulous parsnip mash.

This is truly interesting, hugely enjoyable modern food, both light and satisfying, a perfect retake on gourmet cooking for a contemporary audience. Desserts continue in the same vein, with delicate sorbets, innovative patisserie or a delectably light, cinnamon-rich version of a traditional apple *tarte à l'ancienne*. As well as informal, L'Epicerie's approach is also very flexible, so that even at busy times there's no problem at all with ordering just one or two courses. And, as an important last-but-not-least point, this restaurant is extraordinary value. Even the house wine served in *pichet* jugs has been carefully selected, and goes down so well with the food that there really doesn't seem to be much point in spending any more.

Touring Around

St-Malo has a substantial 19th- and 20th-century sprawl, but its heart is still the walled city, and the best way to get an idea of it is to take a walk around the **ramparts**. At regular intervals they are interrupted by giant gates and bastions: the natural starting point is the **Porte St-Vincent**, with the arms of St-Malo and Brittany above the gates on its outer façade, which has been the old city's main entrance since the 18th century. In the pedestrian passageway alongside the main gateways is a tiny barred chamber where anyone who tried to enter the city after the ten o'clock curfew, in force until 1770, was locked up for the night.

To the left of St-Vincent, looking towards the city, is the **Grande Porte**, formerly the principal entrance, with two massive 15th-century drum towers. The long, straight south side of the ramparts that crosses the **Porte de Dinan** has great views over the ferry terminal and the Aleth peninsula, while the **Bastion de la Hollande** on the seaward side of the walls contains the kennels of the famously ferocious watchdogs that were released on to the beach every night in the 18th century to deter nocturnal interlopers. The **Porte des Bés**, the next gate along going clockwise, has a large round tower next to it, the **Tour Notre-Dame**, and makes a good point to pause as it is the only gate with a crêperie on top (Le Corps de Garde, *see* p.364). At each corner of the ramparts there are statues of doughty St-Malo seafarers, and there are different views at every point around the walls: by the main gates you overlook the basins of the modern port, with its yacht marina immediately below; further round, you can look across to the harbour islands and the green shore of Dinard across the bay, which give the scene its variety and make the Rance estuary one of the most beautiful in the world.

The broad and sandy **beaches**, where people paddle, swim and windsurf, extend around the west and north sides of the ramparts, continuing into the long **Grande Plage** along the modern sea front. On the west side, the **Plage de Bon-Secours**, there is a walled-off saltwater swimming pool. Water buses to Dinard leave from the **Cale de Dinan**, by the southwest corner of the ramparts. Another favourite excursion is to paddle across at low tide to the **Fort National** (*open June–Sept daily; times depend on tides; adm*), one of the small bastions built on a rocky outcrop: slightly further out (so, once again, keep an eye on the tide), is the island of **Le Grand Bé**, with superb views back towards the city. This is the burial place of the writer Chateaubriand, the archromantic, sometime Foreign Minister and egomaniac who demanded to be buried here, and was given a virtual state funeral by his home town in 1848.

The present shape of the ramparts is due to Marshal Vauban, the great military engineer who was a ubiquitous presence in the innumerable fortifications put up around France under Louis XIV. Whether through conventional trade, slaving or piracy, St-Malo had become France's most important commercial port, and in 1689 Vauban was sent here to provide the city with a comprehensive system of defences. It is among his greatest work; interrupted several times by ferocious Anglo-Dutch attacks, building was only completed after his death by one of his assistants, Siméon de Garengeau. The old city was considerably extended, especially towards Porte St-Louis in the southeast corner. Another major change was due to the city council, who after a disastrous fire in 1661 banned the use of wood and made stone – usually granite – obligatory for all buildings within the walls. It is thanks to this, and the plain, severe lines favoured by Vauban's soldier-architects, that St-Malo sometimes has the look of a Gallic Aberdeen. Good examples of the military-looking *hôtels* erected during that era, built unusually high to maximize space within the ramparts, can be seen in Place Chateaubriand, Rue de Chartres and Rue des Cordiers, near the Grande Porte.

However, old St-Malo today is not really as the 18th-century architects left it. Look twice at many of the buildings *Intra-Muros* and you see that the stone is too clean, the edges too sharp, for them to be that old. The modern walled city is, in fact, a very clever replica. In August 1944, when General Patton's army broke out from Avranches across Brittany to the Loire, several thousand German soldiers retreated into St-Malo, determined to deny the Allies the use of the port. They were led by one Andreas von Aulock, a caricature of a Prussian General complete with monocle, who during truce negotiations both infuriated and astonished his American opponents with his super-cilious manner and habit of being immaculately turned out even at moments of terminal crisis. He did have the good grace to order the civilian population out of the city, saying 'I prefer to have my enemies in front of me'; this, though, only encouraged the US commanders to try and batter their way in with all the means at their disposal, with bombardments from artillery, aircraft and ships offshore. Even so, it still took two weeks of ferocious street-by-street fighting before Von Aulock finally gave up resistance, in suitably Wagnerian style in the castle of the old city. By then, an estimated 80 per cent of *Intra-Muros* St-Malo had been destroyed and the port so comprehensively sabotaged that it would be unusable for months – although Vauban's ramparts withstood 20th-century technology as well as they had repelled cannonballs. Photos in the castle museum show the extent of the devastation.

Post-war, the city fathers of St-Malo did not tinker with any modernistic reconstruc-tion plans, but with great determination set about getting their city back as they remembered it. Any buildings that could be were painstakingly restored; others, irre-deemably lost, were replaced with new creations in matching style and materials. The resulting restoration is remarkably successful, and a model of its kind. *Intra-Muros* St-Malo doesn't feel like an artificially preserved city, and even locals can be hard put to identify which buildings are genuinely old and which are not. Its cobbled streets remain atmospheric places to wander around, and you can discover corners such as the **Cour de la Houssaye**, near the meeting-point of Rue de la Corne de Cerf and Rue Chateaubriand, with a relic of St-Malo from before Vauban's time, the **Maison de la Duchesse Anne**, a fine 15th-century Breton stone townhouse. In Rue d'Asfeld, near Porte St-Louis, there is one of St-Malo's must-sees, the **Maison de Corsaire** (*guided tours Feb–11 Nov Tues–Sun 10.30–12 and 2.30–6, July and Aug also open Mon; adm*). Built in 1725 for the Magon de la Lande family, then one of the wealthiest in St-Malo, it's a rare surviving example of the mansions put up for the city's merchant dynasties with their (often ill-gotten) gains. It was long ago converted into apartments, but the owners of the lower floors – distantly connected to the Magons – have opened them up as a very unusual private museum, so that you can take guided tours through several of the remarkably unchanged rooms, and the extraordinary cellars, built to receive shipments from across the world and with secret entrances so that goods could be landed out of the sight of Customs men or the Magons' competitors. The owners are hugely enthusiastic about their house, and their tours are full of fascinating details of the eventful history of the house and of St-Malo (with plenty on pirates); the full effect is only available in French, but tours can be arranged in English.

The streets of *Intra-Muros* also attract thousands of visitors, which can make the main squares overpowering in high summer, but other streets stay more tranquil. The old city has a quite trendy nightlife, with two hubs around Rue de la Corne de Cerf and Rue de Dinan; a less fashionable crowd gravitates to Rue Jacques Cartier, while all and sundry meet up in Place Chateaubriand. By day the old city still hosts vigorous **markets** that are great for stocking up on every kind of food (*see* p.362). More static shopping is focused around Rue Broussais and Place du Pilori, with fashion and food shops, and plenty of opportunities to buy Breton knick-knacks and other souvenirs.

Here and there in the old town there are sections that retain a raffish, port-city air, such as the waterfront bars of Rue d'Orleans, which blend into the lines of touristy restaurants set into the ramparts along Rue de Chartres and Rue Jacques Cartier. The main social focus of old St-Malo, however, is **Place Chateaubriand**, site of a clutch of grand cafés that are prime places to secure a table for an afternoon, and well justify their slightly-high prices with 19th-century interiors that post-1945 were restored more lovingly than the city's (not especially striking) Gothic cathedral. Around the corner, at 3 Rue Chateaubriand, is the house where the great writer was born, in 1768.

Overlooking the cafés on one side of the *place* is the castle, now housing the **Musée d'Histoire de la Ville et du Pays Malouin** (*open April–Sept daily 10–12 and 2–6; Oct–Mar Tues–Sun 10–12 and 2–6, closed Mon; adm*). A visit lets you explore the inside of the castle, built in the 1420s and modified by Vauban, and take in the great views from the top ramparts, with their low galleried roofs. The museum collection is a corker: it makes scarcely any concessions to progressive notions of history or modern museum techniques, and is for the most part an unabashedly old-fashioned, gung-ho celebration of local heroes, especially mariners and pirates. Piracy had long been an 'interest' of the seamen of St-Malo, but it was in the 1660s that Louis XIV's minister Colbert followed England and Holland in authorizing French captains to engage in privateering – that is, attacking foreign ships so long as they belonged only to the country's enemies, and a part of the booty was passed on to the state. For much of the next century, privateers employed as many men in St-Malo as conventional trade, and their profits did much to build the post-Vauban city (St-Malo ships also played their part in the slave trade, which the museum conveniently ignores). The legendary *corsair* captains are fully commemorated: there's **Duguay-Trouin**, who plundered Rio de Janeiro in 1711 and ended up one of the town's wealthiest citizens; **La Bourdonnais**, taking Madras from the British in 1746; and **Robert Surcouf**, who privateered for Napoleon and seized HMS Kent in 1803. Needless to say, these Gallic seadogs have never rated much of a mention in British history books. Also present in the museum are less martial heroes such as the explorer Cartier, the inescapable Chateaubriand and the Catholic writer Lamennais, and a mixed bag on aspects of St-Malo's history such as the lives of fishermen, local customs and reconstruction after 1945.

There are also attractive parts of St-Malo outside the walls. From any of the gates on the harbour side of the ramparts, turn right and walk around the quays, past the ferry terminal. Cut right at Rue Clémenceau and Rue Dauphine, and you will come to the **Plage des Sablons**, a sheltered beach on a neatly arc-shaped cove that's now full of yachts and dinghies. Beyond it, clad in trees and standing out into the estuary, is the promontory of **Cité d'Aleth**. This was actually the site of the first city of St-Malo, a Gallo-Roman and then an early Breton settlement, and contained the hermitage of Maclow, or Maclou (from whence comes St-Malo), a Christian monk and mystic, believed to have been Welsh, who came here from Britain in the 6th century. However, the erosion of the peninsula led to the main community transferring to the *Intra-Muros* area in 1146. There is a beautiful walk on the Corniche path around the Aleth peninsula, with great views of Dinard and the Rance. At the other end of the path, winding, narrow streets and snug, rocky inlets create the feel of a small harbour town in the St-Servan district – and indeed, this, like several other outlying parts of town, was only incorporated into St-Malo in 1967. On a spit of rock stands the **Tour Solidor**, a 14th-century fortress that now contains St-Malo's other main museum, the **Musée International des Cap-Horniers** (*open April–Sept daily 10–12 and 2–6; Oct–Mar Tues–Sun 10–12 and 2–6, closed Mon; adm*), dedicated to the sailing ships of all countries that went to fish the Newfoundland banks and to round Cape Horn.

St-Malo also has another nautical attraction, the **Manoir de Jacques Cartier** (*open June and Sept Mon–Sat 10–11.30 and 2.30–6; July and Aug daily 10–11.30 and 2.30–6; Oct–May Mon–Sat, tours 10am, 3pm; adm*) at Limoëlou, on the eastern edge of the city in the suburb of Rotheneuf. Cartier discovered the St Lawrence river, and founded Montreal and French Canada. The house is a little hard to find – probably the best way to get there is to follow the beach road and Avenue Kennedy straight out of St-Malo, and then look for signs when you get to Rotheneuf – but this plain little Breton manor house, with its drains, marriage chests and simple kitchen, gives a fascinating insight into the life of a none-too-prosperous gentleman of the time (none of the articles actually belonged to Cartier, as the manor-farm had passed through many owners before its restoration by a Canadian foundation in the 1970s). Cartier first sailed to Canada in 1534, and again the next winter when he lost most of his crew to cold or scurvy. Before his third voyage in 1542 he was told by François I that, as a commoner, he had to go as second-in-command to a nobleman; the irascible Cartier refused to accept this and sailed off in his own ship, hoping to reinstate himself with the King by returning with some gold given to him by Indians. However, this turned out to be no more than iron pyrites or 'fool's gold', and Cartier retired to his basic house in disgrace. He died of the plague in 1557; it has been believed that he was buried in St-Malo cathedral, but during restoration of the house a body was discovered buried beneath the kitchen, so he may in fact have been buried here.

East of St-Malo, beyond Rotheneuf, the D201 coast road will take you past headlands, lighthouses, and a succession of beautiful coves with open seas and scudding surf to the fishing harbour of **Cancale**, a favourite holiday town of Colette, and famous throughout France for its oysters. On a good day, there are also views all the way across the bay to Mont St-Michel.

Shopping

There are **markets** in *Intra-Muros* on Tuesdays and Fridays: Place de la Poissonnerie is still a fish market, and there are street stalls in Place du Pilori and a large covered market, the **Marché aux Légumes**. Markets outside the walls are in Paramé (*Wed and Sat*), and St-Servan (*Tues and Fri*).

As well as fish, seafood and crêpes, St-Malo's food speciality is its traditional confectionery – *spécialités malouines* – produced in a bewildering range of shapes, sizes and ingredients.

St-Malo ✉ 35400
Cash Wine & Beer Supermarket, 24 Quai Trichet, St-Servan, t 02 99 82 37 06, *cashwine@tele2.fr*. A discount drinks outlet handily located a short way from the ferry terminals (in the opposite direction to the old town). As well as a big wine stock it has plenty of spirits and liqueurs. *Open daily.*

Cave de l'Abbaye St-Jean, 7 Rue des Cordiers, t 02 99 20 17 20, *caveabbayestjean@wanadoo.fr*. Excellent, individual wine merchant in an old storehouse near the ramparts, with over 1,000 French wines, plus local ciders, beers and other specialities. The young staff (several of whom speak English) are very helpful.

Estran Décoration, 5 Rue Gouin de Beauchesne, t 02 23 18 03 67. An attractive contemporary household shop on a quiet square, with a diverse stock of lamps, ceramics, tableware, accessories and some very pretty tablecloths and other textiles.

Maison Guella, 8 Rue de Porcon, t 02 99 40 83 43. St-Malo's most renowned *chocolatier* and confectioner: it's not actually a shop but a giant stall, running the length of one end of the cathedral. On show is every kind of *spécialité régionale* in chocolate, nuts and sugar – highlights are the buttered caramels and the *patates malouines*, little fried balls of potato, almond and sugar, which seem a little dull at first but get more interesting as you work your way through the bag.

La Savonnerie, 12 Rue de Dinan, t 02 99 40 30 20. Utterly French little shop selling fragrant soaps, gels, shampoos, body milks – all handmade using fine natural ingredients – and plenty of other gift ideas.

Taffin Chocolatier, 4 Rue Broussais, t 02 99 40 93 53. A more tranquil purveyor of chocolates and sweets than Maison Guella, with its local specialities – Breton *gâteaux*, *Kouign Amann* (puff-pastry cakes), homemade ice cream – on show in gleaming cabinets. There's a whole range of ornate gift boxes.

Where to Stay

St-Malo ✉ 35400
Hôtel Elizabeth, 2 Rue des Cordiers, t 02 99 56 24 98, *www.st-malo-hotel-elizabeth.com* (*double rooms €80–165*). A charming hotel in one of St-Malo's oldest stone buildings, from 1558 (year of the accession of Elizabeth I of England, hence the name). It's on the landward side of *Intra-Muros*, near the ramparts: rooms at the top (there's a lift) have harbour views. The best rooms in the old building are large, luxurious suites; rooms in an annexe alongside are more conventional, and cheaper. Even so, all are spacious, and the opulent décor has a look of the 17th century. Breakfast is served in a wonderful cellar, where an early owner of the house, a dealer in Canadian furs, used to store his stock.

L'Ascott Hôtel, 35 Rue du Chapitre, t 02 99 81 89 93, *www.ascotthotel.com* (*double rooms €105–145*). Outside the old town in the quiet district of St-Servan, south of Cité d'Aleth, this distinguished 19th-century townhouse has been carefully restored to become a very chic modern boutique hotel. The ten rooms have been individually designed in cinnamony and deep purple colours, and are seductively comfortable; facilities – bathrooms, electronics – are superb. On the ground floor there are equally striking lounges and a residents-only *salon de thé*, and around the house there's a neat, secluded garden for summer breakfasts.

La Malouinière du Mont-Fleury, 2 Rue du Mont-Fleury, t 02 23 52 28 85, *www.lemontfleury.com* (*rooms €70–100 for two, €120–130 for four*). A really lovely B&B in a grand 18th-century *malouinière*, one of the mansions built around the city by St-Malo's pirate-merchants to show off their wealth. It's in the villagey district of Le Petit-Paramé, south of the main town; owner Bob Haby, a former airline pilot, is an especially congenial host, and the beautifully restored house has a bright, comfortable feel. The four guest rooms have loads of character: each is attractively decorated to a different theme – maritime, oriental, African, American – and two are big duplexes with space for four or five. A great place from which to explore St-Malo, and great value.

Hôtel de France et de Chateaubriand,
Place Chateaubriand, **t** 02 99 56 66 52, *www.hotel-fr-chateaubriand.com* (*double rooms €63.80–85.50*). St-Malo's most historic grand hotel, lovingly rebuilt after 1944, retains a great deal of period charm and brio. The lobby, Second-Empire dining room and terrace are all stunning; the 80 rooms have less character, but offer traditional plush comfort. Their attractiveness and price vary according to what you see from the window: those with a view of the sea or the *place* are lovely. The smart **restaurant** (*menus €12.90–32*) serves opulent versions of classic local cuisine, with Breton lobster and mussels dishes as specialities.

Hôtel de l'Univers,
10 Place Chateaubriand, **t** 02 99 40 89 52, *www.hotel-univers-saintmalo.com* (*double rooms €58–81*). Forming a corner with the France et Chateaubriand on the square, the Univers is less a monument to the 1860s than to the 1890s, the *Belle Epoque*, with a wonderful dining room. The 63 rooms have an old-world stylishness, but have all been well refurbished in the last few years. They come in several different sizes, and nine have views over the square. The restaurant is equally enjoyable (*see* p.364).

Hôtel San Pedro, 1 Rue Ste-Anne, **t** 02 99 40 88 57, *www.sanpedro-hotel.com* (*double rooms €52–60*). A hotel with a really individual feel, thanks to the energy and enthusiasm of owner Mireille. She has travelled a lot herself and has a keen understanding of travellers' needs, and treats all guests as friends. The 12 rooms have been refurbished in stylish modern colour schemes, to make the most of the light. The building, near the ramparts and Bon-Secours beach, is one of the most bizarrely narrow of old St-Malo's towers, a tight spiral with just two or three rooms at

each level (there's also a lift). The top-floor rooms have great views, and are worth paying a little extra for; downstairs, there's a convivial breakfast room. High-season rates apply July–Sept. *Closed late Nov–mid-Feb.*

Hôtel-Restaurant de la Pomme d'Or,
4 Place du Poids du Roi, **t** 02 99 40 90 24, *www.la-pomme-dor.fr* (*double rooms €46–59*). A long-running, old-fashioned hotel, with 13 well-maintained rooms and fine harbour views from the top floors. The atmosphere is cosy, and regulars hold it in great affection. There's a similarly comfortable **restaurant** (*menus €14.30–35*), with good fish and seafood. *Closed Jan.*

Hôtel Le Nautilus, 9 Rue de la Corne de Cerf, **t** 02 99 40 42 27, *www.lenautilus.com* (*double rooms €44–56*). A distinctive, hip little hotel in one of the most vertical towers in this vertical city (with a lift to the topmost floors). Some of the 15 striking rooms are in bright modern colours, some are more traditional; some are tiny, inserted into the eaves, but all have good facilities. It's in the middle of town, so none of the rooms have views, and first-floor rooms can be a little noisy; the Nautilus also used to have a buzzing bar, which could be noisy too, but this is now residents-only. This makes things a bit more sedate, but the hotel still has a nicely friendly atmosphere, and is excellent value.

Hôtel d'Aleth, 2 Rue des Hauts-Sablons, **t** 02 99 81 48 08, *cunningham@wanadoo.fr* (*double rooms €36–60*). A good-value budget hotel next to Plage des Sablons beach, south of the old town. The 10 rooms are simply decorated but comfortable, and well equipped, and the location is a huge plus: five rooms have great views over Sablons harbour. Downstairs there's a lively bar, open late, that's one of St-Malo's most popular. The same owners also have the much plusher **Manoir de Cunningham** (**t** 02 99 21 33 33, *www.st-malo-hotel-cunningham.com*; *double rooms €80–180*), on the other side of the same square. Modern but in half-timbered style, it has 13 rooms and suites that are very large, if a bit bland; their major attraction, again, is the location, as all rooms have harbour views. Rates at both hotels vary a lot by season. *Hôtel d'Aleth open all year; Manoir closed mid-Nov–mid-Mar.*

Eating Alternatives

Like the rest of Brittany, St-Malo has lots of *crêperies*, which offer savoury *galettes* and often salads as well as sweet *crêpes*. Note, though, that while *crêperies* generally open all day, they often close early in the evening.

St-Malo ✉ 35400

Le Chalut, 8 Rue de la Corne de Cerf, t/f 02 99 56 71 58 (*menus €22–49*). The Chalut doesn't stand out at first sight from the other bistros along Corne de Cerf, but this is one of St-Malo's premier seafood restaurants. Chef Jean-Philippe Foucat's menus vary continually to make the most of the best fresh fish and shellfish each day; main courses might include brill pan-fried with coriander and a langoustine sauce, or John Dory with *girolles* mushrooms. A highlight is the special 'all lobster' menu, for €61. *Closed Mon and Tues.*

Hôtel de l'Univers, 10 Place Chateaubriand, t 02 99 40 89 52, www.hotel-univers-saintmalo.com (*menus €12.50–35*). The terrace and 1890s dining room of the hotel (*see* p.363) are among the most atmospheric places to eat on Place Châteaubriand – and also good value. The fare covers a comprehensive range – from refined local cuisine and generous *plateaux de fruits de mer* in the more elaborate menus to crêpes, *croques*, salads and other crêperie-brasserie favourites for a light meal, and even a vegetarian menu.

La Corderie, 9 Chemin de la Corderie, Cité d'Aleth, t 02 99 81 62 38, www.lacorderie.com (*menus €16–30*). A restaurant worth discovering outside St-Malo's walled city on the Aleth peninsula, with fabulous views of Tour Solidor and over the Rance estuary to Dinard from its dining room and terrace. The menus and *carte* highlight market-fresh fish and seafood, with fine staples like oysters and *moules à la crème* and light, herby original dishes. It's near the southern end of the Corniche path around the Aleth peninsula. *Closed Mon exc July and Aug.*

Le Bistro de Jean, 6 Rue de la Corne de Cerf, t 02 99 40 98 68 (*menus €14–28*). Owner Jean Trubert is a local character, and his restaurant is hugely popular (and often packed). The fare is Breton-traditional, with

plenty of fine seafood: what makes the difference is the emphasis on market freshness and first-quality ingredients, combined with a very convivial, informal atmosphere. *Closed Wed midday, Sat midday and Sun.*

La Coquille d'Oeuf, 20 Rue de la Corne de Cerf, t 02 99 40 92 62 (*menus €10.50–23.50*). An attractive modern restaurant in one of the most characterful streets of the old city, with pale décor and a bright, fresh feel. The food style is also light and contemporary, with interesting salads, pastas, vegetarian options and light fish, seafood or meat dishes. It's very good value, and service is friendly and efficient. *Closed Mon.*

Le St-Louis, 13 Rue de Chartres, t 02 99 56 58 80 (*menus €13.50–18.50*). A handy stand-by for anyone making a night of it in St-Malo. Not the most elegant restaurant in town, but the St-Louis is a friendly little bistro that serves bargain set menus of local standards, meat grills, *moules-frites* several different ways (c. €11), omelettes and light dishes until late at night. *Open 6.30pm–1am; closed Tues.*

Le Corps de Garde, 3 Montée Notre Dame, t 02 99 40 91 46 (*dishes c. €2.20–8.50*). A pleasant little bar-*crêperie* run by a friendly young trio that has the special attraction of being the one and only place in *Intra-Muros* Saint-Malo where you can eat with an invigorating view out to sea – because it's actually on top of the walls, in a former guardhouse above the Porte des Bés, hence the name. The food includes sweet *crêpes* with the full range of fruity, chocolaty and nutty fillings, and savoury *galettes* that, as an unusual touch, may feature Spanish chorizo as well as standard local ingredients.

Crêperie Ty-Nevez, 12 Rue Broussais, t 02 99 40 82 50 (*dishes c. €2–7*). The longest-running traditional crêperie in St-Malo, owned by the same family for over 40 years. It offers wonderful crêpes and savoury *galettes* made with great fresh ingredients, including delicious speciality *galettes* such as *aux champignons* (with mushrooms, garlic and parsley), and crêpes like the *Quic-en-Groigne* (strawberries, walnuts, vanilla ice-cream and Grand Marnier). Breton cider features among the drinks. And, it's remarkably cheap, even more so than other St-Malo crêperies. *Open 12–7.30pm. Closed Wed.*

Glossary

The full French culinary vocabulary is
enormous, and several pocket guides are
available that give extensive lists of the many
terms and phrases. The following should
provide some of the necessary basics. For
more information on specific dishes and
cheeses, see chapter 2, **The Food and Drink of
Northern France**, pp.3–12.

Useful Phrases

I'd like to book a table (for two/at 12.30pm) *Je
voudrais réserver une table (pour deux
personnes/à midi et demie).*
lunch/dinner *le déjeuner/le dîner*
Is it necessary to book for lunch/dinner today?
*Est-ce qu'il faut réserver pour déjeuner/dîner
aujourd'hui?*
Waiter/Waitress! (to attract their attention)
*Monsieur/Madame/Mademoiselle! S'il
vous plaît.*
The €15 menu, please *Le menu à quinze euros,
s'il vous plaît*
Which are your specialities? *Quelles sont les
specialités de la maison?*
What is this dish, exactly? *Qu'est-ce qu'il y a
dans ce plat, exactement?*
The wine list, please *La carte des vins,
s'il vous plaît.*
Another bottle of wine, please *Une autre
bouteille de vin, s'il vous plaît.*
water (from the tap, perfectly good in France,
and usually given as a matter of course)
une carafe d'eau
mineral water/fizzy/still
eau minérale/gazeuse/plate
coffee (espresso) *café*
white coffee *café au lait /café crème*
That was wonderful *C'était formidable/
délicieux.*
We've enjoyed the meal very much, thank you
Nous avons très bien mangé, merci.
The bill, please *L'addition, s'il vous plaît.*

Poissons et Coquillages (Fish and Shellfish)

bar sea bass
barbue brill
bigorneau winkle, sea snail
bulot whelk, large sea snail
cabillaud fresh cod
calamar squid
carrelet plaice
colin hake
coques cockles
coquilles St-Jacques large scallops
crabe crab
crevettes grises shrimps
crevettes roses prawns
daurade sea bream
écrevisses freshwater crayfish
escargots snails
espadon swordfish
flétan halibut
fruits de mer seafood
gambas king prawns
hareng herring
homard lobster
huîtres oysters
langouste spiny lobster or crayfish
langoustine Dublin Bay prawn
lieu pollack or ling
lotte monkfish
loup de mer sea bass
maquereau mackerel
merlan whiting
morue salt cod
moules mussels
mulet grey mullet
ombre grayling
oursin sea urchin
palourde clam
pétoncle queen scallop
poulpe octopus
raie skate
rascasse scorpion fish
rouget red mullet

St-Pierre John Dory
saumon salmon
saumonette dogfish
sauterelles shrimps (in Picardy)
sole sole
thon tuna
tortue turtle
tourteau large crab
truite trout
truite saumonée sea/salmon trout
turbot turbot

Viandes, Volaille, Charcuterie (Meat, Poultry, Charcuterie)

battis/abats giblets/offal
agneau (de pré-salé) lamb (raised on salt marshes)
andouille large sausage made from offal, served cold
andouillette smaller than an andouille, eaten hot
ballotine boned, stuffed and rolled meat (cold)
biftek, bifteck steak
bœuf beef
boudin blanc white pudding, a sausage made with veal, chicken, pork
boudin noir black pudding
caille quail
canard, caneton duck, duckling
cervelas garlic pork sausage
cervelles brains
chapon capon
chevreau kid
chevreuil roe deer; also venison in general
civet stew (rabbit or hare)
colvert mallard
daguet young venison
dinde, dindon turkey
dindonneau young turkey
estouffade braised meat stew
faisan pheasant
foie liver
foie gras fattened goose or duck liver
galantine meat stuffed, rolled, set in its own jelly
gésier gizzard
gibiers game

jambon ham
jambon cru salt-cured, raw ham
langue (de veau, de bœuf) tongue (veal, ox)
lapereau young rabbit
lapin rabbit
lard (lardons) bacon (diced)
lièvre hare
marcassin young wild boar
merguez spicy red sausage (North African)
moëlle beef marrow
navarin (d'agneau) lamb stew with spring vegetables
oie goose
os bone
perdreau young partridge
perdrix partridge
petit salé salt pork
pintade guinea fowl
pintadeau young guinea fowl
porc pork
poularde fattened chicken
poulet chicken
poussin spring chicken
queue de bœuf oxtail
rillettes potted meats (of duck, goose, pork, rabbit, etc)
ris (de veau) sweetbreads (veal)
rognons kidneys
sanglier wild boar
saucisses sausages
saucisson salami-type sausage, cold
tête (de veau) head (of veal)
tripes tripe
veau veal
venaison venison

Meat Cuts

aiguillette long, thin slice
carré (d'agneau) rack (of lamb)
châteaubriand double fillet steak, usually with a Béarnaise sauce
contre-filet, faux-filet sirloin steak
côte, côtelette chop, cutlet
cuisse leg or thigh
entrecôte rib steak
épaule shoulder
escalope thin fillet
gigot (d'agneau) leg (of lamb)
jarret shin or knuckle
magret, maigret (de canard) breast (of duck)
noisette (d'agneau) small round cut (of lamb)

onglet flank of beef
pavé thick, square fillet
pieds trotters
râble (de lièvre, de lapin) saddle (of hare, rabbit)
rôti roast
selle (d'agneau) saddle (of lamb)
tournedos thick round slices of fillet steak
travers de porc pork spareribs

Cooking Terms for Steaks and Grills

bleu very rare
saignant rare
à point medium rare
bien cuit well done

Légumes, Herbes, Epices (Vegetables, Herbs, Spices)

ail garlic
algue seaweed
aneth dill
aromates aromatic herbs
artichaut artichoke
asperges asparagus
aubergine aubergine
avocat avocado
avoine oats
badiane star anise
baies roses pink peppercorns
basilic basil
betterave beetroot
blette Swiss chard
cannelle cinnamon
carotte carrot
céleri celery
céleri-rave celeriac
cèpes cep (large, brown, fleshy mushrooms)
cerfeuil chervil
champignons mushrooms
chanterelles chanterelles (wild, yellowish mushrooms)
chicorée frisée curly endive (lettuce)
chou cabbage
chou-fleur cauliflower
chou frisé kale
chou de mer sea kale

choux de Bruxelles Brussels sprouts
ciboulette chives
citrouille pumpkin
cœurs de palmier palm hearts
concombre cucumber
coriandre coriander
cornichons gherkins
courge pumpkin
cresson watercress
échalote shallot
endive chicory
épinards spinach
estragon tarragon
fenouil fennel
fèves broad beans
flageolets white, dried beans
frites chips
genièvre juniper
gingembre ginger
girofle clove
girolles same as chanterelles
haricots (rouge, blanc, vert) beans (kidney, white, green)
laitue lettuce
laurier bay leaf
lentilles lentils
maïs (épis de) sweet corn (on the cob)
marjolaine marjoram
menthe mint
morilles morel mushrooms
muscade nutmeg
navet turnip
oignons onions
oseille sorrel
panais parsnip
persil parsley
petits-pois peas
piment pimento, hot red pepper
piment doux (poivron) sweet red or green pepper
pissenlit dandelion
pleurotes oyster mushrooms (soft-fleshed wild mushrooms)
poireau leek
pois chiche chickpea
poivron sweet red or green pepper
pomme de terre potato
radis radish
raifort horseradish
riz rice
romarin rosemary
safran saffron
salade salad (often just lettuce)

salade lyonnaise green salad together with eggs, diced bacon, shallots, fish (herring, anchovies) and maybe sheep's trotters or other meat cuts

salade niçoise substantial salad: a combination of lettuce, tomatoes, hard-boiled eggs, tuna, potatoes, olives, capers, artichokes and anchovies, with a herby vinaigrette

salade verte green salad

salsifis salsify

sarriette savory (the herb)

sarrasin buckwheat

sauge sage

scarole escarole

seigle rye

thym thyme

tomate tomato

truffes truffles

Fruits, Noix, Desserts (Fruits, Nuts, Desserts)

abricot apricot

amande almond

ananas pineapple

banane banana

bavarois egg custard with whipped cream

bombe ice-cream dessert in a round mould

brugnon nectarine

cacahouètes peanuts

cajou cashew nut

cassis blackcurrant

cerise cherry

charlotte dessert in a mould with sponge fingers

citron/citron vert lemon/lime

clafoutis black-cherry tart

coing quince

corbeille de fruits basket of fruits

coupe ice cream cup

crème anglaise very light custard

crème Chantilly sweet whipped cream

crème fleurette double cream

crème fraîche sour cream

crème pâtissière custard filling

dattes dates

figues figs

figue de Barbarie prickly pear

fraises (des bois) strawberries (wild)

framboises raspberries

fruit de la passion passion fruit

génoise sponge cake

glace ice cream

grenade pomegranate

groseilles redcurrants

macaron macaroon

madeleine small sponge cake

mandarine tangerine or mandarins

mangue mango

marrons chestnuts

miel honey

mirabelles small yellow plums

mûres mulberries, blackberries

myrtilles bilberries

noisette hazelnut

noix walnut

œufs à la neige light meringue in a vanilla custard, floating islands

pamplemousse grapefruit

parfait chilled mousse

pastèque watermelon

pêche peach

pignons pine nuts

pistache pistachio

poire pear

pomme apple

prune plum

pruneau prune

reine-claude greengage

raisin grapes

raisins secs raisins

sablé shortbread biscuit

savarin ring-shaped cake, in rum- or kirsch-flavoured syrup

tarte Tatin caramelised apple pie, served upside-down

truffes chocolate truffles

General Terminology

aigre-doux sweet and sour

allumettes strips of puff pastry or potatoes

amuse-gueules, amuse-bouches appetisers

à l'anglaise plain boiled

barquette small pastry boat

béarnaise classic sauce of egg yolks, white wine, shallots, butter, tarragon

béchamel white sauce of butter, flour, milk

beignets fritters

Bercy similar to a *beurre blanc*, but thicker

beurre blanc reduced sauce of butter, white wine, vinegar, shallots

beurre noir browned butter, lemon juice, capers and parsley
bisque thick soup, usually of seafood
blanquette thick creamy stew
bouchée tiny mouthful, or *vol-au-vent*
bouillon stock or broth
brebis ewes' milk cheese
braisé braised
brioche sweet bread or roll
(à la) broche spit-roasted
brouillé scrambled
brûlé caramelized ('burnt')
chasseur white wine sauce with mushrooms
chausson pastry turnover
chèvre goats' cheese
cocotte round ceramic dish
confit meat cooked and/or preserved in its own fat
confiture jam
coulis thick sauce, purée
court-bouillon stock
croustade savoury pastry case
(en) croûte in a pastry crust
cru raw
cuit cooked
demi-glace basic brown sauce, reduced meat stock
diable peppery sauce: mustard, vinegar, shallots
Duxelles mushrooms and shallots sautéd in butter and cream
émincé thinly sliced
épices spices
farci stuffed
(au) feu de bois cooked over a wood fire
feuilleté flaky pastry leaves
forestière with mushrooms, bacon and potatoes
(au) four oven baked
fourré filled or stuffed, usually sweets
frappé with crushed ice
fricassé braised in sauce of white wine, butter, and cream
frit fried
friture mixed platter of small fried fish
fumé smoked
galette buckwheat pancake
garni garnished; served with vegetables
gelée aspic
glacé iced
grillade mixed grill
hachis minced or chopped

hollandaise sauce of egg yolks, butter and lemon juice
jardinière with diced garden vegetables
marmite small casserole
matelote fish stew
meunière floured, fried in butter, with lemon and parsley (fish)
mijoté simmered
Mornay cheesy béchamel
mousseline hollandaise sauce with egg whites and whipped cream
moutarde mustard
(à la) nage poached in an aromatic broth (fish)
nature, au naturel simple, plain
panaché mixed, a mixture
pané breaded
(en) papillote baked in buttered paper or foil
Parmentier with mashed potatoes
pâte pastry, dough
pâte à chou choux pastry
pâte brisée shortcrust pastry
paupiettes thin slices of fish or meat filled, rolled and then wrapped before cooking
paysan, paysanne country-style: with bacon, potato, carrot, onion, turnip
poché poached
poêlé pan-fried
poivrade peppery sauce: a demi-glace, wine, vinegar, vegetables
potage thick soup
primeurs early-season vegetables
printanière garnish of spring vegetables
quenelles dumplings made with fish or meat
râpé grated, shredded
rémoulade mayonnaise with capers, mustard, gherkins, herbs; often used with celeriac
roulade rolled meat or fish, often stuffed
sabayon whipped up wine, egg yolks and sugar (zabaglione)
salé salted, savoury
sauvage wild
Soubise white onion sauce
sucré sweet, sugared
suprême boned breast of poultry; fish fillet; a creamy sauce
tiède lukewarm
timbale small pie cooked in dome-shaped mould
tranche slice
(à la) vapeur steamed
velouté white sauce flavoured with stock
Véronique garnished with grapes

Index

Main page references are in **bold**. Page references to maps are in *italics*.

Acknowledgements

Sincere thanks go, first and foremost, to all the chefs and restaurateurs featured in this guide, and to their families, for their enormous hospitality, courtesy, enthusiasm, generosity with their time, knowledge, recipes and, of course, their cooking. My appreciation, too, to all the hosts of *chambres d'hôtes* who welcomed us into their homes, and to the many hotelowners, shopowners, museum staff, farmers, food-producers and others mentioned in this book, for always responding so well to sometimes-tedious questioning from a dumb foreigner. Warmest and very special gratitude is due also from the publishers and myself to the representatives of the various Comités Départementaux du Tourisme and other local authorities for indispensable assistance, and for their unfailing courtesy, professionalism, friendliness, interest in and knowledge of their areas – in particular, Diana Hounslow and Nicolas Célie of the CDT Pas-de-Calais; Delphine Bartier of the CDT du Nord; Dominique Chaillot of the CDT de la Somme; Sandra Parnisari of the CDT-Seine-Maritime; Capucine d'Halluin of the CDT-Eure; Armelle Le Goff of the CDT-Calvados; Isabelle Chollet of the CDT de la Manche; and Cécile Mathiaud of the CDT Haute-Bretagne-Ille-et-Vilaine. Extra thanks go too to Chantal Atamian of the Office de Tourisme and Martine Bailleux of the Musée Louis-Philippe in Eu, for their especially warm enthusiasm and helpfulness. In Britain, I have to thank Chris Laming of P&O Ferries, and Marie-Thérèse Smith of the Maison de France in London.

Many thanks also to Elspeth Anderson for her careful and patient work, to Angie Watts for the maps, and to Natalie Pomier and all at Cadogan for their continuing support for the guide. And most of all to Ethel, for coming along with me, identifying herbs, picking up on things I never even noticed, and for everything.

Short Breaks in Northern France touring atlas

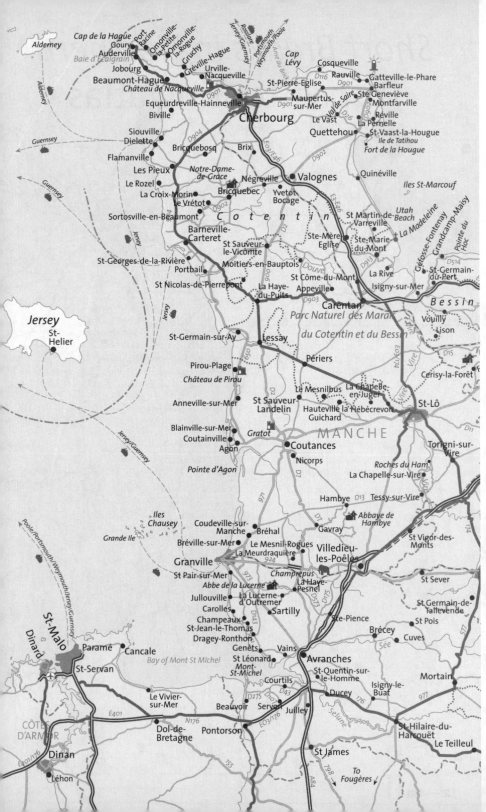

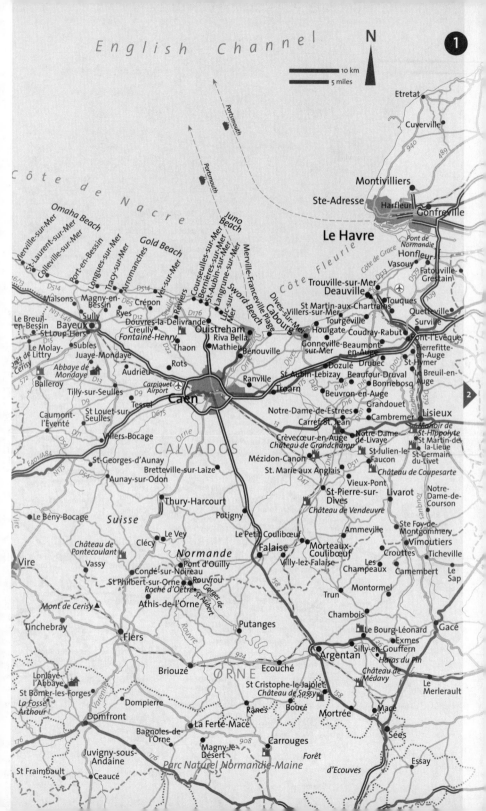

N

10 km
5 miles

English Channel

Côte d'Albâtre

Veules-les-Roses

St-Valéry-en-Caux
Mesnil Durdent
Ingouville
Château Mesnil-Geoffroy
Les Grandes Dalles
Cany-Barville
Sassetot-le-Mauconduit
Ermenouville
Notre Dame de Salut +
Ouainville
Grainville-la-Teinturière
Fécamp
St-Léonard
Valmont
Doudeville
Yport
Ganzeville
Oherville
Etretat
Angeville-Bailleul
Héricourt-en-Caux
Bennetot
Cuverville
Goderville
Fauville-en-Caux
Bréauté

Pays de Caux

Beuzeville-le-Grand
Yvetot
Montivilliers
Bolbec
Maulèvrier-Ste Gertrude
Betteville
Lillebonne
Abbaye de St-Wandrille
Ste-Adresse
Harfleur
Gonfreville
Caudebec-en-Caux
Pont de Brotonne
Tancarville
Villequier

Le Havre
Pont de Normandie
Pont de Tancarville
Notre-Dame-de-Bliquetuit
Aizier
Forêt de Brotonne
Jumièges

Seine

Honfleur
Marais
Vasouy
St Opportune-la-Mare
Vieux-Port
Hauville
Côte de Grâce
Foulbec
Grande Mare
La Haye de Routot
Routot
Fatouville-Grestain
Vernier
Trouville-sur-Mer
Fourmetot
Deauville
St Martin-aux-Chartrains
Beuzeville
Appeville-Annebault
Touques
Villers-sur-Mer
Quetteville
Pont-Audemer
Houlgate
Coudray-Rabut
Surville
Tourgeville
Martainville
Le Bec-Hellouin
Gonneville-sur-Mer
Beaumont-en-Auge
Pont-l'Evêque
Campigny-la-Futelaye
Lieurey
Brétigny
St Eloi-de-Fourques
Drubec
Pierrefitte-en-Auge
St-Hymer
Blangy-le-Château
Brionne
Beaufour-Druval
Le Breuil-en-Auge
Harcourt
St-Aubin-Lebizay
Bonnebosq
St Victor-d'Epine
Fontaine-la-Soret
Beuvron-en-Auge
Grandouet
St Aubin-de-Scellon
Nassandres
Victot-Pontfol
Carref. St. Jean
Cambremer
Lisieux
Carsix
Beaumont-le-Roger
Notre-Dame-de-Livaye
Manoir de St-Hippolyte
Thiberville
St Martin-de-la-Lieue
Crèvecœur-en-Auge
St-Germain-du-Livet
Bernay
Forêt de
Château de Grandchamp
St Clair-d'Arcey
Mézidon-Canon
St-Julien-le-Faucon
St Quentin-des-Isles
St Aubin-le-Vertueux
Beaumont
Ste-Marie aux Anglais
Château de Coupesarte
Vieux-Pont
Livarot
Orbec
Broglie
Beaumesnil
St-Pierre-sur-Dives
Notre-Dame-de-Courson
Pays
Château de Vendeuvre
La Ferrière-sur-Risle
Ammeville
Ste Foy-de-Montgommery
Montreuil-l'Argillé
Morteaux-Coulibœuf
Vimoutiers
Notre-Dame-du-Hamel
La Neuve-Lyre
Villy-lez-Falaise
Les Champeaux
Crouttes
Ticheville
Camembert
Le Sap
d'Ouche
Trun
Montormel
La Ferté-Frênel
Rugles
Chambois

Caen
CALVADOS
Ouistreham
Riva Bella
Mathieu
Bénouville
Ranville
Troarn
Bernières-sur-Mer
St-Aubin-sur-Mer
Langrune-sur-Mer
Luc-sur-Mer
Merville-Franceville-Plage
Juno Beach
Sword Beach
Cabourg
Dives-sur-Mer
Portsmouth
Bretteville-sur-Laize
Potigny
Le Petit Coulibœuf
Falaise

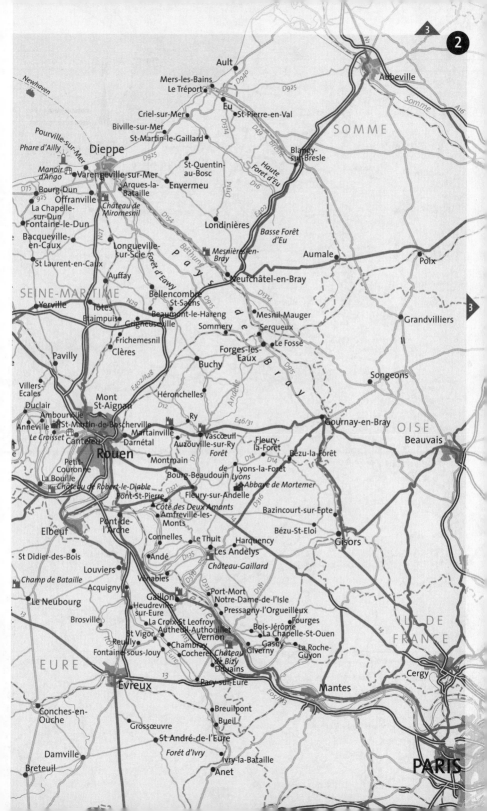

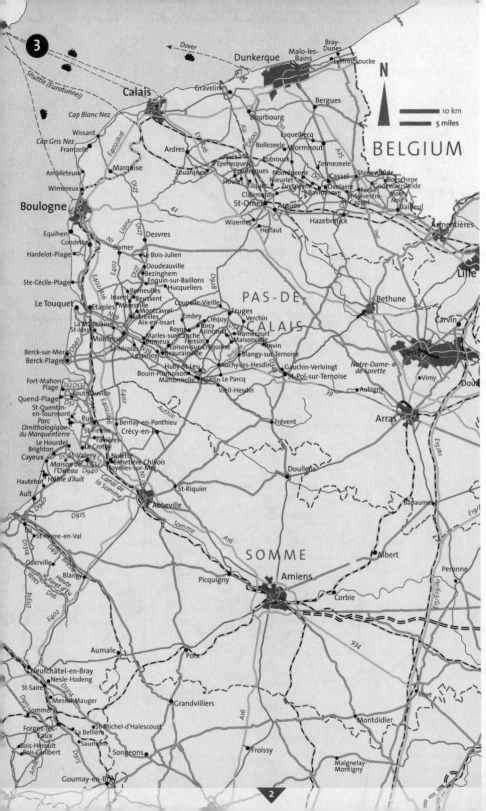